HOOSIER HEAVEN

*From Suffering to an Enlightened Understanding
of What Causes that Suffering*

DAVID McCASLIN

...Fitting the human condition into the human experience...
Changing the nature of the human mind...
The most primal expression of living art

Contents

PART 1

SUFFERING KNOWS NO PREJUDICE

Part II
SUFFERING IS A LIVING EFFECT

PART III
THERE IS A LIVING SOLUTION

Part IV

FIND HARMONY YOUR WAY

The Art in Being Human

How we LOVE art...Another's vision showcased...cloaked somewhere in their chosen media...a hall pass for the ego to tip-toe-venture from the left side of the brain to the right...from thinking with the head to feeling with the heart.

Art stimulates resolve in mankind's melting pot of possible life answers. New pathways emerge that might help route safer passage through the spiritual minefield that links a truth-savvy deeper consciousness to a hesitant free will that cowers to an uncertain ego.

Art cleaves open the spiritual abyss leveraged in between life notions cognitively tethered to an adopted faith...born blind to living validation...made conditional by a god above and life designs unconditionally secured by an intrinsic core faith steadfastly woven into the primal fiber of the human condition that's stirred up and rekindled by the insight-inspiring bright light that shines in the wake of actual experience.

As the blindly trusted should-be soundness of intellectually brewed cerebral concoctions rubs up against the gut-sourced intuition felt during each individual's freehand pillage for life's truth, art unchains the free will for personal insight to grow toward that bright light for some and to better posture the ego for others. How does one secure lasting awareness on this mystical pitch that art keys the way to?

The Hoosier Perspective

Each Midwestern locality is shaped by a unique melting pot of interrelated forces and dynamics. Each area's rolling countryside, humid summers and cold winters, population density and makeup, industrial development and job availability, average income level and the quality and focus of education, and spiritual/religious preferences are just a few of the variables that affect and shape the area's collective worldview. These reality cocktails leave their own unique authenticity footprint in how each of the area citizens chooses to realize or ignore their potential in this ever-transforming cosmos. To best describe what the effects of these life forces are like in any of these regions, it's necessary to have lived in and actually felt the ebb and flow of these sensually recorded causal forces as they have their real-time effects.

An ongoing tug of war over the Midwestern pocketbook strings comes from world-renowned cultural meccas on each of the opposing US coastlines. This creates a very unique "chic motif" counterbalance that helps keep the aging area's deepening lines of maturity puffed out with the Botox of freedom of choice while corporate America lets them know what they should want to buy. It seems to work. These modern trends then strike a unique breadbasket balance under a candy-coated icing of conservative morality.

Some might say there has really been no significant Midwestern contribution to the advancement of the US spiritual/religious zeitgeist since MLK Jr. helped lessen the pain coming from mankind's ignorance over human rights prevalent in the '60s or how young Ryan White's more recent fight for equality helped pave the way for the recognition, acceptance, and treatment of AIDS worldwide. Not much else has been able to escape the suffocating black hole effect produced by the thought-jamming static noise echoing from the thumping beat of widespread Bible Belt fundamentalism. This might sound a bit overstated, but really, who's to argue? The area's distinctive demographics influence relative differences in how the human condition perceives the human experience. While residents adapt to the local assortment of pluses and minuses, the area psyches brew up their own assortment of fleeting reactions that spell out their own unique Midwestern cookbook of addictions.

Spanning farther out, broader cultural differences enter in. It's true that some parts of the world have a happier populace than others. Some have less respect for human rights. Some parts of the world spend their present moments under unbearable oppression or suffer from hunger or even face daily the genocidal tendencies of neighboring clans.

Different cultures have different means of invading and regulating a native's access to their own free will. They have different ways of stealing away an individual's early-life innocence. This affects any individual's angle on how they view and define their freedom and if and maybe how they decide to chase it.

The worldwide applicability of this writing's theme is definite … people are people. However, with the differing varieties of governmental, religious, educational, and family structures and their huge influence on the realization of personal freedom defined by their different ways of limiting personal free-will parameters, any attempted widespread applicability could be somewhat diluted, obscured, or maybe could seem just a bit twisted.

The truth cuts deeper than mere social politeness or even political correctness to say that people are people no matter where they may be born. However, to expect meaningful results when comparing the psychic health and spiritual maturity/aptitude/nature of one area randomly to the next would be foolish. It would be as meaningless as comparing apples to oranges.

The richness of meaning found in any comparative conclusion would be incessantly diluted by all the necessary assumptions, compensations, and checks and balances. The concessions made to keep tempered the rising shadow of doubt and uncertainty inspired with the sudden arrival of each newly recognized area difference would water down the strength of any conclusion.

To best satisfy a truth seeker's due diligence used to sift out a most refined understanding of how local denizens relate to finding their true freedom, it's necessary to speak from the platform where an unpolluted awareness of the ever-turning wheels of the true freedom of ongoing change grind against the community karma coming from the area's uniquely conditioned ignorance of how our reality's nature of impermanence affects the way things are. It's on this plateau of understanding where the waking community consciousness tainted by this miscued and mismatched conditioned perception of what is happening intersects with the unavoidable relational justice that's being demonstrated in what is really transpiring in the transforming process of our multidimensional cause/effect reality.

Only through accumulated hometown life experience is it possible to successfully anticipate where the friction in this relationship begins to draw heat. This heat comes from the locals' misaligned collective worldview founded in misguided prior conditioning unique to the effects of the size and shape of the area's reality footprint.

The seeds of suffering planted in this community-based garden of misunderstanding are then watered by the everyday dedication of the human constituents to servicing their personalized collections of addictions. These addictions come as the "trickle-down effect" of the community vision.

The way each area deals with the resulting suffering becomes apparent in the collective effects on how each citizen expends all their energy just trying to service their ego-protected illusionary accounts of what seems to apparently represent reality...how they chase their design of what freedom is. They piece together select mental snapshots of their past, and along with unfounded hopes for the future, they customize something they can cling to for security while forging unprepared through the unexpected misunderstood naked change that hits them with the arrival of each new unchartered present moment.

With the lack of sensual memory residue from hands-on actual area life experience, there would be much guesswork when designing a method to perform the due diligence to effectively understand the plight of an individual's pursuit for freedom.

This essay is written in reference to the Hoosier experience because that's exactly what it is. The writing reveals what unfolds to actually be a self-help motivational memoir on finding the right path to heavenly enlightenment using the available tools carved out of a Midwestern upbringing.

The writer was born and raised in Central Indiana and has lived there for most of fifty-seven years. While speaking only from actual experience to greatly minimize the presence of any assumptions or guesswork, the level of realism is high. The honest simplicity of this rather no-nonsense approach should allow an increase in the readers' ability to relax their defenses and identify with the intended message while hopefully sensing a bit of the compassion that fueled its writing even if they're not from Midwestern USA.

This writing was influenced by living many days in the Midwest USA. Its attitude and style reflect some of life's walls that were built as a result. This writing applies personal observations on the art of passing each present moment in the confines of the human condition while living through the changing times and conditions unique to the Indiana human experience.

For most Hoosiers, their unfettered free will lies smothered and unrecognizable under layers of misguided prior conditioning, ground-in social custom, local beliefs, and religious riddles. It can only be hoped that their waking realization of what problem the pinprick of present moment suffering actually is, will draw the needed bead of blood to sponsor their pursuit of the healing provided from living the life of a truth seeker.

Chances are the majority of these individuals will never exert the due diligence needed to consciously see how threads of suffering are weaved someway into their each and every passing thought. They will fail to generate the insight needed to see and admit this suffering has a cause. They will not see and knowingly realize that as alive and real and internal as this suffering is, so must be its solution. The suffering exists. It has a cause. The cause has a solution. They can find the path to that solution. For the apathetic, the order to this pathway will never be realized.

Most Hoosiers mentally hover in an ongoing state of unrest and dissatisfaction, unaware that the simple suddenness of real-time suffering wrapped in a religious blanket of intellectual explanation is itself a generic sort of suffering. This is thought to be the normal way of life in their region. This stagnation of humankind understanding hides the magic. It prevents any collective awareness from making any integral working contribution to advancing the overall spiritual maturity of the Hoosier living experience.

In Indiana as everywhere else, access to the meaning of the truth about what allows present moment suffering is a primal right of the human condition. This access can become stifled and muted by the fear of the unknown, wrapped in many sorts of fundamentalist views.

Some understanding generated from religious/spiritual writings is sacrificed through the unavoidable use of foreign languages. Through recorders' mistakes, translators' misinterpretations, language-to-language losses of meaning, the multiple translations, while adapting to changing or new languages stirred up over millennia of time, misconstrue or completely lose the subtle nuances in the intended meaning made by the original teacher. The simple truth's living application is kept suppressed, lifeless and unrecognized, by an ongoing apathy synthesized from the imagined unfamiliar, intimidating, and distancing mystique of far-away Eastern cultures.

Social attitude toward the importance of recognizing the present moment suffering that exists in the Hoosier lifestyle seems to be kept just out of practical reach. People just don't seem to have the courage or the genuine interest to ask "Why?" or shout "Prove it!"

Mental images like what God or our Source might look like, the pearly gates, or angels floating in clouds sidetrack Hoosiers from recognizing the true spiritual connection in light of the sensual dialogue needed to understand these presences well enough to later be able to put into words what our Source's true living incarnation felt like.

This mystic aura seems to distract the imagination and fog the bearing set for any purpose based on mental pictures taken from today's religious text accounts of ancient times. It further fogs up any real-time present moment orientation to associate it with the original intended message taught by our enlightened ancestors from so long ago.

This lifeless, sterile state keeps distant the relaxed communion of thought enjoyed between individuals while sharing common truths of the human condition—truths lost in projected illusions of a somewhat skewed reality that includes unnatural miracles and ascending spirits. Dogmatic attention to pious ritualistic behaviors has developed as society slips its bookmark into its potential for spiritual advancement while grasping at the hollow emptiness of a time that is said to have sacrificed on the cross mankind's only ever walking connection to the almighty male god named Jehovah.

Worshipping imagined forms hosted by illusionary ideas allows for the collective procrastination of standing up and asking "Why?" or shouting "Prove it to me!" at the sources of these unverified claims at explaining heavenly enlightenment. Their untouchable remoteness leaves looming doubts questioning their religious promises.

They would need to merely show a living sign verifying the promise from above that's readily touchable by all anytime anywhere, not requiring any spoken language or having any other restrictive barrier. The collective Midwestern free will that originates these questions has been stunned to hang spinning and tasered by the very ignorance where its mental unrest originates.

This writing documents an example of Midwestern due diligence to uncover and acknowledge the inborn human awareness of the primal truth describing the nature and intended purpose of the source of this cause/effect reality.

The ongoing manifestation of life itself is the living sign from above that demonstrates this truth. It's the universal DNA binder that holds the change-initiating cause of one second to the effect to become the cause of the next.

It's an awareness that's realized from a subtle level of the deeper consciousness. The pathway to it is learned or taught. The steps in the process of realizing self-awareness, of letting the understanding of the truth rise up an individual's spirituality link from deeper to waking consciousness, can be learned as taught by our enlightened ancestors. The process has to be experienced individually using the same sensual dialogue demonstrating the same transforming nature as during those days of our ancestors.

The living truth exists in and emanates from every coming and going bit of energy that defines the pulsing outline of things and objects as the flow of their changing processes passes through the range of perception detectable by the sensual equipment that comes as part of the human condition. The relational justice in this coming and going sensual testimony reflects the right understanding that writes the book of wisdom needed for an individual to graduate from the universal school of hard knocks they attend daily throughout their lifelong tour through the human experience. After consciously seeing the truth of change in action, the unchanging omnipresence of its dependable consistency serves as the foundation that seeds the growing warmth of the steadfast faith in the relational wisdom it points to as it initiates unchanging change throughout its infinite outreach.

Preface

This writing was inspired by a long-overdue insight of how intellectually founded religious theology shows its face in a living reality. The intended message and form were distilled from the amassed piles of nightstand notes and research that followed in its wake.

It develops early-life impressions originating fifty years back when the peaceful sanctuary of childhood innocence was infected with indecision about what life source or god is responsible for the human condition. This writing is a transparent example of one Hoosier's due diligence to discover and describe our Source and to understand its nature and intended purpose.

Sharing it in written form came from the desire to illustrate to friends and family the shared interconnectedness and interdependence of Midwestern religious/spiritual beliefs. It tries to sufficiently illuminate the paradigm of how real modern life just doesn't happen in the biblical sense. It modernizes and breathes life into understanding what the real-time sensual incarnations are of the intellectually sketched spiritual signposts spoken of in today's 2,000-plus-year-old rendition of tunic-and-sandal-clad religious theology.

Hopes are to develop in readers the desire to recognize and seek to understand the ways of our reality's impermanent nature. They'll be better able to recognize and associate intellectually stored religious/spiritual images that comprise their personally tweaked perception of religious theology's cast and concepts (Source, Holy Spirit, faith, heaven, hell, salvation) as they make their unnoticed present moment cameo appearances in the individual's real-time sensual theater.

This writing demonstrates how it's possible, when afforded an eye that's focused on finding the truth about life, for anyone to realize they don't have to suffer through life unhappy with mental unrest. They can muster up the courage to break free from daily ritual and give up their self-inflicted dedication to a nonfulfilling dogmatic lifestyle and perform the necessary due diligence to uncover the pathway to realize an enlightened understanding of their heaven during this lifetime.

The quoted sources and related ideas are readily available through any individual's normal due diligence in today's world of technology. When the comments from these various sources are viewed in light of an eye wise to the ways of ongoing change, the points of friction can be determined, at which the differing claims of science and religious/spiritual disciplines attempting to describe our Source's nature and intended purpose intersect. They all climb the same tree of wisdom in search of life's primal truth.

Hoosier Heaven navigates through the primal signposts that are, by nature, the core spiritual ingredients of the human condition. These markers are characterized by the symptomatic behavioral mannerisms that reflect to what degree an individual is in touch with their internal source of altruistic compassion in the poorly mapped chapter of the human experience that recognizes and confronts the cause of present moment human suffering.

Signature emotional indicators manifest their presence in the behaviors that characterize the different stages along the continuum of self-understanding. This continuum of spiritual maturity spans from the state of unrealized insipient suffering to that of wisdom-enriched awareness with full understanding of what causes the ignorance that allows the addictions that host suffering the frustrations and mental unrest that define the present moment reality of most individuals.

While performing the due diligence in researching the broad topic of what lies in between suffering and enlightened awareness, there were translated or interpolated interpretations of many individuals that stood out. S. N. Goenka teaches Theravada Buddhist philosophy. Thich Nhat Hanh teaches Mahayana Buddhist philosophy. Don Miguel Ruiz is a Mexican Toltec shaman and has written several books about their very insightful way of seeking relief from the cause of suffering.

Lau Tzu's book of wisdom, *Tao Te Ching*, actually provides the Cliffs Notes explanation of how to, in this lifetime, become enlightened about what causes the ignorance that allows human suffering. Peter Merel's introspective rendition of *Tao Te Ching* was used in this writing. He used seven popular modern translations of *Tao Te Ching* and summarized what appeared to be their shared meaning. Siddhartha later gave the self-discovered details of the same process. Biblical accounts of some of Jesus's insightful teachings were also included.

The inborn genius of Mr. Siddhartha Gautama was really in his ability to put into words how he self-trained himself to be able to gain the wisdom-enriched knowledge that enlightened him about the ignorance that allowed him to spend his present moments suffering. There are others who have achieved this same end. He effectively described how to self-train the process step-by-step and explained how the self-command is continually nurtured along. He knew how to describe in intellectually defined terms how to pursue and appreciate the sensual experience. As a lost soul becomes more enlightened, their intellectually sketched theological maxims become more associated with sensually realized signals.

Other enlightened people were or are unable to effectively pass on to others the process they used to reach enlightenment for one reason or another. Some lived in a society that had no ear or patience for their gifted teachings. Others probably had no available way to leave the details of their experience...the scribes to write it down or the material to write it on. This presented a major problem two millennia ago.

Siddhartha's story was passed along orally for six hundred years before it could be written down. It took a few hundred years for the selected accounts of Jesus's teachings to be written and over three hundred years for Rome to decide what accounts of Jesus's story the Romans should be allowed to hear.

Others were/are enlightened during more modern times with society having no eye for recognizing and associating the spiritual state of the individual's radiant genius as being enlightened, in the same way intellectually defined and dated in the theological sense, like in the times of Jesus or Siddhartha. There were different kinds of heavenly prizes or goals that didn't center on present moment nirvana or the absence of human suffering in the present lifetime.

An intellectually pictured theological heaven is different from a sensually defined spiritual heaven even though each offers a plan to foil suffering. The intellectually captured theological heaven extends to some unknown never-seen place up in the sky. The nature of its existence allows for the continual unchanging presence of the things and objects that make up this reality. It draws no real importance from distinguishing otherwise.

The heaven that's discovered sensually is patterned from the transforming world that extends farthest from human perceptive abilities in the other direction. It extends down inside into the cause/effect patterns of the coming and going bits of energy that define the human-perceivable shape of the things and objects of this reality. These are the same things and objects that others may fail to recognize the changing nature of. It's the nature of the sensually witnessed heaven inside to recognize all things and objects to be ever changing as are the ephemeral bits of coming and going bits of energy that define the shape and form of their seemingly continual existence.

After becoming enlightened about the cause of his ignorance that made him blind to bliss and susceptible to suffering, Siddhartha taught how the sequential self-training methodology he developed that worked for him could be used by any truth seeker. He discovered in all his time teaching how the order of presentation also helps maintain the listeners' interest in the subject matter.

To achieve this end, he took the natural cause/effect rhythm of our reality and reversed it. To help assure student interest in the process of becoming enlightened about the cause of ignorance, he first presented the effect (suffering is the effect).

If an audience showed interest in the effect of something, they would have interest to know its cause.

This writing's arranged theme presentation follows the sequential four-point rhythm similar to that used in Siddhartha Gautama's teachings detailing what he learned through his experience to be the four noble truths that a truth seeker will encounter on their journey from suffering to becoming enlightened about what causes that suffering. It starts with one truth presenting the problem (the effect of a cause) to stir listeners' or readers' interest, and then the next truth (the cause) that solves it. In the long run, the cause/effect rhythm reversed allows someone to see and understand the problem and then change the cause. The order of these four noble truths repeat this effect/cause rhythm twice. Thus, this writing is presented in four sections.

The phases of self-trained development found in Siddhartha's teachings that came to be known as an eightfold pathway to enlightenment helped organize the third section of this book on affirming that there is a way to eliminate the ignorance that allows suffering. He broke it down into eight stages of development arranged in three phases of self-training.

The targeted body/mind harmony self-trained in this writing's third section is the same harmony that Lau Tzu taught in the writing *Tao Te Ching* and will defeat the self-ego to allow becoming enlightened about the ignorance that allows human suffering. It's the same pathway to freedom from ignorance no matter what enlightened entity describes it.

In arranging the section presentation order of *The Four Noble Truths*, Siddhartha felt that before an individual first opens their eyes to seek enlightenment, they have to realize there is a problem (that they are suffering) and it must have a cause (human ignorance). They need to be stricken by the primal drive to develop their understanding of their suffering after identifying it as their present moment problem.

The ideas that suffering exists and what its cause is, are covered in this writing's sections 1 and 2. A truth seeker should then want to discover if the causing ignorance has a cure and how to attain it.

This writing describes Siddhartha's second interesting effect from *The Four Noble Truths* being that there is a solution for the cause of this problem of suffering in section 3, "There Is a Solution...Primal Ignorance Undone." Then, to cause this solution to the problem to happen, section 4 discusses finding harmony your way.

What's discussed in each chapter of the four main sections shows more detail on how the section subject relates directly to modern-day life as experienced living in Midwestern USA.

There are other approaches to explaining what lies in between suffering and enlightenment that are considered. All the claims to providing heavenly enlightenment from the cause of the ignorance that allows suffering have to be considered. Any properly designed effort of due diligence will consider as many views and beliefs as needed to be able to triangulate in on what the intended collective message describing the path to their enlightenment might be.

All approaches at explaining the human way of dealing with mental unrest attempt in some way to organize and explain the nature and intended purpose of the source of our ever-changing cause/effect reality. By actually citing these different views and beliefs, it becomes clearer what understandings or common ground is shared between their differing explanations and where their interpretations crisscross and how to finally derive the most comprehensive answer.

To provide some sort of mental organization for those who, as they grow older, feel the pressure of mounting mental unrest, many individuals will adopt some organizational order to handle their own personal impressions of what reality seems to be. Those less insightful or those who place confidence in social opinion might use an updated stenciled approach bearing the stamp of one of today's religions.

Religious pathways to freedom from suffering focus importance more on who or what entity claims credit for this reality and the importance of enforcing behavior compliance to a list of often loosely worded commandments. Not obeying God is the cause given for eternal suffering, not mankind's ignorance about how the human condition perceives the human experience. And for this group of people, there's always the soul-prodding presence of the often-repeated warning of what happens to a follower if they fail to obey their god's commandments that stirs up their deep primal fear for the safety of their soul.

For the forty-five years after Siddhartha realized his enlightenment about the ways of this reality he lived ignorant to, he communicated with others about nothing other than what worked for him in realizing his own wisdom-enriched self-awareness. He taught how to eliminate the human ignorance that distances an individual from the joy and happiness found when living in a state of altruistic compassion.

The recorded volumes of written accounts of his sutras are quite massive. The main fiber of his intended message of how he reached heavenly enlightenment by eradicating his ignorance that allowed his suffering is directly addressed. The parts relevant to this search were all considered.

Siddhartha said in his final words that it's up to everyone to be diligent in their search to better understand our Source's nature of ongoing change to eliminate their ignorance of this ever-present state of impermanence to experience a world of compassion that's free of suffering. This writing exemplifies how it's possible through applied due diligence for a truth seeker raised in the Bible Belt state of Indiana to gain insight into their ignorance of this reality's natural laws through personal awareness that's inspired during focused concentration into the give-and-take cause/effect lessons being tapped out in time among the unimaginably tiny pieces of coming and going bits of energy, the building blocks of our reality, that make up the flesh of the human body.

This writing demonstrates how it's possible for an average individual to realize that it's their ignorance of the truth of ongoing change and their unfamiliarity with the wisdom relating to the relational justice inherent to the cause/effect process of this reality that allows them to suffer present moment mental unrest. It makes it clear how this cause can be eliminated during their lifetime and how to selftrain themselves to find the pathway to this end. This writing exhibits how a truth seeker's successful efforts of due diligence in securing an understanding of this knowledge through gaining self-awareness provides them with the very primal answer that satisfies the ongoing, usually unrecognized human longing for the freedom from the control this ignorance has over their experiencing ongoing happiness, which allows them to suffer.

This writing brings to attention how to distinguish and recognize in real-time sensual imagery what the characters and contributing factors described in the religious theology that individuals are taught about as children and learn to store in their cerebral memory, look like or appear as in the real-time sensual world. These characters and factors are the cognitively etched mental imagery that gives illusionary form to the never-seen God trilogy (or our Source), the Holy Spirit, and our way to salvation.

This writing gives depth to the understanding of what making it to heaven means in terms of real-time sensual life participation. It helps readers understand what their sensual definition is and gives the living texture of life to those intellectually captured ghosts that float around in the spiritual world melting pot of undefined notions lodged in between the inaccessible all-knowing deeper human consciousness and the limited human waking awareness.

It's difficult to shake the deeply implanted and highly undefined biblical notion of being "saved from our sins" or maybe the feeling of debt owed to Jesus for "dying to save everyone from their sins" that's fortified by centuries of followers dating clear back to John the Baptist. The Midwestern take on this blurred notion and the means for any spiritual relief come envisioned as wearing the robes and sandals and speaking with the King James "thou/thine" accent imagined of our ancient ancestors. This separates and distances associating these biblical directives with the modern real-time living involvement concerning the intentions and behaviors that might compose a sin, in its highly undefined status, from their mentally stored enigma of an old religious maxim.

This writing distinguishes those generalized religious mantras of being "saved from our sins" and that "Jesus died for our sins" by detailing what it is that brings about the nature of mind that feeds and nurtures the present moment ignorance that allows the attitudes and behaviors that result in the suffering that defines mankind's present moment hell. These are the attitudes and behaviors (sins?) that allow us to behave in ways that are unwholesome toward establishing the mind control to gain the wisdom-enriched awareness to live the present moment in a state of altruistic compassion.

The transparency of this writing exposes how an average individual can ask the right questions, listen and decide for themselves which information sources have the verifiable answers while progressing down their intellectually outlined, to-be-experientially-discovered pathway to becoming enlightened about the cause of their ignorance. This writing's citing of some of today's most world-renowned religious/spiritual sources allows any doubting Thomas the chance to compare this writing's overall theme to today's widely known religious/spiritual standards. This helps support the credibility of this writing's observations, views, and suggestions.

When requesting copyright holders' permissions from the publishers to use excerpt quotations from their works, the author or their representative of the book *The Art of Living, Vipassana Meditation*, which inspired this author's insight to write *Hoosier Heaven*, declined permission. The publisher would only divulge that the author or their representative felt like this author needed to refer more to the original sources that they had used when writing his book. So, be it that the Theravada Buddhist spiritual discipline is still very well described, this book contains fewer quoted excerpts from outside sources as other theological disciplines may have. The author's intended meaning in *The Art of Living* is very well articulated and many excerpts had been borrowed to add more clarity to the factors that influence how an individual builds their belief system that are described in this book. It helps those with the anticipated mentally sketched intellectual apparitions explaining the details of their religion's deity and the biblically described court to connect and recognize what the real-time sensual manifestation of those intellectually defined characters is when their living incarnations make their real-time walk-on appearance.

Up until the last few decades, performing the due diligence to gain the self-knowledge to understand the ways of this reality was very difficult for anybody, let alone an average individual who works and has a family. It would require much reference research to find original sources with the needed material to answer questions that the researcher might not have even known to ask. Hoosier mysticism and superstition would be very hard to crack through.

This would be nearly impossible for most. They would choose to pass their present moments in a safe, unthreatening USA environment alongside their neighbors as they fetter away their daily energy trying to maintain the frail framework supporting their ego-managed illusionary renditions of what reality apparently is while making no real effort to get a bearing on what the truth is and to seek it. They wouldn't know where to begin.

This is not true with today's technology. The deepest of research can be done at home. The researched sources used to fortify this writing's material are the same types of information sources that Hoosiers can easily see or listen to every day. Seeking a deeper understanding of our reality's impermanence is much more possible for anyone with the right direction or primal drive to do so.

There are citings from referenced newspaper and magazine articles, TV programs of all kinds, songs, spoken poetry, movies, religious and spiritual seminars, and of course there are quotes referenced from different books. The claims made from this variety of sources are built on insightful understandings common to the same tree of wisdom that relate to the relational justice exchange of the cause/effect change that defines this reality. This writing includes a variety of those sources an individual might consider when attempting to hush their ignorance. These are sources any typical Hoosier of average resources living an average lifestyle could be exposed to during any typical day. If not for the diverse subject range and broadcast capabilities of today's satellite radio technology, hearing the material that switched on the mental lightbulb that lined up this author's stale cognitive impressions of Hoosier religious theology with the actual heartbeat of living spirituality would have probably never happened. Just catching the last part of an announcement on an obscure satellite radio station fueled the insight leading to the theme of this book. It instantly hit a nerve.

Shaking off fifty years worth of the doubt-and-uncertainty dust that had accumulated from misunderstandings of how this cause/effect reality works resulting from internalized misguided prior conditioning, to free up the author's primal link connecting their truth-savvy deeper consciousness to their uncertain waking awareness required quite a sudden jolt. This split-second association cracked the cover to this writing's most influential outside resource. The life-changing event that makes this writing a memoir happened twenty-five years prior.

William Hart authored the informative book titled *The Art of Living (Vipassana Meditation As Taught by S. N. Goenka)*. Up to this point in time, Theravada Buddhism was unknown to this Hoosier. A brief initial study of Buddhism that included one reading of Herman Hesse's *Siddhartha* summarizes the frame of reference available to draw from.

Looking back, the Theravada meditation technique details given on the radio advertisement mirrored the self-discovered technique closely enough to jar loose and bring back from sensual memory something that had never really been discussed with anyone else or dwelt upon or thought about for over twenty-five years. At that earlier time, no religious/spiritual associations had been made that connected the author's life discovery-exploratory technique with communicating with our Source or Creator. He found it very effective in putting him to sleep at a time when his thoughts were lost in confusion and worry about the changes brought about by his recent accident.

Who would have thought notions of the ancient catacombs of religious theology could have anything to do with today's living reality? After hearing the radio description of the Buddhist meditation technique, the connection was made. It was not thought that something actually experienced in this sensual world could be the living incarnation of practice that a world-renowned spiritual group used to involve the mysterious ways of the intellectually learned/remembered side of the author's brain. Left side of the brain meets right side? Making this association meant replacing the existing intellectually imagined pictures detailing the biblically founded religious imagery depicting a god/source and the Holy Spirit with what was encountered and recognized in the living now to be the real-life present moment incarnations of those cognitively conceptualized spiritual markers.

Reading *The Art of Living* helped clarify how the personal effort made twenty-five years earlier to sit down and simply find out what real life felt like by focusing awareness into the living flesh of the body actually paralleled Theravada Buddhism's way of finding the mind/body harmony to sustain the right concentration to allow self-training the mind to pick up the insightful understanding of the wisdom gained through attaining self-knowledge to reach heavenly enlightenment. It is said that of the two main fractions of Buddhism, today's Theravada process has been handed down directly by word of mouth from the enlightened Siddhartha's teachings.

The description of the Theravada meditative approach wasn't just similar to the self-discovered methodology; it was exactly the same thing, from the body scanning methodology clear down to sharing the same intended purpose of sensually witnessing what it actually felt like just to be alive, the tingle in the flesh. This author's relationship with newly discovered Theravada Buddhism was founded in suspicion—how their approach to sustained body/mind harmony compared to the one personally discovered. This greatly helped overcome any intimidation that might be posed by an ancient school of spiritual discipline with a history touting billions of followers. It was assumed that the Buddhists couldn't be sued for patent infringement, being that this author hadn't yet filed for a patent for his self-discovered methodology.

No matter what reputation an individual has developed or when they live, he or she is really nothing more and nothing less than one wave in the sea of humanity. Even though Siddhartha now has billions of followers, he made it known that he claimed no affiliation with any religious or spiritual movement. Jesus wasn't a Christian.

After physically healing from the crash and without the author having made any association between the sensual dialogue consciously noted when their mind/body awareness was focused on the physical coming and going sensations to feel what being alive was like and the intellectually sketched images of spiritual theology that the world saw as training the mind or seen as meditating by the Buddhists or Taoists, the self-designed method of mind/body analysis was forgotten. It wasn't for twenty-five years until hearing those few words on the radio describing the theme of that wonderful book that the association was made.

It's interesting how the intended meaning of our ancient enlightened ancestors' religious/spiritual messages hang suspended in layers of secular confusion unrecognized and untouched...distant to all. The fruit of their intended meaning is like the mysterious filling of an unviolated piñata hanging untouched for over 2,000 years...an undefined mystery. Believers build their towers of Babel to reach it to crack through its shell to expose the answer that pins down their thoughts of freedom with ongoing present moment uncertainty.

Siddhartha's first noble truth of suffering ...Suffering does exist

PART 1

SUFFERING KNOWS NO PREJUDICE

...Joy and pain only need a heartbeat

1

Who Has the Floor?

Open Mental Forum

So here we are as fate has it, born into this world. We're born suspended by our five senses in an environment of constant interplay between degrees of hot and cold, light and dark, loud and quiet, and sweet and sour. We attend preschool, kindergarten, and grade school. We begin a lifetime of discovery. We emerge from our age of innocence and begin to assume responsibility for our actions and worry for our souls.

We enhance our belief system on a daily basis as our maturing worldview eagerly searches for posture. Individual belief systems are conditioned and shaped by all the ideas and beliefs the free will agrees to internalize or is possibly coaxed or fooled into believing.

Decision by decision, each individual's worldview is conditioned to take on its own unique perspective of the human experience. New ideas, beliefs, and concepts are embraced as each individual decides how to best fit into the changing flow of this reality.

As people age, many find it very difficult to relax into that good novel they've heard so much about as their thoughts uncontrollably drift from the story line. They just can't help having such a short attention span. Their mental focus wanders through an uncontrollable stream of changing images pulsing through their head.

The voice stream they hear inside their head might include voice bits quoting parental advice, schoolteachers, their best friend, or maybe their greatest critic. They may feel like they're singing karaoke as they let the ideas planted inside their head by others turn them into confused parrots or mockingbirds of social protocol.

Many people pass their time perplexed with ungrounded thoughts that point randomly from unrelated topic to unrelated topic. Their inborn quest to find something to anchor down their unrest stands ready at constant attention.

They may lie awake in bed at night with their thought patterns stuck in an uncontrollable spin, ruminating over their imagined notions based in fear and uncertainty or maybe guilt from past times or uncertain worry about future predictions. Their ongoing doubt casts a mounting threat to their future peace and security. They take a sleeping pill to help temper the echo in the open forum of their waking mind. Yet still, there are those who drift off to sleep with thoughts relaxed in rhythm with life's unchanging beat. They're patiently aware and satisfied as their body reports being tired from a joyful day spent compassionately expressing their life purpose as they let their light shine.

Many struggle to find the "crispness of thought" to separate the objective truth from an illusionary conception of how to fit into the passing present moment. It seems as though their free will has lost its ability to stand up and assert the direction of their passion or even an interest in something they're not sure of. It lacks having any feel for having any genuine intent.

Their free will's been stunned, tasered by the reluctance of self-doubt. Their indecision has stripped them of their ability to sincerely, respectfully, and confidently form and voice their opinion. Any steadfast faith felt in their sense of genuine objectivity has been lost in the uncertainty that follows self-doubt.

Are they truly aware that they're not the same person they were when they got out of bed that morning? Can they find joy in knowing that because of their compassion-based actions they've helped others and at the same time changed themselves? Do they go to bed a bit wiser, a few steps closer to their idea of heavenly enlightenment? Are they yet humbly aware that they're still no more and no less than a maturing human being, one day closer to needing a haircut? Many people live day to day, moment to moment suspended in between the causes and effects that unite to make up the present moment of their human experience that's heckled by their self-inflicted indecision and hesitation. They experience different degrees of struggle in their milieu of self-crafted demons of self-doubt and self-devaluation. Most people spend their waking hours reacting to life's constant flow of transformation with behavioral intentions

servicing many pet addictions.

What is it that everyone, regardless of race or religion, has in common? They suffer from the mental chatter that consumes their ability to think clearly. They suffer the frustrations and disappointments of when expectations of what reality seems to apparently be doesn't measure up to what's actually evolving. Their confused, lonely, and often desperate belief systems stand ungrounded to any solid foundation of experiential dependability in which to develop a steadfast faith. Everyone suffers from the ignorance of not knowing why this is.

Most human beings seek to quiet the unrelated voices in their heads that are constantly shouting out unrelated claims that service and share no common end. The supporting latticework of logic that verifies the different truths of the different internalized claims making up their worldview recognizes having different natures of reality to allow their claims to find its truth or have its effect. The natures of different claims fail to service the same primal truth of life. They don't all need the relational justice of the ephemeral nature of this reality for the purpose of the claim to find its effect.

Their stream of mental headlines changes from one present moment to the next. They have yet to realize that having this state of mind that's consumed by claims not pointing at working toward a common end is like having their own self-maintained petri dish for suffering.

The Mitote/Maya Thought Filibuster

Other cultures recognize this state of affairs in a like fashion. Don Miguel Ruiz, a shaman of the Mexican Toltec, uses an excellent analogy in his book *The Four Agreements: A Practical Guide To Personal Freedom* to describe and exemplify the effects of the mental agitation resulting from a compromised belief system that develops in the waking mind of those who will spend their waking hours servicing their own uniquely construed illusionary version of what they think reality apparently should be.

> Your whole mind is a fog which the Toltecs called a "mitote" (pronounced MIH-TOE-TAY). Your mind is a dream where a thousand people talk at the same time, and nobody understands each other. This is the condition of the human mind—a big mitote, and with that big mitote you cannot see what you really are. In India they call the mitote maya, which means illusion. It is the personality's notion of "I am." Everything you believe about yourself and the world, all the concepts and programming you have in your mind; are all the mitote. We cannot see who we truly are; we cannot see that we are not free.[1]

An individual's present moment mind-set can migrate into becoming an unreined thought factory. There can be no control over the thought process...a thinking filibuster. He describes how the uncontrolled internal conversation common to the mitote/maya state of mind eats away at the sanity of an individual, like how a parasite eats away and diminishes its host.

It plays the roles of both judge and victim. It eats away at their sanity while speaking in tongues about its many unprioritized internal expectations and desires. It recognizes a weakened free will that has no shield to guard it, and it feeds off the indecision. It judges what they've done and what they should be doing and is their hardest, most feared, and most respected critic.

To the judge's ridicule, the victim reacts with a "poor me" attitude, all inside their head. It stifles free will with doubt and more indecision.

Bernadette Vigil, an initiated Nagual woman of Toltec self-mastery and working partner of don Miguel Ruiz, writes:

> The Parasite is a function of your mind that develops through the domestication process and is based on the belief system. It is most easily identified as the constant conversation-taking place in your mind. This inner "voice" generates all those little words you hear when you are thinking about things or interacting with others. It helps to create and intensify your emotional wounds, and it leads to unhappiness.[2]

One of many examples that Ruiz relates is one that anyone can identify with of the judge in action and the victim's response:

> If we make a mistake in front of people, we try to deny the mistake and cover it up. But as soon as we are alone, the Judge becomes so strong, the guilt is so strong, and we feel so stupid, or so bad, or so unworthy.[3]

Ms. Vigil recaps with her observations:

> You will learn how the domestication process of the Dream of the Planet alienates you from your true self and from freedom, peace, contentment and love...you will see how the Judge and the Victim, which are parts of your own personal Parasite, function in your life, perpetuating discontent and the illusion of what "should" be...about the many "hooks" in life, which grab your attention and make you lose your direction. You will see how your wounds are created by the agreements given to you by others in the Dream.[4]

Reason For Body-Mind Cosustenance Never Realized

Signs of a numb and confused free will, will show up in outer physical symptoms. Rumor has it that an individual's body is the temple for their soul. Most individuals who spend their waking time ungrounded in an illusionary reality of the mitote/maya they've created lack having any direction in recognizing and developing their unique talents to best express their inner life potential. They're indifferent about taking care of the only vehicle that could take them to that goal...their physical body that takes shape in proportion to what and how much of what they put into it.

Conversely, when there's a life goal in sight, there are individuals who realize how important it is that their physical condition doesn't limit options on achieving their goal to the fullest. They find satisfaction in maintaining their body's well-being. With a focus bent on realizing the truth about the human condition, the truth about the conditions affecting how the human body best fits into the human experience can't be ignored.

If a truth seeker can't appreciate why their mind must be responsible for providing a healthy living experience for their body, they will never see the reason why both mind and body must be in top form to be able to unite their body and mind in a harmonious state to let the mind sensually witness what happens in their only access to the world where living reality manifests itself, that their material body provides.

They will never be able to self-train the enriched knowledge of self-awareness that can conquer their self-ego that oversees and helps arrange the suffering of their present moment mitote/maya unrest.

In Indiana over 30 percent of the people are obese. That's a gradation of body fat beyond being overweight. Hoosiers have one of the highest smoking rates in the USA. Diabetes II is skyrocketing. Children's life expectancies are now shorter than their grandparents'.

People living in their own illusion of reality have a mental freeze on the reality of their actual physical/mental presence. There's no real connection between their physical/ mental presence and their preoccupation with their god that is believed to have created it. There's no thought that maybe he would want them to take good care of the body he gave them. The biblical statement that their "body is their temple" has no associated relevance to how they fretter away their present moment.

They use the best brand of motor oil in their SUV and are able to tell you why but have no clue what a blood glucose level means, let alone what theirs is and what foods influence this. TV commercials expose onlookers to their crafted human behavior to establish what should be the normal way of taking care of arthritis pain. By taking an over-the-counter anti-inflammatory drug to mask the pain, the individual is choosing to just ignore the reason the joint hurts. The problem is still in the joint. How long till there's absolutely no joint padding left? This misleading information fails to say how feeding the body the nutrients found in different foods will fortify the body's immune system to stop the problem before they have the soreness and joint deterioration.

Most Hoosiers will never reach the understanding of how directing the humble attention of their mind to what is going on inside their body as it manifests life itself, is how they can consciously create the mind/body harmony to eventually undo their ignorance of this reality's relational justice that results in their present moment suffering.

Suffering Anesthetized In The Midwest

Many individuals don't realize how the intrusive effects of a growing mitote/ maya state of mind progressively numb their once bold and protective free will. They lose sight of finding and developing their true passion. Their purpose-directed involvement in the passage of time is lost to indecision over what-ifs and maybes. They get caught up in an eddy of self-doubt. They fail to sort out and plan for the ongoing change that now blindsides them constantly.

Instead of moving forward, they spend their passing moments perplexed in the hell pit of suffering. They waver in endless rumination over notions fed by fears that point at guilt-ridden past regrets, and they freeze in their tracks with worry over future uncertainties. Their waking mood fosters an endless assortment of unfounded thoughts ruminating over what might be or what should have been. "Counting the roses" just doesn't work for them.

Their stagnating confusion may be diagnosed as a condition coming from today's still generalized and undefined pool of depression. Maybe their condition is an anxiety disorder, or maybe it will be diagnosed more as a fear-related imbalance having to do with panic phobia or a post-traumatic disorder of sorts.

A doctor will likely determine that the individual needs some pills to relieve the symptoms. Today's assortment of new antidepression medications are too easily prescribed to new patients who the doctor or psychiatrist may not know well enough to treat with a more personalized and effective recovery plan. They try the different drugs out one at a time to see which one best fits. They try to find the one that causes the least harmful physical side effects.

This impersonal state of affairs can in turn increase the patient's feelings of abandon and hopelessness. Many give up and accept the generalized label "clinically depressed" or maybe to be loosely diagnosed as being bipolar. Lithium's been around for ages.

Or could it be that for many, depression is largely a learned behavior? Could it be that the chemicals that their brain lacks are lacking because they've never learned how to spend their time with their body and mind involved in something to naturally cause their body to make those pain-calming chemicals...maybe exercise?

What about their role models? If their parents spent their time in a state of depression, they could have learned this behavior as the way to handle certain situations. This could be their learned way to give order to the unavoidable change that they greet unprepared second by second. They live incapable of acting in "normal" ways typically learned during childhood.

Pills meant to help suppress depression further numb and distance the sufferer from having a healthy free will that questions the questionable. They will artificially pharmaceutically activate or suppress the mind chemical serotonin designed to naturally occur as a healthy free will's response to some action involving an individual's heartfelt passion. Normally, an alert and active free will naturally pushes the right buttons for the chemical's release as a natural part of experiencing life while an individual lets their light shine. Many, many too many individuals are diagnosed as being clinically serotonin deficient.

Many miss their calling and wander day by day lost, taking their Prozac or Cymbalta to numb their pain, or a Lunesta sleeping pill to quiet the 1,000 voices fighting for their mental podium. They can't figure out what causes the misalignment between their understanding of what seems to be the present moment reality and what is really going on.

They think in an inclusively haphazard way that surely the long list of possible harmful reactions and side effects given in the drug's disclaimer that takes up over half of the drug's TV commercial doesn't really apply to them. They'll pick the antidepressant that affects them with the least number of side effects.

In just a few months after seeing these commercials, they'll see on TV an attorney's new commercial instructing all who've taken these drugs and suffered from something from a list of resulting life-ending or life-threatening effects of the drug to call them to get their share of the billions in escrow from the class-action lawsuit the drug company lost and is now liable for. They suffer.

In the movie *The Awakening*, Robin Williams's character, Dr. Sayer, summed it up well: "The human spirit is more powerful than any drug and that's what needs to be nourished."

2

What We Want

We Want Freedom to Pursue the American Dream

An individual's right to have the freedom to pursue their dreams is a basic pillar of American pride. Exactly what the American dream is, has no real definition. What the American dream is varies from person to person...to become president, to say or print what they want or to worship any god (or devil) they decide to follow, etc.

Freedom's a word that brings sentimental tears of love and appreciation to most any American's eyes and is usually coupled with short stories reminiscing their ancestors, friends, and relatives that have died for its sake in one of the wars fought when this right to freedom was threatened...American or not.

When sighting down the branches of the typical American family tree, it soon becomes clear that paying for the cost of freedom is something most American families have made a dear contribution to. Brief reminders of how are etched in gravestones in most every American cemetery. Having protected First Amendment rights registers a deep-felt sigh of appreciation in America's collective consciousness when reflecting on the ways other parts of the world choose to limit or deny individual freedom.

The pride and security felt while living under America's umbrella of protection emanates from every US citizen's smile as each will tell of the wide variety of life pursuits that having their personal freedom has made possible. Many cultures envy America for its freedom and the perceived power it supports and helps to generate.

Modern technology has greatly broadened worldwide awareness of the First Amendment freedoms allowed American citizens. Social networking websites have helped inspire the public motivation for several Middle Eastern countries to pursue a more democratic government, more favorable to recognizing human rights.

On the surface, the laws and statutes ensuring each person's freedom are really no more than loose reins holding together the process of humans interacting with other humans. As long as behaviors don't violate the laws of conduct, there's no problem. The laws don't really delve into the intentions behind the actions, as per First Amendment rights, just the behaviors.

Under the First Amendment's unbiased protection, some choose to run devilishly wild while others will work under its protective shield to do good for others. It provides USA citizens the freedom from suffering undue outward oppression or unjust governmental control of their outward behavior. They have the freedom to realize their individual talents on their trek in pursuit of their dreams.

Preteens can't wait until they can enjoy an anticipated increase of freedom recognized at becoming thirteen and then sixteen to become eighteen and then twenty-one. It's programmed in socially and biologically to seek social conditions with minimal constraints on physical actions as well as the consciousness to be responsible for one's own actions. Maybe one of the appreciated freedoms recognized in Western culture is the freedom to be openly wrong or at least different. It could be called the freedom to pursue one's own personal illusion of reality. It doesn't matter what an individual recognizes the nature of this reality to be...they can bet all their money on how they have been conditioned

to understand how this cause/effect reality works.

The dreams pursued by most take root in their perception of what reality seems to be. It centers on how their worldview interprets the relational justice or how the behavioral physics between the various forms, shapes, ideas, and beliefs should line up. This is what the individuals' egos will choose to support, defend, and rule.

Freedom from the ignorance that allows an individual to be living trapped in a misguided illusion of reality could be a deeper form of freedom to pursue. Having behavioral intentions coming from a belief system based on a misguided perception corrupted by faulty prior conditioning causes much suffering. These individuals live in the ongoing unrest of a mitote/maya mental state.

The collective purpose of intent of an individual's belief system is a summation of their internalized beliefs and ideas. If the many internalized beliefs could be peeled apart to reflect the contributory influence of each of the purposes of intent of each of the adopted claims being made by those internalized beliefs or ideas, it would become clearer why the individual supports the worldview they support and how they recognize the nature of this reality.

A more subdued and deeper analysis of this mental state might suggest that freedom from the ignorance about things relating to the true nature and purpose of this reality would be an even more beneficial and desirable freedom to pursue. A waking awareness of some standard to keep in mind of how to pick through the various claims about the truths of our reality before being internalized or believed would be a place to start.

We Should Want Freedom From Ignorance

It could be said that having freedom from the ignorance that allows the formation of worldviews blind to the wisdom of living in this cause/effect reality would be the freedom individuals truly long for. This ignorance binds us to suffering, enslaved to the security of our own unique personal repertoire of ongoing addictions.

What would an individual have without their addictions? Servicing addictions is all that people really know how to do to organize and deal with the barrage of change that time continually dishes out. It's what's been practiced and perfected. Each individual has addictions originating from both wholesome and unwholesome or contributory and noncontributory intentions.

This freedom isn't freedom that originates in outside behavior control. It involves undoing the internal confusion that limits an individual from identifying and unlocking their unique genius potential. It's their freedom from self-imposed limitations on developing their ability to express the primal potential of their inner being they must find the key to.

Some might call this freedom a freedom of religion, yet Christianity doesn't cite an individual's ignorance as the cause of their suffering. They say it's rooted in disobedience to God's law. It's a common religious belief that it's largely our behaviors that send us to hell to suffer eternal fire and brimstone, like when breaking one of the Ten Commandments. That's as far as they really delve into where the cause lies. Christianity presents a rough sketch of what not to do and stops short of telling why not.

The US Constitution provides for a social environment that is "Ten Commandments friendly." Citizens have the behavioral freedom to do what they feel necessary to maintain a living environment conducive to attending a church of their choice. This makes it possible for church members to be educated on seeking freedom from their idea of what they must flee from.

Their peace may come through the grace of a particular god they elect to have blind faith in. They will pray to him for his forgiveness and ask him to lessen their suffering from the effects of their addictive behaviors and plea to him to help them stop the behaviors that the Bible says will result in their eternal suffering.

The US Constitution provides for an environment that allows for individuals' open search for internal wisdom.

America has an environment that's calm enough to allow frequent use of quiet personal retreat into relaxed mindfulness centered on life's essence as it manifests to advance the level of self-knowledge and increase awareness of its derived wisdom and the resulting growth of steadfast faith in its omnipresence to bring one closer to heavenly enlightenment to realize freedom of the soul from the ignorance that allows suffering.

For most people, should the social environment not be free of unwelcome outside intrusions, they would have already climbed up a fear-generated tree of denial, blind to the truth of what's happening around them. They'll spend all their waking time in knee-jerk reaction to outward stimuli or experiences and never grow in spiritual maturity. They concede to marching to the drums of others found in the unrelated claims of the 1,000 voices shouting at once from their very confused belief system consumed in a mitote/maya state of waking consciousness.

Conversely, there are those who, no matter what the outward living circumstances might be, don't suffer from the ignorance that allows the misguided purpose of any claim to gain entry into their belief system to create the confusion of a growing mitote/maya state of waking unrest. They've been able to maintain the unfettered status of their free will. They can reflect a deeper understanding of the relational justice that holds together their understanding of the relational cause/effect interplay defining this dimensional reality. They step back mentally and think before they act. They can still find the "freedom to let their light shine."

Victor Frankle was a famous psychiatrist that survived the Holocaust in a German prison camp. Even under the horrendous conditions that imprisoned his human body, his free will remained free to give the wings of freedom to his human spirit to recognize the beauty even in the poor prison conditions he lived in. He even saw this love and beauty in the fish head floating in his bowl of fish soup.

Is the freedom that people seek really the freedom from being under the control of others? Is America only seen as a safe haven from outside oppression? Or, do people seek freedom from the suffering delivered at the hands of their own ignorance of the nature and purpose of our Source, coming from their misguidance during the vulnerable stages in the development of their belief system?

If you think about it on a deeper level, isn't America really a place of least outside resistance for an individual to openly untangle their personal web of ignorance?

We Group-Search for a Generic Brand of Freedom

Many people will fetter away their time vying for sanctuary through peer acceptance. Some might even think they're looking for freedom from themselves … from the way they are. Deep down inside, they're actually looking for freedom from what it is within themselves that blocks their being "who they really are."

Toltec shaman don Miguel Ruiz makes an observation about how individuals exercise their freedom before they get around to being what best suits their unique set of personal talents:

> The freedom we are looking for is the freedom to be ourselves,
> to express ourselves. But if we look at our lives we will see that
> most of the time we do things just to please others, just to be

accepted by others, rather than living our lives to please ourselves. That is what has happened to our freedom. And we see in
our society and all the societies around the world, that for every
thousand people, nine hundred and ninety-nine are completely
domesticated.

The worst part is that most of us are not even aware that we
are not free. There is something inside that whispers to us that
we are not free, but we do not understand what it is, and why we
are not free.[5]

There's something in the status quo they want to be free from, but they can't
tell what that is. Or maybe there's something from the status quo?

They're knowingly or unknowingly looking for freedom from what it is in
their thought process that causes them to do things that keeps their joy and happiness subordinate to what makes them and those around them suffer. They want
freedom from their ignorance about what it is that really makes their clocks tick.
They seek the freedom to develop the awareness to understand the human condition and not leave their behavior to the disposal of the mitote/maya bondage
they've somehow allowed to infect their present moment.

Clubs, churches, temples, or any sort of fellowship, brotherhood, or sisterhood
is made up of individuals knowingly or unknowingly looking for freedom from
the ignorance about what's allowing them to suffer the frustration and indecision
that plague their passing present moments. Most haven't yet consciously identified
finding and eliminating their ignorance that allows their present moment suffering as their primal problem.

Many are more comfortable being around other truth seekers, looking for this
freedom in the same way they are. They coagulate in groups with similar understandings of what the nature and intended purpose of the source of this reality
seems to be. Maybe some of these people just want to drag others into the same
pit of suffering they're in. There are a vast number of church congregations that
validate this observation.

Those with no answer find some calming patience in the fact that so many
fellow humans are likewise poised looking for direction. They just don't know the
difference or even consciously recognize their state of idleness. It seems like a normal day to them...quite natural.

Of course, all seems OK until their primal fear of the unknown resurfaces
when asked if they're afraid of dying. Maybe they think of death as being a state
of permanence, for eternity, an illusionary interpretation of reality that allows no
more change.

They'll behave the same way when together and adhere to ritualistically doing things that seemed to work for someone they might worship from the distant past. Most don't consciously know what this true freedom is they're longing to realize and will probably never find.

The Harley Davidson movement in the USA is a group that openly seeks life's truth while exhibiting nonattachment to the system. The group's logo, Harley, and the appropriate-looking clothes support a peaceful way for a group of like-thinking individuals to express their longing collectively through realizing a free-to-fly-in-the-wind freedom that looks upward, saying, "Here I am, open for the answer." This is not to say some of the group has not yet found it.

They're credited for having a "rebel" attitude...openly longing for what is not. Harley's 2009 spring attitude expressing the rebel attitude mixed in with the stirring USA economic crunch ran NYC ads saying, "Screw it, let's ride." One of their sayings was "We don't do fear." It's a safe bet that they have different definitions of fear.

There's an unspoken desire for freedom from the consequential trickle-down greed-generated stress from corporate USA's subliminal intentions and anything else that suggests a subversive threat to the American freedom to live free from outward oppression that hinders our pursuit of our dreams. Understanding our inner nature and purpose is a dream we all long for. It's part of the human condition.

3

What We Do
With Our Present Moment

We're always getting ready to live, but never living.
—Ralf Waldo Emerson

We Do What Humans Do

At the end of the first millennium, a prominent Buddhist monk, Atisha (982–1054), answered a Tibetan royalty request and with much difficulty was able to travel to Tibet to redefine the Tibetan Mahayana Buddhism that had been suppressed for over seventy years to help pacify the citizens. He left in Tibet his sixty-eight-verse interpretation of the enlightened Siddhartha Gautama's message on attaining enlightenment. His purpose was to provide guidance in attaining enlightenment to relieve the suffering inherent to ignorance-imposed cyclic existence.

At that time the position of the Dalai Lama was created solely to pass along a living account of Atisha's interpretation of the Buddha's message. This was to help preserve the authenticity of its intended meaning as things can get twisted from generation to generation. The fourteenth Dalai Lama is now serving that purpose.

Siddhartha's message is said to teach the pathway back to a state of mind kindled only by altruistic compassion. Atisha's message teaches that the way to the enlightenment about the origin of human suffering begins with a belief system embodied with compassion founded in altruism.

Geshe Sonam Rinchen offers in his book *Atisha's Lamp for the Path to Enlightenment* very interesting and insightful observations describing the human condition. *Atisha* categorizes waking human spiritual awareness into three levels of spiritual maturity. The groupings are tiered based on their relative level of conscious awareness of the truth of impermanence. Midwesterners, being the humans that they are, fall into these three categories.

14

Verse 2: "Understand there are three kinds of persons. Because of their small, middling and supreme capacities. I shall write clearly distinguishing their individual characteristics."

Verse 3: "Know that those who by whatever means seek for themselves no more than the pleasures of cyclic existence are persons of the least capacity."[7]

The rock-and-roll band Rush describes this second group of people who proudly admit to having this mind-set in their song "Live Now, Pay Later."

Verse 4: "Those who seek peace for themselves alone, turning away from worldly pleasures and avoiding destructive actions are said to be of middling capacity."

Verse 5: "Those who, through their personal suffering, truly want to end completely all the suffering of others are persons of supreme capacity."[8]

Mr. Rinchen comments on these three groups when he writes:

> Does everyone fit into one of the three categories? We all have the potential to do what Atisha describes, but most of us don't try because we are still completely involved in the concerns of this lifetime. Those of least capacity are divided into three kinds of people.
>
> Certain people in their quest for pleasure and happiness do many harmful things and may even gain pleasure from the use of deceit and violence. Others use nonviolent secular and spiritual means to accomplish happiness in this lifetime. Most of us are in pursuit of present happiness and fall into this category. Neither of these two kinds of people are authentic practitioners of the least capacity.
>
> Only someone who is concerned with the happiness of future lives and uses spiritual practices alone to accomplish this is a true practitioner of the least capacity. How can we arouse an interest in future lives and overcome our strong preoccupation with this one? Thinking about the preciousness of our human life and its impermanent nature counteracts our obsessive preoccupation with this life.[6]

Atisha's three groupings of human spiritual maturity also reflect an individual's conscious awareness of their need for spiritual development. He observes there being those of the highest level of spiritual ignorance or those of the smallest/least capacity that seek short-time pleasure with disregard for the consequences of their actions and are blindly numb to recognizing the suffering caused. It seems that individuals of the smallest/least capacity might consume their present moment in a struggle, trying to outsmart the basic behavioral guidelines of the Ten Commandments.

Individuals of the middling capacities perceive many things in ways that allow their imagined future enjoyment to be a temptation against their better behavior. The urgency the tempted experience for the taste of a low-fiber high-saturated-fat pepperoni pizza can still be just too much for an individual who's just had part of their large colon removed due to colon disease. Even though they've had the truth of the matter told to them several times, their lack of ability to see the truth that will set them free from suffering prevents them from appreciating the very avoidable harm this diet has on their aging body.

This shows a lack of ability to recognize and then equate in real-life terms what appears as an intellectually learned and understood biblical temptation into the actual sensual display of its present moment incarnation. People of this level of spiritual maturity will become gluttonized by food and become foodaholics while they refuse to sit at the same table with people they recognize as being alcoholics. There are truth seekers of the middling capacity seeking awareness who try to fashion their behaviors after a religious code. Most of these individuals will spend their entire life walking a crooked path as not to miss pillaging anything in their effort to find the answer they've not found yet answered using in any religious code. They try out new ideas and beliefs while their intellectual conception of "the straight and narrow" provides no shortcuts in the pathway they manage to piece together.

And there are those of the highest capacity that are aware of the truth about our Source's nature and intended purpose to initiate ongoing change. They live their lives in an effort to understand this truth on the sensual level, while devoted to compassionately helping relieve the suffering of others. They avoid attachment to things and ideas as they, to some degree, understand the ephemeral nature of our Source.

We Battle The Seven Deadly/ Cardinal Sins

Both the spiritually immature individual who can't quite grasp how many of their activities they view as bringing happiness are actually making them suffer and the individual of the highest spiritual capacity where altruistic compassion motivates everything they do, face the modern-day incarnations of the temptations to sin warned against in biblical times. With early society's reflection on the aftershock of suffering caused by certain human behavior, mankind's collective wisdom finally surfaced in that early day's social consciousness to condemn those behaviors to being classified as sinful.

The negative effects of their earlier behavioral manifestations were collectively recognized and morally outlawed. It's believed that their social taboo status was finally flameetched in stone as the Ten Commandments around the time of Moses.

Lust-gluttony-greed-sloth-wrath-envy-pride is the ten-syllable thought chain denoting behaviors that date clear back to the beginning of mankind that created much of the moral/ethical agitation that resonates yet today. This centipede of sin breaks down into seven short segments, each depicting age-old behavioral taboos. Their ancient lure has, like infectious viruses do, adapted to change.

The adaptive sorts of fleeting reactions they inspire in today's cause/effect reality define each of their modern-day presences. There are seven groupings or combinations of these sensual perception packages that are known today as the seven deadly sins or the seven cardinal sins.

The aftertaste of each of these sins resonates in an individual's present moment waking awareness while remaining unshakably affixed to their must-redo list. Once experienced, the lure and preoccupation with each is sometimes very hard to resist as individuals put up progressively less resistance to their repeating the behavior until it earns the status of being one of the fleeting reactionary habitual behaviors that makes up an individual's personal list of addictions.

Individuals become attached to the security they find in having this behavior being something they are used to doing. They're familiar with dealing with the cause/effect package the behavior brings. Even if their free will is strong enough to question the appropriateness of a behavior, their character probably doesn't have the courage to try other behavioral options.

These categories of sin are very much alive and evolving. When threatened by society's detection of their harmful nature, their lure has the ability to mutate into a derivative state that will continue to work against mankind's spiritual health. Their incarnations mutate to squeeze through any modern-day attempt at harnessing them to eliminate their destructive prowess.

They have the ability to evade being pinned down by any effective behavioral statute or mental antidote. Weeklong summer revivals directed straight into the bowels of their sinful temptation have proven ineffective in eliminating their true cause but effective at fulfilling the misunderstood passed-along ritualistic obligation to have more religious revivals.

Today's ministers or preachers will piece together a series of Bible verses to supplement with millennia-old authority the logic in their intellectually developed lectures, showing how the modern-day implications of the ever-evolving mutant versions of the seven deadly sins are still frowned on by God. The logic of the intellectual reasoning might make sense to an audience during the time of a lecturer's message and may receive many hallelujahs and promises of future conformity, but once the flock leaves the building and the fresh intellectual wisdom concedes its mental floor presence to considering the more pressing causes being shouted in their heads by each of the unrelated 1,000 voices of their personal mitote/maya, the preacher's string of intellectual logic is soon to be forgotten.

The source of the disruptive influence on mankind's ability to maintain ethical/moral standards has seeped undetected through the cracks while the Roman Catholics, in trying to keep the Ten Commandments current, update their list of modern taboos. The Pope issues updated lists of new-age sins defined only by the sinful behaviors. Their analysis misses how the new sins are mostly the mutated incarnations of the old-time biblical taboos.

The Roman Catholic Church's earthly link to God doesn't offer guidance on eliminating the ignorance that allows the sinful behaviors to uproot the cause of the temptation that leads to the listed sinful behaviors. The idea of directing proactive attention to stopping the ongoing process of the deadly sins' adaptive change seems obvious. Yet it seems that even the more detailed objectives based in behavior modification quickly become obsolete as time moves on. The tentacles of temptation mutate around and choke out any effective mental vaccine aimed at stopping their harmful effects on mankind's spiritual advancement.

These addictive behaviors help feed the parasitic internal guilt-inflicting judge and victim of self-blame as described by the Toltec shaman don Miguel Ruiz. The harm of the disruption caused to one's ability to control their mind in lieu of the mental distress caused by the counterproductive nature and residual effect of conceding to any of these temptations can further deaden or at least distance a sinner's conscious connection with their once-unfettered free will.

This spiritual advancement stutters on, trying to maintain moral/ethical standards. The religious train doesn't move on to self-training the thought control to become enlightened about what it is that mankind is so ignorant about that underlines all the suffering from the behaviors that the Ten Commandments outlaw.

To most, identifying and sizing up the actual real-time modern-day incarnations of the age-old seven deadly sins with only the mental pictures held of their intellectually stored descriptions is unlikely. The cognitive picture of the sandal-and-toga sins they sketched with their intellectual pencil seems somehow foreign and unassociated to their sensually recognized incarnations. Yet, the real-time appearances are the very same thing represented by those intellectually recognized religious maxims of long ago. The old descriptions don't size up to their present moment sensually realized incarnations.

Gluttony is one of the deadly sins. This word encompasses several variations of harmful eating profiles reflecting ulterior agendas for using food other than to provide healthy nutrition.

Saint Thomas Aquinas lists six ways to commit gluttony. They include eating too soon, eating too expensively, eating too much, eating too eagerly (burningly), eating too daintily (keenly), and eating wildly (boringly) (Internet, *Wikipedia*: Seven deadly sins).

In the Midwest, it seems like there's a race at each family dinner to see who can be the first one to lean back in their chair away from the table, undo their belt, and brag about how they just couldn't stop themselves from having the second or third helpings. Letting out one's belt after Thanksgiving Day or Christmas dinner to sleep off their overindulgence seems to be the body language showing one's appreciation for this American tradition. It's an accepted way to compliment those who prepared the meal in this northern part of the biscuits-and-gravy/breaded-tenderloin capital of the world.

Many mistake their pressing emotional or spiritual hunger for physical hunger. They will keep eating while not generating the wisdom that will enrich their waking consciousness with the emotional understandings that satisfy the spiritual hunger they long to satisfy. Others might try to satisfy this emotional hunger with endless shopping.

An individual with their present moment attention tied up in the involvement in any of these deadly sins is not actively devoting present moment intended purpose in pursuing a goal of becoming enlightened about what allows their suffering. An individual having no effectual soul-satisfying end in focus is easily weakened by harmful temptation.

Temptations from untested, unverified outside promises or claims to what the future might hold will overtake any belief system weakened by having no eye focused toward developing an envisioned effectual soul-satisfying end. This is suffering with no end in sight. This is endless suffering.

An individual's mitote/maya mental state of having 1,000 voices shouting their unrelated intentions all at once, trying to gain control of an individual's behavioral intentions, causes the individual great present moment mental unrest and suffering. They will in time somehow take action to organize and understand their present moment turmoil.

We Experiment for Perspective to Understand Our Journey

Mix a teenage dare to be cool with the unavoidable ongoing natural push for self-understanding and expect confused behavior trying to satisfy both. This socio-psycho recipe can create just the right flavor of adventure that draws many of today's youth into experimenting with today's Molotov cocktail of drugs and alcohol as they look for the common answer. They end up comparing their life perspective when viewed from different mental platforms to possibly triangulate in on a clearer answer to who they are.

Having a youth's physiological state altered by an outside chemical cocktail such as a few beers or a joint or a hit of LSD allows them to weigh the difference in how they feel or maybe to take note of how others react to an alteration of their normal persona. They get another perspective to help paint a more detailed picture of their inner perception of the only person they can never actually see from the outside...themselves.

It provides an opportunity to better understand themselves as they glance at the expression mirrored on an onlooking friend's face. They can weigh their perception of their altered presence against those from other times. Most don't realize this to be an underlying incentive for drug experimentation, but after years of reflection, this Midwesterner's experience says it was, at that time of life, an unrealized driving force.

To some, being cool includes being able to experience unusual states and still maintain the balance to function normally and remain in control. They'll try studying material for a class at school after getting high and compare it to the effectiveness of studying after drinking coffee or with no sleep.

Many try to bring clarity to their understanding of how or where they fit in, relative to socially established standards. They will partake "party" and then size up and compare their sensually defined high to the adjectives used in the descriptions seen in daily media exposure describing how you're supposed to feel under those circumstances.

They want to experience for their own sensual reference how it actually feels to have a 0.07 blood alcohol level. They want to know how their sensed feelings involving coordination and rationality size up to the MAD-influenced socially defined continuum of what's agreed on as being too drunk to drive.

In a way, they will know a bit more about who they are or at least how others might see and judge them to be and how those present moment feelings fit into their established definition of normal. In an odd way, it helps them to understand how they fit in.

Some will push it to the limit and then look back and compare what their affected states were like to times without the influence of the variant. They push it as far as they can, ideally not far enough to do any physical harm or get arrested.

Many find the wisdom through considering the examples of others who've not turned back to being drug-free of how the users' lives lack any real direction to guide them through the ongoing everyday change that they must face. With repeated decisions to do the drugs, their behavior soon develops into a fleeting reaction that requires no consideration.

Lacking a strong free will to consider and resist temptation and not having the mind control to find the mind/body harmony needed to inspire the insightful understanding of their actions will put many into the clutches of habitual reen-actment. This repeated behavior soon morphs into a habitual unplanned sensually triggered reaction that has an uncontrollable influence on the waking consciousness. It's become another of their addictions. They have formed another attachment to craving the temporary gratification of changing the status quo in hopes of stumbling across the answer to what causes their suffering.

We Craft Our Own "I Am"
to Calm a Mitote/Maya State of Mind

We do not see things as they are. We see things as we are.

—The Talmud

Everyone is gifted at birth with a unique combination of physical and mental abilities or talents that, with wholesome coordination, will culminate into each individual's distinctive form of genius. Everyone is born with the right tools, but most can't read the language the Source-given owner's manual is coded in to identify and use them. They have no direction or clear vision of their intended purpose or passion to inspire the unfolding of their potential...of letting their light shine.

As present moments pass by, individuals must try to organize and maintain a balanced state of mind. As today's youth emerge worldwide from their age of innocence, they tap into their mental collection of internalized beliefs and ideas that have conditioned their belief systems and craft their own personal designer version of "I am." If the individual has had no introduction to the truth about the nature and intended purpose of the ultimate reality and can't appreciate the wisdom of change, they piece or string together a unique self-representative collage of mental snapshots they will use to paint a picture in time of who they think they are or maybe who they want to be.

It's difficult to know what's influenced an individual's prior conditioning. Who really knows what religious leaders they've trusted, or could it be that one of their parents is an atomic scientist? Maybe they still cling to images from the movie *Moses,* they saw with Charlton Heston, when it came out back in the '60s. Maybe their last name is Darwin?

The individual will refer to their pieced-together package of views, beliefs, and to-be addictions and develop an ego-managed "I" or "me." They create and carry a visionary picture in time of "I" in their mental wallet, laminated in pride and proudly postured up against their perceived status of other individuals.

They will construct a self-image from the best of the fixed-in-time mental pictures they've snatched from the imagined continuity of their life. They create a materialistic profile of what might represent or best establish the characteristics of the sought-after illusionary free spirit they think they are or long to be.

They highlight what they see as the good traits in their profile while leaving out some of the others altogether. They see what they want to see reality as being, not what it really is.

It doesn't matter what nationality or religious sect an individual might be; they still have that feeling within that seems to rely on the existence of an "I" or "me." The natural drive to protect the part of the material world that each individual's body comprises is necessary and helps explain the self-protective tendencies an individual has. Still, most people don't see the person that will be here next year as being any different from who they are now.

An individual adapts their own personal ego to oversee and administer the illusionary kingdom of their waking consciousness. Their self-ego is the caretaker of their illusion, crafter and protector of their self-image.

We Become Attached to "I Am" and Anything Related

Most individuals identify their human body with its five sensual ports as something separate from its surroundings...as a special thing. Let's face it—our physical body is the Human Flesh Grand Central Station, where our sensual perceptions that we act and react to all originate. This cause/effect reality is constantly rearranging its furniture, and everyone's physical body is a part of that. People can't really see it happening, but it's a truth that if not understood and allowed for will produce a lifetime of suffering. Most people live their lives taking this primal truth for granted.

That's really big stuff to someone who does not see the interconnectedness of all things. When individuals look at things, because of the limits of human perception abilities, they can't see the constant intermingling of the tiny bits of coming and going energy that bind everything together. Things appear as different shapes and forms, so people perceive things as being disjoined, separate entities.

Those unaware of the consequences of not making the knowledge that things constantly exchange bits themselves and that nothing stays as it was the main tenet of their belief system become attached to their sensual port-bearing body as they imagine its ongoing seemingly independent continuity.

They fail to recognize their body for being the process of change that it truly is. It's true that it houses the spirit, and it's wise to protect it and keep it healthy. But it must be understood that it is an ongoing process of transformation, no more and no less.

The truth is that the human body is an individual's spirit's sensual connection that channels the sensations of the human experience on to be perceived by the human condition. It's where the physical awareness of the human condition and the mental perception of the human experience meet. It's the only real material connection an individual's spiritual awareness has to the materialistic world on the outside of their skin. It's the material classroom where a truth seeker comes to understand the state of change that typifies this reality as it continually manifests from within.

An individual's physical body makes available the sensual evidence to their perceptive mind that testifies to the existence of the other transforming objects and forms that make up this reality. Their body channels a sensual glimpse at the comprising coming and going particles of energy as the pulse of their manifestation passes through the sensual spectrum range that's perceivable by the human condition.

Individuals that have created their own ego-managed apparent reality centered on their illusionary "I am" will develop the same sort of attachment to anything or belief that helps establish and support the perceived authenticity of their "I am" pseudo reality. In an attempt to establish and manage some form of mental balance, they will also cling to this "I am" concept to anchor and shield them from the whirlwind of unanticipated ongoing change.

Many have been flash-blinded by a cultural backdrop or perceived safety net held together by some religious plan to salvation from eternal suffering. This outlook will serve as the foundation for their faith in untested, unverified theories that are blind to the nature of the impermanent rhythm of the cause/effect relationships that make up this reality.

They prioritize maintaining the continued unchallenged presence of any ego-sanctioned items and beliefs that shore up, support, and ensure the secured longevity and balance of their illusionary account of their apparent reality. An individual's adopted religious belief falls into this category. Its fundamental assertions are used to shore up the integrity and constitute the discriminating righteousness of their belief system. Whether or not true to this reality, the fundamental assertions shore up the believers' worldviews.

We Are Trapped Defending A Conditioned Empty Void

Our greatest pretenses are built up not to hide the evil and the ugly in us, but our emptiness. The hardest thing to hide is something that is not there.

—Eric Hoffer

When no understanding or feeling of familiarity is cultured regarding how the cause of something changes into its effect, a great feeling of emptiness fills the gap. This can happen when only taking somebody's unverified word for how a process works or a truth manifests its purpose. Whether the described relationship is true or false, the emptiness in knowingness exists, shaded by the feeling of uncertainty and doubt.

It's a void that robs short any understanding of the cycle of completion. It's a void that rules out developing the steadfast, gut-felt faith in how the entire cause/effect process comes and goes. This compromise plants the fertile seed for a lifetime of primal uncertainty. Assorted fears of the unknown and stemming addictions develop to best manage the resulting pain and suffering that fill an individual's lifespan of present moments.

As an individual goes through their days internalizing untested, unverified claims that explain different aspects of this reality, they distance themselves from the secure and comforting feeling realized in understanding the related process by sensually witnessing or experiencing each of its developmental phases.

Eventually, after young individuals are coaxed from the protection of their early-life innocence, many will want to hide this primal ignorance. Many try to posture their imagined special importance unopposed to make it appear that they have their life well under control. They want it to appear that they have the answer that completes the human dilemma of uncertainty. They choose to wear masks to cover up this emptiness.

Donna Bernadette Vigil summarizes well how individuals cope with a reality they don't understand. She clearly explains how people often wear masks to posture themselves into what they imagine to be a good life while we silently long for the answer to fill the emptiness of the void inside.

> You like every human being, become a master of the mask, but it is not the mask of sincerity or impeccability. It is whatever mask you believe will get you what you think you want. Ultimately you pay a price in life for wearing the masks. Learning to wear masks begins in childhood, through the domestication process. This is how children become such good manipulators. When you were a child, you realized that if you put on a certain mask, you could get what you wanted in life. Your mask may have been being cute, the good girl/boy, the funny child, the tough guy, or any number of other possibilities. You quickly learned which masks worked for you. As you grew into an adult, you learned to wear more and more masks and to become masterful at them.
>
> Saying that you are a great lover is one of the biggest masks in the Dream of the Planet. And sex, like relationships, is one of the biggest hooks. You may want to be lovers with someone desirable in the Dream and then walk away and say, "I not only had this special person, but I was the greatest lover they ever had." Another big mask is the mask of wealth. You may want to wear the mask that you are wealthy by driving an expensive car, living in an expensive house, or wearing designer clothes. These may be way above you budget, but you buy them just to look like you have money or are well off.
>
> You have so many masks that are part of your everyday life because the masks keep you from having to look at your true self.

Putting on a mask is as simple and routine as deciding which dress or suit you are going to wear that day. One of the most common masks is the one you wear around your friends. You decide every day whether you are sincere around them or whether you are going to be fake, putting on a mask so you will be liked and accepted. Not only children and high school kids do this.

You put on masks regardless of your church, your environment, or your culture. As an adult, you put on masks to get the greatest partner, to be looked up to by members of your culture or community, and to be accepted in whatever social circle you try to be in. You change masks like you're changing your clothes. You get so lost in the separation of yourself from your true nature that you never look at your soul. Meanwhile, you feel empty and sad inside, and are always searching for something to fill the emptiness.[9]

Individuals with a life purpose clouded by an illusionary explanation of our reality will continue to suffer the discomfort and unrest from misunderstanding the cause/effect dynamics of many situations. They struggle to find mental balance as they teeter in between deciding which of their self-created masks to wear in an effort to present the impression they feel they need to fit into each changing situation. On many occasions women will paint their face, and many men will select the necktie to best neutralize or exploit what uncertainty they fear they're going to face next.

They grasp unknowingly at things to gain anchor to stabilize the ongoing change they take for granted and don't understand. They get tangled up in the strings of time.

They clench to things and ideas that in this transforming reality don't really exist while standing unprepared to face each new unexpected present moment. They don't know that by not being wise to the natural laws imposed on the human condition inherent to this state of reality, they will always entertain an ongoing present moment struggle to explain and keep up with what just happened. They spend their time always looking back and not planning ahead.

They strive to somehow fit everything they perceive within the boundaries of their idea of "normal." They struggle to find inner peace with no real knowledge of what media to turn to or where to look to find the real-time incarnation of the primal truth that balances the scales of inner justice.

We Cope

There's a countless variety of coping methods people use to help them sedate their challenged free will as its intuitive nature shouts in objection to the many short-sided decisions that hold together the illusionary reality it must try to conform to. Coping skills become personal as they're honed to balance the differing shades of fear and uncertainty they originate from.

It's all too common that someone assumes something without investigating it or wrongly takes something personal. They suffer. Self-pity parties are all too common and wear many different masks.

When an individual's inner mitote/maya judge bangs the gavel of guilt, the inner victim's present moment consciousness takes on a thought-jamming interference pattern that leaves the individual sitting and staring into the distance, wandering in self-pity or locked up in self-doubt, pondering over what's wrong with them. They might be thinking "Poor me" or maybe seeing themselves as a bad, defective, and lonely human being.

They let opportunities to express the uncensored questions that accompany childlike curiosities pass them by. Their "I am"-centered mental block causes them to misunderstand their own reality as well as miss out on showing sincere interest in asking about and understanding the reality of other people. They probably have much trouble when trying to spell compassion.

In any life illusion, to better suit the targeted agendas and to appease any fear-based biases, many individuals will regularly change hats. This can help them satisfy the imagined criteria they need to feel somewhat included.

There can be conflicting protocol they face coming from the different masks they wear. There's the politically right thing to do and the politically wrong thing to do with each mask application in their imaginary apparent reality. This imagined protocol conflict creates yet another ever-present cause of stress in managing conjoined social lives.

How can someone with a waking grasp on reality that's wrapped up in illusion really identify with and understand the real pain another is going through? They're on no path to understanding the nature of their own suffering or the source of its true cause.

The mental states of many are so fogged up by confusion and uncertainty that they can discern no scale to distinguish what's wholesome and unwholesome within their own reality. They're so backed up by their own indecision and fear that they remain lost and guarded on the inside.

They can't begin to put themselves in another's position to consider what it's like looking out from inside the other person's decision-making process. They don't know where to begin to muster up the compassion to empathize with another person's situation. They can't walk in another's shoes until they can tie and untie their own.

Wearing an illusory mask to project the impression that says they truly care misrepresents their true internal state that feels no real connection or concern.

Their pretended mask of compassion can cover up their inner feeling that they're just glad the misfortune didn't happen to them. Secretly they feel content that there's no way their secret malintent can be discovered as long as they wear their false pretense mask of concern while apathetically hiding behind the mask's pair of concerned eyes.

Some individuals become "masters of the illusionary twist" (justified white lie). They're masters of manipulation. They try to manipulate things to happen as things should according to their vision of what reality apparently should be. They have different masks to slip on when matters slip into a different illusionary perception of present moment.

Accounts of real events are tailored to fit into the "spin" of their apparent reality. They adjust their illusionary interpretation of what reality apparently is to allow the undeniably existing yet unexplainable to fit. The cause/effect relationships are deciphered and diluted by their needed illusionary twists in an attempt to fit the square peg of the events' causes as they happened into a description of the effects that fill the round hole of their imagination, keeping their illusionary castle's fragile framework from crumbling. They just want to make the pieces fit as to not endanger upsetting their imagined base for what supports their misconception of how things really should be.

They're foolishly fearful of the possibility of others' accusatory interpretations of their behavior or possibly the divulgence of their imagined guilt about something. Maybe they're fearful of having their uncool, unhip naivety exposed and revealed by someone's objective account of the same social interactions.

Unknowingly, their self-depreciation has become habitual. It's become a signature of their presence. Is it possible that in later years, their handcuffed free will that's been muted most their life will give up and package up the internal struggle and hand their black-and-white view of the present moment reality of their human experience over to dementia to oversee and manage?

In all the present moment confusion of trying to keep their illusion afloat, their free will never manages to develop an eye that's searching for the truth explaining their ignorance that allows their suffering from the ongoing unrest. They never perform the due diligence to figure out the primal truth that explains their mess. Many never learn that option even exists. They just continue to fretter away their priceless present moments, blindly hoping for the answer to sometime float to the top and find them as they continue to suffer. At the heart of their pain is their blindness to the path to the freedom from their ignorance they intuitively know exists.

They deepen and widen the protective mote surrounding their illusionary self-ego castle, built to fortify and preserve their illusionary apparent reality they hide themselves within, all alone, silently waiting to be united with the answer that will "save" them from the unexplained discomfort and frustration they find in the present moment of the life they have to live. They unknowingly wait for the truth resting in their deeper consciousness they somehow know exists to find them and save them.

The truth describing the nature and intended purpose of our Source emanates from every bit of their being. It emanates from all, free to the asking. It radiates a subtle tone and code most don't yet hear, and even if they did, they can't recognize it for what it really is and understand it.

In the back of their mind, they want the answer to find them while they wait day by day, turning the pages of undefined change, hoping the next page will spell out the answer. They just don't know how to recognize the sensual frequency to tune into, to hear broadcasted our Source's ongoing ever-present real-time life pulse.

In the Midwest USA, it's common to label somebody who one might fail to make a connection with as being a snob or say they're stuck up. The missed-out communication can be taken personally. Things get assumed from unspoken exchanges.

It could be that much human suffering comes when an individual assumes something without investigating it and then taking their assumptions personally. It could be that they have a fear-based inability to just open up and speak to strangers that brought about these misunderstood and missed opportunities of communication.

Even though the individual may be king or queen of their own illusionary castle, they can feel lonely and lost, unprepared and socially naked in many types of open engagements. They're not aware of or able to consciously find joy in the common thread of life that all share.

One justification cop-out that can help secure mental balance in the wake of the unexplainable unguarded silence from not knowing what to say to someone and feeling awkwardly quiet is where the tongue-tied individual claims spiritual superiority by thinking of the stranger as being a "sinner," someone they probably shouldn't associate with anyway. They stand pretty sure that the individual is not a member of their unique strain of Christianity, as very few are, that are going to heaven. They feel they should pity their lost soul.

The illusionary self-supporting ego reminds of how extensive their biblical knowledge is and the depths of their godly wisdom. They think how they're above the other individual's sinful lifestyle and write communication off as they poke their nose back up in the air of their illusion and walk briskly away, only to react the same way again as soon as a similar fainthearted situation arises.

A well-known version of this persona is the prima donna, royalty in their own lonely castle. When stressed by a confrontation and while lacking an unfettered free will to evaluate the social situation with a balanced detached awareness, like during many prior similar confrontations, the background fear of the unknown and doubt that lines their belief system shadows the likelihood of there being any worthwhile social interaction. They forget the importance of listening with an unbiased, curious, investigative open mind to what's happening in real-time or of maybe walking in the other person's shoes. They check out and drift back to an earlier time in their life where in their illusionary reality they had their fifteen minutes of fame. This re-strengthens their egotistical bliss-hiss.

When lacking in the compassion needed to venture into the life experience of others, any conversation made will be on the safe side. It will be full of non-specific questions or questions with known answers. This will help minimize the air that's full of the fear of uncertainty that can come with silence.

Much of their behavior is the product of fleeting reactions signing off on intentions that march to the drums of faulty prior conditioning. Maybe this attitude began "once bitten, twice shy." Some event scared them. They continue to suffer in an ongoing ever-changing emotional drama set in the illusionary fixed-in-time infrastructure of an imagined apparent reality.

The more times this avoidance is repeated, the tighter becomes the noose that's choking out what was at a younger age their unfettered free will that operated in a present moment reality where situations were met with equanimity and dispassionate consideration. The likelihood of unraveling the mental mess becomes more remote with the repetition of each occurrence.

Then again, maybe the individual who's judging another to be a snob, might just be expecting all people to notice and give recognition to their special "I am" when there's really no worthwhile topic to give attention to. Maybe their insecurity requires that they're recognized by others to establish their value...a value based on what they're not sure. Maybe they think others owe them something.

There are many who adopt a set of fundamental beliefs about something they don't understand well enough to discuss and become more comfortable and familiar with the cruxes that establish the premise of the claim being made that the fundamental rules apply to. They will find refuge behind this fundamentalist shield and become emotionally inaccessible to those around them.

We Shop Till We Drop...Feeding Emotional Hunger

Many just don't feel comfortable living in their own skin. Maybe there's comforting refuge found inside a new outfit that mimics the shell a favorite movie star lives in.

Many shop for the unknown item that will in some way bring us a bit closer to being complete. Either way, anyway, as humans, we find some contentment in just satisfying short-term gratification itself, regardless of how or with what. When judging by the complete variety of material possessions that never get used, it becomes self-evident how many Midwesterners spend their time acquiring things just to acquire things. With the 1,000 unrelated mitote/maya voices in their head shouting out the things they want that point to no common end, it's a confusing and expensive job satisfying them all.

And who's to say, maybe one of the newly acquired things will help satisfy that ever-prodding, longed-for answer explaining how the human condition fits into the human experience in the informative detail and direction that religious claims are unable to deliver that won't keep listeners guessing or assuming or reading between the lines in hopes of finding meaning. This is a natural behavior, in the healing sense, that a truth seeker's deeper consciousness waits ready to link up its inborn awareness and understanding of the nature and purpose of our Source with their waking consciousness.

Shopping sprees are common occurrences. "Shop till you drop" is a familiar Midwestern chant. Just walking through the malls looking with nothing in mind to buy is a common way many spend time. It helps keep an individual's subconscious want for a revealing change in the status quo satisfied. The shopper has it in their power to buy most everything they pass and ponder. It wouldn't be the first time they only paid the minimum monthly payment due.

In a way, they have perceived control over the unavoidable ongoing change that confronts them as they consider the material presence of a few of their mitote/maya endless wants. What new item might bring them closer to finding their undefined Shangri-La?

The only real need for the continual buying of want items on a national scale is that this behavior is what funds capitalism. The media manipulation of public intention is best described as being horrific in between Thanksgiving Black Friday through Christmas. The comparison of the expected yearly sales to those in the past is a regular part of any news broadcast and the subject of special programs. People testify how they rob Peter to pay Paul to find money to buy more gifts.

Out of ignorance we gratify the inborn human need to know the truth about the human condition, with satisfying the short-term wants of the 1,000 mitote/maya voices. This occupies the passing time of many individuals' lives. We attempt to quiet the internal unrest of our unique, one-of-akind mitote/maya state of illusion. Our longing for change from the status quo where we don't know the answer is veiled by our naivety. Its real-time presence is met by our lack of training in how to understand and have control of our minds as the unchanging flow of ever-changing real-time present moments flows by.

In our waking consciousness we have a primal craving for the awareness and understanding of this ongoing constant change whose significance goes unrecognized. Our Source's living presence goes undocumented. For most, it passes by unnoticed. All humans have a primal spiritual hunger to know what our Source's purpose is...what our purpose is. We have an inborn longing to know how to align the two. We need to know how to find the harmony to let them flow together, as ancient teachers have spoken of and a few have taught.

How can endless shopping to satisfy an endless array of up-popping wants begin to satisfy an individual's emotional hunger that Dr. Deepak Chopra has classified to include love, social connection, purpose, and balance?

What are those that love to shop really shopping for? Many admittingly say they just like to go looking with nothing in mind. Are they trying to settle that longing of the human condition to know where they're from, who they are, and who's in control of where they're going?

We Wander Through Real-Time Led By Our Ego

The greater majority of those living in the Midwest wander distracted through each passing present moment trying to fortify any fragile claims they've internalized over the years to how reality works and that support their unique perception of their "I am." As an individual's self-image inflates, it floats them into an illusionary dream world that's highly sensitive and emotion-driven. With time, it becomes more distant and harder to defend.

Individuals tightly adhere to their conditioned idea of what they think reality apparently seems to be. They avoid that which is in conflict with their views and are drawn to things similar.

This self-made illusionary apparent reality can consume the individual's waking consciousness. There's a part of their conscious mind dedicated to defending and preserving this imagined entity, and that's where their ego resides. It's the prison in which their ego confines and limits the expression of their inborn passion.

While an individual is lost in and blinded by their own adopted version of an apparent reality, in their thinking they will mismatch and confuse the real effects felt in their life with dreamed up illusionary causes. They will have unrealistic expectations for unrealistic effects or results they mistakenly attach to real non-causes. The intrapersonal misguided misunderstandings "caused" by this conflicting cause/ effect mismatching, confusion, or inability to understand the causation/ correlation aspects of cause/effect relationships have the "effect" of much suffering. The consciously unaware have no direction, no active plan of pursuit to lead them to the truth of ongoing change and away from the suffering its ignorance allows. They have no soul-felt destination to spend their present moments finding direction to.

This waking state unwise to the misunderstandings associated with illusionary expectations is at the root of the over 50 percent divorce rate in the USA. It's the misjudged expectations, where illusion and reality don't match up, that start the divorce process. Partners get frustrated and disappointed when their illusionary expectations of what a partner should or shouldn't do or be don't match up to what they actually see their partner as being or doing in real-time. After attempting to look deeper and seek counsel, many will sign their divorce decree. They will still have no waking recognition of the mismatched realities for them to then find the insightful words to describe the perceived disappointment while forging the courage to present those feelings while waving the white flag of honesty to their partner.

Wearing tunnel-vision blinders, "I am" will be defended and fed a steady diet of things to sustain its illusionary strength. The manager ego will ensure that their carefully constructed illusion will stand tall and at the front of the line with others of the most important and always-correct egoguarded dreams in the universe of illusionary worldviews.

Many individuals become obsessed with proving their views as being right and others' as being wrong. This trait is honed from our acquired skill of competing at a younger age.

The ego will make sure the body of "I am" will always have the trendiest of food, clothing, car, and house and be seen among the most prominent of people with the highest of taste. If any of these things fall short of expectations, it's up to caretaker ego to at least make it seem otherwise to others. In this image-obsessed society, many try to develop a self-image that will please everyone.

Donna Bernadette Vigil voices her understanding about belief systems tied up in illusion:

> The belief systems of the Dream of the Planet teach you that there are certain things that mean you have a "good" life. You may carry these beliefs in the form of internalized expectations and desires, such as "I want to have the most beautiful house, with a pretty white fence; my husband is going to be so perfect; I will have beautiful children and they will eat white fluffy bread."[10]

It's common to see someone park their new car at the back of the parking lot. They don't want someone else's car door to take a chip out of their TV-instilled image of them driving that four-wheel-drive SUV some sunny afternoon from some off-road location that looked so cool. The new vehicle will be parked there most of the day as they put in hours at their second job needed to make the monthly payments.

It's a fact that an individual's physical body's the only material thing that their soul/mind has to take reference from that share and relate to the actual unalterable pulsating beat of the universe. As individuals become attached to the "I am" illusion of material permanence, they build a world around it and protect it to all ends, from the barbs that threaten it, both physically and in conversation. It's a fact that the body is the only material connection that our souls/minds have to support the actual existence of the material world where their human condition does the dance of the transforming human existence.

During the time of an individual's present moment ego dominance, their ego-free deeper consciousness will sit back, free will handcuffed and gagged, wanting the Sourceinstalled inner-born truth to find its way up through all the misguided prior conditioning to surface to become clear to the individual's ego manager of the intentions of their waking consciousness. They want to find the inner body/mind harmony to have balance between their human condition and their human experience. It's the harmony that will enable their self-awareness to surface to undo their ignorance that allows their preoccupation with their addictions and mitote/maya unrest.

People don't realize how their ego-in-charge fetters away all of their present moment time and energy while saddled to various addictions. They suffer the resulting unrest. They will unknowingly wait for the longed-for answer to appear. Yet, they have not a clue as to what the answer's real-time present moment recognizable characteristics might be. They're not quite sure what the right question is. Yet, they know it's there, somewhere.

Who really knows what the sign from above will be like? There are many accounts of seeing something sent from God. But, doesn't it seem like there should be an ongoing sign that's available for anyone to see at anytime, a marquee of sorts, easy to find? That's got to be the best way to bring in believers. Midwesterners have no idea how to recognize our Source's nature and intended purpose as it continually manifests in today's passing present moment.

They really have no idea what's fueling their drive or where nature's unavoidable, unalterable ongoing change will take them. By not being alert to its nature, they're not at all wise to its presence. They spend their present moments doing the ego dance, head tilted back, touching their nose, trying to walk a toe-to-toe straight line, drunk with imagined self-importance while their internal judge slams down its gavel, interrupting any sense of mental balance with lightning bolts of guilt.

Individuals are drained of their energy when reacting to all the misunderstood forces of change they posture themselves up against daily. They spend much of their day pumping their life energy into supporting the illusions they've pledged their allegiance to. They have just enough life left in them to survive each day.

When not alert to our Source's nature, individuals are not at all wise to what their own nature is. They don't consciously recognize that they are also no more than a process of ongoing change. They see themselves day by day as the same unchanging entity. As something separate from the whole, their apparent reality can be very lonely in its wet blanket of falseness.

Many have a dice-rolling, hope-based, knee-shaking blind faith that their illusion is the way. They're among the unaware that have a belief system that's tolerant to the perception of things and beliefs with a nature that denies or doesn't address the ongoing change of our multidimensional time fueled cause/effect reality. Their worldview condones the existence of things and ideas that host an illusionary nature of permanence that allows them something imaginary thing to become attached to.

They hope this will bring some sort of balance and order to their unsettling mitote/maya state of mind. The different theories, ideas, and beliefs they've allowed into their belief system will keep them awake at night as the different claims internally argue the unverified logic of their unrelated intended purposes one against the other as they shout out all at once the stories of their unrelated wants and desires.

Is an individual's initial first-glance awareness when meeting up with someone, devoted to trying to perceive what the acquaintance might think of them? Is their initial curiosity centered on validating their perceived social or situational acceptability in the eyes of others? Is their conscious attention focused on "what they think of my hairstyle or makeup?" Or conversely, does the intent of an altruistically-born purpose cut right into their doing something not reflecting their ego's wants, that's compassionately targeting someone else's situation? A switch from using the ego as the platform to tender present moment awareness to one that's lined with altruistic intent and conveyed with a compassionate purpose, an individual can find the guidance to change the nature of their mind.

We Always Have an Eye Open for the Better Way

In Midwestern USA, it really doesn't matter how devout a citizen says they are to a religious or spiritual discipline. It doesn't matter in what direction their religious affiliations or spiritual tendencies might appear to point. Still, they will skim through a magazine or web page article, listen to a TV special, or maybe tune into a radio station featuring what they suspect might give rise to or better highlight the boundaries defining a more grounded answer to their uncertainty-prompted primal question in search of wholeness and balance. They unwittingly seek a more conclusive understanding of exactly how and where in time their human condition and human experience intersect. They long to find it and take refuge in its heavenly peace.

In guarded curiosity, they might lower their defenses during a coffee shop conversation with their most trusted of friends and let their dialogue venture into their newest theory of what life's all about. They might give thought-out personal justification for whether or not they want to be cremated. They might even wager their best-friend credentials against confidentiality when opening up to spout off about noted behaviors that just don't make sense within the local congregation of their chosen religion...like if their pastor might not have a hidden agenda involving their church's altar boys.

Could it be that they're just not able to consciously realize the nature of this latent deep-down ageless question well enough to put it into words? They cannot recognize and associate their intellectual concepts of the mentally sketched spiritual markers drawn from Bible-found descriptions relating to ancient times with their present moment incarnations of those same spiritual signposts when they appear as part of their present moment sensual dialogue.

For the truth seeker focused on defining and undoing their ignorance that allows their real-time suffering caused by their mitote/maya state that dominates their mental status quo, the bare-bones explanation of "when, what, where, why, and how" lies dormant just a primal link away from their conscious awareness. This rusty link can be recharged to unlock the inborn answer vault in their deeper consciousness to satisfy the primal human longing to consciously recognize and associate the modern-day presence of the age-old religious maxims in their real-time present moment sensual incarnations.

We Pillage and Quick-Scan Through Life Looking for the Answer

The imbalance brought on by an individual's mitote/ maya mental state silently prods them into actively hunting for the antidote to their suffering...whether they know it or not. Most people think the answer to their lack of happiness is lurking somewhere on the outside of their sensual presence.

They stand unfulfilled and lost with no alternative but to find ways to hide or disguise their emptiness and ongoing lack of direction and purpose and their basic internalized fear of the unknown. They have built-up frustration, uncertainty and doubt of what if anything can really explain or get to the root of the anxiety and indecision that shadows and mutes their free will's wholesome participation in their present moment.

While in search of the path leading to this answer, the direction of the truth seeker's inner drive is demonstrated in their daily pillaging of the endless wants, desires and ideas of the 1,000 talking heads of their mitote/maya infected belief system. An ungrounded individual will pillage through many unneeded and unfounded activities hoping to stumble across the key somewhere in their status quo where the antidote to the cause of their suffering stands clear. Or, maybe they'll come across something that will better define the question that keeps pushing them along?

This personal need for a sufferer to settle their mitote/ maya state of mental unrest nudges what's left of their ailing free will into scanning each newly acquired thing or belief for the undefined feel of that unknown "answer" that will put a stop to the longing. The US culture has created a pillar of social belonging defined by a clique-relative minimum quota of new things to buy. It helps finance capitalism. It helps disguise the primal human attachment to the inborn human addiction of gaining gratification from craving more gratification by mislabeling it as being normal behavior in this culture.

Daily behavior in Midwestern USA is geared to satisfy our society's addiction to craving the gratification found in mere craving itself. The strong social message of how using credit is a good thing and how advertisers push for the sale of items people don't need perpetuate and shield its causing allure. The more neat things someone owns, the more money they make, the bigger their house is, the more refined the reputation of their private country club is, the more important and powerful they are, the more guarded and safe their ego feels. Just like their role models, individuals stay suspended in their illusion, free will numb and spinning.

Individuals are unable to satisfy their addiction to constant craving...the longing for what is not that will provide what is missing from what is. This state of dissatisfaction with the status quo is deeply infused into the area's behavior. Until the individual is aware of what's going on within the anatomy of their belief system, this motive manipulates the decree of each behavioral intention coming from their belief system to involve trying out something of new form, shape or a new idea or belief and to continue searching on.

Their unfamiliar constantly unfolding "becoming" nature continues to manifest itself in them, as they become a desperate pillager searching through one day's new things and ideas to the next. They hope to stumble across the answer they subconsciously crave that will calm their unfounded thought riddled mitote/maya belief system.

Should the longed-for undefined inner satisfaction of the unknown answer not become apparent...just pop out, be sensed or detected by the individual during the fun they have using the new thing or idea? The individual subconsciously deduces that the new toy or idea does not have the answer to the question they're not even sure of. They get tired and bored with it. The individual will keep the item in their Museum of Wants for that possible, yet totally unscheduled future use at which time the longed-for answer might reveal itself. Or, who's to say, maybe they'll keep it because maybe it'll satisfy a want they haven't even came across yet, that they might have sometime.

There's the latent hope they will stumble across the answer the next time they use it. This answer would allow them to see and understand their addiction(s) and would be the thing to end their uncontrolled longing for what is not and to explain and give them satisfaction with what is.

We Talk Sports

A deeply felt desire of the human condition is to be wise to the relational savvy derived from the interplay between the factors of the cause/effect change that defines our reality. Understanding the truth that details life transformation is literally built into the human condition. We are what the truth is. Manifestation of the truth is what we are. Its truth just can't find the right words to verbally express itself. The truth uses the sensual media to tell its story.

Many sports fans will channel that universal human passion to develop insight inspired wisdom into an insightfilled analysis of the sports events they watch. The goal of their conversation is to show how they can make perfect strategic sense of the factors and the rules that comprise the sport. They'll analyze the interplay between the players, the team game plans and even the weather to exercise and maybe show off their inborn ability to recognize, analyze and decode wisdom from something in this reality.

Sports related topics are safe conversation for those who can't relate to topics that engage and describe topics more closely related to the facets of the nature and intended purpose of the human condition and of our Source. They might have to bare their soul or let their guard down.

Sports related topics are safe in situations where society's deemed it unwise to discuss politics or religion or when getting to better understand another individual's not a priority. Sports related topics are good for those uncomfortable about not having anything more life-relevant to discuss.

4

We Seek Direction

The only thing worse than being blind is having sight but no vision.
—Helen Keller

We Long for Mental Balance

The ever-passing present moment brings to every human being an ongoing assortment of new things to evaluate and manage. This ever-fresh array of sensual stimulation that weaves together a person's life experience has to be emotionally perceived and processed. The effect of unbound change is too vast for the guidelines and statutes that society tries to collar it with. Intentions and expectations miss their mark.

Individuals have to deal with this living transforming reality if they wish to be alive. Everyone manages what's inside their head, themselves. They live in their thoughts. Many can't process unexpected change. It comes at them too quickly. They suffer.

While becoming consciously aware of how life's perceived lows can actually define a living hell of biblical proportions, an individual recognizes that it's really the ongoing pinprick of present moment frustration and unrest that hosts their frame of mind they recognize as suffering. To maintain mental peace, they'll try to somehow put to order their tangled worldview.

Their intuition tells them to gain a sense of balance. They'll try to establish a sense of priority amid the misunderstood relationships among the ever-changing jungle of conceived forms, objects and unrelated ideas and beliefs that have come to populate, stimulate and give character to their emerging, unique and too often threatened worldview. Those wanting to overcome the uncertainty of the unknown will eventually grab for answers by trying to toss a controlling lasso of sorts around the undefined boundaries of their preconditioned belief system. To organize and give controlling order to their unrest, they might attempt a mental roundup of their unfounded beliefs and ideas coming from the unrelated intended

purposes of the unverified claims they have internalized and stored in their belief systems. They might draw an intellectual picture that explains their impression of reality that becomes apparent to their waking consciousness that ripens from their current level of understanding. Its creation is left open to the vast range of
undefined possibilities of their imagination.

They might unknowingly fear the myths they've heard describing the bigger picture or that their chosen god might resemble a monster guarding some vision of hell. Or maybe their vision of the bigger picture will have the temperament of an angelic savior sitting on a cloud...or whatever suits the need of the mood they're in or maybe the mood of the particular unrelated voice from their unique mitote/maya that has the cognitive stage at the moment in their mental theater.

We Use Intellectual Hues to Color Spiritual Worldview on Sensual Canvas

Most Hoosiers are conditioned from early childhood to believe there's a god outside their body that created them, watches over them, and in return for complete unquestioning obedience, will provide an eternal paradise after death. They're taught that if they ask this god for forgiveness and promise their soul to Jesus and live their life up to Ten Commandments standards they can spend eternity in this paradise, free from all suffering.

If they internalize Christianity's unverified claim about the truth of these biblical teachings, chances are that the individual's actual present moment recognition of the spiritual events of the intellectually sketched promised reality will become lost in or short circuited during any cognitive-to-sensual translation when the real-time living incarnations of these intellectually coded biblical markers are actually displayed and coded sensually in the passing present moment. Chances are the incarnations will slide by totally unnoticed.

Their understanding, verification and internalization of the religion's claim, the description of its cast members and their characteristics eventually become the religious maxims this individual visualizes when the thought of what they consider as spirituality comes up. This entire religious regime is all communicated and remembered intellectually. It's remembered intellectually in the outer part of the brain and later accessed using an intellectual card catalog. In this sense, it's always held at a distance from practical application and sensual association when the real thing actually enters their present moment sensually recognized reality.

What's sensually relayed during actual occurrence doesn't match up with what's been intellectually depicted. The intellectual depiction should occur at the same time the sensual signal is being felt or the two will roam disconnected. The intellectual conceptual understanding will remain distant and have no sensual anchor in their transforming human experience.

An individual takes this intellectually gathered information and pieces together their own unique intellectually configured image of what the promise and promise maker are. This configuration takes on the unique form of their own unverified cognitive illusion or cognitively painted picture of sorts.

While wakingly trying to find spiritual relevance in the intellectual's retained picture of reality, the individual cannot recognize the true spiritual signposts as they happen to their human condition in the passing of the sensual reality, throughout the present moment of their human experience. They miss finding the sensual pathway to understanding the ignorance about their human condition that allows their suffering.

When a spiritual event is perceived in real-time sensual dialogue, its true significance passes by unnoticed as they have a mentally preserved rendition that they have their spiritual eye expectations open for that's written in intellectual ink. They're watching for spiritual signposts that appear as once described in a King James versed intellectual dialogue. They have no direction to seek the wisdom and ways of impermanence and this prevents them from maturing in a spiritual sense.

They hang stiff to the flow of change that is continually banging up against their present moment. It's in the wind of present moment change that their spiritual reality waves at them...unrecognized. They suffer.

We Try Blind Faith Shortcuts to Sooth Mental Woes

We take sources at their word and internalize too many things without first verifying their living truth. We blindly believe what we're told without first better understanding the factors involved in making something true.

Without guidance in recognizing what real-time spiritual markers are and what they mean, individuals remain lost in confusion and fear. Many choose to blindly leap into the promising arms of a heavenly god whose presupposed power has become legendary to their culture, for centuries now. But still, it's their choice.

From lack of having any vision or direction, many individuals decide to adopt their society's age-old mass-serving template to organize their personal reality. It comes in the organizational form common to a religion. This public program comes offered through an unverifiable and untestable claim describing the nature and intended purpose of our Source being to provide a future paradise free from suffering. It doesn't address how a believer can become enlightened in this lifetime about the cause of their suffering to unlock the compassion, joy and happiness that exists in this present moment reality that they perceive all their suffering in and are promised future freedom from.

The religion claims rights to being that source of life. Its dialogue describes what behaviors are needed to gain the Source's exoneration from a sin they were born with. The actualization of the religion's promised protection from suffering requires the believer's blind faith.

With no better options available, this choice does give some form of perceived security to the individual while they pillage through life's material objects, ideas and beliefs, unknowingly in search of a better answer. It does offer a stenciled-in rank and file answer to help organize and establish priority among the mind-revolving subjects of their cognitive unrest until they get the proper guidance or find the ability to take it upon themselves to recognize suffering for what it really is, find its cause and how to undo their lack awareness of its conscious understanding.

The time-gathered influence of the intellectually centered power of religious theology has managed to overcome the cause/effect message of real-time sensual feedback. The truth attached to sensual feedback has taken a back seat. Religious theology has accumulated the collective power to tell the story of what reality is... regardless of the story told by sensual feedback.

Sigmund Freud addresses this paradox in his writings on monotheistic religion:

> Among the precepts of Mosaic religion is one that has more significance than is at first obvious. It is the prohibition against making an image of God, which means the compulsion to worship an invisible God. I surmise that in this point Moses had surpassed the Aton religion in strictness. Perhaps he meant to be consistent; his God was to have neither a name nor a countenance. The prohibition was perhaps a fresh precaution against magic malpractices. If this prohibition was accepted, however, it was bound to exercise a profound influence. For it signified subordinating sense perception to an abstract idea; it was a triumph of spirituality over the senses; more precisely, instinctually renouncing the satisfaction of an urge derived from an instinct, accompanied by its psychologically necessary consequences.[11]

Other members of the animal kingdom act mostly on instinct. What a human has mere intellectual opinion of can often overrule the truth of what they've sensually been exposed to. Their sensual understanding of the truth in a cause/effect exchange outcome can be overridden by what they've heard elsewhere and believed, blind to any experiential validation. They suffer the consequences when the expected causes and expected effects don't line up.

Many boldly take pride in proclaiming how they'd mustered up enough blind faith confidence to bet their soul's eternity on the soul management plan of their favorite religious fraternal order. Many will then call it their duty to ridicule or even sacrifice the character or lives of others in its name.

Maybe it's from their want for the promised protection from the soul-saving promisor or maybe from their angst over the alternative fire and brimstone if they dare to call his bluff that they'll try on a quickset faith. They blindly leap over their free will's First Amendment right-protected inborn responsibility of self-preservation to willingly internalize the suggested nature of the alleged Source and the ventured heavenly claim of his soul-saving promise.

Often, it's pressure from peers, friends and family that will coax many prebelievers into giving unearned trust to the living realness of a messenger's account of what a soul-saving messiah had allegedly made known to the world 2,000-plus years ago. The claim's only verification flag planted in this present moment reality is in the believer's scripture-sketched, ego-embellished mental incarnation of a god figure and his promised after-death, post-redemption day, suffering-free state of reality for those that adhere to his commands or the fire and brimstone after-death hell for those who don't.

Many people are swept up in the social current of modern-day fundamental interests. Many new believers become assured by the mass number acceptance of how fundamentally absolute the unverified claim to a future paradise and everlasting salvation from suffering must be.

How could all those people be wrong? And if it doesn't work, really it can't be all that bad because look how many people will be in same boat to divide the "wrong" between. An unspoken feeling of camaraderie helps seal the deal. But really...let's face it...we're born alone and we die alone. We all really do go through the same processing process after death, regardless of how some choose to emphasize how only their religion's brothers and sisters will go to the promised paradise that they've had never had any sensual association with.

In the Midwest, the local culture's religious template is the prominent most popular way for lost or cognitively unsettled individuals to organize their perceived reality of misunderstood cause/effect relationships that ongoing change confronts them with each passing present moment. The believer can find a group of individuals using the same religious template to meet in hope of better understanding their confusing perception of ongoing change. They can hover together in wait for direction in securing the inner peace that unknowingly waits internally gagged in a subtle region of their deeper consciousness, just an insight away. In this state of denial, many mistakenly wait their entire lifetime, silently hoping that it will somehow find them.

We Find Comfort in Fundamentalist Boundaries

With a worldview tethered to the guidelines pulled from a religion's ancient writings without ever having formed any personal experiential tie-in to verify the present moment living participating presence of anything representing the purpose of the religion's claim to salvation from suffering, rigidity might set in and the believer's mind will likely remain closed to other explanations, ideas or views that address other options to reaching heaven. They're too occupied with learning the ways of the written word of their god. They don't want to accidentally break a rule or formalized function attached to the religion's unique sets of rituals. They've publicly promised their unyielding blind faith-secured reverence and now have to provide it as members of their religious group are always on hand to judge and remind them of how bad eternal fire and brimstone must be.

They must learn to rote memory many of the religion's behavioral rituals and memorize scriptures when there may be no real spiritual benefit that the effects of the ritualistic actions may have toward enriching their enlightened awareness about what keeps them from happiness and joy and allows them to suffer. But, that end isn't a goal taught in the Christian discipline.

A new believer has to justify to themselves this spiritual path they've taken that some will say amounts to no more than an individual mortgaging their perception of what their soul's future will be to an outside unknown entity in return for the perceived security of a promised future paradise free from suffering. They have no choice, as they blindly believe the religion's story line without first understanding the living tie the factors involved in making its purpose true, has to the present moment living world they live and die in that's the same present moment pain and suffering they pray to their god for relief from.

It would take real courage for them to step outside the circle and follow the muffled questions their free will is quietly shouting from their distant mind. Still, they can't delve into how their feelings justify the intentions of the religious claim because their present moment sensual feelings that represent their present moment waking reality have never experienced the living inclusion of any of the entity's factors in real-life circumstances. They can't define it or feel its truth in present moment sensual terms.

A mind hardened in this way lacks the openness of objectivity and this confuses the individual's sincere interest in understanding other soul-saving concepts as they secretly keep an eye cracked open in hopes of seeing some kind of sign from above. Or maybe they'll catch a glimpse of something that hints to a better answer or something that will make clearer to them what really the right question they need to ask in the first place.

Their mounting impatience might eventually result in their acknowledging having seen something that was half imagined. Or maybe they'll see something that their limited knowledge doesn't provide them with the existing explanation for and they'll call it a sign from above? Maybe their god talks to them in their sleep. These instances would be experiences totally unique to their living experience...something that's not available for all to see anywhere at any time.

They can be very sensitive to criticism or any questioning related to the modern-day relevance of their ritualistic behaviors. This is made evident in trying to talk to a person whose resistant mind's imprisoned in the dangerous confines of fundamentalism.

Out of fear of the unknown, an ego will defend the existence of the fragile framework of the self we patch together and perceive as being separate from the rest of reality. It doesn't know where else to turn. We're conditioned from childhood to support what we pose as being the truth.

As a believer is continually confronted by the ongoing change of this reality and feel compelled to keep it organized, many situations come up that threaten the blind faith secured bond of their loyalty to supporting the existence painted by the religious claim. Even though they may feel a tinge of doubt, many feel that the security experienced in supporting the pretenses of the religion's claim is surely easier to deal with that what might erupt if they step out and start asking challenging questions. They settle back into the comfort and safety found in conforming to the fundamentalist boundaries that define the scope of their chosen religion.

We Build Our Towers of Babel

While in our own communities there are many people who are homeless and hungry, instead of using the untaxed weekly collections to cloth and feed fellow humans in need, many religious groups will use those funds to finance building the most elaborate type of buildings produced by humans to meet in to perform their weekly rituals.

Many truth-seeking humans build elaborate structures topped with elaborate steeples pinpointing up to their god to rush to his attention a focused projection of the holy intentions spawned within its elaborate walls. The lands mankind has inhabited over the past few millennia are littered with these tributes...massive cathedrals that harbor an air of holiness. They have giant walls of the most detailed stained-glass windows. The gothic hallways reach up to spectacular heights and boast the most advanced architectural design that amaze today's designers.

They've learned from their ancestors that trying to build the actual structure up into the heavens to God will not work...such a silly idea. Still, they build their tribute.

They use the best materials. Their design takes on a gothic nature that God's followers gamble will better satisfy a god whose presence has been mentally sketched from ancient accounts of his actions.

The cross on top symbolizes how God's son died for their sins. Maybe these crosses are skeleton keys that open the doors of heaven? It's hard to see how this use of funds is going to help fellow humans better understand why they suffer present moment hell and how to overcome its cause in this lifetime.

We Design a God to Walk in Our Shoes

Individuals experience the present moment in an emotional state that reflects how they've been conditioned to perceive reality. They arrange the world to find a balance that best suits their personally honed form of sanity or insanity. Everyone fashions their conscious understanding of their environment in a way that they're most likely to find joy and happiness, as they understand it and to not suffer. For lack of direction, many must scramble for these answers.

In the Midwest, the faceless anonymity that characterizes Christianity's god allows each person to choose from their collection of mental pictures cognitively sketched from the assortment of Bible-related stories read about, told about, or maybe seen on TV the image of who or what characterizes the most fitting protector and/or judge to handle or explain the emotions that fill in the gaps in their understanding that connect the causes to the effects in the assortment of life's changing barrage of challenges that arise in the dust of the continual variety of passing situations. People can do no better than bow to their notion of the god or source that lives in their cognitively painted picture of reality that they feel most compatible and comfortable with.

People customize their god to meet their needs and possibly fulfill their wants. It's a god with the powers that prove to be a suitable and appropriate match for their level of spiritual maturity.

Their god will tie together the ends that don't meet or match up to their suspected causes, that don't make sense, that don't arise as the product from what their understanding of the process of relational justice says should be. Many of these unexplainable cause/effect relationships are justified, rationalized, or simply excused as being the sorts of things that happen only by the grace of God or maybe the explanation might simply be that God works in mysterious ways. When the true pulse between causes and effects can't be understood, just being a part of God's mystery can serve as a suitable explanation.

Each individual's spot along the suffering-to-enlightenment continuum recognizes different types of needs corresponding to where their unique level of spiritual maturity meets up with their illusion of an apparent reality. These needs will gel into a corresponding push for satisfaction from the god they ask for support or expect punishment from.

A god is as compassionate or punishing as the individual is conditioned to imagine. There's a direct correspondence between a god's gifts and punishments and the conceptual limits of an individual's conditioned worldview.

Almost one-third of the world's population, over two billion people, are Christian. The modern-day zeitgeist of the Bible could be seen as an intellectual kaleidoscope of evolving modern-day interpretations of its edited multitranslated ancient message. It's very rare to find two Christians that agree on what Jesus's intended meaning was meant to be from within any of the versions of the ancient text's many translations.

The Eastern spiritualist Dr. Deepak Chopra also recognizes this default setting of the human condition. He also ventures that many humans fashion a god to have characteristics appropriate to satisfy their particular judge/jury protection/punishment needs they have to best placate their present moment perception of the relational factors representing their unique illusion of an apparent reality...like creating a god in the image of the individual.

When what reality serves up doesn't match up with illusionary miscued expectations, something divine, all-powerful, and out of this world is needed to explain the unexpected and make the ends meet. This helps them keep their free will sedated, or maybe gives them a much-needed divine kick in the pants?

In his book *How to Know God: The Soul's Journey into the Mystery of Mysteries*, Dr. Chopra suggests that there are seven basic versions or stages of God that can be associated with different aspects of different faiths. It follows that these different stages of God recognition reflect varying levels of spiritual maturity.

Dr. Chopra suggests that individuals at the lowest level of spiritual development or maturity will turn to a deity figure capable of the most devastating forms of punishment or reward that are bound only by the individual's conditioned world of imagination. The different stages of God recognition will progress up to the illusion of a god that encompasses all possibilities that come to the awareness of an individual that has a more wisdom-enriched understanding of the relational justice inherent to the impermanent nature of this reality.

These described incarnations of a god created in our own image are very interesting and do a wonderful job of bringing to words one theory of the diverse range in what's needed to keep corralled the wide range of illusions people create to explain and weather the emotional reactions coming from their unique perceptions of this cause/effect reality. These are examples of what people living in an illusionary apparent reality will create to help give organization to their uncertainty and use to inject the missing relational justice needed to fill in the gaps and bring balance to their misguided views and beliefs.

An individual's illusionary reality needs to be able to call on an appropriate phase of a god to deal with the type of misaligned internal misunderstandings that arise between illusionary causes and their mismatched effects to be ready for the sudden appearance of the real ones. Their particular internal unrest may turn to a god to reward, punish, grant a wish, console, understand and tolerate, help create, cure an incurable disease or situation, or just watch over all things in an omnipresence that's been read about, but that relationship with the living present moment cannot quite be understood. It may take a god with powers that transcend those an individual has experientially witnessed during their lifetime to somehow apply the relational justice they know positively somewhere in the subtle region of their deeper consciousness exists. Until they wakingly uncover their link to this inborn source of truth, they must conjure up and trust a faith that's actually blind to the actual source of this truth.

The variety of illusionary apparent realities ranging from individual to individual is probably somewhere around six billion. There could be a countless number of god-conception possibilities characterized by what is needed to balance the belief system of someone spending their present moments stuck in an illusionary apparent reality. Dr. Chopra's possibilities represent another's vision of grouping and arranging the needs of the human condition and explaining the human experience.

It could be said that everyone's mental conception of their heavenly god lives within the boundaries of and watches over and rules their inner abyss of uncertainty that's void of any sensually defined familiarity or recognition. People will call on their god to reward or punish them in the way they feel he would want to for their own deserved good. Many figure that when this life is over, when the void filled with uncertainty is gone, somehow, so will the suffering it brings them.

Instead of fashioning a god to walk in one's shoes, individuals need to realize that they walk in the shoes of our Source or what it is that continually recreates us. Knowingly or unknowingly, this is what everyone does, and there's nothing they can do about it. Why not try to understand it in this lifetime? Become enlightened about this living process.

Individuals need not talk to their hopeful intellectual conception of a god whose feared presence is somewhere in the sky where he sits quietly watching over their shoulder, in hopes he will hear them and not be mad at them and ignore their wishes. They must be still and with the greatest level of humility excuse their self-ego to open up to experiencing our Source's ever-present message and with all their attention sensually listen and witness the presence of what is real and true as are the coming and going vibrations manifested from within their flesh, from which all relational wisdom originates and is revealed. This is the key to start understanding the ignorance that allows the addictions that cause the many forms of human suffering.

There's no need to make the process of finding our Source so mystical. There's no need to make such a pious ritualistic deal out of the process of understanding the path to becoming enlightened about the ignorance that results in human suffering. Everyone has the potential to perform the due diligence to understand this. Like Siddhartha on his deathbed and the Nike saying suggests...just do it!

5

What We Get

We Get Affluencza and a Want Museum

Affluenza, n. a painful, contagious, socially transmitted condition of overload, debt, anxiety and waste resulting from the dogged pursuit of more.[12]

Today's media buildup that convinces the public of what its artificial needs are is needed to keep this capitalist society financially buoyant. Between the sway of misleading copy and the injected impulse from seeing pretty people in staged events, it's easy for those who get paid to market manufactured items to convince society how much they need something that without the media plug might rate no higher than a curious want.

Lost in their unique illusion of reality, an individual might dream of how while owning or using some certain thing or idea, they might somehow own or capture the object or TV-injected mood of their newly stirred up fixation. What tenders this fire is the deep-down urge to somehow stumble across the answer to the unknown question that keeps them turning stones to find. On the way down this path, there are many who will be sidetracked when their ego butts in and in trying to improve their illusionary idea of neat or cool or having what the Jones have, tales control.

The Midwest is full of hoarders and pack rats. Their behavior is a symptom of them having an "I am" attachment. What and how much a person owns helps reveal how uncluttered and interrelated their intentions are...how vulnerable they are to falling into the wraps of addictive behavior.

How many belongings haven't been touched for six months...for one or two years? Do these items fill a storage shed in the back yard? Can they park their car in their garage? Do they have an extra job to help pay for a larger house that provides additional storage space? Do they have a new pole barn to store these unused dusty relics that are kept to possibly fulfill some unimagined future need? Where was their head when acquiring the different items hanging in their closet with sales tags still shouting, "BUY ME!"?

Which mitote/maya voice was shouting its unneeded want related to one of many unrelated ends, has possibly now been forgotten. Another filter has been added to further deaden their waking access to and the strength of their free will. With the addition of each additional unneeded item, any focus on a future path to spiritual maturation they may have had motivating their belief system is now a bit more blurred and indistinct.

When an individual clings to and fails to release unneeded items, they further define and prolong their payless career choice as a Want Museum curator. They continue to be slave to all the pointless ritualistic care responsibilities of the unneeded items. They continue to suffer life's present moment frustrations and disappointments associated with all the unneeded activities they waist their present moment time on while their unique inner talents are busting to be discovered and developed to instead allow the caretaker to one day let their light shine. Way, way too many Midwesterners just don't see this.

The always-changing assortment of mostly unrelated Want Museum to-dos keeps its curator tethered nearby. The attached responsibilities of these unneeded items chase them around all day prodding them to take care of the needless, unrewarding and unfruitful duties on the items' dowered to-do lists. The additional individual details that each item contributes to the collective bundle of responsibilities fades into the background to support a growing sense of knowing that something's going to need attention soon. Many curators eventually choose to take refuge in their own self-crafted zone of apathy.

Their present moments are consumed by unnecessary responsibilities. Their thoughts are not free to allow them to anticipate new change and joyfully bend with the passage of time. Their mental state that possibly appreciated the moment involving the unneeded item's acquisition has grown stagnate and clouded by their clinging to the physical relic reminder.

The curator's field of vision is full of things that add no value to the future. Their use potential is dead or totally undetermined. This aura carries over into their daily activities and future plans. They chase after a vacation to get away from this instead of doing something that fulfills a related part of their future end purpose to undo their ignorance that allows their suffering.

A cluttered home means a cluttered mind. This proverb of sorts states the truism of how a cluttered residence reflects the design logistics of a cluttered belief system. By an individual not having a plan of action to selectively stock their belief system with tested and end-related claims wise to the savvy of ongoing change and a feel for what their plans do not include, they will accumulate wants and whatifs that will gradually fill any material or mental storage space they have.

In the specter of owning things, they don't consider how if an individual has everything, they have everything to lose. This paradox accompanies a worldview that recognizes the permanence of material continuity and it will lead to suffering from attachment and craving. They'll ride by homeless individuals casting thoughts of pity of with how much better off they are because of all the responsibilities they can afford to support.

Was their motivation to hang on to their want relics directed by intent representing a contributing part of a greater purpose? Was it merely one voice of the 1,000 unrelated voices of their mitote/maya state of mind, which had the floor at that time mirroring the wants of friends/family, or social clique they just happened to be with at that time of acquisition?

Maybe their free will had been bypassed when making the unneeded acquisition that actually served the financial end of some corporate entity disguised by a crafty marketing technique? Was it a voice shouting the faux need of its misguided purpose duplicating or copying some aspect of the superficial veneer of their favorite cultural icon their ego was grabbing at or craving to be like or have?

How attached are they to these items? Can they not release any of these items due to some imagined future use being projected by one of the uncontrolled possibly subliminally inducted purposes of some internalized claim serving the well-being of another entity that has no sensible application or practical probability? Does the item's imagined future use represent some unrelated fancy of another entity's self-serving ego?

For someone whose time is spent bowing to addictions and want-serving causes that share no common end, do the items' functions contribute to any real common passion? Do they point to endless suffering or suffering endlessly?

They may wonder if at least part of the answer to their peace of mind and happiness resides in one of these objects or ideas. They'll play it safe and cling to all the items to give the answer a chance to resonate at some undefined future time. They'll hang on to all they can to keep unthought-of possibilities open to satisfy the untamed 1,000 voices that rule their mitote/maya mental state, not knowing which may have the unknown answer to the unrealized question explaining the cause of their ignorance that causes their present moment unhappiness and unrest.

Maybe playing with or using one of the relics one more time would help uncover the unknown answer to their deep longing to settle the ongoing mental stir caused by their mitote/maya state of mind. If they get a brief glimpse at the unknown answer, maybe they'll understand what the unknown question is they long to satisfy?

Nostalgic sentiment causes suffering in any individual's illusion. Freezing in time and clinging to what may seem to be the memory of the emotion or spirit of that past moment creates a kink in the natural ongoing flow of time and thought in an individual's transforming cyclical life/death process.

Each time this happens it results in a mind that's progressively becoming a little less able to handle the change perceived when the next possibly fruitful new and fresh present moment presents itself. It's a mind less awake to appreciate moments of indefinable love.

Clinging to this behavior creates a process-stopping cog in the ever-turning wheel of their life's ongoing natural process of maturing change. Clinging to the material relics associated with a mental library of past events "gunks up" an individual's ability to radiate and perceive change and present moment creativity. Maybe at times it's an unforgotten self-imposed guilt over a forgotten event that stages the clinging to a material reminder that's to blame?

If an individual already has too many unneeded items, they tend to want and acquire more. The more someone owns, the more resistant to change they are. They're stuck in the dream-memory times of the clung-to "want museum" items.

Their belief system remains infected with the virus spreading the illusion of the imagined solidity and permanence of ideas, beliefs and things that allows having something permanent to cling to wanting more of or to be aversive to. Maybe their free will's been numbed into silence by the tempting lure of promised future happiness while misguided purposes of infected claims continue to shape their intentions into grabbing at the unrelated wants of their unfocused ego seeking to satisfy their addiction to having a continual ongoing flow of the simple gratification gotten through acquiring something new?

If an individual has no idea of all the physical items they have and what ideas and beliefs they stand for mentally, then they don't really know where their life's at or where it's going. It's defeating and mentally tiring to be surrounded by the changing responsibilities of hosting the possessions maintained simply for their reminiscent histories or because of some possible unknown and unlikely future use. The items' functions and purposes probably share no common source or direction.

The time of their real use or functional value may have already passed. This feeling is blinding to the museum curator and the lurking presence of the upkeep and storage space responsibilities will feed and help sustain an untouchable and often purposefully ignored unrest deep within.

Being "young and carefree" is an expression used to jokingly show amicable envy of the limitless possibilities a young person's future holds. A deeper analysis of this thought reveals that the adage implies the truth that they are free of caring for the responsibilities inherent to unnecessarily owning unneeded things. Not being old enough yet to have acquired things makes up for being older and not having the sense to know when to release unneeded items.

The terms young and carefree are grouped together because in the greater US society, if one doesn't yet understand the problems that come with being attached to things, it's necessary to be young. After an individual stops growing they begin accumulating more and more items such as the clothing that they, as adults, haven't and will no longer grow out of.

A teenager discards and replaces clothing because they outgrow it. There's no reason to keep it. Their wardrobe is minimal because they probably can't afford to buy a lot of new clothing.

They may want to own many adult toys like their role models, but have yet to acquire them. For most, the process of the accumulation of unneeded things along with their addiction to clinging to things to populate a Want Museum has just begun. This motivational bug has probably already bitten their role models. In this Midwest US society, they stand little chance of sidestepping the temptation of its infective lure.

Some responsibilities are based on needs and are necessary in the pursuit of the freedom from the ignorance that allows suffering. Those based only on wants or uncertainty must be released. There are enough responsibilities connected to actual needs to occupy one's time. Unnecessary responsibilities dull one's life and overbearingly smother out their free will.

An individual must know the difference between a "want" and a "need." It's wise for an individual to be thankful for what they have and not to be preoccupied thinking about what they don't have.

Enough is Never Enough...We Find No Need to Release

Most individuals have possessions they can cite no real reason to keep, but likewise find no apparent reason to let go of. They pass their present moments suspended in a type of uncertainty-caused indecision that's culturally common and joked about by many. Clearing out the cobwebs from material possessions and making room for needed-only items correspondingly makes for more mental room for new thoughts and ideas to feed into realizing a more focused life direction.

Individuals who haven't consciously realized what aspect of their human experience has true value might use their collection of toys to pump up the seeming importance of their "I am." In the Midwest, many judge an individual's importance by what they own. They joke about the ongoing battle between the Smiths and the Joneses.

When deciding on what to release from their Want Museum, an individual needs to recognize the life purpose they intend to pursue. They should define their life priorities and focus.

It's easy to find reasons to keep things and ideas. In deciding on what items will contribute to the pursuit of an intended purpose, they are defining what their intention of purpose represents. This isn't so easy. They release everything else. This helps them define who they are and who they are not.

It's tough to find the courage to make a commitment to release something even if its release involves something recognizably proactive in nature. To stop and say "I don't plan on doing anything involving the utility offered by this item" can seem limiting and making the decision can be easily deterred or procrastinated due to a hidden fear of the unknown. Things needed for future pursuits are kept and things that have served their purpose need to be let go of or any related suffering persists.

The ungrounded unverified internalized claims of misguided beliefs responsible for the acquisitions of these items in question are going to tug strongly against their release. The mitote/maya voices that sponsored internalizing those misguided claims will try to interrupt any mental coordination to understand why they are being either needed or unwanted.

Strong sentimental attachments can leave echoes of guilt in thoughts that something's being lost forever. Betrayed loyalty to a passed family member or friend might be felt. To cling to items or memories because they bring memories of something or someone does not involve the same emotions or reasons on hand when gifting the item or why the experience was originally performed. It doesn't replicate or capture to fix in time the same love or joy involved during the present moment of the past when the intended purpose represented by the item initially was felt.

After releasing an object from an individual's Want Museum, the item's functional value can be easily regained. There are other options such as renting or borrowing something if need of the released item's functional utility unexpectedly reappears. The Smiths or the Joneses next door probably still have theirs and will loan it out?

During the weeding-out process it may be discovered that one of the retained items rekindles a forgotten passion, allowing it to resurface. The recognition of its purpose had been smothered out by the weight of the caretaking responsibilities of other unneeded items. It can be life changing. The new vigor can result in future involvement helping relieve the suffering of others while helping them along their path to heavenly enlightenment. That's all Siddhartha did for the decades following his enlightenment about his ignorance that caused his suffering.

Great things such as weight loss or relief from depression come from understanding the ignorance that allows attachment to addictions. Letting go of the material possessions that represent mental attachments while focusing one's intended purpose on eliminating that ignorance that allows this misguided thinking frees the Want Museum curator from unnecessary mental responsibilities, bringing them closer to the freedom to train their mind to realize the wisdom derived from waking awareness of our Source's nature and intended purpose.

In comparing apples to oranges, the faint residual feeling of disappointment from not getting what was wanted following times of exercised self-control over the needless buying of wanted things is short-lived. This resulting disappointment is not nearly as mentally painful as the ongoing mental ache of being in debt after thoughtlessly writing both mental and material bad checks in the illusionary apparent reality created by a confused ego-managed belief system that is ran by too many chiefs. A long-lasting feeling of satisfaction from exercising self-control replaces the aftertaste from needless wanting coming from the misguided belief system that generated the needless want.

Precious time is fettered away daily while idly trying to decide which of the 1,000 voices to listen to while reacting to a controlling ego by letting it push the "buy this" button. It's easy for this uncontrollable urge to last throughout one's entire lifetime.

There are so many Midwestern role models whose life style demonstrates ongoing toy accumulation that it actually seems like the right thing to do. It's mistakenly perceived as a way for an individual to define who they are. The more items an individual owns, the harder it is to tell who they really are. True self-definition disappears and passions go unrecognized. To refer to a childhood Bible school song refrain, the toy collector's true life-light is held under a bushel or completely snuffed out.

In the Midwest it seems to be expected for parents to die with a house full of things representing as many memories as possible. It's almost customary to pass on the responsibility to their children to sort out the things they couldn't find the time, inspiration and courage to deal with processing. They didn't fulfill their responsibility of seeing the full life cycle of those items through their use or timely disposal.

Geshe Sonam Rinchen remarks on this in his book *Atisha's Lamp for the Path to Enlightenment*:

> At death nothing at all but our spiritual practice will be of any use to us. That is the only thing worth doing—everything else is a futile waste of energy. We tire ourselves for the sake of reward and reputation and in our search for the kind of companions we prefer, but we can take none of these with us when we die. They must be left behind and only the imprints of negative actions we have performed in the process of trying to acquire them accompany us to our next rebirth.[13]

When an individual realizes the importance of the ever-evasive present moment, they'll want to keep it uncluttered and open with room for new things and thoughts.

Debt...A Most Taxing Possession

It's disruptive for an individual to owe the fruits of their future present moments to some other entity. Debt creates an undercurrent of expectations and obligations that work in establishing the individual's default setting for the mood they most easily slip into when just passing the time.

Owning debt creates a new reason for going to work. The American Dream used to be to be able to buy a new house because you've worked to earn its luxuries. With the emergence of home mortgages, the American Dream's been morphed into being when an individual has a job and a good enough credit rating to convince some outside entity to loan them the money to one day, maybe in thirty years, be able to own the home instead of the promise to pay for it.

Their daily plans have to be built in a way that allows for not disrupting their obligations to provide a constant stream of cash to pay for something they already use. At this time in history this country's flipped upside down on what's owed and how it's going to be paid back.

We Get a Fat Camel

In this Midwestern society, the thought of having only the items that are really needed is considered to be a worthy goal. Yet, it receives a rather casual acceptance and it goes mostly unobserved.

Owning things has been pounded into Midwestern heads from birth and on throughout life. An individual's misguided attachment to things and non-things comes from their misperception of the nature of the ongoing relational interplay among the cause/effect factors that populate and make real the passage of each of their present moments. There's no real sense for the difference between something that's wanted for some endless reason and something that's actually needed to contribute to the life purpose they have in focus.

The blinding effects of want affect people today, just as back 2,000 years ago. Jesus described in a parable how having great possessions will keep one from realizing heaven. A young man was telling Jesus that he did not murder, commit adultery, steal or bear false witness. He had honored his father and mother and loved his neighbor as himself all his life. He had followed the Bible's moral/ethical guidelines.

> The young man saith unto him, all these things have I kept from my youth up: what lack I yet? Jesus said unto him, If thou wilt be

perfect, go and sell that thou hast, and give to the poor, and thou shalt have treasure in heaven: and come and follow me. But when the young man heard that saying, he went away sorrowful: for he had great possessions. Then said Jesus unto his disciples, Verily I say unto you that a rich man shall hardly enter into the kingdom of heaven. And again I say unto you, it is easier for a camel to go through the eye of a needle, than for a rich man to enter into the kingdom of God. (Matthew 19:20–24, King James Version)

Jesus tells the young man that he needs to sell what he has, give to the poor and to follow him. One is left to wonder what's wrong with owning things. The recorded account of what Jesus said doesn't go into detail. In the King James translation the young man's tie to his Want Museum was so strong that even Jesus's warning couldn't lessen his attachment. Of course, Jesus wasn't yet a martyr with a religion named after him as he has today. But still, the truth is the truth, no matter who brings it to attention.

There's no biblical reference made to break it down to what the responsibility of owning things does to one's present moment to affect or distance their realization of heaven. There's nothing said that occupying one's mind with the full-time job of managing possessions, prevents them from having the freedom of mind for making the right effort to make the right concentration to find the body/mind harmony to enrich the right understanding of life-in-motion and better focus on the path to reach heaven or enlightenment. It's just that if an individual understands the nature and intended purpose of our Source, they will understand the harmful effects of being attached to clinging or being aversive to something when in reality, is no longer exists, only its memory as fashioned in the illusion of the individual.

The moral here is not about the goodness of giving to the poor that sets things right with owning things. Not to imply that giving to the poor is bad, but giving too much to the poor, if it's not something they need, could set the poor up for managing their own Want Museum and blind their present moment of the fruits of finding the way.

In explaining Atisha's Tibetan Buddhist declaration on the subject of the craving of attaining possessions, Geshe Sonam Rinchen noted the same sort of effect caused by hoarding want items when he said:

> The greed of wanting everything we see, and the lack of contentment whereby we want more or something better make it hard to practice purely and complicate our life, whereas the disposition of the exalted simplifies it and makes pure practice possible.[14]

The intended message of Mr. Richen's commentary on Atisha's message and Jesus's comments were basically the same. Even though rooted in insights stemming from the Christian and Buddhist schools of thought, they both take reference from the same, and only school of wisdom.

Only Mr. Richen's account goes into detail as to why the procurement of and the responsibilities inherent in the ownership of unneeded items will keep one from reaching heaven or enlightenment. He says that the disposition of the individual with his higher described level of spirituality realizes that hoarding preoccupies the mind, as would any moral/ethical difficulty an individual is having. It's a preoccupation with a person's mental attention to some degree, like an individual has after breaking one of the Ten Commandments.

Doing away with their want museum makes it impossible for a truth seeker to self-train their mind in the right concentration to pursue being self-trained in attaining the wisdom-enriched enlightenment about what they are ignorant about that allows their suffering. This is realizing the same goal that Jesus and Siddhartha taught about...how to eliminate the ignorance that denies a reality of joy and happiness and allows suffering. Mr. Richen's described exalted individual sees this connection.

We Miss the All Too Obvious, Self-Evident Truth

Anyone will acknowledge without thinking about it that there is a passage of time. It can be seen that as time passes, so does the material structure of things. In modern society, science documents this pictorially, clear down to the coming and going particles of raw energy that comprise the structural formation of things and objects that appear in the human range of perception.

Humans become attached to clinging to their memories of the things and ideas they perceive as time passes. They don't consciously recognize that as things and ideas change, they turn into something else...that what they hold in their memory no longer exists. Memories are edited by the ego to preserve a desired perspective.

The only thing or concept that does not change is that this change does not stop. Reality continues to constantly change. This uncontrollable unalterable and unstoppable thing about this reality is embodied in the coming and going pulse of life as it manifests itself.

Each human has only one place where they can actually access this phenomenon, and that's within the confines of their own physical body of material flesh. This is their own growing garden of flesh that their soul/spirit has the duty to tend to. It's been said that their body/garden of growing flesh is the temple of their Source.

The manifestation of living change that's focused on that's within this window to the present moment will be the same ten years from now and it was ten years ago. It's the very same state that's happening now. The present moment is the present moment. It's all there ever was and all there will ever be.

We Grow Old

Many individuals never really find the answers to their self-prodding questions about where they're from, where they're at, or where they're going. Their internalization process is responsible for the development of their mitote/maya mind-set that eventually allowed them to be lured from their early age of innocence.

Like Adam and Eve in the beginning, the woes from their free will's concession to the tree of knowledge in developing their belief system alienated them from living their life in the grace of our Source. Their chosen path of conditioning's led them to miscalculate the nature and purpose of our Source. Their present moments have been full of question, uncertainty, fear and the resulting unrest.

Their present moments throughout the day are spent fulfilling and servicing the many contracts or social expectations they've agreed to. For most Midwesterners, this seems to be the normal state of affairs. People's life energies have been mortgaged away and they wear the golden handcuffs of a job or career to satisfy the financial part of their responsibilities. For them, satisfying this load of responsibilities is an end in itself. It consumes their life.

For those who have no real passion driven direction, their daily itinerary is satisfied in just finding something to do as they unknowingly pillage through life searching for what's missing from their current perception of life. They have an inescapable longing for the answer to the unrest.

Five days per week, time is spent in slow traffic coming and going to work. They think about the factors relevant to the mortgage or car payment(s) they must pay on time each month. They have contracts on their new super-functional cell phones and another one for their air card for web access on the road. Their laptop's beginning to lock up on them and they're not sure if their service contract's expired yet. They feel relieved they were able to make their periodic house, car and health insurance payments on time this month. They wonder what their friends think of their accomplishments. They fear that sometime they won't be able to make those obligations like some of their friends. Their cortisone level rises as they watch a cigarette butt get nonchalantly flipped out of the car in front's window at the stoplight.

They'll report that they are happy if asked. But, the truth is that their daily time schedule is mostly promised to staying caught up on prior obligations relating to unrelated wants that live in their waking conscious mind. It's conditioned into the USA capitalist lifestyle.

As most individuals grow older with their waking consciousness stuck in the deep ruts of a lifelong illusion, they still lack the needed guidance and courage to break free this and their deeper consciousness where the truth lies will concede and gradually go to sleep. While unknowingly having the soul-saving truth of our Source's intention to initiate ongoing change just an insight away for so long, they eventually become so bored with games and wasted energy that their ego-managed waking consciousness puts it through, it slowly shuts down.

Their ego-managed waking consciousness slowly loses reason to wear all their identity masks. They no longer try to inflate the perception of their social status in the eyes of others. It becomes less likely for them to remember details about certain situations that were at the time nothing more than the pursuit of an unneeded ego-managed want related item directed at no end. They were of no consequence then, there's no real reason to remember them now.

Could a belief system that has allowed a lifetime's accumulation of unrelated purposes turn to dementia for relief? Is dementia hereditary? Or, could dementia be passed on simply because its behavioral conditioning is passed through life example and not actually through the DNA?

Many who are unaware of the nature and intended purpose of our Source will reach a point where they stop searching and become totally numb to being alive. They give up, old and tired while uncertain and afraid to experience life and by lacking the awareness to feel the truth they are numb to its presence and in surrender they forfeit to and invite death's gradual arrival.

We Suffer

Mankind struggles with troubling thoughts that involve some phase of guilt or regret over the past or worry about the future. It doesn't matter what creed or color, the meat from these seeds of suffering tastes the same.

Suffering shows no prejudice. We are all tied to the same whipping post. We all bleed red blood. The hurt feels the same. It feels the same today as it did 2,000-plus years ago and how it will feel 2,000-plus years from now.

Yet, many humans don't understand what suffering really is. Most of mankind is still trying to get its head around the moral/ethical standards outlined by the Ten Commandments. Many continue to mistake feelings of insipient suffering for happiness.

Mr. Rinchen comments:

> We all regard physical pain and mental pain as something unwanted. It is much more difficult to recognize contaminated pleasure as a form of incipient suffering. Our search for pleasure preoccupies us and takes up most of our energy, yet it is doomed to failure from the start because none of these pleasures can give us the real and lasting happiness we crave.[15]

When an individual becomes attached to something or some idea they perceive as having a permanent continual presence, they develop expectations involving the snapshotin-time item or idea. When things don't work as expected, disappointments, let downs and other forms of suffering are bound to follow.

Wants, once gotten after suffering through the wait time, may not turn out to be as wonderful as expected. Even if they are, at some time their greatness will end. It will be time to sell that wonderful houseboat that provided many days of peaceful retreat. The wait time can seem like eternity. For some, the process can seem like torture.

They are not savvy to the idea that the only thing or concept that does not change in the boundaries of this reality is the demonstrated purpose of our Source...to unchangingly provide ongoing change. In this primal truth, mankind can develop an unshakeable steadfast faith. This faith strengthens hand-n-hand with the growth of their inspired insightful wisdom-enriched understanding of the relational justice defining this primal truth of ongoing change.

Many cling to religious riddles that provide an explanation of our reality for them to organize their worldview within. It gives them answers to explain the misunderstood and unexplainable. It helps them give structure to their unexplainable mental unrest with a plan to reach a nonviewable heaven free of the degree of suffering they don't understand at a future time in a place somewhere they have never seen, promised sometime after they die.

Most individuals don't understand what the original sin that wraps itself around their free will is if they're ignorant to our Source's nature and intended purpose and how not understanding it can undercut and infiltrate all the real-time present moment decisions they make and the suffering it allows. The repetitive real-time emotional storms individuals experience are visible proof of this ongoing ignorance. Most people fail to see the forest for the trees.

Most individuals cannot see deep enough into their presence to be wakingly conscious of how their reactionary emotional episodes that bring present moment unrest come from the way they choose to perceive the presence of various sensual packages that trigger these emotions. They don't see how these misunderstood sensory perceptions come from their worldview that's been shaped by faulty misguided claims they've agreed to internalize into their belief systems during times of their prior conditioning.

Many of those who've taken the leap of blind faith don't really identify or link the suffering they are experiencing in real-time with the intellectually stored images of the hellfire and brimstone suffering read about in the Bible that they are promised after-death salvation from. They see no living evidence or living sign of any of the socially introduced gods/ sources that are here, now. So why should they be able to connect their real-time feeling of suffering with a promised undocumented god whose presence is only registered intellectually? Open-ended uncertainty has been in this society for a long, long time. It's considered to be a normal state of mind.

There's no heartfelt god-human connection developed in times when an intellectually recognized god gets included in the material reality where there is no heartbeat evidence of their living one-on-one communion. The individual's mental image of the god that was sketched with an intellectual pencil has much trouble being recognized and associated or sized up with its real-life incarnation when perceiving the brail-like signals of the coming and going sensations of each sensually realized present moment. Any common ground ever shared between the individual's intellectually based Sunday morning sketched cognitive illustrations of their spiritual reality and the real-time sensory signals of the spiritual signposts that sensually appear in their present moment goes by unrecognized.

It's during the real-time in the present moments of mental hell that guidance is needed to find out what this Godpromised state of heavenly life is like in terms that lead to relief from today's suffering. But the self-depreciating thinking somewhere in their guilt-instilled mind that "even if what's promised is real, my being such a born sinner, the soothing salvation is probably not deserved or has not been earned" keeps their present moment thinking and behavioral intentions consumed by wondering how and what to do to better please their god...often doing good for others is a forced deed for the anticipated reward of acceptance in this promised heaven-to-be and not really so the other will actually be better off...purely from altruistic intentions being for the good of the other. This falls short of the altruistic compassion that truly opens up a present moment to joy and happiness.

This mind-set comes with a hollow inner wall of questioning doubt that stealthily nags with an echoing air of fear-spawning uncertainty that chaffs a believer's present moment with tight-lipped, dare-not-to-be-asked questions. As socially programmed, the masses vie to consider their state of ignorance-generated suffering to be the normal life they must endure till death, to then gain salvation from any more real-time fire-and-brimstone mental pain.

These individuals stand blinded, like a deer-in-headlights with their fee will stunned by missing the details of their inadequately tested and verified internalized belief about what suffering is and the path to their safety away from it. They hang suspended in an intellectually stored traditional illusionary explanation of reality. It's illusionary because it can't be tied to real experience and its mental picture is bound only by the limits of the human imagination. The free will of their waking consciousness remains blinded on the intellectual side of their thinking capacity and they fail to gain the courage to loosen up and take an introspective look at the real-time present moment reality of their human condition.

Judging by the number of people who make this choice, it stands to reason that the majority of society reasons that following a religious plan is probably the right thing to do, or at least as close as they can come at the time. They'll make the choice and keep the membership charter intellectually stored, while keeping a truth-seeking eye open for a more fulfilling answer.

Any religious spin has a plan requiring no creative mind development. Religious plans call only for mental discipline to first believe and then the mental obedience of following a set of behavioral guidelines such as the Ten Commandments. Religious entities have no universally recognizable real-time living involvement (signs from above) in our reality to experientially base an individual's journey toward attaining a real-time living heaven. Religious claims promise an enlightened heaven after death in an unexplored land of uncertain illusion limited only by the confines of each individual's imaginative design.

Religious believers hover in this unknowing state of undefined uncertainty. Religion is where they will hang their mental hats until they finally realize that the present moment frustrations and unrest that rule their living waking consciousness is what suffering really is. They must find the courage and confidence to step away from measuring suffering in terms of fire and brimstone.

It's when they realize what the suffering is replacing that they can fire up the motivation to do the due diligence to start asking the right questions to figure out its undoing. A truth seeker yearns to know what life feels like...what it is all about. It's the kindling for the fire of their unstoppable curiosity. Figuring it out will leave space in their passing present moment for nothing but generating behavior founded in the human condition's factory setting of altruistic compassion.

As their fear-related uncertainty mounts like that accompanying an unbalanced checking account, they must find the due diligence to uncover its cause and how to eliminate it. They will then be ready to investigate the Roots of Suffering. Religious believers continue to wonder unsatisfied, pillaging blindly through any on-hand information source that might hint at the hidden answer to an unknown question or maybe to finally give them a glimpse at the entity they've been giving their faith blindly to.

Suffering is a Choice...The Head or the Heart?

Who understands the world is learned.
Who understands the self is enlightened.
Who conquers the world has strength.
Who conquers the self has harmony.

—Lau Tzu, *Tao Te Ching* verse 33, 16

Sticks and stones may break my bones, but words will never hurt me.
—Childhood Retort

Unrest taxes the present moment peace of mind of most people. Human suffering's the toxic residue that infects the human condition in the wake of human ignorance. It's the afterbirth following each newborn thought born from a misguided prior conditioned understanding that's supported by the miscued logistics of how the cause/effect factors that write the story of time-spawned change actually line up. Suffering is mental inflammation. Suffering is compassion potential... oxidized.

Human suffering is very much alive and shows no prejudice. Its mind-seizing effect can slow down and magnify an individual's perception of time passage to where a single second seems like an eternity of agony...fire and brimstone agony. An individual can feel trapped in a pit of misery where the churning stomach tolerates no appetite. A sufferer may spend their day isolated, sowing a garden of bitterness. An ongoing unyielding guilt-rapt rumination over what's too late to take back or change may inspire a deep-down-felt assurance that there's no way out...the desire to end it all. Suffering rides in on the coattail of ignorance and the pain it ushers in lives only in the present moment. It has to be confronted and conquered on the sensual battlefield of the present moment.

To escape suffering's clutches, an individual needs to know who and what they are. They must feel comfortable in their own skin and learn how to best blend their worldview into sync with the rhythmic flow of the relational justice inherent to the nature of a reality that's truth depends on the ongoing passage of time.

Ignorance of the true nature and purpose of our Source spawns a fear-based venom that eats away at the groundwork of every individual's belief system. After subduing the free will and numbing an individual's freedom of thought, ignorance's caustic effects emerge as a product of an individual's compromised worldview. The effects are detectable in how the individual acts or reacts in everyday situations while using their skewed prognosis of reality. The often-unusual unfolding of suffering's irregular details serves as a popular source of subject matter for discussions and giggles around the water cooler at work.

It may seem a bit trite and maybe a little shallow to parrot the old childhood retort about how sticks and stones can unavoidably break bones and how to an individual with a properly conditioned process of perception, corrosive words have no real (emotional) hurting power. No matter how gnarly an insult might be, it's the receiver's perception process that generates and allows any hurting. It's an unavoidable truth that it's in the living arena of mind laid perception that real suffering exists and flourishes. Suffering's endless array of chameleon-like incarnations infects its victims in the present moment world of feeling.

Any emotional suffering coming from something said is a result of how the listener's prior conditioning poorly prepared them to interpret and perceive the relationships between the causes and effects in this reality as our source's natural laws of relational justice dictate. Credible emotional conditioning makes the suffering avoidable.

The skewed prior conditioning of any suffer-to-be, flips the cognitive switch that turns on the physiological process that brings on the ill physical and psychological effects their belief system stands ready to accept or believe are to come... making it real. It's what they perceive as normal. Eliminate the ignorance of the relational justice of the cause/ effect event and eliminate the suffering.

Suffering's nails are dug into an individual's compromised understanding or misunderstanding of the naturally occurring relational justice among the causing factors that become the effects in any situation. Suffering comes from a present moment state of mind built on imbalanced perceptions of the relational justice involved in how the human condition fits into the human experience.

Suffering works like a viral infection that feeds on the unsure fear-frozen thought patterns of those with an unguarded numbed free will that's allowed the sufferer's belief system to internalize misguided beliefs and ideas to hone an imbalanced worldview. It endlessly bestows an ever-changing assortment of viral recipes to affect a boundless menu of human misery. The sensual theater of feeling is the only true battlefront on which the cause of suffering can be tracked down, confronted and excused in mind-toheart-to-mind confrontational combat.

How each individual chooses to face life's challenges will determine their success at sidestepping suffering's present moment stranglehold on their happiness. Above in Peter Merel's interpolation of several of the most popular modern-day translations of *Tao Te Ching* verse 33, Lau Tzu asserts an insightful Cliffs Notes contrast comparing the two most basic ways people acknowledge life...intellectually with the head or sensually through the heart.

As time evolved and early mankind's population grew, overlapped and interacted more, the earliest arrangements of today's seven cardinal sins appeared to converge and edge out any shared compassion that may have existed in those days. In the emergence of mankind's collective moral/ ethical consciousness, the poison of the sins' presence and the destructive nature of their repeated effects finally registered in mankind's collective state of awareness.

Like how the appearance of the Ten Commandments, fire-blasted in stone, as they had no paper at that time, on Mount Sinai 2,800 years ago, did in first bringing from humankind's collective inner consciousness to its open forum of collective waking consciousness, the first publicly recorded regime of the do's and don'ts of human relations, the Taoist master Lau Tzu brought to light from mankind's same wisdom-rich deeper collective consciousness to its slowly maturing waking conscious awareness, a most insightfully wise distinction between how each of the most basic life recognition options, when chosen by the human condition to adapt to the human experience, affects the individual's spiritual well-being and spiritual maturation potential.

Verse 33 was probably the first time this inspired life-insight was ever pulled from mankind's collective deeper awareness, brought to social visibility and written down in the timeline of human development. His discriminating observation reasons that when an individual attempts to reconcile and integrate their human condition into their human experience, a differing intrinsic core value originates and resonates from each of the differing life approaches where an individual uses either their head or their heart.

The cerebral approach to attaining life-strength is fostered up from an individual's learned, intellectual understanding of how to relate to reality. Whereas in the heartfelt approach to acknowledging life, strength grows while experientially attaining self-definition by bringing to wakeful awareness the insightful understanding of our physical reality that waits consciously dormant and uncultivated in a subtle level of every individual's deeper consciousness.

In verse 33, Lau Tzu infers that when an individual recognizes and internalizes the world intellectually and then uses that cerebral knowledge as a tool or maybe even a weapon to conquer the world, they will amass a power reserve reflected in some form of personal strength...perhaps a hollow hardedged and brittle shell of power? When this person thinks of spirituality, they will look up, away into the sky, as they've never consciously witnessed its presence in their heart.

How this life approach is developed is recounted in this book's section 2, "Suffering Is a Living Effect, It Has a Living Cause." It considers the way life seems when living in a reality you know. It looks at human suffering's real-time cause and at its elimination in this lifetime.

In immediate contrast to approaching life intellectually, Lau Tzu goes on to point out that when an individual acquires life strength through understanding and internalizing life by attaining and using the mind/body harmony needed to achieve self-discovery, they become enlightened about the relational justice of our Source's natural and primal law of impermanence. Their wisdom-enriched awareness of our Source's impermanent nature and purpose to initiate ongoing change conquers the individual's need to create a selfego to manage and represent their worldview.

Sensuality is suffering's chosen media-of-present moment transfer used to spread its pain. Sensual report is the language of the tangible internal world theatre of human feeling, the heartland of both suffering and joy. By doing the due diligence to learn how to speak this language...body language...to navigate the sensual media used to communicate pain in the physical theater of the self, suffering's cause can be felt out (hunted down), contemplated, understood and forgiven.

The suffering it provokes will subside in the wake of the altruistic compassion it inspires.

Within the next few centuries, Siddhartha teaches how this life approach worked for him. He stories the detail of exactly how through self-trained harmony, he reached the level of enlightenment that Lau Tzu had pointed at a few centuries earlier. He tells how the human mind can be self-trained to reach this end of an enlightened understanding of what causes the ignorance that allows all of human suffering. In his teachings, he describes how he did it.

It's disappointingly simple. Midwesterners are intimidated or distanced by their perception of its ancient eastern grandeur. It makes it seem untouchable to them. It's attainment has no record of life history in their human experience.

There's no one alive today or even in centuries past that they know of that's officially considered enlightened. The vast majority haven't yet formed any working conception of what enlightened means. The range of accounts of what it was that Jesus was enlightened about would be vast.

The composite biblical account of Jesus's intended meaning of Jesus's later-provided like-approach was intellectually castrated by its third century Rome-serving creation and edit to leave its millennia of readers hanging at the start of the same process Siddhartha describes in complete detail. Christian believers are never to know where to turn for the detail of actually witnessing our Source's sensually realized sign from above and following it to their wisdom-enriched enlightenment about what it is that they don't understand that culminates into their real-time suffering.

In our Source-provided world of feeling, a self-trained mind can understand the sensual display of real-life physical markers to reveal and develop a steadfast core faith in knowing what the true nature and intended purpose of our Source is. A truth seeker of today needs to understand where the spiritual signposts pictured that preconditioned their intellectual fix on ancient religious theology meet up with the sensually emanated incarnations of those same religious maxims in the real-time present moments of today.

When these sensual signposts are recognized and associated with or linked to the intellectually sketched religious notions, their sensually witnessed presence unmasks and inspires the way to tap into the source of insightful wisdom that brings waking clarity to the nature and intended purpose of our Source. Siddhartha describes how he became fully enlightened about the object of his ignorance that allowed his suffering. That's all he ever talked about for the decades following his enlightenment.

This knowledge/awareness-gaining process works for anybody exactly the same today...2,500 years later. Advancement in spiritual maturity achieved by linking self-knowledge experientially from the deeper to the waking consciousness...

letting intellectual theology find sync with sensual reality...is nurtured from the inside and founded in the sensual experiential discovery and realization that every aspect of this reality is completely transitory. The dynamics of this life approach are considered in this book's third section, "There Is a Living Solution...Primal Ignorance Undone."

This process undoes the ignorance that preoccupies and indefinitely delays finding the unique purpose felt when human passion finds and unlocks human potential. It's the same ignorance that sponsors the same lack of understanding that underwrites all of human suffering. Soughtout wisdom-enriched awareness changes the nature of any human mind that's been locked in the myth of material permanence...a worldview acknowledging attachment to craving and aversion. It allows seeing beyond the ego to embrace and embody newly inspired insightful wisdom that overwrites and undoes its ignorance.

Each of Lau Tzu's two approaches to contemplating life finds a truth seeker at a present moment plateau of awareness somewhere along the continuum between suffering and enlightened awareness. To near the state of enlightenment, an individual has to find how to remove the shades of faulty prior conditioning for an enriched understanding of this reality's relational justice to shine through from the inborn ageless wisdom imbedded in the deeper consciousness. The deeper consciousness flows with the living rhythm of our reality well enough to commandeer forming a scab over a cut in the flesh and to remind the heart to pump life-blood through the human body without a reminder from the waking consciousness.

Of the same accord, that same deeper consciousness longs to heal the aching soul by making transparent to the waking consciousness its wisdom-enriched understanding of the relational justice appropriate for ruling this impermanent reality. Their confused ego-managed waking consciousness can then eliminate the ignorance of the impermanent nature of this reality that allows their ongoing inclusion in the circle of suffering. The human free will finds it depressing to be lost in the turbulence of change and having no direction toward understanding it well enough to be free of the paralyzing numbing effect of its controlling current.

When approaching life through the heart, an individual lives in a reality they feel. A soul-deep steadfast confidence surfaces in the individual as they develop a sensual record, defining a gut-felt familiarity with the truth of change that gives meaning to the passing of each passing present moment. They stand assured of our Source's omnipresent ability to sensually demonstrate the truth of its primal promise to provide unchanging change at any time that any individual points their curiosity at witnessing the reassurance of its omnipresence.

With all the humility they can muster, a truth seeker self-trains their ability to fine tune the harmonious coexistence between their making the right physical effort in guiding their sustained mental awareness to find and free up their awareness of this answer. They sensually tune their harmonious mind/body awareness into witnessing life as it manifests within their flesh. They relate their ebb to its flow. This is our Source's ongoing free-to-all message-of-life broadcast. It's our sign from above that manifests from within. Our Source speaks to us through our hearts.

An inspired insightful understanding of this release of life will undo the ignorance that allows present moment misery. A truth seeker's passing day can be filled with moments of sudden inspired insightful revelations of how their surrounding reality makes sense.

They can wakingly feel the insightful revelation. It's relaxing and they can consciously attribute that shade of mental peace to their conscious awareness of its intuitive existence. Ask them to put this great feeling into words and they will struggle to find the words and most won't be able to. The meanings that are perceived and felt in the heart aren't the same as those built in the mind. It's necessary to do the due diligence to translate one into the other.

When those using the heartfelt approach to acknowledge life think of spirituality, they look inside where they've witnessed the making of its truth.

It's clear that suffering through a living state of present moment unrest and confusion is what plagues the waking consciousness. Being that this suffering is an effect from something that happens in a living reality, does it have a preordained cause or a living cause that can be shaped and eliminated?

PART II

SUFFERING IS A LIVING EFFECT

...It has a living cause...The root of human suffering

Suffering's Not Satan-Sent

If human suffering is a living part of the present moment makeup of today's transforming reality, it has to have a real-time cause in today's living world. The cause of human suffering simmers undetected as part of the belief system conditioning process that generates mankind's present moment thought patterns. These thought patterns trigger the physiological reactions...sweat, increased heartbeat, etc. that document its lurking authority. Just the hollowing stir of its ignored presence is needed for it to have its way with undercutting how each person perceives the time-wrapped ever-flow of interacting factors that create each cause-into-effect present moment.

What it is that inspires human suffering is what it is that keeps its living presence updated. Like a virus, it mutates what's effective now in causing suffering into what makes ineffective any recently heard superficial statements of intellectually stored borrowed wisdom designed to attack suffering only at the behavioral level. It has a wide assortment of fleeting emotional states developed in individuals to rouse up and back into their mood through how they over time, develop their belief system. Look at the average Hoosier waistline and realize that many devout Christians fail to recognize the true spiritual tie-in of the mental push and pull from thoughts of whether or not to eat something they know to be unhealthy as a temptation.

Human suffering hosts a cadre of perception possibilities for any living being to develop. Suffering's antithesis involves experientially gaining the conscious awareness of this reality's nature and intended purpose. This knowledge undoes the ignorance that allows suffering to circle in time. They gain wisdom-enriched knowledge of how this world works by finding and self-training a spiritual understanding of the ongoing sensual dialogue that shouts its story from their flesh-bound human condition.

That's all suffering is. It's a living effect. It has a living cause. It has a cause that can be neutered by anyone that performs the due diligence to uncover the pathway to understanding the modern incarnation of its cause for what it really is. By following the self-discovered path to the bright light that highlights the other end of this present moment, an individual learns to find and live within the silver lining that invalidates mankind's cloud of fear.

There are a few documented accounts from 2,000-plus years ago that describe how a few individuals managed to unraveled their sequence of suffering. It's a process that works anywhere for anyone, with guidance in any language. A truth seeker must consciously gain sensual sight of what the difference between suffering and happiness feels like to them. They must recognize that they experience suffering and that it's not necessary and that it's not ordained. "You dig your own grave...make your own bed."

They must realize for themselves that suffering is not Satan-sent. Suffering's not just a philosophical notion or something to deal with or manage at a later time. Each present moment is an unauthored state of now that's open to the effects coming from the underlying purpose of an individual's causing intentions.

A truth seeker must direct their efforts at discovering what compassionate love is to then realize that one of the effects of this discovery is that once discovered and owned, that suffering's pulse fails to return and rule the state of their waking consciousness. It's important that a truth seeker's focus is directed at understanding the nature of their mind, so they can change it to allow their thought patterns to flow to the same rhythm as do thoughts coming from a state of altruistic compassion and not just blindly swinging wild to fight off suffering. They must sight forward toward establishing blissful awareness and not back focused on aspects of suffering.

1

Hoosier Roots Conditioned

Born Suspended

So here we are, as fate has it...born into this world. We cross life's threshold curious, suspended solely/souly by our 5 senses in a reality of transforming give and take dynamics...a whirlwind of ongoing change. The human condition lives in a multi-dimensional reality that takes time and mass and at the velocity of impermanence, mixes in an infinite number of appearing and disappearing bits of energy to produce the forms and shapes perceived within the perceptive boundaries of human sensitivity. Humans bend to their perception of the ongoing cause and effect interplay between the varying degrees of hot and cold, light and dark, loud and quiet, sweet and sour. They develop likes and don't-likes to the differing combinations of sensual buzz.

Individual's each develop personal preferences to what stimuli combinations they want and don't want to feel again. They share the same playing field with over six billion fellow spirit-occupied human shells...all from the same factory...all burning the same gas...all bound for the same recycle bin.

Young human minds naturally teem with early life questions. An ageless unanswered wonderment about all the mysterious aspects of the newborn exposure of the human condition to the human experience is quickly recognized in the trusting sparkle of curious infant eyes.

They're born armed with the vulnerable beginnings of an unfettered free will that allows them to evaluate the intended purpose of any new explanatory claim encountered from an endless array of information sources to feel for and verify the living nature of the truth of its claim before internalizing the intended purpose of that claim as being true.

These interpretations assign some degree of yes-no like-dislike meaning to the many combinations of new sensual messages encountered. This freshly forming unfettered free will evaluates and learns to determine what ideas and beliefs to internalize to characterize and shape the maturing belief system used to voice their ever-developing youthful worldview.

An unfettered free will guides an individual as they recognize the potential of their inborn and unique-to-their-mindand-body talents. They uncover and release their passion in effort to realize and give being to their life purpose.

Their unfettered free will taps into their inner strength as they let their light shine. Some say a young individual's free will has its first real public coming-out at around two years when their newly realized ability to firmly plant a vocal flag and their phonic ability to firmly articulate "NO" coordinate and fuse into one as they boldly stake claim to their newly coordinated personal independence.

Family and friends wait on hand to lovingly help bridge passage into the new cause/effect reality set in this multifaceted, multidimensional, ever-changing climate. They eagerly share their perceptions of society's dos and don'ts. They describe needed behavioral skills relating to everything from giving and receiving love to potty training and developing sandbox etiquette.

The true inborn nature of a young curious mind mirrors the nature of our Source from which it was conceived...created in its ephemeral image. Their body is merely a breathing wisp and living fiber of the omnipresent all-encompassing present moment essence of the ever-changing interwoven multicolor fabric of reality crafted via our living Source.

Each living soul shapes and directs a unique mind/ body combination of talent potential. Each individual has a responsibility to the whole of our Source to realize their inborn talent potential for mankind's united advancement toward the enlightened understanding of the human ignorance that will eventually reset the human condition collective waking awareness to the present moment factory setting of love, joy and happiness they came from. It's the human ignorance that sponsors the common strains of suffering for every black, white, yellow, Christian, Muslim, Islam or whatever oriented human being.

The youth's glow of untested innocence reflects from the eyes of their admirers...a glow that will fade with the passing of time. It becomes the aging youngster's life-task of self-discovery to rekindle their internal flame and restore the glow of their inner child.

Early Conditioning and Steadfast Faith

An infant's conscious awareness of the sensual input coming from each of their five senses grows daily. Family, friends and other ad hoc teachers compete for the child's attention. They want to pass along their construal of society's values beliefs and traditions to the child as accepted ways of interpreting and cataloguing perceptions of these new sensual experiences.

They want the child to share the same understanding of life that they have chosen. In some instances, selling the child on their life philosophy reaffirms to them what they've decided to be the truth. Or maybe it allows them to see in others how or why their philosophy's flawed? They want the reassuring nod of approval from another fellow human that they see things as they do...that their picture of reality makes sense.

Many new claims that offer explanation or interpret certain aspects of this reality are accepted into a child's belief system uncontested. The validity of these unquestioned unverified claims is supported only by that attributed to cultural mass acceptance or through the child's total confidence in the source of the news like an infant would have in their mom or dad or sibling or teacher or any authoritative grown up.

There's a continual bombardment of countless stimuli on each of the child's five senses. Having the young learner's focused attention is needed to influence their perception of these new experiences to have the child internalize the interpretations of any related claims into their belief system to shape their worldview. These early-internalized beliefs establish a child's collective purpose, seeding their developing life purpose that accounts for their intention-inspired behavior.

Don Miguel Ruiz, a Toltec people shaman, comments on this idea:

> Attention is the ability we have to discriminate and to focus only on that which we want to perceive. We can perceive millions of things simultaneously, but using our attention, we can hold whatever we want to perceive in the foreground of our mind. . .
>
> By using our attention, we learned a whole reality, a whole dream. We learned how to behave in society: what to believe and what not to believe; what is acceptable and what is not acceptable; what is good and what is bad; what is beautiful and what is ugly; what is right and what is wrong. It was all there already— all that knowledge, all those rules and concepts about how to behave in the world.[1]

People are very impressionable at an early age. This is especially true when any new information, views or beliefs are presented by an adult authority figure. There are so many new things to absorb. The child may lack the maturity to come up with logical inquiries. New ideas, views and beliefs are agreed to and internalized before being questioned or before the young individual could consider other options.

When a country's religious logo "In God We Trust" is stamped on all the monetary currencies as well as on many of the license plates of its citizens and when a country's national pledge of loyalty is made to the religion's god in the same breath as is the pledge to the nation's flag, the religion's individual acceptance is highly likely. Citizens are pressured to internalize these canonized religious understandings and behaviors because they represent the country's socially recognized religious/spiritual beliefs. These symbols are a part of the citizen's reality from the when they can first understand what their country believes in and what their relatives have died for.

An adult explaining a fact to a child that there's a supposed religious/theological order that determines reality's cause/effect relational justice can stun and dampen the child's healthy inquisitive nature. Just like they are told about their desire for the opposite sex, they are led to blindly believe that it will all make sense to them when they get older...accept it now and understand why later. Blindly accepting a religious ideology can flash-freeze a child's willingness to question and consider.

This should be the time to nurture the child's conscious acceptance of their undeveloped competence and confidence in understanding the true nature of this reality...why things and situations really work as they do. They're actually at the best time in their life for developing a steadfast faith set in their conscious awareness of the omnipresent consistency of the relational justice in this reality's day-to-day cause/effect rhythm.

As an infant, sensual awareness increases daily and then one day they begin to recognize the independence and voice of their budding unfettered free will. Their free will bravely exercises its inner purpose of questioning the authenticity of things and ideas. As their vocabulary develops to put to word their inner felt questions fueled by their great desire to learn, they will openly question and openly challenge the claims made by any authoritative adult figure.

They will question just about anything their attention spans across. Mommy and daddy are replaced with "no" and "why" as being their most favorite words. These words are repeated on each occasion until their inner felt questions are answered or quelled by a substitute, bribe or some sort of threat to the inner felt freedom of their free will. Many noble young questioners of authority will suffer multiple time outs, grounding sentences, restrictions from TV, computer or texting privileges. For many it's the start of a lifelong process of
losing touch with their unique self-protecting curiosity.

Open expression of the free will helps to develop a child's ability to recognize and reflect the voice of their inner self. Their maturing free will has no hesitation to shouting "No!" or in asking "Why?" This prods the person making the claim they'd like the tot to believe to prove the truth to satisfy the tot's inner-felt uncertainty questioning the practicality of the truth of their claim.

For now, the young child's awareness of this analytical ability of their unfettered free will is being sharpened and honed day by day along with the size of their vocabulary. These qualities will come into sync as their sensual awareness becomes more focused, but at this very young age, their bare trust will have them naively adopting most any claim they're told they should adopt while forming their fragile worldview.

Don Miguel Ruiz makes these observations:

> It was not your choice to speak English. You didn't choose your
> religion or your moral values—they were already there before
> you were born. We never had the opportunity to choose what
> to believe or what not to believe. We never chose even the
> smallest of these agreements. We didn't even choose our own
> name.³ As children, we didn't have the opportunity to choose
> our beliefs, but we agreed with the information that was passed
> to us from the dream of the planet via other humans. The only
> way to store information is by agreement. The outside dream
> may hook our attention, but if we don't agree, we don't store
> that information.²

Even at the very young age when a child first begins eating solid food, if they
don't like the taste of something, there's nothing that can be said that will change
their mind. Even though they can't yet talk, their free will's evaluated their sensual
experience. It's determined their liking or disliking of the food and is leading their
behavior in the way it sees best and safest. They try to gain more of something
approved or move farther away from something sensed to be unpleasant for the
human experience of their human condition.

They unintentionally begin to develop a genuine yet steadfast faith in the
dimensional physical consistency in this reality our Source has provided for the
human condition to live in. They come to understand that gravity that holds them
to their chair today will also hold them to their chair tomorrow. The wisdom of
how to best negotiate their chair today will hold true tomorrow.

They feel confidence in how their sensual port set in their taste buds will
evaluate and perceive the relational justice among the interacting factors that their
saliva transports from the food they've previously tasted. They develop an unrecognized comfort in our Source's omnipresence. As they grow older their steadfast
faith in this truth grows deeper.

They naturally assume that the next time they taste this food the cause/effect
factors in this time-fueled reality will be the same. So, they feel confident that the
next time the unpleasant food's presented to them, it will taste the same and again,
they will refuse it. Even at this young age, their experience-based-faith-supported
unfettered free will's looking out for their well-being.

Rivalry Conditioned To Support And Fortify Self-Ego

We learn how to get what we want and how to live our lives. Behavior to
avoid punishment and to get rewards is learned. Avoiding punishment and getting
rewards become intention motivators common to all. We become attached to the

behaviors that get rewarded as well as the behavior that is effective in avoiding punishment. It begins in the primal gardens of each and every human being where their seeds of intention are planted daily.

As we grow, we will compete for people's attention in search of the rewards or notoriety we've been exposed to and grown fond of. Picture a child as they shout, "Mommy, Mommy, look at me and look at what I'm doing!" This early aspiration for praise and recognition generates a spirit of competition that will continue into adulthood.

We will compete for the attention of our peers and others to pass along the information making up our personal belief systems. It helps solidify, strengthen and add base to the claim of the idea or concept that we support as being part of society's accepted and adopted collective belief system as well as strengthen our particular tangent of that belief if that be the case.

The spirit of competition is nourished and gains strength in repetition while developing into a defining personality trait. This competitive spirit will be used to gain belief and acceptance of our views and beliefs and to discredit the views of others as we defend our ego-managed illusions of "I am" from notions that will minimize our calculated legitimacy.

Gagged Free Will Accumulates Impending Doubt

Early-age skepticism or rebellion to accepting or internalizing society's passed-on claims usually lacks the effectiveness of a coordinated well-articulated probing and the analytical reasoning ability to push the objection up to level two. Thus, the objections are usually not strong enough to win. The adult presence of parents and teachers tentatively draws the kind of respect that will often gag any freewill protest. Pure intimidation is at times a factor.

Repeated surrender to under-challenged questionable internalized claims that had questionable unverified credibility associated with the claimed purpose of their claims sets stage for a mounting after-taste of uncertainty, doubt and self-questioning. If there was no opportunity to experience a true heartfelt validation, like when tasting food, of the claims made by the questionable internalized explanations, the amount of latent cumulative doubt buried in the back of someone's mind will accumulate over time. Many individuals decide that it often becomes easier to just not question question-worthy claims.

No longer consistently using their unfettered free will to test unverified new claims, the individual will have less truly felt steadfast confidence in the dependability of the effect of the claim's suggested causing purpose to be replicated in the dependable cause/effect relational justice of our reality. Their sensual feeling of validation has yet to be realized in relation to the living plausibility of the purpose of these unverified claims.

The true intended meaning is lost as the experiential unfamiliarity negates any steadfast faith in the natural connection of the cause a claim avows to and its promised effect, so any assurance to the purpose of the claim is fragmented by uncertainty. No matter how well described the sweetness of chocolate is, it's not truly chocolate-sweet until it's mixed with saliva and ran by the individual's sensual port that's physically equipped for tasting.

It's regretful when anyone's naturally compelling drive to question is destroyed or quelled by their exposure and repeated submission to pressured surrender. In most people, the effects of repeated surrender are realized to the point of their submissive gullibility that sterilizes their free will of its inborn leadership and self-protection qualities.

Impending doubt can become entrapped in an eddy of mental rumination. Our society conditions us to ruminate over bad events. TV news comes on at all hours of the day and is designed to review in the deepest detail the worst happenings that happen. "Breaking News" is the bait that keeps the news staff racing around to out-scoop their competitor news organizations. Switch from channel to channel and the same stories are reintroduced and reviewed...over and over. We've learned how to let our ideas bearing guilt or other negative emotions set the stage for our present moment state of mind.

Midwestern churchgoers can spend their entire lifetime under the religious umbrella and don't question what the living application of the religious mantra that Christ died for our sins is.

Why are certain behaviors classified as sins? If we don't know what makes a behavior a sin, how can we avoid other behaviors that might display similar bad effects or originate from similar thought patterns?

Do these sins cause suffering? At this point, any meaning to this question is lost in loose ungrounded definition. Does the generation of these sins have a cause? Can this cause be affected by an individual's efforts? Is there a way to eliminate this cause? What is the way?

They become so tired of questioning and being shut down, it seems it's just not worth the trouble so they just "go along with the crowd" or become a social nuisance with an unfamiliar, uncontrolled purpose directed anywhere other than society's well-being that is probably harmful to others.

Questioning Authority

Questioning what doesn't make intuitive sense is a basic tenet of self-preservation. When something just doesn't gel between the conditioned collective worldview of an individual's belief system and what is being sensed or perceived from an ongoing situation, an individual should take action. They need to revive their subdued free will and reconnect with the child in them who's inner nature is wanting to stand up and shout "No!" or at least plead "Why?"

Regardless of the implied credibility of the claim's source, Siddhartha taught the necessity of questioning anything that carries some degree of uncertainty. Until an individual knows directly that a claim's supporting factors are verifying the truth of any newly encountered claim represented by someone else's expressed view or belief or of any source of information, having a steadfast faith founded in the dependability of the ongoing transient nature of the bigger picture to warrant the existence of the same dimensional reality for the continued validity of the relational wisdom associated with the claim's current validity in question helps allow an individual to stay involved with focused direction in the present moment. This helps keep their inborn talents honed to the nonillusionary reality happening in between the causes and effects making up the ever-passing present moments in their life. They're more consciously in touch with the development of their talents.

If everyone sincerely questions things they don't feel secure with, in the end they will all live in harmony, bound to a common focus. The end answer is the same for all. There's only one shared truth, one shared intention to initiate the ongoing change of the ultimate reality.

An individual either lives with conscious awareness of this world's impermanent nature, or they live lost unknowingly spinning in an illusion that they live in a reality where things can have a nature to exist in a state of nonchanged where the nature of their expectations doesn't match up with the nature of reality. This makes them suffer.

They live through each present moment with the inner imbalance that brings to their minds a subliminal agenda to be looking to find mental balance. Or, maybe they'd just be looking for a way to restore what they experientially remember having mental balance to have been like earlier in their lifetime?

Not having mental balance reminds them of the calm sort of present moment that comes with a balanced state of mind. They inwardly sense its absence and are unknowingly longing for it while looking to sense it in the essence of whatever their present moment introduces them to.

The Academy Award-winning Hollywood actor Morgan Freeman expressed his feelings on life when he said: "You can't just go hiding and hoping that something is going to save you. The only way you can measure your life is by testing it" (*USA Today* December 19, 2007, D1).

It's also important for an individual to question the quality of the types of experience used by the sources of the claims to establish the truth of the claim they're considering blindly internalizing. Progress toward an enlightened understanding of the human ignorance that inspires their suffering is realized when an individual gets past doing things because it's something that cool people do and they try to realize on a personal scale what it is about the activity or situation that draws cool people to it. Break it down to an active sensual analysis of the situation and weigh the level of appreciation for the perceived sensual messages of the event on a personal unbiased scale versus a reflection of how other people react.

Free Spirit Domesticated and Desensitized

Don Miguel Ruiz made an interesting and somewhat obvious observation that human beings are animals, and like animals or pets, they are domesticated. It's a part of belief system development. Individuals learn the difference between good and bad, right and wrong. They use these markers to set the boundaries of what they like and dislike. Rewards and punishment of sorts are used to fashion expected compliance.

Many behaviors are learned to help an individual to best fit into a society. This can interrupt a normal healthy growth and development process. Role models and teachers take a child's honest expression of how they really feel and teach them to abridge it with what they think is needed to fit into a popular societal worldview structured around an unverified illusion of what reality appears to be.

While they're being swayed from their childhood innocence, they patch together a worldview that's to some degree miscued by faulty misguided conditioning. Many are lured into believing in an illusionary conception of the cause/effect relationships that make up this reality. They might imagine nonexistent properties and priorities that support a conception of what a reality based in continuity would apparently be. They lose touch with their free will that protects their inner child.

It's here where their free will lives in their belief system, where the true experiential feeling that sensually ties their intended actions to the effects of those causing behaviors, are frequently lost or sacrificed to an illusionary explanation secured by a blind faith to the claim maker's living participation in today's present moment and where the expectation of the relative justice in certain cause/effect relationships finds its balance. An illusion-inspired interpretation helps find a temporary mental calm. It helps front to the waking ego an explanation for the mental confusion that feeds their mitote/ maya mental state.

They drift into a reality where a heartfelt connection between the cause and effect disappears to be replaced or lost in the chatter of the 1,000 voices of their growing mitote/ maya mental state that's hijacking their belief system. Their conscious awareness is in a state where causes and effects continue to happen with each passing present moment, but the cause/effect relationships become lost confused and misunderstood causing much suffering as they struggle to keep their illusionary bubble from popping while having nowhere to turn.

Autodomestication

Individuals eventually learn how to judge themselves and others by the justice inherent to the ideas and beliefs they've agreed to internalize that comprise their belief systems and worldview. Don Miguel Ruiz's metaphoric parasitic inner judge that individuals create for themselves enforces prior conditioning with the old learned feelings of good boy and bad boy. For many, there's an elderly white-robed bearded man up in the sky, looking over their shoulder, whispering, "Heaven or hell?"

Individuals are auto-domesticated by this time. They no longer need external judgmental commentaries on their behavior. They automatically punish and reward themselves, based on what their internalized beliefs have conditioned their idea of right and wrong to be.

Don Miguel Ruiz suggests that when an individual's true inner nature goes against faulty prior conditioning, they'll still perform in line with their misguided prior conditioning because going against the book of agreements used to write the charter of their worldview makes them feel unsafe and uneasy. They enjoy the safe feeling they get from staying securely in line and not breaking any of these rules.

This sort of cowering reaction can become habitual to any inner-confrontation involving the unknown. After much repetition, it acquires a fleeting nature...a reaction requiring no conscious thought. It can become a defining part of their addictive personality. It's something recognizable to others.

These individuals lack the strengthening steadfast faith that can be developed alongside their fine-tuning of their conscious awareness of the primal truth of ongoing change...a faith strong enough to support their standing alone to question anything society blindly says is so.

Their faith is not a faith that's surety has been established in their experience. It's a faith that's blind to providing the courage needed to stand-alone or to even just stand against what the masses might swear by that's backed only by a history of acceptance by the masses.

They will say nothing about what their true inner nature might be questioning. People become like sheep on the way to the market. They acquire a herd mentality.

In response to this prodding mental tension, as don Miguel Ruiz suggests, the parasite judge changes into the inner victim and, while feeling the guilt and blame, will also feel shame and self-pity. The victim can punish themselves for this daily for the rest of their life.

The human being is the only animal that repeatedly punishes themselves for prior mistakes. Cattle ruminate the cud they chew while humans ruminate their thoughts of guilt and worry over things they blame themselves for or over things that are yet to come.

The extent of self-punishment and self-depreciation can be horrific. The inner victim doesn't feel good, attractive or smart enough. They feel unworthy.

They suffer because of their ignorance about the primal nonsecular self-evident truth of our Source's nature and intended purpose to continually initiate ongoing change. They suffer because too many layers of faulty prior conditioning obscure their inborn awareness of the savvy of how things relate and prioritize in a reality of ongoing change that resides in their deeper consciousness.

They've lost sight of the resident truth they were born with. The simplicity of the innocent truth shone through unobstructed until their unfettered free will allowed their belief system to eat from the tree of knowledge to then be infected by misguided untested unverified by the illusionary nature of claims that only find their truth in a reality with a different nature than this impermanent cause/effect reality. This has created their fog of mental unrest. They suffer.

Diffused Passion

As long as people are domesticated to live in a reality founded partly on society's faulty conditioning, attached to the cravings and aversions of an illusionary reality, they're going to march confused in a crooked line to the drums of others' undefined self-serving purposes. Their intentions will reflect the thought patterns generated from a compromised worldview.

They lose sight of any direction they might have started to develop at a younger age that highlighted any special talents they might have had. They lose contact with the internal switch that allows them to let the light from their Sourcegiven talents shine.

They'll live in disconnect from their inborn link to sensing and expressing what's truly felt in their heart. The factory setting of their unfettered free will is becoming fettered. They've not yet, at least intellectually, became aware of our Source's nature and purpose of intent to unfailingly initiate ongoing change.

Self-love is founded in the faith in the ongoing consistency of the cause/effect relationship savvy afforded by those who give a want-defined definition to the ongoing change of this reality. When so many individual's can't see deep enough to grasp the truth behind this deceptive giveand-take, it's no wonder inter and intra personal love runs so thin in our society. It's no wonder so many Hoosiers blindly live day to day overweight killing themselves with a diet of white flour and sugar while nonchalantly flipping their cigarettes out their car window at stoplights as they miss the light while talking or texting on their cell phones. Their heads are planted deeply in the sands of denial on the beach of ignorance.

It's no wonder so many Hoosiers can sit back and hear about people in other cultures who are being totally stripped of their freedom of expression and not feel as though it's their brothers and sisters who are being so ravaged. Their view of humanity can't even penetrate the color of the skin to appreciate the warmth of the soul.

If an individual's not been introduced to a way of realizing the primal foolishness in becoming attached to craving and aversive thoughts, the 1,000-voice disharmony of a self-trained mitote/maya reality will set in. It begins gradually in the early years as it shorts out their waking link to their deep-down inner prescription to freedom of the spirit.

Forty-plus years ago, there was an eighth grader whose first favorite author back in first grade was Dr. Seuss. He had eagerly read all of Dr. Seuss's collection that the school library had. He gave Dr. Seuss 100 percent of his attention when reading. This individual's present moment ability to focus their mind had since changed from that initial passionate immersion to one he suddenly realized in the back of their eighth grade social studies class to be full of mind-drifting unfocused indecision. He couldn't stay at all focused on the subject of what he was reading.

His cognitive attention was floating untethered, lost to all that he read. Even if he were reading something interesting, his mind would soon uncontrollably drift. He would just wonder when his attention would again be hijacked and the concentrated effort of following the story line of the reading would be lost.

He had realized there was no real conscious awareness of where his mental focus should point or why it was out of his control. He was unsure what criteria were needed to qualify something as worthy of his interest. Why did his mind roam with no real direction?

Another unsuspectingly subdued free will had lost its power to protect or even identify its host's life purpose of intention. All true passion was being diffused into the random unfounded interests of misguided prior conditioning.

This individual's ongoing ever-changing reality had no realized direction. His belief system was lined with uncertainty that shadowed all the present moment decisions of the teenage phase of his human experience.

Individuals amass internal agreements to how they decide to perceive the purpose of outside claims to the answers of how different causal factors relate to each other. They determine how their reality makes sense. They develop a personal belief system that's fronted by a worldview they've developed that expresses who they are and what they feel, how they act and what they believe. If internalizing misguided conditioning has tainted it, their purpose is diluted and their focus on their passion becomes diffused.

2

Herd Mentality

All Onboard the Sheep Wagon to Market

The more people that are involved in something, the sense of person-to-person exchange is minimized. The compassionate feeling of walking in someone else's shoes is replaced with the fear-fed greed of fattening the reserves to protect the ego-managed "I am" from the uncertainties of the unknown.

It could be said that the USA as a nation is being desensitized to the difference between a want and a need. Its citizens are being conditioned to suffer en masse. Benjamin

R. Barber, Kekst professor of Civil Society at the University of Maryland and a Distinguished Senior Fellow at Demos in New York City, insightfully interprets what he views as civic schizophrenia to be what is happening to our capitalist society in his most recent of twelve books, *CONSUMED How Markets Corrupt Children, Infantilize Adults, And Swallow Citizens Whole* (W. W. Norton and Company, Inc. 2007). He suggests that society creates an air or ethos of beliefs to assure its continuance.

For a profit-based society to continue, it masks needed consumer consumption behavior as moral or religious to perpetuate spending and injects it into society's current of perceived normalcy. He reasons how our society finds ways to sell overproduced silly goods in a society that has relatively few genuine needs.

> The idea of an infantilist ethos is a new twist on an old concept: that capitalism as an economic system demands certain reinforcing cultural attitudes and social behaviors in each of its stages of development, and that such attitudes and behaviors can be inculcated in a society through a value system that takes the form of a society-wide moral or religious ethos.[6]
>
> The perduring American myth that associates worldly success and wealth with godliness and that led Andrew Carnegie to write in his *Gospel of Wealth* that not evil, but good, has come

to the race from the accumulation of wealth by those who have the ability and energy to produce. It also continues to be visible in American pop religion, pop therapy, and pop culture—televangelism, twelve-step therapy programs, and many of the more meretricious (and hence successful) get-rich-quick schemes.

Much of the pop-cultural literature apes Puritanism's mood even as it debases its currency. It preaches sobriety (twelve-step programs) while encouraging indulgence (advertising and marketing), calls for temperance of character (conservative cultural critics), even as it molds behavior into a consumerist mold (conservative support for market capitalism). It demands leisure for consumerism (shopping malls as surrogates for town centers) but turns leisure into a kind of work (the imperative to shop) since the ascetic ethos is conserved not in an obligation to produce, but in a new obligation to shop and consume. Greed becomes a form of altruism, indulged not out of love of love of self but out of love of capitalist productivity. When President Bush wanted to find a metaphor for normalcy in helping Americans find their way back from the nightmare of 9/11, he seized on shopping—imploring Americans to show Al Qaeda its patriotic backbone by going to the mall and getting on with the business of consuming.[4]

Subliminal Thought Engineering...
Mindless Obedience

Along with the acceptance of society's accumulation of history-tried-and-true beliefs and views, there are beliefs that are much more unfounded that manage to ride into individual belief systems on the same acceptance cart as the other time-enduring customs, views and beliefs. It's common for this type of new information to receive very little resistance in Midwestern USA.

"Sweet tooth" is a sort of pet phrase to help justify going against what is healthy for one's physical body. It's been said that when deciding on the safety of eating new untried foods long ago that sweetness was a sign of its more probable safety. However, there is no sweet tooth. Sugar feeds the bacteria that fill the human tooth with cavities. There's a section of the tongue that's sensitive to sweetness. This cute little phrase has had quite a collective impact on the level of health problems regarding human dental and physical reality in the Midwest. Yet, the phrase has greatly helped justify the consumer behavior that supports the bottom line of sweet-related industry.

Society's collective free will is held hostage by advanced methods of subliminally suggestive advertising. It's advertising that subversively hooks individual's attention to sneak their untested unverified self-serving purposes around the claim-analyzing function of the individuals' free wills as subliminal implants.

The purposes of their subliminally injected intentions come from their collective corporate belief system and resulting greed-driven worldview with desires for capital gain more than any altruistically engendered compassionate concern for society's collective well-being. The fundamental point underlying broadcast TV is to instill dissatisfaction with an individual's lifestyle, so they will feel a need for different stuff.

The media silently injects into society the need to buy things. When did the Christmas "giving incentive" change from being a gift handcrafted and appropriate to compliment an individual's life routine to something the gifted has no use for and will have to add to their museum of needless wants for feeling too guilty to give it up or dispose of it. The giver is satisfied merely with being able to check off the receiver's name from their friends and family gift list that they must somehow find the time to make token purchases for.

In modern times, the daily news gives constant updates on what's expected and anticipated for holiday sales every year. "It's the American way," they say, the Americans' duty. The thousands that line up hours early on the morning of Black Friday following Thanksgiving to get an item that's out of stock elsewhere or that the store has a reduced price on is unbelievable. Caught up in the craze, people from the back of the lines will storm the doors at opening time. Some eager shoppers may see the rest of the day from a hospital bed. People who don't read the fine print in the advertisements will not know that the store only has ten of these reduced-price items.

Now that Internet time purchasing has begun to represent a significant amount of consumer spending, the Monday after Thanksgiving is now known as Cyber Monday. It's advertised to represent the busiest day of online shopping each year. The opinions of marketing experts are revealed as to what buyers are thinking and why or why not they're going to buy online. Spending is presented as being more than a responsibility. Spending is presented as the natural American thing to do.

This media behavior creates a kink in society's collective process of reaching the white light. It's known as greed; a derivative form of craving. It deceivingly gums up society's collective progress in insuring the liberty and freedom of its citizens to understand their ignorance that causes their suffering and develop and express their life purpose.

Once individuals have internalized these infected intentions of purpose of the illusory corporate claims into their belief systems, the subliminally injected purpose silently influences the individuals' future related action-bound intentions and behavior.

This indoctrination suffocates and numbs an individual's free will by unnaturally and deceivingly bypassing their free will's right and responsibility to verify and establish the information's validity before accepting or internalizing the purpose of the claim into their personal belief system.

The behavior-shaping claim of the message from the outside entity has been unfairly mainlined into the individual's belief system. The functional utility of the individual's free will is being numbed and denied to the individual's unaware and naive waking consciousness. The outside entity has its way with the individual's purposed intention to unduly influence their behavior.

Companies invest millions of dollars to find the most effective way to inject into the onlooking individual the desire to do what their advertising is vying for. These corporate intentions are nothing short of being seditious to the concept of individual liberty and the true freedom of self-expression. Today's advertising is designed to convince watchers to purchase the product or service of the entity that pays for the ads. They're not going to spend their money to advertise to people anything that makes it less likely that their interest will

do anything but bring in more profit.

They will tell half-truths...the good half that benefits their product or service. They will use actors to play short commercial roles without telling the audience that the beautiful person is really an actor. They will exaggerate or tell outright lies about their services and products. Even the most "honest" ads play truth jujitsu within the scope of objectivity.

Ahem...What was it that I Needed?

A society with a collectively numbed free will, lacking direction that's caught up in the whirlwind of ongoing change actually wants to be told by corporate America what is cool, modern or chic so they can fit in and be normal. Without knowing how to find their way and not really knowing where they're going, they want to be told what's needed to be accepted into the illusionary cliques nurtured by the media to generate money to fund corporate interests and keep the economy rolling.

Rome wanted its Romans to feel they had to turn to Rome for answers when they edited out Jesus's teachings to groups of higher spiritual maturity where he addresses how to look inside to find balance. They will spend much of their time, money and energy spinning their wheels, dealing with their self-trained mental state of mitote/maya. They will pillage through these suggested items that are unrelated to any path to becoming enlightened about why they suffer or find temporary bliss while hoping to blindly stumble across the way to this peace love and harmony they subconsciously know exists.

Mr. Barber highlights corporate America's self-righteous attitude toward the willingness of buyers' to lay down their guard, allowing corporate manipulation of their reality:

> For all the power of marketing, consumers are too often willing subjects of manipulation. It is less the efficacy of advertising than the frailty of shoppers that renders resistance so problematic. For in the absence of real wants and genuine needs, consumers often seem to invite the producer of goods and services to tell them what it is that they want. The cynical slogan behind which earnest marketers hide when faced with the tawdry, the harmful, and the meretricious proclaims "Don't blame us, we just give people what they want!" Yet when skeptics reply "It is you, however, who tell the people what they want!" marketers offer the ingenuous response, which contains a seed of truth that "Yes, to be sure, but the people want to be told what they want!' They need to be shown what they need!"[5]

The Midwestern mind-set follows this paradigm. The Midwestern mind-set that falls prey to this methodology for selecting the products marketed to satisfy corporate interests will in the same way bend to social suggestions on how to best calm their spirit.

Christianity requires an individual to take a leap of blind faith. They are told they need to act now to secure personal freedom from the clutches of afterlife suffering to live in an afterlife paradise. New believers are told that as soon as they commit, they are saved...no matter what sort of present moment mitote/maya mental state they have to deal with.

Having sights set on relief from a present moment hell is not a main directive. The citizens haven't thought it through that deeply before they blindly commit to having faith in the religion's philosophy. It's through God's grace that relief from everyday suffering is attained...period.

This blind commitment is founded in a religious claim that has no experientially based substance to build a heartfelt steadfast level of trust on. The religious claim doesn't come paired with a living sign to demonstrate the truth of its account of what our Source's nature and intended purpose are.

The internalization of this asserted claim lacks the inner-felt validation of having been there, done that, like the sensually defining experience a baby has tasting their food that they later will eat again or will refuse to eat again...a sensually sealed yea or nay experiential surety.

This creates a void of uncertainty that rocks the soundness of the believer's belief system and worldview. There's the latent feeling of uncertainty in the believer's deeper consciousness having seen no living sign verifying that the claim's promise maker and suggested purpose is alive and participating in the ongoing display of reality. In leaping from hearing a claim straight to believing it, their free will's been zapped with the stun gun of looming doubt...even if all their friends and family belong to its member list.

Fundamental narrow-mindedness seeps in and its unbending nature allows the experience-lacking void in their belief system to fill with doubt, uncertainty and fear. It carves an emotional void in the completeness of their personality. They enter back into this void anytime the theological topic is revisited.

With this indecision, they gradually give up their ability to make up their mind. They lose touch with what they really need versus what they want. Still, they use their present moment energy trying to keep their ego-managed illusionary account of apparent reality hip to what's perceived as popular.

Their numbed free will has developed no relationship with our living Source to derive relational wisdom concerning the cause/effect factors of our transforming reality. Midwestern symptoms of this state are visible in the unending amassing of personal possessions. Other outward symptoms of this mentally imbalanced separation are seen in how citizens have developed no real concept of why or how their own physical body should be cared for.

They cope in a makeshift illusion about what reality is and what matters. The difference between their actual needs and wants is out of focus in their illusionary apparent reality with no internally felt direction to set their own priorities by. They'll read this page and say: "This state doesn't exist in me"... denial.

Faux Needs to Sustain Market Demand

In this capitalist society, the citizens have most everything they need to live a healthy physical life. If they understood and could appreciate this state of affairs, society's demand for new items would disappear. It's would be like tying a tourniquet around this economy's aorta. This would be very bad news for our economy's survival.

Corporate America must continue selling products to stay solvent...to pay its employees to continue living out a variety of ego-managed illusions of reality. Corporate America, partly through deceptive advertising, creates many new uses for many of the new items they're producing to be thought of as being something the average citizen must have and need to buy.

Mr. Barber elaborates:

> The infantilist ethos generates a set of habits, preferences, and attitudes that encourage and legitimate childishness. As with Protestant asceticism in its time, infantilism reflects broad attitudes and general behavior that mirror the age, beyond the specific concerns of capitalism. But it also serves capitalist consumerism directly by nurturing a culture of impetuous consumption necessary to selling puerile goods in a developed world that has few genuine needs. As the earlier ethos helped explain and shape the leadership of capitalist producers such as Jacob Fugger and John D. Rockefeller, but also Bill Gates in our own period, the infantilist ethos helps explain and shape the behavior of capitalism's marketing executives and ardent consumers in our era.[9]
>
> For the ethos is impressively efficient in creating market demand by encouraging the manufacture of faux needs in the affluent world, thereby assuring the sale of all the goods and services capitalism is zealously overproducing. Infantilization aims at inducing puerility in adults and preserving what is childish in children trying to grow up, even as children are "empowered" to consume.[6]

There's an ongoing display of TV ads maintaining an ever-changing menu of corporate-sponsored faux consumer needs. They show actors using the item as though it was a part of their everyday life. This does make a mental impression that floats in and adds color to the illusionary stage plays existing in consumers' minds when walking through a store with intentions set on shopping.

There are different styles of toilet bowl cleaners based on the angle the cleaning pad's connected to the handle and the ease of disposing of the dirty pad. Is this something that is really needed? There are lawn weed whackers that should be bought because of the ease the user finds in reconfiguring the handle attachment to allow easier access to pesky weeds in situations requiring a slightly different angle of cutting action that might prove useful. This is a faux need being created to help the companies maintain their bottom line.

This is legalized modern-day free-will genocide. It's a tangle or snag in humanity's collective quest for enlightenment about what's replacing mankind's joy and happiness with suffering. The cutting-edge of the cause stays sharpened on mankind's apathy toward the ignorance that allows its suffering.

During the credit crisis of 2008, the social norm of maxing out credit was treated by the media like it was a common, unquestioned truth. It's bad to have a low credit score, yet to have a high credit score that a borrower could use to extend their credit was a good thing. Having a thirty-year mortgage and a low interest car payment is now the American dream. The dream used to be to save up the money to buy and own a house, not to mortgage away thirty years of your future to a bank to meet their time schedule and guidelines to one day pay off their note to then actually own the house. Initially, the dream-seeker may say they own the house, but actually all they truly own is the obligation to repay the debt for living in a house that the bank owns, not the house.

This mind-set blocks an individual's forward momentum. Don't be misled. This is really anything but the American dream of finding personal freedom from the cause of the ignorance of our Source's intended purpose to initiate ongoing change...the ignorance that allows them to unknowingly suffer through their list of addictions in search of the joy and happiness they once knew.

Brand Name Over Sensory Report

Selling the public on how what's really a less significant facet of a product's true value might really be a need and not just a want has proven effective to help keep the USA economy moving on. Another way to sell a product based on what's not really such an important faculty of the product's true value is to convince the masses to buy their manufactured products because of who made them instead of how well they fulfill their designed utility.

It's become poetically cute for consumers to say how they love to "shop till they drop." It's very interesting how Mr. Barber recommends that the prevalent "ethos" of our times place the freedom available in a democratic republic second to insuring that the citizens buy things "made in the USA."

> The identity politics of the twenty-first century is then part and parcel of the infantilist ethos. It mistakes brand for identity and consumption for character while treating Americans as consumers of Brand USA rather than as the free citizens of a democratic republic.[7]

Children are especially vulnerable to these subversive efforts and there seems to be no mercy shown. Advertising that is misleading, twisted or simply untrue is very common. Some untruths are realized by revealing only the half truth about something.

And then there's the Internet. Picture the ever-evolving science of actively devising ways of sneaking, jamming and spamming advertising in your path when surfing the worldwide web. No authoritative source needs to be cited here, as everybody knows the truth of this through experiential association as it's certainly happened to anyone who's used the Internet.

Youth in poverty will spend money they don't have to be wearing the latest style of Air Jordan tennis shoes. This unneeded want has fueled the misguided intentions responsible for theft and even murder.

In a recent Stanford University study measuring the effects of advertising on children, the study author Dr. Tom Robinson said the kids' perception of taste was "physically altered by the branding." The Stanford University researcher said it was remarkable how children so young were already so influenced by advertising. (8/07 Archives of Pediatrics and Adolescent Medicine was funded by Stanford and the Robert Wood Johnson Foundation.)

"Branding trumps sensory input," said Susan Lynn, a Harvard University Medical School psychologist on an August 8, 2007 MSNBC *Today Show* commentary dealing with a recent study on McDonald's child-targeted advertising being analyzed on the program.

Some people call this brainwashing. The subliminally installed claim's purpose aimed at controlling these kids' future intentions to affect choosing the McDonald's products was unfairly main-lined directly into their young vulnerable and still developing personal belief systems. It denies their fair unbiased consideration of other food options that are less likely to lead directly to adolescent diabetes and overweight problems. It damages an individual's free will, stunting the growth of and lessening resistance to future unauthorized belief system intrusions.

Their free wills are being further numbed and choked out by each additional unethical invasion of their young developing personal reality. This is true anytime another entity, unknown to the host, seeds the host's belief system with the outside entity's self-serving intentions designed to determine the host's future decisions. It's especially unjust to scar such young naive unsuspecting free wills before they have had time to become acquainted with realizing the justice in the wisdom originating in understanding the relational justice in the impermanent nature of our Source and to actually be able to see the whole picture.

With all the corporate bidding for our attention and the documented control it has over the collective whole of our Capitalist society, every person in our society suffers individually to some degree. We're domesticated into a social haze where if not armed with the savvy awareness of our Source's truth of change acquired through self-knowledge we're bound to march to the drums of others. We are being conditioned in a way that is gaining access and control over our free will through various subversive free-will-numbing tactics.

There are so many people that are being subdued by these conditions...very few stand up to question it. This is normal in the Midwestern USA. People use all their energy treading water in this challenging Midwestern social current.

They're too individually wrapped up in the collective movement following the overall illusion, like sheep on the way to the market.

Hollowed Promises

Individuals can become upset when some event outcome is not what their perception of how things coexist and interrelate had envisioned it was going to be. They have trouble understanding how or why different causes produce certain results or effects. Or, maybe they just have trouble trying to figure out where certain effects originate. Either way, they suffer the confusion.

Suffering is compounded when it's realized that something turns out not to be what was expected because they were purposefully led to believe the product should be something else and that some concealed unforeseen result serves to benefit the deceiver's hidden agenda. People often react with anger when they feel others care so little about their well-being to outright lie to them or not tell them the whole story about something and then take their money...or maybe even take something more personal.

Unfounded promises, half-truths and total misrepresentations are often given to people to encourage them to believe a misleading claim made about a product. After buying into or believing the promise of the claim and actually using the product, reality creeps in. In today's economy in far too many instances, the promise greatly overstates the reality of the promise made by the advertised claim of the manufacturer or whomever the entity is that gets the money. As the reality of the other half of the truth becomes apparent and the illusion of what was promised has been shattered...the person suffers the feeling of betrayal or lost trust or from foolish for blindly having faith in what they heard. Just put any TV infomercial to the test.

In Midwestern USA, this type of supplier letdown stands blameworthy for much suffering. Replace an unquestioning public naivety with an alert public free will demanding controlled verification or validation for what it's being presented and this type of public disappointment will soon disappear. This would force corporate subliminal planners to find other ways of tattooing their self-serving footprint on the individual belief systems of unexpecting people to underhandedly influence the intentions behind the buyers' shopping behaviors.

The disproportion between what products really turn out to be and what's promised in advertising could be described as a true source of our society's imbalance. This is a kink of misrepresentation forming a tangled knot of injustice in society's quest for the sense of balance found in seeing the true justice and having the clarity of understanding what it is that glues the cause to the effect in ongoing change. A society's sense of an ongoing balance of justice is what keeps it stitched together.

There's nobody to try to fool or please. The truth is the truth. What is is what is. Let's get on with it. The confrontation between corporate promise and consumer reality creates an imbalance that interrupts the cause/effect rhythm that is characteristic of a social awareness immune to attachment. The ignorance of how this attachment operates is the deep rooted and primal cause of suffering in Midwestern USA.

Sunday Morning Televangelizing in Hoosierland

Many Midwesterners satisfy their socially imprinted biblical directive to pursue inspiration from the scriptures by listening to the inspired insights from reading the Bible their pastor has prepared during the week to present during the Sunday morning lesson. No figures were found to indicate the percentage of the churchgoers that actually study their Bibles through the week. Many satisfy their conscious fix with TV.

It's interesting how practically all the TV evangelists viewed on Indiana TV sport the accent of a Bible Belt Southern drawl. Maybe it helps ensure the ratings? The odds against it being that only southern accented people can preach the Bible are pretty high.

Maybe the common southern draw of Sunday morning TV preachers is meant to mimic the famous southern draw of the honorable gospel preacher Billy Graham? Maybe the spoken message here is accent-flavored to help it slip-in unquestioned by any doubting listeners, into their belief systems, on the similar sounding coattail of Mr. Graham's socially proven credibility? Maybe an intrigue or unanswered mystique wraps around the TV message if it mimics the southern twang of Mr. Graham that seems to draw that sort of interest? What better way to keep people from changing their channels?

It's diverting attention and focus from the message to the messenger for better ratings? It's a mistake to believe the message because of the tone of the message rather than the content of the message. Either way, it really should be about the message and not what it sounds like.

For over 2,000 years the recorded accounts of different enlightened souls' teachings have been subjected to mankind's evolving interpretations of what the enlightened teachers' original intended meaning was actually meant to be. These contemporary renditions of what message was originally intended are coming from individuals who are not enlightened and are also soul-searching. They assuredly venture their subjective interpretations of the written translations of the enlightened ones' ancient oral teachings as though they're hitting the nail on the head, assuming there are many people who believe it to be so. While actually they only represent a voiced guesstimation, hoping for a gathering of peer verification and acceptance.

Dr. Robert Schuller, a well-known-to-the-Midwest Sunday morning TV evangelist, said on a cable TV program about the Gnostic Gospels that he needs only to understand the "biblical masterpiece" ...that there's no need to even consider the Gnostic accounts of Jesus's life story. It has to be noted that Dr. Schuller did not specify which of today's translations of the biblical masterpiece he had full blind faith in. Dr. Schuller has a flock of weekly TV watchers numbered in the millions.

The purpose of Dr. Schuller's intention to ignore other accounts of his savior's life was probably unquestionably internalized by many of his listeners. The inborn unfettered nature of their free wills have been previously reduced by their earlier choice to have untested and unverified blind faith in the Christian religious claim to the nature and intended purpose of our Source.

Dr. Schuller has seeded their belief systems with the intentions to deny consideration of any explanation of heavenly enlightenment other than that of the Rome-edited masterpiece.

In the same program, biblical experts recommended taking biblical classes or reading other books to enrich the intellectual understanding of the Bible. Referencing the intellectual knowledge of other believers falls short of self-training the ability to cultivate a wisdom-enriched enlightened understanding of the cause/effect relational justice of the impermanent nature of this reality to excuse the ignorance that allows suffering in this lifetime.

Wisdom enrichment is gained through the sensual experiential understanding of what makes up the self—i.e., self-knowledge or self-awareness. It involves sensually dipping into the internal factory of change itself, witnessing it through the sensation of contact...where the mind meets the body. It's the only material contact the spirit has with this physical reality. It's a sustained sensual focus into the cause/effect flow of life itself being manifested. An intellectual understanding of the nature and purpose of our Source merely seeds the process of self-training a waking awareness of the wisdom-enriched experiential understanding of the nature and intended purpose of our Source.

Most of the Christian orators of the many Bible related TV programs or specials go to lengths to describe what they think Jesus meant by what they read in the scriptures. None make any tie-in to any detectable living coexistence of the Bible's ancient God in the present moment heartbeat of this reality. Any construal of Jesus's intended meaning is always subject to a very wide range of interpretation.

Time and time again, it would be asserted how Jesus died for our sins and made up a third of the royal God trilogy, but what that had to do with the eradication of ignorance-allowed suffering and attainment of joy and bliss in this lifetime was never explained...only the assured promise of heaven or hell after death.

A Biblical Agenda...A Kaleidoscope of Intellectual Rumination

After hypothesizing and accepting an intellectual concept behind a religion's experientially unfounded guidelines, there are many offshoots of illusionary interpretations that segue from one spiritual signpost to the next. They fill in any perceived blanks. With the sketchy framework of the ancient story, it can't be avoided. Sermons can get very suppositional and imaginative when based only on individually hypothesized interpretations of the written accounts of the particular biblical translation that's been studied. Midwesterners listen and then just round off the edges to allow a square peg to fit into a round hole.

Believers sketch with their imaginations a uniquely compiled mental rendition of their intellectually registered concept of heaven and its supernatural components and characters. No two believers describe the heavenly promise the same. Even Rome's priest-picked gospel authors all describe Jesus's experience differently.

Believers have trouble seeing the forest for the trees. They can't get past arguing and splitting up over the details to get a feel for or a scent of the whole of his intended message.

Christian speakers quote scriptures and give lessons describing their unique interpretation of what they've gathered from repeated readings of their Bibles or other religious materials. Many lessons deal with some aspect of following the Ten Commandments by leading an ethically and morally postured life. There's dialogue on what an individual's emotions should be, how compassion is needed and how good morality is needed to replace the bad. There aren't lessons that explain how an individual can make that replacement other than to pray to God and ask him to do it for them or for God to give them the strength to do it.

What does it feel like when God gives someone strength? How is it inspired? Answer these questions in terms of a present moment sensual experience that would document God's living existence in real-time that's free of any church atmosphere. This experience would be something for an individual to use to register God's sensually detectable involvement in real life. It could serve as something tangible to anchor their cognitive sketches to in their mind that they've made from all the written biblical accounts they've studied and heard about.

The living involvement of the unverified religious claims is unfounded in the present moment living environment. It opens the podium to the personal interpretation of anyone who decides to unravel the meaning of the scriptures.

Preachers describe how and why their worldview makes sense of their intellectually gathered religious timeline of events. There's usually a deeper interpretation offered by Christian speakers that reads between the lines of the scriptures to tell what was really meant by God, Jesus or maybe one of the apostles.

Of course, that deeper interpretation would also depend and be influenced by which of the many translations of the scriptures being analyzed. With the many different ancient religious/spiritual texts, there's an ever-changing variety of evolving interpretations.

Compare interpretations on what Paul meant in his messages to the Corinthians or what John meant when he was exiled and he put to pen his visions of how revenge might find its way to his persecutors in the Book of Revelations. In preparation for giving a Sunday morning lesson, a teacher will ruminate and ruminate over the scriptures while searching for an intriguing angle to present their understanding of the written word, as per their chosen translation format of the Roman's selected accounts of Jesus's life and lessons. They are intellectually reasoned interpretations because religious claims to what this reality is and who runs it have no verifiable sign that demonstrates the living truth of the claim about what and where they say heavenly salvation is. None are tied or relate to laws of impermanence, even though the wisdom they parrot was taken from the pool of wisdom that floats a reality with this nature and intended purpose.

They are not grounded in any type of physical sensual experience, notable in the perception range of human beings. So, there's no dialogue comparing what actual physical feelings might represent in the process of maturing spiritually. Describing what is meant in the interpretation of the written scriptures is like somebody reading or hearing about what "hot" means that's never held their finger to a flame and then describing what it feels like. A religious believer will have blind faith or take the messenger at his word for what hot means and then when they encounter it in real life, they won't recognize it.

When allowing for what were in biblical times considered unexplainable miracles and by having no window of experiential history defining what reality will actually allow, the range for imagined interpretations here is huge. There is no personal experiential basis or dependable footing in the practical limits of present moment life present to build a shared objective understanding on...to found the fiber of a common intrapersonal faith in that can be understood and orally shared interpersonally.

Turn on any religious TV channel and observe varying interpretations of any and every scripture's message. Religious speakers pose their intellectually calculated notion of what God's intent was behind any scripture they read.

When the very popular television evangelist, Joel Olsteen's Sunday morning TV evangelical program airs, he begins his lesson by instructing the packed stadium to hold their Bibles in the air and literally parrot a pledge of allegiance to the Bible. It is "what they are and what they are about."

Mr. Olsteen asserts it is necessary to use God's word to break addictions. Mr. Olsteen makes no reference to which transmuted meaning of the many translations of God's word should be consulted to break addictions. He also suggests referring to one of the publications that his enterprise sponsors for a deeper biblical understanding. There is no biblical guidance for an individual to actually allow our Source to surface for them to witness the truth sensually explained to then understand the forming of the uncontrollable fleeting nature of the habit energy of addictions to affect releasing their list of accumulated uncontrollable reactionary behaviors.

There are no practical suggestions offered on how to retire the ongoing mental agitation or unrest coming from a mitote/maya state of mind inherent to anyone with a numbed or smothered-out free will that plays nursemaid to an addictive personality. Christian teachers say only to not be that way. There's no guidance on how to remove misguided faulty prior conditioning to give suppressed thoughts of true altruistic compassion the room to breathe.

In a popular modern book, *A Purpose Driven Life* by Rick Warren, just open the cover, and it says on the inside cover very plainly the answer to our suffering is found on the outside and warns against looking inside. One must make the leap of blind faith and not expect any living verification or a true sign from our Source to verify the claim made about what our Source is and what will bring an end to our suffering.

By accepting religion's unverified claim explaining our Source, the new believer leaps over a newly created void in their belief system that's missing having their free will experience some living evidence to properly verify that the claim of how the stated cause of an individual's attainment of heaven (the religious promise) actually is connected to that effect (salvation from suffering).

This protocol leaves the believer's natural self-preservation process in a state of uncertainty, depending solely on a faith of hope. This faith of hope is founded solely in the believer's comfort with the assumed integrity of the messenger of that religious claim. Hopefully they didn't misunderstand it before passing it along and they have what the claim maker intended his message to be.

There is no living real-time present moment "heavenly" sign to support any Christian religious claim. Mr. Warren's book had a high media-driven social acceptance. Flockfollowing conformity is a common facet of the human condition in Midwestern USA at this point in time. Millennia of generational mass acceptance could also be viewed as a form of undue influence...a touch of bullying.

With the countless number of religious claim interpretations and no real in-this-lifetime heavenly goal to aim at, individuals get antsy while they wait for something to happen.

Biblical interpretations lack having a grounding factor that comes from having a sign of validation demonstrating the claim maker's living presence.

Their details lack having any present moment validation from any conjointly experienced sign to collectively be calmed by, discussed and built on. If this easy-to-access available-to-all living sign were there, there wouldn't be such a wide variety of imagined accounts of what the unverifiable reality is.

3

Free Will Compromised

...If The Inner Voice of Intuition Is Ignored...It Will Die

Unfettered Free Will Stages a Resilient Belief System

We're born human, our lives a mere synapse in the cause/effect process of our Source's living network of ongoing change. We share DNA in the larger spectrum of living creatures, a human shaped pod of Source-like potential.

Everyone is born into this ultimate reality with an inborn unique genius. It's an inner potential that comes special to their unique size shape and inborn abilities. They have the right and responsibility to determine what collection of views, ideas and beliefs they internalize into their belief system to best unlock, develop and realize those special talents to, in a general sense, benefit the collective advancement of humanity's quest for enlightenment about the ways of an impermanent reality.

What something or someone becomes depends greatly on how well they consciously discover, recognize, and align their intended purpose with the rhythm of our image-reflecting Source...free of all illusionary attachment. To live in waking awareness savvy with the relational justice of the interactions among the coming and going bits of energy making up the sub-microscopic world and how it affects the rhythm of their time-released packet of potential, gives their free will the foundation to do its job free of the spirit-encumbering duties common to a curator of an endless want museum. There needs to be enough mental dexterity and latitude to take the appropriate steps to highlight one's distinctive qualities and exhibit open tolerance void of prejudice to different ideas and beliefs.

Behavior-producing intentions are products of an individual's collective purpose of intent. They surmise the intra-influence of the internalized claims comprising the mental reservoir of ideas, views, beliefs and concepts gathered throughout one's life that make up their belief system. An individual's belief system becomes their tin of paints they use to color their worldview, which color-codes the unique defining traits of their personality.

Alanis Morissette said on a PBS Travis Smiley show that there was nothing better than finding her vocation of writing songs...of being a vessel. She feels fulfilled and that she has found her niche by being able to be accurate in expressing what's felt in her belief system. She discovered this gift through her ambitious free will. It taps into the genius of her potential...setting free her focused passion and intended purpose.

Our evolving foothold in what we perceive as reality is reflected in our belief system. Its breadth lies in all we've experienced and its level of strength is reflected in our ability to access our free will and the type of faith that holds it together. Its evolving web of consistency exhibits its trustworthiness and its integrity is sensed in how often the feeling of compassionate fairness flavors its intentions.

Our Free Will Holds Key to Unlock Potential

An unfettered free will is needed to effectively filter what claims an individual decides to internalize as being true to their worldview. It verifies whether or not the cause/effect transformation the claim takes credit for recognizes an impermanent reality or one that is continual. It looks for the sensual verification that the cause a claim initiates is causally connected to the effect the claim is explaining how to get. It helps the individual through the process of self-training their energies to link the self-knowledge stored within their deeper consciousness to their ego-managed waking consciousness.

When healthy, the free will protects an individual's conscious mental facilities. It serves as ID checker and club bouncer protecting the anatomy of an individual's belief system from unwholesome intruders and headlines as the star of the show in expressing an individual's worldview.

An unfettered free will ensures the integrity of the claim-verification phase of the belief system claim-internalization process when an individual considers believing any new information from any new information source. It tests and verifies the natures and causal link between the intended purposes of new outside claims and the resulting effects before believing and internalizing them to affect their maturing worldview. An unfettered free will goes beyond believing some claim merely because an information source said it was so.

The intended purpose of each new claim internalized into one's belief system further shapes an individual's collective purpose of intent that fashions their worldview. An individual's free will makes the final decision when they make up their mind. It's a free will's humankind right to the freedom of expression that's protected by the First Amendment. It's an individual's duty to understand and protect their free will so to always be able to test and validate the nature and cause/effect causal link of claims vying to be internalized into their belief system. It's an unobstructed unfettered free will that allows individuals to freely let their light shine and contributes to mankind's united quest for liberation from the collective ignorance that allows human suffering. It's an unobstructed free will that has the wisdom to recognize the justice in allowing others an equal chance to let their own lights shine.

It's up to each individual to contribute to the collective realization of worldwide compassion during their earthly presence, within the boundaries of their human shell. We are ambassadors to the future with the responsibility of doing what is best for the entire inter-related interdependent ever-changing ultimate reality and to grace all things with a sincere expression of compassion to help lessen worldwide cyclic suffering.

Be it said the human free will represents the most fundamental and primal part in the expression of the human condition throughout its human experience. It's our open tie to the sea of humanity, the source and signature of our expressed intent.

An unfettered free will makes possible a truth seeker's finding and following their path to the enlightenment that exposes the roots of their suffering by linking the truth explaining the self-evident ephemeral nature of reality waiting in the ego-free regions of our deeper consciousness to their conscious wakefulness.

As we age, our primary duty of vigilance is to maintain and care for our minds and bodies. A healthy mind is needed to shape a healthy body and a healthy body is needed to support the physical soundness of a healthy mind to sustain an adaptable unfettered free will.

A healthy unfettered free will is needed to maintain an uncluttered mind capable of uniting in harmony with a sensually alert body, to humbly listen with total sensual focus to the subtle language of our Source for the living message to inspire the insightful wisdom enrichment that makes clear the story of the human condition going through the human experience. It works as point guard on an individual's pursuit of heavenly enlightenment.

Free Will...Belief System's Protector and Spokesperson

Having just an intellectual glimpse at the truth of ongoing change will begin loosening the chains of uncertainty that confine a deadened free will's unfettered status. Its role of testing and verifying the truth savvy and nature of new claims is being reawakened. A truth seeker's vision to recognize and solve inner-felt uncertainties involving claims that are questionable is gaining clarity. The courage to step out and follow up on satisfying those feelings is strengthened.

With the awareness of our Source's truth of initiating change realized through self-discovery and the wisdom it inspires sensually tattooed into the belief system, an individual has an unshakable foundation for supporting a growing inner strength that will weather all storms and serve resolute to a sturdy and growing regime of steadfast faith. This bridges any existing void between cause and effect with understanding. It delivers an enriched awareness and full dose of anti-ignorance.

An unfettered free will channels the intuition that manages to distill up from the same deeper consciousness that understands the details of how the human condition fits into the human experience. The deeper consciousness supports the healing of both the body and the mind as it instructs the formation of scabs over abrasions to the flesh and the spirit. It has a built-in timer that keeps the human organs, hormones and the interacting life supporting body systems functioning in time with the Source-guaranteed ongoing change that continues to evolve. The deeper consciousness makes no room for "bad" conditioning or misconceptions about the relational justice among the interacting cause/effect factors that make up this reality.

An unfettered free will filters the new claims made by new ideas, beliefs or concepts. It filters out the claims with natures that allow their cause/effect transformation to occur in a reality with a continual nature.

When an individual loses touch with their free will, they lose their focus, direction and ability to realize their potential. They become more naive and a victim of uncertainty. They turn inward. To quote a Bible school song, their life-light gets hidden under a bushel.

They suffer while not understanding the nature of the mind they're lost in and a stranger to. Their free will has lost its soul.

The underlying nature of any new claim's intended purpose is the defining characteristic that determines the claim's validity. The nature of the claim's intended purpose is the underlying aspect of the claim's purpose that an individual's unfettered free will tests and verifies. When the free will senses that a claim's purpose has a nature that allows attachment to craving or aversive intentions, it will not be internalized. The claim's intended purpose is directed at something or idea that's remembered presence is really only an imagined figment of the past that recognizes life continuity or an imagined state of nonchanging permanence.

Those states are illusionary and will cause misalignment between an individual's pieced together account of an apparent reality and the real-time cause/effect transformation. There will be attachments or addictions relied on to help cope with all this misalignment. They're ignorant as to why. They suffer.

Whenever possible, an individual seeks experiential verification of the claim's purpose before believing and accepting the influence of the claim's underlying purpose of intent into the collective purpose of intent that represents the individual's worldview. They seek the living evidence to demonstrate the living truth of its purpose...to feel the flame of the claim as described, to truly understand what the claim really means by "hot."

There are claim validations done by the free will that are of an intellectual nature and can't really be experienced sensually. In those situations, the enlightened Mr. Siddhartha Gautama suggested that the claim's wholesomeness, blameworthiness and relationship to harm and suffering are considered in light of acquired wisdom before internalizing the new claim. How wise individual's felt about the claim should be considered.

If verified, the validity of the new claim's purpose of intent is then supported by a corresponding steadfast faith. The claim's verified truth has strength-generating faith founded in the confidence that the same time-fueled environment that's allowing the documented sensually witnessed manifestation of ongoing change will later exist to ensure the same continued validity of the relational wisdom now derived from our Source's exhibition of the truth of this ongoing change. The omnipresence of the same unchanging dimensional cause/ effect reality assures the day-to-day dependability of this truth and the continued steadfast surety in its ongoing presence. It can't be doubted. It was witnessed with the individual's own sensual eyes.

Believing claims with infected natures distorts, corrupts and scatters the belief system's focus. It lessens the mind-calming consistency realized in having a common end shared by the intended purposes that make up a belief system that shapes a worldview. Some have a nature that recognizes the impermanent nature of our reality and some don't. The fundamental difference is very subtle to detect but huge in effect.

The health of an individual's free will determines whether or not the individual will spend their days with realized purpose and focused intent walking the straight and narrow line or living moment to moment listening to the 1,000 voices in their state of mitote/maya confusion that are all shouting unrelated previously internalized intended purposes that honor attachment to the clinging to and grasping at the unchanging ideas, views, beliefs, memories and things representing an illusionary life continuity, with no real common end. They're all related to preserving protecting and strengthening the "I" or "me" pictured in their ego-managed illusionary version of what reality must apparently be. Their wants and needs lack being a contributing factor in the path toward an awareness that undoes the ignorance that allows their suffering.

The confused individual will not know which of the unrelated purposes of the shouting 1,000 voices to focus on. Not having experienced awareness or sensually seen at least a glimpse of our Source's truth of initiating change in action, the individual has no historical foundation of sensual recognition and appreciation of the most basic and primal of truths.

Unverified Claims Choke Out Belief System

Time will pass as they wander aimlessly in an illusionary apparent reality lost, insecure and lonely among the looming doubt and indecision that shadows their behavioral intentions coming from their misguided belief system and worldview. With the lack of questioning and claim nature/purpose verification by an unfettered free will, infected claims easily gain entry into their belief system to distort their worldview.

The growing mix of internalized claims that make up an individual's belief system with unrelated natures and untested cause/effect relationships between what the claim says it will do and what it actually does do, don't share a common core direction with the claims' cause/effect purpose leading to an end that supports in one way or another the relational justice of this ever-changing reality. This will further distort their belief system's existing focus on finding direction or purpose aimed at recognizing and releasing their inborn talent potential. Any existing common end of purpose of intent or direction of purpose the individual might have become a bit fainter and less defined with the internalization of each infected claim that might have an illusionary purposeless unrelated end.

They will lead their life pillaging through the different items and notions they come across while looking for the answer to what nags at the peace and sanctity of their present moment. They will yearn to find the answer to their unrest and discomfort with life.

Individuals either are developing an eye for the truth to understand the ephemeral nature of the ultimate reality or they're not. Both cases will appreciate and try to recognize the impermanent transforming state of things while focusing their life direction to flow to its becoming rhythm or they ignore its natural ongoing cadence and swim against the current while clinging to the imagined rock of apparent reality with a non-change-allowing nature of continual permanence.

Being able to seize or capture and hold the essence of ever-change in time is nothing but an illusion. Insightful wisdom derived while gaining self-knowledge (knowledge of self through sensing one's further creation as it manifests) recognizes that clinging or grasping at permanence can be nothing more than an illusion.

Taking the final step to verify things before internalizing their claims helps immunize the belief system from internalizing misguided, misleading or false claims that emit the free radicals that lead to a diseased belief system harboring notions that incite attachment to thought patterns that spell out clinging and aversive intentions. Claim verification helps weed out the claims that have a nature to respect the notion of nonchange.

This is the knowledge of the truth that's derived insightbased wisdom makes sense of the human condition that otherwise resides suppressed in the human deeper consciousness. Everyone has a responsibility to the other members of the interconnected whole of our shared Source to carry their weight and to seek and discover this truth and live by its derived wisdom for the collective sake of the whole.

As an individual's free will validates and internalizes only claims with purposes of intent stepping in time with our Source's truth of purpose to provide ongoing change to constantly be transforming into something else, the individual is able to lead a life with a forward tilted focus and defined end purpose. They can have a well-lit path on the road to becoming enlightened about the cause of the ignorance that allows their present moment suffering. This process is supported by their steadfast faith in the ongoing dependability and continuance of the conditions that make possible its cause/effect truth, giving rebirth again and again to its derived wisdom as the cycle of cause and effect continues to echo throughout the universe.

Free Will Bypassed

After an individual gets a sensual taste of the mental peace that awaits when they gain awareness of the primal truth spelling out the relational justice involved in the coming and going pulse of the present moment, their free will reassumes more of its natural role. It's an awakened free will, alert and as speculative and analytical about a claim maker's true agenda, as a woman can be right after a guy gives her his best pickup line introduction.

It's the ignorance of the relational savvy coming from this truth of ongoing change that eventually cripples the free will and leaves the individual at the mercy of an unfiltered belief system confused while marching to the drums of others to a disturbing array of endless rhythms.

Any untested unverified claim vying to be believed and internalized into an individual's belief system with a purpose of intent that actually gets internalized unverified, will have bypassed the free will's prescreening process. This unverified internalization widens any preexisting void that lacks the experiential understanding developed from sensually linking a claim's described cause to their observed effects. This weakens the claim verification phase in the anatomy of the individual's belief system. It's missing the real-time present moment sensual validation of the claim's type of nature and cause/effect causal link.

A misled individual might end up having their behavioral intentions directed at serving the interests of some hidden agenda of an outside entity after internalizing their misleading untested/unverified claim. Often through subliminal thought engineering, the outside entity's interests are projected while falsely inflating the importance of the imaginary self in the listening individual's illusionary apparent reality.

The individual's free will is numbed a bit more and the void of understanding in between new claims' described actions or causes and the results or effects widens with each new untested/unverified claim they believe as their focus becomes progressively a little foggier. Their ability to interpret reality becomes increasingly weakened and probably a bit more self-serving.

They become a bit less in touch with what their true feelings are. They become number about feeling life and living in the present moment. The individual becomes more of a social pushover...a puppet of society.

An individual's free will is that little voice in the background. When the belief system becomes overran with misguided conditioning, what the individual's true inner unbiased nature is saying can become but a mere whisper. They lose their sense of identity. Their personal priorities are reshuffled and rearranged by outside pressures. Their ability to see the reality of the situation fades. This eats away at their self-esteem and erodes their confidence in their self-belief.

Their free will has been stunned. The unfettered free will's First Amendment right to speak what it feels is being unethically smothered out for the interests of other entities voicing their untested claims by fooling people into believing them. The free will's human right to actively maximize the individual's self-preservation by questioning anything has been silenced as they wear the mounting assortment of chains from untested claims.

The individual's belief system has become infected by the highly contagious virus spreading the recognition of an illusionary reality with a continuous nature that allows the attachment or clinging to the permanence or perceived continuity of things and non-things.

The virus gradually piggybacks its way into an individual's belief system on various agreements internalized with inadequate validation due to the unaware, unsuspecting, numb, smothered or choked out claim testing/validating function of the free will. Internalizing any more unvalidated, untested infected claim further strengthens the hold on the belief system of any other previously embedded claims that don't share the same impermanent nature as that of our Source. Resistance to believing future infected claims is weakened a bit more as the free will becomes a bit number and its influence a bit less respected and a bit more faint.

The grip of the dark side has been tightened and is choking out the part of the individual's free will that tests new information and makes decisions relevant to the needs of the individual. The individual's belief system is being occupied rent-free and the real-time moment-to-moment behavioral intentions emitted from it are at least partially controlled to serve the interests of the imposing outside entity.

These misguided purposes of intent are backed by a faith that's blind to having any sensual history verifying the impermanent nature and cause/effect causality of the claims' described purposes. This is a faith of unfounded hopes blind to sensual recognition and void of any steadfast confidence. The truth of a claim with a continual nature cannot be experienced for validation because of the absolute primal truth of the counter claim of constant change. Any religious claim to our Source's nature and purpose of intent can offer no real-time present moment living "sign from above" that the religious claim's completion involves factors that represent something that is workable in an impermanent reality.

Individuals with their life purpose lost in an imagined apparent reality will fritter away their time and energy servicing the purposes of an endless (claims directed at no end) mixture of unrelated misguided claims. Due to their unawareness of our Source's nature of initiating ongoing change and its working properties they can't conceive how fruitless their clinging and craving to fixed-in-time concepts or things to adorn, preserve or defend an illusionary "I" or "me" is and the suffering it causes.

They will continue passing their present moment servicing their own unique menu of addictions. This leaves the screech of uncertainty-inspired fear-of-the-unknown echoing faintly from the depths of their personality in the language few have learned to recognize and understand.

Science...Mankind's Free Will Guardian and Spokesperson

Science without religion is lame. Religion without science is blind.

—Albert Einstein

Science will be around for a while because it gives humankind the light to see what the eye cannot. Science's demand for experiential verification about all the interrelated parts of this reality's state of impermanence, lights humankind's pathway to an enlightened understanding of its collective ignorance that causes human suffering.

All of mankind shares a common goal. Everyone seeks the truth to know where they came from, who they are and where they're going. They seek the feeling that they are OK where they are. Religious, spiritual and science-minded groups have always been in search of the same thing. All want to understand the ultimate reality, their god, or whatever it was that's responsible for this reality and how it works. It's what protects them and brings them safety in from the unknown.

Religious claims to what our Source is lack having any real-time living experiential verification of the living participation of its god. Religions cannot figure out where to point the unconverted to see living verification that what their claim purposes and intends goes beyond the realm of being conceptual and has anything to do with the heart beat or rhythm of the passing present moment. Religion's living presence just doesn't happen in the real sense of "happen" that's recognized during the normal passing of the day.

For the past five hundred years a particular group of individuals has wanted to see the living experiential proof for any claim made attempting to make sense of our reality. They call their pile of verifying facts Science.

Like religious leaders, scientists are human beings that come from the pool of humanity that wants to identify and understand the nature and intended purpose of our one and only Source. The difference is that those with the mounting pile of verifying facts refuse to take the leap of blind faith to skip over the proof and blindly believe that this reality's origin, past, present and future is the work of one of the still remaining external gods.

They insist on experiential verification for anything that proposes to contain a part of the truth to our reality puzzle. They insist on having the purpose of any claim verified before internalizing it as something that helps give order to the puzzle.

Science wants to see the real-time living experiential proof of what is to be accepted as the truth. If it's a sign from heaven, it must be perceivable to anybody equally, with the credibility of a repeatable double-blind study. Science protects mankind's first amendment right to question anything, regardless of its origin.

Science doesn't blindly accept some explanatory claim just because a very trustworthy person says so. Empirical evidence is called for.

Since the scientific process involving claim validation emerged there's been religious nontolerance for the scientific way. Religions allow for blind faith while science demands the experiential evidence of no less than double blind testing standards...a big difference and thus the conflict.

Yet, both disciplines long for the same answer. They both try to unravel the same tree of wisdom that puts order to the relational justice that makes sense of how the impermanent human condition fits into the transient human experience...they just see it from different points of view.

What is responsible for creating our reality? When did it start? Religious groups take the leap of blind faith across the valley of void or void of uncertainty where society's collective unfettered free will is numbed by superimposed conceptions of the truth that repels any questions they would rather not try to answer.

If the science community could just see a living sign to verify the god's living contribution to the living part of the present moment, maybe there would be no uncertainty-sponsored fuss.

Science hears and recognizes the uncertainty echoing down mankind's valley of primal confidence that's shouting for living proof of any claim, religion-related or not, to maintain the integrity of the unfettered collective free will of a free society. Scientific evidence produced during the testing period of the scientific process provides the real-life verification of the claim being made. It's that simple.

The depth of the scientific verification of the truth of a claim or hypothesis comes in different levels of trustworthiness. The level of scientific integrity of the scientific evidence varies depending on the testing standards used.

Verification can come from a study based on a survey of only a few people of an entire applicable population up to a randomized placebo-controlled study of various sized tested populations. The randomized placebo-controlled study provides level 1 clinical evidence to the question being tested. This makes sense, as it's tough for a small study to provide adequate convincing verification of what the cause/effect mechanism is.

Scientific proof is not fool proof. For an individual to have sufficient faith/confidence in scientific results, the test conditions must satisfy the intellectual standard they set to demonstrate adequate proof for.

Science can look at things that unenlightened human sensitivity cannot perceive. Upon occasion, as science noses around this reality, it comes to some realization that religion has just assumed what a contradicting legend was about to be true, if acknowledged at all.

Case in point...Science has recently documented and photographed the existence of the tiny coming and going, now-you-see-it-now-you-don't particles of energy...the *kapulas* that Siddhartha described visualizing in his account of becoming enlightened about his ignorance that was causing his present moment unrest and dissatisfaction.

The bits of pulsating energy simply come into existence and go away with no predictable rhythm. Their behavior details the recently discovered metaphysical aspect of this impermanent reality that makes up the sub atomic particles that make up the atoms that make up the transforming forms and objects that humans can sensually perceive.

The seemingly still presence of these transforming forms and objects gets mistaken for a separate entity with a continual existence that most individuals will use to piece together their fragile ego-managed illusions that consume and confuse their waking conscious minds. This is the same reality Siddhartha experientially defined within his own flesh with no electron microscope or other modern scientific equipment. Through his self-trained discipline, he sensually witnessed it.

The experiential aspect of Siddhartha's self-discovery stands as the basis for his conscious understanding of the impermanent nature of the coming and going *kapulas*. It's at the primal core for his enriched waking awareness that the nature of our reality is one of impermanence. His understanding of this is the primal answer that undoes his ignorance that allowed his suffering.

Sensual Mind-and-Body Tie-in Essential

Even though the scientific evidence does provide experiential association of the cause and effect involving the claim, it fills the experiential void of uncertainty only in the belief systems of the members of the scientific community that experienced performing the experiment and not for those who didn't make the applicable hands-on scientific investigation. The scientists' experiential witnessing was aimed more at verifying the existence of the coming and going bits of energy, not to understand how the natural laws that rule the cause/effect relationships of those particles tap out the relational justice in the push/pull of everyday relationships on the larger scale.

The scientists and anyone else who reads the applicable new studies might intellectually know about the new scientific verification of the existence of these *kapulas*. The discovered coming and going nature of mater was realized and filed away in an intellectual reservoir describable by language and mathematics.

But, are the investigative scientists all enlightened? No, the scientists' understanding of this proven fact about the nature of this reality is based on intellectual knowledge only. They've never witnessed it through the sensual microscope that brings into sensual view the actual manifestation of change itself to gain inspiration to insightfully unravel its simple truth. Like this example, their religious theology has never been realized in the language of sensuality.

4

Trusting Claim Sources' Credibility

...Our Free Will's Nemesis

Knowledge and Wisdom Sources

Word of mouth can often be biased and misleading for many reasons. Individuals can never be sure about their information source's known or unknown inner agenda or whatever might be distracting or at least diverting or sidetracking the information source's attention while presenting the actual subject matter of the claim their sharing with the listener.

When possible, it's a good idea to see the purpose of any claim in action. People often end up feeling betrayed, should they ever realize the truth. When they look back on the experience, they're angry with themselves for not questioning its truth in the beginning. Hurt and disappointed people have different ways of expressing this anger.

Unsuspecting individuals unknowingly get unmonitored information introduced to the free-will verification process of their belief system from many places. Perhaps through something they've read or watched on TV without their awareness they receive subliminal messages that unsuspectingly influence their intentions in the direction of the information source's interests. Unchallenged information often floats into an individual's belief system unquestioned as part of cultural lore, from schoolroom blackboards, religious pulpits or from many other places.

An individual's internalized acceptance of this unquestioned information sets the stage for future frustrations and suffering when conflicts arise between what their misinformed illusionary configuration of what a cause/effect situation should be and what actually happens. Expectations not matching up with actual results bring unrest.

Generally speaking, the intended purpose of any claim either reflects the relational wisdom derived from insights taken from real-time experience with what happens in between the causes and effects of our Source's impermanent present moment or it doesn't. Any claim purporting the idea or reference to an object or non-object as having an ongoing sustainable continual nature of solidity to become attached to and crave will cause suffering.

It doesn't matter whether the expressed purposes of a claim of an idea or belief is heard, read in a newspaper, textbook, or Bible, viewed on TV, learned in school or church, seen written in the sky, or overheard in a café. Something they believe may be part of their society's passed-along tradition. In William Hart's book *The Art of Living*, it's said that at Theravada Buddhist meditation seminars, Buddhist teacher S. N. Goenka teaches how the human condition is set up to absorb the wisdom that best helps it navigate its way through the human experience in three basic ways.

An individual can receive or borrow their wisdom from others as just listed. Or they may take what they've received from others and intellectually make their own abstract calculation of what the effects of the claim should be on reality. Or they might have personally experienced the truth of the claim's purpose.

Too many people don't appreciate the importance in how they verify the truth of a claim. They aren't sensitive enough to detect the difference in credibility and reliability inherent to different types of information sources. They're too quick to put similar confidence in anything, no matter the source. Very often it's the information's source's reputation that determines believability of the information rather than a free will's examination of the workability of the new claim's living purpose to determine the actual viability of the claim's living nature.

Many individuals will often have faith in the truth of a claim based only on their personal trust of their information source's credibility and are blind to having seen a living incarnation of the purpose of the claim. They also trust their information source's character-judging ability to evaluate the credibility of the source they heard the claim from and trusted blindly if they might have verified the plausibility of its truth themselves. And who knows how far back in generations this chain of unverified blind trust could stretch?

This behavior is so common in this culture that its naive nature is thought to be normal.

This behavior has a deadening effect on the usefulness of the free-will...further numbing its sensitivity. The weakened belief system will fall easy prey to the self-serving, non-compassionate purposes of claims crafted by outside entities targeting things totally unrelated to the well-being of the effected individual.

The answers and explanations that an individual may come across that inspire them to develop and define the purpose of their passion in this ultimate reality come in many different packages. They each carry a different level of inherent reliability. When finally agreed on and internalized, the trusted claims become the backbone of the individual's worldview and are supported by either a steadfast faith in the claim's witnessed living presence or a faith blind to its verification.

This steadfast unbendable confidence is founded in the ongoing omnipresence of the consistent relational justice of this multidimensional reality for the recurring relational interactions among the transforming bits of energy in the tiny universe that demonstrates time and time again our Source's purpose and intent.

Faith in an unvalidated claim is blind. Blind faith is having confidence in things even if their claim has not been validated experientially.

Sometimes it might be acceptable to have blind faith. This might be when a camp counselor tells a child not to jump into the fire, as it would burn them and they might die. This is heard or borrowed wisdom and very good advice.

Blind faith based on received/borrowed or intellectual knowledge is good and useful if it serves as a catalyst for testing the issue at hand to develop the heartfelt steadfast faith found through the personal experience of actually feeling the flame of the claim. This child will verify that intellectually known claim someday by holding their finger near a flame to give experiential life to the intellectually stored warning.

Intellectual Picture is Forerunner to Experience

Received or borrowed wisdom from the camp counselor to the child about fire hazards will later serve as a catalyst for the child to convert their borrowed wisdom to experiential wisdom and test the validity of the claim made. This will help them justify the blind faith they had in the councilor's fire hazard warning. They will test for the living evidence of the borrowed wisdom and experience it directly... sensually. They will feel the flame of the claim.

In the same light, it's the child's intuitive questioning that wants to fill in their belief system void of uncertainty left in the wake of their blind faith-backed internalization of the claim created in the camp councilor's fire danger warning. The child will hold their finger close to a lit match just to experience the sensation and feel the affirming sensual signpost that verifies and validates the councilor's intellectually registered claim. The hands-on test will create a sensual tie between the cause and the effect. The living truth of the relational justice made by this claim about the flame will be figuratively burnt into the child's experiential memory.

This direct sensual involvement gives the borrowed or intellectual knowledge an experientially acquired sensual reference. The faith is no longer blind. The child will stand with a steadfast faith in the day-to-day validity of the relational truth of this cause/effect sequence. As long as our dimensional reality doesn't change, those curious testers can have steadfast faith the same interplay between the cause/effect factors will continue to produce the same kind of hot during future present moments.

In the anatomy of this child's belief system the experientially void intellectual realm of uncertainty between the intellectually described cause (flame) and the effect (burning sensation) is no longer void of the feeling verification as the sensual signal is perceived by the child. They've experientially tasted the relational justice between flame and sensation that the intellectual picture lacked.

This is the relational wisdom that gives rank and file to the impermanent nature of this cause/effect transforming reality. Given the child's newfound experiential awareness of the intellectually retained description of hot, they will naturally develop a bone-deep steadfast faith that this bit of wisdom-based advice will continue to stand true in the future.

So, when in a situation involving proximity to a flame again, the child's free will sets intentions based on their own tested and verified experiential wisdom drawn from actual sensual messages their conscious awareness has had burnt into its sensual memory through actual experience. The intention to avoid the flame will be repeated enough to eventually generate a reaction formed by habit energy and then into a fleeting reaction. It will precede the mental chatter involved in trying to reference and cognitively Google the intellectual recall library for the book, chapter, and verse used for accessing the slower-to-access and sometimes forgotten mental files of borrowed or intellectual wisdom swimming in the ego-managed waking consciousness in the outer catacombs of the newer part of the human brain that warns of what to do when around a flame.

When the child brought their finger near the flame, the truth of the flame describing the heated effect resulting from the interplay between the cause/effect coming and going factors in this reality was undeniable and unquestionable. The truth was seared into primary knowledge making it available on a sensual recall pre-intellectual basis.

It's very doubtful the individual will show any hesitation that a flame will be just as hot at any time in their future. They will never imagine the dimensional properties of this impermanent reality to change in a way to make that flame feel any cooler. One flame will be the same kind of hot as the next. They have a new naturally developed steadfast faith in this. This insightful wisdom is guarded by experientially verified steadfast faith.

This experience brings sensual awareness to the conscious mind of the relational truth in this cause/effect relationship, from flame to feel, by means of the only mind-to-material tie available...the body's sensual experience. The wisdom-enriching methodology of this example follows the same protocol for when a truth seeker generates wisdom-enriched awareness through gaining self-knowledge.

A truth seeker learns of self-knowledge with mind and body harmoniously focused within the flesh of their human shell. They've self-trained their moral capacity to self-train their mind control to sustain their conscious mind/body awareness within the essence of their physical presence to then self-train the conscious ability for the right thinking to eventually inspire the insightful wisdom-enriched enlightened understanding of this impermanent reality to repopulate their present moment with joy and happiness. It's what's needed to eliminate the ignorance that allows their suffering.

Borrowed or Intellectual Wisdom Begs the Question

Using intellectual knowledge is like mentally seeing or maybe like exercising cognitive vision. In normal conversation, someone might excuse themselves, saying: "I have no real experience with that, just what I've read and heard." You know the expression: "Oh yeah, I can see that. That makes all kinds of sense." Here, a flow of intellectual logic that has been pieced together from one end to the other... from the cause through its effect to make theoretical sense.

Intellectual knowledge is not experiential knowledge that you can "feel in your bones" where the truth about the cause/effect relationship in a situation has ever actually left its sensual footprint. Intellectual knowledge offers only an explanation that makes cognitive sense.

When the intended purpose of a new claim is vying to be internalized into an individual's belief system via a borrowed, received or intellectual wisdom format, an alert and unfettered free will should hold the intended purpose of that claim at bay until experiential verification is possible.

Borrowed or Intellectual Wisdom Seeds Experience

Why is a star athlete a star? Is their winning form based on how they've read or been told their sport technique should be performed or does it come from their developed muscle memory from fine tuning a new skill? Their winning technique may have originated from what they had read or how they'd been intellectually taught. But, their winning behavior came through making corrective adjustments while repeating their experience of finding mind/body coordination with their mind focused on how to best move their body.

They learned what behaviors didn't work and allowed the effective ones that best fit their body/mind composure to evolve into their own style. In gymnastics, should a competitor discover a unique movement combination, their sport will name it after them.

Their winning skill came from the practiced experience that helped coordinate transforming the physical movements initially patterned from the mind-consuming right effort of focused mind/body harmony into being an unthought, fleeting reaction...it's become their natural response.

Their winning behavior is backed by their unspoken steadfast faith and confidence in being able to repeat their trained skill, given that the dimensional constraints of our reality remain constant. The initial borrowed or intellectual wisdom of how to perform the technique served as a catalyst to develop experiential wisdom through actual experience.

In Indiana, basketball is a premier sport and serves as a great example for developing experiential knowledge from borrowed or intellectual knowledge. A child wants to become a basketball star. They study or are taught what physical movements make for the most effective technique and how to develop skill in their technique through practice.

The borrowed or intellectual wisdom alone will not produce someone who can effectively be point guard on a team that's in contention for the NCAA championship. It's not until the student has acted to practice the most appropriate technique suited to their physical and mental makeup that they will develop the skill level needed. It's been practiced so often that it assumes the nature of a fleeting reaction.

They compete with peers to gain the court time so they can become a basketball star. The borrowed and intellectual knowledge served as a catalyst for developing basketball wisdom based on personal experience.

A new marital artist will consciously decide to act and painstakingly practice and repeat the physical motions they need to affect the right body/mind harmony or technique. Being new movements, they need to be consciously aware of each one until they've done it so many times it becomes a fleeting reaction that their muscles are addicted to reenacting that will be performed automatically when the conditions call for it. It's not until they receive their black belt that these concentrated-on actions assume their addictive status and this is when they say a student is ready to demonstrate their learned martial skill as an art. Realizing this mind-into-body harmony summarizes the spirituality aspect of martial arts.

Did the athlete learn how to be a good athlete or how not to be a bad one? There was probably more learning required to learn what moves not to use as to learn which ones worked best.

When Michael Angelo was asked how he could possibly have carved his Statue of the David that killed Goliath from a block of granite, he said that David already existed in the granite, all he had to do was chip away the unneeded stone to set him free. Like so, the athlete just had to eliminate the moves that didn't work toward the targeted end effect.

The star athlete had no blind faith that the ability to perform was simply going to be gifted from an unfamiliar outside source. Their steadfast faith in their skill purpose developed right along with their competence in the skill itself.

For the athlete to deserve the honor of being able to perform as a master of the sport, they must pay their dues and walk the path of experiential learning alone to gain the related mind/body wisdom to do the feat. They must feel it in their bones through real-life experience. This enables them to also lead others along their own paths to experience the personal trainings to perform at this higher level of athletic maturity and to then become a coach or (master) instructor. To acquire intellectual knowledge and experiential training is why children go to school. A hospital intern may have been at the top of their class all through medical school, but will not be a good doctor until they've had years of experience.

Cerebral-Based Worldview Spawns Ideological Inflexibility

A cerebral or intellectually based worldview where the decision-making processes is rooted mostly in a certainty standard that doesn't reflect that much on any experience related intuitive gut feeling will form an ideological inflexible shell. The individual will have to stick to the more fundamental elements of the purpose of the newly internalized claim. When the intended purpose of a claim of borrowed, received or intellectual knowledge goes untested by an individual and internalized blindly to then represent the intended purpose of their worldview it can lead to the inability to consider ideas or options requiring more imaginative and adaptive lateral type thinking. The individual has no reel for what constitutes the truth of the purpose of the untested claim.

The new believer in the claim lacks the experiential reference of how the contributing factors of the claim combined to affect the claim's purpose to freely understand its nature. They were never a part of the living experience demonstrating the claim's truth of purpose in action. Their description of the claim's truth has to come from how they've read or been told it came to be...thus book, chapter, and verse. Care must be taken not to venture future thinking outside the intellectually understood boundary outlines.

By not having experienced the feeling of what happens between the cause and effect of when the new claim's purpose affects its promise, the comfort of having sensually witnessed the true nature of the relationship between the factors involved, feeling the heat of the new claim's flame, has never been realized. An individual gets stuck on parroting the "broken record" description from the received borrowed or intellectual understanding they have of the new unverified claim.

They're not really capable of having the type of faith that comes from having sensually witnessed the claim's truth. They lack having any steadfast surety in what they feel when its cause/effect outcome is based merely on what they were told should come about.

The individual's sensual association with the formation of the truth of the claim's purpose will repeatedly slide by undetected, if it ever appears. The intellectually understood cerebrally stored English language version of the issue's actual sensual incarnation will not detect or perceive the sensual incarnation when it actually happens, if it ever does. The real-time sensual incarnation of the spiritual signposts from intellectually retained religious theology will pass by unassociated.

They have no feel for or felt understanding for the situation to have experience-based faith-backed courage for considering even possible variations of the involved factors. They have no feel for the cause-allowing factor that actually links the cause and effect to openly consider and tolerate possible variations. By not having a felt association for the cause-allowing factors they cannot analyze to compare and consider other options or variations of the factors that make that cause/effect relationship happen. They have no foundation to anchor a comparison.

All they can do to explain why something is the way it is or the way it should be is to give book chapter and verse. With no real understanding, the tolerance to allow entertaining other explanations disappears. The constraints imposed by only knowing the truth of a claim as it was explained or intellectually calculated to be can serve as a form of bondage to the free will.

It's essential to develop an understanding of reality that visualizes change and matures under the watch of an unfettered progressively wiser free will. Openness to tolerance is not merely a better way to deal with people in daily life...it unlocks an individual's worldview to allow visualizing the much-needed optional gateways for acquiring a more balanced realization of the pathway to an enlightened understanding about what's happened to an individual's joy and happiness.

In considering other possibilities, an individual might come across insightful wisdom from a different claim and with their current understanding triangulate on a still better understanding and bring their intellectual knowledge closer to finding the most effective self-training to give their intellectual knowledge an experiential reference.

If individuals don't continue to expand the boundaries of their understanding, they'll be imprisoned by their views and unable to sort out the way to an enlightened understanding and freedom from their suffering. Forced belief in borrowed wisdom numbs the mind with the fearful uncertainty of unanswered anticipation. An individual cannot recognize the real truth.

To allow one's becoming nature to unfold in a way to best realize their unique talents and skills, to best expose their inborn potential, they must have an open mind to new ideas that can bring a more enriched understanding of the ways of our transforming reality to expose and best use talents they may have and don't understand.

They must have the internal faith-backed security to admit their ways of doing things could be improved. They must not be stuck in a too-often practiced response that's turned into a fleeting response that characterizes an addiction to fundamentalism. This would prevent their open-mindedness and forward movement toward a higher spiritual maturity.

The honorable Buddhist teacher Thich Nhat Hanh shares his thoughts on this subject in his book *The Heart of the Buddha's Teaching:*

When we hear a Dharma talk or study a sutra, our only job is to remain open. Usually when we hear or read something new, we just compare it to our own ideas. If it is the same, we accept it and say that it is correct. If it is not, we say it is incorrect. In either case, we learn nothing. If we read or listen with an open mind and an open heart, the rain of the Dharma will penetrate the soil of our consciousness.[9]

The Importance of Sensual Retort

Can anyone make the claim that apple pie is one of their favorite foods based only on a friend's mouth-watering description of what it tasted like to them without ever tasting it themselves? Even if the friend used the best-suited descriptive words possible, can they have a faith beyond one that's blind to any real-time validation from a sensual taste test? Is it worthwhile to have an inner confidence blind to experiencing the living incarnation of the claim's promise that gives life to and connects the effect (the taste) of biting into the pie (the cause) that mothered it?

The cause/effect taste relationship is going to remain subjective to the internalized expectation influenced by each individual's prior conditioning. The subjective nature of any imaginable reality is open to the limitless expanse of illusionary account when unfounded in the real-time range of possible effects coming from real incidents. If they haven't actually tasted apple pie, the imagined taste formed from their cerebral interpretation of someone else's description would be limited to and no more than anything concocted by combining the sensual memories of the tastings of prior similar things that any prior tasting reference may have been experientially conditioned by.

Can soul-felt meaning really be passed along verbally? Wouldn't the claim of delicious be sounder and more defendable if backed by a bone-felt faith solidified in the sensual verification of having actually tasted the pie? How do an individual transfer the meaning of sweet without sensually witnessing its experience?

Can "flame-hot" really ever be more than conceptual when transferred verbally? Can you really ever know the sensual meaning of "hot" without ever approaching a flame?

Faith based on sensual knowledge developed through a mind's actual experience can't be compromised (given the individual has an unfettered free-will capable of realizing how the host feels and the courage to express it)...even if countered by reputable friends or other reliable outside sources. Without actually tasting the pie, the individual would have an experiential feeling void in the anatomy of the internalization process of their belief system. There's no sensual history to base an objective opinion of taste on. There's no sensual evidence to establish truth between the causing pie flavor and the effect on taste it becomes.

After actually tasting the pie, the felt experience is there to more objectively validate the truth of the friend's claim to the pie being delicious. An individual can decide not to jump over the burning bush because they have previously felt what is meant by hot. Its truth savvy is felt and realized/ documented experientially to register in the belief system with a primary sense that relays its full sensually implanted meaning even before any intellectual reference could be conjured up.

Here, there is no blind-to-experience void of uncertainty in their belief system between the hearing the cause and realizing the effect. The would-be void missing the experiential association is instead filled with an immediate sensual reference to their experiential association made with the claim-verifying feeling.

An intellectually constructed version of a sensual-experience that lacks a previous sensual report of what apple pie tastes like would be totally illusionary. It would be a belief of taste in which the individual would lack the very strong steadfast faith-felt-to-the-bone they would have developed and defended had they actually had prior apple pie tasting experience.

By testing any questionable information sensually before internalizing the claim being made, it straps to each tested concept, idea or belief in the developing belief system the sensual experience testifying to its truth...the plausibility of its claim's described cause/effect relationship. Confidence in this truth comes from the same foundation primed by the steadfast faith established when sensually witnessing our Source's truth of ongoing change during self-discovery. It's the same base of constant omnipresent consistency.

It's a deep-felt discovered faith that the cause/effect dimensional reality will continue to exist and will allow the recurrence of the same dimensional support for the interplay among the cause/effect factors that was earlier experienced. There can be steadfast faith in believing that as long as there's no change in the dimensions that hold together what is perceived as reality, this interplay will happen again, just as experienced...the very same agenda for the coming and going bits of energy to push forward and give definition to the passage of time.

5

Language...

The Shorthand Cliffsnotes of Intended Meaning

By and large, language is a tool for concealing the truth.
—George Carlin

Linguistic's Inherent Limitations

The recording timeline from the original manuscripts that shows the linage of translations relates directly to the credibility of the accounts of Christianity or Buddhism or any other "-ism" or "-anity." Anyone who's betting all their spiritual marbles on any of these beliefs should really be interested in recognizing the negative filters to understanding found in the recording transformations and the inherent dilution or muting of the enlightened teachers' original intended meanings that result.

There are many language limitations and cultural differences that add filters between the enlightened teacher's intended meaning and the understanding of today's truth seekers. There are limitations to the human condition that reach in between the initial listeners of the spiritual founding fathers teachings and their recorded understandings of the teachers' intended meanings. Much of the intended meanings were lost, diverted misunderstood and mistranslated during the transformation of the original messages to what we have today...2,000-plus years later.

In considering the handicapping limitations that are inherent to using the word formulation process for transferring an originating source's intended meaning to an interested party, the use of linguistics as a chosen media isn't really much more than transferring diluted approximations of intended meanings. The act of converting a gut-felt intended meaning from the sensual media of understanding to the written word of a chosen language, in itself auto-crafts a compromised purity of meaning.

The process of transferring a spiritual teacher's intended meaning is best suited to having a comparable spiritual ripeness between the teacher's intended message content and what the listeners can intellectually grasp. There should ideally be no outside static of sorts to sidetrack the listeners' decoding or understanding that's attributable to the message media itself.

Language is a social agreement. From culture to culture there's often a difference between one culture's intended meaning and another culture's conditioned interpretation of the same message. The audible tone and inflections of a speaker can affect their intended meaning. Different people from different cultures can interpret the same message quite differently.

With Jesus's primary language of Aramaic, known to be a language of few words, there might not have been the right words to express the intended meaning of a newly identified level of sensitivity that had never before surfaced or been channeled from mankind's deeper consciousness through the waking conscious mind of one of its human elements who goes on to express its intended meaning through a verbal language.

Any word used is going to misrepresent or clip the wings of the intended meaning's conveyance to some degree. The intended meaning of any thought transcends linguistics. D. T. Suzuki, a great Japanese author of writings on Buddhism, Zen and Shin made this observation:

> The contradiction so puzzling to the ordinary way of thinking comes from the fact that we have to use language to communicate our inner experience which in its very nature transcends linguistics.[10]

The author of *The Tao of Physics*, Fritjof Capra, explains how Zen Buddhism attempts to transfer intended meaning without the crippling effects of linguistics:

> Zen Buddhists have a particular knack for making a virtue out of the inconsistencies arising from verbal communication, and with the koan system they have developed a unique way of transmitting their teachings completely nonverbally. Koans are carefully devised nonsensical riddles, which are meant to make the student of Zen realize the limitations of logic and reasoning in the most dramatic way. The irrational wording and paradoxical content of these riddles makes it impossible to solve them by thinking. They are designed precisely to stop the thought process and thus to make the student ready for the nonverbal experience of reality.[11]

It Was Centuries Before Written Accounts of Anything Appeared

There have been 2,000-plus years for the intended message of the enlightened ones to be diffused and diluted. Every imaginable type of human influence on their original utterings have had time to have their way with what the enlightened ones meant in their teachings. The writings have been passed back and forth from area to area...language to language...culture to culture. Some of today's individuals and sects choose to follow their interpretation of a modern translation of their religion's Bible word for word?

There have been a few thousand years for the written accounts of the original human interpretations of the intended meanings of the enlightened messengers to be divided among the many unenlightened differences in worldview that bounce echoing from wall to wall down the halls of mankind's collective confused mitote/maya state of mind. Step back and shake off any fundamentalist halo.

Humans can only be humans. It can't just be said that what's in today's Bible is here because God meant it to be that way. After texts reach a certain age and are passed down through enough generations, they seem to take on an air of being sacred. The ancient writers lose their contemporary persona and what they've written assumes the illusionary passport visa showing their credibility has received the stamp from above.

The different Buddhist Canons are massive in size. They individually consume up to five feet of bookshelf space. The Vatican secret archives have fifty-two miles of shelving.

Both Christianity's Bible and Buddhism's Canons were not recorded till long after the deaths of their enlightened originators. The gospels of the Bible began showing up fifty years after Jesus's death and continued during the next few hundred years.

Siddhartha's sutras were passed down orally through a time of about five hundred years before being written down on palm leaves. Buddhism Canons are a product of various monks' passed-along memorized accounts of his verbal sutras. The diamond sutra is the oldest dated manuscript known to mankind. It was dated AD 868. It wasn't discovered until 1907 in a cave on the edge of the Gobi desert.

The main differences between the published product of the Buddhist and Christian founders' accounts is that Mr. Gautama's sutras had not been selectively edited by the Romans or any other power-hungry force like the Bible had been edited to serve the interest of the Roman Empire.

Buddhist teachings document their deep analysis of the infrastructures of both the human waking consciousness and the ego free deeper consciousness and have them amazingly well mapped out. To understand all the divisions, groupings and lists is beyond the capacity of the normal individual. It would surely take an enlightened individual to understand all the outlined thought pattern switchbacks and brain wave spaghetti bowls.

The Vietnamese monk and Buddhist teacher Thich Nhat Hahn shares his interpretation of the details of the early recording of Mr. Gautama's sutras. He recognized the influence of human prejudice in transferring intended meaning.

> For four hundred years during and after the Buddha's lifetime, his teachings were transmitted only orally. After that, monks in the Tamrashatiya School (those who wear copper colored robes) in Sri Lanka, a derivative of the Vibhajyavada School, began to think about writing the Buddha's discourses on palm leaves, and it took another hundred years to begin. By that time, it is said that there was only one monk who had memorized the whole canon and that he was somewhat arrogant. The other monks had to persuade him to recite the discourses so they could write them down. When we hear this, we feel a little uneasy knowing that an arrogant monk may not have been the best vehicle to transmit the teachings of the Buddha.[12]
>
> The transmission of the teachings of the Buddha can be divided into three streams: Source Buddhism, Many-Schools Buddhism, and Mahayana Buddhism. Source Buddhism includes all the teachings the Buddha gave during his lifetime. One hundred forty years after the Buddha's Great Passing Away, the Sangha divided into two schools: Mahasanghika (literally "majority," referring to those who wanted changes) and Sthaviravada (literally "School of Elders," referring to those who opposed the changes advocated by the Mahasanghikas). A hundred years after that, the Sthaviravada divided into two branches—Sarvastivada ("the School that Proclaims Everything Is") and Vibhajyavada ("the School that Discriminates"). The Vibhajyavidins, supported by King Ashoka, flourished in the Ganges valley, while the Sarvastivadins went north to Kashmir.[13]
>
> ...The third stream of the Buddha's teaching, Mahayana Buddhism, arose in the first or second century BCE.[14]

The factor of human error must be considered. To have someone of Atisha's described smaller or middle capacity of spiritual maturity trying to make record of a lecture directed at an audience of supreme spiritual capacity is like having someone in the sixth grade taking notes at a college philosophy class. This affected both the Bible and the Buddhist Canons. And beyond this, recorded accounts of teachings were all filtered through the subjective perceptions and were generated subject to the personal likes and dislikes...the unavoidable spin of the recorder's belief system and worldview.

> Even during the Buddha's lifetime, there were people such as monk Arittha, who misunderstood the Buddha's teachings and conveyed them incorrectly. [Arittha Sutta (Discourse on Knowing the Better Way to Catch a Snake), Majjhima Nikaya 22.] It is also apparent that some of the monks who memorized the sutras over the centuries did not understand their deepest meaning, or at the very least, they forgot or changed some words. As a result, some of the Buddha's teachings were distorted even before they were written down.[15]

There's been message fragmentation resulting from making a religion's charter bend to the wants of powerful humans. In the early 1500s, England's King Henry VIII broke away from the Roman Catholic Church to be self-proclaimed head of the Church of England to accommodate his desire to remarry. To this day, England worships God under this royal's reinterpretation of what had been postulated to be the intended message of God's law.

Considering a shorthand-like translation history since AD 1500 that today's Christian Bibles have gone through. This is just a portion of the linage of translations today's incarnations of Rome's Bible has gone through, taken from a PBS special program on Bible translations.

> It's a Greek Bible...The Tindale Bible of 1500...The Martin Luther Bible...the Church of England based on Henry VIII's desire to have a church that would allow his divorce. The Mathew Bible. The Cramers Bible, largely Tindale's with an English translation from Latin...took away some power from the clergy...not recognizing the Pope...Tindale and Cranmer burned at stake. The Geneva Bible...The Puritan Bible...got rid of bishops...the Duea Bible...The Bishop's Bible...King James came along after Queen Elizabeth...called a conference...bishops won out over Purns...a new Bible was produced under King James for a church that all could use, 1630 Massachusates the New England Experiment, Bay group created new church...King James Bible was at heart of their faith...It's thought of as being the voice of God...1700s North Hampton Mass, Johnathan Edwards...the great awakening...evangelical movement...Puritans couldn't tame it...pursue salvation! Many types of churches resulted...People want to read and interpret the Bible for themselves (PBS TV SHOW April 25, 2007 PM).

It's been said that storytelling is how we pass along our history from generation to generation. There's a party game in the Midwest that makes light of the unavoidable change to the intended meaning of a statement when passed verbally from one individual to the next. The exercise starts with one person whispering into the ear of another a detailed story of some sort. The listener then whispers the same story into the ear of another person. After the story has been silently passed between all the guests, the last person to hear the story tells the story to the group. The final account of the story is always far from the original. The more participants, the more entertaining the final account is.

Intended Meanings Lost in Translation

The Bible is the most translated book in the world. It has been translated into over 380 languages. Based on the subjective nature of the battlefield of human opinion alone, it's really impossible to determine how much disintegration there's been of the original orators' intended meanings.

The human spin and error factor over the lengthy 2,000plus years passage of time brings to question how well the founders' intended message has been preserved. The serious and prudent individual should consider all the available accounts and try to better recognize through triangulation the heavenly founders' intended message.

Many Christian believers whose biblical conditioning comes from studying the King James Version of the Bible think they have to use that language dialect in expressing their wishes and requests to God. It's often thought that using the same type of terminology as used in this version of the Bible they are familiar with will possibly help keep their hopes and wishes classified as holy to increase the likelihood of having them fulfilled? The prayers are full of "thees," "thines" and "thous."

The language used in the King James Version of the Bible sounds antiquated in today's world while it was a language of the future back during the days when the Jesus walked the earth and when Bible was written and first recorded. It was a newer language to include more words that reveal a deeper understanding of concepts that 2,000 years ago were just emerging in mankind's waking consciousness as distant theories yet to be developed.

Jesus spoke Aramaic, a language of few words. There are no recordings of any of his teachings in his native tongue. It's hard to imagine how the true intended meaning presented in an oral presentation done using a language of few words could ever be captured and related to other people in writing or orally.

Preserving his intended meaning in his teachings would be greatly enhanced by witnessing his body language as he spoke his ideas. Jesus taught about new angles on subtle aspects of spirituality that were probably no words for yet.

There are no Buddhist recordings of any of Siddhartha's sutras in his native tongue, Ardhamargadhi. There was a loss of their intended meaning from the start from the early lectures of both enlightened ones. It mattered how the recorder interpreted what they heard and passed it along and how those remembered accounts were finally recorded centuries later for the first time.

> We have to remember that the Buddha did not speak Pali, San-skrit, or Prakrit. He spoke a local dialect called Magadhi or Ard-hamargadhi, there's no record of the Buddha's words in his own language.[16]

There are no copies of the original manuscripts of the Bible. There are only copies of the copies of copies. Since none of the oldest copies are identical, it's impossible to know which ones are correct or at least present only the errors of the most reflective accounts.

If written accounts of the books that were chosen to make up the Bible didn't begin appearing until after fifty years past Jesus's death, how could the authors remember exactly what Jesus or any other of the biblical characters said when presenting their statements in quotation marks? It was five hundred years before Siddhartha's sutras were written down.

Those original 2,000-year-old recorded impressions have been translated into languages that didn't even exist back in the day. There have been translator assumptions made to expand in translation the original meaning into the more deeply defined meanings of languages that have since evolved because of the need to expand mankind's developing cognitive understanding for a more meaning-sensitive detailing of older beliefs and concepts.

As time passed and mankind had more opportunity to give more thought to the meanings of the words used to describe the original revelations or inspired insights about the human condition in the human experience that came to mankind's collective waking awareness, a richer vocabulary evolved to tie down the later more defined meanings. The later translators having the greater selection available of the more meaning-sensitive words had to decide which words to use to best channel the enlightened orator's intended meaning. It's like fitting a round peg into a square hole, and making it expand to fit.

It sounds practiced and a bit trite when the fourteenth Dalai Lama says in English how we need self-confidence and less fear and stress and that as universal values we need compassion and the spirit of forgiveness. It's a true and good answer in the general sense. His answer to what we need is much more focused and pointed when he answers the question in his native Tibetan tongue. Even so, the meaning of that answer is a hand-me-down from the original dialect from earlier centuries. Still, the Dalai Lama's Buddhist function is to provide a passed-along living interpretation of Atisha's recovery of Siddhartha's process of gaining enlightenment that he reintroduced to Tibet at the turn of the first millennium. We need to understand the layers of limitations caused by labeling intended messages with the limitations inherent to using the words of any language.

In 2007, when teaching his interpretation of Atisha's writings while in Bloomington, Indiana and speaking in English, the Dalai Lama described his idea of meaning in his native tongue through his long-used interpreter. The Dalai Lama wouldn't be able to secure the intended meaning within his command of the English language. Still, the intended meaning is further diluted by its exposure to the inherent limitations of human communication and the step down into the limitations of the English language in having descriptors appropriate to support the deeper meanings associated with spiritualism that the language of Tibet covers much more thoroughly.

Jesus's Intended Message? Apples to Apples, Bibles to Bibles

Try to imagine all the unintentional variances or twists in the Bible's authors' versions of the enlightened ones' intended meanings that did occur when the authors made their written accounts and have come to follow over the past 2,000-plus years. Think of all the culturally-bent intellectual spins and inherent human error that have affected what is read today that's taken as being what the orator meant by what they originally said. It's believed today to be the channeled message from God above? Today, the total number of versions of the Bible is enormous.

It only took a bit of due diligence and an Internet connection to discover this following example showing the skew of intended meaning that exists between some of the different biblical translations of the biblical message in Proverbs 4:7. The intended meaning of this verse captures the need to get wisdom and with that get understanding.

Here are but a dozen varieties of today's Bible translations being used. Of the several websites that offered multiple translations of the Bible, Biblehub.com was used to view the following biblical excerpts.

> New American Standard Bible: "The beginning of wisdom is: Acquire wisdom; and with all your acquiring, get understanding."

> God's Word Translation: "The beginning of wisdom is to acquire wisdom. Acquire understanding with all that you have."

> King James Bible: "Wisdom is the principal thing; therefore, get wisdom: and with all thy getting get understanding."

American King James Version: "Wisdom is the principal thing; therefore, get wisdom: and with all your getting get understanding."

American Standard Version: "Wisdom is the principal thing; therefore, get wisdom; yea, with all thy getting get understanding."

Bible in Basic English: "The first sign of wisdom is to get wisdom; go, give all you have to get true knowledge."

Douay-Rheims Bible: "The beginning of wisdom, get wisdom, and with all thy possession purchase prudence."

Darby Bible Translation: "The beginning of wisdom is, Get wisdom; and with all thy getting get intelligence."

English Revised Version: "Wisdom is the principal thing; therefore, get wisdom: yea, with all thou hast gotten get understanding."

Webster's Bible Translation: "Wisdom is the principal thing; therefore, get wisdom: and with all thy getting get understanding."

World English Bible: "Wisdom is supreme. Get wisdom. Yes, though it costs all your possessions, get understanding."

Young's Literal Translation: "The first thing is wisdom—get wisdom, And with all thy getting get understanding."

Differences in translator spiritual maturity or in their style of expressing the same intended idea is obvious here in the different translations of Proverbs 4:7 that deal with finding wisdom, understanding, knowledge, intelligence and prudence and the way these concepts interrelate. The variety of translator perception seen within these translations exhibits some of the differences in human expression touched by spiritual maturity or maybe just the style of acknowledgement. The authors have to find the right words to express the meaning they're trying to consciously channel from the feelings coming from deeper within.

These different translations are all meant to relate the speaker's intended meaning of their original expression of the message in Proverbs 4:7. This comparison demonstrates what happens after the intended meaning of a message is processed within the subjective confines of a translator's worldview to then be processed by the translator within the set guidelines associated with a differently particular language to best reproduce the original teacher's intended meaning without having personally witnessed the teaching.

The projected meaning of the translator's translated message is filtered through any biases acquired from their prior conditioning. It's exposed to their level of intelligence as well as the amount of knowledge they have available to be processed at their relative level of spiritual maturity.

The main directive of the verse varies throughout these translations of the original recorder's written understanding of the actual teaching listened to or the account of it they were told about from over 2,000 years ago. This verse had already been translated many times through several languages spaced throughout scores of lifetimes prior to the versions of its diffused meaning shown above.

The general consensus of most of the translations seems to be that wisdom is the starting place...to get wisdom and with that an enlightened understanding. This process is exactly what Siddhartha dedicated his lifetime to realize and teach about...spreading the word of realizing this process of gaining wisdom through self-training right understanding.

This is as per the New American Standard Bible, King James Bible, American King James Version, American Standard Version, English Revised Version, Webster's Bible Translation, and Young's Literal Translation. There are minor variances in the story lines, but they say close to the same thing.

The God's Word Translation leaves it in the air as to whether the understanding comes from all the wisdom you have or all the worth you have. The Bible in Basic English does the same thing as the God's Word Translation, yet it says to pursue gaining knowledge not mentioning understanding. Having knowledge and understanding are two different things. One can have knowledge and not have the right understanding.

The Douay-Rheims Bible is more explicit about not how to get knowledge understanding or intelligence, but prudence. It says basically to sell what you possess to purchase prudence...that by getting rid of all one owns they become prudent.

The Darby Bible Translation says that intelligence comes from gaining wisdom. Maybe it has the process backward? Maybe wisdom helps an individual make sense of their intelligence? Its line of thought fails to realize that intelligence is needed to recognize or have an insight about the attributes of the interplay between the factors involved in a time-fueled cause/effect relationship that demonstrates the ongoing change of our reality.

The World English Bible says to get wisdom and in the same breath it says to give up all possessions and with that gain understanding. The conclusion is rather illusive here. Does giving up all possessions bring wisdom? It seems a truth seeker needs the wisdom to understand why they need to give up their possessions...that managing their possessions consumes the peace of mind needed to self-train the mental control to sustain the right concentration necessary to develop the wisdom of understanding our impermanent reality. When Jesus asked his followers to give up what they owned and follow him, did he mean to literally follow his footsteps or to follow the way of the wisdom in his teaching?

Are wisdom and understanding synonymous in the mind of the translator of the intended meaning of this scripture? Did their relative level of spiritual maturity really qualify them to translate from one media to the next the original orator's intended meaning?

The various translations of Proverbs 4:7 are easily found by using any Internet search engine. This makes due diligence easier for any truth-seeking individual's normally apathy-stricken mind to change the historically proven normal behavior of following blindly only one translation, version or account.

In times past, the different biblical versions were available, but access to them was just too much trouble. In the Midwest, using the King James Version is just taken for granted and never really questioned. The intended meaning's just second-guessed. Just check the desk drawer of any Midwestern hotel room. By reading the variety of different interpretations of the same message, individuals will begin to wise up to the inherent dangers of not asking questions.

By considering the Gnostic Gospels of Thomas, Judas, or any of the others would give a fuller and richer understanding of what Jesus's original intended message was. It's also in the 2,000-plus years of humanizing that Jesus's intended message has had that makes the wisdom of blind reliance on a single translation very questionable.

Meanings of *Tao Te Ching* and Bible are Interpolated

There are many different translations of the Bible. In each of the different translations, the four gospels each offer slight variations about the story of Jesus. It's up to the reader to sort from their perceptions of the meanings which of those accounts lean more toward the originally intended message and, with respect to each account, interpolate their own final meaning. They must synthesize the various factors into what makes the most sense going by how they've allowed their worldview to be conditioned. Many will consider, side to side, the different translations.

In the book *Tao Te Ching*, like with the Bible, the meaning intended by the messenger of wisdom has also been translated by hundreds of different sources. Peter A. Merel has reviewed several of the most popular modern-day translations and synthesized what appears to be the common meaning shared by the translations of Lau Tzu's recorded insights into his 1995 interpolation of *Tao Te Ching*.

> This document attempts to draw the texts of several popular
> English translations of Lao Tse into a consistent and accessible
> context. It is based on the translations of Robert G. Henricks,

Lin Yutang, D. C. Lau, Ch'u Ta-Kao, Gia-Fu Feng and Jane English, Richard Wilhelm and Aleister Crowley.

This work is not a translation, but an interpolation. It does not represent the original text; the original, if there was an original, has been jumbled, mistranscribed and reinterpreted many times over many thousands of years, and is here cast into a language that is incapable of presenting its poetic structure and philological connections.

Even an original text, translated as faithfully as possible, might remain inaccessible to the modern reader unable to place it within its original context. The intention of this work is to construct a document that closely corresponds with the best modern translations of Lao Tse, but which is blunt, easy and useful to read within a modern context.[17]

Word Semantics Vary from Culture to Culture

Different cultures generate their own assortment of words reflecting the different impressions reality's distinctive footprint has left in their region. Culture to culture, the same words may have different intended meanings.

Comparing language to language, French and Italian have several more words that convey additional meanings of the word "love" than does the English language. Eskimos have nine words that give a more differentiated understanding of different types of snow. The eastern languages have a much larger selection of words to convey more focused notions relating to the topics of spirituality than does the English language.

Some intended meaning is compromised when translating a well-defined insightful spiritual concept from one language into a language with less words relating to the more developed insight into spirituality. It's necessary to choose a word with a different and possibly more general meaning than needed.

Some intended meaning is compromised when translating from a language with less available words to a language with a more available selection of words defining the topic or idea. The translator might have to decide which deeper meaning the intended message had. Maybe the teacher in that earlier instance wasn't aware of the more distinct meanings at that later time? Either way, it's up to the translator's discretion as to which way of meaning to go when expressing the teacher's intended meaning.

There's a rounding-off effect on the intended meaning in both situations. An avenue of focused attention may be selected that was not the original meaning intended. The intended meaning gets misdirected or is totally lost. The life of the message can be consumed by compromise.

When considering individual spiritual maturity levels, the effort to find a word to express a concept that's not so well understood will cause the speaker's intended meaning to be lost or altered. This happens when converting languages from any written account of any oral presentation, oral account of any written presentation, oral account of oral presentation or written account of written presentation. The odds are against an accurate account of what meaning was originally intended.

Jesus's native tongue Aramaic is an old language of few words. To secure Jesus's intended meaning, a student really had to be there to hear and watch his body language. It would be left up to the subjective decision of the individual who actually witnessed the animated expression of his intended meaning to choose what descriptive and feeling-focused words to use to describe their heartfelt perception.

Translations of intended meaning were also exposed to the weakening effects of an original listener's lower level of spiritual maturity or that of anyone in the translation process. They wouldn't be able to express in writing the intended meaning of a spiritual teaching they were listening to when the message is beyond their level of spiritual maturity. Don't forget the accidental, intentional and unintentional subjective human input and errors that come with anything.

Speaking in Tongues

Could speaking in tongues possibly be a way to transfer the heartfelt emotional meaning that exceeds the capability of any spoken language? There are those who believe this to be the case. Could the unstructured nature of its undefined phonic and grammar formats allow for the better transfer of the messenger's intended meaning?

Consider Jesus's language Aramaic, an ancient tongue of few words. At one of his lectures, there might have been individuals representing different language dialects in the audience, who would have had a lessened understanding of his spoken word. For Jesus to convey a pressing thought for a new concept or consciously unexplored level of spirituality that hadn't yet floated up into mankind's collective waking consciousness to even allow speaking about, when the sought-after words were lacking, a sound plus the expressed visible body language was what was possible to best express the inner message. Could it be that from this combination, new words evolved?

Jesus taught mankind about the subtle truths of life that were only beginning to surface into mankind's cumulative waking consciousness. He taught of new insights to enlighten mankind's waking awareness as to what the cause/effect truths are that rule God's creation. How could he use the few-word language of Aramaic and accomplish this? He had to have used parables and body language to express these truths.

It could be similar to what a oneto two-year-old child does when they try to express a desire...a combination of blabber, finger pointing, eyebrow raising, hip shifting and eye intensity. Parents can often understand the intended meaning of their young children as they speak in tongues?

In the '70s, on many of the music billboard's record sales charts, Led Zeppelin's song "Stairway to Heaven" sat at the top for quite a while. This is not a documented fact, but it's safe to estimate that 95 percent of the listening audience can't understand to recite all the words, unless of course they're reading the lyrics. Yet, where the music and the lyrics fuse there's a sound that articulates a message the listeners like to hear.

Maybe traditional poetry passes a bit closer to the speaker's heartfelt meaning as the message's relaxed cadence and intent seem to find that common chord. Indiana's great poet Robert Frost seemed to create his own dialect of English in his poetry. His laws of written rhyme soff'n the flow of thoughts into its own phonic rhythm, a feng shui–safe marriage of short'nd syllables, missin' vowels, an' crafty punctuation tha' jus' tickle da new thoughts as dey roll off the mental tongue.

The Rich Language of Mathematics

Arguably, the intellectually based language that reaches beyond any regional dialect to best communicate in poetic truths, the relational justice between the different factors that make up this cause/effect reality is mathematics. It was the language used by Einstein in 1915 to make known his inspired insight into our dimensional reality through his theory of general relativity of mass, time, and space...$E = MC^2$. Those who understand the meaning of the symbols can be led to understand the meaning of his insight...at least intellectually.

The mathematics of engineering is responsible for the completed construction of a countless number of things that are built from following sets of plans... bridges, cars, trains, airplanes, spaceships, roadways, homes, and everything else that makes up the skylines of our beautiful cities, to name only a few things. People speaking different verbal languages can unite in coordinated effort to reach the same end when they have a well-prepared set of blueprints.

One reason going to a big city captivates people is subliminal and never realized by most. People celebrate an unnoticed sense of human accomplishment in the coordination of discipline, patience and having the ability to follow the same procedural order. The sort of extroverted sense of stepping out and working in harmony of effort with unknown others in the completion of such an immense challenge such as to build a one-hundred-story building has to be felt by any onlooker at some level.

Like how many Midwesterners are drawn to the sound of a French accent or the potentially seductive accent of a southern belle, individuals are drawn to the powerful accent of applied and accomplished purpose that radiates from the language of mathematics as written in a set of blueprints or maybe in explaining how time relates to the speed of light.

When this coordinated effort is over time multiplied by twenty-five square miles of similar results that span several generations, it's no wonder people like to go see the big city. It can be calming, relaxing and through the scale of its presence, it can be thought inspiring. Visiting a big city shows one's pride in the potential stored in being a human...most often unrealized or at least unappreciated to the waking mind.

All of this is made possible by the power of the language of mathematics to articulate precisely the intended purpose of the designers that planned the layout and dimensions of that huge ongoing project that can extend beyond a normal lifetime. They offer their trust as they pass much of their contribution on to be completed by future generations.

Just visit the pyramids.

6

Religion Identity

Labeling

After realizing that suffering exists, that it has a cause, that the cause can be eliminated and then wanting to find the way to do just that, one thing that will delay the journey is to become part of an "-ism," an "-anity," or any specific group that wears the handcuffs of blind faith. This can begin to prejudice a truth seeker away from the purpose of their search and start to kindle the early flame of fundamentalism. A label means that the labeled suddenly is something, but what's more important, it also means that the labeled is not open to being something else.

Once labeled, a religion follower has to jump through the hoops of a limiting fundamentalist dogma. Anytime an individual wears a label, it puts a strangle hold on their possibilities.

Calling Jesus a Christian would mean he is not a Buddhist. Calling Siddhartha a Buddhist would mean that he is not a Christian. With the goal of both groups being to attain the riches of eternal joy and happiness with freedom from suffering, it would be best to leave Jesus's or Siddhartha's depictions as being those who share the same goal...not to insult their cause by making access to their all-inclusive brotherhood seem foreign, privileged, restricted or biased.

Jesus was one of the many religious proclaimers that had a following before his death, but there was no recognized Christian religion until Rome allowed it. Jesus of Nazareth was not a Christian. Christianity wasn't legalized until more than three hundred years after he was martyred.

Siddhartha was not a Buddhist. He was a Buddha, just like everyone has within that has yet to be realized. He didn't make any claim about owning or being founder of anything having to do with what he referred to as the law of nature.

Christianity and Buddhism did not exist when both the founders were alive and found enlightenment. They both represented the truth they understood and were trying to share guidance to its Source for others. There's not a restrictive

Jesus's way or Siddhartha's way. They both walked down the same path at different times in history.

Intended Message Lost in Religious Rite and Ritual

Christian worshipers have been given no self-training guidance on where and how to direct their present moment intentions to become enlightened about what it is that causes their suffering before they die. Following the Ten Commandments and praying to God is about where it stops. It doesn't take much time before an individual's waking mind becomes bored or challenged again by their mitote/maya confusion that they seek relief from.

There's no hint given about how to harmoniously unite the mind and body or even what that accomplishes. Siddhartha tells how to unite the mind and body in the harmony that Lau Tzu says will enlighten the individual with the knowledge that will conquer the self. Christianity stops its soul-reckoning guidance at what behaviors to do or not to do without explaining why or why not.

The outward expression of a religion's rites and rituals seems to be the important thing when a congregation comes together. If an individual is nodding off to sleep during the sermon, communion, or a song, they're missing the essence of what they're supposed to be there to worship. Religious worshipers become attached to the setup of the religion and leave their quest for spiritual advancement naively unattended.

A loosely defined salvation promised by the god being worshipped loses its presence to the present moment sensual awareness or feedback of performing the rituals themselves. Believers easily develop attachment to the ritualistic nature of the actions that after a few millennia of repetition seem to only pay tribute to the object of worship more than to accomplish any spiritual ends.

Most learn to see the ritualistic behaviors and dogma as an end in themselves. The ritualistic behavior was originally performed years ago and were then used as a means to a spiritual end and individuals since think that perhaps repeating the behavior will keep them closer to the yet-tobe-understood end the original millennia-old performance was directed at.

Actions become reactions through repetition. The repeating of any type of religious ceremonial rite becomes habitual, especially when there's no end purpose felt in the heart while engaged in the act. In what eventually becomes mindless repetition they lose their original intended purpose of the behavior? Like people become attached to habit energy's fleeting reactions developed from prior conditioning, attachment to the repetition of religious rites and ceremonies form into a ritualistic shell that defines that particular religious sect.

This is a pattern of behavior that leads to the real-time suffering the truth seeker seeks salvation from. The ritual has no real end in mind other than a loosely understood salvation or sorts? It requires no real application of the mind, so while performing the ritual, their mind wonders preoccupied from voice to voice of the 1,000 separate voices talking at once in their mitote/maya mental state.

Most people spend their lives mesmerized in a vacuum wondering about life's answers. They spend their life wandering about in an apparent reality they've created that never touches on and stirs up their inborn awareness of reality dormant in a subtle region of their deeper consciousness. This ritualistic behavior is common in most cultures, done en masse and goes unquestioned as it has always been that way and that's as deep as most people think about it. Its presence is a stone in the path of society's collective advancement to the happiness joy and compassion of heavenly enlightenment.

Geshe Sonam Rinshen expresses a Tibetan Buddhist view in his commentary book, *Atisha's Lamp for the Path to Enlightenment*:

> Our intention makes an enormous qualitative difference. We may do something quite unremarkable and ordinary, it may even appear frivolous, but if the kindhearted wish to help all living beings is present, it is the practice of a Bodhisattva (enlightenment-bound individual). On the other hand, we may engage in what appears to be spiritual practice, but without the right kind of motivation it is nothing more than a worldly activity.[18]

Many view versions of religious piety to be superstitions. This leaves many afraid to step outside the ring of socially prescribed behaviors. Just the same, individuals become addicted to their formed reactions that deal with circumstances involving the related stimuli.

Living in the apparent reality with an undying attachment to the illusion of the "I" extends to include one's possessions, views and beliefs, religious promises and practices. The ignorance of the nature of this reality's nature that underwrites this process is what allows an individual to suffer present moment frustrations and disappointments.

Eventually we become moms and dads' passing on these beliefs in line with our society's adopted beliefs. This helps explain the dysfunctional nature of many families...unable to communicate as their thoughts separately drift from internalized misguided purpose to unrelated misguided purpose being shouted all at once by the 1,000 voices in their individual belief systems to have their human host act on the endless purpose they shout about. Topics of thought can amount to no more than twinkling aspects of differing illusionary accounts of reality that go unmentioned, misinterpreted or misunderstood between family members around the dinner table.

Does Religious Claim Confront the Cause of Suffering?

The true test for any religious or spiritual belief is how effective its claim describing the nature and intended purpose of our Source is at identifying and addressing suffering's cause and providing for its removal. Does the discipline's charter address the ignorance founded in the void in an individual's belief system that allows the smorgasbord of addictions to clinging and aversive behaviors that contribute to an individual's suffering?

Human suffering is human suffering...regardless of any religious/spiritual fraternal membership. How do they define and address its cause?

Is there a sign from above to verify its omnipresence? Is there a living essence of the maker of the religious claim to be sensually verified that provides a secured foundation for a more steadfast faith in the witnessed effectiveness of the claim being made? Does the presence of its living truth shine through to the truth seeker's waking awareness in a way that they will stand up for and defend?

Does it give a truth seeker an experiential look at their Source's recognition and compliance to the self-evident ongoing change that leads us all from birth to death? Is the claim's truth something that has to be read about and intellectually remembered and quoted to defend?

Cultural Intimidation

Technology has opened up many new sources offering very descriptive analysis of the Bible's origination. Not long ago before all the recent technological advancements, with the biblical lands so far away, hidden and out of sight, the information was far away and completely out of mind...making the local version of the Bible's translation the only option considered for explaining the events 2,000-plus years ago, a pillar of Midwestern cultural fiber passed down through so many generations.

Cultural unfamiliarity intimidates many Midwesterners when they consider the tenants of Eastern based spirituality. The lingering thought of some aged white-haired eastern guru with a long beard who speaks languages Midwesterners do not understand stunts the pursuit of most non-Christian pathways to paradise. Do flying carpets really exist?

The imagined guru might actually be farther along the path of understanding life's truth, but the primal truth is just as true and as readily available for any Midwesterner at this time as for any Eastern guru. It needs no eastern stamp of authenticity. It's just as available to understand and gain insight about in Hoosier land as for any guru posed in full lotus position in India. It's totally available in English with no Indian accent.

The guru, however, might be more in tuned to the self-training process effective in gaining the insights to realize wisdom. It was in this region that the way to realize enlightenment was first written down in a way that made it through the sea of translations to service today's state of curiosity.

The guru might have available more appropriate borrowed and intellectual knowledge sources in his life circumstance than Hoosiers do to serve as the intellectual catalyst and guide for developing the experiential knowledge that lights the path to the enriched awareness that earns them the title guru.

The limited Midwestern availability of the borrowed, received and intellectual knowledge information that originated in the East makes it easier for a Midwesterner to be intimidated and to perceive the guru's presence as being lofty, foreign or too deep for their non-Eastern persona to grasp or understand. The Midwesterner will often bow to fear of the unknown and not ask questions. They will easily depreciate their holy-worthiness due to their generic surroundings with a history lacking any competing spiritual-based lore.

Unfamiliar Eastern terminology distances the insights and masks other theological answers behind what Godfearing Hoosiers see as possibly being another religion that their god will punish them for considering. For way too many, fundamentalist walls go up to block any possible investigative understanding.

When someone's explaining the basics of suffering, people listen, and then when told this aligns with one of the "-isms," they close their ears dumbfounded and distanced due to their prior conditioning associated with attempts to absorb the many different foreign religions from times of their past. The reaction of many is to quit trying to understand, as it's just another very detailed religious philosophy.

Foreign sources describing any religious or spiritual theology directed at reaching enlightenment will break a listener's concentration by going into detail in describing foreign words and their derivations. This alienates the Midwestern reader. It bores them and breaks their train of thought and distances the concept.

They wonder if it will help. Is it necessary to learn these terms of Sanskrit or Pali that were used in these ancient canons? They don't stop to think that Siddhartha also did not speak these languages. The message of truth is simple, nondiscriminatory nonsecular and does not have to be disguised by or coded in Pali or Sanskrit.

It puts the path to enlightenment under the shadow of foreign origination. It can make it seem that the derivation of the foreign words must be understood so not to break the paper trail of the concept. It creates a new information tsunami too large and too distracting for the comprehension of the average mind.

It's not clear to the truth seeker that they are seeking the truth of life that's not hidden in the meaning of foreign words. It truly distances the truth's availability, in a way. To them, the pathway to the enlightening truth that they're now looking for, was once uncovered by a person from a different culture of long ago and told about in an ancient book. This vision of reality confuses the end result of finding an enlightened understanding in the obscuring means to that end. There are no known enlightened Midwestern role models of today for the Midwesterner to refer to?

Many Midwestern believers unconsciously feel deep down inside that actually coming across any living incarnation of what they imagine the read and told about Christian heaven to be is rather unlikely. For one thing, there're no biblical descriptions about what the presence of the Bible's interacting entities and forces are like in twenty-first-century terms.

In having the physical proximity of eastern religion's home-based so far away really lessens the probability of it drawing many Midwestern followers. Their world seems mystical with so many divisions and interpretations. It's possible that religion from foreign lands is not taken quite as seriously. Individuals hear of so many famous people who've spoken and studied under gurus and their lives turn out to be as full of suffering as their own.

It's a fact that the way to enlightenment in this lifetime was experienced and recorded by easterners. The accounts of guidance offered by Jesus were edited by Rome before Rome's publication of the Bible. Siddhartha's guidance was finally recorded even though the Buddhist tradition had already split many times.

In the Midwest USA, up until recent times, available guidance has been very difficult to find. There haven't been truth seekers who've known to look inside to find the source of their present moment unrest. The technological advancements of modern times is making due diligence much easier and these Eastern disciplines are becoming much more available.

Religion's Adaptive Evolution

Many say that super-human superstition adjusts to present moment shifts in the real-time picture of this reality as social opinion matures in the wake of science's advancements. Religion's interpretations of many of yesterday's no-nos have changed and adapted to the times. They have to, or the religion dies out. Religion's future gets tripped up over fundamentalist restrictions and narrow-mindedness.

Nicolaus Copernicus, who died in 1543, was an astronomer who first theorized heliocentric cosmology where Earth revolves once a day and circles the sun once a year. Both seventeenth-century religion and science didn't accept this idea at the time. Before the time of the father of science, Galileo (1564–1642), many things like having the Earth at the center of the universe were a part of the Catholic doctrine. Mankind used to think the world was flat. With time, human due diligence led to discoveries that proved those notions to be totally illusionary.

Today's new pope of the Roman Catholic Church is laxing up on the church's engraved standards to help insure the continued existence of the perceived reality of the Church's theological story to sway in the way of the progressively better understood rhythm of the true reality their God claims to have created. He's making changes in how the church recognizes gays. The Bible's comments on marriage and relationships between two people are being interpreted in a much more liberal sense to allow the church's condoning of homosexual lifestyles.

Change and scientific development go hand in hand. As time passes, new scientific discoveries are made that confront established norms and beliefs. Science further unwraps to better understand nature's gift of change. Scientific proof will often reduce these norms or beliefs to being filed away on the shelves of superstition.

As mankind approaches a collective awareness of how the effects of ongoing change manifest in the range of human perception, there are legitimate questions that arise...questions that rise to the top through mankind's conditioned mitote/maya state of social confusion that can't find focus into its collective all-knowing deeper consciousness.

If a new issue is not agreed on, the issue stays in the front of society's mind and is not yet stored in its collective belief system. The issue might be a topic for a presidential election debate. Issues are questioned and discussed to society's satisfaction and are in time finally internalized adding a new or modified facet to be remixed into society's collective belief system. This questioning process accounts for a countless number of positive changes to mankind's collective worldview.

As time has demonstrated, once society collectively accepts a new discovery, religion will then have to make its adoptive change and reform/adjust its blind faith claims to allow for the newly experientially verified evidence tested by science. For the most part, religion keeps the boundaries of its field of mysticism within science's evolving boundaries of proven fact. They must be careful not to suggest or support the relational interplay between the cause/effect factors of this reality that have been shown to no longer be valid...now shown to be mere superstitions.

Many older religions have gone by the wayside for such oversight and inability to adapt. Still, there are Evangelical Christians who blindly adhere to the seven-day creation of a 6,000-year-old Earth and blindly take pride in denying the existence of dinosaurs. They're creationists that support this theory of creation called creationism.

World religious leaders are usually thought of as being unbendable to the lore of times past. Buddhism is an "-ism" per se, but it is not a god-worshipping religion.

The fourteenth Dalai Lama expressed these feelings when questioned about what he does when a Tibetan Buddhist belief is confronted with a new development in modern science. He said he considers both and usually sides with modern science in the movie *Conversation with the Dalai Lama.* Being aware that the truth of our Source continually initiating ongoing change is its nature and intended purpose continually feeds the insight that change is inevitable.

Science questions the factors of this cause/effect reality and produces tested explanations describing the natural laws that govern the relational justice between the causing factors of ongoing change. The existence of gods that once were used to explain these phenomena then becomes obsolete. It's through scientific insights unraveling and revealing newly discovered understandings of the cause/effect truth that many religions claim the right to that accounts for mankind's overall advancement and the disappearance of ancient religions. It's the search for the truth and its forward tilted resurfacing to mankind's waking consciousness level that's resulted in the disappearance of earlier religions.

Mankind no longer worships the Greek gods. They are no longer taken seriously unless maybe when the power of their myth fronts an athletic team to having an unbeaten record. Their once believed strengths are revived now only in effort to gain their superimposed or suggested mystical protection or strengths and a crafty edge on marketing products or services. The existing religion of many gods, Hinduism, appears to be on its way out. Its numbers have fallen drastically as have its pledged national allegiances.

To this day there remain groups that believe Satan's at battle with God for the souls of mankind. Some say his defying stance is founded in his anger for being cast out of heaven. The way mankind's unfettered free will (modern science) is questioning the new topics that today's change is producing, it's hard to tell when today's surviving religious traditions will be absorbed or phased out or maybe combine to watch each other's backs.

Traditional Christianity's numbers are falling. The wave of modern-day Evangelicals is an attempt to involve the youth in Christianity's revitalization. Buddhism also has an ongoing renewal of ways to interpret the volumes of recorded sutras of its ancient canons.

Modern Day Clarity to Ancient Mysteries

Today's scientists are recognizing a deeper understanding of the present moment effects of the cause/effect relationships of our surrounding reality that the Old Testament authors had once freely attributed to having been effects caused by the wrath of God. Through analysis of available mummies of the time and comparisons of biblical descriptions to the symptoms of known historical plagues, it can now be seen that smallpox, typhoid, scarlet fever and the bubonic plague are a few deathly sicknesses that were unknown to our ancestors and how the compared descriptions easily correlate and align with the biblical descriptions of God's wrath.

Whenever there was an epidemic outbreak the public would look to the leaders for answers. To blame a major decision of a leader or the leader of an enemy with going against God's will gave an explanation that could be understood while not inciting social division or blame. God's wrath was cited as the reason for spreading of a plague in times were infected members of a community would travel to surrounding communities, unknowingly spreading the bacteria responsible.

The metaphysical insinuations of today's scientifically noted interactions between mental activity and biochemical changes are undoubtedly bringing mankind's collective waking consciousness closer to recognizing how humankind can control their path to heaven or better understanding the true nature of our reality from scientifically understood internally generated right concentration, right thinking and right understanding. It's getting down to counting the alpha waves.

Scientifically seeing how mind and body can meet in harmony to overcome the uncontrollable interference of the 1,000 talking voices of an individual's mitote/maya state during right concentration is coming nearer.

The vision that parallels present moment enlightenment with after-you-die heaven is still too foggy. The meeting of minds between mankind's collective understanding of how the intellectually prescribed religious maxims of religious theology and reality's sensual testimony to the nature and intended purpose of our Source have a ways to go. The vision that parallels wisdom-enriched awareness of the truth of ongoing change with present moment heavenly enlightenment is still too foggy. The understanding that guidance from scientifically inspired intellectual knowledge could be equated to this religious/spiritual mystic thing is still too foggy.

The new way revealed will be totally free of any associated labels or names of previously enlightened individuals such as Jesus or Siddhartha Gautama for their guidance offered in the highly edited accounts of Jesus's teachings or the passed along versions of Siddhartha's sutras.

Mankind has always looked to the heavens for answers and still does. The search for planets in other solar systems has found many other planets that are capable of supporting life, as we now know it. In the search for evidence of there once being water on Mars the space probe Phoenix has verified that there's water on the planet Mars. Martian soil has the nutrients to support life. What happens to religious explanations if it is proven real that there was or are living organisms on Mars? Could God's creation assume relevance beyond Mother Earth?

The Roman Catholic Church has recently agreed to consider the possibility of there being life of foreign planets. The Pope insists however that this would have no effect on its religious claim to the God trilogy.

A new space probe returned amazing Kepler space telescope high-precision images in August 2009 of a new planet, HAT-P-&-B, orbiting another sun 1,000 light-years away. That's about 5.9 quadrillion miles. What if it's found that this planet could support life? How can one conceptualize what a quadrillion is? This is only 1,000 light-years away. What about other galaxies that are millions of light-years away...or billions? Can anyone really conceptualize how far light can travel in 1 year?

On the other end of the unobservable spectrum, the smaller scale galaxies within the scope of metaphysics are also yielding discovery by leaps and bounds. These are leaps and bounds that are receiving experiential verification. There is no void of uncertainty in the belief system of the scientific process of scientific discovery. Science's goal on the most basic of levels is to document exactly what it is that ties a cause to its effect.

New Technology Attempts to Give Life to Biblical Accounts

Hollywood has progressed by leaps and bounds with its new technologies to bring to vision what centuries of past generations have only been able to picture in their imaginations as being real biblical history. Mankind's creative imagination is boundless. A sample of the vast array of visual possibilities is demonstrated in the production of the many films that are meant to document times described in the Bible.

The parting of the sea in *The Ten Commandments* (1956) with Charlton Heston as Moses...*The Ark* (2014) with Russell Crowe with the incredible monsters that crushed the negative forces depicted in the Bible are just a few productions displaying imaginary depiction of how God delivered justice to those opposing his plan.

These visuals can leave much of an audience in wonder when they think of the power of God. These visuals can leave much the audience in doubt when they think of the living presence of a God who operates in such a fashion that they have never seen or experienced.

It's easy to minimize the significance of what can be left up to the imagination. It's easy to just give it the benefit of the doubt. But when trying to put into real proportion the biblically described details of what was supposed to be real back in the day, it can be hard to find a way to make it appear as though it fits into today's living impermanent reality.

Born-again Christians, Evangelicals or those who support the 7-day creation get upset and object to movie productions' best attempts at giving tangible detail to what is described in the Bible. They site the movie depictions as being inaccurate. The movie creators try as best they can to replicate in real life terms what depicts those Biblically described instances. It's really impossible to set limits to the range of possibilities to the human imagination. It must be asked, how it can be replicated. What changes could possibly make their attempt at duplicating what's depicted in the biblical message seem more tangibly accurate?

7

Due Diligence in Action

The Buddha's last words on his deathbed are characteristic of his worldview and of his attitude as a teacher. "Decay is inherent in all compounded things," he said before passing away: "Strive on with diligence."

—Fitjof Capri[19]

Due Diligence at Midwestern Fingertips

In Midwestern USA the introduction of non-Christian viewpoints in understanding the bigger picture began as a very slow process. It was jumpstarted when the Beatles met with the Maharishi and transcendental meditation became a popular new word and mental toy in the '60s. The presence of Buddhism and other Eastern religions seemed to be held at a cultural arm's length. They seemed to be only for truth seekers that wore robes and sandals and had the nickname Grasshopper.

There were layers of cultural, language and time barriers that kept an effective appreciation or application just one magic carpet ride or incense stick away from the typical Midwesterner. There was always the deep-seated fear-instilled taboo of going against or even considering anything so foreign to the culturally stamped Christian way of life. A few interpretations of Eastern religion have slowly trickled in ever since and with today's technology, have a much more available and easily accessed presence.

It's arguably true that the hidden pull from the main objective of the human experience involves finding the longed-for answer that explains how and maybe why the human condition is best meant to fit into the human experience. It's a natural form of self-protection for any individual to want to define and understand the unknown before venturing out to live in it.

The human condition has to reflect on the human experience to sort out and question anything that's not understood in defining the source and status of everything here. It only makes sense that to understand the unavoidable state of ongoing change or decay, a truth seeker must go into the essence of change or decay itself and sit quietly baring each sensual gateway to sense its story.

As the enlightened Mr. Siddhartha Gautama said before passing, it's up to every person to give their due diligence to arrive at this end of understanding and to wakingly appreciate what ongoing change or decay is and what it implies about the passing relational interplay between the interdependent yet independent living expressions of this reality to undo their ignorance of it.

Primed with this sort of life-maze should seem exciting. It's up to each individual to perform the due diligence to discover for themselves what this ongoing transformation or decay is all about. They must self-train their capability to gain waking awareness of this primal truth to restore their joy and happiness and eliminate the ignorance that allows their suffering.

Performing the due diligence is needed to answer any doubts about any claim explaining this grand mystery before being internalized into the belief system. The answer to this question reflects on how the individual views the nature of this reality and serves as the foundation for their worldview. The means of performing due diligence are very different today than they were back a few thousand years ago in the times when our publicly recognized enlightened ones lived that we still try to emulate today. The spiritual drive's the same. The questions that generate the spiritual drive are the same.

Back in the early days there was basically only word of mouth to do the investigative research. The available intellectual knowledge resources of today completely warp what was available back in of those days.

Siddhartha had to sensually figure out and internally picture the coming and going *kapula* that modern science finally has on film. But, it's in sensually realizing the experiential picture of that random coming and going sensation that Mr. Gautama found enlightenment and is why having only intellectual knowledge of this truth leaves today's truth seekers or scientists living in a world they merely know the nature of intellectually.

Modern up-to-date more comprehensive information is available from nearly everywhere worldwide. There're Google's instant answers, Internet news and encyclopedias, History Channel, National Geographic Channel, public service radio and TV, newspapers, magazines, books, lectures, classrooms, water coolers, teachers, preachers, coffee shops, friends and relatives that are readily available to find answers...to only name a few.

Information technology has polarized the world. It's instantly available, more systematic and less policy related. People from different corners of the world are getting to know each other. It surely won't take long to straighten out many of the ageless wrinkles that are holding back worldwide progression to the white light of altruistic compassion. Look at the early 2011 changes in Middle Eastern government. Egypt's long held power regime was toppled by three young free-dom-minded people that made their plight known on Facebook. That immediately spurred likeminded demonstrations and change in other nondemocratic governments.

There are many social networking sites that have millions of worldwide users who are mostly teens and twenty-somethings. Facebook is a social networking Internet site with millions of worldwide users. Twitter's around to keep interested people up to date on their chosen role models' every movement and thought. U-tube adds instant publication of short film clips to the world's available access.

People are unbound by geography in making new friends and passing along personal information in everything from emails to digitalized pictures and movies about what life is like in their culture. Information access that was unheard of five years ago is one click away today.

The transparent readiness and availability of cultural details worldwide will be the undoing of the inhuman policies of once isolated cultures that minimized human rights and personal freedom. Cable and satellite TV offer cutting edge documentaries on absolutely everything that mankind's free will...science...poses as a question needing a fully felt answer to.

It's possible to collect information, rich in detail covering any angle of any topic or question. There's ample information dealing with every imaginable aspect about religions and spiritual beliefs. Libraries have a goldmine of free information in all forms of media. The fear of the unknown has a newly energized challenger. Still, an individual has to have the courage and sincere drive to get up off the couch and venture out beyond the boundaries their religious doctrines set for them to face the monsters they're warned about.

A Truth Seeker Must Generate the Right Questions

And I say unto you, Ask, and it shall be given you;
seek, and ye shall find; knock, and it shall be opened unto you.
—Luke 11:9, King James Version

Everyone's interested in where they came from and the truth about how and why things work and how to be happy and joyful and eradicate the pain of suffering. Far too many individuals have been infected with the mitote/maya virus that cripples the belief system and numbs the unfettered free will.

Like sheep on their way to the market, local citizens wait and watch while their present moments slide by, apathetic and lost among the 1,000 voices talking at the same time in their head about unrelated ego satisfying short-term purposes that they, out of fear, use all their energy to satisfy and defend. Hopefully there's enough child-like curiosity and enough remaining remnants of an unfettered free will to actively follow one's inborn curiosity and desire to ask the right questions to know the truth. Purpose-directed due diligence is essential.

In not understanding the nature of our Source, which everyone is a united part of, individuals stand bare to the truth about their true nature. Their behavior finds sync with its natural rhythm at odd times and it calms them. They go to the gym, to a martial arts class, to play basketball, to go for a good walk or whatever to bring their mind and body closer to finding harmony in effort and awareness together on the same pod of time. If they only knew what this harmonious involvement accomplished, they could knowingly pursue it and the results would multiply much faster than they do by accident.

They're finding satisfaction in the effects of an unknown cause. While they think it's a good workout that calms them, they don't understand that it's the feel of the mind and body working in harmony, that's satisfying their soul.

Even with all the sources of information made available by modern technological advancements, most individuals fail to find the needed curiosity to make a sincere effort to perform the due diligence needed to address the cause of their ignorance that allows their suffering. Not finding the right source for guidance in what questions to ask to end up understanding how it all fits together eliminates most of those who might have the curiosity to try to figure it out. The fire's burning inside, they just don't know what it means or how to effectively cool it.

It takes a truth seeker's unbiased curiosity matched by their due diligence with an eye focused on finding the source of what gives them happiness, joy and peace of mind and calms their present moment unrest. They must ask themselves the questions that address these feelings yet have no ready answers. It's essential that they answer these questions in a way that they understand on a sensual level of acknowledgement and not simply taking someone's word for. They must devote the time to dig for the answers.

8

"And Now,
The Rest of the Story"...Paul Harvey

The Life of Jesus Before Age Thirty

The biblical accounts of Jesus began when he was around thirty years old. There are no real accounts of what happened earlier in his life.

There was a story of his preteen visit to the Jerusalem temple, where he sat in the midst of doctors, listening to the teachers and asking questions. The teachers were surprised at his level of spirituality. This was before Christianity. There was no mention of his teaching them about the kingdom of his father, God and the Holy Spirit as has been rumored from many a Sunday morning pulpit (Luke 2:41–49, King James Version).

Just a computer keystroke away is much information dealing with where Jesus was from his teens until returning home which is where the New Testament starts. One account of this missing time zone has been well summarized in *The Lost Years of Jesus: The Life of Saint Issa*, translation by Notovitch (12-19-06 Internet writing from The Reluctant Messenger).

> Ancient scrolls reveal that Jesus spent seventeen years in India and Tibet. From age thirteen to age twenty-nine, he was both a student and teacher of Buddhist and Hindu holy men. Brahman historians recorded the story of his journey from Jerusalem to Benares. Today they still know him and love him as St. Issa. Their "Buddha." (Introduction)

Nicolas Notovitch published a book called *The Unknown Life of Christ*. During his travels researching his book he journeyed through Afghanistan, India and Tibet. He stumbled across ancient records of over two hundred verses of the life of Jesus known as *The Life of Saint Issa*.

153

There were skeptics who returned to the area to either find the ancient documents or to prove his fraud and disprove his writings. One was Swami Abhedananda. He found a Bengali translation of the same document Notovitch had found a Tibetan translation of in a different Buddhist convent.

In 1925, Nicholas Roerich revisited the place Notovitch found the verses and made his own diary of Issa's travels.

> After having perfected himself in the Pali language, the just Issa applied himself to the study of the sacred writings of the Sutras.
>
> Six years after, Issa, whom the Buddha had elected to spread his holy word, had become a perfect expositor of the sacred writings.[20]

It doesn't matter if Jesus learned from Siddhartha's teachings or if the truth about our Source was written on a post card, the primal truth about living is what's important...not who said it, when it was said, what language it was said in, what clothes the messenger was wearing, how they died or anything else. It's a human being's way of finding enlightenment. It was Siddhartha's way or Jesus's way of teaching the way. They were both enlightened teachers who's discovered paths to enlightenment were documented in some fashion.

The Gnostic Gospels...Selftraining Mind Control and Wisdom

The Kingdom of God is inside of you, and it is outside of you.
When you come to know yourselves, then you will become known,
and you will realize that it is you who are the sons of the living Father.
But if you will not know yourselves, you dwell in poverty,
and it is you who are that poverty.

—Coptic Gospel of Thomas, Saying 3 of 114

When Constantine saw that Rome could have a greater populace control by having Rome sponsor a religion, he ordered writings and representations of all the other contending religions of the time to be totally eradicated. He also ordered all Christ-related texts that were not chosen to be a part of the Roman Bible to be totally destroyed. They had the detail on self-training the mind control and wisdom that Constantine didn't want Roman citizens to know existed.

Rome's priests selected from the available accounts of Jesus's life story those that didn't teach about individual spiritual autonomy, leaving present moment control of any reader's life decisions more in the hands of the Roman government. Only the written accounts of Jesus's life story that involved the initial steps in the process of reaching enlightenment about the impermanent nature of this reality, when a truth seeker self-trains their moral and ethical standards were selected. The selected accounts all highlighted living life by the moral/ethical standards of the Ten Commandments as being an end in itself.

Jesus's teachings relating to how a truth seeker selftrains their mind control to be able to self-train the wisdom to reach enlightenment about the nature of this reality were all ordered destroyed. The Romans didn't want their populace to realize that they were actually in control of their future and happiness as Jesus taught. A few were missed and it's taken centuries for them to be discovered.

The Gospel of Thomas gives an account of Jesus teaching that God's kingdom is everywhere. To know this, he says an individual must get to know themselves. It's the same self-knowledge that Lau Tzu and Siddhartha pointed at.

In this passage Jesus is assuring the audience that our living Source's nature and intended purpose is here everywhere in everything. They will become aware of the living Source by sensually witnessing its living nature as it lives to release itself in their body...their only sensual link to the present moment. We must learn to look into life's manifestation itself...living itself, to find mankind's living Source.

The level of symbolism and the deeper message in this teaching suggest the author's orientation called for a higher spiritual maturity to understand. Individuals must learn to merge religious theology with reality and recognize what part of the passing present moment represents the living father Jesus spoke of that Thomas wrote about.

Nearly fifty early Christian texts that were supposed to have been destroyed by Rome were uncovered in 1945 in a cave in Nag Hammadi, Egypt. There have been versions of several of these texts recovered elsewhere as far back as 1890. The quote above is from the Gospel of Thomas. It's thought by many that the Roman-published Gospel of John and the Gospel of Thomas were very interlinked.

It's thought that the Gospel of John was a questioning refutation to the Gospel of Thomas. It's like when someone who can't quite grasp the deeper more subtle meaning of something voices their questions in anticipation of an expected answer in the response. This is what John and Thomas's relationship represented. It's thought that John was the original person that was doubting Thomas.

Both gospels taught of Jesus as being the divine light of the world. John's interpretation of Jesus's message was that Jesus, the man, was the lone divine light among us. Thomas understood it to be that all came from the same divine Source and all have equal access to that Source, as Jesus did.

Thomas understood that it was the message Jesus carried that was the divine light of the world, not his human body. Thomas's message was that the Christ was the word that delivered the truth, the divine light of the world.

The intended messages of many of the recovered Gnostic understandings targeted a higher level of spiritual maturity...possibly instances where the teachings were directed more at audiences that Atisha described as being of supreme capacity. It's unavoidable that the crowds had varying levels of spiritual maturity. They were able to see and hear the seed sown by the teacher in Jesus's parable of the sower. The lecture content of lessons of higher spiritual maturity would parallel the upper folds of Siddhartha's eightfold pathway that dealt with self-training mental focus and self-training the mind to realize wisdom.

Yet, even the Rome-approved gospels Matthew, Mark, Luke, and John that were accounts of Jesus's basic teachings addressing the right speech, right action, and right livelihood level of spiritual advancement of the small and middle-capacity populace had leaks referring to the inner salvation or inner existence of the inner kingdom.

> Know ye not that ye are the temple of God, and that the Spirit of God dwelleth in you? If any man defile the temple of God, him shall God destroy; for the temple of God is holy, which temple ye are. (1 Corinthians 3:16–17, King James Version)

> Do you not know that your body is a temple of the Holy Spirit, who is in you, whom you have received from God? You are not your own: you were bought at a price. Therefore honor God with your body. (1 Corinthians 6:19–20, King James Version)

When becoming familiar with the nature of our Source as it gives sensual texture to the omnipresent dimension of time that the individual perceives as it fuels the coming and going energy pulsing through their body, they realize that it too is their nature as they are one with our Source, a part of material makeup of this reality. There's no bias, prejudice or level of self-devaluation that can take that away.

Their material and mental presence is a living ever-changing part of the process being addressed in the cause/effect ongoing relational interplay fueled by time's progression of ever-change. Actually, knowing yourself, physically on the metaphysical degree, opens one's waking eyes to the truth that explains the manifestation of change as one cause (of material change or as Siddhartha would say... decays) transforms into its effect.

In the Gospel of Judas, Jesus shows his favor of Judas above other disciples by saying, "Step away from the others and I shall tell you the mysteries of the kingdom," and "Look, you have been told everything. Lift up your eyes and look at the cloud and the light within it and the stars surrounding it. The star that leads the way is your star."

It is thought that Jesus recognized Judas's spiritual level to be more like Atisha described as being of supreme capacity and more capable of comprehending the progression of behavioral trainings described by Siddhartha as the self-training of one's concentration and the self-training the thinking and understanding in developing one's wisdom. The Gospel of Judas asserts that the other disciples didn't know or understand the true gospel or depth of Jesus's intended message.

Based on the belief that the human body imprisons the spirit; the Gospel of Judas says that Judas acted out of obedience to Jesus's instructions and not out of betrayal. Jesus's being handed over released the spirit of Jesus from its human flesh confinement. It can then be said freedom from the human shell is what motivated him to cause his own death.

The Gospel of Judas states that Jesus told Judas: "You shall be cursed for generations" and then added, "You will come to rule over them" and "You will exceed all of them, for you will sacrifice the man that clothes me." "Text might be hidden, Gospel of Judas" (CNN, April 6, 2006).

The Gospels according to Thomas and Judas were two of the accounts of the teachings of Jesus representing the Gnostic view of salvation where Jesus's teachings offered guidance to the insight-inspired wisdom attainable through knowledge of what the self is about that's accessed from within one's living body.

For the sake of an individual's tolerance of other accounts that go against their illusionary reality of what they think reality should be, they should check out this information and draw their own conclusions. They should make their own extrapolations of intended meanings and do their own due diligence.

Jesus spoke on different levels of spiritual maturity to different audiences and tightened the range of spiritual maturity through use of parables—i.e., he taught high school material to audiences of high school intelligence and kindergarten material to children. For the most informed intellectual understanding of Jesus's teachings, it's necessary to have all the accounts of what happened and what was taught as readers all have different levels of spiritual understanding.

The Buddhist monk Thich Nhat Hanh voices this same opinion when considering how to best understand Siddhartha's teachings:

> Often, we need to study several discourses and compare them in order to understand which is the true teaching of the Buddha. It is like stringing precious jewels together to make a necklace. If we see each sutra in light of the overall body of teachings, we will not be attached to any one teaching. With comparative study and looking deeply into the meaning of the texts, we can surmise what is a solid teaching that will help our practice and what is probably an incorrect transmission.[21]

It was over five hundred years following Siddhartha's passing that his lessons had been first recorded. They had been passed down orally through generations of Buddhist monks. By then, Buddhism had divided many times over opinions of what Siddhartha's intended meanings were. There had been generated three main streams of thought. Mr. Hahn relates a truth seeker's need for the interaction of all three sets of the recorded interpretation streams of the Buddha's lessons.

> These three streams complement one another. It was impossible for Source Buddhism to remember everything Buddha had taught, so it was necessary for Many-Schools Buddhism and Mahayana Buddhism to renew teachings that had been forgotten or overlooked.[22]

An open mind is necessary. Familiarity with as many angles to the original event is helpful especially when there's been 2,000-plus years of passing present moments to diffuse and dilute the intended meaning.

> When an archaeologist finds a statue that has been broken, he invites sculptors who specialize in restoration to study the art of that period and repair the statue. We must do the same. If we have an overall view of the teachings of the Buddha, when a piece is missing or has been added, we have to recognize it and repair the damage.[23]

Rome's purpose of intention to control the actions of its populace resulted in selective adoption of the accounts of Jesus's teachings that told about living a life that minimized social and personal disturbances, but stopped short of what to do after becoming a spiritually stagnant law abiding citizen to find personal peace, enlightenment about ignorance or heaven. This made it easier for the government to control the anticipated direction of confused public focus to be one looking to Rome for guidance and leadership.

Rome Chose Biblical Accounts Targeting Audiences with Elementary Depth of Spiritual Maturity

The spiritual maturity levels of both the authors and the translators of the accounts of Jesus's message are important factors to consider in understanding how well they captured and reflected the depth of Jesus's intended meaning in his teachings. The degree of spiritual maturity Jesus chose to use when wording his teachings to most effectively communicate with audiences of varying collective levels of spiritual maturity has to be considered. It was common for Jesus to use parables to help get across his intended meaning.

The spiritual maturity level of the written accounts of Jesus's teachings was a determinant for whether or not the Roman bishops selected them to support Rome's political agenda behind making the Roman Bible available to the Roman public. It wasn't directed at the spiritual well-being of the Roman citizens. It was engineered to neuter and pacify the Roman public. Constantine who authorized Rome's acceptance of Christianity as its religion from the many available, didn't accepted Christianity as his religion until on his deathbed...just in case.

Except for the scriptures where hints pointing toward the inner kingdom were missed and not filtered out, the content of the Rome-approved Bible consists mostly of accounts of Jesus's teachings targeted at audiences at lower levels of spiritual development or authored or translated by those of limited spiritual depth of understanding. It's targeted depth of spiritual development ended with the development of the more basic moral and ethical guidelines...the same right actions, right speech, and right livelihood Siddhartha spoke of in his first level of self-training leading to a truth seeker's spiritual enlightenment.

The Beatitudes would be an example. In the Beatitudes, Jesus spoke of the award coming from living a life founded in humility. Humility is the foundation for effective communication with our living Source. It's the most basic of understandings. Humility is the key that unlocks the door for witnessing our Source as it manifests change in real-time.

With a steady self-trained moral/ethical foundation coming from adherence to the Ten Commandments, the humility of the meek is essential to generate the mind/body harmony to defeat the ego-self. Lau Tzu speaks of it and Siddhartha details how to cultivate it.

This allows a calm minded truth seeker to then self-train the mind control to self-train the wisdom to have eyes open to inherit or recognize and appreciate the becoming riches of life's actual manifestation that comprises what we collectively perceive as being Earth. It's needed to self-train the mind control to self-train a wisdom-enriched awareness of our Source's nature and intended purpose that's alive and present in everything.

Rome's editing didn't allow the accounts of Jesus's sermons (gospels) into their published Bible that related to the spiritual truths as found in the self-training guidelines of Siddhartha's eightfold path where a truth seeker self-trains their mind to sustain the concentration to understand the activity that the right awareness of their right concentration is focused on so to derive the insightful wisdom to attain enlightenment about what robs them of their happiness and allows their suffering-causing ignorance.

It's also true that all of Siddhartha's sutras were not about higher spiritual guidelines. Both he and Jesus spoke to their audiences on a level appropriate to address what they felt their audience could identify with. Atisha's breakdown of human behavior into three different levels of spiritual maturity progression; small, middle and supreme spiritual capacities is an example of identifying differences in the depths of truth seekers' spiritual understanding.

The enlightened teacher would speak to an audience of small spiritual capacity about the more basic level of spiritual development involving ethical and moral standards or the aspect of life they were still coming to grips with. The spiritual content of each sermon was gauged to target the different spiritual understanding capabilities of different audiences of different combinations of social strata.

It's fruitless to teach college level philosophy to a group of young children. Both Jesus and Siddhartha would target their sermons or sutras with an audience of supreme capacity to the more advanced guidelines of mental focus and body/mind-united analysis while in pursuit of the experiential truth. They would speak to audiences of the highest spiritual aptitude about how to experientially link our Source's truth of impermanence that resides in a subtle level of the ego-free deeper consciousness with the waking conscious mind. Jesus's close apostles also fell into different levels of spiritual maturity...from Peter or John to Judas or Thomas.

Both Jesus of Nazareth and Mr. Siddhartha Gautama personally made insightful observations from their times of harmonious mind/body deliberation while focused into the coming and going presence of the coming and going bits of life-giving energy felt manifesting within their bodies. They interpreted their wisdom-enriched understanding of the truth into parables to help those of lower spiritual maturity to better understand the deeper felt intended meaning of their message. They both had occasion to humbly surrender their harmonious mind/body awareness into their internal chamber of life transformation-in-process for marathons of forty days and forty nights.

Their sustained right concentration (meditation) focused into the interplay between the uncontrollable coming and going sensations in the living fiber of their bodies helped inspire the insights leading to the wisdom so brilliantly taught through the use of their insight-invoking parables. They listened to the universe as it spoke to them through their body to learn its subtle truths.

What else could a truth seeker do with their mind if they were to meditate for forty days and forty nights? During each of those present moments when Jesus meditated for forty days and nights or when Siddhartha sat under the Buddha tree, where were their thoughts directed? Their mental language was a sensual one, far beyond the scope of an intellectually crafted verbal language. They humbly listened and deliberated. Surely there was no need for Jesus to speak to his heavenly father in Aramaic, a language of so few words, when sensuality is on hand and knows no limits.

The same principles of the wisdom they arrived at could be used for an endless number of parables to get the same point across. It's like someone saying: "Here, let me give you an example," when trying to make their point to someone not quite grasping the gist of what was being said. They found a way to communicate the meaning of the relational principles that govern our cause/effect reality to their listeners of any spiritual maturity.

> And the disciples came, and said unto him, Why speakest thou unto them in parables?
>
> ...Therefore speak I to them in parables: because they seeing see not: and hearing they hear not, neither do they understand. (Matthew 13:10 and 13, King James Version)

Jesus said in the gospel according to Matthew when asked why he spoke in parables that some just cannot understand what they see or hear. He was likening it to sowing seeds where some seeds will take and some will not. He was saying how the group he was speaking to had been waxed gross by their care for this world and the deceitfulness of riches. Their hearts were waxed gross to hearing or seeing the truth that's being spoken or is visible right in front of their faces. The parable relays the same intended message, only dressed in different clothes.

Being that most individuals couldn't yet understand or grasp the meaning of the more subtle areas involving the self-training of mind control/right concentration and wisdom and that self-training a sound moral/ethical standard was of primary importance, Jesus always made clear the basic necessity of right speech, right actions and right livelihood in effort to prepare the individuals for understanding the more conceptual self-trainings. This was the same as Siddhartha's first of three levels of eight in self-training to achieve personal enlightenment about the ignorance that allows human suffering.

Constantine's selected bishops chose those accounts of Jesus's life and teachings written in a way that was geared more for the understanding of those of small or middling spiritual capacity, not quite ready to be taught about self-training their mind control and self-training the wisdom-enriched understanding to defeat the ego. Those sermons centered more on following the Ten Commandments, like Siddhartha's first three folds of his self-training of basic ethical/moral standards, not on developing the personal independence that Rome saw as a threat to the social obedience Rome depended on to remain a world power.

The Bible says in Psalms to get wisdom and with that to get understanding. The written accounts of Jesus's teachings with details on how to actually get the understanding of wisdom were edited out of public accessibility after AD 312 when the Bible was authorized and its production financed by Rome. Constantine ordered all religious material other than the selected texts to be obliterated at that time.

Christian believers have taken the leap of blind faith and missed the teachings that detail self-training mind control and wisdom enrichment explained by Jesus to those who could grasp the meaning. Some of these teachings were uncovered in the recently discovered Gnostic Gospels. The present versions of the multitranslated and rewritten 2,000-plus-year-old Bible promise a joyous life after death to some and hell to others. The details on how a truth seeker prepares their soul now to conquer these issues in this life/ death cycle were edited out.

Rome Drafted and Published its Bible to Control its Taxpayers

It had been over three hundred years since Jesus had been martyred, and there were many Romans who saw him as a savior and god. Regardless of possible persecution if caught, many still worshipped him. By this time, in different areas there were different written accounts of his life story that the citizens would secretly meet to study.

Constantine orchestrated the parameters of Rome's first edition of the Bible to establish a uniform statewide moral/ethical regime for citizen behavior and to gain control of his followers. He gave the citizens public access to a portion of what they had been getting secretly. He had most of those accounts of Jesus's story destroyed.

By legalizing and recognizing Christianity as Rome's religion he made it openly available to the public, but in editing a Bible to publish for the followers, he also selectively removed many of the written accounts being followed by many of the followers. He greatly limited Jesus's intended message by removing so many of the written accounts.

It could be the case that people, who once worshipped Jesus through an account from an author in their area, were denied worshipping that part of his message. They would be persecuted because they didn't worship Jesus as described by Rome's Bible. Constantine put blinders on Christianity from the start by selecting the accounts of Christ available for Rome's Christians' Christian guidance. It has to be said that Christianity was neutered at birth.

His religion-related actions were intended to maintain a mass of Roman Bible-disciplined Romans looking for direction. His limited message left the Christian Romans looking to the government for guidance.

He managed to give the Romans a religious promise that gave them what they wanted, but one that couldn't be found in their living world. It was a religion that gave them an unimaginably, untestable paradise, after they were dead. Until then, while alive they would pay their tribute and taxes to Rome. They would follow Rome's leadership while they lived by the moral/ethics of the Ten Commandments. He did not want them to have any hint of inspiration to look inside to find the common ground with their Source and be capable of self-training the understanding of the wisdom of the relational justice that allows them to determine their own direction.

Christianity Was Selected...It Made The Most Sense

At that time in history, there was a vast assortment of different claims made by representatives of different unrelated gods trying to satisfy the needs of our ancient ancestors at the time Rome's government decided to become fully vested in Christianity...just Google it.

To name a few, there was Mytherus, whom the Roman soldiers held as the god of gods with a similar story to Jesus of being born to a virgin, who shared the same birthday and was also resurrected to return to a heavenly god.

Isis, the Holy Mother of God, was considered the queen of heaven...the holy mother of the gods. She had a similar story to Jesus, and the Romans did not outlaw her worship until AD 500.

Christianity went through innumerable changes and difficulties in its early years. When it was separating from Judaism around the first century, it was seen as basically being no more than a superstition.

Throughout his life, the emperor who legalized Christianity, Constantine, was not a Christian. He held to Mars the God of War and Apollo the God of the Sun. He tolerated Christians as his mother was one and was later consecrated as Saint Helena. He recognized the importance of Christianity to Rome's administration. Christians were literate. They had to know how to read to be able to interpret the scriptures.

When he took control of the empire in AD 312, Constantine gave Christianity Rome's sanction and support. Christianity was declared the state religion of the Roman Empire. He had political reasons. Christianity was viewed as a major force to be suppressed and integrated. He ended persecution of Christians and granted them freedom to worship in public. He made available money to build churches and financed making the copies of the Rome-selected collection of gospel transcripts.

He had his eighty-year-old mother travel the path of Jesus to collect material relics associated with the life of Jesus, giving Christians material objects to worship and to help solidify the religion into the Roman populace. Constantine lived in sin and converted to Christianity on his deathbed.

The scriptures of all other contemporary religious claims supporting different gods and the accounts of Jesus deemed unacceptable for inclusion in the Bible were ordered destroyed. Some of those ancient manuscripts that divulged the true source of authority that Constantine eliminated have been recovered in the past one hundred years. The outlawing of other contemporary religions and the circulation of the approved Christian Bible caused other religions to fade into the past.

With Rome's sanction and support, Christianity lost its independence and freedom of speech. Christians had to conform to Rome's approved theology boundaries or be persecuted. Church leaders made effort to suppress Gnostic Christians. Their accounts of Jesus were declared heresy. Many of the forbidden gospels had subject matter addressing a higher level of spiritual maturity and understanding. They told of Jesus's teachings of the personal freedom and independence found within. This more spiritually advanced subject matter was taught in the disincluded gospels to crowds from areas Jesus felt to be more spiritually advanced.

From Many Accounts to One Story

The selection process of the Bible of today took a very long time. It is a library of smaller documents. In AD 325 Constantine handpicked bishops to select the accounts of the gospel appropriate for Rome's tailored spiritual theology.

A counsel met in Nicaea in Bithynia to gain consensus on the Christian Church. The first uniform Christian doctrine was called the Nicene Creed. It first unified all of Christianity. The decision was made there to make the perception of Jesus to be half man and half God. They also decided when to celebrate Christ's resurrection. They organized the first biblical canon to be used by all.

A limit of only four gospels was selected. The head bishop romanticized that like the four directions of the compass, the four directions of the wind came the four pillars of the gospel. These gospels were written on the same level of spiritual maturity yet they didn't totally agree with each other.

Constantine's bishops edited out accounts of the gospel that were more focused on how Roman citizens could find their direction coming from anywhere other than the outside, or Roman rule. He had to ensure citizens' loyalty to Rome's control and not let them think they were responsible for their own destiny through the subtle reality that Jesus had pointed out was to be found within. It's the same place that Lau Tzu and Siddhartha pointed at. Constantine's priests selected the accounts of Jesus's teachings that shaped the Bible's message in the way needed to best secure and serve Rome's interests.

It's possible that Jesus was killed to put an immediate silencing to the idea that average individuals have the power within to find their own freedom...to control their own destiny during their lifetime before they died and went to Rome's approved illusion of heaven.

What he was saying must have really been hurting Rome's citizen control when they decided it was better to give him martyrdom than what the Romans were being introduced to. It was that important to stop his teachings. It only took a few generations to have the cap secured cutting off those who actually heard the original message delivered in Jesus's Aramaic language. An individual just has to wonder how much of Jesus's intended meaning was altered and lost throughout this process.

The Roman priests' then selected the available written accounts of Jesus's life message that favored the author interpretations that were directed primarily at followers learning at the basic level of spiritual maturity...like spiritual school kindergarten. A truth seeker must first calm their mind by assuming a moral/ethical character like directed to by the Ten Commandments. Jesus taught this, as did Siddhartha.

None of the selected accounts offered the guidance on right concentration and developing wisdom as Siddhartha's teachings went on to detail. The same more detailed message is found in the forbidden gospels.

Constantine's priests left out the written account of Jesus's teachings by Thomas that's older than the chosen four gospels. He didn't include the account left by Judas or the book by Mary and others. The interpretations that gave account of Jesus's teachings given to audiences of higher spiritual maturity, like to students in spiritual grad school were not included.

Authors with higher levels of spiritual maturity possibly wrote these accounts of Jesus's life story. They better understood the final stages of what Siddhartha detailed as a process of self-training the mind control to realize the wisdom to conquer the self-ego to understand the ignorance that robs individuals of their joy and happiness and rules the misery of their present moment. They could make better mental sense of it.

Rome's citizen control scheme included quelling citizen self-detection of direction to initiate the due diligence to understand what's missing from the status quo and where to find it. Constantine definitely didn't want his citizens to develop the ability to focus their mind beyond the ego-inspired hopeful verbal chatter up to a god in heaven. The published accounts of Jesus's life in the Bible gave no direct guidance on what the media of human-to-Source message exchange is and how to hear or witness the message to inspire wisdom coming from our Source.

The Old Testament is where the Roman citizen goes to get guidance on the relational justice in the present moment. That's where one finds a god of wrath to be feared.

In Rome's composite Bible blueprint, the path to heavenly enlightenment stops with God's burning-bush-searedin-stone order to blindly follow his Ten Commandments and not why or how to use the resulting calmed mind. This is like the first of three phases of Siddhartha's pathway to enlightenment is to self-train living within moral/ethical limits to calm the mind for spiritual advancement through self-inspection. Even so, self-training the mind to self-train wisdom is unavoidably hinted at in the priests' selected accounts of Jesus's basic teachings they used to populate the Bible.

Jesus really had unbearable living conditions for teaching the meaning of emptiness. He had no choice but to become martyred with his teachings to then be miscued to suit his killers' likings.

For a government with an economy structured in a way that allows the infiltration of greed to power the decisions that tailor how and where power and money are distributed among its citizens, the level of spirituality reflected in Jesus's teachings that was targeted by Constantine's priests from the available gospels, works wonderfully. It was well planned.

Rome's Bible sets the bar for mankind's spirituality high enough to at least establish an expected plateau of moral/ ethical standards. Rome's recipe to control its citizens still works through the religion that Constantine decided to let his unsettled discontent citizens have to coral their natural spiritual longing in this unsettling world of ongoing change.

The Roman Bible weakens their free wills' resolve by calling it a heavenly blessed plan and uses guilt and the fear of a never-seen almighty god's wrath to help enforce it. It stops short of teaching its believers how to figure out what is at the root of their suffering and how it saps out their life energy that should be directed at understanding our living Source to allow their living in mental peace. The same recipe works well in many parts of today's world...like in Midwestern USA.

Same Tailored Message Corrals the USA

President Obama carried over his 2008 election slogan to be used again in 2012...to provide undefined change. Change is naturally all that ever happens anyway. It's the only thing that cannot be avoided. Ongoing change is our Source's nature and primal promise and the Obama promise is to keep providing it...what a naive society. As a president, his job is to campaign the direction he's going to lead that change. He was unable to do this. He never tried.

Obama-change is undefined with no direction, and so, it's just like Rome's. Obama wants the government to make all the decisions for the individuals. Obama's direction points a God-fearing society blindly into undefined hope so the government can control those looking for it...exactly like Rome did. Most present moment trends follow in the wake of society's government-approved pattern of social dogma...the want for the shell of religious routine to hide the kaleidoscope of painful feelings coming from a mind scared by a boo from the misunderstood present moment...ritualistic religious routine...the great socio-opiate stabilizer.

In a society based on the Roman religion that stops offering direction on how to secure mindful satisfaction at the basic plateau of finding moral/ethical balance, with no direction to the source of mindful satisfaction, simply finding short-term gratification becomes gratifying in itself. We shop just to shop. We shop till we drop. We pillage blindly 'till we die. Then we can go to heaven to realize what our present moment dream of happiness and joy is to be...even though we no longer inhabit a sensual body to witness its message.

Most blindly and unwittingly pillage and plunder through life hoping to randomly stumble upon the inner direction their primal inner being instinctually knows to be there to discern the answer to what's missing from their status quo. They try personal relationships, grown-up toys, sports activities, shopping, volunteering, traveling, religious clichés while unknowingly hoping to by chance stumble across the answer to a question they're not even sure of.

Today, the Ten Commandments still set the infrastructure for society's moral/ ethical grid. USA laws and statutes are centered on the ethical/moral groundwork laid out in the Ten Commandments. It's control-through-ignorance style worked then and it continues to work today. Today's Pope issues a Ten Commandments annual updating of bad, in light of new incarnations of old bad thought patterns, instead of depicting the source of the unwholesome thought patterns that generate the miscued worldview.

It's the same moral/ethical pattern that's seared into the USA legal system. It deals with the relational justice that's spelled out in the nature of life itself as it manifests moment by moment. The relational justice is blind to labels as it equally affects atheists as well as followers. Saying there's a god that endorses it helps establish its ground level position. The basic relational justice recognized in the ancient ten-count statues prove the timeliness of the truth they represent as like 2,000 years ago, they form the foundation for keeping this highly impulsive modern society in order and looking to the government to provide the leadership through our Source's ongoing process of change.

9

The Hoosier Condition

Pieced-Together Life Tapestry in an Animated World

Humans perceive the characteristics of things they recognize with their five senses as what must apparently be this world's makeup. Human perception capabilities fall short of being able to recognize the existence of the metaphysical world that gives composure to what they can normally recognize.

By recognizing only the seemingly unchanging characteristics of these things and objects, they see them as different. This is a reality with a continual nature. Individuals will form preferences that will lead to choosing favorites or nonpreferences that they will become attached to the craving of or possibly develop an aversion to.

From this assortment of impressions, individuals intellectually knit together a tapestry of selective mental snapshots taken from remembered moments from past times and name it "I." This helps organize and quiet their mitote/ maya state of mental agitation and helps give structure to the unexpected ongoing change that continually confronts them. They struggle to bring the unrecognized ongoing manifestation of change into sync with their illusion of what reality apparently seems to be.

Ignorance of Impermanence Breeds Illusion of Self...
Preserving Self Takes Present Moment Priority

An individual's attachment to their idea of "self" will consume their energy in each present moment as the cling to ideas they want to posture themselves into becoming. Individuals will build a protective bubble to live in until they find the missing link that connects their wandering-wondering waking consciousness with the inner knowledge they unknowingly long to find. It's the answer to the question they have yet to learn how to ask.

While living with an illusionary worldview, most picture their body as a special separate entity relative to everything else. Yet, their body is an included part of the greater picture's process of transformation and shares the relational truths of coexistence. All material objects are constantly swapping the tiny coming and going bits of energy that make up the interconnected matrix of material reality. The degree that an individual's waking awareness understands what these relational truths of this reality actually are designates where their spiritual maturity falls on the continuum between suffering and heavenly enlightenment...between seeing a present moment with a nature of continuity and understanding a present moment elusive with impermanence.

The thought that an individual can go to bed at night as the same person they were when they got out of bed that same day is not an accurate understanding of reality. Any claim that any perceived thing or non-thing could be recognized at a later time, as the same thing it was at an earlier time is illusionary. Individuals will allow miscalculations of the ever-transforming cause/effect sequence of this reality such as these to affect their fix on reality and this makes them suffer the dissatisfaction and frustration from the seemingly frequent mental-burns coming from these miscalculations.

A human being is a flowing process in action like a river is made up of flowing water particles. Both are in a state of constant transformation.

Ignorance of the relational justice inherent to the process of ongoing change causes suffering anytime an individual grinds their worldview projections dependent on a reality with a continuous nature against the cause/effect role that ongoing change plays in generating the makeup of this reality in each passing present moment.

Not having a worldview in tune with the relational protocol of our cause/effect reality causes anyone to ponder the resulting miscalculations between what they think should be happening in their illusionary idea of what reality apparently is and what actually happens in real-time. The ignorance of our Source's nature and intended purpose to initiate ongoing change causes individuals to suffer through their frustrations from misalignments between their illusions of an apparent reality and the unavoidable relational justice of the natural laws that keep balanced the forward-rolling present moment wheel of time.

This ignorance keeps separate one's waking consciousness and the ongoing clock of change their deeper consciousness uses to time their heartbeat and tell their pancreas when to produce more insulin. The awareness of this truth of cause/effect change exists in everyone. In most, its awareness-link to the waking consciousness has been buried deeply by internalized faulty prior conditioning, leaving much confusion and uncertainty in its wake.

When reality's steady cadence of ever-change causes their hair to begin graying or lines to form in their once young complexion, they suffer the frustration that this cause/effect life process is actually affecting them. They feel slightly dismayed and a bit lonely on birthdays at their receding timeline instead of enjoying their ride on time's magic carpet while not finding it comforting that everyone else is just as much older as they are. Their suffering is the outward symptomatic manifestation of their ignorance.

Fundamental Ignorance

The thought that anything or any idea can rest unchanged in time is basic primal ignorance. The only original and level one fact is that after the current present moment has expired and the next present moment has arrived, whoosh—the cards are all again reshuffled. This is more than important. It's not what everything is about. It's all that anything is.

What was the next present moment, the effect that its prior presence caused has now became the causing agent to affect another next present moment. There is really nothing that remains unchanged to become attached to. The only thing remaining is a memory that pulls out special parts of the passed present moment to fondle in thought...that will also change.

This is Buddhism's concept of emptiness...that there's nothing remaining. The self-evident and obvious simplicity of this primal fact doesn't justify knowingly ignoring it, taking it lightly or excuse overlooking its importance. The reality of its truth hollows out any notion condoning the ongoing continuity of anything or idea in this transforming cause/effect reality.

What Buddhism refers to as the fundamental ignorance involves a person viewing reality as having a continual nature...remaining unchanged into the future. At the core of this fundamental ignorance is a distorted view of grasping at and clinging to the idea of selfhood. At the heart of our afflictions is our believing in the true existence of things instead of the essence of perceived things, grasping at a misconceived illusionary perception of the lasting state of solidity of shapes, forms or beliefs.

The unavoidable self-evident fundamental truth explaining the human presence in this reality is that it's a living interwoven part of the universal transformation process. An individual living in a world they know intellectually recognizes no real level of importance in how the fact that everything in this reality is transforming sets the stage for human recognition of the laws of nature that we live by and how this fact set to a metaphysical beat of action demonstrates the relational guidelines for how things exist among each other during the change of time. Siddhartha saw it in his enlightened understanding of reality 2,500-plus years ago and science is taking pictures of it today.

Without having established a waking relationship with their deeper awareness of our Source's nature, an individual will not be privy to the process of developing the relational wisdom that allows the release of faulty prior conditioning. Primal ignorance is perpetuated and its removal crippled and made unlikely by the resulting interference from the individual's mitote/maya state of ongoing mental agitation.

They lack having self-trained the focus and concentration to develop the wisdom to be enlightened about what allows their ignorance. The unawareness results, much of the time in their being a parrot of the wisdom of others as they don't understand or cannot feel the process of its derivation. Many quote the Bible to describe the logistics of how they plan to reach a state of love joy and happiness that's free of suffering. The outward expression of their life purpose is not rooted in their waking desire and efforts to gain a conscious enlightened awareness of our Source's truth of impermanence.

Attending to their self-preservation agenda builds up, fortifies and hardens their ego-managed self-image. It lines the gaping void in their belief system making it more set in its ways. The individual will spend their present moment energy defending and strengthening their perception of "I" to protect it from the unknown monsters that live somewhere in this gapping void of uncertainty that their religious leaders warn them not to delve into. It remains a mystery to them what might lurk inside there.

Incasing their conscious awareness in a protective cocoon spun from their self-posturing ideas lessens their waking involvement in shaping a worldview that will best allow the release of their inborn potential through their recognizing and developing their inborn special talents. They will lack the experience-backed faith of vision to underwrite their courage needed to generate the insight-inspired wisdom to be their own keeper and to let their light shine.

They will make decisions along the way that will disrupt their smooth transition through school and into the job market or maybe in selecting a mate. What they expect reality to be just doesn't size up with what the police department or a College's entry office thinks it is. They might wonder why they seem to choose mates who abuse them or drink excessively. Conversely, there are those who anticipate change, plan for it and better understand the relational justice that makes the impermanent society of an impermanent reality flow smoothly.

They pass their waking moments in ignorance, clinging to fixed ideas of what they think really should be. To be saved from this suffering, an individual needs to change the nature of their mind that underwrites their point of view and understanding of the living process.

Their intended purpose needs to be cleansed of notions allowing the attachment to craving and aversion. To do this they must remove their ignorance of the impermanent nature of this reality.

Inner Genius Development Suspended

Unaware people live their days with their undeveloped talents unknowingly suspended in their untested inborn potential. Their direction of purpose remains tangled up in the confusion of their ego-managed web of ignorance.

They've developed no consistent rhythm for using their free will's test valida-
tion-verification function when screening the belief of a new claim before internalizing it.

This verification fulfills satisfying the middle phase of the three-step procedure
needed to successfully believe something and not be blind to the nature of what's
going to influence shaping the nature of the worldview. After a claim is heard, it's
verified then it is internalized. A searcher first hears the religious claim of gaining
relief from eternal suffering. Then they verify that the claim maker is part of this
living reality and that the claim they make has an impermanent nature void of
illusion.

Sensually tasting the presence of impermanence with at least an intellectual
understanding of how it fits into this reality should serve as the foundation for
building their worldview and for sprouting the roots of a steadfast faith to grow
alongside their enriched understanding of the truth. There's no gut-felt glue present in any faith that's blind to having experienced the connecting of the cause to
its effect for a believer in any religion's intellectually based theological explanation
of the Source question.

Unaware, agitated and confused minds are full of 1,000 unrelated voices all
shouting their unvalidated and unregulated claims of purpose at the same time in
effort to initiate a behavior-producing intention to satisfy a needless want of the
misguided purpose their claim represents. The random nature of the flow of their
mental activity eliminates any sustained attention span...whether in meditation or
thinking at work about the details of a project. Chances are they have a low level
of mind control. They probably have trouble staying focused and absorbed when
reading the interesting plot of a good book.

They have not practiced introspective reflection in patient contemplation while
their focused awareness is immersed of the essence of the ongoing time-fueled
change that's alive in the coming and going sensations of their flesh. Their thought
patterns have too much unwholesome, thought pattern-interrupting activity that
infiltrates their right effort to sustain right awareness to attain the right concentration to gain inspiration from the interplay between the sensually detected cause/
effect relationships among the streaming uncontrollable coming and going bodily
sensations during their attempts at self-discovery, for their insightful enlightenment about the nature of impermanence.

They fail to display the ability to prioritize the needs that service a common
end where a lifetime of change-savvy-validated internalized purposes of intent are
focused and meet. This missing self-trained ability to sustain concentration is what
they need in order to realize the insight-inspired wisdom to understand the formation of their habit energy and fleeting reactions to then unravel their ongoing
mental unrest and addictive tendencies.

Ignorance of our reality's state of impermanence that defines our Source's nature and intended purpose results in an individual's inability to understand what they don't understand that causes their uncontrolled addictive behavioral tendencies. They are numb to inspired insightful wisdom enrichment coming from growing awareness of the truth of change to help them understand the nature of their thinking and how to freeze habit energy and step back and think to then act in response to those same sets of sensations that arise from the variety of unwholesome mood or thought patterns that make up their every day present moments that they, out of ignorance, allow to feed their indecision and addictions. The unaware individual will simply react with a practiced behavior that's formed the fleeting habit energy that scripts their life story riddled with addictions and suffering.

The unaware don't realize the middle validation step is missing since they've never been aware of ever consciously experiencing the calming unifying effect of sensually communicating to some degree with the ever-fleeting presence of the essence of ongoing change. Its intellectually held spiritual significance has never been parleyed into being realized in the terms of the sensual language that it appears in. They make do and try to add organization to their mental mitote/maya by adopting an unverified faith, blind to having witnessed the living involvement of the claim's intended purpose, because society tells them it's normal. All they have to catch them when they fall is a forced faith of hope in a god with whom they have never established a real-time tangible personal relationship that's founded in a sensual experience where the individual listens to the god instead of telling the god what they want.

To unsolder, reopen and fill the void created by the missing (feeling) step of the belief system anatomy, the fear of the unknown that currently fills the void is floated out by sensually experiencing the claim-validating effects felt during self-discovery. One feels the flame of the claim to become aware of how the purpose of intent of the Source of the bigger picture is to forever initiate change. This intention is reflected in its nature transparently demonstrated everywhere in everything each and every passing present moment.

Whatever special talents were born to this individual remain locked up within their misunderstanding of the relational justice that's involved in this cause/effect reality. They must undo their web of ignorance and find the clear head to realize the potential of their inborn genius.

Scurry For Mental Order

Those who choose the cerebral approach to viewing life will somehow weather their unpreparedness to meet the challenge of ongoing change. They try to manage their inability and frustration at matching up real-life causes in the passing present moment with the actual effect that will appear in the next new and unexplored present moment.

Often due to lack of available options and from feeling pushed by the panic of a lack of time, distressed individuals will entrust their soul's eternal future to the life rhythm and set of priorities offered by a societal organization template that at that point in time is the most suitable to meet their need for mental file management. They figure it can serve as proxy until they somehow figure out what's wrong with or missing from their status quo.

Confused, they scurry to establish a system of mental organization to find rhythm and set priority for the continual influx of raw unexpected change involving things and ideas they already have on their plate along with the novel things and ideas they've never before encountered. This all appears in the wake of the unanticipated naked change that confronts them at the onset of each new present moment.

These individuals try to cope with and counter the confusion coming from their unrealized lack of conscious awareness of the natural order of things while coexisting in the living rhythm of the primal truth of ongoing change. In so doing, their behaviors exhibiting foolish patterns of clinging for the security of the memory ghosts that shadow their illusionary mental patchwork of continual existence. They lack the self-confidence and courage to seek out and consider other different mind-set organizational options.

10

Taking the Leap of Blind Faith is a Choice

...An Intellectual Adventure

There is a fifth dimension, beyond that which is known to man. It is a dimension as vast as space and as timeless as infinity. It is the middle ground between light and shadow, between science and superstition, and it lies between the pit of man's fears and the summit of his knowledge. This is the dimension of imagination. It is an area which we call the Twilight Zone.

—Intro to Rod Serling's '60s TV series *The Twilight Zone*[28]

Blind Faith Breeds a Primal Void of Uncertainty

Like in the visionary realities of Rod Serling's TV series *The Twilight Zone*, having a worldview that's founded in nothing but intellectually inspired images of the imagination leaves an individual's perception of their life experience vulnerable to the ways of whatever creatures they choose to create in their fear-filled uncertain imagination. Mankind develops perceptions from life impressions of times experienced and frets over finding the way of least resistance to organize it all to maintain sanity in lieu of perpetual confrontation from time's new unexpected and misunderstood change.

Most individuals are fooled into thinking their answer to this challenge might be realized by way of their spoken or written language. Everything about sensing and perceiving their life experiences happens in the part of the brain that's much older than the part that handles speaking, reading and hearing. It happens before they have time to subject the experience to their intellectually calculated opinion of it. The old brain in the middle that coordinates exchange between the physical senses and the mind is really where their answer of least resistance lies.

The sensual world is where the mind and body meet. A truth seeker will find success when they let the mind and body unite in common purpose with a shared focus so the mind can sensually witness what the body has to say about the coming and going impermanent reality it is a part of. It's the only contact their mind will ever have with the material reality to learn about the nature and purpose of our Source that continually pumps it full of life.

When a truth-seeker becomes a religious follower, they chose to force-fit an age-old seared-in-stone answer to finding their soul's eternal peace through their belief system to further shape their worldview. Then they must stitch shut the newly formed void in the heart of their belief system by weaving into their on-call intellectual memory the prescribed details that lay out the rules and special circumstances of the claim made by their soul's new and eternal landlord (mortgage holder for some). They must keep these details on hand to give the book-chapter and verse to answer questions from those that still respond to their free will's curiosity about why they do what they do.

The void interrupts the natural flow of their belief system's chain of understanding. It's missing the experiential binder...the sensual evidence verifying that the claim's cause (religious plan) is causally linked with the claim's effect (getting heavenly enlightenment). It must be the nature of any internalized claim's cause/effect process to find its truth in a reality with the living pulse of an impermanent present moment. This constitutes the fiber of their worldview.

An unfettered free will determines whether or not it's in the nature of the considered claim to have any living participation in the realm of reality it's claim promises to initiate its described cause/effect sequence in before internalizing the claim to allow its nature to further shape the nature of their worldview. An unfettered free will verifies if the nature of the contemplated claim finds sync with the impermanent rhythm of this cause/effect reality to ever make the claim's purpose anything but an illusion. Sensual evidence of its impermanent nature should be there to verify if the claim maker has any present moment living presence (looking for the sign from above) for the cause/effect claim to ever be anything other than a dream or an illusion.

This new void in the individual's belief system replaces what should be their free will's sensually gathered evidence normally found when testing whether or not the cause/effect transition promised by a claim actually happens. It's in this sensual experience-based assurance that comes after initiating a claim's cause (adopting the claim's plan) and sensually witnessing the transition to when the effect (heavenly enlightenment) kicks in that the experience-based-gut-felt steadfast faith takes seed. Christianity's claim to religious cause/effect transition tells of an effect (attaining heavenly enlightenment) with a promised paradise that even provides a chariot-escorted escape on the final Day of Redemption from the present moment mitote/maya state of reality on Earth that generates their ever-nagging unrest and the hell they need saved from.

In a general sense, when an individual believes a claim they've heard or read about without knowing the plausibility of its truth, they've created or widened a void in their belief system. The nature of the claim being considered may engage a reality that allows a state of continuity to exist or it may recognize a state of reality with a nature of impermanence. After internalizing a claim, any thought or idea-building that's done assuming the truth of unverified claim's nature and intended purpose will be shadowed by a looming degree of unanswered uncertainty stemming from not first learning about the nature of the claim's purpose.

This primal void of uncertainty represents the gap or interrupting break formed or widened in the natural sequential flow of one's belief system self-protection/preservation protocol. It's affected when blindly adopting or internalizing a new claim's relational characteristics. Whether its nature is ever-changing or nonchanging, if not tested, the uncertainty still leaks in to dilute an individual's gut-felt confidence regarding their worldview.

This paradigm holds true for any claim made regarding the nature and purpose of our one and only Source...the designer and maker of our reality. This void is primal because it is directly tied to the most primal of truth understandings explaining the ongoing change that the relational wisdom relating to our cause/effect reality is generated from. Mankind's ignorance of the wisdom encasing the cause/ effect relational truths that tie together our present moments are at the root of all human suffering.

Individuals who have taken the blind leap of faith by internalizing the nature and purpose of a blind-to-experience (unverified) claim without verifying that the claim's purpose of intent has a nature in sync with the impermanent nature of this reality have burned the bridge of experiential understanding that spans between when a truth seeker hears a Source-contender's claim and when they decide to internalize their claim, blindly accepting the nature of its promise.

Anytime a potential believer has internally agreed that they have no need to see any hard living proof or living sign to document the realism of the workability of a claim's nature...the void of collective uncertainty in their belief system has been added to and widened. Their unobstructed access to the testing power of their unfettered free will becomes progressively cluttered.

When an individual doesn't take or make the time to sensually verify the flow of a claim's described present moment cause-into-effect transition, they will not have the sensual memory basis needed for its future recognition. Being sensually familiar with the perceivable constructs that result in a claim's proposed truth coming to pass that set up and support the cause/effect flow that characterizes the event allows its later recognition when opportunity arises to feel it again.

Without having any sensual experience history with a claim's cause/effect connecting link, they will be unable to recognize the true cause of the effect the claim promised to cause when, at an unexpected future time they experience the real-time incarnation of that effect. Even if the individual can recognize the modern-day incarnation of what religious theology explains to be heaven or one of its players, they still won't be sure of what caused it. They won't have any idea what the true cause for something is if they've never sensually linked the cause and effect, even when it's 'cause it's right in front of their face...like in Jesus's parable of the sewer.

Success in sensually understanding the supporting constructs of a claim on this deeper level will leave the individual relaxed enough with their known experience with the subject to allow their curiosity to build to consider other options explaining other causes (religious claims made for the same effect to exist...variations in the means to get the same end effect). That might be another entity's ideas of how to find salvation and thus help eliminate the ignorance that keeps them from heavenly enlightenment that allows their suffering. They have increased confidence in what they've sensually witnessed compared to their level of confidence from what they've had merely had verbally explained to them. The door is more open to increased patience and tolerance.

Cause to effect transition experience is a fundamentalism breaker. The individual understands the details of what supports the claim so they don't have to carry around the written text that replaces experiential reference as the cause to effect link.

Due to the lack of inner-felt familiarity, the views of narrow-sighted fundamentalists can only sight down and use the supporting details describing what they are told by the maker of the claim. They can't waver on the claim-maker's details of what happens between the explanatory cause and the predicted effect (the claim's solution to suffering or being saved). They haven't felt the generator of the claim's truth as being a part of the living present moment. They can't recognize the written Holy Spirit's sensual incarnation in the passing present moment. The new believer must quote the nonverified claim-maker's claim-justifying details to explain their religious rites and rituals.

Wearing fundamentalist blinders, church congregations argue and split over minor wording differences in a multi-multitranslated book that's written in a language that didn't even exist back in the authors' days of robes and sandals. This unfounded anxiety over the means to the end should be a bit more adaptable and forgiving when allowing consideration for the differences in the material reality of today compared to that of 2,000-plus years ago.

Believers in religious claims that have a nature of permanence that allows attachment, have to cauterize shut the belief system void that formed in between when they heard the information source's description of their religious entity's claim to provide eternal salvation from suffering and when they decided to believe it, making it part of their worldview. If a claim has a 2,000-year-old history of being believed by the masses it's very easy for today's individual, even though they may feel questions prodding from the inside, to feel unworthy to question its power by numbers and to go ahead and roll the dice...the same set of dice that's been used for generations in their family.

Is the effect of reaching enlightenment about why joy and happiness have been distanced by the ignorance that causes suffering, linked with the outside source's suggested cause (religious claim) of reaching its after death eternal joy and happiness and absence of suffering? Can they prove it? Can they demonstrate the living involvement of their god's energy in the right-now present moment real-time change that's going to one-day turn into the present moment realtime change when Jesus comes down on a white horse to take to heaven those who conformed to God's rules?

When a new believer takes the leap of blind faith, there's no sensual synchronization found between any claim's permanent nature and the unavoidable self-evident truth that everything is part of the transforming process of change. They can still cling to the imagined nonexistent. The relative importance of the real-life applicability of this unavoidable primal truth of ever-change goes unnoticed and the resulting ignorance will persist until this ignorance has been undone. Purposefully initiating continual ongoing change is our Source's modus operandi during the transformation of reality's cause and effect process where everything is becoming something else.

Suffering present moment discontent due to the ignorance of our reality's nature of impermanence is realized in many ways. The individual suffers through not understanding why the effects from a causing behavior aren't the effects that their belief system expected. They may look at some condition and attribute its development to causes that their misguided worldview understands to be possible that in reality don't line up.

The familiar saying that "God works in mysterious ways" is a quick way to give up on understanding how to link up a cause to an effect and just accepting something as being the way it is...the way it was planned to be. It adequately appeases the confusion of most about developing an understanding working sensual relationship with what happens in the middle...between a cause becoming its effect.

Dreamed-up seemingly real illusionary explanations of what our Source is can easily be relied on in a pinch to explain unexplainable real effects when perceived, but not understood. Attributing the occurrence of bad events as being punishment from God is still very popular in Midwest USA. Borrowed or intellectual knowledge or memorized wisdom can be used to provide a second-rate validation tier of its own type of authenticity or truth. Any faith in this type of staged truth must be blind.

From the past claims as to why the god Thor threw lightning bolts from the sky to today's innumerable opinions of what the day of redemption will appear as when it comes are examples of cause/effect relationships that lack the experiential understanding to base their predicted truths or causes on. Illusionary structural supports are necessary to explain and justify these projections. Just try to imagine the level of uncertainty and look-over-the-shoulder fear resident in the worldviews of those who believed in those earlier sets of gods? The poor Hindus...Almost everything has its own god...yikes!

Sensually witnessing the purpose of any claim in action, religious or nonreligious, to verify that it has a nature that finds rhythm with our Source's nature of ever-change is important. Having blind faith that the cause/effect transition process of any claim's intended purpose has the nature that beats to the impermanent rhythm of this reality creates the void of uncertainty and doubting fear that freezes any truth seeker into a fundamentalist state of ego-managed (I am) self-defense.

An Inner Compass that's Lost its Polarity

This reality is real and living. Blind faith pulls an individual's conscious involvement with that living world away to the intellectually created and nurtured world of an unchanging lifeless claim explaining the role of the human condition in the human experience. Blind faith in a religion excuses the mind to look the other way and let God take care of it. It excuses their laziness to not get involved and ask questions about what's affecting the life in real-time. It gives the believer a socially accepted reason not to face many things about their personal reality head on.

Without an unfettered free will that's wise to recognizing the nature of a claim and unrestrained to effectively guard an individual's belief system from internalizing new claims with intended purposes that service cause/effect processes with a permanent nature, the individual will internalize some explanatory claims that have intended purposes pointed at end goals that fall somewhere in the endless variety of illusionary ends with natures that allow or accept as real the cause/effect transfer state of a continued permanence that leads to all types of illusionary attachment.

The individual is losing touch with their intuitive push toward sensing the difference between a need and a want. They will second-guess their chosen direction in the light of right versus wrong. This is where wants are often sought over needs by an individual just to stop the waving of the mental flags that point to nowhere in their mitote/maya state of mental confusion—i.e., a paycheck is spent on a sweater like one worn by an idolized movie star instead of paying utility bills and buying diapers.

With the internalization of each new unverified claim, the widening void of uncertainty in their belief system is filled with more reserved doubt and question. Their worldview becomes more littered with claims that support an endless array of unrelated purposes and goals with cause/effect transitions that support conflicting natures of reality. This conflicting noncongruence feeds their mitote/maya monster of mental confusion while each unrelated claim vies for the host's action. They each shout to gain the highest position on the individual's priority tree. Actual needs and superfluous wants become indistinguishable.

The individual doesn't know which way to turn. They long for direction.

If a claim has a purpose that is not geared for impermanence, it must relate to an unfounded untethered end of an imaginary unfounded cause/effect relationship. There are a countless number of illusionary unfounded ends with continuous natures and miscued intended purposes that sidestep the beat of the relational justice of our reality's impermanence.

These notions are born from illusionary accounts of our reality due to the individual's lack of guidance in recognizing reality's impermanence in the present moment. Claims either have natures with impermanence savvy or they don't. The only thing all the totally unrelated ends from imagined states of reality have in common is that they all deal with a subject that exists in a constant state of permanence that an individual can cling to with thoughts of wanting more or less of. This is how idols of worship are formed.

The unfiltered internalization of explanatory claims that fortify ungrounded ends with natures that fail to recognize and flow with the impermanent nature of our reality will gradually populate an individual's belief system...like corrupted programming slips by computer antivirus software to eventually lock up the hard drive.

These are frivolous claims aimed only at supporting stagnant mental snippets of an illusionary facet of an ego-managed worldview that through ignorance lives their present moments mind-numb to situations that are pointing at eruptive ends that are figured to recognize a reality with a permanent nature. Over time, the resulting thought patterns of decision compromise weave a cataract over any objective focus, warping one's ability to maintain a balanced perception while riding the waves of a transforming reality. The ensuing frustration and anxiety are examples of the consequential mental unrest that plagues humanity.

Actions motivated by intentions supporting ends aimed at attachment to craving more or less of something have a continual nature. When the behavior is repeated to the point where they become habitual actions, their repetition will acquire the fleeting nature of a reaction that occurs before conscious thought is given. These trained addictions give definition to the individual's personality that characterizes their physical presence.

Faith Blind to Unverified Divinity Remains Ungrounded as it Echoes Through the Void of Uncertainty

At this point in history, older religious theologies have matured into accounts of god(s) from above with unverified claims that fail to clearly define what their main purpose is in everyday terms. They don't touch on what suffering is in present moment terms and what their plan has to do with it, let alone provide a living plan to end it. These are claims that come with no present moment living "sign from above."

They require a leap of blind faith that the promise will come true at a future present moment in time. He watches every human, everywhere, every second of the day and requires his believers to address him in prayer, yet offers no physical contact and only listens in prayer. But, that's just God's way.

This leaves the claim's credibility subject to uncertainty and the questioning-doubt that can scar the claim-believing individual's intentions and actions with the crippling limp of unyielding hesitancy. The claim's truth is really no more believable than the credibility of the claim's borrowed or intellectual knowledge source.

Blind faith does not help a religious believer develop a stronger sense of faith. Increased age shouldn't be mistaken for a deepened relationship to something that has no way of being sensually referenced. Increased age just means that the believer has maybe divined a greater assortment of ways to creatively rationalize a justification for the way something works out when it goes against what was anticipated.

It lacks any bone-felt tie-in to bite into when expressing confidence in the nature of something's dependability...its known ability to participate. It's like always being held back at arm's length when wanting to sit down and get to know somebody better. Believer or not, steadfast faith in this reality's omnipresence will enrich the individual's waking conscious with experienced-based wisdom from the life they've lived. This level of modern-day spiritual maturity might earn them an elder's seat in their local congregation.

Blind faith lacks the gut-felt direction coming from an internal compass that's tuned into the sensual heartbeat of our Source. A truth seeker can park their awareness into that heartbeat, sit back in deep reflection and it can inspire their thinking to have an insightful wisdom-enriched enlightened understanding of the time released relational properties of ongoing change. Armed with an unfettered free will that's guarded by a steadfast faith with roots reaching into the truth seeker's personal experience with the manifestation of ongoing change itself, they can learn to sense what newly encountered claims have a permanent nature and lead to the attachment to illusionary notions and the resulting suffering.

When not actively on topic in an individual's waking attention span, the supporting strength of the blind faith disappears and the person is thrown back into the realm of their dreaded mitote/maya state of mind. The nature of the religious claim's intended purpose is not related to what their human experience deals with in the real present moment of their ongoing transformation through the ongoing generation of new life found in the ongoing change that ties one present moment to the next. Blind faith has no automatic regeneration of a gut-felt surety that's there without an unprimed presence.

A blind faith will draw out dreams that test the boundaries of its conjecture. Blind faith's stature is founded in shifting sand on an unchanging shoreline.

Every thing and non-thing knowingly or unknowingly is marching to the drums of Father Time totally preoccupied and wrapped up in the moment-to-moment process of changing into something else. This includes non-things like the variety of religious riddles that have evolved, changing in purpose and intent as they dodge evolving scientific insights that have nipped at the heels of their credibility every time when asked for a material sign verifying the religious entity's living participation in this organic reality...ever since mankind first saw the need for religious theology.

An unverified religious claim's state of being is far too transitory...the solidity of its stance is far too debatable and its day-to-day nature is far too unpredictable for an individual to ever have bone-felt confidence or experience-based faith in its future consistency. There has to be some sort of witnessed ground performance to start having faithful confidence in what someone says they will do in the future. This is different than having faith in a claim-maker's intentions after having experienced their work history.

There's nothing concrete or experientially defined to justify having any confidence as part of any present moment expectations when considering any internalized belief founded in nothing but blind acceptance. Conversely, an individual can self-train their ability to witness change itself by catching our Source in the act as it manifests itself within the flesh of their bodies. Any truth seeker can build a faith, steadfast in the undeniable truths inspired during focused awareness in this physical arena of change.

By sensually experiencing the truth of our Source's claim to unchangingly provide ongoing change, a truth-seeker has personally seen in action the living proof of the change that's being promised and that they have steadfast faith in being there. The religious claim to conditionally end suffering by allowing some to go to a heaven and the rest of God's children to go to hell describe a future reality with no signs of detectable involvement or living presence in this reality's cause/ effect present moment.

Heaven's Reality Built to Different Dimensional Specs?

A believer has to blindly accept as true that time will end and then there will be a reality that is subject to another schedule of time-passage (a future heaven in the sky). This could mean there's another dimensional reality with another book of relational wisdom? Could it be that the future heaven will have a nature of continuity that allows permanence of things and ideas? Good and bad emotions would have to have different recipe schedules. What if the transforming nature of today's reality, suddenly stopped?

There would begin a new schedule of relational justice suited for the different nature (impermanent versus continual) of the new reality. For something to be a sin would take on different characteristics than those sins in the dimensional composition and with the relational justice suiting for today's impermanent reality?

Even if the future heaven has an impermanent nature, a believer has to develop illusionary images of theological maxims they will carry in their intellectual memory that will make it difficult for them to realize what real heavenly enlightenment is if their attention is ever drawn to a realtime waking glimpse of its real-time incarnation. Its sensual spiritual signpost will slide by unnoticed...unappreciated for what it really is.

The mental picture formed depicting this futuristic state of heaven is open to undefined illusionary expansion. With a continual nature, there would be no cause/effect change from one present moment to the next present moment to allow joy, happiness and compassion to be realized as is during the energy flow of the real-time present moments of today's impermanent material reality. Yet, it's this real-time joy, happiness and compassion that are being promised in this future heavenly reality.

The steadfast faith in the dependability of any religious/ spiritual claim to accurately depict what the true nature and intended purpose of our Source is rests on the time-fueled pace of our cause and effect reality being the same tomorrow what it is today. This ensures that the relational wisdom derived from tomorrow's inspired insights into the relational interplay of the cause/effect factors will be the same as those observed today.

The claim's truth should have inspired the insights to derive the wisdom to map out or recognize a state of justice within the web of the relational infrastructure that relates cause to effect. The truth of our Source is demonstrated in the essence of its manifested presence that resides in, holds together and creates the sequence in between a cause and its effect. The house rules and playing field have to stay the same for a poker player's game strategy to have consistent day-to-day success.

It's the same reality for everybody. It doesn't matter to which religious fraternity an individual may belong. One key to the credibility of any claim's attempt at explaining the longed-for answer that lays out detail to our Source's nature and intended purpose depends on the day-to-day unfailing consistency of its nature and demonstrated played out purpose of intent as time fuels our journey from one elusive present moment to the next. Its demonstrated nature should prove self-evident and unchanged, traced all the way back to the beginning...the start of the transforming reality its claim seeks to explain with its particular synthesis of the truth and thus the seed for a faith steadfast in the unshakeable "I've been there and done that" resolve.

Unpredictable change is natural. It defines us in exactly the same language and media as our Source created us in. It would be quite foolish for an individual to knowingly set foundation to build expectations or place confidence or have a faith in anything or non-thing other than our Source's demonstrated and unfailing intended purpose to initiate time-fueled unalterable-by-man constant change or to deny the wisdom coming from an enriched awareness of the sensually witnessed interactions that make this reality so self-evident. In this present moment cause/effect reality, every other thing or non-thing demonstrates nothing but brand-new constant change.

This unquestionable primal truth precedes any supposed subjective truth of any religious unsupported guarantee. It can't be denied. An individual must achieve a waking awareness of relational justice...the savvy of the relational principles relating to this one primal truth and then, if it feels appropriate, go ahead and join any religious or spiritual dogma that's popular in the changing face social life that their inner faith supports.

Every event is the effect of a cause that then transforms into the cause of another effect. It's OK. It's what it's all about. It's the plan. It's a nature shared between every human and their Source. Its essence is the coming and going push that connects one present moment to the next.

Intellectual Lore is Religious Claim's Sole Living Link to Future

An example of insightful wisdom suddenly rising from the deeper consciousness to the waking consciousness is when it suddenly dawns on an individual that any belief or doctrine is really no more than a product of a perception generated during a living person's life span...from their physical birth to forming their world-changing contributory insight to writing it down to dying. Formulating their perception of reality has no more time to mature or age than the length of their human life span. It's true that new insights can build off of the realized insights of our forefathers, but still, the percolation time of its development to an individual's conscious recognition to social injection is limited to the time duration of that individual's human life span.

An individual's worldview mirrors the collective purpose coming from their experiential living experience reflecting internalized claims from borrowed, received/intellectual and sensually registered information sources. Any worldview really has less aging and seasoning than an old bottle of wine.

Religious promoters offer their interpretation of what evolving religious claims that started about 2,000 years ago have changed into over the millennia. The cultural acceptance of the religious doctrine's viability becomes further seasoned by every new generation of questioning and testing and ends up being revised by more informed interpretations over centuries of human life spans, but one only has so long to interpret and induct into their belief system their subjective version of the handed down lore they see fit or are fooled into internalizing to represent their ever-unique and ever-maturing worldview.

Today's religious doctrines reflect their updates to their religion's soul-saving claim to adapt to and stay abreast with the scientific discoveries that are slowly undoing the mystery of our reality. All religions evolve until their illusionary fog disappears from the heat of some new unquestionable proof of their futility. That's been time-proven. Ask anyone from the retired god Zeus's courtyard.

The passage of centuries may point more toward a religious belief becoming more of an unquestioned part of the society's charter. Its lack of need for an individual's initial authentication becomes stronger with society's unwillingness to question something our ancestors said was true. After its logo has been printed on the society's currency and flags, it's the reputation of the belief, not the truth of its claim, that mistakenly assumes the credibility of an entity or truth that's been around alive for centuries.

This ageless presence stuns society's free will and cripples it from seeing present moment suffering for being all that it actually is. It sedates humankind's natural curiosity and wrongly lulls it into believing it has to wait to die to finally have a chance at realizing the truth of their god's claim that he will keep them safe from suffering the same mental unrest or hell they experienced while living. The only living part of these unverified religious claims is that their reputation and the need for its truth's verification has been hushed by the passage of time and quelled by an ancestral validation of sorts with safety in growing numbers.

The reputation of the claim being voiced is the only connection to a living entity the purpose of the claim has to offer. To maintain its presence in the living world, a religious claim will leach onto the belief systems of the living. This is how the religious claim to a purpose of intent that has never shown a living sign in the present moment flow of life that all can see stays associated with and a part of society's life flow.

The void-of-life purpose of the religious claim rides into the individual's belief system when they willingly take a leap of blind faith and vow to adhere to the legion of fundamental ground rule expectations, rituals and dogmas common to those who believe in this untestable claim. Its uncertainty fills the void created in the wake of the new believer's blind acceptance.

There's no part of the religion's claim to ending mankind's suffering that's visible in living form today, only the miscued worldviews of individuals attached to the promise of its illusionary dogma.

It's passed on down through time...blind leap by blind leap...living soul to living soul...generation to generation.

Jehovah's Heaven-Above Finds Life Only in the Imaginary Designs of Each Believer's Unique Void of Uncertainty...It Waits Nestled...Fed by Host's Fears...Their Judge and Jury

Mankind from times long past would gasp in awe at things they didn't understand. That's still true today, but human understanding of the dimensional lattice-work supporting this reality has advanced exponentially over the past five hundred years, since the times of Isaac Newton.

Besides raising mankind's conscious awareness to the presence of gravity, he and his contemporary Edmund Haley helped break mankind's fear of the heaven's unknown relationship with the Earth. The first map of the magnetic field was drawn up. It was figured out that the planets orbited around the sun and their pattern...simply genius. They calculated the distance the Earth is from the sun. Imagine how these unknowns would further enhance mankind's mystery-fueled uncertainty and wonder about their place and their safety in the bigger picture.

Our ancient ancestors were aware of many unidentified and misunderstood qualities of the surrounding reality that their parents might have warned them about that even they didn't understand. They kept in reserve a looming uncertain sort of fear that few understood or questioned.

This is also true of mankind today even though Mankind understands so much more about the impermanent nature of this reality than it did five hundred years ago. It's hard to believe that any human could have learned to understand it to the point where they were at one with its nature, two millennia ago. We have ancient written records of a few that did. It's a wonder how many might have realized an enlightened understanding of the nature of this reality in the thousands of years before written record was possible?

The early Egyptians made the revered and feared crocodile of the Nile a god and named it Sobec. His image appeared standing guard, projecting its unknown powers with its carved image overlooking the various public places of Egyptian government and was carvingly stamped onto many of the other things that represented the pride of their culture. Hinduism has made separate gods of most living things in reverence to the visibly apparent yet mysterious presences of life they perceived in each.

An individual's belief system's void of uncertainty that results from their internalization of misguided beliefs or understandings about the relational justice in this impermanent reality without first getting experiential verification of the claim's nature and witnessing the link between how the effect of a claim's truth is born from its cause represents what's become today's incarnation of ancient mankind's inner kingdom of uncertainty. Forming this void at the heart of understanding what the presence of the claim's truth feels like when the truth of the claim's effect actually does transfer from its cause relates to the validity of any claim being internalized, not only to those related to religion. They are all built on the mere merit of intellectually acquired and retained knowledge that's consciously oblivious to the nature of the beliefs that comprise the nature of the worldview they set the stage for, due to haphazard internalization.

Christianity says that mankind has an inborn weakness to opt for using intellectual knowledge as a means of interpreting the world. This state of conscious neglectful ignorance could be thought of as mankind's original sin, Adam and Eve's downfall? Ignorance or lack of appreciation for the impermanent nature of this reality leaves individuals unready for the naked change that confronts them in the passing of each new present moment. Jehovah personally warned Adam and Eve.

Like the Egyptians and our ancestors and their ancestors did for things they felt fear of, they gave this mystified and awed region of their waking conscious uncertainty a god to organize and rule over the fearful unrest their ignorance of the nature of this reality generated. Today's incarnation of how our early ancestors and their ancestors chose to deal with their fears from their void of uncertainty has been handed down from generation to generation and that's how its legendary life is preserved as it adapts to and dodges Science's speculative progress from discovery to discovery. It's been handed down in spite of science's experiential verifications of newly recognized primal certainties that religions have had to dodge or agree with and adapt to.

Each individual develops their own personalized version of this void of uncertainty. Its awe is realized it terms of inner unrest from the uncertainty generated as this void develops in their belief system. Some individuals try to categorize and understand this reality by being a believer in a religious philosophy.

The individual's ignorance or conscious obstinacy (Adam and Eve) about how they choose to develop their belief system allows their ignorance of or a conscious disregard (?) for our reality's impermanent nature to affect the nature of their worldview. That's what made God mad and Lau Tzu warns against in verse thirty-three of *Tao Te Ching*. This hollow abyss in an individual's belief system that's void of sensual record of having been there and done that fills with uncertainty in the absence of this invaluable experiential knowledge. As an individual becomes a believer, their trusting faith in the unverified claims they daringly internalize, convinces them to hog-tie their questioning free will and to accept and believe notions that stand true to the purpose of claims having a nature of continuity and permanence where the evils of attachment thrive unchecked.

It's an abyss of imagination and illusion with an infrastructure supported and strengthened by each additional unverified claim that may have a nature of continuity that the individual internalizes. Their internal distress intensifies with each misguided understanding, miscued interpretation and miscalculation of the unavoidable relational justice in this reality. There's a frequent clash between what these misguiding beliefs, that's shaped the nature of their worldview and what this reality's unavoidable schedule of true relational justice determine to be a cause/effect outcome. This is all that's needed for each individual's personal and unique living hell to germinate and proliferate...now in each present moment of this living lifetime.

Christianity avows that humans are born with the original sin. Buddhism believes that people are born into the circle of suffering. Out of ignorance or maybe a little ignorance mixed with a little obstinacy, individuals allow their belief system to internalize knowledge before being experientially verified to form their worldview. The lack of hands on experience in how the causes of some of the claim's they internalize actually do become their effects, creates the belief system abyss of uncertainty that shapes a worldview primed to perceive a reality of a continual nature by not really knowing any better.

Every individual creates their own inner void of uncertainty. Most follow their cultural lead in finding a way to explain and organize the unrest and angst their void of uncertainty generates. Many individuals become religious believers and force fit the stencil of their chosen religious soul-saving plan over the inner unrest coming from the fear generated in their own unique void of uncertainty. Their plan for relief from eternal suffering floats unanchored to any experiential ties in a region of their conscious mind where they have no means for changing anything into what could be founded in gut-felt steadfast faith.

Today's Christian teachers are afraid to enter what they fear to be inner darkness. They tell their followers to look out and up to God.

Everyone's living reality is what they perceive it to be within their own conscious mind. The primal truth is that everything on the outside (as well as inside) has to demonstrate impermanence to be a part of this reality. There are no gods in the sky that demonstrate their participation in crafting the living experience in this reality's impermanence that they were supposed to have created. Their presence or their Holy Spirit's should be alive and felt in the essence of each present moment.

Just ask a practitioner of any religion to give their description of the Holy Spirit, the Day of Redemption or maybe what eternal heaven is or where it's located. Let them take you on an air balloon tour, tethered only to their intellectual interpretations of the particular translation of Rome's Bible that they studied or their shared hearsay with another believer. You'll float untethered to anything of familiarity, through their imagined conceptions of what they intellectually surmise the important aspects to be while speculating what they think God meant by what was said in the written text.

Eliminate the void of uncertainty from a believer's belief system and eliminate the unique conception of heaven they know and understand heaven to be. Change the nature of what their conscious mind understands the nature of this reality to be and change their understanding of heaven.

11

Religious Rite

*...Unearned Trust in the Untested Promise of a
Conceptualized Supernatural Promise Maker*

*Striking up a blind faith in any professed truth can help secure a makeshift sense of
balance in times of pressing anxiety over any related unknown.*

—Anonymous

Is Claim's Purpose Geared to Work in this Reality?

Is the listener wise to the nature of this reality? Learning about living in this reality is an ongoing process. Many individuals far too often venture far too much trust in the credibility of their information sources. The nature and truth of many new claims represented by those different information sources were never really tested or verified by these individuals.

For many different reasons, people often knowingly or unknowingly decide to believe and internalize new claims made by different sources of information at face value. Not first seeing the truth of a claim in action leaves a belief system gap of uncertainty between accepting the belief as a part of an individual's worldview and when the claim's promise actually comes to pass. There's no feeling of familiarity that gets sensually registered while experiencing the claim's work-in-process. They're ignorant to becoming familiar with the nature of the claim's cause/effect process itself. Does the cause the claim initiates, as the source described, actually bring about the effect or result that it stands for?

Does the interacting chemistry of the underwriting factors that combine to bring about the claim's purpose represent a reality that has an unchanging continual nature or one that's fixed in an ongoing process of transformation to make true the cause/effect promise the claim makes? In these two types of reality presence, there would have to be different sorts of relational justice between the factors involved in creating the claim's cause for it to bring on its effect.

Having different networks of relational justice would call for different wisdom configurations to explain the insightful shortcuts that interlink and makes sense of the relational justice between the contributing factors making up the claims that answer to these differing systems of relational justice. Which type of nature of reality presence is the listener's worldview geared for?

Are they even aware of the difference? It's true that out of ignorance, humanity does assume that there are different types of reality presence...impermanent and continual. However, it's interesting that all the different religious/spiritual and science disciplines seek life truths from the same tree of wisdom. Seems then that this reality really only has one type of presence?

If the listener's not aware of there being any difference, they would live in the confusion and suffering that comes from their ignorance that allows expecting the cause/effect relational justice connected to a continual presence of reality for the truth of a claim to come true in. But what effects they get will reflect the cause/effect relational justice of this reality's impermanence. It's not even on their conscious mind that there's a difference?

Does a claim have a miscued purpose designed to realize its truth in a reality with a continual nature where the give and takes of its purpose might be designed to create a feeling of attachment? Essentially though, no matter what they think, the purpose of any claim that the listener internalizes will have no choice but to find its promised truth in this reality's impermanent nature. Imagine all the kinds of disappointment and confusion this can create.

Different listeners have different resulting emotions that demonstrate the sorts of suffering that result from this sort of miscued worldview. This dilemma underlies the human ignorance of this subtle truth that most people aren't consciously aware of.

This individual's worldview stands in restless confusion when they become attached to something mistakenly thought to have a continual nature when the nature of this reality is actually in a state of constant change. It's very important for an individual's conscious ability to experience joy and happiness to have a worldview that recognizes how the nature of the claims they internalize is designed to fit into the impermanent cause/effect cycle of this reality.

On a scale reflecting the degree of impermanence savvy that rates worldwide spiritualist/religious disciplines, with Buddhism Taoism and Confucianism, there's recognition of this reality's impermanent nature and how the human ignorance of this presence causes so much suffering.

Religious theology's collective belief system ventures unfiltered into differentiating the type of nature the essence of this reality is. They struggle with finding direction, as their vision is fogged up and they can't see clearly where to go.

Tree of Knowledge or Tree of Wisdom?

To take it one step further, not only do many individuals take a messenger's message at face value, many will believe that the claim maker that the messenger's message is representing exists even if the essence of his presence has never been confirmed to be a part of the real-time present moment. He lives in writing and in the lore of the ancient past.

His living essence has even been given the name of the Holy Spirit and is said to be here today, yet even this can't be cornered for all to see. Its intellectual description is presented in writing, yet its intellectually registered description finds no connection with its sensually realized present moment incarnation as it arises in real-time. There's no intellectual-to-sensual association recognized. Religion's reality just doesn't happen in a recognizable real-time sensual way.

He's told of in books and people swear blindly to their faith in his plan, yet in his plan there's no part describing how to make contact with his living presence in a detectable sensual way. If this is his reality as his claim projects, where is he? What's he doing? Who's tending the fire that continually manifests new life? It seems that some entity's got to be here to explain and take credit for all this very real transforming energy that comprises everything that makes up all the present moment cause/effect activity in this universe.

Does his doctrine recognize the significance between an impermanent reality and a continual one? Adam and Eve partook of the fruit of the tree of intellectual knowledge. That event had significance. The godly warning against relying on internalizing the deceptive fruits of intellectual knowledge was one of the first points that God made in the Bible. It's a truth that goes all the way back to the beginning...either fourteen billion or six thousand years ago.

Today's rendition of Rome's Bible also speaks of the need to pursue the tree of wisdom that supports the relational justice of this reality. Having a worldview that relies on intellectually knowledge is quite different than one that's built from personally witnessing the transforming experience of impermanence...of life itself transforming. Did those Roman priests that determined which of the many gospel accounts of Jesus's life to include in the Bible they were publishing and allowing its citizens to rely on, decide to leave out the accounts of Jesus story that told of how to recognize the possible evils created from an individual basing their worldview on the fruits eaten from the tree of knowledge that God warned of in Genesis? Relying on intellectual knowledge leaves an open door for internalizing beliefs with purposes that depend on this dimensional reality's relational justice existing in a continual world.

Constantine's priests decided to leave out the gospel accounts of when Jesus explained how to, with due diligence, self-train the wisdom-enriched understanding of this reality's impermanent nature. Did Jesus tell how to make it from living in the hell of present moment suffering to self-training an enlightened awareness of the nature of impermanence that undoes the ignorance of what it is that makes suffering through the present moment happen...in this lifetime?

Siddhartha's account of how he did this wasn't edited to the standards of Rome's tyranny, as was Jesus's story. His story's much better documented. It's the same truth presented in a more complete way that's much less confusing and misleading.

A Premature Gamble to Put Blind Trust in Another's Asserted Soul-Saving Intellect

Some individuals trust taking another entity at their word for the validity of a claim they're representing. Others prefer to trust only what they've actually experienced before internalizing it to hone their worldview.

Does the purpose of the claim made by their information source find its truth in a reality with a living transforming nature or does the purpose of the claim they represent rely on the illusionary relational justice common to a reality with a continual nature to make true the promise it represents? The purpose of a claim needs to be experientially validated to determine what's the case here.

An individual's tale of reality needs to originate from an experiential awareness enriched with the wisdom that's savvy to the relational truths that guide the coming and going bits of energy that give form and texture to the sights and sounds of this impermanent reality. Taking the leap of blind faith means an individual becomes a believer, acting on someone else's opinion while either knowingly or unknowingly hoping the messenger has something substantial to back up their soul-saving claim. The soul's fate is important.

The believer has blind trust in their messenger's surety of the claim's truth. They're blind to any experience with the claim and the actual claim maker that the messenger has accumulated to establish their steadfast, substantiated faith in its truth, if they ever did so. In believing the claim to the future of their soul, the believer is blindly trusting that the said entity making the promise that they've never seen or met does have a living existence and will carry through with their promise.

To substantiate the truth of a claim that a promised state of reality will exist sometime in the future, that promised state of reality has to be have existing factors that have living substance in the present moment to interact at sometime in the future to be the cause that produces the future effect of the promised state. Otherwise, with nothing living to relate to in this reality, this promised state will remain the dream state that it currently is.

To have a faith in the existence of a more powerful entity is a basic tenet of membership in today's religious charters. The pattern is to have faith in a theological force that's deemed worthy of submissive worship and unquestioned obedience. Many faithful believers radiate with a seared-in pride in how they've shown the courage to blindly trust the future of their soul to a theological force that can't be sensually touched or identified in this reality. Many citizens are eager to conform to this unwritten assumed societal mainstay. How can it not be true? They sense safety in the millennia's-worth of numbers?

Individuals make the mistake of erecting a pseudo faith before they know what having a true inner-felt faith really means. They'll lower their free will's inborn intuitive protective shield to question and experience to validate the nature of the intent of any claim's purpose before deciding to internalize its message into their belief system to further hone the collective intent of their worldview.

The inborn verve of an unfettered free will to verify what its host allows to be internalized often reduces to shallow trust when weakened by intimidation, luring promise or social pressure. The form of faith that secures this process becomes a common crutch shared by others who also leap blindly from dare to belief without first feeling the living heartbeat of the unseen promise or promise maker that's responsible for connecting the claim's causing factors to its promised effect.

New believers will rise from their Sunday morning pew after the call to repent and surrender to the front and with blind trust they'll pledge their soul's future to the heavenly promise they just heard. They bow to the biblical promise of protection from after-death suffering that Rome authorities oversaw the publishing of 2,000 years ago. Many see premature blind faith as being a healthy cultural habit as accepting God's promise or surrendering to Christ is something pictured in the Bible and happens today in churches everywhere. It's seen on Sunday morning TV.

Their mental picture of the promisor is sketched from the borrowed/received wisdom from outside intellectual media. They'll use images from their earlier life experiences to patch together its imagined physical appearance and the mood they're in at the time will affect their god's type of tolerance.

Are they doing this because their friends did it…or maybe their siblings? Is it because their parents are making them do it? Are they running away from or are they running to something?

From selling snake oil to shouting "Heil Hitler," it's an ageless practice for representatives of outside entities to force-feed individuals an unverifiable claim to what they swear to be in the best interest of the listener. A religion's claim to salvation is a claim explaining the most defining aspect of someone's existence and involves the nature and intended purpose of our Source. With a claim where the nature of its intended purpose cannot be tested for its orientation to the impermanent nature of this reality, comes the attachment-friendly nature of blind faith that sanctions a believer's waking ignorance about the nature of our Source.

Any individual who blindly adopts having faith in the nature and truth of an unverified claim will be blind to recognizing and enjoying the inner-felt steadfast faith in the unquestionable future performance and omnipresence of the ever-consistent dimensional properties defining the reality created by our one and only Source. It's assumed by many that true faith can be founded in the shallow trust of something that was just heard or read about or maybe just seconded by a trusted friend...not needing to be founded in personal experience. It's a faith that doesn't reach deep enough in an individual's experience to anchor any gut feeling founded in experiential confidence.

A mystical godly entity whispers an intimidating unchallengeable boo at potential believers by threatening any disobedience to his untestable recipe for salvation with an afterlife eternity of hellfire and brimstone. This scares some into prematurely taking the blind leap of faith before trying to seek living validating evidence that the claim-maker breathes life into or is at least a contributing factor to the present moment pulse of the living change that defines everything about this reality.

It's the same impermanent collection of coming and going bits of energy that make up today's impermanent reality that the godly figure used long ago to enact the stories written about in the Bible. If the Christian god was alive in the present moment in those days, his presence should be notable in today's present moments?

The allure from the promise of an earned spot in an eternal after death heaven of joy love and happiness will coax others into blindly believing in the version of the many possible religious claims they were exposed to. This state of unfounded conundrum is the breeding grounds for the fear of uncertainty that drives from the backseat driving of a believer's worldview that's hesitant to step into any unventured territory.

They will struggle to find the courage to even recognize, let alone attempt expressing soul-felt honesty in the face of peer ridicule. The reference for their faith to turn to does not come from an experienced based intuitive gut feeling inside, it comes from what they can reference that's printed in the Bible.

Given that Christianity's religious claim beckons with the introduction that Jesus died for your sins, there can be much confusion in what the meat of the intended purpose of the religious claim being made really is. Reciprocation for Jesus's altruistically based compassionate deed of the highest level might sway some into taking the blind leap. With all due respect, watching any of today's movies showing the cinematically amplified torturing death that Jesus suffered through before dying on the cross will probably help many more make the belief system jump to blindly agree to have faith in Christianity's religious claim.

The fact that there are still many surviving religious theologies that had different Earth-bound representatives that make similar basic claims to providing outside saving powers has to create a deep-down questioning doubt factor in the minds of the different faiths' believers, especially since the claims have permanent continual natures and the intent of their religious purposes aren't grounded in their new believer's experiential association. How can the believers of the different religions really be sure that their personalized outside god is the right one?

Maybe it's just OK with some individual believers because there are so many people riding the same sheep wagon? In the back of their minds, they know that they'll end up in the same place together with all of humanity after they die anyway. They'll pay the same price for their state of apathy toward performing due diligence as all the others with the same level of commitment?

Blind faith takes root in the sands of denial that the unaware bury their heads in. It supports their apathetic naivety as they live their lives whirling in the spin of their illusion. They suffer with worry and indecision in situations that hinder or prevent them from realizing that they are a developing process trying to express the talents of their inborn potential. Every aspect of their present moment and the outcomes of future present moments caused by the current passing present moment are affected by their increasingly fear-based apathetic laziness and delusion.

The individual has a relationship with their chosen religious entity that's not founded in having any sensual history documenting any evidence of the living truth of the intended purpose of the religious claim they've internalized. The truth to any claim that has a continuous nature doesn't really exist in a reality where time breathes the Holy Spirit of life into present moment causes to transform them into their effects. A nature of permanence doesn't breathe with time. Any believer or truth seeker should be aware of this difference before expecting to make any spiritual progress. It's ground rule number 1.

A believer manufactures a premature faith in the truth of the claim representing some belief before trying to actually feel the flame of its claim and feeling the heartbeat of the living truth of the intended purpose of its promised claim. They've decided to take a leap of blind faith over the newly formed void its unverified claim left in the understanding process of their belief system. Their free will's intuitive protective shield's been lowered.

They've taken a leap of blind faith over the claim-validating step in the anatomy of their belief system's internalization process that deals with feeling the truth that allows them to feel and verify the ongoing feeling connection between the effect and its cause. For most, learning to find, separate and understand this connection on a personal level can take a lifetime, if ever.

Instead, they've decided to cauterize together the intellectually drawn cause of giving themselves to Jesus, to its unverified effect of gaining the promised future state of heaven. There has to be a pitted doubt left sealed by the scar inside the newly formed or expanded void of uncertainty that fills their belief system.

There's no living sign or verifying experiential evidence that the cause of committing to Jesus will affect the effect of the claim's intended purpose of providing a state of eternal peace. The cause and effect share no living bond. The way the relational interplay between the real cause and its real effect actually transpire does not make familiar sense. Sometimes individual's will manipulate the perceived cause/ effect factors of the situation to have the relational interplay of the cause and effect match up to satisfy the constraints of their illusionary apparent reality.

This step forcibly glues the cause to a mentally staged and possibly illusionary effect or vice versa. A believer cannot really question it, as there is no real glue holding the cause/effect transpiration together other than what someone or some source relayed intellectually.

The eagerness to fully commit and go to bat for some unverified claim's suggested purpose like this could for some reason seem quite commendable. It does seem that many find honor in casting aside any attempts at reason and hesitation to take a giant leap across this void in their belief system's free will validation process to then proudly make the claim to having unbendable inner faith, confidence and strength of character based solely on what could really be no more than their inner faith in the imagined reliability of the messenger's credibility to support this claim. They don't really understand what having true steadfast inner fait means. Many boldly demonstrate bragging pride in just being able to venture so much barefaced surety.

There are those that will die with their chin held high in wonder, bloated with pride for something they have never actually witnessed as they have seen others do it and really have nowhere else to turn. Then there are those that will die for something because it represents a truth they have personally witnessed and know internally that it can't be denied.

The first group must have extreme confidence that the information source of the claim is right, even though they've never experienced its imagined truth to have the true feeling of the worth of sacrifice. They put great confidence in the messenger's reliability as they venture their trust in the claim's existence and the unchanging presence of its ability to do what the messenger says it will do to build their blind faith in. They have a blind faith of hope directed at the existence of an entity they've been told to be the source of the unverified claim explaining the nature and purpose of our reality. It's a claim that the outside entity actually is our Source...the planner and creator of the human condition and sole director of the human experience.

The unverified untested claim's no stronger than the believer's confidence in the credibility of the borrowed received or intellectual knowledge source they heard the unverified claim from. There can be no internal sensually recorded surety verifying the truth of the claim.

Taking the leap of faith leaves one's free will with no verifying test results to go by. In only trusting the credibility of the source of their borrowed or intellectual knowledge, they will live in hope and uncertainty. They pray to their unseen god in hope that their god is listening to them as they make effort to communicate in an intellectually spawned verbal language.

They don't see the god or source or understand him well enough that they can tune in to him at any time and listen to what he, our Source, has to say to inspire their insightful understanding. Instead, the believer talks to him, hoping he's listening. They then wait and hope and watch for results...unless maybe until their mind moves on.

Even though it may be true that a believer might have a reserved doubt about what they're doing with their faith, they're afraid to move on. It's the best they've got. They have absolutely no idea about where to turn.

Vague Heavenly Promise with No Living Sign From Above

The Rolling Stones advise in their song "Blinded by Love" for an individual not to mortgage their soul to a stranger. In modern times, some entity that an individual has never had the experience of personally meeting is usually considered to be a stranger. It's best to first develop a knowing relationship.

Any promise made about the future of the human soul that shows no living inclusion in the heartbeat of the present moment is an illusion. It should be verifiably evident that the Holy Spirit that's described in the religion's promised heaven-free-from-suffering afterlife is the same one that creates the life in the passing present moment. The nature and purpose of a promised reality without a sensual sample of its living participation in this reality's process of transformation leaves the details of its definition wide open to the unique imaginary flavors of each individual member of mankind's collective imagination.

In the Midwest when something happens where an individual cannot connect the event to any causing factor, good or bad, it's common to hear the statement that God works in mysterious ways. There's no denying that the event happened. There has to be some comment that links it to God since God's all knowing and responsible for everything.

It's the human spirit that's to suffer here when kept in the dark. Wouldn't a god of love want his followers to be at peace? Transparency is a must. But yet, the Christian god keeps it mysterious and makes it difficult to understand.

To many, the reality of there being a god is no more than a vague notion. Would-be believers look up into the sky or out into their surrounding environment for a sign from above to give them convincing experiential verification of the real-time presence in this reality of the promise maker. In staying in line with Christian theology, they fail to recognize the life manifesting within their human condition as being the Holy Spirit image of their Source and as being the sign from above reflecting the living proof of our Source's presence in the present moment.

An individual might wonder why a god of limitless power would not offer real present moment verification to the validity of their claim-to-salvation so an individual can hold their finger to its flame to feel the warmth of its truth. Instead they make necessary a faith blind to witnessing the living presence of the proclaimer of the religion's claim's truth that keeps his believers guessing so.

Cinematic accounts of biblical stories are as close to seeing a living incarnation of Christianity's god that its believers will ever come. The scene in the movie *Moses* where Charlton Heston receives the tablets written in stone from the burning bush represents the perceptions of many who've seen the movie when they think of a living god.

That is as close as Christianity's god comes to making a living appearance in this living reality. It's the visual image that will pop into the minds of people who've seen the movie when the subject of the Ten Commandments comes up. It's one of the few examples of Christianity's god making a living appearance in this reality that is available for anyone to witness.

Many Christians take pride in firmly stating how they are God-fearing believers in his doctrine. Leaving an ancient biblically verified footprint that leaves its readers with an impression that they should fear is disappointing when the Bible says it's all about love. Imposing fear on an entity of lesser spiritual maturity brings question to the intended purpose of the entity with the ultimate degree of spiritual maturity. It brings to question how good of a role model he's being to leave this impression of being such a bully. Where's the compassion here?

Believing someone on TV, for example, when they swear that God appeared and talked to them in a vision is resorting to believing borrowed or intellectual knowledge to document the sign. Many others credit any inspiration they may have that effects what they do in the future to God's personalized leadership. Not to question the truth of an individual's testimony to what they give testimony to, the living sign should be available to any human's perception any time of the day. It shouldn't require twisting God's arm to be shown a unique and special sign that has to be described to others because its occurrence is now over and in the past. We're talking about an individual betting the fate of their soul on this.

There have been many near-death and some reports of after revived from death experiences where the individual sees a bright white light that beckons them with a complete feeling of peace. There is no intent here to question whether or not this is true. In one-way or another, these claims probably are true.

However, in the recounts of these encounters, it's being assumed that there's a god who is responsible for the white light. This might be what the human mind perceives right before the thought-producing brain synapses finally shut down. What happens to the energy of the human mind after life has left the body and after the white light has consumed it remains as quite an intellectual poser. To hear the answer while living, it would be an intellectually remembered answer. What about sensual assurance?

Besides, this happens to everyone. Were those who've given their account of this white light evidence all Christians of the particular faith that God is going to offer heaven to? Or, some say that souls go to a waiting place until the Day of Judgment.

Any sign from above should appear via a communication media that helps minimize any of the staling effects coming from the huge time gap in between mentally sketched images of times of long ago and the present moment waking consciousness used when talking to a friend. Did God really expect people 2,000 years past Jesus's death to base the future of their souls on what they read in the fragments of stories collected and edited by the Rome-fearing Romans?

But then, it's a Christian Catch-22 sin to question Jehovah's intentions while at the very same time our primal Source's intention to initiate ongoing change is openly available and begs to answer any questions from any of its human models that care to find the humility to ask and listen. Shouldn't biblical wisdom have a common denominator centered around or rooted in the relational justice between the causes and effects that write the natural laws that define our reality's nature of ongoing change? It was in the impermanent theater of this reality that the stage was set for every story that transpired back in biblical times and was reported to have happened in the Bible?

Why should God choose to disguise and leave mystically up to the human imagination a plan that's supposed to be based on compassion and love? Why not update it at least once every 1,000 years? Why use fear of God's Old Testament wrath to hold today's humanity's free will hostage? Why would a god of love dangle a carrot of an undefined after-death heaven in front of its children while they suffer through a lifetime of present moments, ignorant as to why?

Why would a living god allow those who want so badly to know him and worship him to find out that their fourteenyear-old child has been sexually abused by his spokesperson, their congregation's minister? Many would say how that's just God's way? He works in mysterious ways?

Love thy enemy as thyself...at least until judgment day when they can be kicked down into the fire and brimstone of hell...because we're right and they're wrong...because they didn't do what they were told to do or not to do...because they had the strength to want to understand and looked up into the heavens and shouted why?!

Does compassion just disappear once the earth is gone and the impermanent dimensions that hold this reality together change into those that will hold heaven together...into dimensions with an ongoing continual nature...purely illusionary... like those that warp today's impermanent reality?

How could God use Job by trying his patience by mercilessly taking all he had just to prove a point to Satan? Why did he argue with the devil at Job's expense? What natural right did he have to do that? True godly love for Job, who God admitted deserves it, would have instead resulted in those present moments that Job was undeservedly suffering through, to instead be resulting from the effects that Job's sinful actions had caused to happen...not undeserved effects coming from God's spat with Satan? God seems to be propping up his ego here with his self-serving use of Job's present moments?

What if all the sudden, the Holy Trinity appeared in the sky with all the bright lights and awesomeness? As visual witnesses, all would see the entities that are going to protect us after we die. They'd see the entities that have been read about performing miraculous feats 2,000-plus years ago. Still, there'd be nothing witnessed that the entities would be doing besides appearing magnificently in the sky for a short time.

How are these gods contributing to or helping the process of present moment transformation that they created? Is it really fair to make the subjective suggestion that some unlikely, hard to explain occurrence as being God-sent? Where's the living sign that nobody can deny that that is what it is...available for all to see... anytime...anyplace?

It's cruel for God not to simply provide living evidence of his present moment involvement in this reality and openly work with his believers. His world exists in an afterlife promise somewhere untouchable outside sensual reality. Believers have to create an illusion ignorant to the savvy of the self-evident truths of the ongoing energy of time as it pushes their human condition through the human experience of constant incoming naked change. They suffer throughout their lifetime because of their ignorance about how this works.

Believers suffer in their blind effort to cover the sensual void created in their belief system between the unverifiable claim of providing selective salvation and any living evidence verifying his promised after-death salvation. To have substance, why wouldn't this unverified religious claim have real-time present moment living verification?

Every believer's illusionary picture of how the whole heavenly trinity system is set up has to differ as it exists only in each of their senses of imagined order and material composition...the Father, the Son and the Holy Ghost. Do angels exist? What or, better yet, where is the biblical Holy Ghost...described in line with how its biblical incarnation would be perceived in today's sensual menu? It gets so complicated trying to make sense of a concept's possible implications that float untethered and untraceable into the endless boundaries of an illusionary intellectual understanding.

These understandings are not based on any life commonality or any illusion-limiting practicality that follows actually feeling the purpose of the claim's intent to establish an afterlife heaven in the sensual limits of real life. Thus, no two intellect-based descriptions of the biblical heaven or the day of reckoning are the same. Listen to the variety of biblical interpretations from the evangelists on TV. Absolutely no two are alike. They are all expressions of what the speaker thinks they mean and wants their listeners to believe.

Doesn't sexing the god as a male take away the yinyang duality an omnipresent god should represent as is evident in many man/woman or husband/wife relationships? Aren't there facets of the human condition that the female point of view is better equipped to understand and fulfill? Where's the deserved justice in duality here?

After one is baptized (saved for afterlife), what do they do until they die? While spending all their daily energy attending to their addictions, they repeat making the same mistakes because they have no relationship with our self-evident Source to allow their own self-trained development of their own understanding of the relational wisdom in this impermanent reality that we all must bow to? They are told by most Christian teachers to shut this pathway out. They don't recognize, let alone understand the Source of experiential wisdom to decode its message to let their joy and happiness replace their suffering in this lifetime.

The connection between an individual's conscious awareness and the underlying primal truth explaining the nature and presence of the source of this reality shouldn't depend on any cerebrally acquired, borrowed wisdom transferred through any form of intellectual medium. It's in what each individual is here and now, living. The challenge is learning how to understand and recognize it in its camouflaged world of faulty prior conditioning. An individual must learn the sensual definition of the intended messages left by the impressions set by the descriptions that formed their cognitive images of ancient present moments.

Fundamentalist Mindset Weakens Self-Confidence

Developing a worldview that stems from a baseline intellectual decision to blindly trust the credibility of another source's knowledge to have the trustworthiness of a truth that has been experientially verified weakens the free will's level of self-confidence. An individual having the security of their soul depending on the promise made by unverified religious theological hearsay settles into the depths of what supports their worldview and trickles down as an influence on all their future decisions.

It allows a tinge of unspoken uncertainty and doubt to unknowingly shadow all decision-making. Allowing the decision of their soul's security to be based on something that cannot be shown to have any present moment functional participation in their life that's been demonstrated to fit into the relational justice necessary to make this cause/effect transforming reality work, undercuts having an understanding of other cause/effect relationships involved with the cause/effect relationships of other events. The individual can have trouble realizing what is real in this reality and what's not when trying to understand what might be the cause of something or what the effects might be coming from some interaction.

Having to refer to what's written in ancient scriptures to intellectually articulate what's the right way to live in these modern times and what's in store for the soul's future leaves the ability to trust oneself in making important decisions founded in one's own modern-day determinants greatly compromised. Sequestering any doubt or questions related to the scriptural account of the truth injects that feeling of doubt about being able to determine important things. Hands are tied.

It can reach the point where they carry such a background lack of steadfast faith in what seems obvious and real. By ignoring and second-guessing science's truths throughout life and operating on a blind trust as to what's true, the individual can develop a complete lack of trust in what they decide makes sense. Following directions on using a simple devise can be riddled full of unreasonable doubt.

Forced Faith Blind to Experiential Truth Breeds Confusion

The conscious struggle to force-live a belief about the nature of our reality that's based in an abstract picture of reality that's blind to the gut assurance gathered during experiential validation that's not a natural flowing part of the living picture of present moment reality, saps will power or self confidence in having the ability to make a decision that's backed by a definitive level of confidence in the justifiability of the wisdom chosen to make the decision. The comforting intuitive gut reassurance is missing.

Being accustomed to relying on looking in the Bible for the documented right way to live, with its wisdom expressed in terms relating to an abstract and removed ancient culture, in itself distracts associating the life forces of present moment reality with the spiritual well-being of the soul. What's happening now isn't really connected to or tied in with the picture of spirituality needed to satisfy an imagined paradise in life after death.

A lagging doubt tugs at each decision made during the day. When mixing having no conscious feel for the trustability of a decision made with the desire to outwardly demonstrate individual intelligence, more bad decisions will be made. Having developed the feel for having to look elsewhere for life's wisdom to live by lessens any tie-in with relating the thought of biblical spirituality to the spirituality living in the present moment airs of life. Spending time worried that the man looking over the shoulder won't approve of decisions being made takes free will away from focusing on the give and take of real cause/effect life forces.

A blind faith that's not a faith held steadfastly grounded in the self-evident experiential truths felt by the human condition allows a believer to lose touch with differentiating between what's make-believe and what's not. A believer with their confidence in what makes this reality tick that's guarded only by the assurance from their level of confidence in the interpretation or vision of reality from where they heard or read about the unverified truth of religious theology will eventually not be able to appreciate the difference between the workability of what's real and what's make-believe. The individual will grow tired of the present moment unrest that never seems to go away even when trying to walk the religious theological path. They concede and allow their developed indifference to underwrite a state of apathy and laziness that replaces ambition towards making sence of the real things that are a part of the flow of any day.

Culture Blindly Lingers in Notion of Religious Promise

There are many who see a religious prescription to heavenly enlightenment as being no more than a hallucination of the masses, founded in superstitious. Any faith built solely on an intellectual interface with an unknown nature that an individual's never experienced is a faith built on a foundation of shifting sand.

This is a faith in what's unfamiliar and untested. It walks blind while offering no inner-felt confidence that the Source's omnipresence will be there tomorrow to in fact make valid the same wisdom that makes sense of the same relational justice of the same change-producing dimensional framework to a reality that makes possible the same impermanent cause/ effect process that the claim's truth testifies to today.

With over six billion people on this planet it's estimated that over a billion and a half are Islam followers while well over two billion are Christian. That alone is a very large number of individuals that have taken a leap of blind faith concerning the destiny of their souls. This number doesn't include those people who might bow to other gods or superstitions of which there are many.

These large numbers provide convincing support for the idea that many individuals settle to follow their local religion's template for reaching an afterlife promised heaven for their eternal protection from suffering. The memberships of the different disciplines grow regionally, depending, among other things, on family, culture, nationality and geographical divisions. The influence from those factors is more of a key than the theological content of the charters of the different religions in determining what particular religion the different individuals choose to follow. Today's pattern of decisions seems to have passed from generation to generation for centuries by our ancestors.

For most, the established religions or their modern-day incarnations seem to be the trusted path to follow and the soul-saving plan to build their worldviews around. Religious conformity is a cause for which many have killed those who doubt the validity of. They still do today.

It dislocates and rebuilds a wall between one's true identity with nature's self-evident truth that emanates from what's right on hand and what is perceived through ignorance as being real. Yet, these regional beliefs are definitely a safe place to hide in ignorance, as long as you live within the boundaries of the culture they're nested in.

A believer sees many of their peers going through the many manifestations of present-day suffering and they still don't stand up and question the religion's proficiency at restoring the love, joy and happiness that's been replaced with suffering. Hush-hush conformity is so much easier and it doesn't draw attention from those who may challenge any opposition. It becomes OK to let their peace of mind take second seat to a bit of background mental uneasiness about the uncertainty of their future in hard times. Over time their present moment uneasy states of mind meld together to make what they learn to recognize as being a normal day.

The undefined imagined illusionary implication of an unverified hereafter clouds their perception of their unique Source-given talents with underlying uncertainty and a shadow of delayed doubt they have to visualize reality and think through. They're afraid to jump off the social sheep wagon and ask why or shout "Prove it" or to try anything else to make things better. They're blinded by indecision from finding a worthy cause to pursue.

Blind faith is a hopeful, uncalculated faith seeded in fear of uncertainty reaching out from the void the claim's internalization has created in an individual's belief system protocol from never securing a feel for the living presence of a religious claim's truth. They have no familiarity with the nature of the claim. Their blind faith has no solid predictable and dependable foundation to grow from. It calls for and requires unearned unwarranted trust.

Blind faith is not a faith that finds the individual. It's a faith of the individual's favorite designer creation that adapts and often bends to give reason for the unexplainable facets of their life situation. It supplies backing for things that have no reason.

With no available-to-all transparent living affirmation of the claim's truth to start from, there's no available common sensual experience that would allow different truth seekers to share their accounts of the experience to help their brothers and sisters to recognized inspired insights they might have missed recognizing to better understand the spiritual meanings and significance of their common-shared experience. Individual's could discuss any sensually recognized spiritual markers noted that other individuals could identify and focus on.

In a spiritual journey supported by blind faith, there's no shared common sensual experience to tether the imaginations of different individuals when the different individuals could describe what the experience actually felt like. A religious believer has to rely on their intellectual reasoning, logic of deduction and on their confidence in the reputation of their information source to intellectually validate the spoken-of religious claim's viability and truth.

Not finding the answer to explain what's wrong with "what is" after a lifetime of searching will push some into forfeiture compliance. Just as Rome's Constantine who legalized Christianity in 312 AD did on his deathbed years later, many people decide just to be safe in case there just might be some unfelt reason the unverified religious claim might be true, they take the leap of blind faith and join the religion.

With time, the frustration from not understanding this chain of events and unexplained mental turbulence brings a feeling of giving up or depression in many. Time is spent ignorantly bound to addictions, dissatisfied with the way things are or "what is" while longing for "what is not" without a real answer or clue on where to look. This is living in a world they know and not a world they feel; they suffer. Their blind faith is not a user-friendly faith.

Mistaking Mental Rumination in a Prayer of Hope for Soul Enlightening Mind into Body Meditation

Matthew 6:6

New International Version
"But when you pray, go into your room, close the door and pray to your Father, who is unseen. Then your Father, who sees what is done in secret, will reward you."

New Living Translation
"But when you pray, go away by yourself, shut the door behind you, and pray to your Father in private. Then your Father, who sees everything, will reward you."

English Standard Version

"But when you pray, go into your room and shut the door and pray to your Father who is in secret. And your Father who sees in secret will reward you."

New American Standard Bible

"But you, when you pray, go into your inner room, close your door and pray to your Father who is in secret, and your Father who sees what is done in secret will reward you."

King James Bible

"But thou, when thou prayest, enter into thy closet, and when thou hast shut thy door, pray to thy Father which is in secret; and thy Father which seeth in secret shall reward thee openly."

Holman Christian Standard Bible

"But when you pray, go into your private room, shut your door, and pray to your Father who is in secret. And your Father who sees in secret will reward you."

International Standard Version

"But whenever you pray, go into your room, close the door, and pray to your Father who is hidden. And your Father who sees from the hidden place will reward you."

NET Bible

"But whenever you pray, go into your room, close the door, and pray to your Father in secret. And your Father, who sees in secret, will reward you."

Aramaic Bible in Plain English

"But you, when you pray, enter into your closet and lock your door, and pray to your father who is in secret, and your Father who sees in secret will reward you in public."

GOD'S WORD Translation

"When you pray, go to your room and close the door. Pray privately to your Father who is with you. Your Father sees what you do in private. He will reward you."

Jubilee Bible 2000

"But thou, when thou prayest, enter into thy chamber, and when thou hast shut thy door, pray to thy Father who is in secret; and thy Father who sees in secret shall reward thee openly."

King James 2000 Bible

"But you, when you pray, enter into your room, and when you have shut your door, pray to your Father who is in secret; and your Father who sees in secret shall reward you openly."

American King James Version

"But you, when you pray, enter into your closet, and when you have shut your door, pray to your Father which is in secret; and your Father which sees in secret shall reward you openly."

American Standard Version

"But thou, when thou prayest, enter into thine inner chamber, and having shut thy door, pray to thy Father who is in secret, and thy Father who seeth in secret shall recompense thee."

Douay-Rheims Bible

"But thou when thou shalt pray, enter into thy chamber, and having shut the door, pray to thy Father in secret: and thy Father who seeth in secret will repay thee."

Darby Bible Translation

"But thou, when thou prayest, enter into thy chamber, and having shut thy door, pray to thy Father who is in secret, and thy Father who sees in secret will render it to thee."

English Revised Version

"But thou, when thou prayest, enter into thine inner chamber, and having shut thy door, pray to thy Father which is in secret, and thy Father which seeth in secret shall recompense thee."

Webster's Bible Translation

"But thou, when thou prayest, enter into thy closet, and when thou hast shut thy door, pray to thy Father who is in secret, and thy Father who seeth in secret, will reward thee openly."

Weymouth New Testament

"But you, whenever you pray, go into your own room and shut the door: then pray to your Father who is in secret, and your Father—He who sees in secret—will recompense you."

World English Bible

"But you, when you pray, enter into your inner room, and having shut your door, pray to your Father who is in secret, and your Father who sees in secret will reward you openly."

Young's Literal Translation

"But thou, when thou mayest pray, go into thy chamber, and having shut thy door, pray to thy Father who is in secret, and thy Father who is seeing in secret, shall reward thee manifestly" (biblical excerpts from the Bible Hub, hub.com/matthew/6-6.htm).

From the twenty-one different translation interpretations of Matthew 6:6 listed above, it's tough to tell exactly what God's intended meaning was about praying. There was no mention of what the reward was, and more importantly, it was sketchy on how he will present his award, externally through the mail or intrinsically through a bit more wisdom-enriched awareness of what the believer was asking for in their prayer dialogue. Or maybe the believer should just keep their eyes open after each time they pray for the next few days and ask themselves when something they perceive as being good or bad happens, if maybe the event represents God's answer to one of their prayer concerns about doubt X or worry Y.

This state of affairs needs deeper consideration by those who are ready to mortgage their souls' future for the present moment peace of mind that's anchored only by their blind faith in the unsubstantiated promise of afterlife peace and happiness from an invisible god. The feeling of camaraderie attached to two millennia worth of past believers makes this type of faith in blind trust acceptable and seemingly normal. There really should be a living sign for anyone to witness anytime, anyplace, showcasing the living nature of the religious claim's truth for new believers to build a heartfelt steadfast faith in that's blind to any second-guessing or childlike doubt.

Many people agree to put their fate in the hands of an unfamiliar unknown power they never get to at least shake sensual hands with to create a living relationship. The god Jehovah is humanized, sexed and given an omnipresent, all-knowing capacity of hopeful, yet unfounded problem solving. His flock is happy with simply internalizing the understanding that "The Lord works in mysterious ways?" This gives quick reason for cause/effect relationships there's no ready explanation for. It uses the assumed power of a higher authority to justify times when the effect of a cause/effect relationship seems unfair or unjust.

God's frequently asked to prevent or solve a problem, not asked how he does it so as to allow independently doing it in the future and thoughtfully saving him the time and trouble. Christianity teaches that mankind is created in his image.

Ask a Christian what that means and see how it takes to get a duplicate answer. Man should be able to recognize the same relational flow of this reality's cause/effect truth if his was the image of the Source that created it?

Christianity's god is assumed to have unchecked access to our inner being. He understands it far better than its host and he can monitor/control it. It's said by some that he's responsible for instilling their inspired insightful ideas. There are many who frequently look back over their shoulder to see if he's watching.

Acquiring the enlightened understanding of this reality that comes through attaining self-awareness holds no real priority in the realm of blind faith. The religion's fortitude of dependability is backed only by the believer's unquestioning acceptance of what happens during their present moment, understandable and mysterious, as being the expression of God's way.

Believers must live in a waking awareness fashioned by what satisfies their ego-managed consciousness. They're warned against trying to get to know or understand their inner self. They have to give their inner self the blind shoulder. Under the fancy robes and inside the magnificent church buildings, pointing up through their steeples to God, crafted from top quality materials are people who only see the side of the material reality they choose to see.

While in a state of blind faith awareness, it's believed that the wisdom that understands suffering originates from God above and not something that's shines from within. In a reality you're trained to intellectually conceptualize and not feel a believer makes effort to communicate with their god in their native verbal tongue.

They've not developed the sensual ear to be quiet and seek quiet introspective contemplative deliberation with awareness focused into our Source's message of ongoing wisdom-inspiring sensual dialogue. When trying to learn about something, there's a time to talk and there's a time to listen. This is the time to really understand what humility means.

When a religious believer calls upon their idea of the Source of this life force, this person-to-Source conversation is one-sided...human to god instead of god to human. Their ego's finger is stuck in their sensual ears while their mitote/maya voices originating from faulty prior conditioning shout out special requests all related to "me" or something or idea that is attached to "me." Their thought patterns that determine what they say in their monologue to their god usually involve rumination over past or worry about the future. Some pray for the success of the basketball team they drew at the office.

By the time the believer's thought patterns that carry the intended meaning of their prayer are mentally paired with the available words in their language to express those thought patterns, the primal feeling making up that intended message has probably been compromised or approximated to some degree to fit into the accepted meaning. The words that are used to relay the message to God represent how their language can best represent or approximate the original felt meaning that generated the topic of their prayer's request to God. By the time their felt concern's been distilled down and put into the verbal media, the inspiring concern's been diluted or maybe completely lost.

As the believer mentally chats in prayer through what's on their present moment mind, the prayer dialogue comes secured by a faith of hope that their god's in a good mood, not angry with them for some unknown thing which their internal judge keeps shouting "Guilty!" ...that they repeatedly blame themselves for.

This god's always held blameless for creating the situation for the suffering that's being prayed for relief from. Bad situations are excused as being his will that's being inflicted for some reason he might have that will work out good in the end or maybe it's that the believer's receiving their deserved punishment for some prior disobedience. He's held blameless for allowing the believer's perception of the situation, the way they look at it, to be one that causes them to suffer. God's held blameless for them seeing the glass as half empty instead of half full.

Often when nonbelievers or even believers are really involved in a sudden present moment fix, they'll openly beg to their god for mercy. They admit to the Guy upstairs that even though they don't deserve it, if only this one time, they'll never sin again if he'll just undo what bad thing might happen in a coming present moment of this waking lifetime. They'll worry about life after death later. It's probably better to ask him to undo the upcoming bad thing than to yell at him for letting it occur under his watch in the first place? Believers usually don't hold something bad against him until after its happened and they just can't see any relational justice in it at all.

They don't know how to listen to our Source's ongoing sensual message containing the key to the wisdom of life's truths and answers to their questions. They fail to realize any inspiration to recognize intuitively the relational insights from which to derive the common wisdom to enrich the waking awareness of what ongoing change does to the cause/ effect inter/intra-factor relationships in our reality.

There's no biblically suggested way to get God to do the talking and for them to be able to just sit back and learn during times of prayer. Rome's edition of the Bible gives no detail of how self-trained wisdom enrichment was accomplished 2,000 years ago. How could this process possibly be understood in today's Christian world?

After praying, a believer can only hope he heard their intellectually formulated and projected wishes. They can only hope that none of their deep feelings were lost as they selected the right words to describe their soul-felt thoughts while praying to God.

They will have to wear fundamentalist blinders now to avoid letting other explanations of our Source's nature and intended purpose slip into their belief system and challenge the delicate untested structure of what they've been told to be their illusionary account of what reality must apparently be. They must maintain the illusionary strength of the intellectual legs that support the original unverified religious claim to salvation from suffering. To start questioning any of the constructs of the bigger picture claim will start knocking out or weakening the crossbars of attachment that fortify its unchanging legs of support. They walk on eggshells.

Their decision to trust their fate to intellectually based truth verification standards shows that it's cool in their worldview to not be shown a living-in-this-present moment sign from above to verify the truth of the claim they've decided to internalize to explain the nature and purpose of our Source. In willingly taking the leap of blind faith they're agreeing not needing to be shown a personal living sign that the spark of life that will make true the religious claim's promised cause/effect sequence (religious theology opens up heaven and ends suffering) is alive and visible in the pulse of the present moment. This would allow a faith that's literally heartfelt and steadfast in our Source's omnipresent consistency to build in their worldview.

If a new believer is willing to venture out and trust their soul's destiny to the maker of an unverified religious claim and if that source promises to save their soul, why are they not given the secret as to why they suffer as time passes while they are living so they can undo it and spend the rest of their days living happily? There's still no saving buffer between the ignorance that allows suffering and the present moment unrest that results.

A steadfast faith grows from experiencing the sensual witnessing that strengthens an individual's awareness and allows them comfort when considering other religious theologies. They have strength to stand alone in its support. They understand how the religious claim's cause/effect sequence transpires as they've personally experienced it in action. A faith with no sensual grounding to establish willing and open confidence in exposes the human condition to the human experience unprotected from the unknown, still cautious of any confrontation.

Instead of going 'round and 'round in inner conversation about silent rumination that's directed at another entity for them to handle, self-train the mind control to end the rumination and better understand the problem so it's not necessary to have blind faith that another entity might handle it. Then better understand the twelve-step program serenity prayer about being able to accept what cannot be changed, to have the courage to act on and change what can be, and to have the wisdom to know the difference.

Those satisfied with a blind faith have to put up with the hell of everyday life for lack of options. Many still pray to God for relief from the pain they suffer in the present moment while believing or hoping they've already earned their promised future salvation.

They wait for some undefined future present moment to come for the same joy and happiness that's unknowingly available now if they would just develop an eye for the truth and seek guidance down the path of right moral behavior to self-train mind control to eventually self-train the wisdom to be enlightened about the ignorance that allows their suffering. The outside, unverified promise has coaxed hundreds of Muslim youth into ending their life by murderous suicide early to enjoy their teachers' promised worldly after-death pleasures.

Mistaking God's Promise for God's Wisdom

Christian believers trust that the main crux of Christian theology describing how Jesus died for mankind's sins to allow those who trust and believe in God's word to earn an afterlife free from suffering, to be God's wisdom. This unverified supposition is no more than a promise. Wisdom comes after an analysis of the cause/effect relationship in interactions between established elements of this reality.

The causal factors in this paradox have vaguely defined descriptions and the produced effect has no track record to reflect on. The proposed soul saving chain of circumstances has no verifiable experiential history that demonstrates any credibility of the claim-maker's ability to eliminate human suffering. An individual can really have no more than blind faith in the proposed causal factors actually producing the suggested effect of earning an alleged judgment day heaven free of suffering...whatever that untested reality might feel like.

Wisdom pertains to the interaction between causing factors and the resulting effects. Wisdom makes sense of or points out the best way to approach the latticework of causing constituents to best affect the desired outcome. The assessment process of expected effects is based on the analysis of an observed history of previous interactions.

The Christian mantra that Jesus died for mankind's sins to allow those that believe in God's word to attain an afterlife free from suffering doesn't have any historical reference. It has no record of ever being a part of the life force creating the present moment that's experientially verifiable in a way that any mature human can realize. It's a promise of a future event that's founded solely in a faith that's blind to understanding how a cause produces its effect or how an effect is linked to its cause. It calls for having blind trust in the borrowed wisdom of an unverifiable claim maker.

An Age of Blind Hope

A faith in the intended purpose of a claim while having no personal experience that in real sensual terms documents the living truth of the claim's intended purpose to help seed steadfast confidence in, is a faith that's blind to any personal understanding of what the effects of the cause (religious promise) should really feel like (heaven or not). This type of faith's secured by no more than an unfounded free-floating hope that something is going to happen that has at this time developed no history of any involvement in this reality's cause/effect process of living transformation.

The faith is based more in intellectual pride and not in sensual surety. The faith lacks having the soul-calming attribute gained from having been-there-done-that. It lacks the savvy for recognizing and knowing that the cause/ effect factors involved in the claim's living presence will come to pass, as its living involvement works toward future present moments. Any living involvement has yet to be documented.

The unaware individual guarded only by a faith founded in hope will continue through the day, fundamentally stiff to ongoing change with an infertile mind that's blind and inflexible to recognizing the benefits of working toward a productive change in the nature of their mind that generates their present moment intentions during their daily routine. As many others effectively release their potential through their special talents for the good of others, the frozen unaware are doing the sea of humanity a disservice. Furthermore, they don't acknowledge and probably cannot even recognize the good others are doing for the good that it really is. These observations make for excellent conversation starters.

They're not trying to be rude. They just don't think to support others on doing certain things that they don't take the time to realize as being important to the other's progress. The beauty in constructive change with effective leadership wise enough to recognize the direction to go will not come as quickly to an individual who pulls their faith out of their intellectual hat.

Blind Faith is a proud name for a misleading label that disguises an uncertain hope. It's a displaced trust. It has no sense of reference to any reasonable scale of proportion or rational probability to recognize the boundaries for what's really going too far to hope or ask God for. There's nothing to inspire real insight as to how a cause actually goes about changing into its effect. There's that void of uncertainty they have to cope and deal with.

Not founded in any real-time present moment living experience, a claim taking responsibility for our reality is wide open to illusion. It requires illusion. It allows individuals to pray for and often place a numbing present moment hope for the occurrence of a miracle...a rearrangement of reality's building blocks that only a god could do. The kind they've read about, yet probably have no living reference to.

The unsupported truth this blind faith is founded in has no detectable experiential premise on which to establish, back up and assure its future presence to serve as foundation for a faith in its dependable constancy and reliability. Christianity's claim to salvation has been caught up in an ongoing continual tweaking process since its Rome or Constantine OK'd its inception as the only permittable religion in AD 312. It changes right along with the political times and scientific advancements. It has no warranted constant to serve as foundation for the needed dependability base upon which to build a steadfast faith of vision.

Today, there's really no worldwide prevailing common understanding of what is meant by doing something for the greater cause. While viewing mankind's current presence, it's dissected regionally, ethnically, religiously, culturally. It's financially and physically separated by the compassion-proof borderlines of separate cultures and countries. During these times, humanity's not viewed as being made up of equal members from the same sea of humanity.

The now retired head of Rome's Catholic Church, who many actually believe to have a special connection with God himself, Pope Benedict XVI at the end of a weeklong trip to Australia, told 350,000 young pilgrims at a Mass in Sydney to shed the greed and cynicism of their time to create an "age of hope." The pope said it was up to a new generation of Christians to build a world in which God's gift of life is welcomed, respected and cherished—not rejected, feared as a threat and destroyed. The goal is "a new age in which hope liberates us from the shallowness, apathy and self-absorption which deadens our souls and poisons our relationships" (*USA Today* July 21, 2008, 7A).

Nondirected hope is what USA president Obama used as a campaign slogan in both elections he won.

A focused vision aimed at gaining awareness of the relational wisdom coming from our Source's intended purpose of initiating ongoing change is what's needed in liberating humanity from the shallowness, apathy and self-absorption which deadens our souls and poisons our relationships. Proactive behavior is needed to be directed at training mankind in the right ethical/moral behavior to allow self-training the right mental control to inspire the insightful wisdom to unlock the door of self-imposed ignorance to liberate humanity...understanding what's wrong or missing from the living present moment that allows the shallowness, apathy, greed, and self-absorption. This will not be found being led by a blind hope pointing skyward.

An age of hope is where those who've had no sensual glimpse at the present moment light that shines now as it did in the beginning look for answers. The sensually unfounded claims of religion corral these people as they wonder-wander. It gives them a set of commandments to help minimize and organize the living chaos that prevails within their collective mental state of mitote/maya unrest.

Believers Fail to Honor Their God and Attend to the Details of His Intelligent-Design Divine Intervention

Any consciousness preoccupied in blind faith, ever-pondering for an ever-more balanced understanding of the written abstract standards defining the posed truth of a god's unverified promise, lose touch with how important and relevant the role the state-of-life status of their mind and body actually is in securing the protection from suffering they stand locked in silent rumination to better understand.

—Anonymous

Should it be that a separate god entity created a human-occupied Earth among a countless number of galaxies and maybe even multiverses, it only makes sense that mankind would respectfully honor their god and show their appreciation by taking care of what he created...starting with themselves. It seems like there would be some tie to taking care of his handiwork in order to earn his approval to live with him up in heaven.

Just look at the collective waistline of Midwestern Christians.

Science comprises the fraction of humankind that has the gut-felt courage to query "Why?" or "Prove it!" Science represents mankind's free will. It wants to see proof before legitimizing any claim made about the relational justice inherent to our Source's unchartered coming and going bits of energy that give form to the ever-changing picture of life within the range of human perception that those who don't any better will form personal attachments to and suffer for.

God would surely appreciate mankind's understanding savvy with how things work in the transforming reality he created 6,000 years ago. This knowledge about the relational justice inherent to the cause/effect flow of this reality would enlighten his people with the conscious awareness about what it is they are ignorant about that makes them suffer. This accounts for many of the daily incidences they pray to him to lessen their suffering on and help them make it through.

This relational justice that echoes up from the interactions among the bits of energy in our subatomic world that give the perceivable shape to the forms and objects in this ever-changing reality holds true regardless of what entity gets credit for creating it. Should it be that there is a god in an elsewhere environment that mastered the creation of this cause/effect reality, his believers should honor his creation, as told to in 1 Corinthians 6:19–20, King James Version.

That due respect starts with their physical body they are told to respect as being their temple of the Holy Ghost. There is a difference in the minds of believers between the Holy Ghost depicted in religious theology and the one that is alive and sensually detectable as it's manifested within their human flesh. Believers can't connect their cognitive suppositions with what they experience in their waking reality. The intellectual vs. sensual tie-in's not there.

The imagined mental picture of a god up there overlooking all below has a nature of presence that doesn't change. The nature of the moment-to-moment sensual presence the true existence human bodies endure sends to the brain sensations that relay the feel of bubbling life. The body is no more that a process that's continually transforming into something more mature.

The cognitive depiction and actual sensual presence are different and not really associated together. Humans aren't built to connect or associate the different natures of existence together. They're not the same. One's recognized in an ever-present tingle and the other's conveyed through mental recall. In ignorance, they unknowingly build their worldview around one or the other while most are insensitive to there being any difference.

Thus, with many, there is no connection between their living bodies and the cognitive notion devoted to the security of their soul among all the uncertainty they experience that's associated with the ignorance they suffer through. Most proceed to treat their body with disregard.

As per modern-day religious guidelines, ignorance-reflecting gluttonous intentions, eating white flour, sugar, etc. don't really register in the Midwest as a Ten Commandments type of sin. These processed nutritional concoctions weren't around back in the day and even for those who had much food available to their liking, the food was organic, free of pesticides and nonprocessed.

The misguided thought patterns that signal the mouthwatering lure just aren't realized as being the same biblically described temptation that kept our ancient ancestors tied to the gates of hell centuries ago. They're everyday reality that lacks the grandeur of something ancient that played a part in our ancestors' life experience.

To playfully justify overeating when a friend might be watching, an individual might suggest how "nobody can eat just one," even though they might not be uncontrollably splurging on Lays potato chips.

A self-protecting unfettered free will would see more the value of being educated about nutrition and its relationship to the bigger picture. This due diligence is so easily satisfied in today's quick-to-access jungle of available information that's just a computer click away.

A modern-day term, binge-eating, has been coined that describes someone that's lost control over their eating habits. Many believers fail to recognize this urge to eat more and to ask themselves what it is they are really hungry for. Before overeating, do they stop to reflect on what their body is telling them? Does their body really need nutrition or are they attempting to satisfy an emotional hunger? Do those who recognize the benefits of healthy eating merely for the health benefits or do they couple it with the thought of respecting God?

Many individuals can tell you exactly why they need to use the new synthetic motor oil to help preserve the life of their car's engine, but have blocked out considering how the life of the engine of their body depends so greatly on what types of oil they run through it. An unfettered free will would perform due diligence to know the baseline, nonsubjective truth about what something does to their body. God would appreciate this.

An unfettered free will would choose the feeling of being healthy over having to loosen the belt and take a nap only to satisfy a fleeting reactionary addictive want of the misguided foodaholic voice in their mitote/maya ruled head. Most have no clue about what "food addiction" is. They may refuse to have dinner with someone who is a known alcoholic without considering who really does the most physical self-harm at the table...a foodaholic or an alcoholic?

Alcoholics have earned the bad reputation because alcohol used out of moderation does do harm to the physical body that God created. Many blame alchohol consumption for the release of an individual's demons that result in their unacceptable behaviors. Many Christians completely abstain from drinking any alcohol and that is a sort of overkill, as it's known that moderate amounts of alcohol can be healthy. Jesus condoned the drinking of wine as he on occasion changed water into wine. Over the ages this truism tagged to the abuse of alcohol has turned alcohol consumption into being something that is considered by many to be bad overall and shunned. In today's world, it has no real basis. Complete abstinence has developed into a sacrificial ritual of sorts that's aired in a state of hypocritical blindness?

Believers don't recognize the biblical wrongness of how the poisonous foods of today have the type of harmful physical effects attached to alcohol abuse. They don't associate the modern-day incarnations of the don'ts of biblical theology when they appear in present moment living. They don't associate their irresistible desire to eat today's concoctions of salt, fat and sugar on the same plateau with their intellectually registered understanding of what a biblical temptation or a biblical sin might be.

When the harm to the body that God created that's done through the misuse of food is considered, it quickly becomes clear how many more people die from heart disease, diabetes and cancer alone than from cirrhosis of an alcoholic's liver. These diseases are caused largely through food abuse.

Awareness of just this one religiously minimized modern-day truths would help to free an individual from the suffering caused by the ignorance of its ways. Instead, they choose to develop a belief system muffled by the intellectually calculated and rather apathetic notion that their god will relieve their suffering after they die with the comfort from a promised, yet never experienced heaven with a vaguely described nature that's foreign to their life experience. Until then they blindly deny and choose to remain ignorant about the change-related truths that threaten the stability of the illusionary supporting agenda of their ego-managed apparent reality.

When a believer's truth-assessment willpower is locked up by a fundamentalist worldview, biblical life and real-time present moment life are quite disjointed. They continue living day-by-day, suffering in the ignorance of how our reality actually makes perfect cause/effect relational sense.

Many fundamental Christians don't associate their god and the expressions of his power with being the living part of their real-time presence...thus they don't invest the same conviction to taking care of their physical body as they do to memorizing the verses of one of the translations of the Bible.

Religion's Realm in the Human Experience Doesn't Register in the Primal Region of the Human Condition

The presence of religious theology is purely a phenomenon of the conscious mind, and it doesn't contribute to the heartbeat of truth that it makes claim to. Religion's presence in the conscious awareness of the human condition is no more than an incarnation of a type of suffering caused by blindly internalizing the purpose of an unverified claim that's purpose isn't designed to find its truth in a reality whose nature is to be in constant motion. It needs an illusionary reality with a nature that allows things to have a permanent presence.

In this state of waking consciousness, the consideration of mind and body involve different states of consciousness application. Believers with blind faith in something they have no real-time experience with have thoughts that are formed from percolated illusionary notions of some anticipated future outcome that's wrapped around their confidence in the continual presence of something. Religion's expectations are just one form of expecting and anticipating results that can't happen in a reality where nothing ever stops. A believer's expectations end up being miscued when reality really happens, and they suffer.

A Disclaimer is in Order

In these modern times, more disclosure and transparency are being offered to make unnecessary the need to make assumptions about what's going on. To help answer any questions an involved party might have at the time of exchange will help avoid problems at a later time down the road. Open disclosure of the details of how a deal transpires from cause to effect, sort of warranties or at least helps make clear a process's inner workings. It gives the involved party a feel for what's going on.

There needs to be an objective disclaimer attached to any process that requires a believer's trusting faith that leaves them blind to understanding the hows and whys of the workings of the intermediate process that connects making the promise of what reality is, where it came from, and where its future lies with when the promise actually comes true.

Any unverifiable religious theology needs to specify that anyone who internalizes the life after death purpose of the religious claim needs to understand that it has no sensual evidence to validate the purpose of its claim...its truth. It needs to warn that for the claim to have its described and promised effect, the dimensional characteristics of the reality must have a continual nature to allow the attachment the claim inspires. For the religious claim's cause/effect process to transpire, it has to allow for the attachment to things and ideas that's not possible in an impermanent reality.

Most who live today in this impermanent reality imagine this illusionary attachment to be possible. They create an illusionary world, and their ego manages their experience of suffering through all miscued intentions and reactionary emotions...like the guilt this theology inspires. This is the ignorance they need to become enlightened about.

The disclaimer should warn of the danger or risk of internalizing this claim that's backed only by the integrity of the source of the claim, that there's no experientially realized evidence of the living presence of the religious claim's suggested maker. It should warn that blame for the claim's nonperformance should lie solely in the believer's act of believing its premise. It should go on to inspire the reader with how the cause of the suffering can be highlighted, quarantined, understood and eliminated in this lifetime.

Religious Mind-Set Typifies Haphazard Learning Aptitude

This writing is not trying to bully Midwestern Christianity. The promise made in religious theology is just one example of the type of claim that's believed and internalized without first verifying that the contributing factors that produce the claim's purpose can work together to manifest the claim's promise or truth in the relational justice inherent to this impermanent reality...that it doesn't inspire some form of attachment. Wholeheartedly believing something to be true without first substantiating that what it says it can do can actually happen in this impermanent reality is a mistake many people make when accepting as true and internalizing the belief about the claims made about many things.

The soul-saving claim made by a religious discipline is just one example of this. At one time or another, everyone is too quick to believe something, but the mismatched cause/effect results are measured on a much smaller scale. Religious theology's relevance stands out because of the effects it has on this world's stability. Its relevance involves the legacy and eternal future of an individual's soul. The religious mind-set warps the entire global mind-set.

12

Crippled Free Will
Uses Fundamentalist Crutch

Mum's The Word Breeds Dogmatic Inflexibility

When an individual decides to be labeled Christian, they are agreeing to minimize the importance and ignore the significance of never having experienced the conscious awareness found when sensually witnessing the living presence of their god. This experience demonstrates the living relevance and supports the blind out of their blind faith in the likelihood of him fulfilling his promise to send his followers to an eternal heaven free if suffering.

This demonstration should be in a way that's available for all to see and not just a special few. This leap of faith muffles the free will's urge to get a firsthand understanding of what the sensual incarnate of the Holy Spirit is at this very moment. It's replaced with holding on to a mental sketch from an intellectual description of how the Holy Spirit is described in the Bible.

Believers are consenting to live by the book of established moral/ethical rules that evolved from mankind's collective deeper consciousness around 3,000 years ago when it was realized that these actions that might up front appear to be pleasurable, actually caused suffering that really benefited nobody. Religious followers say their god etched his demands in stone on Mount Sinai. It doesn't really matter how the human perception of the effects of these taboo behaviors congealed into public policy or what entity gets credit for it.

It's a fact that Rome's Bible was pieced together and selectively edited by humans under Constantine's watch...God-inspired or not. A new believer is agreeing to deaden their free will's protective function of doubting and questioning what's not understood to defend the purpose of an unverified religious claim that explains how it will account for and eternally watch over their soul.

Religions' behavioral/moral standards attempt to corral the masses. Terrorist organizations hide behind religious causes. It's clear that with their said barebones fundamentalist interpretations, they make use of their religion to mask their treachery. Any religion's charter-rules provide an untestable claim to reaching a heaven with salvation from suffering with an intellectually defined path to follow. Individual interpretations will vary.

Religious fundamentalism serves as a hardcore antidepressant/antianxiety pill meant to put a safety cap on the need for answers to the muffled questions that arise in the absence of firsthand evidence. The uncertainty-based fear that internalizing the religious promise creates can be detected in the believers' tight clenched fists when faced with a challenge from outside doubt.

Some consider this kind of hard-nosed unforgiving rigidity administered from the top in this way to be fascism. Maybe that only applies to human regimes? After choosing not to further question the explanation offered by the religion's claim defining who we are, where we came from and where our souls are going, the void of feeling left in the new believer's belief system is filled with a fundamental set of book-chapter-verse Band-Aids to ward off and seal out outside challenges to the purpose of the religious claim that remain unanswered deep within the new believer.

After being warned by popular religious personalities, not to look inside, most believers decline to make any attempt to further understand their deeper consciousness. In Christianity, after the Roman Bible's edit and mandated destruction of all accounts of his other teachings and those of competing religions, believers have no record to follow for guidance of any self-exploration technique taught by Jesus. An illusionary understanding of reality maybe better left undisturbed and unquestioned, so not to awaken any old demons?

It was brought to attention earlier how using borrowed, received, or intellectual knowledge to shape one's belief system is restrictive to spiritual advancement. Having only blind faith when internalizing, accepting or believing received or mere intellectual knowledge at face value without first verifying the living validity of the truth and the nature of its claim experientially, lets the knowledge become a form of bondage and a barrier against really learning our Source's truth experientially.

It could be that the original sin Christians are warned that mankind is born with is the human tendency for an individual to shape their worldview from a belief system trained at the hand of intellectually acquired and founded, experientially unverified knowledge. The weakness is continually nurtured by continued eating of the fruit from the tree of knowledge, like Adam and Eve. Actions coming from intentions based on unverified misinformation acquired from misguided prior conditioning unwise to the folly of any notion that entertains activity in a reality with a continual nature that allows attachment stands as a barrier to lifting the ignorance that causes present moment suffering.

The Vietnamese Buddhist teacher Thich Nhat Hanh offers insightful wisdom concerning the effects of having one's reliance only on knowledge and views attained solely through borrowed or intellectual knowledge. He observed that this is an obstacle to true understanding and insight and that this ideological inflexibility puts at a distance where the truth about our Source lies. It's the source of dogmatic fanaticism.

> The Buddha regarded his own teaching as a raft to cross the river and not as an absolute truth to be worshipped or clung to. He said this to prevent rigid dogmatism or fanaticism from taking root. Ideological inflexibility is responsible for so much of the conflict and violence in the world. According to Buddhist teaching, knowledge itself can be an obstacle to true understanding, and views can be a barrier to insight. Clinging to views can prevent us from arriving at a deeper, more profound understanding of reality.[21]

...Skirting The Question

Most individuals don't care to understand how they're plagued with suffering's present moment thorn in the side state of unrest. They've convinced themselves that the life they live is normal. They don't see how ever-present their suffering is and how its premise leaked as the effect coming from the ideologies their worldview has about life in this reality and how these ideals fail too often in matching up with the rhythm this reality insists to work into all cause/effect outcomes.

They have nothing to motivate them to discover the process of identifying and eliminating its cause. They will elect to take refuge in their unique mental sketch of a religious promise to have an eternal suffering-free life after death awarded for following a set of behavioral guidelines without knowing why these guidelines were chosen or how the relational justice in mankind's real-life interacting generated them. There's no travel brochure giving real detail to this promised Shangri-La.

Even so, the stick-in-the-side festering wound never heals. In recognizing their life as normal, some will learn to mistake their uneasiness with the trials and tribulations coming from unexpected change for modern-day happiness. Following a religion's behavioral manual, they will strip their free will of its built-in questioning function.

It will have them living by rhyme supported by no reason. They crawl into their human shell, blind to understanding their human condition that's alive inside, waiting for a promised heaven to bring love, joy and compassion to their human experience.

...Social Belonging Secured

When someone feels the significance of their social belonging threatened, one fundamentalist defense that helps reassure the believer of their self-confidence and realitive social self-worth is when they silently remind themselves of how many biblical scriptures they have memorized. They think that no matter what the situation may appear as, they can take much pride in knowing that they are probably a comparatively much wiser person than the others present, secured by the magnitude of their biblical memorizations.

One interaction option is for them to choose to bully those with whom they might be discussing something with, with a related meaning found in the Bible. They offer an unbending configuration of the meaning they imagine the fine details of the story described in the version described in one of the thousands of different Bible translations to be. They usually can't offer any real adaptive meaning or real tie-in between their biblical wisdom and present-day situations. They prove to be incapable of compromising any of the security they gain from what they imagine the meaning to be.

When the threatening discomfort from social awkwardness can't be shaken any other way, a fundamentally bound believer might rationalize that the others present aren't members of the same branch of the church as they are and don't adhere to the same biblical wisdom. They have to be sinners and there's no real need to communicate with them, as they don't see things the right way, as does their congregation.

Over time, this state of mental isolation will be secured only by their blind faith in their calculated explanation of this unverified, poorly defined abstract world of promise of future mental peace, made in the times of the remote past. They lose touch with appreciating the justice found in the simple beauty found in real-time living.

They've built an impenetrable and unyielding fundamentalist firewall that isolates them from the fair exchange of heartfelt ideas. Family and friends will dread entering into one of these totally one-way broadcasts where any sincere eye contact gets replaced with one full of a threatening yearn to understand and agree. The knowledge that this is unlikely, taken from past experience, only fans the fire. There are impassable constraints rooted in a uniquely tailored fundamentalist opinion that hover over all the decisions made by family members. Present moment life in the Midwest just doesn't happen in the biblical sense.

...Rocking From Pitch to Pitch Perpetuates Imbalance

Religious fundamentalist thinking follows a written script set in a non-defined futuristic dreamland. With no living link to connect this scripted religious panacea to the sensually alive present moment, an individual mentally sketches a picture that depicts living in their god's after-death land of bliss. A personalized intellectual rendition that describes this heaven is all there is to relate to.

Having to intellectually draw and redraw or remember this religious pitch after leaving it to attend to a present moment real-life activity interrupts the flow of a believer's mental calendar. It's the type of thing that after waking up in the morning, an individual has to remember and reconstruct the details outlining the religious promise instead of waking up and just knowing it. They have to remember it, then wait to see how it effects the mood they're in. Then they remember what they last thought about it and rationalize how they now feel about it.

The believer is riding the ups and downs of the sensually recognized present moment to then have to jump back into a nondescript intellectually filed religious reality. This leaves them standing in the sensual present moment looking to the promise of an ultra-state of reality when they need answers to living in the present moment state of reality. They could really use a more aware perspective to better understand it.

After an individual loses touch with their free will's inborn ability to verify the nature and real-time living presence of a claim's purpose, they're doomed to coping with a mitote/maya state of mind that's full of notions with purposes of intent having continual natures laced with inclinations toward attachments to clinging or aversion. Their free will is numbed insensitive from allowing the uncheck internalization of too many unverified claims. Their self-confidence in their prowess with questioning things is crippled with a growing self-doubt they never felt when they were in the innocence of their younger years.

...Living in an Emotional Illusion

The underuse of an individual's much needed claim verification process results in having an infectious ignorance-spreading virus concerning our Source's nature and intended purpose of providing unchanging ongoing change. This virus of ignorance piggybacks its way into an individual's belief system every time their free will allows the purpose of an claim that's not privy to the savvy of ongoing change to further hone their worldview.

It makes one blind and insensitive to the relational relevance of the truly impermanent nature of our Source. Their mental platform will entertain an ongoing open party line conversation between 1,000 unrelated voices making havoc within their mind...confused and undecided. Their present moment will lack direction and be dominated by a fleeting form of frustration.

Having not yet recognized that this reality is in an unchanging state of impermanence and not having developed a spiritual appetite to better understand what this truth means, an individual often chooses one of the available religious/spiritual templates to internalize and center their worldview around...they bite their lip and take a leap of blind faith.

They tell themselves they should believe one of the many religious claims describing our Source's nature and intended purpose. The leap of faith these religious groups prescribe is a leap over a void of questionable uncertainty created in their belief system's anatomy by not having any personally witnessed experiential evidence of the religious claim's present moment living involvement in the same reality that will one day be host to Jesus as he comes down to Earth to save the obedient individuals and send the rest to

spend eternity in hellfire and brimstone.

Taking a leap of blind faith between any claim and its resulting effect leaves open a newly created void-lapse in the anatomy of an individual's belief system. Between hearing any claim that offers explanation to any causing factor and the effect of believing it, there's a void missing any assuring feeling of its living truth. This spawns a guarded unanswered uncertainty, loyal to the claim that has so daringly been internalized. They remember how their friend they respect enough to believe their account of this religious claim seemed to take pride in professing their blind faith.

There is no causing claim-to-resulting-effect connection signaled by any living sign to affect any feeling of the claim's right now real-time present moment involvement they can sensually witness. The religious claim's only involvement is the intellectual promise that's been internalized while the believer then hangs suspended in their illusionary intellectually understood abstract adaptation to what reality should apparently be like after death...as imagined in the intellectual regions of their waking consciousness.

...Touchy and too Skittish to Adapt

It can take a lot to admit to being wrong on any decision...especially when involving the nature and purpose of the Source of our reality. After committing to religious claim, a blind faith believer can be very insensitive to any alternative explanations describing our Source.

Until this lock on lateral thinking is removed, the individual will not be able to ask the right questions to understand that it's the present moment suffering they experience that defines the present moment hell they've been promised protection from in the present moments after they die. Until they realize that, they will be unable to recognize and mentally navigate the pathway to undoing the ignorance that allows it.

In the Midwest, many Christians take pride in having the guts to put their cards on the line and dare to take the leap and have a blind faith harbored in their belief system. They're so spitefully sure what they did was the right thing to do... some would, in needless defiance or uncertain wonder, defend it to their death.

Christianity's defenders quote the scriptures to prove their truth. There are some verified correlations between times and events found in the Old Testament that have been established. Guarded by a waving Bible in one hand, they'll stand stubbornly determined to shoot down any and every objection questioning their resolute. They assume it to be real because it's written in the scriptures and the scriptures are true.

This assurance sees them through day after day, year after year until the realization surfaces that when they die, no matter how loud they shout halleluiah or what their projected protocol is for how their soul is to be dealt with, they consciously realize that, really, everybody is going to be dealt with in the same way. They have no experientially based pitch to stage their religious projection on.

Their frail surety wavers when the thought involving their unavoidable death brings them down to a more practical view of reality. They react to surfacing pinpricks of uncertainty and unfamiliarity. Deep down inside, in the same subtle region of their deeper consciousness that house their awareness of the truth of impermanence is the gut-felt awareness that their waking explanation is but an illusion.

They took the leap of blind faith in effort to bring organization and calming order to lessen their state of mental unrest caused by their unique and growing mitote/maya state of mind. Part of their adopted illusion included the attainment of their imagined description of a promised heaven after death if they recognize the Holy Trilogy or a hell after death if they don't. Just ask any Christian what heaven or hell is like. There will be no two descriptions the same. It all comes from an unfounded illusionary pool of intellectually founded imagery.

They drift into an illusionary reality...an emotional dream minefield embedded with their own unique collection of addictions. This fix on the present moment helped them bide their time while searching and pillaging through things and ideas to meet the ever-changing and endless demands of the 1,000 voices of their resident mitote/maya state of confusion while unknowingly keeping a sensual eye pealed for a connection to the truth their deeper consciousness silently longs to release into their unaware waking consciousness.

...A Searching Hope Subdued by Fear and Uncertainty

Fear warns of danger. It might be a recognized threat coming from a similar experience. It might appear as caution to the untested parameters of an unfamiliar situation. Fear of the unknown is a most basic and soul-rattling state of fear. It's primal to the human experience.

There's an immediate sort of deep-down discontent with the present moment and a knotted-up hope in search of its relief. Religious dogma is centered on this very searching hope.

Fear's presence brings an instinctual code red signal that highlights a threat to human self-preservation. Fear is the physiologically generated warning sensually perceived that comes with an apparent threat of physical harm or thoughts of a future with undefined and untested parameters. It's the comingling of an anxious mind and an alert body.

Fear of the unknown comes when a child thinks there's a boogieman under their bed or in their closet. As a child grows older and through their due diligence they're assured the conditions just aren't right for an undefined boogie man to be a cause within the ring of real circumstances to result in their feared effects. With a more wisdom-enriched understanding of the true reality, their fear of the unknown has been minimized.

Fear of the unknown comes if an individual neglects their due diligent questioning of the intended purpose of a new claim that was mistakenly believed to be true and internalized, like the notion of there being a boogieman. Fear from uncertainty comes when unknown factors remains at bay.

They have never actually held their finger to the flame to get a sensually felt experience of the claim's living participation in the passing of time as it fulfills the promise its intended purpose is supposed to provide...heat. A claim's verified purpose of intent leaves an experiential imprint of what happens between the cause and its effect to tie them together...the feeling of hot between striking the match and the sensation of the flame. No promised purpose of intent that's only intellectually justified can effectively explain the sensual adventure unleashed by the flame of any claim.

By having a claim's purpose of intention experientially burned into their experiential files, like that of a hot flame, they can feel secure in understanding what the claim's purpose is about. When different religious or spiritual theories explain different means to reach the same end (suffering-free heaven), if they've experienced the journey down the road from the claims promise to realizing its effect, they can then dare to discuss these other means to that same end. They don't have to reference written material and pull reason from their intellectual memory files... they have experiential files on hand or in hand to refer to. They speak from their hearts and not from their heads.

Their belief systems are not waxed gross, wearing blinders, consumed by narrow-minded fundamentalism. They can pass an essay exam on the subject at hand without having to quote any book, chapter, and verse as when justifying the cause/effect validity of something that has never been experienced.

For many people, their present moment attempts at taking action to find direction falls short, leaving them suspended in a cloud of perpetual hesitancy, reluctance and doubt, dangling in a primal void of uncertainty inspired fear of the unknown. It's a state of having one's purpose or cause locked up in the ignorance of how things really work in an impermanent reality and being afraid of what the real truth is that's hiding in the dark unexplored regions of their deeper consciousness. Maybe the real truth looks just like that ole boogieman?

This fear compromises the entire belief system of any individual or society it infects. Their spiritual progress is numbed by ignorance and can't see the wisdom of the true relational interplay in between a cause and its effect. Those sleepwalking down the intellectual pathway of a world known intellectually will repeatedly stumble over their mind-numbing blanket of fear of the unknown as it blurs the visionary possibilities available when living in a reality they can feel.

Their fear of the unknown that over time fills the void of uncertainty in their belief system is the breeding ground for their apathy that infects the potential of every passing present moment. Their free will can become completely deaf to any outside plea to listen to other claims about the intended purpose behind the bigger picture. At the best it's very unlikely they will be capable of hearing any alternate message with an unbiased ear. This fear feeds on the ungrounded uncertainty making it a moment-to-moment ongoing presence in their waking reality that is reflected in all their thoughts and behavior.

...Mind Waxed Gross to Seeing the Truth

Today's assortment of causes to fuel spiritual confusion has added depth and grown much more interlayered since the days of Jesus and Siddhartha. There are now all the developed religious vindications to sort through with the confusing "-anity" and "-ism" conjectures that lay claim to it all.

Still, in those days, as today, individuals had to contend and struggle with the curse of human ignorance concerning our Source's, our reality's nature of impermanence. This seemingly inborn human perpetuity to develop ignorance about the nature of the reality they live in could almost be considered the original sin? Today, like in the days of chariots and crucifixes, the ignorant suffer and long for the answer.

Since the long-ago times of our spiritual icons that they make movies about today, people have had to effectively sort through and realistically deal with more layers of societal membership expectations to maintain the unfettered nature of their free wills. Today, there are many more kinds of media involvement to distract and depolarize an individual's internal compass.

Many companies who use the media spend a lot of money to learn how to best attract the attention of people to convince them to buy what they're hired to sell to them. Many tools are used ingeniously...greed...pride...guilt...etc...In the Midwest, older citizens who are used to the days when it wasn't necessary to lock their doors are blindsided by salespeople who know what mask to wear to best play their trusting nature to legally con them out of their money. With today's economy the way it is, it's a safe bet that nine out of ten person-to-person sales situations fall into this category.

The greatest mind hypnotizers, the love of money and trying to second guess the ways of the world have more ways of possible involvement in today's world than that of those from long ago who offer guidance on reaching heavenly enlightenment. Recognizing the truth relating to what living is like in an impermanent reality when one of its present moment incarnations comes to an individual's attention is less likely today. They can't decipher its significance, even when it's right under their nose.

Today's society pressures its citizens to be content members of one faith or another. Indiana doesn't charge its Christian citizens for specialty license plates that voice their trust/faith in God.

Jesus used a parable to best relate his message about the significance of what motivates the inner mind and how an individual's eye for the truth can be blinded. He taught of how a mind waxed gross keeps human awareness at bay to the truth.

Jesus tells of a sower and how they chose to use their inborn potential failed to be the one that was the best for letting their light shine and releasing their inner genius. The most productive behavior failed to be perceived by those with their minds waxed gross, preoccupied by worldly interests while being misled by the deceitfulness of riches.

> And in them is fulfilled the prophecy of Esaias, which saith, By hearing ye shall hear, and shall not understand: and seeing ye shall see, and shall not perceive:
>
> For this people's heart is waxed gross,
>
> and their ears are dull of hearing, and their eyes they have closed: lest at any time they should see with their eyes, and hear with their ears, and should understand with their heart, and should be converted, and I should heal them.
>
> But blessed are your eyes, for they see: and your ears, for they hear.
>
> For verily I say unto you, That many prophets and righteous men have desired to see those things which ye see, and have not seen them: and to hear those things which ye hear, and have not heard them.
>
> Hear ye therefore the parable of the sower. When any one heareth the word of the kingdom, and understandeth it not, then cometh the wicked one, and catcheth away that which was sown in his heart. This is he which received seed by the way side.
>
> But he that received the seed into stony places, the same is he that heareth the word, and anon with joy receiveth it: yet hath

he not root in himself, but dureth for a while: for when tribulation or persecution ariseth because of the word, by and by he is offended.

He also that received seed among the thorns is he that heareth the word; and the care of this world, and the deceitfulness of riches, choke the word, and he becometh unfruitful.

But he that received seed into the good ground is he that heareth the word, and understandeth it; which also beareth fruit, and bringeth forth, some an hundredfold, some sixth, some thirty (Matthew 13:14–23, King James Version).

Jesus taught of the mind-arresting effect that being mused by the world and mislead by its riches has on one's ability to be objectively open and perceptive to hearing and seeing the truth when presented it. Someone with their belief system tied up in an illusionary apparent reality after being deceived and mislead by worldliness and riches will have a heart that's waxed gross to hearing or seeing the truth even when its glow shines directly on their faces.

Today, even if they somehow could intellectually recognize primal truth criteria, they would lack the steadfast faithbacked courage to step outside their religious definitions of what truth is and voice their questioning objection among their peers.

They choose to exist in the discomfort they're familiar with, rather than to step into the void of unfamiliarity and uncertainty to stand-alone. This is a silent dilemma of the heart the vast majority of the Midwestern culture has grown accustom to. There's no eye for the truth or courage needed to open up to look inside where it manifests itself to witness it...unbiased by predetermined expectations.

In today's world, many people confine their spiritual quest to the politically safe realms of the local religious claim explaining heavenly freedom from suffering. The unaware individual's belief system and worldview have been waxed gross and are too unsure to say or even think anything different than the intellectual prescription they've decided to ingest and for many, to choke down.

They've taken a leap of blind faith over a necessary step in the anatomy of their belief system calling for the living and experientially verified proof of a claim's cause/effect connection. Ideological inflexibility results as they have nothing to base their related actions on other than the written plan that accompanied the untested unverified claim. This is another coat of wax to make more obscure the individual's inborn ability to self-train their ability to develop a wisdom-enriched understanding of our Source's nature of impermanence to undo the ignorance that brings their suffering.

Their mind's been waxed gross to recognizing the truth explaining our Source's nature and intended purpose of providing ongoing change not only by worldly interests and the deceitfulness of money, but now in today's world, also by their involvement in an "-anity" or an "-ism" that's developed over the past two millennia. In blindly believing the promise made by a religious claim, they've crawled into a religious shell of fundamental stubbornness that can be really hard to crack.

...Spinning Blindly in Fundamentalist Denial

There were no figures available as to what percentage of Christians have the Ten Commandments memorized? Yet, they pave the pathway to heaven. How much confidence do they really have in this religious plans effectiveness? Is their religious option really anything more than the best option they can recognize in their life circumstance? Doesn't the conflicting natures of an eternal heaven with no real defined state of presence and a changing real life consciousness separate the two?

The religious believer's inner compass spins nonstop, wanting to reset to its true north. It seeks direction. In their heart they want to consciously realize the passion that will expose their unique genius while they are still living. Their excitement will motivate the needed development and give meaning and definition to their life. Their passion and behavior can meld.

They coil up tighter and tighter after deciding to "blind" their free will's foresight ability. They must sacrifice valuable thinking-time energy to sustain an on-alert cognitive readiness, the scripted behavioral boundaries of a pseudo soul-security promise they've sworn allegiance with.

They entrust their soul's eternal future to this state of blind trust. They're no longer as relaxed and ready to feel a reaction to something now that their mind's using nervous energy to stay cognitively clinched to the details of the religion's written word when any related soul-related topic gets mentioned.

A lifestyle energized by a belief system and worldview now branded, as "God fearing" is one lived by God's chosen ones who plan to be saved from the sensual agony of an entire eternity spent in hellfire and brimstone. This is believed to be a good normal lifestyle.

There's a true primal justice found in the relational interplay between all cause/effect factors in this reality that we all answer to that's misunderstood and unfamiliar to most. To make some sort of rational sense of this reality, many adopt a religion's claim to how things fit together. This sets into motion a dogmatic spin that will continue to unfold. It grows into a whirlwind that soon assumes its own force that's too strong to break free of.

An individual trying to cope while piecing together an illusionary worldview based on anything but the truth of how life's cause/effect trade-off actually fits together, poses a challenge similar to fitting a square peg into a round hole. It just doesn't match up. The heat from the friction continually burns away at their peace of mind.

It's usually the objective perspective of reality that gets pared down, bent into shape and convincingly rationalized to a fitting size. The true connection between cause and effect gets dusted with illusionary magic powder, tweaked by the spin of seemingly harmless white lies that allow reality to bend a bit to make it fit into and become consistent with a believer's illusionary account of how the certain cause and effect factors of a situation should be tied together.

If an individual is faced with natural facts that deny one of the imagined facets of their religion-imposed illusion that now defines their worldview, bending toward the natural fact would necessitate real change that could completely upset the fragile balance of the scales of justice that weigh their compromised or rationalized self-understanding of who they are and how important they may seem or simply how they fit in.

The older their illusionary castle, the stronger their ego manager objects to any change. The individual spends their days' energy just trying to maintain any equilibrium they imagine exists in their personal rendition of what reality is.

The resident internal judge, as described by Mr. Ruiz that sits gazing over the individual's shoulder into their mitote/maya-ruled illusionary apparent reality, continually and unforgivingly raps the gavel of guilt on their free will's forehead. Their self-belief is protected only by a spot-on blind faith of hope. The victim in this illusionary reality courtroom shrinks back into denial, quick to rationalize and completely incapable of objective focus on the true interplay among the actual real-time facets of the cause/effect situation.

Their mind and body remain complete strangers to each other. They don't appreciate the common ground of impermanence shared in harmony between their physical body and their aware mind...how one actually depends on the other...the potential beauty and rhythm of it all. The potential for finding their enlightenment by understanding the impermanent connection between them with sustained concentration focused into the naturally harmonious coexistence of the two is miles away from becoming a conscious possibility. Their spiritual vision is cut short and blinded by the white noise of the mental chatter of their mitote/maya they've allowed to gradually drug their free will and take hostage their belief system.

They have no truly suffering-free end in focus. Without removing the cause of their suffering, it will continue to reappear. Changing their worldview is threatened by their fear of the personal and public exposure that would reveal how weak, average, and vulnerable they truly are.

The deeper conscious awareness of the self-evident truth of impermanence remains obscured by their unsettled waking consciousness. It's weighed down by the unanswered loose ends coming from misguided prior conditioning that's endless assortment of unrelated claims rules their belief systems while they string together an illusionary worldview. They have developed no eye for finding the key to unlock the doors of denial to let surface their inner awareness of the truth of impermanence. Their wall of fear is too tall...too thick.

They need to first begin at least intellectually, the gradual process of recognizing the nature of their thought patterns and releasing those of the prior conditioning that condone the ignorance allowing attachment that allows their suffering. They must synthesize an intellectual understanding into the experiential wisdom that unveils the awareness of the truth of our Source's nature and intended purpose to initiate ongoing change.

Individuals in denial are comparatively slower at getting the connection when discussing the everyday interplay between relationships in this time-fueled cause/effect reality. They get lost in or have to work around and find compromise with various misleading unverified beliefs, ideas or concepts they've chiseled down to represent and support their worldview.

Sometimes they never do get the point as its objective account will just be neutered, stored, and categorized as just another denied or misunderstood facet of this reality. This only compounds the growing imbalance between their idea of how things should be and how they really are. They simply deny the truth that stares them in the face as they slide naked into the unforeseen surprise offered by the next unanticipated upcoming present moment in time.

...Frozen from an Enlightened Understanding of the Nature of this Reality

Denying The Self-Evident Truth That Ties the human condition into being a part of this impermanent reality that proven-evidence documents as being our Source's historical path of change separates the fundamentalist believer from consciously participating and appreciating the truth of our Source's nature to change. It builds a wall between the truth their deeper consciousness knows they are a part of and their conscious mind that's too full of fear of the unknown to develop a wisdom-enriched understanding of the cause/ effect justice it enforces.

A fundamentalist view locked in blind faith to a religious theology that denies the proven evidence of this reality's timely historical development will distance the believer from associating their living presence with the actual source of this reality. Having the relaxed recognition of this reality to develop an understanding awareness of its impermanent nature is stopped short by the static coming from the denial of its developmental truth.

The believer drapes a film over their perceptive awareness. They consciously tie one side of their brain behind their back. It becomes blind to the plethora of sensually coded explanatory knowledge, attainable within its coming and going presence that pulsates as the essence of their physical presence. Being able to squander up enough mental reserve to self-train the mind/body harmony to venture into that inner lecture hall just won't happen. They forcefeed a religious parody into their belief system to support some degree of an opinionated and insensitive worldview.

There will be no self-training of an enlightened understanding of the ignorance about this reality's impermanence that brings on suffering. If an individual cannot recognize, acknowledge and respect something's origin, there's no way they will let themselves develop a conscious understanding of its nature. This is evident in how different races treat each other.

Helping to support dwindling membership figures, there's a renewed movement of Christian tradition. Its modernizing regrouping and approaching the media united under the name "Evangelical." Their theory of six-day creation goes under the name Creationism.

Some Evangelicals profess the earth is 6,000 years old and was created in seven days, as described in Genesis. There are religious fundamentalists who deny that our sun is 14 billion years old as documented by science's ability to deduct such facts from the natural evidence found in today's version of our changing reality. They blindly deny that our sun will in about 5 billion more years will burn itself out and become a nebula star and drift apart. They affirm the biblical account creation to the point of saying that our sun's around six thousand years old. They lead tours taking children through Chicago's History Museum boldly denying the scientific evidence that the earth is a bit older than that, dinosaurs and all that.

To satisfy those of the Evangelical movement and assure the inclusion/representation of their religious claim right alongside of Darwin's claim to mankind's origins, the name "God" has been removed and replaced with "Intelligent Design" or "Divine Intervention." This also allows the theological claims of other religious groups to be included in the same movement.

By including the reference to the unknown, those who lack direction can feel like they are caught up with the others in search of the answer. It gives the issue a more politically correct generic flavor.

Endless volumes could be written recounting the colorful array of creative twists (white lies, etc.) individuals in denial use to piece together and find sync between their illusionary picture of an apparent reality and what reality truly appears as...the way they interpret and make known their version of what should be a true account of what's going on...an apparent reality.

They will medicate the mental scars that develop with sleeping pills and anti-depressants as their illusionary balloon gets blown around by the wind of time-fueled change with no steadfast faith tie-down anchored to their awareness of the only thing that doesn't change...the Omnipresence of this reality's state of change itself and the relational wisdom derived from the constructs that make up its truth.

The deep-seated fear of their long-time worshipped god/judge watching over their shoulder is devoutly etched into their belief system. The uncertainty-generated fear felt by their waking consciousness of what the nature and boundaries of the real verifiably living yet unknown answer may be that unknowingly resides in their deeper consciousness is compounded and further teased by the guilt generated fear/dread of this god/adjudicator's absolute brick-wall ruling on the day of final judgment to whether or not they made the final cut.

Those living in illusion may hear the truth, but like those in Jesus's parable of the sewer that have the seed of truth sown directly into their mental garden, with vision blurred by their miss-focus on worldly concerns, will never hear or see it. They don't know how to best use their available resources.

They've established no experiential association or link to the truth savvy relating to ongoing change to take root in. As Atisha observed in his insights grouping human behavior with spiritual capacity, there are those that find full satisfaction in spending their present moments absorbed in contaminated pleasure, fully blind to the fact that the effects of their efforts, thought to bring gratification actually inspire insipient suffering.

...Fundamentalist Denial Bleeds into Apathetic Mind-Set

A blind faith believer becomes too dazed to seek out core answers. Religious surrender signals a frame of mind that settles for an iffy path for their soul's fate. They lead a life of compromised concern initiative...settle for second rate solutions and lack the self-confidence to trust that they can ask the right questions to make things work.

When a believer cuts off the childhood curiosity that had them trying to figure out the details of the things alive in this reality to deny any recognition of the proven evidence of the development of this reality, they neuter their conscious ability to solve everyday problems. They gradually lose touch with their ability to ask why about things.

A believer will give up on trying to understand how other processes work. Fixing simple things around the house will become scary challenges that get put off. Procrastination will eventually turn into no action taken at all. Their self-confidence will suffer while they live by their fundamentalist rulebook and life will lose its meaning.

...Persecuted in the Name of God

Many Christians take pride in a crowd's pressing questions as being a form of the expected, the promised persecution as they stand-alone. They stand alone just like those in their mental picture of their robed Christian ancestors being stoned as they stood alone, sandal-clad preaching God's word?

Take note that this is different than standing alone protected by steadfast faith while voicing an unpopular yet to be explored insight into one of the kinks in mankind's collective pathway to enlightenment. Today's persecuted Christian stands supported by their cognitively pictured collection of persecuted Christians remembered from movies seen or taken from the folds of a Gideon's Bible seen in a motel desk drawer. Or maybe they've seen other Christian's preaching in the yard of a local college. There are enough to fill an entire ageless arena in their illusion of reality, parroting a book, chapter, and verse, waving their biblical flag waiting to be shot down...martyred.

For many this denial-spirited blindness is a basic part of fundamentalism. The individual is so eaten up with uncertainty-spawned fear of the unknown, they're afraid to make use of life's tools of survival. They're blind to seeing and too fearful to open their upcoming present moment to consider the different sides of anything that hints at being contrary to their church's charter to their religious ideology. The limiting effects of inflexible theology mixed with the blindness inspired through denial, finds individuals imprisoned in a view of life sighted through a window of reality that's been glued shut by fundamentalism.

...Ritualistic Hovering in Divine Anticipation

As time passes for many that are deaf and blind to the reality of ongoing change, the natural inner longing to restore peace of mind remains on standby. Individuals spend idle time unsettled, thinking this state of inner peace is not to be found in things as they are. Somewhere within they know that the answer exists. After finding no other option in their search they will reach out in exhaustion to various religious or spiritual groups or networks as they seek guidance on forging their way.

They will find common ground with the group of people clinging to the closest most similar type of uncertainty or misunderstanding of the purpose of nature's greater plan as they have. They congregate with other people that have made the most similar illusionary compromise. They'll meet together to reinforce their explanation of what reality apparently must be as they become piously fixed in some unique collection of dogmatic rites and ritual. Hopefully, they're not looking for believer's who choose to suffer in the same way...to the same set of rules.

They spend their present moments wading in protocol. Hopefully, patience will prevail in those situations where their congregation might argue over the wording of some scripture and their congregation chooses to split apart. Hopefully their fundamentalist views will entertain a tolerance to at least this extent.

The internalization of any of the religious claims to our Source's nature and purpose of intent comes with the same caveat..."travel at your own risk." There's no history of any experiential claim verification available for developing a living relationship with the intended purpose promised by any religious claim fixed in a continuous reality.

There's no way for the claim believer to put their finger to the flame of the religious claim allowing the ultimate reality to sensually demonstrate for them in a living sense...in a sensual dialogue defining the living involvement of the religious claim's intended purpose to watch over them as promised. They stay suspended in pious ritualism waiting for him to show them a sign while silently and subconsciously still hoping to find hints to the answer as they pillage through the ideas and toys of everyday life.

An ongoing state of perplexed impatience permeates the hovering ranks of Bible-carrying Christians. They want something to happen to verify biblical prophecy. There's always someone interpreting the warning signs given in the Book of Revelations into the cause/effect realities of today and prophesying the second coming of Christ into their misunderstood and feared tomorrows. Dates are set; reputations are defended.

Most have no vision-directed pathway allowing them to relax as they breathe in—breathe out while finding and releasing their inborn potential. Even though they are all basically good individuals agreeing to be collared by the constraints of the Ten Commandments, they still have no guidance on developing their mind to understand the unchanging change.

The answer waits hidden, veiled by ignorance. They have nothing but unguided biblical directives to be happy and joyous and a list of sinful behaviors not to be involved in. There's no guidance on changing the nature of their minds to actually release and realize those heavenly states of mind in this waking lifetime experience.

Some stay forever connected with the religious group or culture they were born into. In today's world in Central Indiana, extreme religious segregation continues to describe the makeup of the great majority of all Christian congregations. In the larger cities, churches are emerging that claim total acceptance of all religious beliefs.

They stay true to the collective belief system in search of the longed-for answer of truth. They develop reliance on and become lost in ritualistic behaviors week in and week out. They hope that possibly by performing the same or similar "holy" actions that are copied from available biblical accounts in hope, some related dust of righteousness will settle on them.

With pious dedication, fundamentalists pledge to wait while they hover in the observance of rites and rituals until their god Jesus thunders back to Earth to take some individuals with him back to the reality of heaven and mercilessly send the once sinless children...now hopelessly sinful, once warned adults remaining behind to be shuttled to a hell of fire and brimstone. They're not taking steps along their individual pathway to enlightenment, as they have no guidance.

They're trying to adhere to not breaking any of the Ten Commandments and to do unto others, as they'd wish to be treated themselves while they wait. However, it's true that many just can't keep their hands out of the cookie jar.

Ritualistic behavior does not recreate the conditions of the original first-time situation when that certain repeated action-turned-ritual was appropriate for the sought-after liberating result. The chances are that the repeated behavior doesn't recreate the same effort, awareness and concentration directed at the same purpose of the first application of the action.

The ritualistic washing of one's feet had its time and place. Two thousand years ago washing someone else's feet would be a great showing of hospitality and respect as their feet were openly exposed to the dust coming from dirt paths. There's really no reason for this today. In those times, one's feet would become dirty from dust and sweat. This service had a purpose. To do it today is unnecessary. Try to experience this even on today's mostly paved pathways. Wear sandals with no toe or heal around outside for a few days without washing your feet. Those days are now gone.

The material objects originally used long ago could only be one of many available tools used to affect the purposed intentions of the original performer's belief system. Today, during ritualistic activities, minds wander into other realms of thought and lose focus of any intended spiritual purpose. It becomes just an action performed out of habit with lost expectations of any results after repeatedly seeing none. The action's utility effectively serves as nothing more than an expected time-filler to consume part a Sunday morning religious service. Add a full oration of Latin into the mix and it becomes difficult for some to keep their eyes open. It seems like Aramaic would be more appropriate anyway?

The unexplained mandatory obedience of the Ten Commandments domesticated into a person's personal belief system does not alone in itself help the individual advance toward an enlightened understanding of their ignorance that keeps their joy and happiness at a distance and allows their suffering. It's a religious belief that through religiously following these ten mandates, that a believer earns the ticket to heaven after their human condition has expired.

It's not taught by Christians that these commandments were made to help provide a calm unobstructed mental presence to allow the use of the right effort, awareness and concentration to wakingly understand the related wisdom to become enlightened about what they don't understand about the impermanent nature of the human experience and to in turn, liberate them from the living cause of suffering. It's by not having any guidance on developing thought awareness and control that individuals are unable to knowingly seek the enlightenment by developing the kind of wisdom that while gaining self-awareness or self-knowledge reveals the most basic of life's insightful truths.

A part of these religious rituals includes over-repeated and lazed intentions that accompany scheduled church attendance and pious participation in religious rites, ceremonies and prayers to please him and assure acceptance into heaven after death. Pious ritualistic ceremonies and rites are maintained, argued about and slept through every Sunday morning in the Midwest.

After so many repetitions of the same physical actions and Latin words with no significant religious effects, individuals give up and yawn, think about mowing the lawn, the nice SUV they want, how much they'd like to have their hair done like some movie star or about something they'll have to tell the pastor about during their next confessional. This is boredom typical of ritualistic hovering... while unknowingly waiting for the answer. Their intentions of seeking the source of happiness, joyful bliss, and compassion are naturally unavoidable. It's just that their journey's misguided.

While in this haze of reality centered on a promised future heaven through obedience, it's really present-day pain and suffering that Christians' prayers are directed at. They want the truth. They want relief from today's hell. They impatiently wait for a living sign. They need to see with their waking eye that their god is here and occupies an actual living thread of the present moment that's alive in the same cosmos of transformation that can relieve the pain and suffering they address in their prayers of hope.

They don't have proper reference or guidance into developing the wisdom needed to realize this truth. Their true path to enlightenment is put on hold and they wait for a sign pointing them to the answer.

Pious religious rituals and rites lose their attraction when an individual's point of view is suddenly altered through gaining sight of how to attain conscious awareness of the truth of ongoing change. An unexpected wave of inspired insightful realization can change one's point of view, the nature of their worldview. When you change the nature of how you look at something, you change the nature of what you think. The awareness can suddenly dawn on an individual that they are suffering...that it has a cause and a solution to whet their appetite to fully enrich their awareness to realize the solution.

An individual that has spiritual direction with an end in sight for their spiritual pursuit loses their longing for what is not as they finally understand how to be satisfied with what is. For them the truth of ongoing change alive in their deeper consciousness finally has a chance to be linked with and speak to their waking consciousness via sensual media and exercise its first amendment right to be heard. This is an individual who has finally sat down, shut up and listened (sensually) to our Source while attaining the firsthand knowledge of what literally makes up their self.

...Blind Faith Blinds People To Modern-Day Progress

Turning to the Bible for all the answers is what many choose to do. They choose blindness in areas that can eliminate their ignorance that makes them suffer.

Blindly trusting that there is an unverified god with an afterlife heaven to again be alive in and free of suffering for an unknown reason, still fails to shield the living soul from present moment fear of what's unknown. The truth is that there's really nothing about the conceptualized heaven that has been experientially witnessed. Without an understanding of this reality, this reality is unknown. When an individual lives their lifetime confronted by a state of changing unknown, they suffer.

Believers seem to classify the nature of their present moment living ephemeral existence as the same as the after-death living existence spoken of in the Bible. While, after death, their bodies have continued changing and have returned to dust that will still change into something else, in this impermanent reality, it's hard to say what medium their soul will assume to be able to find common meaning in the environment they're consumed by in Christianity's heaven. In this reality, the mind and body meet in the sensation. That's the only way the mind can find the true meaning of the impermanence that defines this reality. The sensation is where the mind goes to gain an enlightened understanding about the impermanence of this reality that's alive in the flesh to undo their ignorance about what this reality is that makes them suffer.

When someone needs help getting along with other people, there are councilors, psychologists and psychiatrists whose help could eliminate the individual's suffering by helping them remove some of their ignorance about their misguided understanding of the relational justice of this reality. There are those in unhappy marriages that choose not to see marriage councilors because of their fear that its association with modern science that might intimidate them.

They might have a fear of drawing attention to themselves. Instead of trying to eliminate their ignorance of why they suffer, they dive into the Bible for relationship advice. Times are changing. It's not so appropriate anymore for the wife to simply love and obey their husbands. The implied unquestioned obedience is destructive in a couple of ways. This is still a part of the wedding vows for many married couples.

There is the religion of Scientology where they outright refuse the medical attention that could cure an affliction because they have blind faith that God will heal them. This is an extreme.

There are those who've spent years of their lifetime proud of their blind faith and have lived in decent health. When they become ill and don't feel well, the last thing they want to do is deal with the fear of the unknown. They feel pressed and perhaps desperate.

They can become blind to help. They are afraid of having to listen to science's modern-day cure for their ailment. The uncertainty about the unknown is immense. They dive into the scriptures and look for an answer.

Many individuals are so stricken by the fear of the unknown and with no guidance to an answer, they become very reclusive and afraid of any attention. It's a step beyond simple shyness.

The thought that there might suddenly be a reason for them to have to take action and do something with their latent potential that would draw public attention to them can be terrifying. Maybe people would make fun of them. Maybe people would be able to easily show how wrong and foolish they are and stupid they look. This individual lacks a faithbacked purpose of intent to, out of love for others, step out and let their light shine.

Their troubled belief system attends randomly to the unrelated intentions of the many mistakenly internalized unverified claims they've deemed acceptable that collectively shape their worldview that now shout disorganized, unrelated wants from atop their soapbox inside the individual's head. The illusionary apparent reality they've created in effort to shield and organize their searching mind shutters at the thought of having its disguised frailty exposed.

Their fear tells them that it will only take a few simple questions to crumble the frail supporting threads of logic that support their ego-built castle walls. The unaware individual is more afraid of living than they are of dying. Numbingfear that's based in uncertainty is very real and affects most everyone to some degree.

After Jesus's death, when confronted by the Romans, Peter and John denied knowing him. Even with the Roman edit of the scriptures, the reason has to be the same. They reacted out of fear. They hadn't developed sufficient mind control yet to tap into their center of steadfast courage. They weren't on the spiritual plateau of understanding with our Source that Jesus had become one with and taught them of.

They were disciples in the process of developing right concentration to self-train their wisdom to realize the strength and the steadfast faith to think and act and to be capable of resisting their uncontrollable emotional reactions to fear.

They were shutting down their primal link to their deeper consciousness for their waking ego-managed consciousness to better hear the truth about living that Jesus had became enlightened about and was trying to enlighten them about.

...Keeping Two Sets of Books

Being Hoosier-raised, an individual gets exposed to a social tsunami of Christian opinion about the nature and purpose of the god who created the earth and mankind. Christianity in Indiana is divided up into many different splinter groups with different names that have their own recipe for the only way to please God to be granted heavenly status.

Individuals that have not developed a personal relationship between their belief system's criteria for verifying a claim's promise and our Source's intended purpose to initiate ongoing change will have an undefined feeling or will lack the feeling of who they are, where and how they fit in. They might be too tentative about the present moment to feel that comfortable in their own skin. Mankind is created in our Source's image, as per the Bible, so individuals also are in a constant state of non-constant. Individual humans have the same nature passed along from our Source. It's too simple and obvious to seem important. It's a given.

In today's world, on the mass social surface, religious tolerance seems to be greater than on the level of individual believers or congregations. Maybe this stems from a deeper felt social caution from not being politically correct? Maybe it stems from wanting to inflate the perception of Christianity as a powerful worldwide spiritual answer.

It's interesting how many of the older fabric traditional Christians still tend to enforce much of the Bible to the letter. The congregation will argue and even split up over the smallest of ritual-related details. They'll split over understandings of re-chewed ideas involving particulars about details in their chosen translations of the written word that really have nothing to do with relieving the human suffering resulting from the human ignorance over living savvy to the laws of ongoing change...the laws of our Source. If a group member doesn't agree with the group's interpretation of the Bible, they may be asked to leave the congregation. Does this mean that they're no longer a Christian? It must matter whose standards are used to answer that question.

However, on a different relational or perceptual scale, when it comes time to comparatively tally up the size of the major religions, only having the label Christian is good enough...like in how "close only counts in playing horseshoes or tossing hand grenades." This inclusion happens even though when viewed through their sectarian fundamentalist glasses, it's only their Christian sect that's to be eventually saved. At least, this is what's preached from many Midwestern pulpits every Sunday morning.

To help purport the grandeur and substance of Christianity as a world-recognized religion, even the older fabric traditional Christians will minimize the importance of the intra-faith squabbles to allow the numeric inclusion of the other sects of Christian believers when comparing the size of the major religions. Still, when it gets down to bare knuckles, they believe that those of differing Christian interpretations are going to go to hell in the end.

Regardless, they wait hovering in performance of Sunday morning rites and rituals. They wait for the answer to arrive. Many believe it will be Christ returning on his white horse to take their sect to heaven as he sends souls who follow different religions or who had refused to deaden their free will to take a leap of blind faith, to an eternal hell of fire and brimstone.

His heavenly father will give them the joy and happiness they failed to develop themselves during their lifetimes on Earth. They will enjoy an eternity in Jehovah's heaven experiencing the emotions that are attainable while alive in the human experience, should they have known how to selftrain their journey to reach them. All these states of emotion require a time-pushed impermanent state of reality to be recognized.

Many believe only their unique interpretation of this cause/effect reality pushes the right sensitivity buttons deemed politically correct in the spiritual world. While on the other hand, differing religious claims all get the same benefit of the doubt when considering the laws of the USA taxing system. This helps preserve that tax-free status for those seeking their god.

When it comes to counting heads, using the looser standards for determining who's saved does help establish the global significance and give background support to fortify the likelihood of correctness for their religious blind faith. Maybe that helps prolong the time until their charter dissolves. Like so many religious efforts in past millennia...their blind faith will be set aside any time their sect's chameleon-like adaptability cannot jive with what new frontiers in relational justice that science has proven to be unquestionably a part of our Source's reality.

...Big White Elephant Somewhere In The Room?

A religious believer sits quietly on a church pew among a room full of fellow brethren who've all agreed to internalize and accept as true one of the many biblical translations of the 2,000-plus-year-old account of humanity's origin and future. They all agree there's a male god that's responsible for all of this and whose judgment will one day determine the future well-being of the same soul they spend their waking time catering to. They can only hope that none of these fellow brethren will rock the boat of its shared unquestioned acceptance by asking the challenging questions that would threaten the continued unchallenged acceptance of its unsubstantiated living omnipresence.

Geshe Sonam Rinchen references how this dilemma existed back in religions' earlier days in his commentary on *Atisha's Lamp for the Path to Enlightenment*. He cites Chandrakirti, a seventh century Indian Buddhist and meditation master of the Mahayana school of thought when he says:

> Unless we rid ourselves of the fundamental causes of suffering, they will continue to give rise to it. Chandrakirti says that if we think there is a snake living in the wall of our room, we are foolish if our fears are quelled when someone tells us not to worry because there is no elephant in the room. This is like understanding the nonexistence of our less subtle fabrications while ignoring the most subtle. [26]

The higher the Christian concentration is in a group, the more likely it is to see religion-related behaviors like saying a prayer before a meal. It's more likely to hear fundamentalist critique expressed about social events or individuals.

Believers sit behind their own unique veneer of blind faith and blind trust. They keep quiet the feeling that their religious mind-set might have a few leaks, but as long as nobody's saying anything, they choose to just look the other way and watch and wait.

The avoidance and inability to communicate that's created has a significant influence on the dysfunctional makeup of many families in Midwestern USA.

...And Betrayed with Ultimate Hypocrisy

Individuals who live in a mitote/maya mental state characterized by the ongoing confusion and unrest brought on by having a thousand different voices shouting different demands, cannot filter out, identify and point toward any internally driven pursuit of any life passion or focused goal. Their life stories are sprinkled with accounts of hypocritical actions. OK, humans aren't perfect and that's why they have turned their souls over to Christ?

They will emit an array of inconsistent behaviors giving in to their culture's common addictions that come from their society's misunderstanding of the relational justice appropriate in our Source's impermanent reality.

At one moment they'll be professing how TenCommandment important it is not to steal and the next they'll be helping themselves to a handful of mints while walking out of a restaurant. They take with them a much larger portion of the owner's bottom line than the owner had intended for showing their gratitude and thanks for their patronage. They'll say how important it is to do unto others and the next second, they'll be saying inappropriate things about their friend behind their friend's back.

When an individual isn't sure what their life purpose is and have no real direction, their lack of conscious self-definition is exhibited through their behavior as they exhibit inconsistent self-expression. They lack direction to consciously sync the nature of their intended purpose with that or our Source.

In public atmospheres, these sometimes-uncontrollable inconsistencies of intention are recognized as hypocritical and phony. This inadvertent hypocrisy is really unavoidable by anyone with a head full of indecision and uncertainty wrapped around a miscued illusion that the misguided individual would possibly defend to the end.

Their behavior testifies to a disguised state of roaming priorities with no real common end or passion to focus on and direct their behavioral intentions to. This affects the behavior of anybody whose life purpose is not focused through recognition and awareness of the primal truth of ongoing change with present moment behaviors reflecting the appropriate and applicable wisdom.

The lack of the waking awareness focused on what it is that makes everything tick leads to diffused behavioral intentions that affect inconsistent reactions to same or similar situations. The ways many individual act or react can be largely dependent on which of the 1,000 voices of their mitote/maya mental state of being has the mental floor at the time and with what, where or with whom their present moment finds them.

Individuals might please the norm of their Sunday morning church group or they might please the norm of their Saturday night drinking buddies. An onlooker's recognition of this hypocrisy is a main reason why many truth-seeking people leave, switch or chose to never join any Christian church.

Wolves dressed in priest's robes represent an extreme example of this hypocrisy that causes great suffering. Many church leaders vow to honor and respect other human beings only to secretly act with intentions resulting from misguided prior conditioning.

Consider the number of Catholic priests that sexually abuse the children in their congregations. Many have been caught. These are child predators hiding in a priest's robe to satisfy a social sickness interrelated to diseased and misguided prior conditioning. It involves an addiction they don't understand how to or even want to cure.

> Nearly 14,000 molestation claims have been filed against Catholic clergy since 1950, according to tallies released by the bishops' conference. Abuse-related costs have reached at least $2.3 billion in the same period...Advocates for victims have criticized the annual reports because the auditors and researchers must rely on information provided by the dioceses and religious orders (*USA Today* March 7, 2008).

To help eradicate this inexcusable criminal behavior, the Catholic Church establishes lists of rules for the priests to follow. How futile this preventive step is. It does nothing to curb the offender's desire to perform the misguided behavior.

It's very unfortunate their religion is unable to turn to Christ in Rome's edited version of Jesus's teachings for guidance in eradicating the ignorance that allows misguided addictive behavior, to undo the prior conditioning responsible for their misguided intentions resulting in the sexual child abuse.

Indianapolis Star (8/11/08) reports the following:

> The Archdiocese of Cincinnati has issued a detailed list of inappropriate behaviors for priests saying they should not kiss, tickle or wrestle children.
>
> The newest versions of the Archdiocese's Decree of Child Protection also prohibit bear hugs, lap-sitting and piggyback rides.
>
> But, it says priests may still shake Children's hands, pat them on the back and give high fives.
>
> ...The Cincinnati Archdiocese says it updates the rules every five years. the latest version issued last week, also mandates background checks for contractors working with children.

At least giving guidance that attempts to control the behavior is a start...like in how the Ten Commandments say what to do and what not to do. However, developing the ability to know why or why not is needed to find true mental peace.

On the other hand, there were no records found of any Buddhist leaders' secret involvement in any activities such as child sexual abuse. They have guidance on finding and realizing the primal truth through self-discovery.

It's true that Buddhism is as fragmented as Christianity. However, Christianity loses guidance to enlightenment after its requirement that Christians develop moral/ethic standards as mandated in the Ten Commandments. They have no guidance on recognizing and self-training the development of the mental control to allow the self-training of the relational wisdom to consciously realize the enlightenment about the nature of impermanence that their ignorance of, allows their addictions and behaviors that cause their suffering.

13

The World's Religious Tango

We use a higher power to encourage us in our lower deeds.
—Roger Waters, May 17, 2012 Serius/XM Deep Tracks interview

All forms of religious theology require a faith that is blind to living verification. Their existence is founded in the abstract imaginative supposition that's been conditioned into each different individual and the enforcement of the religious purpose is fueled by their emotions.

Worldwide Primal Void of Uncertainty Resonates in an Echo of Spiritual Warfare

All societies admit having one or two religion/spiritual disciplines that the majority of their citizens belong to. The development of today's differing cultural worldviews originates in the different groups' collective belief systems having taken their own collective leaps of blind faith.

The groups each blindly trust in the soul-saving claim of a proclaimed creator's untested living presence in the heartbeat of today's reality. The stories of the gods' self-proclaimed religious rights are then adjusted to support the moods of differing local agendas. Unverified culturally internalized claims explaining the nature of our Source, or of a source that only accepts or at least favors them as his chosen ones, have been handed down through centuries of generational tweaking.

Differing religious claims that have been blindly accepted by different cultures sway and distort the individual worldviews of many of the citizens in those different cultures. This leaves a dangerous imbalance in how onlookers' perceive the citizens living in the societies with those collective worldviews.

When needed, societies will warp or twist the collectively internalized unverified and potentially misguided purposes of their creator's religious claims to best make the ends of their infected social opinions meet and make sense. When unable to find a path of logic to make ends meet, they might give their confused collective agenda a religious authorization to account for its seemingly unnatural explanation.

There are individuals or groups of individuals in each society that will claim, tongue-in-cheek, that they have their god's approval to justify the evil intentions behind ghastly behaviors against others. They know that nobody can actually communicate with their god to verify that he has given his approval.

Most world citizens have free wills that are coaxed, fooled or socially pressured into internalizing an unverified claim that bears godly credentials and the seal of the culture's credibility...stamped on their currency as well as their license plates. Many individuals hang loose in the middle and just don't object. Nevertheless, this approved cultural soul train clarifies to other cultures the nature and purpose of intent of the heavenly entity this area bows to in case they want to enter into a relationship of some sort.

They don't really consider the practicality of how their personalized one and only god must also rule over the rest of the humanity. Is it stubbornness or shallow insight that allows them to miss finding a god that's more adaptable to cultural differences and norms...that doesn't favor their race because of some promise or special attention granted back in the days of the Old Testament?

They, en masse, reassign their Source-given responsibility for the eternal accountability of their souls to an external entity that doesn't prove or show himself in true living color for all to see. The presence of the religious heavenly entities is on the outside. None speak through the sensual media, the common sub-dermal language of life spoken within each and every human being, yet understood by only a few. This is another culture that is numb to hearing the truth.

These religious claims represent their culture's best answer for filling the hollowed void in the anatomy of the culture's collective belief system that fails to explain what happens between real-time causes and their effects. The void misses feeling the social awareness to allow linking together the society's problems to their actual causes.

How appropriate is an individual's behavior when based on the borrowed or received intellectually stored accounts of an enlightened ancestor's experientially derived wisdom? On the global scale, the resurgence of war between different societies' collective worldviews shows the lack of true experiential understanding of the interplay among relationships or the relational justice in this cause/effect world. Some societies get so frustrated and short-sided by not understanding cause/effect relationships that they blame their neighbors and send their young to war to die in the name of their chosen god.

Lessons experientially learned during past generations of our ancestors that are no longer there making the decisions, have lost the social sensual ties needed to affect the behavioral intentions of today's world leaders. The frequency of wars supports the effects of decisions made based on reasoning generated from intellectual supposition.

An individual has to have been there for war's related suffering to have been sensually scored in the part of their belief system that underwrites their behavioral intentions for what matters about past horrific results to override and affect future decisions. They've seen what true loss looks like on a picture of the face of a young child looking over the body of their war-slain parent. A front-page newspaper picture can't reveal the heartfelt pain that's there tearing the child's heart out during the present moment the picture was snapped.

World wars repeat themselves. Greed driven behavior craves the imagined pleasures and security of the power-in-reserve afforded by money. There's a worldwide greed for that security. Too many of today's rulers are blind to the truth showing the foolishness of attachment and craving. War waging motivation comes from the fear of uncertainty that generates the craving for the security and power that's blind to the experiential truth defining this wisdom that lies in between the cause and effect pillars of reality. There is no understanding or linking of the causes of the ongoing effects that define the world's reality of the day.

There exists a war-causing inability to come down from the plateau of fundamentalist intolerance alive in their societal illusion to focus and deliberate on historical lessons. There's a societal need to seek inspiration from contemplating the interplay between the supporters of different claims of different entities in similar historical situations and attempt to find the insightful wisdom to avoid those situations that taught such painful experiential lessons to our forefathers.

Even though there might be those who trust the wisdom based on mistakes made and felt by today's forefathers, they create only a minority. The majority that elected the country's leader suffers from the ignorance of a normalcy bias of sorts that minimizes the importance of basing national policy on lessons learned from history that's never been actually experienced by those living. Most people don't know their history and don't care enough to give their attention and have blind faith in to trusting those few that do.

The society's clouded vision stands blind to any answer to help the leaders understand what causes the ongoing perceptual problem from cause/effect misalignment. The ability to explain the society's real-time dysfunction is lost in the void between recognizing the causes of their social problems and matching them with the observed real-time effects that result in their suffering. There is no feeling for what links the cause and effect together. The people of their present society have not experienced suffering from the same interplay among similar relationships of times past. The historical situations are intellectually considered by a few and not real enough carry much weight.

When someone stumbles across a likely solution, most citizens lack the inner strength coming from an experienced inner feeling with what bonds cause and effect...the steadfast bone-felt faith in the consistency of what they've already sensually witnessed to be true. Their decision-making process is numbed by uncertainty and they're too afraid or apathetic to take action.

Fundamentalist blinders will cast shade on any objectively perceptive account of the society's true cause/effect order of things. Religions use the Old Testament for their frame of reference. The media will paint the cause/effect picture that best suits the order of their illusion of what they think reality should be...a subjective view fashioned in effort to increase ratings. It sways interests to the financial benefit to those who control the media.

There are religious fundamentalist beliefs that harbor such extreme lines of thought that individuals become blinder-wearing radicals in their defense. Even if they inwardly think nonviolence might be the better route, they'll too often lack the faith within themselves to step out of line and take action for the best interests of the situation. They lack the bone-felt-faith-backed courage to be a messenger of the truth. They use up their gift of time involved in pious dogmatic ritualistic behaviors that lead nowhere but in endless circles of suffering. They may use a religious screen to justify their harmful actions of hate and prejudice.

The USA electorate united in the 2008 and 2012 presidential elections to elect for president an unproven leader who promised nothing but unspecified directionless change from what is. Change is unavoidable. Proactive influence on the direction of that change is not. Proactive influence is not synonymous with the blind hope offered to win the 2008 and 2012 USA presidential elections.

Unspecified change was the common goal representing what unaware people crave and are always in search of...a change from what is. It's been the defining protocol of Father Time since the beginning. The ongoing change from what is, is our Source's nature and intended purpose-driven order of things. The present moment that reveals the status quo transforms or changes into the present moment effects fueling the next present moment of change.

The mostly Christian US society is frozen in the confines of fundamentalism. Fear and uncertainty echo throughout the media airwaves. Religion is to be kept out of politics. The public mind is waxed gross to seeing the truth related to the ephemeral nature of our world. Its social dialogue spins in fundamentalist denial that only feeds the nation-wide suffering. They've re-elected a leader offering no direction with an administration caught up in stagnant nondirectional hovering and blame dodging.

The World Dream Has No Eye For The Primal Truth

The cutting-edge of mankind's worldwide design for adapting to change in today's human experience is founded in primal ignorance. In the wake of this ignorance there's tremendous injustice, hate, envy, bigotry, anger, greed and lack of trust. These negative forces grow from the prevailing uncertainty and collective fear of the unknown. There's no shared vision of a way to be free of suffering to provide a common direction for different cultures to work toward.

In the Midwest, there's very threatening economic and social problems coming from corporate fear inspired greed. Greed-stricken individuals of power heartlessly set up new homebuyers with deceiving mortgage opportunities. They steal the retirement hopes of millions of their fellow countrymen. An incomprehensively large national debt will remain for future generations to also not be able to pay off. Masses are losing their jobs and homes and millions have no health insurance. Billions upon unlimited billions of dollars are being printed off and pumped back into the economy, monthly, to the advantage of those that mismanaged their part of the economy to cause the 2008 mess...

Hoosier health is falling prey to obesity and sugar type 2 diabetes in proportions never experienced. Our newspaper headlines have daily accounts of young American mothers and fathers who've given their life over in the Mid-East to fight terrorism. All Hoosiers long for the truth and search for answers, but with the worldwide belief system dominated by misguided claims and expectations there's no real connection between the suffering that's being experienced and what causes it. The link between real cause and effect is clouded with conflicting illusionary dreams that result in wars being waged worldwide. There's no eye for recognizing the truth that unifies.

Don Miguel Ruiz summarizes the emotional drama found in today's world:

> In the dream of the planet it is normal for humans to suffer, to live in fear, and to create emotional dramas. The outside dream is not a pleasant dream; it is a dream of violence, a dream of fear, a dream of war, a dream of injustice. The personal dream of humans will vary, but globally it is mostly a nightmare. If we look at human society we see a place so difficult to live in because it is ruled by fear. Throughout the world we see human suffering, anger, revenge, addictions, violence in the street, and tremendous injustice. It may exist at different levels in different countries around the world, but fear is controlling the outside dream.[27]

The same denial that feeds narrow-minded fundamentalism accounts for the pious ritualistic hovering and hypocrisy that defines society's modern-day boundaries and limits of tolerance. Validity by numbers takes over sealing this state of affairs into a world mind-set waxed gross to recognizing and understanding man's commonality in this world of natural change. Mass acceptance of this old mind-set helps to justify and make cultures resistant to changing any societal dysfunctional behavior. This state is the defining tide in today's multinational social current.

This emotional drive train coagulates and is channeled through various religious fronts worldwide to collectively mask the confusion and ignorance. Religious intention is twisted and the religion card is used to justify genocide and war.

There's yet no common grounds of recognition shared throughout mankind's collective consciousness that acknowledges how all humans experience the same suffering together from the same irritating moment-to-moment discontent of not knowing the answer to mankind's origination and destiny. It's an intimate thing that's shared on a primal level.

Being divided by national borders, skin color and language only diffuses this intimate and shared reality. When mankind shares the same recognition of what suffering is, is when it will be able to collectively focus on a united vision to eliminate the shared ignorance that causes it.

Gateway to Tolerance is Rusting Shut

Many of today's societies not located in war zones seem to be supporting an increase in religious tolerance. Are these groups showing willingness to allow groups supporting other beliefs to co-exist even though they know they're going to go to hell after they die? Or, are these groups saying that it's OK, they'll listen, and as they realize that maybe they're not really 100 percent correct. They admit that there might be something they could still learn. Are they saying that maybe there is some truth to be found coming from other perspectives on what explains the mysterious waking zone of spirituality?

Any belief system that is developed primarily through internalizing borrowed or intellectual knowledge from secondary or nonprimary information sources leads to the weakening of an individual's or a nation's collective worldview. The developing willingness to sway with outside suggestions eventually saturates the solidity of the belief system and worldview with uncertainty to then be effectively frozen in denial of anything but what they were told and can't experientially refer to and describe.

There's the underlying fear or uncertainty looming in the background that accompanies any undocumented unexperienced religious claim backed only by a faith blind to actually feeling the heat of the flame of its claim. Religious fundamentalism's rigid presence defines or at least outlines the nation's common purpose or at least the best collective effort that could be coordinated.

The relaxed fluidity or belief system elasticity that allows for adaptation and change over the passage of time comes when there's a felt understanding of the purpose of the primal truth describing our Source. With the conscious awareness of our Source's intended purpose of initiating ongoing change as being a part of an individual's or nation's collective philosophy, change and adaptation are expected and welcomed. This makes room for relaxed tolerance as change is anticipated.

It's OK to consider different means to the same end comprised of the same joy, happiness and love that all humans feel.

This change anticipation is missing from fundamentalist environments. Lacking the fluidity of tolerance, these nations will cower to considering any new belief or idea that may in fact have enlightenment about the ignorance of impermanence as the ultimate purpose but yet have a different means to that end.

When confronted by a different society that has a different worldview they feel equally strong and noncompromising about, both sides will freeze into a defensive stance. The different views deserve to be heard, if not from trying to feel the empathy of compassion, at least out of curiosity.

To conquer an enemy, it helps to understand them. A fundamentalist nation will fail to meet and consider all views and are too afraid and uncertain about the unknown and too frozen in their fundamentalism to consider options. They've built a wall of denial mortared with the fear that only allows for the shallow token consideration designed to mislead onlooking nations. Understanding opens the door for negotiation.

Any society backed by a religious creed energized by a social undercurrent subject to fundamentalism has a line drawn in the sand as to the limits of its tolerance. Numbing its citizens' minds with blind faith in its age-old sketch of the bigger picture with no flame-on feeling to testify to its truth sets the standard for understanding and the limits of patience and tolerance associated with its beliefs.

A short fuse is common with an individual or community mind that's pent-up with unbridled unexplained emotions. Changing any lines of the written script could throw the mounting imbalance completely off...pop the illusionary bubble. Individually and culturally, the long-gone childhood curiosity that fueled an unfettered free will that asks "Why?" or shouts "Prove it!" is capped by the fear and confusion of becoming a mentally or physically executed social outcast and then of course there's always the illusion of eternal punishment in hell for such disobedience.

Midwestern USA is in the northern end of the Bible Belt. Social and family cultural expectations ride high on each citizen as a part of the religious force. Even though other spiritual options are slowly making their Midwestern debuts, the social mentality remains waxed gross to giving way to recognizing and considering any different possibilities or means to the same end. Christianity's claim remains the Midwestern society's social default explanation for what the nature and intended purpose of our Source is and probably will be for quite some time.

A Human is a Human is a Human

All human beings are from the same mold. Aside from a few minor DNA differences, they all burn the same candle. The life-supporting needs are the same.

The emotions of hate, anger, greed and envy all feel the same. The ignorance about where the fear from all those sentiments originate is the same. Love, joy and bliss are the same. The spark of life in each person is the same. Feeling the nature and understanding the intended purpose of our Source is the same for all.

On a worldwide person-by-person preverbal basis, all of humanity shares the same pain-to-ecstasy sensual reckoning with the feelings that they define by using different languages. Their chosen god will lie out a plan that promises to provide good feelings free of suffering on an eternal basis. Suffering knows no prejudice. Everyone realizes it through the same ignorance and the path to a state of nonsuffering is the same for everyone. Life related protocol is the same before and after death for everyone, no matter how many gods mankind has created and bows to. All humans will all be dead in the same way, no matter what religious ideology they bend to.

Humans all enter the world alone and leave the world alone. Their physical bodies will all be equally dead in our Source's ongoing cyclical process of dust to dirt. All Christian, Muslim, Jewish, pre-biblical-time ancient ancestor, nonbelievers and those who've never heard of any of the above clicks are processed together... makes no difference.

Stir in a teaspoon of fear of the unknown with just a pinch of pride in the pot of humanity and end up with some individuals who will do things such as denying others entry into a club or group because of their nationality. When these fear laden intentions are then multiplied by the numbers that make up a society, you'll find societies sending their young to die because another society doesn't see an issue as they do, backed only by their blind faith in one of the religious fraternities.

At this modern-day in history, there's a conceptual kink in the social mind of many of the world cultures, eliminating any worldwide collective effort to focus and have a common purpose defined by altruistic intentions. Societies with their collective free will being choked out by their social belief system's infected views and beliefs are together afraid to question the resulting infected intentions and fast to execute those who do. They vow to wipe out certain human cultures in the name of religion. And their circles of suffering spiral on.

14

The Human Condition

Primal Arena to Witness Life Manifestation

We are all born mind and body to the natural rhythm of this reality's impermanent nature. Everything about the human mind and body conforms to the truth of ongoing change. We are the truth of change. That's all there is...no way to get around it.

The awareness of the human mind, when introspectively focused into the essence of the physical body's presence finds its awareness directed into the sensual arena where life itself is being manifested. While trying to self-train the mind to sustain its focus into this coming and going pulse of life, what could be a better place to find the inspiration for sudden insights about life itself? Siddhartha was able to leave record of how this worked for him.

Human flesh is made from the same coming and going particles of energy that make up everything else in this reality. Everything consists of passed-around shared bits of coming and going energy that have been here for over 14 billion years. DNA analysis shows how tightly all humans are linked together.

The process of swapping parts is a condition of this reality's ever-changing infrastructure that chronicles the makeup of everything. Our minds and bodies are an expression of the essence of the physical application of this truth of ongoing change.

Within, the human condition of body and mind offers the sole arena where the mind can witness our Source demonstrate its living presence. The body is said to be the temple of God, our Source. The interactions among the bits of coming and going pieces of energy that make up its perceivable manifestation is nothing more than and nothing less than each individual's contributory part of our Source's transforming presence.

The Bible says humans are created in the image of their creator. Like all things, the human body is nothing more than a transforming process. But like our Source and unlike most of the remainder of this reality, the human spirit can impose its own calculated affect on directing the pattern of this change to its own agenda. Human thinking has access to the world of abstract.

Seeing the metaphysical details of what actually constitutes the ever-changing state of reality that makes up the human condition to better understand it is beyond the normal perception capabilities of the human condition. This doesn't really seem fair. Not being able to see the details leads to much questioning and uncertainty.

It's no wonder humans develop a concept of a self and an ego to manage it. Individuals will, in their own way, make some sense of this puzzle. They put together an explanation of what the unverified spark or root of this living reality must apparently be. Many look up into the sky and cry impatiently for a god to show them a living sign verifying his contribution...that he is here...or there.

A closer analysis of the faster-than-lightning flow of the natural chain of cause/effect events affecting this process of life-in-action, making up the transforming human condition will allow amplifying its separate yet totally integrated facets for closer examination. A closer look at how the human mind filters and processes the sensual signals it encounters will help shed light on how the understanding of the resulting perceptions further develops an individual's peace of mind or their addictions to suffering.

The modern-day world of neurochemistry and the metaphysics of quantum mechanics explain what makes up the subatomic particles that make up the objects and shapes perceived in the range of human perception, It allows for an easier intellectual understanding and acceptance of the observations of reality's coming and going that past enlightened souls experientially discovered and brought to mankind's attention. Modern science has been able to record physical images of Siddhartha's 2,500-year-old sensually recognized observations.

Reality is a process of ongoing constant change...the arising and passing away of matter and antimatter. Defined shape undetectably pops into and out of existence, changing of its own unpredictable and totally unalterable schedule. This is what the sensations represent that are focused on while sensually seeking self-knowledge. This mind-intobody awareness gives the hands-on experience of sensually witnessing life's manifestation in process. This exposes conscious waking awareness to the real-time Source of inspired insightful wisdom that gives a relational order to the implications of the coming and going cause/effect activity in focus.

Absolutely nothing is dead in time. Everything's in a state of becoming and has an ephemeral nature dancing away to the present moment metronome of Father Time.

This coming and going swirl of simple yes/no binary relational truths tapped out by the same *kalapas* sensually visualized by Siddhartha and Jesus is the revealing source of the primal knowledge describing the timeless relational truths that fill the pages in every book of wisdom. Their unfolding story telling of this present moment relational justice writes the subject line for the evolving story told over time by all our books of science. Primal wisdom helps give conscious order and understanding to the unbiased justice behind the sensually triggered emotional logic perceived by the human condition.

In effort to better understand what causes the skipping record of religious dogma or sectarian bias, it's appropriate to look at how human beings process the sensual barrage of messages perceived in the changing human experience of this time-fueled cause/effect reality. It's important how each individual chooses to use their free in developing their belief system to shape the nature of their worldview.

Mind and Body Coexist Heart'n Hand

Both mind and body cohost the human condition's journey through the human experience...from ego management to self-acknowledgment. They must be consciously differentiated, then worked together while trying to discover and become consciously immersed in the harmony they share that allows life to transform. The mind's conscious awareness needs to be focused into the essence of the body's presence.

Learning to sustain this focus allows a truth seeker to self-train their mind control. The thinking inspired by the focus into the factor of change itself leads to the insightful understanding that enlightens the individual to what it is that they don't understand that distances their joy and happiness to be replaced with their suffering. They can sensually witness the ever-changing present moment of the greater picture that they are a combine part of and that makes possible the material grid work for them to realize the genius of their special talents to one day let their light shine.

By staying ignorant to the primal truth of ongoing change, an individual can suffer from the subliminal prick of daily discontent and not really know why. Does their unrest originate from their physical actions or from what their mind tends to?

It's important to consider whether or not there's any difference between actions of the mind and actions of the body. It brings to question which part of the human condition the root of their suffering originates.

An individual's actions are fueled and sculpted by intentions reflecting the collective purpose of the claims they've decided through use of their own free will or been subliminally fooled or even threatened into internalizing into their personal belief system. One's belief system cocktail of internalized claims collectively shapes their worldview.

The purpose of these intentions is important in determining the perceived goodness or badness of the resulting behaviors.

Helping an elderly lady to safely cross the street to avoid being ran over which allows her to be healthy to enjoy the rest of her life has a different intended purpose than an intention producing the same physical action with a purpose of intent of keeping her safe so you can take her purse once she's reached the other side. The purpose of intent of the escort's belief system was different in each of these instances.

It is mental actions that are responsible for the external consequences of what an individual does and says. It's important to understand the anatomy of the belief system and how its naive development allows for shaping a worldview blind to the relational justice that's necessary to support this reality's impermanent nature. This will help make clear the cause of the mental actions that reflect the ignorance that allows an individual to suffer life's elusive frustrations. The lacking of this understanding has to be the mother of all naivety...a primal naivety of sorts. An individual's primal naivety goes hand in hand with developing a belief system in a way that allows the worldview to assume a nature blind to impermanence that continually feeds their present moment suffering.

What's missing to complete a sound mental system is certainly the primal awareness of our reality's nature of producing nothing but ongoing change...since day one. Lacking a waking relationship with the ongoing savvy of this truth causes an individual to experience the disappointing results of when things don't work out as expected or when things happen without understanding why or where they come from.

The Flow of the Human Psychic Process

In his book *The Art of Living*, William Hart summarizes S. N. Goenka's descriptive teachings about how individuals receive and process stimuli in light of the roles played by the mind and body and how life experience shapes their worldview that generates their perceptions. This summary does a good job of slowing down the flow of the human mental process for a closer and more analytical look.

The idea is that consciousness is the first part of the mental flow. This just means that the individual is there and something has touched one of their sensual platforms. Of course, in full-speed reality, this process is happening to all the senses at the same time.

Next, the mind identifies or perceives the input and categorizes it as positive or negative, based on prior liking or disliking experiences (conditioning) they've had with that type of input. This process is mentally registering as a sensation from the outside input at this time. With the mental labeling of liking or disliking label, a neutral sensation will be recognized as a good feeling or a bad feeling.

Finally, the mind will react to its lightning-fast evaluation and seek to have or not to have something. Any actions related to liking or disliking something might eventually take on fleeting nature of a reaction that no longer takes consideration.

The reactions that come from actions taken based on a misguided understanding of the relational justice that runs this impermanent reality like drinking too much or taking drugs will be viewed as being an addiction. However, it's also true that actions that become habitual based on an accurate understanding of what balances the cause/effect scales of relational justice appropriate for running this impermanent reality would also be addictions. Things like having a healthy diet, getting plenty of exercise, stopping at stoplights, obeying the speed limit, or maybe not smoking are all behaviors that need no twelve-step programs to gain control of.

Consciousness, perception, sensation/evaluation and reaction happen so rapidly that distinguishing their separation can only be theorized. Slowing down and disjoining the mental process into functional zones allows the theoretic partitioning of the anatomy of human sensation processing for a more detailed examination.

The integrated duties can be conceptually highlighted to help dissect the thought patterns that sway the formation of intentions. If an individual doesn't understand the lightning-fast process, the process of forming behavioral intentions can easily assume a fleeting reactive nature that eventually skips over considering alternative actions such as understanding and gaining control over resulting reactions to change them into actions coming from considered deliberation.

It must be kept in mind that human beings can only perceive sensations to the degree or the relative scale that their development of recognition sensitivity allows within the physical limitations of their nervous system. The human anatomy doesn't come equipped with the makings of an electron microscope.

This ability can be further developed by effectively self-training mind control. People untrained in mind control have trouble perceiving the coming and going appearances of the totally unmapped "now you see it and now you don't" particles of energy described by the various modern string and M theories. This variety of theories in how to describe the infrastructure framework of this reality sums up mankind's collective effort to make intellectual sense of its impermanence.

Most individuals have trouble with their mind wandering from what they are trying to stay focused on. They've not been trained how to focus their thinking uninterrupted long enough to relax into the world of impermanence for their thinking to be inspired by the life manifesting within the essence of their body. The beat of the cosmic dance can be sensed in its coming and going essence in the space that's filled with the flesh of their bodies. A fully wisdom-enriched understanding of what their ignorance misinterprets would reflect a truly enlightened awareness of what it is that forms and comprises the relational justice that establishes the cause/effecting yin-yang polarity of this impermanent reality.

Even though humankind is a working part of the transforming picture of this reality, one must humbly keep in mind how little control humans really have over any part of the process. Many may think they can control their bodies, but they have no real influence over their involuntary physical processes they rarely give any thought to. And that's not to say anything about having no involved influence or even a clue to what relational truths are happening on the metaphysical or even on the cellular levels.

Individuals may think they are acting in response to or reacting to forces from their external reality. They are actually forming behavioral intentions in response to internally processed positive and negative interpretations of their perceived sensations. Their experiences with these sensations become internally tagged in relation to their likings and dislikings from their prior internal evaluations of the stimuli. Individuals react to their conditioned perceptions of the sensations within them.

Perception is discriminatory. Old likings and dislikings of experienced perceptions of past sensations that have formed into attachments to cravings and aversions greatly influence human behavior. Reactionary behavior coming from misguided prior conditioning distorts an individual's perception of reality and that of their new experiences.

Black, white, yellow, red, male or female...the way different individuals perceive what's on the outside of their skin (as well as the inside) follows the same formula and is subject to the same book of relational justice. Humans realize physical and mental pain and suffering as well as joy and happiness all in the same sensual way. Maybe understanding how this lightning-fast process works will help in understanding a way to self-train having control of how the mind works.

Humans Long to Know What's Missing from Status Quo

It's coded in the human DNA. Humankind suffers from an ongoing sense of craving. In the wake of human ignorance there's a fear-crafting uncertainty that frequently makes us cry, "Uncle." This uncertainty creates an impatient insatiable hunger for our human condition to find a peaceful balance within its human experience.

We long for an understanding of whom and what we are. We want to know where to find our passion. We long to find the answer that details what's missing and defines "what is not now," and because it's missing, it makes us suffer in the what is now.

Likings and dislikings formed from initial interactions will result in assigning preferences to those outcomes. Those preferences result in choosing to act in certain ways. These preferred actions get repeated until their repetition requires no thinking and they become reactionary and habitual. The habitual reactions evolve into the fleeting reactions that materialize as the visible symptoms of an addiction.

It's natural for the human condition to knowingly or unknowingly want to look to see what's around the corner to see what change has in store for them. It's natural for humans to want more of what its human nature, which is the same as the nature of our Source, is going to actively impose on them.

> Tanha is a Buddhist term that literally means "thirst," and is commonly translated as craving or desire. Within Buddhism, tanha is defined as the craving to hold onto pleasurable experiences, to be separated from painful or unpleasant experiences, and for neutral experiences or feelings not to decline. The Buddhist tradition identifies tanha as a self-centered type of desire that is based in ignorance. This type of desire is contrasted to wholesome types of desire such as the desire to benefit others. . .
>
> Tanha is a type of desire that can never be satisfied...
>
> However, tannha, meaning "thirst," is not a chosen kind of desire, it's a reflex. It's the desire to pull something in and feed on it, the desire that's never satisfied because it just shifts from one sense base to another, from one emotional need to the next, from one sense of achievement to another goal. It's the desire that comes from a black hole of need, however small and manageable that need is. The Buddha said that regardless of its specific topics, this thirst relates to three channels: sense-craving (kamatanha): craving to be something, to unite with an experience (bhavatanha): and craving to be nothing, or to dissociate from an experience (vibhavatanha).[28]

It's the suffering from longing for more that accounts for the ongoing human thirst to know what is absent from the what is. This is the mental habit of longing for what is not.

Those who are ignorant of the laws of impermanence and have no answer to what's missing from the status quo will cling to and grasp at any idea, notion or belief that's related to "I AM" as they bide their time wrapped in addictions, wandering unknowingly in random search of the illusive primal answer. On their daily path, anything bringing any form of gratification through liking or gratification through avoidance becomes a possible target of addiction.

There's an unrealized eagerness and primal need emanating from the human deeper consciousness to let the inborn resident age-old awareness and understanding of the truth about our Source's nature and intended purpose surface into the waking consciousness to heal the aching spirit. Like the deeper consciousness knows how to form a scab that heals a cut to the flesh, it naturally wants to allow the awareness of the answer to rise as inspired insights from a more subtle region of consciousness to heal the scars of the waking mind coming from the frustrations and unrest it suffers when the individual's ego-managed ill-construed expectations from their illusionary perception of this reality scratches up against the actual effects of the relational interactions experienced in this reality. This is made worse when their lack of relaxed tolerance shuts down any open-minded questions to better understand why there was no real meeting of expectations with reality.

The task is to engage the body/mind harmony necessary for the inspired thinking to wakingly realize an insightful understanding to further decode the tree of wisdom. This makes clear the savvy of life's impermanence to realize the soul healing that will completes their life. It makes them whole.

By not being consciously aware of this state in the status quo of what is, humans long for a status quo with the state of what is not where they could realize the answer. The individual's waking consciousness remains wrapped up in some illusion of what they might want things to be while remaining unable to find comfortable step with the flowing transforming rhythm of the cause/effect reality of their lives.

This relentless state of longing is unknowingly laced into and reflected from every thought and behavioral intention unaware individuals make. It's subconsciously felt that having the answer would give peace and security. There's an inborn self-preservation instinct to have the answer. It's in the human nature to heal itself and having direction to this answer is necessary to accomplish healing of the mind.

This longed-for answer is onboard...just a mere insight out of reach. Having the inborn answer to our suffering so close is similar to having forgotten someone's name or an important fact. It's like being just on the verge of remembering what something forgotten, that's slipped the mind is...having it just on the tip of the tongue, but not being quite able to bring it to mind. They know it's there, but can't quite put their finger on it. It prods an individual's mental presence from one present moment to the next.

"Searching for the answer" is the common theme that underwrites the storylines for countless poets and songwriters. It's become a common theme with the unsaid understanding that it's just something most people do. It's a trait common to the human condition worldwide.

Today's teenagers individually send/receive over 3,000 text messages monthly. They're addicted to wanting to know another new bit of information that might help them to discover how they fit into this reality.

Many people mistake their spiritual hunger for their physical hunger. They overeat thinking that by satisfying an internal want for physical food, they will satisfy their internal need for spiritual food.

Finding no answer to relieve the cause of their present moment suffering and having no plan or direction to seek out the antidote for human unrest, eats away at the unaware. Their behavioral intentions tend to reflect an innerfelt hollowness.

Not knowing how to confront the issue and pursue the answer, their ego finds different ways to sidestep the primal question in search for the primal answer to what's missing in their recognition of the status quo. A person's unknowing subconscious longs for the state of awareness that fills their belief system void of uncertainty by describing the nature and purpose behind the status quo with the sensually understood feeling of authentication.

The internal flame of the primal question is kept lit by the burning feeling of not knowing what's missing.

People Crave the Simple Gratification of Life's Tingle

The most primal of all human addictions streamlines down to the endless unquenchable craving of craving itself. This unappeasable yearning is an ongoing human attachment to feeling short-lived gratification from attaining any form of short-lived gratification. It doesn't matter what it is.

We crave the getting part of a process. Once we have it, we must turn elsewhere for something else to get. Even though it might not be consciously highlighted, the unrecognized feeling of life manifesting in an individual's body presents its own gratifying pleasure. Individuals who never look inside to develop a deeper understanding of our reality can spend their entire lifetime unaware of this.

Even though they can never see it, it's the only actual inclusion with our Source's ongoing change that humans actually experience to on a personal level. Individuals have an unrecognized primal level attachment to the desire to attain simple gratification from feeling the ongoing spur of life itself as it tingles within their human shell.

Satisfying this constant craving for natural change itself gives short-term gratification. Those unaware don't understand this evolving state of body and mind as it keeps reappearing. They make no conscious effort to anticipate and fashion any direction to understand this oncoming change. They ride it like a wild horse.

An individual may believe that the next adult toy they buy or however they choose to needlessly spend their resources might just contain the key to happiness they cannot find in their present moment unrest. Maybe the next new present moment will have the unknown answer to their mental discomfort? Humans find gratification in the spin of undefined change itself.

Cravings of Liking and Disliking "Rote" into Habit Energy

Individuals develop likings and dislikings in their perceptions of what different sensations or sensual combinations feel like from day one. They establish preferred patterns of behavior in the situations where those sensual stimuli are present to affect getting more of the stimuli or to avoid it. Repeating these actions develops into habit energy that works to cue an emotional signal that eventually will automatically trigger that repeated action, eventually giving the thought-out action a fleeting nature that will further define their unique set of addictions.

In the December 18, 2007 Internet journal *Ask Dr. Mao*, in the article "Dr. Mao's Secrets to Longevity," Dr. Maoshing Ni states that in his medical opinion "it takes 14–21 days of repetitive behavior to form a new pattern in your brain. Once the pattern is formed, it becomes an automatic behavioral response."

Even though these actions may lead to some form of suffering the individual will learn to accept as normal, an individual becomes attached to keeping these behaviors. They will eventually fall within the individual's perceived safety zone. These actions become to be the emotion-driven uncontrolled reactions that define their addictions that characterize their personality.

Individuals perceive sensations that represent their prior conditioning experiences as phenomena that do or do not bring gratification. They get attached to their associated perception of wanting more of or wanting to avoid, cling to or steer clear of certain sensations or certain effects of different causes.

Without much repetition, behaviors conditioned by one's liking and disliking become ingrained in their intention production process to the point where the individual is totally attached to the gratifying effect caused by their chosen action. After a number of repetitions of the behavior the individual has no impetus to quarry their belief system as to what action is appropriate. With time, the individual will eventually lose sight of why they're reacting in a certain way. This habit energy will eventually determine what eventually becomes their addictive behavior when confronted with similar situations.

A free will that's numb to experientially verifying the nature and living truth of the intended purpose of new claims can become unconsciously stuck in between the expected relational justice found in an impermanent reality and the relational justice common to an imaginary reality with a continual nature. They may be hesitant on a fundamental level or even selectively naive to new alternative behavioral options.

Society's bad habits become ingrained through mere suggestion. Without experientially testing or verifying the purpose of the claim, susceptible individuals will learn to settle for nothing more than an intellectual explanation. A socially deemed acceptable safe response is repeated and repeated to soon become a fleeting reaction fueled by habit energy. One becomes attached to the habitual behavior.

At this point, it's become a reaction they're uncontrollably addicted to repeating. They often have unbendable blind faith that the behavior's one that's appropriate.

Even when aware of a response's possibly corrosive effects, on future occasions, the reaction remains as the automatic response. The individual will repeat it. It's the safe expected response. It's just something they do as not to chance the unknown consequences or effects of something different. They're afraid to try taking the other fork in the road.

It could be said that most people have belief systems conditioned and developed in a way that results in their issuing behavioral intentions with these undetected skips. Their acting in situations has changed to reacting...

The individual will mistakenly issue and reissue the same misguided intentions that affect the same incipient suffering over and over. Their behaviors habitually continue to replay like a broken record. Uncontrolled new change continues to draw out their reactionary misguided and confused intentions of purpose that are realized in an individual's unique pool of habitual addictive behaviors.

This suffering gets repeated daily. Hopefully, the individual will become consciously aware of it and their ignorance that allows it. The suffering stops after they've eliminated the ignorance that allowed it to happen...like experienced by Bill Murray's character in the movie *Ground Hog Day*.

Bill Murray's character was ignorant to why he was stuck on reliving the same miserable Ground Hog Day over and over. Until after much contemplative deliberation over his thinking during the repeated daily experience inspired his insights into the relational interplay of the cause/effect factors making up the passing present moments of his repeated day, he suffered the burn of reality's consequences rubbing against his misguided idea of how, in his illusionary vision of reality, joy and happiness was to be found. It was by eliminating his ignorance that he modified his behavioral intentions that were causing him to suffer the present moment frustration and disappointment.

The ignorance in his belief system resulted in behavioral intentions repeating the same behaviors until he finally realized why those intentions were causing him to suffer. He had this inspired insight largely through ongoing deliberation over daily trial and error. As long as his intentions came matched to old ego-serving habit energy tied to his faulty prior conditioning, with the personality he had developed, the cycle of suffering would continue to repeat itself.

It was through his private contemplation and heightened awareness of his real-life experience gained through trial and error as the days repeated that he realized he had to stop, think and then act with behaviors coming from intentions based on altruistic compassion. It was not until he became aware that his intentions should not come from old ego-serving habit energy that he was able to awake to a new day. His experiential wisdom gave rebirth to his free will to question things. Altruistic compassion became his motivator and he finally won the trust of the pretty girl's heart.

Attachment to Things and Non-Things

Individuals need to be wakingly aware that our Source's nature and intended purpose to initiate ongoing change enforces its truth in every passing present moment. This knowledge found through self-examination undoes the ignorance that will change the nature of their mind and worldview to put to rest the formation of the misguided fleeting reactions that contribute to their suffering.

Many individuals decide that it's sufficient to subsist in their illusionary account of what reality apparently seems to be. Individuals become attached to clinging to or wanting to avoid something they've sensually perceived or experienced sometime in their past. If out of ignorance, they recognize this reality as having a permanent nature, they'll unthinkingly assume the item or idea to exist in a state of continuity when considering how to treat or deal with it. They'll choose to treat it like it had a continual unchanging existence through the changing flow of time...a still and lasting presence they can cling and become more attached to.

They might suffer if its lost or even if it's changed in any way. A great many people go to all extents to stop anything from going away or becoming extinct. They need to also look the other way and see what's new and adaptive to the status quo that might be well suited to take its place.

Our Source actively reveals its truth through the transparent sensual exposure of coming and going physical sensations that signal the ongoing manifestation of new life in their host's body...if they would only put on their sensual ears and listen. The unavoidable presence of our reality's unpredictable ongoing change is something completely beyond human power to control or alter.

Out of ignorance, many foolishly try to alter the rate this flow with their imagined control over our Source's ongoing process of coming and going transformation by thinking they can allow shapes and forms to retain their unchanging status to fit into their illusionary account of reality. In following suit, they become attached to their imagined status of their imagined individuality "I am" and anything or idea that comes with it.

Individual's become attached to the ideas and beliefs the images of these objects of shape and form may represent in their illusionary worldview of what our reality apparently is. They become attached to the emotions that have developed that trigger the habit energy-fueled fleeting reactions resulting from repeating actions inspired by their mitote/maya worldview. This attachment to something they're familiar with weaves a security net they cannot seem to find in anything else.

They become attached to gratification of any sort caused by the emotions developed from the fleeting reaction habit energy...good or bad. The heroin addict keeps seeking the sensual gratification of the drug even though they know they're feeding a mind controlling addiction that's destroying their body.

For all practical purposes, suffering and attachment are synonymous terms. Geshe Sonam Rinche sheds light on this fact of reality when he says:

> Only by understanding the nonexistence of what they perceive, by understanding that things do not exist as they appear, by gaining personal knowledge of this and familiarizing ourselves with it can we uproot these misconceptions. There is no other way to get at the source of our suffering. To overcome these misconceptions, we must see clearly that what they cling to doesn't exist. Disliking them may make us want to be rid of them but won't stop them, nor can we get rid of them in the way we remove a thorn.[29]

Sensations Synthesized into Emotion-Driven Addictions

With attachment to uncontrolled habit energy-fueled fleeting reactions, an individual doesn't think first...they've conditioned themselves to just react. Much of their present moment behavior and moods are led by emotion-inspired fleeting reactions.

Red-flagged cause/effect aftershock, creeps in from the world of emotional perception and rings the individual's cognitive bell. It tells its victim to react to the nerve-wired pain potential however their preconditioned perception sees fit to synthesize it. It silently thanks them for unknowingly allowing it the opportunity to elude their free will to thwart their peace of mind and happiness and to sort out their happiness from the suffering it leaves in its wake.

The more these reactions are repeated, the deeper the corresponding emotional triggers become embedded into how they express themselves. This reactionary thinking becomes more of a wall between their current hell and their freedom from their ignorance of nature's impermanence. The emotions become the signature of their moods and personality and motivate the behaviors that define their life style. Their emotions hijack their free will, and their better judgment is swept aside. The more conscious energy that an individual concentrates into practicing and honing these negative emotions, the stronger their hold becomes on their present moment and the more likely that they will be turned to for advice on dealing with life situations.

Bernadette Vigil shares her view on this in her book *The Mastery of Awareness: Living the Agreements*:

> You may not realize that by reacting to situations with strong emotions, you are feeding the energies of these emotions. When

you feed these energies, they expand. They become stronger. As a result, you go deeper into jealousy, sadness, anger, depression, self-pity, and so on every time you react with these emotions.[30]

The basic spectrum of emotions includes anger, joy, surprise, fear, distress and disgust. Each individual's misperception-inspired emotions that are triggering their reactionary behaviors comprise some unique specter of this rainbow of basic emotions. These emotions house a muse of the original attraction/liking or repulsion/disliking feelings experienced while developing their perception of the sensation or combination of sensations that with time triggered the emotions that were automatically reacted to.

Toltec shaman don Miguel Ruiz comments on how an individual transforms what they experience into uncontrollable emotions conditioned from past. He tells of how to control these reactionary emotions, an individual needs to start with controlling what they say and do.

> One function of the brain is to transform material energy into emotional energy. Our brain is the factory of the emotions.[37]
>
> We are addicted to being the way we are. We are addicted to anger, jealousy, and self-pity. We are addicted to the beliefs that tell us, "I'm not good enough, I'm not intelligent enough. Why even try? Other people will do it because they're better than me."[38]
>
> The problem with most people is that they lose control of their emotions. It is the emotions that control the behavior of the human, not the human who controls the emotions. When we lose control, we say things that we don't want to say, and do things that we don't want to do. That is why it is so important to be impeccable with our word and to become a spiritual warrior. We must learn to control the emotions, so we have enough personal power to change our fear-based agreements, escape from hell, and create our own personal heaven.[31]

Individuals will subconsciously grasp at things offering some fleeting gratification and push those away they pair with inevitable discomfort hoping to home in on a good human experience verses one of suffering.

I Swear...I'll Never do that Again

There is no intellectual cure for addictions. No matter how much will power an individual can generate from a crippled and weakened free will contaminated and poisoned by prior conditioning, without guidance they stand a very poor chance of changing the nature of their mind. Any fleeting reactions fueled by habit energy, rote into memory will continue to persist. The more times a reaction is repeated, the deeper it becomes ingrained into their present moment persona.

Chances are great that any behavior an individual just "swears they'll never do again!" will happen again within the next few appearances of similar situations. To change behavior that results in more suffering, it's ineffective to simply intellectually swear that the reactions expressing those emotions are "just going to have to stop."

The experience-void in their belief system's understanding of what happens in between the causing stimulus and the affected emotion is filled with ideas and beliefs coming from their state of mitote/maya confusion fed by their ignorance. It's protected a hallowing blind faith in the unknown. With the appearance of the stimuli, the previously established perception of liking or disliking begins the lightning fast process leading to their uncontrollable reactionary response.

Should there have been an undesired behavior they had wanted to change prior to it becoming an automatic reaction they should have recognized the triggering physical symptoms of the behavior, stopped and focused on altering the behavior in its initial stages before becoming automatic. Once it has become an involuntary reaction and after receiving the triggering stimulus, they lack the sufficient understanding of how their mind works to affect the mind control to step outside their train of thought and catch themselves to evaluate the appropriateness of the thought patterns that initiate the behavior.

It's beyond their natural ability to pull up from their intellectual storage a memorized book, chapter, and verse rendition of some stored borrowed, received or intellectual wisdom read or heard at an earlier time in a book or at a lecture to consider behavioral options that may be more appropriate, at least more appropriate in another situation for the source of their memorized wisdom. They have to break it down to the bare nature of our Source to help undo their prior misconditioning and change the nature of their mind and the worldview it represents.

This intellectually memorized book, chapter, and verse might come from readings or lectures that really made sense to them at the time. They may have sworn they were going to begin living by the insightful justice of that read or heard relational wisdom from that time on.

These quips of intellectually stored wisdom could have been memorized from *Tao Te Ching*, the Bible or from another knowledge source of intellectually transferred borrowed wisdom. The instigator of that wisdom had been experientially inspired to have the recorded insightful understanding of the relational interplay of the involved cause/effect factors to originate the inspired insight and to then apply the relational street sense to other situations with similar causal frameworks.

Not having ever stopped their state of mitote/maya, stepped outside to recognize the thought patterns warning of the physical symptoms of the coming appearance that triggered an emotion-fueled response with equanimity and aware-ness will allow the fleeting reactions their stealth existence. Their emotion trigger-ing sensational signals cloak into a nondetectable state and continue undiscovered to feed the individual's addictions.

The free-flow of the primal sensual pathway linking the deeper consciousness and the waking consciousness has to be de-cluttered and restored. The wisdom-en-riched awareness of our impermanent reality derived from one's deeper awareness of life-change-in-action needs to be brought into the focus of the waking con-sciousness. The liking/disliking perception of a triggering sensation has to be rec-ognized and excused to not return along with the unrest that follows in its wake.

If not, any underlying unrest will come to a boil again and seek expression that stirs up the auto-repeated intention that orders the same fleeting reaction. To rein-in the emotions it's necessary to eliminate the root of their cause. Trying to simply control the result will never stick. This only causes a deeper frustration and more suffering. To cool a steaming pot you must turn down the fire that supplies the heat, not just repeatedly blow off the hot steam the fire produces.

This unchecked reflex habit energy will repeatedly result in one's breaking the Ten Commandments or the object of any other sworn-not-to-repeat pledge made. This habit energy is wired into the belief system as a reactionary response. The reflex habit energy is the downfall of many New Year's resolutions and Sunday morning pew promises. The heroine needle gets reused and reused.

When confronted with the temptations of imagined future gratification that come attached to some sensual inputs that result in breaking one of the Ten Com-mandments, this habit energy of attachment beats to the mental starting gate of intention production any intellectually stored direct order from the Bible, *Tao Te Ching*, the *Koran*, or private intellectually made self-promise not to repeat the tabooed behavior even if threatened by hellfire and brimstone in the afterlife for any noncompliance.

The individual repeats the behavior. In other words, the intellectually stored wisdom from these sources of wisdom is bypassed or beat out every time there's a confrontation at the reactionary race starting line. Only by changing the nature of the mind that recognizes what produces those emotions can this emotion-based culprit be defeated.

Reaction overpowers the passivity of cool thinking that allows an individual to pull back and evaluate the situation before then acting on it. It beats out any cool thinking with an emotionally inspired reaction. Finding out why one would allow the emotional process of reacting to control this range of mental states from their attraction or repulsion to liking or disliking will expose the cause of the reacting that allows suffering.

Anything other than pursuing and recognizing the truth experientially means it is merely being approached intellectually. There may be more than one certain way of learning it experientially, but the meaning will be the same as there is only one truth describing ongoing change. An individual has to be there in person sensually to personally hear the message to derive the wisdom to learn how to truly be liberated from the ignorance of its truth.

15

The Human Experience

Suffering's Not Predestined...Bad Karma is a Choice

Each individual bears full responsibility for their actions. They must realize that some of what they may perceive as happiness really satisfies nothing more than a temporary want gratification that sanctions nothing more than their insipient suffering. The juicy steak with a baked potato loaded with butter and sour cream and a few white flour rolls might taste good at the moment. Their increased risk of heart disease and type 2 diabetes is what they can look forward to.

Their ability to realize special talents while pursuing their life passion has been stunted. They must realize what their suffering is and that it's a mental state that's not predestined or predetermined by random fate...that it is avoidable and fixable in this lifetime.

Fate takes care of an individual's basics like who their parents are, their sex, nationality, when they're born, the color of their eyes and how tall they are. Fate sets people up to use their unfettered free will to do their own thing. They use their present moment actions to fashion their own destiny.

In the end, it's the present moment use of an individual's unfettered free will that sets up and determines if they will suffer or not. It must be realized that people do have direct control over what they believe or do not believe while shaping our belief system and worldview. Performing due diligence is a human right of freedom everyone has to answer any uncertainties before internalizing or believing the purpose of any claim.

This is freedom of thought...of behavior. Individuals determine what they say and do in light of their prior conditioning. The choices they make do affect and shape their future reality. While weathering the process of a transforming earthly presence, it's from the wake of an individual's actions that their karma grows.

The first association many Hoosiers had with the word "karma" was back in the '70s when the record store named Karma was a cool place to buy LPs, 8 track, or cassette tapes as well as should-be-illegal utensils fitting to the drug culture that came with just a hint of Eastern mysticisms...adding to its coolness. During the same time era, with the Midwestern infiltration of the eastern philosophies it turned out that the applied meaning of "karma" is really based on the idea that individuals are responsible for their own actions and that those actions generate effects on our environment and those effects on our environment will eventually have effects on us in return.

Karma means that our present reality is shaped by our past actions. We can control our future by controlling our present actions. To suffer is really an optional effect stemming from which courses of action an individual decides to take. Assuming that an individual has no desire to suffer, it's their conscious ignorance of reality's nature that brings on their suffering.

Be it that we can control our karma to the degree we have developed control over our own actions and that our suffering is suited to the karma of those actions, the cause to our suffering must come from what caused those actions. This is the type of cause that can be understood and controlled.

Free Will Meets Sensual Temptation

As a member of the animal kingdom, human beings are especially susceptible to temptation. Other animals usually show greater sensitivity to only one of their senses. Humans are on the watch for gratification from all five. When an individual hasn't developed a good sense for telling the difference between a want and a need, they frequently choose a course of action to satisfy a want to gratify the ego managed illusion of "I am." The confusion inspired by the human mental state of mitote/maya is temptation's best friend.

When you throw in a set of opposing thumbs and no real sense of life direction you have to be careful. Any individual who's not established a sound sense of priority, frequently struggles with their decision-making process. They must deal with tempting thought patterns reflecting wants and needs from all five senses that help bring to life possible imagined future gratification to deal with. Generally speaking, this is unique to the other branches of the animal kingdom where behaviors are naturally motivated more by what is needed.

In his commentary on the writings of Atisha, an eleventh century Indian Buddhist scholar and saint who reintroduced to Tibet the Tibetan Mahayana Buddhism of today, Geshe Sonam Rinchen puts this into perspective.

> It involves ridding ourselves of our present attachment to the sense objects, which is like a chain that fetters us to suffering. It makes us greedy, discontented and unhappy now, and the actions we perform because of our craving bring suffering in the future. Deer are attracted by the sound of the hunter's flute and die as a consequence. Elephants stand still when they are touched gently

and scratched. This makes it easy to attach the iron hooks by which they are controlled. Moths are drawn to the bright flame of the lamp, which burns them. Fish are tempted by the worm on the hook and perish. Flies are attracted to the smell of the cesspit and drown. These creatures succumb because of their particular weakness, but we humans have a weakness for all the sense objects—sights, sounds, smells, tastes and tactile sensations.

Natural and artificial shapes and colors enthrall us, by natural sounds and by music, by natural fragrances and created perfumes, by tastes to the extent that we eagerly eat foods we know are bad for us, and by physical sensations of all kinds. These factors exercise the greatest fascination when associated with human beings: their appearance, the sound of their voice, their smell, their taste and the feel of their body and touch. The truth of this is apparent if we honestly examine our own experience. People are even prepared to undergo painful and dangerous surgery to improve the appearance of this body.[34]

A modernized analysis of this unique array of sensual influence finds that in the industrial countries there aren't many wants and needs that aren't but a few minutes away that our parents or grandparents had to go without, wait a few days for or make for themselves. Finding sensual gratification takes less and less effort with the development of social infrastructure. The readily attainable satisfaction from the objects of sensual temptation is more easily accessible than in years past. Becoming easier to get and seemingly a more common part of the environment, the calls of temptation have become harder to recognize.

Live to Eat or Eat to Live?...Sugar, Salt and Fat...Oh My!

In Central Indiana, just watch how many decide what to eat while in line at a cafeteria. The size of their waste and health of their heart teeters on their nutritional decisions rooted in the uncertainty of a belief system fronted by a deadened free will. They have no eye focused on finding the truth describing the ignorance that causes this annoying indecision.

If they did, they'd recognize these present moment thoughts as the lure of temptation to satisfy the cravings of an overactive sweet tooth or maybe to satisfy an emotional hunger. Their state of mitote/maya confusion gnaws away at their sanity with imagined hunger pains...the present moment incarnation of the same zone of temptation warned about in the Bible. In their illusionary apparent reality, they lack the ability to recognize and associate the intellectual wisdom accumulated from what the Bible has to say about gluttonism to today's present moment sensual reality that this wisdom applies to.

When there's a wall between how an individual intellectually learns about and remembers our Source and how they view the appearance of the living sensual incarnation of our Source, the source of everyday cause/effect life events, there's a huge loophole for unbridled temptation to seep in. It stands unrecognizably disguised, unnamed and foreign to both camps of thought.

When an individual is not conscious of any link to exist, associating their physical body with our Source, there's no spiritual reason for the well-being of their body to take present moment priority. When Source-related thoughts are engendered and remembered only intellectually, the reality of any sensual connection involved in an individual's heavenly enlightenment slides by unnoticed.

Real-time behaviors that harm the body are not recognized as being in the same reality as those of biblical sinful behaviors...intellectually retained verses sensually recognized...sandals and togas verses suit and tie. Religious believers cannot actually define what a sin is anyway.

It's not considered how this eating style results in living in a body that's weakened physical condition leaves the mind less able to focus on self-training the mind control to self-train the wisdom-enriched experiential understanding of the impermanent nature of this reality. The taste-pleasing temptation of eating a self-destructive diet has the same sinful results on allowing the mind to walk the path to enlightenment as breaking one of the Ten Commandments.

It's been proven that salt, fat and sugar are three foods that are as addictive as heroin or cocaine. The processed forms of these three items instantly turn to sugar when they enter the bloodstream after having the protein and fiber constituents removed in earlier processing to be marketed in another way to stretch the profit margin. These three food forms have infiltrated the American diet to the point where at least one-third of the citizens are overweight and type 2 diabetes, heart disease and stroke, just to name a few of the consequences of human consumption of these lethal food ingredients.

Many churchgoers don't connect that uncontrollable urge they feel when confronted with a bag of potato chips, a donut, candy bar or a soda as being the same evil knock of temptation as described in the Bible. If they do realize it's bad for them and for that reason don't partake, it's for the health of their body. The health of their soul is not so much a factor in their decision-making.

To be able to decide what notions and ideas explain or best interpret the sensual perceptions individuals decide to internalize into their belief system to sustain a collective purpose or direction to live by, human beings need full use of an unfettered free will to verify any claim's association to the truth of ongoing change. When possible, claims need to be put to the test and the intentions they're representing verified through personal experience and considered in light of insightful wisdom coming from and backed by primal faith founded in the omnipresence of the primal truth of impermanence revealed through the sensual witnessing of the ultimate reality or bigger picture in action...within oneself.

When an individual's passing present moments aren't met by a mind tethered to a focused sense of direction, their behavioral intentions are much more open to the influence of imagined temptations of an illusionary future. Their mitote/maya state of mental agitation houses all the unverified claims with unrelated purposes of intent they've internalized into their belief systems with many having a nature based on the illusionary notion of there being a reality with a nature of continence. It supplies the grab bag of possible illusionary ends that lead to their suffering.

This feeds their mitote/maya state of unrest that keeps them lying awake in bed at night. Confusion and uncertainty-spawned fear overrides their present moment with a sense of hesitation that's become their norm and the petri dish for their suffering.

The Fruit of the Tree of (Intellectual) Knowledge... And the Original Sin

The modern-day personification of the original sin Adam and Eve were originally condemned for after their partaking of the fruit of the tree of knowledge, brings a matching reallife condemnation for any individual who allows their belief system to form a worldview based on ideas and concepts originating from borrowed, received or intellectual knowledge. It's the same tree of knowledge. They're condemned to a living hell of suffering the present moment frustrations and unrest coming from the misguided perceptions they have formed in understanding how causes and effects relate to each other. They cover their innocence with the leaves of uncertainty and indecision.

They're not using their unfettered free will to call for the experiential verification of the suggested truth of any claim describing anything they question or feel uncertain about. They internalize the truth of a claim even when based only on its intellectual merit. When the purposes of claims they were internalizing, supported the notion that this reality has a continuous flow, they will suffer the hell from forming attachment to their notions about things that really don't exist.

They have not wakingly visited their personal arena of life manifestation to personally witness the ongoing change that characterizes the nature and intended purpose of our Source. It's the beginning point of recognition to build a steadfast faith in the self-evident truth that omnipresent ongoing change is in process. They have a lack of understanding of the living nature of ongoing change on the primal level of understanding that comes from having been there and done that. Any faith they have will be blind to this and dependent on what their outside source has told them it will be.

Christianity alleges that every individual is born bearing the original sin. Each newborn child inherits the blame and is accountable for the primal sin, which arose at the outset of the human condition. It arose in the Garden of Eden when Adam fell to Eve's temptation pitch and was caught by God, fruit in hand, partaking from the tree of knowledge...the tree of good and evil.

Considering any account of whom or what our Source is, it does seem that from the beginning, our god or our Source would recognize the negative significance of an individual's not being aware of and living in tune with the consequential wisdom derived from understanding the relational interactions among the transforming bits of energy in the material world he/it created so long ago. It seems that he would forbid anyone from developing his or her worldview based on unverified received, borrowed or intellectual knowledge endorsing a false reality with an illusionary nature of continuity...of unchanging permanence. It would be a sin because it would impair their ability to self-train their own enlightened understanding of the impermanence of this reality that their ignorance of makes them suffer so.

The truth of impermanence is the most primal and basic level of truth. It defines the material presence of the process that makes up everything. Impermanence's conscious understanding brings on the state of compassion that feeds mankind's intrigue with spirituality.

An individual's knowledge founded only on intellectual knowledge will inadvertently miss the point. They will have a belief system infected with unverified truths and thus, many beliefs the believer hasn't established the feel for what happens between the cause and effect that establishes the truth. Even if the claim's true, the believer wouldn't be able to recognize it's sensual living incarnation even when it's right in front of their face...like in Jesus's parable of the sewer. The individual will suffer a living hell lost in uncertainty, misunderstanding and confusion.

Adam and Eve's story emphatically and symbolically makes the point of how unacceptable Jehovah thinks it is to rely on intellectual knowledge, as represented by the tree of knowledge. Adam and Eve are unbendingly warned-against behavior based on trust in knowledge that's merely intellectual, which eating the fruit represented. Breaking this order took them from their state of innocence as they were flooded with present moment uncertainty and doubt after eating the fruit. They covered the shame of their ignorance...their fear of the unknown about what might happen with leaves. It introduced fear of the unknown and doubt. They put on their clothes.

In *Tao Te Ching*, verse 33, Lau Tzu says that he who understands the world is learned and who conquers it has strength, but someone who has harmony can conquer the self and who does that is enlightened. Jehovah's directing them away from a life of greed and fear to a life of harmony and understanding.

So, for disobeying God, they were dispelled from a garden they perceived as being a garden of nonsuffering into a world of confusion where causes and their true effects don't necessarily line up. They continually suffered the frustrating confusion coming from their ignorance of the true nature of this reality.

Relying on intellectual knowledge creates a sensual void of uncertainty in an individual's belief system. It leads to the present moment discontent and suffering that comes from addictions involving attachment to uncontrollable cravings and aversions. It results in an individual having an illusionary conception of reality that rubs against the balanced relational justice found in actual relationships as their cause/ effect reality unfolds.

Eating from the tree of knowledge, or internalizing unverified intellectual knowledge that may be corrupted with personally unverified misguided claims subservient to attachment to cravings and aversions, may be the original sin, but it's an individual's ignorance of the truth of ongoing change that allows them to commit the sin. Buddhism refers to this as fundamental ignorance. Their conscious ignorance about the importance of their free will and how their belief system shapes their worldview to recognize the nature of this reality allows them to develop this ignorance of impermanence and to be coaxed from their childhood innocence.

It's tough to find a common answer to actually pinpoint what the original or primal sin is. Ask any Christian what the original sin is, and there will be that many different answers, if any at all. The only constant part of the answer will be that it is the sin that Jesus gave his life to save all his believers for.

Is the original sin really just the act of using intellectually generated knowledge to build a worldview? Could it be said that telling others the way to avoid the misguided mistake that defines the original sin, without even really knowing what the original sin is while hiding behind the cover of a religious name, may not be the original sin, but is really almost as bad?

This type of ignorant deception somehow goes beyond mere false advertising. Out of the ignorance it inspires, it inspires truth seeker's to separate themselves from finding enlightenment about why they suffer within their lifetime.

This could be why the Bible instructs individuals to seek wisdom. It's self-evident that true wisdom's acquired only from experiential knowledge. The trick is to realize that this message is not echoing from up in the clouds. The actual message is echoing nonstop from deep down inside the human condition at this very moment.

The Internet technology company Apple represents the modern world's most prolific means of accessing the deepest regions of intellectual knowledge. It's eerie to wonder what inner agenda Steve Jobs may have been responding to when he decided to give his company the name Apple. Did he consider its possible association with the fruit of the tree of knowledge? Had some evil agenda been subvertly conditioned?

In the Midwest, the apple is typically pictured in readings and stories to be the fruit that Eve handed over to Adam in the Garden of Eden, maybe with a snake watching from the tree. The company Apple's logo is an apple that has a big bite taken out of it. Surely the fruit of the company's logo apple must taste very good, for such a big bite to have been taken. It's just luring onlookers to step on up and take another.

Primal Link—Last Physical Feature Developed at Birth?

So. the lungs may not be the last things to develop before birth? If this original sin is something an individual is born with, then it must be that the individual's born with an underdeveloped primal link connecting their deeper consciousness that contains awareness of the truth of their creation, to their waking consciousness that lives in ignorance of this deeper awareness...making their life assignment, like Siddhartha said on his deathbed, to figure it out.

It could be that this primal link is the very last part of the human model to develop? Maybe the chemicals to complete the nerve synapse required for this awareness to flow from the deeper consciousness into the waking consciousness develops in the living individual during their age of innocence while they become integrated into the yin-yang world of experiential and intellectual knowledge.

Maybe the primal link's development is different because it's not a matter of DNA and fate, but more a human responsibility denoted by what the DNA and fate combo was produced to carry out. Unlike the lungs, one of the last features to develop before birth, the awakening of the primal link of spiritual sensitivity between the deeper consciousness and the waking consciousness could be the very last aspect of bringing the development process of the human package to its full rendition?

It would be true that it requires a combination of nurturing and training above and beyond that of tissue formation, physical therapy or learning the ABCs. It's the waking individual's chance to realize the total harmony in what they are a part of as their evolving spiritual mind finds harmony with and within their ever-changing physical body.

The development of the primal link is the calling out for the individual to bring their conscious understanding of the harmony that unites their mind and body into sync with that of their deeper consciousness that keeps their body in time with change. The conscious mind and body must humbly unite in harmony to cross the bridge of sensual communication and witness the story of how the mind and body are a part of the transforming whole to wakingly experience its truth and bring to front the wisdom derived from that truth detailing how they fit into the relational justice of the whole. This is the self-knowledge acquired through self-discovery that Siddhartha Gautama, Jesus of Nazareth or Lau Tzu discovered in their lifetimes.

This process unites the waking human consciousness with the latent knowledge in their deeper consciousness that understands the details. The deeper consciousness is the human vehicle's glove compartment holding the human condition owner's manual. Like it tells the physical body how to mend a cut, it tells the mind how to heal the spirit.

Mankind's Original Sin = Cyclic Suffering Rebirth?

From the Buddhist construal of the living human condition, Geshe Sonam Rinchen addresses this same sort of sin-at-birth dilemma in his commentary *Atisha's Lamp for the Path To Enlightenment*. He points out the view of the Tibetan Mahayana Buddhist tradition that individuals are born or reborn as the result of contaminated actions...a sin or some action not driven by wholesome intentions that will cause the cycle of suffering to restart...being born or reborn to only die (again). So, an individual's life cycle would originate from a contaminated action that will confront them through their lifetime up to their physical death. Suffering is present until the individual identifies its state and undoes its cause.

> Our search for pleasure preoccupies us and takes up most of our energy, yet it is doomed to failure from the start because none of these pleasures can give us the real and lasting happiness we crave. The subtlest level of suffering is the very fact that this body and mind have come into being through contaminated actions and disturbing emotions. This means suffering is integral to our present condition.
>
> Though we may see it, we don't feel the presence of an eyelash on the palm of our hand if our hands have been hardened by manual work. Ordinary people are equally unaware of this pervasive suffering of conditioned existence. For the exalted, who have direct experience of reality, this most subtle form of suffering is a constant irritant like an eyelash in one's eye. They see the urgent need to get rid of it.[34]

Like in Christianity's "born with the sin" dilemma, Buddhism teaches that during their lifetime, an individual has to figure out how to come to terms with this overshadowing sin. It's the same state of suffering described by Christianity resulting from the ignorance about the nature and intended purpose of our

Source to initiate ongoing change. It's just stated a bit differently. They likewise, must develop the primal link from their source of knowledge to their waking consciousness.

Rinchen asserts that our search for pleasure will never affect the happiness or satisfaction we crave or long for. It will never reveal what is missing from the status quo that allows us to suffer. His account points out that those who are unaware of the primal truth of ongoing change will continue to suffer unknowingly. Yet, the exalted, or those who are more spiritually mature, who've had the direct waking experience of sensually witnessing the truth of the reality of ongoing change, realize their dilemma and seek to solve it through becoming enlightened about the cause of their suffering, as detailed in Siddhartha's *Eightfold Pathway to Enlightenment*. They must educate and self-train their waking consciousness to understand and become wise to the subject of their ignorance.

In both the Buddhist born-with and the Christian original-sin dilemmas, the state of resultant suffering is the same. Humans are humans. The solution to undo the suffering is the same. Everybody is in the same boat.

It's an inherent part of the human condition to long for the answer to undo the overriding original sin that humankind is born to deal with. Individuals must establish the efficiency of their primal link to allow inborn truth awareness to surface from their deeper to their waking consciousness. Like Mr. Rinchen points out, most people are unaware that they are suffering as they get caught up in their contaminated pleasure and foolishly mistake incipient suffering for some form of happiness. All need to change the nature of their minds from having a worldview that supports beliefs that this reality is capable of a continual state of existence that condones attachment to things and ideas. They must infuse the relational wisdom resulting from that primal truth into their worldview to live in rhythm with the savvy wise to the nature of an impermanent reality.

Theological attempts to point to human suffering's core cause are removed and confusing. Christianity's original sin and Buddhism's observed cyclic suffering both stem from the human ignorance relating to the primal truth of how this reality is impermanent by nature. In this, Christianity blames it on how Adam and Eve settled for mere intellectual knowledge to shape their worldview. Buddhism believes that an infant's birth is the result of the contaminated pleasure that originates from unwholesome intentions typical of a misguided worldview suffering from the same. One way of describing this real-life paradox of human condition suffering has a Christian accent and the other way of saying it has a Buddhist accent.

We Remain King Or Queen Of Our Castle

When an individual loses contact with their free will they will develop a worldview support system that accommodates their ego-managed worldview like the street infrastructure of an ancient city was designed to best accommodate the ruling castle of a primeval kingdom. All streets lead unconnected straight to serve the castle like the spokes on a wheel support its center hub.

The intended purposes of many of the internalized claims that shape the belief system of the individual's worldview have unsubstantiated unrelated intended purposes with no shared interdependence or supporting ties with the intended purposes of other internalized claims. Some claims have natures or polarities that repel that of the others. They don't flow together.

If any of the internalized claims' intended purposes are blind to the importance of this reality's impermanent nature, it might be that the claim's intended purpose might not be workable if the reality their intended purpose relates to, doesn't stand still. Like a castle's surrounding street layout, a confused belief system lacks having coordinated inter-connecting support between the different intended purposes of the beliefs that together make up the collective content of their belief system.

The purposes of intent of all the different claims they've internalized should relate to and support the complimentary relational wisdom inherent to a reality with the nature of ever-change. The intended purposes of these claims would share interconnecting and interdependent ties that help support the combine effort of reaching the common end purpose. This would afford an interrelated latticework of ideas and beliefs to better support a worldview that demonstrates consistency in influencing the outcomes in the cause/effect issues that make up the ongoing change of this ephemeral reality.

The intended purposes of many of their belief system's internalized unverified claims are wired to be triggered by or made true by or made to happen or take form in a reality with a different nature of presence. This shouldn't happen in a reality that is nothing but impermanent. Some of the intended purposes of an individual's worldview will prove to be untrue in the impermanent conditions of this reality.

If the validity of the intended purpose of various claims go untested and unverified before being believed, an individual will internalize many beliefs with contradictory or non-related purposes of intent, some shortsighted of the nature and purpose of our Source.

They support purposes with intentions directed at ends (results of effects) that probably recognize realities that have different natures of presence...from a continual permanence to transforming change. Some claims entertain the notion that allows for the subject of a memory to retain its material state of permanence as visualized in the memory.

The purposes of many claims are fueled by faulty intentions honoring attachment on some level to notions of clinging to or of seeking avoidance from something that's continual existence is founded in the memory dust of illusionary things or beliefs. The intended purposes made by these claims will point toward ends founded in illusionary things and ideas that share the illusionary nature of solidity or permanence or continuity of form or shape.

They lack having the common thread of supporting beliefs sharing a common savvy that's wise to the implications of what effects ongoing change has on the ongoing cycle of the causal factors and end effects of this present moment reality. All the intended purposes of these claims have in common is their disregard for the relational truths that accompany all aspects of this impermanent reality, where what is perceived, as being now is no longer, as it has already changed into something else.

Having differing perceptions of how things relate to each other as change happens will change the expected outcome of cause/effect relationships. It will change the perception of what is needed to bring about a certain effect or result. It will affect future relational perceptions involving the memories of that fixed-in-time earlier result or effect and might inspire behaviors that will eventually develop the habitual reactive trait common to an addiction.

These notions originate in the edgeless imaginary world of illusion. Here, the understood natures of the impulses that fuel their intended purposes do not complement each other. They lack harmony. In this mind-set, the unrelated ends compete for importance and priority. Throughout their host's waking day, the resonating wants of these unrelated endless beliefs echo their internalized claims from one end of their worldview to the other.

These claims lack the connecting streets or having intended purposes subject to common natures that would add an interrelated cohesion and complementary motivating purpose to support the thinking they inspire. Because their belief system's internalized claims were poorly filtered leaving some of the intended purposes applicable only when subject to different states of reality, they will spend time pursuing those wishes and desires with nonrelated ends. They will result in having misaligned and misjudged expectations between the causes and effects that create the passing present moment of their transforming life situation. They'll suffer different levels or types of present moment frustrations and unrest common to the faulty conditioning leading to their resulting addictions.

Conversely, if the intended purposes of the internalized claims composing the individual's belief system were all related to a common end centered on the relational truths of the natural law of impermanence or ongoing change, there would be an integrated harmony supporting the individual's belief system and worldview and the intended purposes behind the actions and behavior they inspire. Without this they hang suspended in the chatter of a melting pot of unverified ideas, theories and beliefs making up unmatched imbalanced relationships while at the same time they try to realize their inborn talents and potential allowing them to let their light shine.

As all the uncontrolled chatter in their belief system points in different directions, their mental vision will be nothing but a blur. This would be the point where the start of a steadfast primal faith should reassure their free will to find the courage to venture on. It takes firm root in this sensual witnessing and grows in proportion to the development of their awareness of the truth reflecting what our Source actually is through developing their self-trained awareness of what their material physical self actually is as it changes in time.

Their ability to initiate developing a basic primal steadfast faith has been crippled by not having at least a waking sensual glimpse at our Source's omnipresence that demonstrates the truth of ongoing change. They had not personally experienced the primal consistency and omnipresence of the dimensional conditions that allow the ongoing reproduction of the relational interactions of the coming and going particles that writes the book of relational wisdom that lights the pathway to the enlightenment about why humans suffer that's revealed while self-training self-knowledge.

The average Midwesterner sits spinning their wheels in their unique and lonely apparent reality, king or queen of their castle. Their ego-managed worldview is supported by the intended purposes of their belief system's many internalized claims that have no real interdependence or supporting ties like the lone-standing streets leading to service the needs of an ancient castle.

Their walk along the straight and narrow will be afforded no map and their deep inside fear of what the unknown truth may be that they somewhere in their bones know to exist and their lack of the backbone afforded by any steadfast faith will make them resistant to assistance from others in finding some direction along their life path. This is typical of the fundamentalist mind-set of any mind waxed gross and sidetracked by attachment to cravings and aversions or numbed over by the fear of the unknown.

16

The Antidote to Human Suffering

Human Suffering?

The cause of suffering today is exactly the same as it was 2,000 years ago. Most people blame their unrest on something from the outside world... maybe injustice, war, or world hunger. Many pin the cause of their suffering on an unfair boss, an untrue spouse, a physical handicap, an upside-down mortgage, a lost job or the weather. The fact that a neighbor has a better car is often grounds to suffer from harbored envy. Brutally unfair and torturous prison conditions may be viewed as reasons for suffering for others.

The economy of a society with no principal or principle reserves can be blamed for its citizens' suffering. The USA national family is $19,000,000,000,000 (trillion) overspent in actual debt with about $70,000,000,000,000 (trillion) to be owed for promises made in federal programs. They refuse to follow the "don't spend" logic for national debt relief that's advised for solving family credit card debt. There's no doubt this environment creates many situations that can easily be pointed at as being stressful.

Political leaders look to borrowing and spending more money as a way to overcome the problem. The USA just prints more money to artificially maintain the stock market while banks lend the money of its customers to corporations while paying their customers nothing for the use of their money.

The average citizen doesn't even know how many zero's there are in one trillion, let alone how to get their head around how irreparably large a multitrillion dollar debt is. It's like trying to get a mental fix on how far away a galaxy is when it takes the light that it emits billions of years to reach the earth. One trillion seconds would last for 31,688 years!

A string 1 trillion inches long would circle the earth 633 times! One trillion paperclips weigh more than 800,000 Honda Civics!

There are millions of subprime mortgage holders that didn't read the paperwork they were signing to realistically consider how they could be able to make monthly payments on their new adjustable rate mortgages after the rate resets to the higher interest rate outlined. They blindly trusted the corporations and professionals who offered the programs...like others in their circle of friends were doing. Each of these individuals or couples felt some sort of illusionary protection from this sort of thing happening. Nonetheless, they may think this unfortunate turn of economic events is what causes their suffering.

Some religious souls claim that the Devil, living in Hades, the Greek mythological home of Satan, the god of the underworld, oversees the suffering of the human experience just like their god oversees its future relief. These may be things people choose to suffer over, even though really, suffering is best described as the state of mind, the living hell we choose to create for ourselves during this lifetime.

But what is it that allows human unawareness to misappropriate the cause of suffering to things like mentioned above? The answer lies in how the human belief system isn't being used as nature has shaped it to be used after millions of years of being subject to fight or flight conditioning.

Ignorance About The Belief System is the Agent of Primal Ignorance...A Truly Profound Uncultivated Ignorance

Primal ignorance is an unawakened, non-confronted non-constrained ignorance. Its cause stands virgin to conscious recognition. It lingers disguised in wraps of conditioned rationalization, misunderstanding and misinterpretation. It's threaded through an individual's mental network involved in every intellectual decision made concerning the cause/effect relationships that create and constitute their living waking reality. It's an unidentifiable marker of their personality. It has managed to tie a lasso around their future.

Its cause rests hidden in how they've developed their belief system that forms their worldview. Its elimination lies in their ability to self-train their calm mind and living body to unite in harmony to better understand the relational justice of the reality that their living flesh is a part of.

Everyone has their own unique way of deciding what they'll believe and internalize into their belief system to shape their worldview. This accounts for the unique strain of ignorance each human suffers from and maybe it contributes to why even though people do feel the same pain, they might not suffer in the same way over the same thing.

Each individual has their own way of judging the credibility of new claims they hear before internalizing its purpose as part of the belief system that substantiates their worldview. They draw their own lines in the sand. They decide whom they'll let pull their leg when they can tell someone's trying.

Everyone's born with the free will and freedom to ask why or to demand for someone to prove something they might question. They have different criteria for deciding when they just have to see something for themselves before believing it. People have their own way of deciding how high to set the bar before they'll trust in something blindly.

Mankind's collective free will, science, sets the bar the highest. It requires experiential substantiation for all new claims it questions.

How individuals train their belief system is how their strain of ignorance about the impermanence of this reality evolves.

The seed to human ignorance about the impermanent nature of this reality lies in how the human free will loses its unfettered nature for what's believed. Trouble arises when it fails to recognize the erring nature of claims it's verifying which leads to the individual's misguided conditioning. People need to understand how their mind works to initially guard against developing the ignorance about the nature of this reality.

Using the free will to verify the nature of claims before internalizing them is a defensive fight or flight mechanism that helps protect the human condition from suffering down the road as it strives to maintain balance during its journey through the human experience. A claim's nature needs to be verified whenever possible before internalizing the claim's purpose as being sensitive to our reality's impermanence or not?

Is its purpose a part of this transforming reality or is it illusionary? Does it condone attachment to craving or aversive causes that are centered on an illusionary state of reality?

Having a free will that's numb to feeling out any claim validation when considering new information and the mental unrest of having so many mental voices all talking at once with no guidance or consciously felt direction leading to self-discovery leaves an unaware individual hopelessly caught up in the spin of their unexplainable illusion of how things should be. An inborn part of nature's process is to heal itself and bringing home an individual's awareness of whom and what they are does just that.

Securing an unfettered free will that verifies the nature of any claim vying to be internalized to shape an individual's worldview is an initial step in eliminating or avoiding the ignorance about how the relational justice in an impermanent reality affects things verses how the relational justice in an illusionary reality with a nature that's continual does. Conscious awareness of this difference lights the path to the enlightening discovery and understanding of the wisdom related to this sort of impermanent reality.

It's important that every individual understands that it's up to them to develop their own worldview. It's shaped by what they choose to internalize into their belief system. They need to understand and be sensitive to the nature of what they decide to believe and allow shaping the principles behind the opinions that support the philosophies that represent their worldview.

The big problem is that this needs to be conveyed to people while they are very young. Their trust is too great in those close to them and living experience too brief to be able to understand the context of this paradox.

The Root of the Ignorance that Allows Suffering

People need to realize that they suffer. It must consciously dawn on them that because they've come to react to things, that they suffer. Their real-time state of living is corrupted by emotions that don't have to be there.

They react in ways that bring up negative emotions because they don't understand how the nature of the subject involved is different than what they've been conditioned to believe it to be. Their expectations about what benefits or conditions should come with the subject don't match up with what actually does.

The ignorance from not knowing that the impermanent nature of our reality underwrites the relational justice for everything in the cause/effect transitional process that defines this reality is where human suffering begins. A conscious understanding of how it does it brings an enlightened awareness of its nature and undoes the future suffering it might have caused.

Primal ignorance doesn't sense what the difference in cause/effect relationships would be like between a reality with an impermanent nature verses a reality with a nature that's continual. This lack of appreciating the significance of this reality's true state of transformation allows for the possibility of something's continual presence.

It's through the process where an individual self-trains their understanding of their primal ignorance concerning the impermanent nature of this reality that they will eventually undo their ignorance and thus, be able to enjoy the love and happiness it robs them of and nix the suffering it generates. They will recognize and forgive the layers of religious riddle camouflage and other faulty prior conditioning and the answer will surface from their deeper consciousness into their waking conscious awareness.

By gaining control of the mind and eliminating the cause of suffering (ignorance of impermanence), the mind can be freed and the effect (cyclic suffering) can be eliminated.

While suffering, a truth seeker will utter how "things just aren't what they thought they're supposed to be." Their personal illusions making up their apparent reality have unreal parameters founded in the shifting sands of unverified beliefs, many of which have continual natures. Their attempt at intermingling illusionary causes and effects with real causes and real effects result in their suffering an ongoing frustration of not understanding why there's the wearisome repetitive cause/effect mismatching.

Individuals imagine something about an illusionary item that's presence is fixed-in-time and become attached to it...as if it's always there and will continue to be there. The misunderstanding of this relationship ignores change and allows for the development of cravings and aversions relating to these misconceptions and all the suffering resulting from when the effects don't meet expectations.

Individuals need to be aware of how all that is materially real now is a part of nature's real-time ongoing process of transformation and is no more than an ongoing rearrangement of the material composition of the present moment that was just here and how the material composition of the current present moment will affect how it's all rearranged to create the material configurations of the present moments to come in the ongoing flow of this forward tilted process of change. The present moment is a product-in-time of the bigger picture's process of transformation.

It's through the developed presence of uncontrolled fleeting reactions that the misguided purposes of intent of internalized corrupted claims held in one's belief system are able to hold an individual's free will hostage. The unfettered nature of the free will is handcuffed by the internalized beliefs of claims poisoned by their illusionary natures that condone material continuity as their addiction-generating attachments continue. Their present moment spins in confusion as reality is muddled in the spin of their illusion.

It's their continued ignorance that allows the repetition of the reactionary behavior causing the repeated suffering. An individual's "tanha," their "thirst" for craving and self-centered desire, is rooted in ignorance.

> In the first teaching of the Buddha on the *Four Noble Truths*, the Buddha identified tanha as a principal cause in the arising of dukkha (suffering, anxiety, dissatisfaction) ...
>
> It is this "thirst," desire, greed, crav-
> ing, manifesting itself in various ways, that gives rise to all forms of suffering and the continuity of beings. . .
>
> It is the most palpable and immediate cause, the "principal thing" and the "all-pervading thing" ...
>
> This "thirst" has as its centre the false idea of self arising out of ignorance.[36]

Ignorance about our real nature is the root of suffering and it's an individual's ignorance about our true nature that allows an individual's haphazard style of development of their belief system into a worldview that allows suffering to flourish. It's a highly infectious disease of the belief system that is so easily spread to others.

Individuals repeatedly eat intellectual apples from the tree of knowledge and don't do the due diligence to selftrain the insightful wisdom to wakingly realize that it's foolish to perceive anything's presence as being permanent or continual. They don't know how to. The only aspect of this reality that is unchanging or continual is its state of ongoing change.

Finding the conscious appreciation for the difference between the effects a state of impermanence has on a cause/effect reality verses those of an illusionary state of continuity is an early step in undoing the ignorance that allows suffering.

Individuals will suffer frustration, confusion and disappointment while not recognizing and understanding their mental imbalance when the observed effects resulting from the relational exchanges inherent to the impermanent nature of this present moment rub up against their illusionary expectations of what the effects should be like in a continuous reality.

Ignorance of the need for belief system maintenance allows the ignorance. Ignorance allows the suffering. The integrity of the belief system's free will determines the individual's susceptibility to developing that ignorance. Allowing the belief system to internalize claims without first verifying their nature leaves the individual's belief system unprotected from developing an illusionary account of a continual reality. The relational justice that is needed to service, maintain, and keep flowing the ongoing change of an impermanent reality will not unite the causes and effects of a reality with a nature of continuity.

The primal awareness of the primal truth is the primal answer bearing the primal solution to eliminate primal ignorance. It's the primal antidote to ignorance-caused suffering. Sensually verified primal faith-fueled altruistic compassion flavors the intended purpose of an aware individual's behavior as they let their light shine that lights their pathway to liberation from the ignorance of our Source's impermanent nature and intended purpose to initiate ongoing change.

The truth seeker will find freedom from suffering when they understand the relational justice of the ephemeral reality that eludes them. When they are free from this ignorance of change and the craving of attachment it endorses, they will be free from the suffering it inspires.

The Way Life Seems...Living in a Reality You Know

Individuals who decide to trust the credibility of beliefs or ideas that they've read or heard about (intellectual knowledge) without experientially verifying the truth of the claim being made, to help serve as the foundation for their worldview, settle for living in a world they intellectually know. Should they trust in the sustenance of the biblical warning that eating fruit from the tree of knowledge was a no-no back in the days of Adam and Eve, they should venture forward with caution. For not heeding to God's command to not partake of the fruit of the tree of knowledge Adam and Eve suffered his ordered punishment. They were cast from the garden of innocence into the world of doubt and fear.

Claims believed before seeing any verification are unsubstantiated claims. For the purpose of the unsubstantiated claim to find its truth, it might need a reality with a different nature for recognizing the passage of time. All claims where the execution of it causal contributory factors that don't rely on the passage of time for them to find their truth are illusionary. Illusionary misrepresentations of the cause/ effect rhythm inherent to the relational justice of an impermanent reality bring perceptual misalignments between what an individual thinks should happen and what does happen as life unfolds, bringing frustration and disappointment into their lives.

When someone proceeds to structure their worldview with much of their prior conditioning having originated from experientially unverified intellectual sources of borrowed or received intellectual knowledge, they're resting the soundness of many of their future decisions merely on the credibility of the borrowed or intellectual information sources of those unverified claims. They're bypassing their free will's primal right and self-protection responsibility to test the cause/effect relational validity and nature of the intended purpose of any new claim made by an outside information source before they internalize it to help shape their worldview. They pass up developing a conscious familiarity with their gut feeling describing the actual fiber of what's essentially woven into the cloth of time that threads a claim's causing purpose into its resulting effect.

They've left out actually experiencing the development of what's promised by the claim...the journey. It's like they're OK with not taking the opportunity to enjoy the ride while witnessing what happens during the time from hearing a claim to when the effects of its promise become reality. Some say that for many things, the ride's more important than the destination.

By not first testing the nature and truth of the claims making up faulty prior conditioning before internalizing the purpose of the claims, it's unknown if the collective purpose of intent was infected by any claims with a nature blinded by the illusionary notion that time stands still and allows or even encourages the attachment to cravings and aversions for what are in fact nonexistent objects and beliefs. This lays foundation for suffering the restless ongoing discontentment and frustration that nips at the heels of their perception of the present moment status quo.

The real-life truth of ongoing change is verified through personally experiencing what makes and proves true the real-time explanation of what actually happens in the passing synapse of change that connects a cause to its effect. Take away the feeling or sensual witnessing factor and the clarity of the process of a cause becoming its effect can get confused and lost among dreamed up illusionary interpretations of misqued expectations of what the relational justice of reality apparently could or should be...intellectually speaking.

In a reality an individual intellectually knows, the waking conscious mind looks into a carefully constructed and guarded illusionary framework of reality pieced together from memory image snapshots and moments in time clipped from memories of life in process that they cling to. The individual mistakenly thinks that life has a nature that's continual. This allows attachment to aspects of that state of solidity. This keeps at bay any frustrated individual's effort to effectively identify and give organization or put to order the unsettled mitote/maya mental unrest that's invaded their belief system and holds hostage their free will and peace of mind.

Their confused conscious intellect tries unsuccessfully to figure out why their mitote/maya mind state exists and how to be rid of it. To settle their mental unrest, they will make different attempts at finding the answer they silently unknowingly long for. They are drawn to anything that might have the answer. They attend church in effort to at least keep a clean slate until the day of reckoning that many people believe in that's said to suddenly come blaring sometime in the unreferenced future. The fact is that they are drawn to anything that might give them a simple clue as to what the right question is for the answer they're searching for.

What a believer's faith that's blind to the living verification of the claim's living participation in the present moment is founded in, is all their conscious perception of their soul's future has to depend on. This sets the stage for an unfounded faith of hope.

Before internalizing many claims, they had failed to test and ask further questions to work loose any looming freewill-generated curiosity. The success potential for their inquiry skids to a stop at this point, as they have no living feel of any living truth that supportingly demonstrates the factors making up an unverified claim, religious or not. They really have no bone-felt understanding to anchor a steadfast faith in as a starting point for their free will as they venture on to consider other leads to what the question might be for the answer they're searching for.

They've taken a blind leap over a newly created or further widened void in their belief system and have an uncertain blind-to-verification faith of hope in the unverified claim's promised purpose. They must hope the information source of that information knew what it was talking about...that maybe it had some experiential evidence.

The new believer hovers, passing their present moments in pious ritual while wearing blinders that shut out new ideas and blinds them to seeing other possible answers. They have no experientially founded platform of understanding established to consider any claim that threatens the purpose of the claim they've decided to blindly believe.

There are those who strenuously bite their tongues to live daily staying true to the moral/ethical guidelines of the Ten Commandments with no feel for finding the source of the pool of wisdom from which the Ten Commandments finally surfaced from to be fire-scribed in stone a few millennia ago. They have no clue how to self-train their mind to recognize and associate the biblically based spiritual maxims pictured in their mind with the coming and going sensual dialogue that their heart could perceive as being the real-time incarnation of those intellectually filed religious maxims in present moment sensual terms.

Their conscious mind hasn't relaxed and tried to actually take conscious notice on their own terms of our source's ongoing story of the living truth that constantly emanates from each particle of their living body. They've never tried to sensually listen to the life force that transmits in a sensual frequency that they've not yet known they should figured out how to tune into. They don't know how to generate and interpret any inspired thinking leading to insightful life wisdom they might realize with their self-trained mental awareness suspended in introspective contemplative deliberation while focused into their living arena of ongoing change. This draws them nearer to having an enlightened conscious understanding of the impermanence that their ignorance of puts at a distance their joy and happiness and allows them to suffer so.

It's a message truth seekers have to sensually hear themselves. They must visit and experience the essence of the very process of change itself. Most need guidance on self-developing their mind to appreciate the living potential of the unique inborn human talents to realize and develop during their human experience. Even the enlightened souls of Jesus and Siddhartha did this to realize the awareness that eventually crowned their souls with the enlightened answer that undid the web of ignorance that kept their souls bounded to the cycle of human suffering.

By using only the waking conscious intellect to find the path to living in a state of altruistic compassion and in turn, finding salvation from suffering life's discontent, the blind faith believer has no sensual eye opened to find a way to recognize and tap into their deeper awareness of life's truth. Their enlightened understanding of our source's nature and intended purpose is out of sensual sight and out of sensual tie-in to their conscious mind.

This believer has decided to compromise the integrity of their belief system in taking the leap across its free will's realm of claim testing and stands blind to feeling any experiential verification. They will have a forced-faith founded in the hope of actualizing the truth of an unproven claim with a foreign unfelt premise of a promised afterlife that's free of suffering in a place never seen in a time with a real history they've never known. It's a time in future history-to-be that even the maker of the claim has yet to experience.

The human deeper consciousness strives 24-7 to synchronize self-healing...to form a scab over a cut in the flesh...to keep a steady heartbeat...to heal a bruised body...to replenish joy to a bruised heart. There's a muted yearning from the deeper human consciousness longing to rekindle its living link with the lost and wandering waking human mind. It longs to have its instilled and timeless self-knowledge migrate to wisdom-enrich its host's conscious awareness with the relational justice savvy that guides its human condition to better navigate the human experience.

I now realize that the problem of suffering is caused by an individual's ignorance coming largly from allowing their belief system to internalize claims without first verifying the nature of their purpose. They have no real conscious awareness of the impermanent nature of this reality. Is there a solution to this cause of suffering that can be found and self-initiated during this lifetime?

Siddhartha's third noble truth of the cessation of suffering…suffering ceases when attachment to desires cease.

PART III

THERE IS A LIVING SOLUTION

…Primal Ignorance Undone

Never mistake knowledge for wisdom.
One helps you make a living, the other helps you make a life.
—Eleanor Roosevelt

What I am looking for is not out there, it is in me.
—Helen Keller

Any individual should first gain an increased self understanding to allow developing a more enlightened awareness of the nature of this reality to better weigh the contributing factors to any decision that requires having blind trust in any sort of unverifiable theological claim.
—Anonymous

The Way Life Seems...Living in a Reality You Feel

Where an individual looks to find their Source or Creator is related to how they perceive the nature of the reality they live in...impermanent or continual...sensually or intellectually. It's an indicator of whether they look for a proactive angle to approach the things that fill up their day or if they tend to migrate from couch to couch.

Individuals who look up into the sky when they think of our source or creator have yet to consciously witness or feel the real-time living presence of who or what they're looking for. To give order in this sense of lost uncertainty, they live their life through a worldview that's ego-managed.

Individuals pattern their behavior based on what the collective nature and intended purpose is of the claims they've decided to internalize that form the belief system that inspires their worldview.

Whether or not a claim's purpose is true or false under the dimensional constrains of this reality, each internalized belief challenges or relates to our ephemeral reality in 1 of 2 different ways. The nature of each claim made by the different beliefs they've chosen to internalize either assumes the presence of things and beliefs to be continual...or not.

If an individual is unaware of the differences between and the consequences of believing in the presence of each type of relationship with time, out of their ignorance, they will haphazardly allow the undeserved internalization of the unnatural nature of misleading contentions into their belief system to affect their worldview. This ignorance will eventually lead to present moment confusion and frustration as claims with conflicting natures were allowed to shape their worldview.

Individuals who realize and appreciate that our source's living presence emanates from the ongoing coming and going sensual displays of the unending manifestation of life itself, live their life in a reality they feel. These individuals look inside to find their source or creator.

They choose to entrust the development of their worldview only to the credibility of internalized beliefs that are experientially verified whenever possible. They don't just take somebody's word as adequate substantiation for the nature of a claim's truth. They maintain a healthy free will that makes sure they test the ever-changing waters of their human experience.

Through self-training their ability to control what's on their mind, they learn to discern the true difference between wholesome-productive and unwholesome-nonproductive thought patterns. These are thought patterns that either build to a collective common end purpose or ones that interrupt the wholesome chain-of-thought progressions needed to reach an end purpose. Unwholesome thought patterns interrupt their train of thought. They learn to sort out the counterproductive thought patterns. Due to their ignorance, they're naive about the characteristics of the fibreless cognitive constructs that support misguided thought patterns.

These misguided patterns include ones that mistake insipient suffering for pleasure...too many drinks...too much food...going into debt...eating white flour... the difference between a want and a need. They learn to selftrain the enriched wisdom to sense a feel for the thinking that will actually lead them to the nethermost level of their primal urge to radiate altruistic compassion. They will come to notice that this state of being has the effect of being free from suffering.

When living in a reality you feel, a sensually founded steadfast faith in the unyielding dependability and consistency of our source's omnipresence in providing this reality's dimensional parameters to make possible the repeated demonstration of our Source's coming and going dance that showcases its nature and intended purpose will naturally take seed in the individual's belief system. It will shield them through the unstable ignorance-based thought patterns (temptations) associated with attachments to cravings and aversions that bring on and feed the suffering from the particular modern-day human addictions they've allowed to handicap their worldview.

A steadfast faith will naturally grow alongside a truth seeker's wisdom-enriched awareness of the relational justice dynamics of this reality. As a truth seeker's conscious understanding grows in what this reality's dimensional characteristics are and how they remain consistent to ensure the re-occurrence of the same manifestation of new life for anyone to witness so does their instilled steadfast confidence in its day-to-day truth. It's been this way since day one. This is our Source's sign from above. The manifestation of life in action is the Holy Spirit in action.

It's an assured faith of confidence chiseled into a truth seeker's waking consciousness just as deeply as their conscious understanding of the nature of our Source's presence extends. This faith cannot be separated from the awareness of its truth as the individual grows to recognize how the sensually witnessed truth is now far too obvious to doubt or deny.

When an individual realizes in their waking heart that there is no difference between people, there are those that will die defending this truth. Unable to denounce the natural law ensuring racial equality, Nelson Mandela went to jail for twenty-seven years.

This faith finds the seeker. It's a faith generated from within, not blindly bestowed or gifted from an outside source with no observed present moment living involvement that can be substantiated in the passage of each present moment.

An individual living in a world they feel will not be able to separate church and state when assuming that "church" represents the same wisdom they use for making the decisions to run how they choose to live. They may be able to keep religion-ordered behavior out of the state environment that's denoted by ritualistic practices or dogma of their church, but their acquired spiritual wisdom defining the relational interplay between the situational factors of this transforming cause/effect reality that they live by should be the same wisdom that is needed to lead the state or make decisions about the interplay of the state in the cause/effect scenarios of this present moment reality. The spiritual credentials that truly rule an individual's present moment behavioral intentions can't be grouped and separated from their behaviors when they live in a world they feel.

1

Our Source's Nature
and Intended Purpose

Blessed is the one who continually authors creation.
—Jewish verse of praise

Poof...It's Gone...Now, Just a Figment of Your Memory

In the beginning was the creation...the onset of an unfaltering unleashing of ongoing change...Mother Nature's pulse of time. Even though actual creation details remain forever unclear, the deep-seated most basic and primal truth describing what's since happened is that the resulting reality is no less than an unprecedented uninterrupted ongoing time-driven forever cascading process of forward-propelled cause-becoming-effect change. It's a simple and unavoidably self-evident that our Source's nature and intended purpose is to initiate ongoing change. The intent of that purpose is totally unambiguous. Our Source sprinkles the pulsating Holy Spirit sparkle of life into each passing present moment.

This ultimate reality includes every bit of matter and antimatter touched by time. It includes every coming and going bit of energy making up the smallest of ephemeral particles that comprise all the shapes and objects that make up this universe. Without question and beyond anyone's imagination, the self-evident truth is that all the coming and going bits of energy making up this reality are united in an unending process of ongoing transformation...an unending metamorphosis of changing from one thing into another.

All and everything relating to the observed effects of this change are but mere subjective opinion...truth as interpreted when viewed from a different wave of humanity in the flowing river of ever-change. The process of change is what we are and all we are and all that there will ever be as our sensory inputs dance moment to moment to the metronome of time.

Time's passage is nonstop and each pulsating bit of matter and antimatter in this entire universe receives equal floor time and fair passage through time's window into making its real-time cause and effect coming and going presence.

We live in an eddy of change, cyclical and unending. This reality is a multidimensional interplay/intraplay of new life in a state of constant flux. As time passes with the constant tradeoff involved in our reality's unbiased process of becoming, we've all shared common parts of the coming and going bits of energy at one time or another. We are and are not each other.

Ongoing change is a natural process totally beyond the influence of any human persuasion. The change is 100 percent unauthored. No one has ever slowed down or sped up time. This reality is a 24/7 arena of causes becoming their effects.

Our Source uses naked change to oil the present moment stamp that notarizes the real-time release of each individual's intended purpose as they expose or don't expose the unique karma-shaping fate-bending sway of their own inner-born potential to affect the cumulative persuasion left from each of humankind's present moment footprints. Many will savor these flash-in-time instances while not factoring in the truth that the subject's purpose and form no longer exist as they have continued to change.

With or without a heartbeat makes no difference. Everything transforms. Everything has the living pulse needed to change. Living motion is everywhere in all things. Something with a living spirit has the power to affect that change.

The Human Mind And Body. . .Forever Changing

Your body is not a noun. It's a verb. You are not your body you are its creator.
—Deepak Chopra,[1]

Being created in the image of our Source, the human mind and body continue to change. With most people, the significance of time-pushed ongoing transformation goes unrecognized or at least unappreciated. Unchartered change blindsides each of their new unused present moments with the random confusion coming from a fatigued belief system. Their present moment thoughts are riddled with the unrelated remnants of misguided claims that float around ungrounded in their poorly defined, poorly supported vulnerable worldview. They suffer at some level of unrest and indecision.

In others, change is anticipated and welcomed. They periodically focus their awareness into the arena of change itself with a calmed focused mind anticipating inspiration for their conscious awareness to be progressively enriched with the insightful understandings of its impermanent nature that will lead them to a wisdom-enriched conscious awareness that explains their ignorance and releases them from the suffering it inspired.

The human body is an ongoing flow in an unchanging state of transformation. The human mind continues to evolve. Our human experience is constantly affected and forever changed by the input of differing sensory signals through each of the five sensory ports of the human body. The human mind's understanding of reality is constantly affected and changing.

The constant processing of sensual inputs keeps one's mind busy. Individuals go on to becoming wiser, more intelligent, more emotional, more confused, more or less satisfied, sleepier, happier and sadder...whether aware of the ongoing change or not.

The great singer/songwriter Neil Young commented on a July 18, 2008 Charlie Rose PBS TV interview that people change. He said he agrees with the great singer/songwriter Bob Dylan's observation of how he (Dylan) no longer knows the Bob Dylan who wrote his earlier songs. The mental inspiration that wrote the lyrics to his earlier songs has come and gone. He said that you don't own it (the inspirational message). It comes to you and passes through you.

People's minds transform and change. Individuals channel inspirational insights from the deeper collective human consciousness tuned into the ephemeral reality shared by all. It doesn't go any deeper than that. Some express its wisdom in their art, to be interpreted by any onlooker or listener. This is a positive, half-full forward moving side of the absolute truth of ongoing change.

Reality's unavoidable code of transformation won't entertain any notion that any illusionary object or thing or idea or belief is not changing...that the purpose of any claim's intent has a nature that entertains imagined life continuity. It's foolish for an individual to become attached to a mental impression that clings or shows aversion to any imagined nonchanging existence. This is ignorance on the most basic and primal of levels.

Exponentially Grand Expose of Ongoing Change

Our 13.7-billion-year-old universe is expanding...tumbling outward in an ongoing process of constant renewal. Maybe our Source just can't make up its mind as it keeps rearranging its bits of coming and going furniture? Is it an endless search for the right versus wrong universal feng shui...impermanence due to impatience?...surely not.

This universal state of affairs is real. Preferred naivety to the grandeur of this truth is a symptom of fundamentalism. Recognition and innocent surrender to its majesty breathes the sweet life breath of humility.

Our universe is thought to extend over 150 billion lightyears across...edge to edge. Space itself is expanding at an increasing rate. Galaxies are distancing themselves from each other at an accelerating speed. This is thought due to newly discovered dark energy that science doesn't at all understand.

It's said to make up over 70 percent of space. Dark matter is said to comprise 25 percent of space. Science really knows very little about this reality either. It's known that dark matter bends light coming from far away galaxies with its gravitational pull. It's like looking at a penny in the bottom of a shallow pond of water and how the light will bend once it enters the water.

In effect, what mankind bases all the relational justice found in its laws of physics is demonstrated by the coming and going bits of energy that give form to everything detectable in the human range of perception which pertains to the remaining 5 percent of what makes up the remaining space, as we know it. There's a hidden universe out there that we know very little about.

The Earth has been thought of until recently as being the center of the universe. Nineteenth century astronomers believed the Milky Way galaxy made up the entire universe. Our modern space telescopes have documented that there are more galaxies in the sky than there are grains of sand in the ocean. Each galaxy contains hundreds of millions of solar systems. Just stop and try to begin imagining this. This is real.

Just in our Milky Way galaxy, there are estimated from 100 to 200 billion planets. Science is discovering how some have the combination of natural conditions that could possibly support life in some form. And now they're hypothesizing a multiuniverse reality.

Our 4.5-billion-year-old planet is located in the suburbs of a disc shaped relatively tiny 6.4-billion-year-old Milky Way Galaxy. During one light-year, light will travel over 6 trillion miles. This scope is beyond normal human imagination. Yet, it's true that this entire melting pot of energy, matter and antimatter, detectable and nondetectable all come together to form this transforming cause/effect reality.

It's through science's study of the life cycles of other solar systems that it's been hypothesized that our sun will become a nebula star in about 5 billion years. At this time, our sun's at its half-life stage. The hydrogen and helium inside that creates its gravitational mass will burn out and the sun will expand out, consuming its planets in the process.

Human Perception Blind to Wee Metaphysical Role Models

It's the relationships between the tiny particles of come-and-go energy that create this world as we know it and it's their undetectable interactions that author the laws of nature that underwrite the wisdom needed to find peace in compassionate joy and happiness.

—Anonymous

Nothing stands still and unchanged in the wake of time's unstoppable forward tilted momentum. For most, the perception of the ongoing manifestation of this reality's objects and things is mistakenly recognized as having a nontransitional presence with a nature that is continual. For all practical purposes, the object doesn't change. The importance of its transforming nature isn't really recognized as being important let alone as having any significance.

The human spectrum of recognition doesn't include the sub-atomic metaphysical reality where the relational exchanges between the coming and going bits of energy give substance to those objects and things. These interactions tap out the relational laws of how causes transform into their effects because they do just that on the most primal of scales. The limits in sensual latitude of the human range of perception lead unsuspecting individuals to a mistaken assessment of what seems to be a still world picture that's actually a spinning whirlpool of change.

This primal level miscalculation can end up costing them a lifetime of frustration and unrest when their worldview keeps confusing what they think really ought to be with what actually is. They get attached to and cling to illusionary bits and pieces of what has become their dream.

Misaligned interpretations of cause/effect situations that are in reality governed by the laws of relational justice of ongoing change create great friction within worldviews that are attempting to find focus in an illusionary framework of nonchange. It's the ignorance of this most basic of truths that seeds all the suffering known to humankind. Where do we turn when diagnosed with a sickness or disease? What has helped mankind discover the cures to what was previously a mysterious illness? We pull out a microscope and look beyond the range of human sensual perception, closer to where the relational truth stamped out by the coming and going bits of energy exist. The cause/ effect relationships on the cellular level are analyzed to find out what the cause/effect relationships are that rule what happens to the forms and objects detectable in the range of

human perception.

In this reality, there is actually nothing. Today, science intellectually recognizes the fact that the nature of this reality is impermanent. Only those who were experientially enlightened could understand the depths of its meaning 2,000-plus years ago. Scientists today see it intellectually and those enlightened understand it sensually.

These tiny bits of coming and going energy are the Lego set of molecular physics. Their uncontrollable unpredictable movement creates the noted characteristics of the subatomic particles detailed in quantum physics. These coming and going bits of energy in this tiny metaphysical world react within the dimensional networks that tighten the girdle of the bigger picture.

They work within the dimensional properties of the various cosmic singularity theories. There are five different string theories that overlap and describe different views of coming and going arrangements of energy. These theories assert that matter emanates from tiny strings, not particles. It's like musical notes, when plucked, constantly arising and passing away. In this theory, with the oscillating strings there are now ten dimensions to our reality.

There's the super gravitational theory that explains the infrastructure of this reality. It accounts for there being eleven dimensions to what supports what many humans perceive to be solid permanent things with a continual nature.

They give mass to the similar, but differing dimensional wave-like properties of the parallel universe M (membrane) theory. It's a related modern science explanation for the presence of matter. It proposes that our universe is arranged in layers of membrane or sheets of energy, with particles that are constantly arising and passing away.

Science's growing understanding of particle physics, the relational interplay among the tiny bits of appearing and disappearing energy bits, our subatomic truth orators, provides the subject matter that writes our modern-day books of science. It inspires the insights that write the modern physics, metaphysics and chemistry textbooks.

Newly surfaced relational truths continue to write the books that philosophize the wisdom that all religions and science make effort to explain and maybe claim credit for. They are the wisdom strip writers for China's fortune cookie factories.

An individual develops a feeling of unshakeable confidence in the continued validity of the sensually derived insight-inspired relational wisdom they uncover as long as our reality's impermanent conditions continue to remain consistent. The card shark's winning game will be unbeatable as long as the house rules don't change. This unquestionable consistency is what seeds a truth seeker's steadfast faith.

These coming and going bits of energy give the structural definition to the subatomic universe that details every atom that makes up the bigger picture. In the world of theoretical particle physics, there's now strong evidence showing the physical presence of the Higgs boson particle. Higgs boson God's particle is just becoming better understood by science.

Its existence explains how particles accumulate mass as they radiate from their field of origin. Its existence gives symmetry to mathematical equations. Its existence helps explain scientifically how things accumulate their mass.

It further describes the behavior of particles. It helps predict what types of particles something might decay (change) into. That all things decay is what Siddhartha alluded to on his deathbed that each individual needs to become enlightened about to undo their ignorance of to find happiness and joy and escape suffering.

Science can provide an intellectual picture of this reality. It's up to each individual to experientially understand its truth.

The present moment bustle of mankind's most fundamental and tiniest role model is totally outside the realm of normal human waking perception. It goes by totally unnoticed. Few stop to realize that the cause/effect relationships involved in the behavioral physics of human interactions within their environment bend to the same relational justice that's patterned out by these wee role models. The practical applications of the relational justice inherent to the primal truth describing the nature and intended purpose of our Source starts on the smallest of scales and ripples up, through everything in the range of human perception.

The relational justice present in the sensations accompanying the coming and going of the smallest of our role models writes the screenplay that carries one present moment into the next. Primal wisdom details the universal justice that transpires when a change transforms into its effect, as our Source continually makes true its intended purpose of supporting this ongoing cause/effect transformation.

To gain an enlightened understanding and waking awareness of the impermanent nature of this reality, what better place for a truth seeker to park the sustained awareness of their right concentration (meditation) than where there is nothing present but the ongoing emanation of life itself? What better place could there be to be while relaxed into a contemplative deliberation to exercise maintaining the mind control that's trying to just stay focused into this arena of change to be inspired by the coming and going dance of impermanence to realize sudden insights about life's impermanent nature?

Time and Space...A New Concept

Time plays host to and ushers in cause/effect change. It's only been in the last one hundred years that Albert Einstein was able to pry open the collective waking consciousness of that day's religious and scientific schools of thought to allow the collective visualization and public intellectual understanding of the claim that there's yet another dimension to what was thought to be a three-dimensional reality...the fourth dimension of time. He defined the comingling relationship between time and space with his equation $E=MC^2$.

Past time is a measuring stick for the passage or history of change. Its rate of passage is set relative to the limits set by the physical properties of the speed of light. The speed of light is a constant 671,000,000 mph. Space and time adjusts to each other (space-time) to keep the speed of light constant. Isn't everything we see actually no more than a hologram of sorts, fading into the next piece of space-time?

The uninterrupted presence of the flow of our reality's only nonspatial dimension, time, allows change to unfold and present itself in the recently recognized remaining nine or ten dimensions thought at this time to support today's reality.

This accounts for the various configurations of the theorized planes and fields, strings of energy, parallel waves and so on.

It's unknown what will happen to the dimensional count when dark energy, background radiation, antimatter and black holes are better understood. They say dark energy is expanding our universe. Could it be ripping it apart? Black holes are so dense, if the earth were collapsed into black hole size, it would be less than 0.2 inches tall.

Gravity is thought of as a warping of the space-time fabric. The gravity of a black hole is so great light cannot escape. Mankind knows absolutely nothing about the reality within a black hole except that they fulfill a needed role in balancing our reality. Could they be wormholes or shortcuts to other galaxies or maybe other dimensions?

Time and space are relative to each other as velocity approaches the speed of light. Approaching the speed of light, time and space warp into each other, keeping the speed of light unchanging. This effect is negligible within the scope of human perception. For all practical purposes when confined to this planet, time is constant...the only truly unchanging and highly predictable omnipresent dimensional element of the bigger picture. Time is our Source's unchanging and predictable means of initiating change and the unpredictable.

The Blanket of Time

An unchallengeable regiment of the human condition's time metered trip through the human experience is its interwoven reliance and inborn dependence on time's constant change. Humans of all ages cling to their blanket of time.

There's a deep-felt comfort and security enjoyed from the predictability and unquestioned assurance of time's passage as it steadily unwinds our life-clocks. We set our hourly clocks by its time-proven consistency. We take pride in being able to estimate the passage of its presence. We cherish having a close-knit relationship with our Father Time.

Prior to making a solo appearance before a large crowd, many get anxious. Having developed the ability to sense and gauge the rate of time-elapse from actual personal experience in sensing time's even passage gives an inward felt confidence. It gives an inner-felt and sensually recorded history and experience-based astuteness in estimating how many similar like-timed present moments have to roll by before an anticipated public appearance will become an experienced present moment of the past affecting the "right now" karma of a passing future present moment.

Having the written-in-my-bones feel for the amount of time pending this upcoming event minimizes the uncertainty associated with it and possibly helps calm one's nerves for them to more confidently see the event through any stage fright to its completion. It lessens their suffering from preevent anxiety. Waking awareness of time's dependable and predictable presence can act as an anti-inflammatory mind medication of sorts for many.

Individuals who in their expectations understand and respect the bigger picture's controlled pace of time-elapse are considered to be patient. Having recognition and appreciation for time's unalterable continuance is how they establish an internally unchallenged willingness to wait. This is based on wisdom-enriched awareness, realized or unrealized, that our Source's pulse of time is one thing they have no possibility of changing.

The inspiration for this universal wisdom applicable to this state of reality can be experientially discovered as a basic tenant of self-discovery when someone acquiring self-knowledge realizes how they have no control over the coming and going sensations that percolate during the manifestation of new life. It's from the same pool of wisdom common to any religious or scientific formula.

Nevertheless, time's unassuming presence and predictability is so much a part of what humans are that it's largely taken for granted. It's experienced by all but overlooked unattended and unappreciated by most. Time's passage blindsides many who have not developed a personal relationship integrating its time-textured nature of impermanence into the understanding and rhythm of the nature of their belief system that's reflected in their perceptions of our cause/effect reality that characterize their worldview.

Mankind has such great faith and confidence in time's omnipresent consistency we make it a factor in sizing up our universe. When time is factored together with the universal dynamic, the speed of light, man can predict other transforming heavenly bodies to be millions or billions of light-years away. We have confidence in knowing that dependably constant time, times the speed of a dependably constant wavelength yields consistent accuracy in a conceptually graspable means of measuring the great distances in this universe in terms of time travel.

In our reality, the speed of light is also a steadfast faith-worthy attribute of Source-determined consistency. Any calculated change in its velocity is in direct proportion to the passage of time to keep the mathematical relationship $E = MC2$ true. Yet, it lacks the 24/7, 365-day presence that comes with the omnipresence of its counterpart, time.

It's to be noted that the natural forces of quantum gravity, electro-magnetism and the weak and strong nuclear forces share an omnipresence of sorts. However, these forces can be manipulated in the real unchanging time elapse of this cause/effect reality through manipulation of the factors that constitute their presence. For example, it's time's ever-present unchanging presence that enables the cause/effect change that affects light's measurable travel and the effects of the related natural forces to be realized.

Every year, modern society collectively celebrates and gives thanks honoring Father Time's omnipresence on an unrivaled scale of worldwide proportion as mankind openly demonstrates its reverence for the passage of time. Free of all religious ritual, dogma and protocol all nations unite and pay their tribute to Father Time with a worldwide birthday party focused on exactly the same thousandth of a predesignated second in time at the start of each and every New Year. This is the only thing worldwide that never starts late. The Chinese New Year gets its own reverent celebration of similar grandeur...same thing just different heritage. Will the celebrations merge one year? We'll see. Time will tell.

The final seconds of Earth's passing year, if viewed from the moon would show like a global crowd wave in a huge sports arena. As Father Time sequentially blows out his world-wrapped birthday candle display, the lit-up crystal balls in each successive time zone, one after another make their ten second descents through the celebrating fireworks and shouted-out countdowns of the final seconds of each year. Mother Earth spins from the finale of one day into the birth and passage of another day of countless present moments to make continually true our Source's intent to initiate ongoing change.

Some become so inspired by the change into a new year, like changing from the status quo into a new time where the answer might lie, they vow to break an addiction and become a better person. In the Midwest, these are addictions like watching too much TV, poor physical conditioning, weight gain or smoking cigarettes. This New Year's vow usually receives more serious attention than frequently renewed Sunday morning pew-promises to similar ends. However, an individual's lack of awareness and understanding of the anatomy of their belief system will result in the priority of their worthwhile efforts being confused with and diffused by those of pointless-to-no-end ego-preserving causes of their confusing mitote/maya state of mind and their quarantined addiction will probably persist and live on.

"Time is on my side." "Your time will come." "Just give it some time." "It's just a matter of time." "Time heals all." "Time will tell." "Time is our greatest enemy." "Time is our greatest friend." "Time waits for no one." "It's the fastest time on record." "It's the longest time on record." "He's makin' time with a pretty lady." "It's all in the timing." "Time is money."

Mankind doesn't question time's ranking authority and value. Father Time's presence assumes its own identity as a superpower...as a powerful entity with superior unlike human capabilities.

Without time's unfolding, there would be no wrongly perceived life continuity for those who understand this reality to have a continual nature, to snatch snapshot memories and mental images of objects from to mentally stamp as unchanging and something to cling to. They will patch together unchanging memory blankets of illusionary notions they will cling to while being propelled emotionally unprotected through time's unending meteor shower of new unexplored present moments that bring the constant change they don't anticipate or understand and are not ready for.

Finding Sync with Transitory Reality is Key to Joy... Expose Self-Potential and Let Light Shine

Like how the size and shape of a single wave of water is influenced by the push and pull of the entire ocean, the character and purpose of each separate human being finds form to the knee-jerk influence from the ever-changing forces within the sea of humanity. If someone is gaining a wisdom-enriched awareness of the nature of this impermanent reality, they develop a conscious acceptance and pro-active anticipation for the turning of the page.

They might not know exactly what's going to be on the next page, but they're aware that it's coming. Their expectation of unavoidable cause/effect change would better allow them to script what happens in their current present moment to affect what appears on that next page. They can fashion the present causes to have the well-planned productive effects that are best suited to affect the release of their inborn potential for them to let their light shine.

Individuals can develop steadfast faith that there's nothing else to bet on but the dependable predictability of this reality's Source-initiated transforming presence. The consequential tree of relational wisdom attached to the natural cause/effect pull from these omnipresent conditions knits together, makes sense of and sets to balance the relational justice between the contributing factors. Just check the charts of the stars or *The Farmer's Almanac*.

Yes, having wisdom-enriched awareness of the predictable order of the cyclic rhythm of reality's unpredictable budding cause/effect relationships is feasible. But, making any sense or finding any pattern of relational justice in an individual's illusionary notion of an apparent reality where there's no focus that penetrates the effects of unpredictable, not-to-scale and unmonitored cause/effect relationships is quite impossible.

During an individual's lifetime, to satisfy the inborn purpose of the human condition to knowingly mirror our Source's nature to initiate ongoing change, an individual must find the balance and courage to initiate behaviors that actively give creation to the purpose of their unique combination of skills and talents. Misguided prior conditioning leaves an individual's belief system scarred and unfamiliar and likely to misalign and misinterpret the real relational justice in how a particular cause results in its effect.

They will not understand the relational justice that would successfully lead them to knowing what might be the cause of a particular effect they are faced with or what the likely effect might be of an unwise cause they are about to initiate. Their clinging to nonexistent notions of objects forms or ideas leaves them slow to reality. They suffer trying to maintain poise within the imbalance.

Efforts at interpreting illusionary understandings in the world of relational interplay where the individual finds no rhythm or anticipated itinerary to tether their understanding of cause/effect displays to, make the mission of actually linking effects to their true cause or predicting what effects an upcoming cause might bring, quite unachievable. It becomes guesswork that will bring more suffering.

It's frustrating to whatever degree of neurosis or level of insanity one may choose to recognize it on. It should be each individual's responsibility to humankind to realize their talent potential and let their passion bring humanity closer to a suffering-free coexistence founded in altruistic compassion.

2

The Primal Basics

And ye shall know the truth, and the truth shall make you free.
—John 8:32, King James Version

The Primal Truth About Our Primal Nature

Decay is inherent in all compounded things…
—Siddhartha, on his deathbed

It doesn't matter who says it…the truth is the truth. It may be heard in a Goodwill Store TV add saying how this reality is in a constant state of change or the last thing Siddhartha said on his deathbed of how change is inherent to all things. This is the basis for the self-evident truth that enlightened him about his ignorance that caused his suffering. Understanding the truth of ongoing change will set you free of the ignorance that creates a state of mind that replaces joy and happiness with present moment suffering. This is the very truth that testifies to our Source's nature and intended purpose.

Our Source's primal intended purpose is to initiate ongoing change. Our reality's state of impermanence is the most basic and primal of truths. Its ongoing functional presence is conditional to the existence of this reality. Understanding it is functional in enjoying the compassionate joy and happiness in what it provides.

The parameters of our Source's nature and purpose were established in the beginning during the big bang 14 billion years ago or maybe when God snapped his fingers six thousand years ago with the seven-day creation or possibly at the start of the hypothesized expansion-contraction existence of our universe. Solving the creation riddle is really unimportant as today's evidence of transforming life is self-evident, no matter what the suggested beginning looked like or who or what may have caused it. Besides, the claim makers of all the different accounts of creation have ended up breathing the same breath of ongoing change as those with different accounts.

315

A present moment is a present moment, no matter at what point in the past. History's really only an opinion or a subjective perspective anyway. Knowing exactly how it all started or what god gets credit serves no significant role in focusing ahead and reaching an enlightened understanding of its real-time presence.

If there was a beginning, the important thing is that it was at a past present moment that the dimensions of our reality came into sync. It's a dimensional package that supports an infrastructure of consistent relational justice. This comes with the package of applicable wisdom that breaks down and takes objective note of how the relational properties of the infrastructure relate to each other.

It's in an individual's confidence of the omnipresence of this interrelated web of relational properties that they can anchor a steadfast faith. The ongoing cause/effect consistency of this interrelated web makes the relational wisdom of today the same as that of times in the past as well as times of future present moments.

The primal truth details our Source's nature and intended purpose to initiate ongoing change. The truth explaining our present moment comes out sensually coded from the human deeper consciousness. Its story is the sensually channeled experiential key to decoding the relational wisdom making sense of an individual's ignorance of the nature0 and intended purpose of our Source's living presence in this cause/effect reality.

In time, truth seekers learn to decode the wisdom making sense of what happens in the space between when a cause changes into its effect...the truth of what draws and binds an effect to its cause...the fiber in the synapse that holds together each passing present moment.

The ongoing momentum in this reality's impermanence is the gravity or the binding magnetism that binds a real effect to its real cause. The process of gaining conscious awareness of its truth progressively fills any belief system void with understanding and squeezes out any fear-inspiring uncertainty. The self-generated steadfast faith in the surety of its unskipping omnipresence is the primal truth's guardian.

The primal truth is singular straightforward and baseline. Its story is readily available to any roaming ego-managed waking consciousness and is the same for everybody or it's an illusionary impostor. Its role is indivisible and can't be diluted substituted or rationalized.

Just as the primary colors red, yellow and blue serve unchallenged as the primal constituents to the world of colored visuals in the human range of perception, our Source's unchanging, change-initiating omnipresence sets the forever consistent parameters for just normalcy as each individual's becoming potential is released and exposed to fate's karmic paint palate. Primal truth affects the changing hues of the subjective human life experience that blend, color-coding the character of their unique life karma on fate's canvas of undefined limits.

An individual's present moment waking awareness of the primal truth reminds them of who they are and who they are not and all they have potential to be. One's present moment waking awareness of the pillars of our Source's primal truth prompts them of what's illusionary and a waste of their time to pursue.

Our Source, without skipping a beat, boldly and courageously demonstrates its intent to initiate ongoing change throughout everything. It's patently obvious that our Source's omnipresent and eternal role as architect curator and resident artist of the present moment goes fully documented back to the beginning of ongoing change. Our Source continually authors creation.

A truth seeker's awareness of the primal truth puts to order their interrelated, interdependent present moment written-in-time life attributes affecting the expression of the human condition within fate's constraints on the human experience. It completes the dimension and balance that makes real the give-and-take energy of yin/yang duality.

An enlightened awareness of the primal truth bridges and unites the imagined scope of the oxymoron, unchanging change. The primal truth is all-comprehensive. The primal truth shines from everyone, but seems to require 3-D glasses for most to see.

The primal truth's inborn experiential record resides deep in the subtle regions of mankind's primal being. There's only one truth explaining our Source's nature and intended purpose even though through attempted religious exploitations of its true nature, it may have received different names and characteristics from different people in different languages from other times and places. Its abuse and separation through intellectual categorization has warped its meaning and made it unrecognizable to most. Still, there's only one truth and one light to make visible the path to its awareness.

Attempts to label our Source might imply that there's a separate entity or origination source that watches over, controls and guides us from afar and listens to us from above when we pray or possibly appears to us in our dreams. Yet, the actual radiation that warms us to our Source's style and purpose of intent can be kindled and experienced only from feelings within.

The primal truth is binary and nonsubjective— it is or it isn't. The primal truth that everything is a part of the universal swirl of unpredictable coming and going metaphysical sparkles of energy is the unchanging fact of life. It's blind to prejudice and 100 percent nondiscriminatory.

There is really nothing that can happen beyond the present moment, yet the present moment is really a myth. The only thing here at this moment in time is what holds on present moment to the next...never realizing either...the cause that will become the flowing effect of the next imaginary present moment in the plasma of time.

The nature of ongoing change and intended purpose to initiate change that our Source's truth defines reaches out into infinity, encompassing the entire universe...initiating transformation in everything it touches. The truth about the bigger picture's nature and intended purpose sets order to the universe as it enforces the open laws of cause/effect karma on each and every release of human potential.

The Buddhist teacher Thich Nhat Hanh agrees when he says:

> If we see the truth of one thing in the cosmos, we see the nature of the cosmos. Because of our mindfulness, our deep looking, the nature of the cosmos will reveal itself. It is not a matter of imposing our ideas on the nature of the cosmos.[2]

Mr. Hahn affirms Siddhartha's enlightened observation that the same truth of impermanence flows in everything and how it's useless to try to alter its nature.

The primal truth of ongoing change is the subject of revelation sensually witnessed while an individual is gaining primal awareness through the process of self-training their moral behavior, mind control and wisdom development while gaining the self-knowledge leading to their self-discovery. An individual's conscious awareness of the primal truth of this state of ongoing change is gained or realized only through the experiential learning gained with awareness focused in their own physical theater of ongoing change.

The primal truth underlines impermanence as being the fundamental building block of reality's working definition. Its omnipresence enforces the nondiscriminatory laws of karma as interpreted by mankind's ever-evolving bias in defining humanity...as the human condition engages the human experience on life's balance beam of fate.

Christian and Buddhist traditions both speculate about sources with different natures. Christianity allows our Source to have a nature that's continual and doesn't really stress how the relational truths that describe impermanence can be important in their explanation of God's plan. Buddhism underlines impermanence as being the nature of our reality, realizing that since things are always transforming, it's foolish to become attached to memories of what they were once perceived as.

It's like the difference between someone having a worldview coming from a belief system focused on a world they intellectually know and having a worldview shaped by a belief system conditioned by a world they feel. Their temperament projects the steady, calm and relaxed, consistent, dependable, directed and forward moving beat of the drums of Father Time they knowingly and willingly march in harmony with as they become the living expression of their full potential.

The truth of ongoing change was the truth, is the truth and always will be the truth. It's the first and simple truth, primal before and beyond religious ridicule. It's totally binary character is beyond any human intellectual appraisal inspired by any sort of subjective opinion or standard stirred by reason or deduction. It is the obvious unquestionable and self-evident primal truth exposing our Source's nature and intended purpose to timelessly initiate ongoing change.

One Truth...One Reality

What's the nature of the God-hosted reality of afterlife heaven? It can only be wondered if Christianity's place called heaven has the same properties of ongoing change as this reality the obedient Christians would be saved from...and yikes... what about hell? Do these realities have the same scientific relational principles describing their nature?

Since the collective wisdom that applies to this cause/ effect reality depends on each present moment being in the state of transition, the after-death heaven would live under a different tree of wisdom if it has a continual nature where objects and ideas can remain unchanged? It's very important that any relationships that find effect while under a different state of existence would have wisdom-enriched understandings that would apply to a different sort of relational interaction.

Still, the promise of heaven boasts having the joy, love and happiness experienced in this reality. How else could it be perceived of as being so desirable if it didn't identify with the sensual experiences stored in experiential memory? Why would or better yet, how could any human want anything different than the perfectly orchestrated compassion, joy, love and happiness that's inherent to this reality's set of natural laws that apply to the state of the human condition that lives in this human experience?

Why would or better yet, how could it need to be promised in a different configuration of reality? Rod Serling's *Twilight Zone* of the 1950s and '60s hypothesizes how this would work in several of its episodes.

Is it even possible to have a reality that leaves out the progression of time and the change that makes record of its passage? If it were possible, it would be plagued with all the suffering that accompanies all the attachment allowed in the illusionary continual worlds of so many people today. If so, as is in today's world, it's a reality defined within the boundaries of boundless illusionary human imagination. Are there any two preachers who can give nongeneralized accounts of exactly who or what God, the Son and the Holy Spirit are or what Jesus's return well be like and what about the day of redemption?

Calling the primal truth a religious or spiritual truth intellectually prejudices its intended purpose as something special and not a part of that which is not religious or spiritual. The primal truth was around long before the concepts of religion or spirituality came along to point it out. Giving it a theological classification pigeonholes and warps its presence in a humanized illusionary apparent reality where mankind is the center of attention and all things are intended to serve them as the outside universe revolves around tiny Earth.

The primal truth exposes and makes transparent the true source and sponsor of this cause and effect reality. It testifies to the present moment energy of time propelling one present moment into the next at the speed of time-space. It defines the forever-consistent environment for all claims to establish their truth in or for any cause to have its effect. This omnipresent time-fueled and Source-regulated speed of transformation affects all things equally and is totally beyond the control or edit of any individual part of the whole. It's just that most people unknowingly, spend most of their daily energy swimming against its forward moving current. They exhaust their energy treading water in a pool of doubt and uncertainty harboring the ignorance that allows their continued suffering.

The cause-generating property or function of our Source explained by the primal truth is the life-giving, sparkof-life, holy-ghost-like initiative that change's or gives birth. It allows the new life of new cycles to begin. This cause-initiating property of ever-change is what defines the nature of the ultimate reality. It's what sets tempo to and regulates the flow of the uncontrollable stream of physical sensations realized while gaining self-knowledge.

The Toltec shaman don Miguel Ruiz shares his view:

> Life is the force that makes the transformation of energy possible. The force of Life that opens a flower is the same force that makes us grow older. Look at your physical body, and just imagine how you used to look when you were five years old compared with now. It still is you, but the body is completely different. It has changed.[3]

The simple most primal of truths is that nothing stands still in time. The time driven human experience is never at rest. The once childhood persona of a teenager has died repeatedly to be constantly replaced with reborn ever-maturing karma-shaped products of unused developing potential. The teen's present moment persona continues its ongoing process of death to rebirth as the ultimate reality makes real its intended purpose of sponsoring ongoing cause and effect change.

The death of the teen's present moment persona sets premise to cause its present moment rebirth. Its rebirth was the effect of its cause, death. Its rebirth will then be the cause affecting another death to cause another rebirth of a more mature, possibly taller, possibly wiser version of the ever-changing human package of living potential. Given that the presence of our time-fueled cause/effect reality does not cease, this life-death cause/effect transformation process will continue till their body's death causes another rebirth and so on.

Instead of lifetimes spent in other physical bodies, is this strobe-like life imagery of momentary life moments the previous lives that allegedly flash before you just before you die? Maybe it's not a flash comprised of previous lifetimes in different human (animal) shells? Do these the prior lifetimes of reincarnation refer to the present moments within this human shell or those spent in others?

The process of gaining self-knowledge provides a deep level of personal experience-based primal awareness bringing a conscious understanding to the most basic and primary of truths that's fundamental consensus is undeniable and beyond the confines and critique of any religious condescension. Its awareness sponsors a wisdom-enriched understanding that gives order to the interchanges relating one thing to another in the ongoing flow of this time-fueled cause/effect process humans recognize as reality. Our Source's process described by the primal truth is what integrates all causes to the effects they transform into.

The primal truth is our Source's uninterrupted sensually posted notice and mandate to all coming and going bits of energy to mature, to decay, to become something new and different. This primal truth serves as the basis and sets the rules for the perceived truths of all other visions of truth. It anchors any claim recognizing some form of attachment as being untrue because the reality of constant change makes impossible the continual existence of anything.

Primal Truth...Subjective and Tolerant

The manifestation of change never stops. The ongoing demonstration of our Source's ever-changing nature encompasses the entire universe (universes?). It's the eternal life-initiating buzz of the bigger picture.

The time-fueled omnipresence of our Source's uninterrupted continual change is the nonsubjective baseline gift of life each cause has for its effect. Its material transmission is the only available ongoing unlimited medium to support this reality's cause/effect cycle. Its baseline presence is instant and uniform.

Objective truth is subject to an individual's point of reference. An individual watching an event from the front side will describe it differently than an individual with a line of observation focused from the rear.

The sensual combinations an individual encounters and perceives within the scope of their five sensual ports will be different than that of other people and will reflect their subjective interpretation affected by their unique cocktail of prior conditioning. This is true even if it's a sensation that's the effect from the same cause that two people experience at the same time and place.

The same event will receive different reported effects from different people. An individual's present moment interpretation is subject to any internally retained likings or dislikings associated with the subject matter from prior associations from similar cause/effect situations.

Thich Nhat Hanh points out his view on the significance of the role played by an individual's perception:

> The source of perception, our way of seeing, lies in our store consciousness. If ten people look at a cloud, there will be ten different perceptions of it. Whether it is perceived as a dog, a hammer, or a coat depends on our mind— our sadness, our memories, our anger. Our perceptions carry with them all the errors of subjectivity. Then we praise, blame, condemn, or complain depending on our perceptions. But our perceptions are made of our afflictions— craving, anger, ignorance, wrong views, and prejudice. Whether we are happy or we suffer depends largely on our perceptions. It is important to look deeply at our perceptions and know their source.[4]

An example of truth, subject to individual prior conditioning that's related to the claim made could be an opinion of how good a piece of apple pie tastes. The individuals' physical testimonies are subject to their stored perceptions resulting from prior conditioning involving any taste experiences with apple pie. These experiences are affected by outside factors that influenced or shaped their earlier perception to become one of the internalized claims that make up their belief system.

Outside influences of the taste could be Grandma's smile, McDonald's subversive advertising or a head cold affecting that moment's sensual report of taste. The accuracy of this truth remains relative to the subjective influence of the personal likings and dislikings formed during the different individuals' prior experiences with similar events.

Any experience other than that with the unalterable coming and going sensations of life manifesting itself within an individual's physical arena of ongoing change will reflect a history of the individual's personalized perception of one or a combination of sensations. An individual's perception of any experience is a subjective interpretation of what the sensed effects were resulting from the outside cause that's intended purpose transpired into or became the effect being considered. To them, their subjective perception is the truth. Different accounts of the same experience can really be equally true in light of the differing prior conditioning affecting the interpretations of the individual perceptions of the experience. Recognition of this unalterable primal reality

looks the same from any angle. It's the basic primal truth.

Understanding this creates the foundation for making tolerance a welcome part of an individual's worldview. It saves so much unnecessary suffering. Its understanding can help inspire true compassion in times of conflict and lead to a peace-keeping compromise. It helps keep the air open to different possibilities for solutions.

Primal Awareness (of the Primal Truth)

Ongoing transformation is the only state of reality anyone has ever experienced. Yet, the seemingly constant material presence of this always-changing reality is just assumed and taken for granted by the vast majority...big mistake. An ongoing state of transformation is the only thing constant about this ephemeral reality.

Does reality have anything to say to us? It's as much a part of us as we are of it. Or is it that we just stay coiled up in our ego-shell and don't have the courage-fueled curiosity to find direction and the mind control to listen to what it has to say?

Most people don't step out of the picture they've painted of our reality to venture their focus into the omnipresence of what it is that fashions the forms and gives shape to what's detectable within the range of human sensual perception.

The inborn human longing to have a wisdom-enriched awareness of the most basic and primitive of truth's describing the nature and intended purpose of our Source is primal. Attaining a full conscious awareness of this primal truth is a worthy goal of vision. This level of conscious awareness affords the experientially founded enlightened understanding of the relational justice in this cause/effect reality that gives definition to our Source's nature of impermanence.

Reaching this end will allow a truth seeker to live in the joy and happiness found in a state of altruistic compassion. It will relieve them from the suffering they experience from its ignorance.

The living truth of our Source's nature and intended purpose to initiate ongoing change resides totally in the time-energized present moment essence of a cause transforming into its effect...one smear in time merging into the next. When looking back on change...hindsight is no more than reflection on the afterthoughts of once perceived interpretations while looking forward on hopeful or fearful change is no more than speculation. Neither states of conscious perspective echo the real-time push of Father Time's ticking present moment life clock.

Enriching the awareness of the wisdom associated with the nature of the truth of ongoing change fattens and strengthens the primal link between a truth seeker's knowing deeper consciousness and their ego-managed waking consciousness that silently longs for the mental peace they know exists somewhere. The ego mistakenly suspects it to be found somewhere on the outside of their human shell. This is a misguided idea conditioned by a religious society's guidance that's backed by years of acceptance and by its mass numbers.

With the right effort to merge in harmony a sensual body and an aware mind with a sustained focus directed into the essence of their body's presence, an awareness of our Source's nature can grow and the self can eventually be conquered. Inspired thinking yields insightful wisdom and the truth seeker's right understanding undoes their ignorance so their joy and happiness returns and their ignorance-caused suffering disappears. Having a wisdom-enriched awareness and understanding of ongoing change is the antidote to human suffering.

An individual must find the real-time courage to make the effort to face and sort through the next present moment anticipating and accepting the change it brings. They must push to the background any interference in focus coming from prior conditioning that protests the growing clarity of their vision for the truth. These feeble constructs stun their present moment and limit their potential. In realizing that they're an equal part of our Source, any truth seeker has the unprecedented right to know of and to feel their part and understand their role in its presence.

Primal awareness of our Source's nature and intended purpose of initiated change supports a state of mind that's not really discovered learned of taught...it's recovered, realized, and remembered. It resurfaces. Attaining awareness changes the nature of one's mind and gives coherent direction to their worldview. It plants the seed for an enriched conscious understanding of the insightful wisdom about cause/effect relationships in the flow of this time-fueled impermanent reality.

Primal mindfulness focused within to gain self-knowledge will eventually lead to a richer awareness of what the living nature surrounding causes is that occurs in each passing present moment and a heightened understanding of the resulting effects occurring among the interactions of the relevant cause/effect factors.

Having the right sort of awareness or mindfulness needed to reach a wisdom-enriched enlightened mental state is not found in making an ongoing consciously heightened concentrated effort to be aware of everything that's affecting the five sensual ports or making the effort to perceive all sensual signals that pass by...like being in a state of "super alert."

"Super alert" shouldn't be confused with "super focused." For an individual to achieve self-training wisdom, their heightened awareness is focused on inward activity and not on outward surrounding events. Having the right awareness includes knowing what to have a relaxed eye for when uniting an aware mind harmoniously with the calmed body to cross the bridge of communication to the plateau of understanding to witness our Source's message.

Super alert would be nearly impossible to attain, let alone sustain. Focused attention would be directed more toward the outside, not inside where it can generate inspiration to better understand the essence and nature of what it's focused into. If a truth seeker's mindfulness is not directed into the medium where the sought-after answer to the ignorance lies, their thinking will cannot be inspired by its presence and related insightful thinking to a better understanding cannot happen. Wisdom-enriched mindfulness will not develop in this way.

Making the effort to be cognizant of all that's going on without is not the same as being cognizant of what's going on within. Heightened mindfulness of what's going on in the external world would be more a form of heightened alertness and not really heightened awareness.

Heightened alertness consumes too much of the intellectual fodder of the conscious mind. You do not become closer to our Source as a result of this exaggerated effort of intensified, yet dispersed concentration. It may be concentration, but it's not the right concentration that attains body/ mind harmony with the mind control to self-train the wisdom to undo the ignorance-born suffering.

Sustained focused concentration on the senses is part of the process of self-discovery in effort to develop and enrich primal awareness. This state is what allows the inspiring of the insights to eventually change the nature of one's mind. It involves being aware of how things are happening rather than taking inventory of all what's happening. It's through a nonverbal sensual experience that an individual consciously begins to gather insightful understandings to recognize and appreciate the impermanent nature of this reality. This recognition must extend beyond the examination requirements of mere intellectual understanding. Attentive sensual exposure of an individual's alert body/ mind to the primal truth of unstoppable, unalterable constant change allows its present moment understanding to develop in their waking consciousness.

Primal awareness of the essence of ongoing change is like when an individual wants to understand the true implicit meaning of "hot," they'll hold their finger to a flame. The sensually archived memory of "hot" can be described and known intellectually, but its true experiential meaning cannot be transferred intellectually. By holding their finger close to a flame, experiential awareness fills the belief system's experiential void formed between only hearing about the cause (flame) and effect (sensation) when given an intellectual description of hot's sensual meaning. To gain a primal awareness of the truth about our Source's nature and intended purpose of initiating ongoing change, an individual must sensually experience change itself.

Our Source's claim-validating radiation of life noticed during self-discovery validates its present moment real-time living presence through and from the individual's sensual body to their attentive conscious mind. There's truly an unquestionable transforming nature to the living experience. There comes a consciously realized sensual record of what the awareness of the Source-paced presence feels like. This validates that they are a part in action of this shared universal presence.

The conscious awareness of our Source's nature and purpose of intent is attainable by any person at anytime anywhere. It's the same primal truth that was around during the passing present moments of 2,000 years ago and is the same one that will be here during the passing present moments of 2,000 years from now.

The perfect place for a truth seeker to be when they're trying to enrich their awareness of the impermanent nature of our Source is within the factory where new life is made. They have to be able to foster up the mind control to keep away interruptive thought patterns while they try to find the coordinated mind/body harmony to sustain the focus of their mind's awareness into the essence of their physical body's presence.

From here, they put their mind into a state of introspective contemplative deliberation while sensually witnessing the coming and going pulse of life itself as it's being manifested within their flesh. The essence of its presence will inspire the truth seeker's right thinking and insightful understanding will bring their enlightened awareness of the tides of change.

Really, what better place could their waking awareness that's bent on understanding ongoing change to be other than in the actual venue where the process of making new life is staged? From here, their waking awareness will be inspired to have sudden insightful wisdom-enriched understandings of the ways of life's impermanence as they surf in its wake.

Spirituality…The Primal Link Bottleneck Between the Deep and Waking Consciousness

When people think of their spirituality do they look up into the sky or do they look inside? Do they think their spirituality's healing powers are realized from the inside or is it only bestowed from another entity on the outside?

It seems that the concept of spirituality serves as a melting pot for thoughts or ideas pointing to the undefined and mysterious…from the fear-inspired, glass-half-empty, devil-sent, demonic-looking ghosts to the hopeful glass-half-full protection of the Holy Spirit engendered from within or sent down from heaven. What all these conceptions have in common is that they all deal in mystical uncertainty.

This notion-holding think tank ponders the mystique of the undefined that exists between the truth savvy of the subtle regions of a truth seeker's deeper consciousness and the decision center of their ego-managed waking consciousness. This elusive arm's length co-existence between what the primal truth really is and what some think it might be is their zone of spirituality.

Their ignorance about the influence this reality's state of impermanence has on their life is responsible for their present moment misalignments and misunderstandings of the cause/effect process of this reality. Many suffer as they ritualistically fetter away their time.

While sorting through daily activities with quiet reserve always on alert for answers, many will bow to gods while bending to their addictions. They wait idling in their rationalized security for their shoot-from-the-hip approach to somehow take on a more coherent meaning and give them direction to healing what brings on their unique uncertainty that causes them to confuse their priorities.

To find the wisdom to understand the nature of the human condition a truth seeker has to look no further than within their own ever-changing living essence. It's a most obvious, self-evident truth. It's just that only a few recognize its simple genius.

In a reality you feel, there's a living connection or link between the deeper awareness stemming from the primitive brain and the ego-managed and most often illusionary waking conscious awareness on alert in the cognitive brain. This span of supposition, mysticism and sometimes sworn conviction houses the essence of an individual's spirituality. In most people, it's a poorly defined disconnect in between the deeper and waking consciousness.

For most, the concept of spirituality drifts boundary-free. The mainstays that give fiber to its character, origin and give destination to its focus remain undefined. Successfully linking the truth savvy deeper consciousness with the ego managed waking consciousness allows and individual to reach their spiritual potential. Many see spirituality as a mental connection leading from their waking consciousness to a god figure somewhere in the sky instead of down into their sensual heart.

The significance of the role an individual's physical flesh plays in hunting down their spiritual awareness goes unrecognized and therefore, for most unappreciated and disrespected. It's their only coming and going connection to the buzz of reality. The link or tie between an individual's waking mind and their deeper conscious awareness of our Source's ephemeral nature and purpose is primal.

The deeper consciousness has no time but to recognize anything other than the truth of ongoing change that makes the human body's becoming maturation process fit in proper rhythm with the passage of time. The truth seeker fortifies their primal link by increasing the sensual sync between their ego-free deeper consciousness and their ego-managed waking consciousness.

The primal link that houses an individual's realm of spirituality energizes and manages the migration of their growing self-awareness. The path of deliverance originates in the subtle region of one's deeper consciousness where the resident human condition owner's manual outlines exactly how the human condition fits into our Source's process of transformation.

The deeper consciousness hates it when the ego-managed waking consciousness takes the reins and unthinkingly reacts to fulfill the shallow wants of the disconnected demands being shouted from the individual's waking state of mitote/ maya. They bend to temptation. They sin and perform deeds that will further distance the possibility of being able to calm the mind to self-train its ability to recognize the wholesome inspiration that will allow them to insightfully undo the tree of wisdom that will free them from the ignorance that makes them blind to the truth.

The deeper consciousness keeps the physical body on schedule. The present moment streaming of one's deeper consciousness runs regardless of the doubt/ uncertainty/ hesitation-generated ego-managed fear that typically taunts at and confuses the waking consciousness. Even though this schedule is swayed by a waking consciousness imbalance, as conscious perceptions form the foundation for depression, etc., the deeper consciousness does its best to regain the natural rhythm that ensures a healthy existence. It's its nature to change and find the balance to heal.

The heart beats...the brain produces serotonin and dopamine...the lungs process oxygen...cells divide and it commandeers the healing of the flesh when needed. The deeper consciousness is too busy doing what it can to run things in a healing and life perpetuation sort of way. It has no time or energy to devote to corrupting the human experience with misguided influence. It finds no time to play in the illusionary reality that includes an individual's posturing of their importance at social gatherings or trying to please all the people all the time.

In the primal picture of things, a truth seeker sensually witnesses our Source's truth of ongoing change as our Source writes, directs, produces and runs the mixing board of the entire show. It enriches an individual's worldview with street sense. It helps regain a sense of balance from the ignorance-induced imbalance that caused the static between the deeper and waking consciousness.

The Obscurity of the Deeper Consciousness

The thought of becoming familiar with one's own deeper consciousness frightens many. Just learning how to correctly spell subconscious is as much effort many ever make to understand it.

Maybe it's a place where their demons lurk. Many religious teachers forewarn against the demons of the deeper consciousness. They advise against exploring the crags of its depths. They advise to look out and up to God.

The deeper consciousness is the reservoir for an individual's uncensored (mostly consciously unrealized) collective sensual intelligence. It stores an unfathomable amount of consciously forgotten personal history. Yet, it's there with split-second reflexes that are based on those forgotten experiences, when appropriate.

The subconscious comes programmed with a generationally tuned inborn knowledge of the biological rules that must be adhered to just to survive... instincts...intuition.

And who's to say, maybe its stored history of personal record goes back into prior lifetimes? It can be agreed that the deeper consciousness at least knows how to best serve all the needs of the individual's currently transforming human condition. Even when the waking consciousness is asleep it labors on. It's a good thing it does, as what else could wake a person in the early morning to go use the bathroom?

Do these prior lifetimes embody each of the present moment-to-present moment physically changing life-story instances while in this body or maybe undocumentable prior lifetimes spent in other bodies? Which kind of past life is it that flashes before your eyes right before you die?

The subconscious is the ground-zero primal part of the human consciousness lodged in the older core part of the brain where inherited instincts and automatic reflexes reside.

It sees to the functioning of an individual's involuntary bodily functions their ego-managed waking consciousness lacks the ability and knowledge to keep on schedule. If an obligation is out of sight, it's out of conscious mind. It strictly enforces the work schedules of our involuntary systems. The owner's manual for the human body/mind is recorded online in this subtle region of the human computer.

The sensual memory lives in the reflex region of the deeper consciousness centered in the primitive brain. It's queried first for response instructions when a related cause arises. When stimuli meet perception, it offers a gut feeling opinion founded in the central brain sensual memory files collected from past experience.

Individuals' ego guarded waking minds are most often blind to the feeling of how they really feel deep down inside. Often times, their actual gut-felt opinion doesn't really line up with the intellectual reasoning used to justify some cause/effect exchange.

Ego-generated filters too frequently blur important sensual message files. Similar reoccurrences go unrecognized at times of future encounters. They remain in the individual's mental spam to be forever ignored.

The human ego resides in the other end of the human consciousness continuum, managing the conscious mind. The intellectual mind lives in the waking consciousness in the later-developed outer part of the human brain.

It can be totally consumed and spinning, lost ruminating with fearful guilt and regret. The ego's influence often results in misdirected reasoning. Its conditioning inspires an often-skewed explanation for how many causes and effects are related in this reality.

The elusive deeper consciousness is not bothered with the notions of one's waking conscious mind that are knotted up in ego infatuations. As the ego gets all worked up and controls the waking consciousness, the deeper consciousness will slip back into silent remission while emitting an ongoing faint plea to listen to what it has to say. It longs to share its knowledge with the waking consciousness about the ways of the truth of the impermanence of this reality.

The waking consciousness catches wind of this faint cry as the individual turns over everything in their path to find an answer or maybe just to better understand the faint cry. When they're not even sure or aware of what the appropriate question is, they look, pillage and plunder in an uncharted effort to find answer to feed their faint primal longing.

Through the suitable right concentration, a truth seeker's waking consciousness gets a sensual glimpse at the ongoing present moment relational interplay between the coming and going life factors of the subject of their targeted right concentration. The underused primal link from their ego-free deeper conscious to their alert/relaxed conscious mind/body is finally ready for action.

It openly manifests the transforming individual's living nature to change which all humans share. It's the full time production of the bigger picture that's beyond the individual's control as they humbly sit and take quiet audience. An individual's primal link runs the projector at their private screening. Their primal link is their universal web address for the answer to the what is not that is longed for by those unaware of the sought-after primal truth.

The great musician Neil Young's May 18, 2008 PBS *Charlie Rose* show appearance found him saying that he respects "the Source." He awaits its inspiration.

This is an example of an individual who knows our Source is there, but has not yet discovered their primal link to bring to their waking consciousness awareness what our Source is. They might not even recognize and associate the present moment Source they refer to above as being the same intellectually isolated Source recognized by religious theology.

The primal link unites the subtle regions of one's truthaware deeper consciousness with their unaware waking consciousness. Initiating the primal link completes a truth seeker's life. It makes them whole. Confidence, faith, understanding and compassion all take seed and the free will is unlocked and revived.

Finding the primal link that connects the deeper and waking consciousness is what makes an individual's spiritual ends meet.

The Primal Harmony Needed to Conquer the Self

Everyone applauds the inclusion of harmony in any situation. It's a word that implies a state of balance. Just its mention seems to round off any unforeseen rough edges. It implies working together.

It can be harmony between two organizations, among individual people, between a human and an animal or any separate factors in any situation. It can be the perfect harmony of a well-conducted orchestra.

Harmonious cooperation between the mind and body of a single individual makes it personal. The harmony that conquers the ego-self involves finding the sync between two things that could be working to separate agendas.

An individual could be meditating with thoughts tied up focused on the thought of an object or a mantra or whether their pose is correct or a million other things. They could be sitting full lotus with body ready and waiting, but their mind is thinking about anything other than the essence of the presence of their body. The mind and body have to be pointing at the same end otherwise the harmony will just not be there. They might have a very relaxing meditation experience, but it will not effectively bring them closer to having a wisdom-enriched understanding of the impermanent nature of this reality that can undo their ignorance of it that replaces their joy and happiness with suffering.

The most basic and primal expression of harmony is when the awareness of an individual's mind can be focused into the living essence of their physical presence. The body doesn't need to move. It sits motionless. This puts an individual's conscious mental awareness where the thing they want to fully understand lives.

This is just making the right effort to make the presence of its essence available for mental prodding from their mind's awareness of it. At this point where the coming and going activity in their body is emanating and where their mind's awareness is fixed, is where the mind and body meet...in harmony.

Their thinking gets inspired while their mental awareness sits watching what it wants to better understand. This inspired thinking primes the mind for the coming of wisdom-enriched insightful understandings of this transforming state of reality.

The mind and body are working together in harmony for the mind to better understand what the body is showcasing. This is the only place a truth seeker can go to better understand the transforming material world their body is a part of. But what could possibly be better?

When the attentiveness of the conscious mind strikes awareness of the coming and going essence of life as it manifests within the flesh of the body, the potential is there for the individual to self-train a wisdom-enriched enlightened understanding of the true nature and purpose of this reality and defeat their self-ego. This undoes their ignorance that allows all their present moment suffering.

With physical effort and mental awareness combined in what Siddhartha calls right concentration, the mind and body meet in harmony on a sensual plateau of understanding...mental heart in physical hand. The key is to have both mind and body focused together with sustained attention tuned-in to sensually witness our Source's sensually channeled story.

The Answer's on the Tip of the Tongue

Developing a conscious understanding of the longed-for answer explaining our Source and destiny that waits in the deeper consciousness is like trying to satisfy the nagging stir to remember something from a forgotten personal experience that seems to be just on the tip of the tongue'. The more the individual thinks about the forgotten experience, the more of it will resurface and come to mind over time. In like fashion, a truth seeker realizes this buried knowledge about the human condition bit by bit, over time as they selftrain moral/ethical behavior to allow self-training the mind control to allow consciously shaking up the deeper consciousness to allow the answer to surface and become part of their waking awareness.

Not living in tune with the primal truth of ongoing change unknowingly bothers people. They suffer for it. Down inside, in a subtle region of their inner being, they are familiar with the answer as it's what constitutes every transforming metaphysical bit of coming and going energy that populates their existence. The truth of their existence sways to the beat of the impermanence that it is, even if their waking mind, out of ignorance, might recognize and process cause/effect relationships under a different set of expectations.

This answer of sorts is something they're sure they're familiar with, but can't quite nail down. Many people spend their lives with the answer just out of reach, suffering the frustration. Most spend their lives not knowing what the question is.

When this inborn curiosity surfaces, an individual must feel the push to do the due diligence to sort out the answer. With this they become a truth seeker.

Each time a truth seeker practices self-analysis they have to avoid falling into any sort of pious ritualistic pattern. They must be driven by the desire to feel and witness the presence of life itself in the present moment. There has to be an organic inner push to point their present moment attention in the direction of understanding what it is that makes them so miserable. It must be the subject of focus for their mind's eye.

They have to stay focused on the reason they're doing the mind/body analysis, not on what they were told the proper physical technique, the proper place or what the proper time of day to perform the mind/body analysis is. Having a preoccupied distant mind voids the needed attentiveness necessary in making the right effort with the right awareness to find the right concentration.

A pseudo effort at having some sort of right technique just to meet ritualistic criteria like spending a preconditioned amount of required time confuses the priorities. This attempt at the right effort lacks being grounded in true humility and proves ineffective.

There's a world of difference between falling into the ritual of seeking body/mind harmony simply because it's the predetermined time to do it and wanting to because of being so grateful to just be alive wanting to touch it, feel it, witness it, understand it. An empty ritual of sitting down and letting the mind wander will not affect any better understanding of the very mind that's wondering about the same mind that's wandering. A desire primal to the curiosity about the pulse of humanity itself has no room for showing political correctness to ritual or hearsay.

The truth seeker needs to become saturated with the present moment. They have to offer their stripped-down sense of genuine humility common to any relationship built on compassionate love. They have to have the courage while accepting and being prepared to get hurt and feel pain as they face the fear of uncertainty that comes from the void of uncertainty in their belief system as they sensually unwrap the answer to what they've always longed to know. This answer is the medication that their deeper consciousness wants to release to heal their aching heart.

They will have to step outside of the boundaries of protection offered by fundamental naivety. It's the answer they've longed to know since being coaxed from their childhood innocence in their earlier years.

It's new to them. They're confronting naked change without their developed defenses to protect their ego in their unique illusion of what reality apparently is.

As self-knowledge increases over time, their growing steadfast faith will stand progressively stronger supporting their courage and fortifying their humility needed to discover what the next time-manifested present moment has to offer.

It's a relationship of love. It's a new way of approaching the unexplored realm of the future. It has to be fed by the primal desire of wanting to taste what life itself feels like.

Primal Faith

Time passes. Its steady advancement never stops. The impermanent nature of the reality it sets the pace for and its stable presence never changes. The perpetual presence of this oxymoron constant change assures that causes will always have the steady push of time to bring about effects. The passage of time and change are self-evident...not open to debate. On this solid foundation, a primal steadfast faith develops to support the internalized beliefs of an individual's evolving worldview.

Time-fueled change is the life energy for the boundless cause/effect interplay that pushes this transforming universe from one present moment to the next. A truth seeker's primal confidence grows in the dependable presence of the consistent change-perpetuating factors of this Greater Picture. The multidimensional characteristics of this ever-present environment remain consistent for the moment-to-moment transformation to unfold within.

The cause/effect interchanges of the tiny transforming bits of energy seem to momentarily unite to form the picture of this reality perceivable by humans. It's a given. People assume this truth of reality because it is all that has ever been perceptually understood. Everyone has steadfast faith in this...even though because it's so obvious, most don't consciously realize it.

Applied steadfast primal faith is the fiber that strengthens an individual's human condition as they accumulate wisdom on their trek through their human experience. Its inspired confidence envelops and protects their belief system.

It begins naturally when an individual develops an eye for and knows where to look to gain primal experiential awareness of the primal truth of the ongoing change that defines this reality. Its roots are deeply entrenched in the experiential memory of the primitive core of the brain.

The inner-felt assurance of the unending omnipresence of the only unchanging dimension of our present moment ultimate reality, Source-paced time-fueled ongoing change, serves as the foundation for an individual's regime of steadfast primal faith. The truth seeker has a developing "out of sight, out of mind" surety that the relational justice of the truth they have sensually witnessed will prove true again...day after day...same relational justice statutes...sensual package relationship from sensual package relationship.

An individual develops a feeling of unshakeable confidence in the continued validity of the sensually derived insight-inspired cause/effect relational wisdom as long as our reality's impermanent conditions afforded by the coming and going bits of energy that made possible those insight inspiring coming and going relationship patterns that inspired their insightful awareness of the wisdom of this truth remain consistent. The card shark's winning game will be unbeatable as long as the house rules don't change.

Steadfast faith vies that in this reality, the yin/yang duality of this oxymoron "constant change" is a universal dimensional dynamic that can truly be depended on to be here "as is" tomorrow, energizing the steady continuation of our unpredictable "becoming" cause/effect reality. This unchanging omnipresence ensures confirmation of the sustained validity of any inspired wisdom derived from the insightful implications from any noted internal relational interplay among a truth seeker's observable sensual dialogue from the real-time cause/effect flow of our ever-passing reality. It's in this deep dependability that an individual forges their true and steadfast faith.

It's a gut-felt assurance they don't have to take somebody's word for. They are their own primary source for this knowledge.

This fundamental state of reality finally becomes clear to them. They see it and they become consciously aware of its ageless presence. The surety of this time-less presence adds strength to a growing unwavering faith in the dependability of what our Source continually promises all of humankind...sealed with its omni-presence. It's the very faith that someone might be referring to when they say that they could feel it in their bones.

An individual's conscious awareness of the interwoven significance of time's presence as Einstein identified in his space-time comingling equation, $E = MC2$, for the omnipresent consistency of this island-of-reliability, constant source of initiated change, in the smooth flowing stream of time is the only unwavering solid ground available for an individual to anchor the forging of a well-founded, justly balanced, and stable belief system and worldview. It's consistent throughout humanity. The constant living state of its presence is self-evident and unquestion-ably true.

It's simple. It's right in front of everybody's face. Who says it has to be some-thing difficult to understand that people should have to argue about?

With deeper consideration, it becomes apparent that blind faith in a divine power still relies on the believer having the confidence that the divine power will show consistency in how he decides to manipulate the matter that composes his material world...at least until he allows for something to happen that mankind's not really seen before that they will absolve to just being a miracle while knowing that God works in mysterious ways.

A steadfast faith is a faith in the omnipresent consistency of what individuals have experienced for themselves. To their perception of the experience, they stand steadfast, as the truth of its existence is unquestionable. It's not a blind faith built on an assumed confidence in the source that told them about it with no sign of the unverified claim's living relevance or presence that leaves them groping when questioned about specifics of details or when asked for some sort of proof of how it's nature affects today's living world.

The unfailing laws of natural change are inherent to the transforming envi-ronmental conditions that change in sync to the unchanging tempo of ongoing change. This state or condition is the only thing or non-thing that will be here tomorrow unaltered to secure today's steadfast faith that gives one the courage to stand for the lasting viability of any time-warranted wisdom, popular or unpopular, that supports the relational interactions characteristic of the purposed claim of any view that's true to today's relational justice.

It's the time-fueled ongoing presence of the sensually detected unalterable unchanging essence of coming and going streams of physical sensations within one's body that sensually frames the undeniable claim-validating evidence of what our Source's nature and intended purpose are. It's a sensually stamped receipt verifying the real-time presence of this ongoing transformation that cannot be denied or banished from one's waking consciousness or neutered by some ego-managed intellectual caveat after once being sensually identified.

The truth seeker is strengthened and guarded by their steadfast faith in the timeless nature of the wisdom derived from consciously experiencing the truth of our Source's nature to initiate ongoing constant change. They think forward, openly and in fearless humility taking responsibility for their future present moments while articulating their passion for the purpose of their worldview. The new recognition and awareness of their shared source of life changes any previous notion of loneliness into one of shared common inner-independence.

A conscious faith, the gut assurance, of the consistent presence of the supporting cause/effect factors for the continued existence of the same flow of life manifestation that was sensually witnessed alive and constantly changing, unregulated and transforming from sensation to sensation in any truth seeker's human essence remains in an individual's experiential memory during every passing second. It stands guard against their internalizing foolish notions with natures that recognize a continual physical presence that all attachment, craving or aversion to the real emptiness of an imagined stagnant-in-time object, form or idea that is really no more than a process of ever-changing renewal.

It stands guard over unwholesome thought patterns that serve to swerve their right mental effort to establish the mind/body harmony to sustain the right awareness of their present moment that inspires the right thinking to have insightful understanding of the subject of their awareness to decode the exposed tree of wisdom that undoes the ignorance that keeps at a distance their living in a state of joy and happiness and allows their suffering.

This awareness is the foundation that altruistic compassion love and joy take seed in just as the omnipresence of the truth of ongoing change itself is the foundation of their faith.

A steadfast faith is a faith that can't be intellectually given or taken away. An individual can't be talked into believing its premise. It's a faith in what's been sensually verified. It's a faith that's earned and that an individual doesn't have to think about to convince themselves that they have. They're comfortable with the rhythm of its cause/effect justice and instinctually follow the rhythm of its lead.

Differing Types of Faith Suited for Differing Types of Relational Justice Fitted to Differing Types of Reality

It's important to bring transparency and clarity to what an individual knowingly or unknowingly recognize the nature of this reality to be...continual or impermanent. When thinking of spirituality, does an individual look up into the sky or inside into their heart?

There are different ways people choose to acknowledge and relate to the unavoidable relational justice that determines and characterizes the cause/effect rhythm of the coming and going presence of the metaphysical bits of energy whose pulsating presence pumps life transformation into the veins of this reality's multidimensional framework. Human beings weather through their passing moments either in unsettled frustration or with some degree of an enlightened understanding of what others don't understand about the ways of the status quo that strips away their joy and happiness, allowing them to suffer in their ignorance.

There's a difference between having a faith that's blind to what bonds a cause to its effect and having a faith that's steadfast in supporting an individual's experiential frame of reference in understanding the cause-to-effect tie-in of a claim's stated purpose. Midwestern religious theology is a classic example of an unverifiable claim and how blind faith is necessary when believing and internalizing its assertion to further shape a believer's worldview. The purpose of a religion's claim requires a reality with a nature that is continual for it to find its truth.

Closing inquisitive eyes in blind faith allows the claim to make the cause it says it creates to actually be the effect the claim promises even thought it might take illusionary conditions to work out the logistics of the promise of the claim for it to take form. These are claims that have purposes that forget to factor into the interaction of the supporting conditions of the claim the undeniable relational truths that support the fleeting nature of everything in this reality.

An important factor in how an individual develops their belief system that shapes their worldview is the degree to which they verify the purposes of the claims they decide to believe and internalize into their belief system. It matters what sort of reality-serving relational justice is needed for the collective purpose of their internalized claims that support their worldview to find its truth. What's expected and what's actually fitting are different when expecting an illusion and getting reality.

The nature of a reality where the passage of time supports an impermanent coming and going dimensional latticework of physical incidence is different than a reality where things can assume a continual presence as time passes, as the human range of sensual perception leads the unsuspecting to believe. One is founded in illusion, and one is founded in living truth. A reality with a continual nature would allow an illusionary attachment to things and beliefs that don't really exist in an impermanent world where a thing is nothing more than an ongoing process that's doing nothing but transforming into something else.

The effort it takes to maintain this confused mental state pushes joy and happiness into the background, and the individual spends their time and conscious energy trying to maintain an ego-managed pretense of "I AM." Many cause/effect outcomes are illusionary and don't match up to what reality offers. They suffer.

When a truth seeker recognizes this dilemma and selftrains their mind control to sensually observe the actual living evidence to inspire the insightful thinking to develop a wisdom-enriched enlightened awareness of the impermanent nature of this reality, it makes the ignorance of its truth and all the suffering it inspires unnecessary.

Awaken to suffering...Catagorize illusion...Keep it personal

3

Start Here...
Where Theology Meets Reality

Real life just doesn't happen in the biblical sense, recognize intellectually store religious maxims in the sensual texture heartbeat of every day life experience.

Real life just doesn't happen in the biblical sense...Recognize intellectually stored religious maxims in the sensual texture heartbeat of everyday life experience

Awareness of Mind and Body Presence Involve Different States of Mental Application

In an individual's state of waking consciousness, the consideration of mind and body can involve different states or types of mental priority. Belief in religious theology allows the mind's spiritual wellbeing to be trusted to a power with an unchanging nature outlined in ancient writings while the physical body has its sensual tie-in to the present moment that interrupts the intellectual volleyball with present moment needs.

Many religious believers spend much of their present moment in the still land of their imagination. They stand isolated and loose touch with the reality their body is a part of. Many don't register the time-distant fixed land of the Bible and the sense-activated land they adjust to for survival as being the same.

Invoke the Human Condition First Amendment Right!

Every human soul's born into this reality due to the intentions of two other human beings. They've been given the gift of life? OK, but what sort of a gift is this? Why should a new soul have to come with an attached rider saying that the new soul is a corrupted soul that must be saved and that another person had to have been sacrificed 2,000 years ago to make this possible?

What does the sacrifice satisfy? From what is the soul saved? Finding two religious believers explanations that are detailed the same is more than a challenge. Anyway...a truth seeker must take the driver's seat and put all this into perspective.

They must demand that whom they see to be their maker clarifies how its living essence they've heard about from the Bible or other religious media dialogue is sensually perceived in today's transforming world. The biblical accounts refer to present moment times of a seemingly set (yet totally transforming) reality set in an environment from 2,000-plus years in the past.

The presence of the living transforming nature of so long ago loses its priority after such a lapse in time with so many transitions and changing traditions that it's been subject to. So many unknown people from so many foreign cultures have handled its intended meaning over so many years that it becomes very impersonal and assumes a feeling distant to that of Midwestern USA. A truth seeker must find out where in the coming and going pulse of an individual's life-manifesting tingle is the sensual present moment incarnation of the biblically described Holy Spirit as well of the other biblical cast members?

The Bible says the Holy Spirit deals with the transformation of life. The sensual incarnation of the Holy Spirit should be detectable anywhere where the life in transformation is being manifested in today's reality at this very moment.

This transforming of life thing happens in the present moment as life is manifested within each cell of the truth seeker's body. Their material body's their only true connection with the sensual presentation of the reality that they've read about in the Bible and in the reality that they sensually filter and react to in real life. These perceptions should register with the same sense of spiritual urgency.

The truth seeker could go one step further and take the imagined middleman wedged between them and the beat of life out of the picture. Blame for responsibility shouldn't be placed on an entity that's never been sensually seen, felt, heard or tasted. A truth seeker needs to go out there and identify the sensual incarnation of the Holy Spirit's life transforming sensual presence them self! The creator's supposed to be within everything anyway?

Take the responsibility. Undo the ignorance about the obvious. Become enlightened about what it is that explains the ignorance that allows humans to live in the circle of suffering by becoming aware of what's true about the unknown. Stop suffering. Figure out what the present moment incarnation of the conditioned biblical impression of how life actually feels like as it happens in the real-life sense. Make the connection.

We have ancestors who've done it and have tried to tell us how they did it. Feel the burn of due diligent desire...not the burn of living hell.

Imbalance Between Theology and Spirituality

In today's different forms of relaxation techniques, therapies or work out programs that target attaining some degree of mental calming, there's one crucial thing missing...the individual's awareness of the activity's tangible tie-in with actually realizing the joy, happiness, and compassion in this lifetime that's promised in their religion's life-after-death itinerary. Most humans have no conscious understanding of what heaven really is.

The various techniques lack having forward vision trained on gaining an enlightened understanding of the imbedded primal ignorance that allows their misconceptions of reality that causes their suffering. Siddhartha's first noble truth...realizing that suffering exists, is the answer to the first gut-generated question he asked himself to find clarity on his pathway to his enlightenment about what caused his suffering.

Many assume after hearing much religious propaganda that the process of becoming heavenly enlightened during this lifetime isn't really possible. In the Midwest it's not really given much thought. They don't understand what it means to become enlightened or how or that it even has anything to do with their suffering. They don't have enough insight on the subject to allow them to even intellectually connect the dots.

Like most, they've given up before trying. This was probably pounded into their Midwestern worldview at an early age. They've taken on their society's view that a god must do it for them after they die. They see all that happens to them in the living present moment as totally separate from the dusty old biblical times told of from past millennia.

Back in those days, as told in the Bible, religion played a living role in daily life. It was alive in the people who taught it and in those who tried to destroy it. God spoke down to people from up above. Miracles happened. And for Christ's sake, Jesus was a carpenter. Who or what is it that's assumed those roles in today's living reality?

When an individual ties their mental concept of spirituality to a god or separate entity that they've never felt real-time living involvement with, they're tying their concept of spirituality to a feeling of unrealizable expectations. Its promise is a hope that dangles from the white cotton clouds up in the heavens like a carrot for tempting a horse might dangle from the end of a stick in front of their nose.

They reserve a special time on Sunday morning or when their Bible's open at home to make what they see as having a spiritual connection. This dislodges from their daytime waking mind any purpose in directing their workout energy at realizing body/mind harmony and the inspired insights that can result in enriching their understanding of what that feeling of life emanating from their body means...in a consciously understandable way.

There's a subtle background pulse of coming and going reality that they've probably never even given much attention to throughout their life. It's always there and who's to question it? It's something most take totally for granted.

When they experience something truly spiritual that's coded in sensual dialogue like the emanation of new life each second, that's waking definition is only recognized as it was cognitively sketched in intellectual religious shorthand, the sensual signals are never recognized as having any form of relevant spiritual tie-in. They totally miss out on the possibility of the spiritual connection.

Being that the gist of the purpose of a believer's chosen religion has not been sensually/experientially validated by their free will in the present moment, they will have a unique intellectually-drawn-up-patchwork of a concept of what any personal religious encounters are. There is no recognizable experiential reference or sensual history tie-in of any past present moment involvement of this nature.

This creates an intellectual category, a mental folder of religion that is so unrelated to real everyday affairs that it can be capsulated, extracted and separated from government involvement or from talk around the table in situations where meeting new people to make sure things are kept politically correct. It's a religion that's insulated from the living encounter describing an individual's real-time human living and transforming experience.

It's versed in a memorized and set intellectual dialogue that is something the believer has become attached to and craves in times when needed to defend the view of the religious claim to salvation being made. It stays preserved in an intellectual account of what reality apparently should be.

How can something real that's actually felt and realized in the present moment ever size up to that intellectually retained cognitive sketch that's totally unassociated with any living experience? It's not comparing apples to apples. The real-time incarnation of the intellectually sketched spiritual notion will always be held unassociated and at a distance from the intellectual idea. Real-time opportunities or sensual marker tie-ins for spiritual advancement will go unrecognized unless the illusionary impressions are somehow recognized for what they really are and represent in this cause/effect reality.

The individual will not realize how a true spiritual advancement in today's sensual terms is actually as close to a heavenly connection to our Source's message they will ever realize in this cause/effect reality. As they watch for Jesus to break through the clouds on a white horse, the thought of recognizing an actual heavenly connection is much too obscure and undefined.

Its true realization hides behind their illusionary cognitive golden idol of how salvation will one day come thundering down from the heavens. It's tangled up in the many different Sunday morning interpretations of Paul's account of the Revelations we must all await in fear for. Its true recognition will slide by unrecognized with each pulse of our Source's life clock. The individual hasn't seen any living role model accounts to intellectually reflect on or personal accounts to experientially associate with.

They have no referenced sensual definition to draw a recognizable outline around that's experientially associated through prior conditioning to equate what's recognized as our Source's message to being a religious message. Actual buzz of life being manifested from the believer's flesh goes by unrecognized as being the Holy Spirit's life sign from our Source.

And even if the meaning were to be associated or equated, it's not a safe social stance for most. They must recognize the steadfast faith drawn from witnessing the self-evident truth of the factors making up the cause/effect interplay in question for the individual strength to withstand objections from those who don't see the light.

The truth is that any realized insightful wisdom is a piece of the web of truth that holds together the overall puzzle. If their conscious waking mind does not have an eye for uncovering the truth of impermanence, they'll never see it. They have to be looking for it. It's the answer describing what the feeling of being alive actually means.

They have not yet developed enough of an eye for the conscious awareness of our Source's impermanent nature to slow down the skipping nature of their confused ever-changing mitote/maya-controlled frame of mind to make these associations between the intellectually described spiritual maxims and their real-time essence when they consciously witness their transforming incarnations versed in the experiential sensual dialogue recognized by their deeper consciousness. There is no conscious association recognized to allow understanding them well enough to remove the ignorance that allows them. An individual has to recognize and associate what's sensually witnessed as being what the intellectually understood components actually feel like within their own present moment human experience to recognize, give meaning to and excuse any injustice of their real-time presence they experience while suffering through the various addictions they inspire.

Having to take the cognitive time to bring to memory to mentally resketch the cognitive image held depicting the image of a theological maxim takes time. To then be brought into the realness of the impermanent present moment and readjust awareness more to the flow or wave of time can bring imbalance to an individual's cognitive consciousness.

Sometimes a psychological shakeup or slap in the face of sorts can pull an individual out of the safe confines of their illusionary and totally ignorant view of the relational interplay between the coming and going cause/effect factors in this ephemeral reality. Losing a loved one or a major physical injury would be examples that could inspire a truth seeker to suddenly sit back and realize that there has to be more to it all than they choose to recognize at the present time.

They must see that they live their present moment suffering from a general state of ongoing frustrating dissatisfaction or unrest during the passing of their present moments. They must be on the ball enough to ask themselves these internal self-questions to realize Siddhartha's first noble truth that suffering exists.

An individual needs to realize that they have all the reason to unlock their free will to find the pathway to uncover and free up the hidden truths that explain the dimensions of life that are surrounding them as they stand, that they yet stand unready for and naked to...that blindside and loses them in the transforming plasma of each new present moment.

With this realization they will begin assuming the task of investigating subjects that just don't normally get discussed during the passing of their typical day. They set practiced expectations aside and find the courage and vision to follow guidelines such as the Ten Commandments and quiet the voices of their mitote/maya. They can then self-train the mind control to find the mental dialogue to challenge our Source of the approaching present moment with much enthusiasm while humbly requesting: "Take me to your leader." They can self-train a wisdom-enriched understanding of their ignorance.

They have given direction and purpose to their future. Their due diligence can now find what their free will can test and verify to assemble the puzzle and they can change the nature of how they view things and in doing so change the nature of their mind and what they think.

They can align their motivational intent of how they are behaving in their present moments with what's needed to satisfy their life passion. Confusion and unrest subside.

They find sleep much easier to slip into at night. They'll learn much more about compassion other than merely how to correctly spell it or how to wear a mask and intellectually fake its presence.

In the Presence of God...Our Present Moment Source?

The perception of a heavenly relief of suffering that is intellectually conceived and cognitively constructed is different than one that is sensually discovered and defined. One source of the elimination of suffering extends out to some unspecified place...most imagine it to be the sky. The other heaven is discovered at the most distant point possible from human perceptive abilities in the other direction...down inside the bowels of each atom that gives shape to the universe. Even though their proponents say they accomplish the same thing, when the living incarnation of the one that is intellectually pictured and anticipated appears in an individual's sensually perceived present moment, the theological reference it was remembered in will pass by unaroused by its sensually activated reality.

Most religious believers just don't know how to intermingle their intellectually scripted idea of a promised heavenly peace during the afterlife with their sensually scripted account of unrest they feel during the present moment. It's like trying to intermingle an intellectual cause with a sensual effect or a sensually generated cause with an expected intellectually conceptualized effect. Real life just doesn't happen in the biblical sense.

What does "in God's presence" mean? With today's modern attitude, traditional theological approaches to recognizing holy presence are conveniently held at arm's length and not included in an individual's thought patterns relating to their moans and groans of coping with what's going on in the real-time that affects their human experience. They might feel the physical moans and psychological groans and then think up into the sky and pray for relief. Yet, they will take no responsibility for understanding the process of healing the cause of their suffering. They could save their god the trouble of healing them when it's in their power to do it themselves. When the Source or God is thought of as being above, he's separated and isn't a real connected living part of what happens down here...right now.

Christianity's god lives solely/souly in the believer's intellectual world as a concept and is called on when their intellectual mind turns to him to provide protection or deal with something that's not understood or feared. Maybe his reference is needed to fulfill a part of a ritualistic practice?

The intellectually held religious criteria representing ideas of biblical sins and temptations don't integrate into the present moment sensually realized incidence of their modern-day incarnation. Telling lies today lines up pretty well with telling lies in the days of long ago, but the subverted temptations to eat modern day's death-defying salt-fatsugar diet that wasn't around during the days of the Bible, slides by unchallenged. Believers that focus on the traditional out-of-body Source from long ago with no sensually documented present moment tie-in are not in position to relate modern-day cause/effect manifestations of "should I" or "shouldn't I" to their spiritual tight rope that's stretches from one side of their waking consciousness to the other.

When not consciously knowing in a primal way as to why to "recognize their body as the temple of their holy spirit," they have no pressing reason to make their body's well being rate all that high on their priority list and to be all that motivated to take conscious responsibility for its well-being.

The media that all humans have in common, regardless of spoken language, comes as part of the human condition. It's the media of sensual transformation. The felt emotions of sad and happy are the same for everyone everywhere at anytime. Different gods promise the same emotions.

With most, the moment-to-moment bumps and scrapes that affect moods and emotions have no real spot-on association with their intellectually understood ageless pillars of heaven they associated with a heavenly god. With most, the modern ways of considering present moment emotional well-being are not at all tied in or understood in line with what's proclaimed to be holy or spiritual while in church on Sunday morning.

God's Truth is Conceptual…Present Moment Truth is Sensual

A religious believer's perception of the sensual effects of the present moment can become the topics that they pray to their heavenly god about. Maybe they ask for relief from some source of pain or apologize for something they think they're being punished for.

Some believers become upset enough over their interpretation of God's biblical truth to leave a congregation if the congregation allows something that doesn't follow their idea of what they interpret to be the right way. They might part ways because the congregation believes it's acceptable to God to only partially immerse an individual when being baptized or merely being sprinkled with holy water. The congregation might think it's OK to use instruments when singing praise to God while others interpret God's truth to mean singing God's praise only with the voice.

These same individuals might then go ahead and knowingly poison their body with the same artificial sweeteners that in terms of the present moment truth, are proven to cause cancer or have adverse effects on their memory. They will order a soda drink while knowing that it has adverse effects on the health of the body they must use to spread God's word. The wrongness of the Sunday morning subjects of temptation and sin don't wear the same red flags when their real-time incidence is cloaked within their sensually realized present moment incarnation.

During every individual's lifetime, they develop their own spiritual window to search for and view the various religious maxims they form an intellectual understanding and acceptance of. They become attached to these conceptions. They won't catch the applicable living spiritual relevance because they won't notice the true spiritual signposts of anything not wearing the biblical clothes intellectually sketched in their mental gallery picturing the old-time imageries.

The concepts of a sexed God, Jesus Christ, the Holy Spirit, the Holy Trinity, and reaching heaven on the road to salvation are phrases representing a few of today's spiritual maxims common to Christianity. People paint mental images of these concepts and hold on to them.

These concepts become icons that believers worship, reread and review on Sunday mornings. Then they leave church and reenter a world of worry, their underlying guilt and fear gets sprinkled with moments of joy and happiness, with no idea how to eliminate their ignorance that's allowing the worry, guilt and fear. They fail to integrate the conceptualized after-death joy and happiness or fire and brimstone with their present moment incarnations.

None of these cognitively sketched spiritual concepts or visions come naturally or are born into the human condition. These concepts and visions are conditioned into their life. They are effectively molded by teachers, preachers, family, and society and such. They're not experientially associated to anything tangible, so these spiritual concepts lay subject and/or prey to the individual's unique and imaginative illusionary constructs.

It's difficult for an individual to recognize a common meaning between their mentally painted illusionary image file of a white man in a white robe floating in front of a blinding white light invitingly motioning the onlooker to enter (heaven) and the actual real sensual feeling of communicating with our Source as its promise emanates from their flesh. In many instances, the intellectually spun spiritual image depicting the white light of heavenly enlightenment has been mentally painted to best replicate the description of an individual's reported real-life godly experience.

During an individual's description of a near-death experience, they will use their intellectually painted picture of this surreal event to document, describe and verify the reality of what they've experienced. Maybe their description will be fashioned to resemble what they've heard from others in similar reported instances? It could be that out of respect for someone who's neared death, that their description becomes unchallenged or at least uncontested in most instances.

Yet, any listeners can't really place themselves in that situation. It's common for a white light to be reported in near death experiences. It doesn't matter, as these instances offer nothing for anyone to see at any time at anyplace.

Does the individual assume there's a god who issues the white light? Could the white light be a naturally occurring phenomenon without the assumption that Jehovah or maybe Allah produced it?

A mental picture's been painted. There's no real way to test and tie in any portion of what these mental sketches represent in terms of a real-time experience. These mental images form intellectually stored religious maxims of epic significance that are very hard to shake. The accounts can change over time.

The woven interdependence of these religious maxims create their own impenetrable scar that heals over and suffocates the part of the free will that normally allows the waking mind to smell the fresh air of the present moment. For the sake of common recognition, age-old religious maxims have to somehow be parleyed into present moment realtime sensual dialogue to be associated with their present moment incarnations.

It's important to be able to learn to recognize and describe intellectually understood and stored religious maxims of sorts developed after a lifetime of hearing them described in the world of religion with the words and phrases that give textural meaning in sensual dialogue when describing the human condition in the everyday human experience.

As truth seekers learn to understand how to distinguish what the living spiritual signposts are in their flow of consciousness and recognize them as being the real-time sensual incarnations of their intellectually stored spiritual maxims, they learn to acknowledge and strike down a number of their unique behavioral fleeting reactions they have become addicted to. This could range from religious dogma and ritual to any belief supported only by blind faith and to have trust in what they've been told to believe to be true in their described apparent reality.

Cognitive Imagery Not in Tune with Sensual Reality... Holy Ghost is the Same Today as it was 2,000 Years Ago

A religion's rhythm set by rites and a ritual isn't something that humans are born with. To attempt to live in its explanation of this reality, a believer must make the decision to learn its intellectually founded promises and ways of paying tribute to its god. It's impossible to learn about its story, sensually. It's easy to understand why notions set by religious theology and the sensual feedback from living reality occupy different places in an individual's human condition...the first in the head and the latter in the heart.

Most believers can't recognize the sensual presence of their theological projections when they are right in front of their face. The Holy Ghost breathes into reality the same present moment breath of life today that was during in the times of the Bible. The process of transformation that defines the present moment of 2,000-plus years ago is the same one that defines the present moment of today.

The coming and going tingle of life as it manifests itself is the same. It has the same feeling inside an individual today as it did when Siddhartha or Jesus tapped into the same theater of wisdom during past millennia.

When the nature of the intent of an individual's passing present moment thought patterns aligns with the cause/ effect justice of our Source...possibly when they experience a sudden life-insight, those who rely on theological imagery to define their perception of spirituality can't pair the experience with its true living spiritual significance. This could be the case with the real-time physical appearance of any of the dated ideas they've formed about heaven-related concepts. The recognition of these intellectually sketched images they cling to that explain the concept of heaven which they don't experientially identify with, clash or just slip by unnoticed, along with the real spiritual significance of what is happening in the passing present moment. The inner anxiety or discomfort that accompanies how they mismatch a cause with its effect becomes normal, real life for them and eventually for those who see them as models for their behavior.

There's a veil of naivety or ignorance that shadows the sufferer's deeper consciousness, where their inborn understanding of the truth of ongoing change patiently lies in wait of its release to the recognition of their waking awareness. Their primal link of shared understanding that extends from their deeper to their waking consciousness has been numbed out as they were edged out of their childhood innocence. Having this veil lifted, if only for a brief time would provide the experience of having at least a sensual glimpse at where the truth lies and is maybe to be found. This can instill the enthusiasm to work up the due diligence to fully expose it to gain its full wisdom-enriched awareness.

For most, there's a surreal illusionary wall that stands in the way of recognizing and letting the true spiritual nature of a present moment sensual event be perceived as such. They have accumulated a sense of spiritual from the religious intellectual context that's formed over the years.

This is a major obstacle in their pathway to heavenly enlightenment, exposing the cause of their ignorance that causes their suffering. It's one that affects people of every walk of life...from those who wear monks' robes to anyone who's seen *The Ten Commandments* and has Charlton Heston's robed image stamped in their mind as what a godly figure would apparently look like.

Society's Positioning of Common Religious Illusion

A child might study to memorize the intellectual meaning of a new word for a spelling test, but they may spend their entire life without ever understanding what the sensual meaning of that word is. What first comes to mind for many Hoosiers when thinking about heaven are the intellectually sketched pictures that religious tradition pounds into their heads and forever sears into their intellectual memory. Some of the mental pictures are pounded out weekly in centuries-old religious rituals that directly target only a promised afterlife state of suffering relief.

This mind crafting helps create an individually unique illusionary mental picture of what something pure, free of sin and empty of bad people that's promised to believers at some time in the future, if they're good, would be. Anything reflecting any real-time earthly texture falls short and lacks the grandeur or the mental images of angel wings, halos and Saint Peter standing at the pearly white gates that typically comes to mind when thinking of a Hoosier heaven.

Any present moment change in an individual's understanding of our Source with true spiritual relevance that anybody feels affecting today's human experience is quite foreign to the religious impressions describing heaven that are left by the various media presentations that take their best shot at creating visual takeoffs from the ancient biblical milestones described in the various religious texts. True present moment indicators of the living truth that are sensually present in the ongoing human condition can't compete with what is pictorially represented and painted with words throughout the book of Revelations depicted in the color pictures in the copies of the King James Version Bible waiting for any curious mind to inspect in any Midwestern hotel top desk drawer.

These mental fixations can sidetrack and totally distort the advancement of the spiritual enrichment of one's present moment. They dislodge the identity and disassociate what represents finding the Source of true salvation from suffering. They help displace, camouflage and distance the answer to where true spiritual enrichment can be found and stand in the way of discovering the way to that end.

Today's Cognitive Imaging of Millenniaold Reality... Religious Maxim Ghosts are Unique to Each Person

Recognize the living reality heartbeat in the notions used to build the unique abstract mental sketch most Hoosiers cling to that describes their chosen path of religious theology. Most Hoosiers have some version of a Midwestern Christian identity that's been filtered through the warping effects of 2,000-plus years of human handling that explain religious or godly or heaven deeply ingrained in their cognitive memory. The illusionary mind-sets and mental pictures making up these religious maxims are forever unique to each individual's imaginative constructs that form to each verbal description they internalize.

Listen to Sunday morning religious programs. There are no two described interpretations of any shade of biblical spirituality that are the same. They all are the speaker's summation of what they thought the biblical character meant in the translated version that they studied.

Many visualize the true spiritual application of the intellectually pictured religious apparent reality as being so different and abstract from their real-time present moment living experience, they repeat the biblical words referenced in their version of the Bible they read like "thy" and "thou" when wording their prayers to the Almighty. Maybe they're just showing humble respect for the almighty they have never met personally and actually shook hands with? They don't think that to realize that this rather broken special and unique prayer-language they use hadn't even been developed back in those ancient biblical days.

In the days of Jesus, they wore different clothes. Their human experience was totally different and is not available anywhere on earth to see today. Today, those biblical lands are so overrun by misguided individuals, it's not possible for Hoosiers to visit them and feel safe...without carrying an M16...or rather an AK-47.

Modern-day Midwestern Christian concepts are so deeply intellectually ingrained with absolutely no experiential, living or real-time personal history to take purchase in. It doesn't seem real. People can't recognize this paradigm and to cope, they will still choose to wear different hats to adapt to different situations.

It remains a sensually unassociated dreamland to anyone unwise to the importance and relevance of what the state of ongoing change adds to the prism of truth that defines our reality. There's a protective layer of blind faith pasted over the waking ego-managed consciousness of the Christian followers that helps explain the mysteries of change while keeping their understanding of the ways of this reality just a few waves of insightful reckoning out of reach.

Spirtualist Disconnect

Like followers of religious disciplines, many spiritualist tradition supporters where the key to salvation is thought born into the human condition, have problems recognizing a real-time experience as being the present moment living incarnation of the spiritual maxim ghost that they've intellectually developed and theorized about.

One of these spiritual maxims might involve the Buddha that many recognize as being Mr. Siddhartha Gautama. Even though Buddhists profess to seek the Buddha that all humans are supposed to have within their deeper being, many worship Siddhartha as being some sort of intermediary or special Buddha, much like Jesus is with God. They both self-trained their wisdom-enriched awareness that undid their ignorance of the impermanence that distanced their compassion, joy and happiness and allowed their suffering, like any human can do.

Asking questions related to these pieces of the process is what will bring one closer to the meaning of the emptiness of impermanence and lead them to discover their Buddha inside. They sidetrack their efforts by worshipping where one individual's walked and the tree he sat under, as Siddhartha feared might happen.

Siddhartha's teachings that comprised the *Eightfold Pathway to Enlightenment* and the *Four Noble Truths*, which offer guidance on self-training the process to eliminate the present moment infecting ignorance of the truth of change, have formed into age-old spiritual maxims for many as they fail to be recognized in real-time sensual dialogue.

Some are bewildered and self-diluted by the thought that so many people they think may be far more spiritually mature than they are have differing ways of interpreting these ancient maxims. When a present moment occurrence of the intellectually described spiritual maxim actually happens, it can pass by them without their pairing the maxim with its real sensual presence. They miss how their mentally painted two-dimensional picture and its true multidimensional sensual incarnation represent the same thing.

These are samples of spiritual maxims that are not sensually recognized for what they are intellectually understood to be when actually being experienced in real-time. It can be very difficult to experientially piece together and recognize in a sensual puzzle what's been cut out using intellectual scissors from an intellectually outlined grid tethered only by the constructs of an individual's imagination.

Many individuals will fail to associate these intellectually stored religious/spiritual maxims with what actually flashes into their perceived reality when what they've intellectually believed to represent is experienced in real-time. When they do encounter a present moment incarnation of one of these religious/spiritual maxims and fail to associate the direct connection of how it fits into their path to the white light, the true spiritual relevance goes unnoticed and any possible spiritual maturation slips by.

It's just another present moment in a day of their modern life...so distant from what they intellectually consider to be spiritual that happened so long ago. They continue to sit and spin in their ignorance that makes them suffer.

This creates a holdup in their trek to securing enlightenment about their ignorance. They need to develop the savvy to recognize how their real-time emotions and states of mind are what are involved and how they represent what's referred to by the religious/spiritual maxims they have stored in their intellectual memory library.

A truth seeker that recognizes the true monumental significance of present moment suffering with an active eye searching for the antidote to its cause, will seek guidance on uniting in harmony the right effort of body and right awareness of mind to form the right concentration to self-train the relational wisdom to enrich their awareness of the truth of ongoing change. It's possible for anyone to sensually smell out the sweet aroma of the baseline primal truth of our reality's state of ongoing impermanence. They just need to know what the sensually subtitled intellectually filmed spiritual signposts are when their sensual hand taps on the shoulder of their human condition in the present moment of their human experience.

Intellectual Soundness Through Abstract Logistics

Believers in religious theology settle for the intellectually generated soundness of abstract logistics to secure their intellectual grasp on a religious claim instead of experientially verifying that the claim's purpose can find its truth in this impermanent reality. Doing this would instill in them a sensual familiarity that strengthens the growth of their fortifying steadfast faith alongside their growing wisdom-enriched understanding of the nature of this impermanent reality.

The intellectual personification and sensual manifestation of anything an individual perceives in the present moment will not share a common understanding if they've not been knowingly associated through sensation, where mind and body actually meet. Abstract logistics engage a zone of intellectual awareness that's different from that acquired through sensual experience.

When Intellectual Theology Meets Sensual Reality... Connecting Intellectual Expectations With Sensual Realities

By Christianity holding eternal afterlife freedom from suffering as the main purpose of its promise, finding relief of real-time present moment suffering becomes, at best, a serendipitous discovery, if ever realized at all. Still, a present moment state of joy and happiness and freedom from suffering's not the main priority.

Even though believers pray to their god for relief from the many forms of everyday suffering, they don't associate developing a wisdom-enriched enlightened understanding of how to eliminate the ignorance that has them swapping their real-time joy and happiness for everyday mental unrest, as being part of the promised heaven of their religion. They don't associate the parameters that set up their afterlife heaven as being the same present moment spiritual signposts that signals what's needed to become enlightened about the ignorance of the ways of the impermanent nature of this reality that will restore in their lifetime the joy and happiness their soul longs for.

They choose to hold at mental bay a promised heaven of eternal life and happiness after death that exists in a type of present moment they have had no experiential history with. All they can do is imagine what it will be like...what the whole process of the day of redemption to everyday afterlife existence will be like.

It's interesting though how so many things on an individual and personal level that are negative in nature can still get associated with the devil from hell of long ago or some form of punishment from the old-time god from above. Seems like modern-day reference and connection to oldtime religious ideas are popular when it means looking over your shoulder to make sure God's not watching with a bolt of lightning or a spear of guilt.

Most religious believers fail to make any connection or recognize any association between any religious maxims they've formed that their religious goal of eternal happiness brings with it and the living embodiment of these maxims in their present moment sensual experience. They're blind to recognizing the spiritual relevance and significance of the actual real-time present moment occurrence of what is really intended by these mentally sketched spiritual flagships when faced with them when they appear in their sensual disguise. There are so many people who don't really know what their intent is when they use the word spirituality.

Awareness of the blinding veil of ignorance must be gained to spur the due diligence to have the effective introspection that will lead to knowing what questions to ask to self-train the ability to allow exposing the sensual definition of these intellectually construed and stored religious or spiritual maxims that have accumulated in their intellectually stored mental folder titled Holy. They need to recognize and give present day meaning to what their sensual present moment incarnations are. These intellectual paintings representing the extra-terrestrial world of religion's after-death concerns can then be equated into the sensual specter of today's real-time living experience.

Successful efforts at reaching enlightenment originate in the wake of the forward focused due diligence of a truth seeker taking action to feel out and ask the right questions that lead to seeking out and finding the awareness of and to self-train the ability to sensually touch the issue that's breaking up their awareness of the transforming rhythm of their present moment that allows them to suffer.

The place where the truth lives must be found, entered and experienced to understand what the truth is. This protocol is of the utmost importance. It's unavoidable. It's fun. It can prove to bring eternal joy and happiness and the eternal relief of suffering...realized during this lifetime.

The process of amassing self-knowledge from inspired insightful understandings while gaining wisdom-enriched self-awareness strips intellectually internalized and stored stoical religious or spiritual maxims cognitively sketched from borrowed descriptions of grand religious events and godly entities of past millennia, of their distant-from-now, remote inaccessible foreign nature. Their association and shared meanings become real to the present moment through inspired insights.

An individual's quiet deliberation while focusing the mental awareness into the zone of natural harmony in the sensual display detected inside their body eventually opens up and gives meaning to the modern-day applied association and relevance of the intellectually filed mental picture depicting their illusionary take of their religious conditioning. There are several aha moments. Through the sensual language that verifies by signing out the intended purpose of the present moment sensual incarnation of the constructs making up the religion's read-about biblical purpose, it clarifies and brings to life a modern-day version of what Jesus described in his ancient teachings. The truth seeker can feel the warmth when actually becoming friends with the living Holy Ghost or Holy Spirit that they hold an intellectual idea about. Injecting transparency into their intended meanings exercises and strengthens the inner link between the deeper and the waking consciousness. This means less ignorance, more realized compassion and less room for suffering. The importance and relevance of life in the now emerges from the darkness.

It could be said that a religious believer's view through their spiritual window of salvation is focused and intellectually trained in an analog wave pattern. They cannot be expected to know how to perceive the real thing when encountering its true sensual incarnation that occurs in a digital format. Being conditioned in only one perception will not prepare an individual to distinguish the other...analog or digital...intellectual or sensual. Intellectual understanding doesn't necessarily ensure experiential recognition/association.

Recognize in today's ongoing sensual display of undisputable impermanence the age-old spiritual-religious maxims that are intellectually clung to in the only place where ongoing life manifestation can be experienced. Replace an adopted faith that's blind to seeing any living inclusion for the references from the religious claim to how suffering will be relieved for a faith that's steadfastly rooted in the omnipresence of the process responsible for the formation and continued living process making up the human condition.

The benefits derived from creating the harmony described long ago by Lau Tzu and later detailed by Siddhartha that conquer the ego managed self to then reach enlightenment still apply to the human condition of today. The same right effort as described by Siddhartha to maintain a sustained right awareness on the sensual dialogue felt in their day that would allow self-training the mind control to then self-train their wisdom, rings true in mankind's modern-day human experience. This progression of spiritual maturity comes after the truth seeker's stroke of insight that associates the intellectually understood and stored descriptions of the spiritual/religious maxims with their living incarnations in today's sensual dialogue.

Internalizing as true some new intellectually received claim to wisdom that explains how some aspect of this reality works will need to acquire an experiential history for the relationship explained by the claim's purpose to be the first perception on hand to benefit the individual's present moment level of comfort. The cause/effect relationship explained by the claim has accumulated no real presence in their karma. Just read a few lines out of *Tao Te Ching*.

Associating the sensual feelings of pain, hate, greed, or whatever with the intellectually retained picture of the described and understood explanation that made so much sense when first heard about will, with time, develop its inclusion in the individual's menu of experientially based recall. With periodic intellectual association, the intellectually registered wisdom will take on an experiential character. Is it possible to see through the ancient perception screen created when reading the holy books? Replace the mental picture of men and women set in the days of togas and sandals with their living descendants wearing business suits and dress shoes.

In the heartwarming Christian poem "Footprints in the Sand", Jesus tells a questioning believer that during those times when there was only one set of footprints in the sand that coincided with the hard times in the believer's life, is when he had carried the individual on his shoulders. How is this kind act of Jesus actually recognized or imparted to the suffering believer in this real-time sensual reality? How does the compassion offered by Jesus actually make its way into the heartbeat of this living reality?

Could it be that the real-time incarnation of Jesus's comforting compassion that was generated from Jesus's kingdom of unknown location, is imparted to the believer through the helpful compassion exhibited by other living souls? Were there living people there that offered compassionate help when the believer suffered? Was their compassion founded in altruism or did they express compassion because Jesus told them to?

Our Source Lives Before Religious Theology is Conceptualized

The decision about which god an individual opts to bow to, to handle their fears coming from misunderstandings about how this reality works is based totally in their prior conditioning. Developing the mind and body connection to better understand the ways of this reality develops an individual's capacity to decide on where to place the security of their soul. They better sense how far their lack of understanding about how things work forces them to have a blind trust in what another entity tells them is so.

Many individuals live standing still in a swirling dream. They stand frozen, too afraid to recognize, let alone peak out and confront issues that come from self-generated intuitive signals about how the answers to their uncertainties might work in modern day terms and the steps they must take to get there. Should their due diligence draw for them an intellectually retained vision of where to find the answers to the incidental questions that riddle their intellectual vision of reaching that plateau of a deeper understanding, they can self-train their ability to develop an enlightened understanding of the ways of this reality that elude them and cause their ignorance that allows their suffering.

They must recognize that they have no choice but to live their life by the relational justice that happens in all the cause/effect transformations that give structure to the passing reality of the world they live in. By developing their understanding of how the reality they live in works by sensually witnessing its nature as it brings life to their body, they can strengthen their understanding of the mysteries that had before inflicted unanswered fear into their passing present moment.

An individual's more enlightened understanding of the uncertainties about the cause/effect justice needed to make this transforming reality's present moment impermanence possible, will eliminate their need to have a trust in anything that's blind to its inclusion in the ways of that relational justice. Through self-training a better understanding of the nature of this reality, they can better decide on what they need to have a blind trust in. Anything that they've previously internalized to secure or sedate their worldview generated from their misunderstandings and uncertainties about the ways of this reality can be reevaluated and set aside.

Lau Tzu teaches that harmony is needed to conquer the ego that an individual forms to protect them against the monsters lurking in their uncertainties about the realty they live in and don't understand. The mismatching of causes to their effects due to faulty prior conditioning brings a feeling of unrest and disappointment to the individual's present moment.

An understanding of the nature that gives life to the subjects of those uncertainties eliminates the ego's need to posture up any conceived self-importance. Mr. Siddhartha Gautama walked that path and left directions about how anyone else can also walk that path.

4

Finding Balance on the Primal Link Tightrope

The Untethered Inertia of Inner Longing

In Midwestern USA, it really doesn't matter how devout a citizen says they are to a religious or spiritual discipline. It doesn't matter in what direction their religious affiliations or spiritual tendencies might appear to point. Still, they will skim through a magazine or web page article, listen to a TV special or maybe tune into a radio station featuring what they suspect might give rise to or better highlight the boundaries defining a more grounded answer to their uncertainty-prompted primal question in search of wholeness and balance.

In guarded curiosity, they might lower their defenses during a coffee shop conversation with their most trusted of friends and let their dialogue venture into their newest theory of what life's all about. They might give thought-out personal justification for whether or not they want to be cremated. They might even wager their best-friend credentials against confidentiality when opening up to spout off about noted behaviors that just don't make sense within the local congregation of their chosen religion...like if their pastor might not have a hidden agenda involving their church's altar boys.

They unwittingly seek a more conclusive understanding of exactly how and where in time their understanding of the human condition and the reality of their human experience intersect. They long to find it and take refuge in its heavenly peace.

Could it be that they're just not able to wakingly realize the nature of this latent deep-down, ageless question well enough to put it into words? It's evident at this point that they cannot recognize any related spiritual signposts in their daily sensual dialogue.

Does their life purpose teeter on how they pillage through things and theories unknowingly in search of the answer to this ill-defined question? Maybe if they just slow down and hear the right answer and contemplate, then maybe the ever-prodding, indistinguishable question will come more into focus?

For the truth seeker focused on defining and undoing their ignorance that allows their real-time suffering caused by their mitote/maya state that dominates their mental status quo, the bare-bones explanation of the "when, what, where, why, and how" lies dormant just a primal link away from their conscious awareness. This rusty link in their deeper consciousness can be recharged to satisfy the primal human longing to consciously recognize the age-old religious maxims in the real-time present moment ongoing sensual signals that will unlock their inborn answer vault.

Running from Suffering or Focusing Ahead on Enriching Self-Awareness?

Look to the future, 'cause that's where you'll spend the rest of your life.
—George Burns

Do truth seekers look back over their shoulders, unknowingly running from their fears and uncertainties while pondering future encounters with more of the same? Or, do they focus their thinking ahead on enriching their conscious awareness of the impermanent nature of this cause/effect reality? How does this affect their present moment happiness? Should they spend their present moment, whether in full lotus or not, ruminating back to rehash suffering or think ahead on unlocking the secrets of life cloaked in their deeper consciousness?

A truth seeker needs to spend their present moment finding and perpetuating the wholesome aspect of living. They can create a good future of present moments with how they use the present one.

Any individual not spending their time trying to discover and develop their unique talents is fading ...their life purpose is dying out. Their direction is side-tracked, drowned out by the mental white noise of present moment indecision.

Many individuals interpret Siddhartha's intended message from his years of teaching to be the eradication of suffering. They don't see suffering's disappearance as just an effect of reaching an enlightened understanding of what it is that they're ignorant about that allows their joy and happiness to be replaced with their suffering.

Removing suffering really shouldn't be the focus here. People can be so preoccupied with their suffering that they just can't get it off their mind...in one form or another. It shouldn't even be on mind.

Mental presence needs to be focused on letting the wholesome emerge. Progress is in enriching self-awareness and in changing of the nature of the source of their perception (nature of their mind). With this, the existing feel for the nature of the present moment changes and the suffering doesn't return. Suffering's disappearance is a wonderful side effect of reaching the enlightened goal of feeling it out.

Siddhartha's *Four Noble Truths and Eightfold Pathway* focus on the means of attaining the joy and happiness coming from developing a mental state that generates altruistic compassion. Many of those who follow his guidance, instead concentrate on how to solve or eliminate suffering. Evading suffering really isn't the intended purpose of his teachings, just one of the welcome benefits.

It matters which direction a truth seeker's thought-consuming concerns point their present moment attention. These two centers of focus point in opposite directions. Like any state of consciousness, each option will dominate the spiritual intention of a truth seeker's present moment mental attention. Attempted right awareness can only be committed to one state of mind at any given time.

To engender the harmony needed to defeat the ego, there has to be a mind-set focused ahead toward self-training the harmony of right concentration to inspire the enlightened wisdom to be rid of the ignorance that obscures happiness, joy and compassion and allows the suffering to exist, not just ruminating over how to eliminate suffering itself. Present moment thinking has to be tilted toward a goal in the right direction to affect gaining the present moment mind/body harmony needed to enrich the enlightened understanding of this reality.

A truth seeker self-trains their mind control by recognizing and eliminating those thought patterns that would make their wholesome focus stray, while strengthening those that don't. A truth seeker seeks out the inspirational right thinking during introspective contemplative deliberation while their right concentration is sensually immersed in the coming and going display of ongoing change in their flesh. They stand ready for the inspired right thinking to trigger the insightfully loaded right understanding of the justice that rules the forces and trade-offs inherent to the impermanence that characterize the nature of this reality.

Present moment focus devoted to eliminating suffering dwells in an aversive thought pattern. It's a mind-stalling attachment in itself. Ironically, it's a part of a truth seeker's menu of primal addictions targeted for elimination. It short-circuits the final billing for their attachment to ignorance. It repeats the cyclic cause/effect pattern that's paid for each time the individual suffers.

Enlightened on What?...Seeing Reality in Living Color

What is it that an individual becomes enlightened about? To be enlightened about something implies that there exists in the present moment some presence to have a wisdom-enriched understanding of...some do...some don't. Not to be enlightened about that presence, there would have to be something standing in the way of an individual's recognition of the subject's presence and their truly under-standing perception of it. This would be their lack of knowledge.

Our Source is busy maintaining an ongoing process of change and the human recognition of that process is limited to the scope and range of human perception. What energizes the material makeup of what's being perceived adheres to the nat-ural laws banged out by the coming and going particles of energy that make up the metaphysical world of all of this material makeup that's totally beyond normal human perception. Self-training a wisdom-enriched awareness of this ongoing state of transformation gives a truth seeker an enlightened understanding of what their miss-matching ignorance of it was that allowed their frustration and unrest.

This universal state of enlightenment-worthy truth exists today as it did during the beginning of time. The nature and purpose described by the truth is the same and the energy particles of change are the same...only rearranged.

The perfection of the universe is already here. Each human is a part of that perfection. The human condition comes enlightened on the truth of this reality at a deeper level of consciousness. This enriched awareness is already there. It's all that's there as it's all that it is. How could it not know what it is?

It's the intrusion of misguided beliefs and ideas into the human belief system that creates the confusion of humankind's waking ignorance and misplacement of this truth. Misguided conditioning of how this reality works weaves an opaque veil over its recognition. Conscious recognition of the truth of impermanence lives muffled out in a subtle region of the human deeper consciousness. It's not about searching the Earth for an outside answer...it's about unveiling and recognizing the answer that pulsates from the perfection within us.

Removing that ignorance and building a wisdom-enriched conscious aware-ness that understands the relational justice misdirected by this ignorance, will pre-vent the ignorance from returning. A wisdom-enriched conscious awareness of the ramifications of ongoing change means that the individual has an enlightened understanding of it.

With each inspired insight an individual realizes from deep within, the scales become a bit more balanced. There's one less assortment of things to develop mental unrest about. The individual becomes just a little more cool...a bit more streetwise.

Enlightenment can be conceptualized as a process of reduction instead of a ladder to climb. It reduces or abridges a truth seeker to their genius. It's conscious recognition removes uncertainty and fear. Being totally secure in one's under-standing of their relationship with this reality's impermanence is the greatest of accomplishments.

Being enlightened with the truth about internalized misconceived beliefs about this cause/effect reality allows present moment time for joy and happiness to replace the suffering coming from the misconceived expectations. Fundamental ideas that helped sustain present moment sanity in a misunderstood world of change disappear and allow a truth seeker to see and appreciate this living reality's full living color spectrum.

Finding the humility to start the process of consciously discovering what makes up the self can unwrap all the faulty conditioning to reveal the truth about what makes up the human condition. Everyone is enlightened with the truth about what makes them real...they just haven't consciously discovered it yet.

Science Slowly Unravels Mankind's Enlightened Understanding of Reality's Impermanent Nature

In gaining an enlightened understanding of the nature of this reality, modern man gets the benefit of all the discoveries made in the last two millennia. This gives man a better understanding, at least intellectual, of the natural physical relationships in nature's forces that help hold together and explain what the constant change in this reality's all about.

The distance in between mankind's collective deeper consciousness and its waking consciousness becomes shorter as time passes. Mankind's free will (science) shows no hesitation in asking the questions needed to figure out how this reality works. Science blindly takes no other entity's word for how things work. It requires experiential proof. As time passes, mankind's primal link glows brighter.

It has to be easier to become enlightened in these modern times about the nature of this impermanent reality than for our ancient ancestors that are recognized as having achieved heavenly knowledge. The understanding of the impermanence that defines the nature of this reality is becoming so much clearer. Science has since questioned and found the truth about the physical and dimensional principles explaining how so many things work. This means that knowing what to look for makes the journey there to experience it much easier. The trick is recognizing what is understood intellectually in the sensual packages that life travels in.

It's mind-boggling how that everything, material and nonmaterial, that we deal with in these modern times is the result of fairly recent discoveries worthy of patents or copyrights. Just try to imagine all the unrest and dissatisfaction from all the misunderstandings that came about before those patented copyrighted cause/effect relationships became clearly understood.

Isaac Newton figured out gravity, one of the environmental dimensions that hold this reality together. If someone wants to talk about bringing the relational justice between cause/effect factors in this reality out into the open, this is a good place to start. Then there's Einstein's E = MC2 that gave conscious intellectual understanding of the relational justice between time, mass and velocity. Earlier man thought that comets were omens relating to human events. Talk about untethered feelings of guilt? Knowledge of the true nature of the universe has come so far.

Science has pictures of the coming and going bits of energy from the metaphysical side of this reality that can be understood intellectually. Siddhartha recognized and developed an understanding of these same bits of coming and going energy sensually. Truth seekers of today can have a more transparent presentation of the state of transformation in mind intellectually to help bring inspiration from what they experience during contemplative deliberation with harmonious mind/body concentration focused into the essence of the presence of their flesh for related insightful understandings.

Must Walk the Straight and Narrow Alone

It's up to each individual to find his or her pathway to liberation. An enlightened leader can point the way. This is not a lonely path as there are many walking this path, but every truth seeker has to forge their own steps.

Siddhartha teaches how it's through each individual's direct experience that they can free their mind of the bondage imposed by their ignorance. No one can become liberated as a result of someone else's liberation. An individual who has become enlightened about their ignorance can inspire others and help them find their way. Yet, each truth seeker has to experientially feel out their own way to acquire the sensual impressions that unlock the wisdom about the ways of impermanence.

The theoretical physicist Frijof Capra reminded his readers in his book *The Tao of Physics* how Siddhartha could only show the way to someone and how it's an individual's own responsibility to do the work to figure it out firsthand.

> The Buddha did not develop his doctrine into a consistent philosophical system, but regarded it as a means to achieve enlightenment. His statements about the world were confined to emphasizing the impermanence of all "things." He insisted on freedom from spiritual authority, including his own, saying that he could only show the way to Buddhahood, and that it was up to every individual to tread this way to the end through his or her own efforts. The Buddha's last words on his deathbed are characteristic of his worldview and of his attitude as a teacher. "Decay is inherent in all compounded things," he said before passing away: "Strive on with diligence."[6]

Actual visual testimony to the present moment circus of ongoing change is out of the range of normal human perception and with the general lack of public awareness concerning the importance of impermanence...it lessens this life truth's relative importance to most people.

In Midwestern USA until recently, it was rare to find any effective agenda to help guide a truth seeker beyond the early stages of gaining self-knowledge. Christianity's guidance stops at helping prepare a truth seeker to realize heavenly enlightenment by mandating behavioral ethics and morals, then it turns to blind faith in God's promise...period. Guidance in self-training the mind control to develop a wisdom-enriched enlightened understanding of the cause of their ignorance has been hard to sort out but, is becoming more available through the outreach of technology. Until recently for most, it's been that any Midwestern efforts at training the upper levels of spirituality have stood alone on the Midwestern beach of spiritual progress up against a tsunami of Bible-thumping fundamentalism.

Guidance is Crucial in Selftraining Process

It doesn't take an enlightened person to know that the farther along the experiential straight and narrow path an individual goes, the less distinct the steps become. Even if a truth seeker were to sense the natural pull toward gaining awareness and make the right turns toward understanding the cause of their ignorance without tying-in it to spirituality, chances are they wouldn't associate their intellectually stored theological ideals when their real-time sensual incarnation of the spiritual signpost when encountered.

There are many chances to make wrong turns. Identifying the right strings to pluck to make the harmony in the human condition resonate requires an experienced ear. Following the proven path as described by someone who's experienced enlightenment will let them know in an intellectual sense that they are preceding along a proven path. They will just need to make the spiritual connection on their own discovered plateau of common understanding. A truth seeker's attention to basic spiritual nurturing like described in Siddhartha's approach to acquiring the basic self-trainings becomes all the more necessary. Those seeking the way leading to full awareness of impermanence might need increasingly more guidance.

It seems self-evident that a truth seeker's efforts and direction for training the mental awareness to sustain their right concentration and what the mind should be concentrating on while training their wisdom is where guidance like Mr. Gautama's on self-training the ability to find the right thinking and right understanding is crucial. The only qualifier an individual needs is that they perceive things in the human range of sensual perception and have self-trained moral/ ethical standards into their present moment.

The types of wisdom that are received from other sources or intellectually rationalized are ineffective at educating a truth seeker about the ways of the relational justice that supports an impermanent reality. An intellectual understanding of the way and an experiential understanding of the way are different. To understand the way impermanence flows, as being an active part of it, is different from only seeing it mentally.

Look at how those that follow a religious theology don't seem to include the upkeep of their body as being a part of their duty to their god. Their intellectual picture doesn't include the living heartbeat of the truth.

The effective method of generating the right thinking and right understanding can be the most difficult sequential step of self-training for one to realize on their own. There are so many ways to be easily sidetracked from the effective pathway. See how many ways the Mahayana Buddhist tradition recommend. It can take such a slight diversion in purpose of attention to then completely lose direction. Making the right concentration a working part of their conscious activity is where fine-tuning is required. It can't be brushed over.

For instance, the Buddhist Mahayana interpretation seems generally unfocused and fails to address pinpointing and eliminating the cause of primal or fundamental ignorance. To understand the cause, a truth seeker has to experience our Source's present moment demonstration of the antidote. The Mahayana interpretation of Siddhartha's intended meaning is not procedurally focused forward toward this part of self-training a wisdom-enriched awareness that's enlightened about the inter-relational justice of impermanence that will free a truth seeker from their ignorance of it that allows their suffering.

Don't Worship the Messenger

If the truth is really the truth that sets one free from the ignorance that allows suffering, does it really matter who brings to the listeners' intellectual awareness this soul-saving insight on how to expose their awareness of this truth? Does the listener benefit from the message or miss the message's intended purpose of explaining what the nature and intended purpose of our Source is, by dedicating their present moment thoughts to worshipping some personal aspect of the messenger?

Siddhartha pointed out how in his teachings he kept nothing hidden from the listeners, and what he taught applied to everyone. His only intention was to show truth seekers the method he used to gain his enlightened understanding the laws of this impermanent reality.

He made clear that he didn't want to be worshipped by anyone, as his personal experience could not register in another as their personal experience. Like Jesus asked his listeners to follow him, Siddhartha only advised his listeners to follow his ways or live like he lives.

The British are coming! The British are coming! It's fortunate the future US citizens paid attention to this message and didn't drop what they were doing to praise the messenger. Paul Revere delivered a message to take action to avoid the what is, the status quo that citizens were eager to end. People then did what was needed to attain the status quo that is not that provided for the collective well-being of those involved...a status quo free from the injustice imposed by British rule.

The antidote to the ignorance that allows one's suffering is the basic primal truth that breathes, undetected by most, through every aspect of the human experience. By crediting its potential healing power to the messenger that only told of its existence, its intellectual validity and the path of focus to discover its true meaning is obscured, devalued and minimized. Finding the truth's experiential value is never realized.

Billions of truth seekers have been sidelined on their trek to find peace. Followers of Christianity hit a dead end at the Ten Commandments. The Bible offers no guidance in self-training the development of the harmony in mind control to acquire the focus and sensitivity for the inspired insightful thinking to enrich their web of awareness with the wisdom needed to enlighten their understanding of their ignorance about the impermanent nature of this reality. With no Jehovah-blessed printed instructions on how to do this, they beat themselves up over the details of the biblically described means to the biblically depicted heavenly end.

The Buddhist teacher Thich Nhat Hanh reminds his students not to confuse the way the message is presented and the purpose behind presenting the message:

> Please remember that a sutra or a Dharma talk is not insight in and of itself. It is a means of presenting insight, using works and concepts. When you use a map to get to Paris, once you have arrived, you can put the map away and enjoy being in Paris. If you spend all your time with your map, if you get caught in the words and notions presented by the Buddha, you'll miss the reality. The Buddha said many times, "My teaching is like a finger pointing to the moon. Do not mistake the finger for the moon."[7]

Ongoing change has been the truth since the universe came to life and took its eternal plunge forward. It's proper to recognize those who may have realized awareness of this heavenly truth and honor them by incorporating their advice as part of the due diligence used in gaining self-trained personal enlightenment.

It's foolish to worship or pay reverence to their memory, time in history, where they lived or what they've possibly touched or wore. Their guidance was intended for leading others down the pathway to where their own personal experientially enriched understanding and awareness of what those intellectual instructions described was gained. The other factors only supported their journey to that end.

Merely having a blind faith in an enlightened one's teachings will not free a truth seeker from the bondage of their suffering. Being able to recite the scriptures left in the wake of an enlightened one's departure will not tie the sensual knot between a truth seeker's conscious awareness and the truth explaining what impermanence is all about that lurks sensually camouflaged in a subtle region of their deeper consciousness. They must practice what their enlightened teacher has left for them in an intellectual medium to eventually feel its described truth in their bones.

It doesn't really matter how a truth seeker gets their training or finds their pathway to an enriched conscious self-awareness. The instructional intent and end goal are the same, no matter who is the messenger that does the pointing.

Feed Someone or Teach Them How to Fish?

A book with insightful bits of wisdom for its reader to intellectually chew on is good, but for a truth seeker, a process that gives them the ability to realize the same wisdom themselves is priceless.

The wisdom offered in the *Tao Te Ching* showcases Lau Tzu's waking experiential awareness of what happens in between a cause and its effect...the unfolding of ongoing change. In this writing, Lau Tzu served an intellectually graspable message telling of some derived wisdom from our Source's truth of impermanence.

Lau Tzu's writings have been interpreted and translated by many scholars, making the interworking of the relational truths he's channeled from mankind's deeper consciousness more transparent for those with a lesser-developed personal relationship with the waking awareness of our Source's truth of ongoing change. For most, the wisdom presented in the *Tao Te Ching* makes perfect sense intellectually. Yet, an individual's memory record of the cause/effect transformation has not been experientially seared into their sensually realized experiential memory.

Once a reader gets their head around it, it rings so true. It's mesmerizing, especially to those who live in illusionary realities and have developed no way of knowingly or purposefully self-training and realizing the same insightful wisdom for themselves.

It's generally agreed that the engendered meanings are relational principles applying to this cause/effect reality that any individual would want to live by. But practically speaking, once the reader's waking mind's moves onto something else, the statement of wisdom Lau Tzu channeled from his connection to the collective deeper human consciousness will not be in their sensual catalog of primary knowledge and not a part of their factory-set knee-jerk reflex knowledge that's developed from personally experiencing something.

A person can pound Lau Tzu's verses or those from any other intellectual source into their intellectual memory, but at a later time, when the present moment comes when a similar relational situation arises, the earlier read relational intellectual wisdom will not be stored, wired in and through the sensual netting that touches their deeper consciousness in their first-to-be-accessed sensual memory archives, for the most rapid recall to better serve the individual. It's been intellectually memorized and stored in the outer regions of the brain. It's not recalled from the more primitive brain.

Any insightfully applied "lateral application" adaptability will be missing when the feasibility of the individual's usage of the memorized wisdom is challenged in similar situations where the same cause/effect principle applies but the possible relevance of any tangent application is not recognized. Their present moment sensual mind can't recognize these situations, as Lau Tzu's sensual experience that inspired his wisdom-enriched insight that they later intellectually memorized did not leave its footprint in their experiential memory zone. Lau Tzu's sensually backed conscious awareness of the cause/effect justice he realized during his harmonious introspective mind/body deliberations while focusing his right concentration into the relational interplay among the coming and going particles of change is missing.

Rapid recall is a needed part of the fight-or-flight defense mechanism wired into the human condition. In future realtime personal encounters with the subject of the intellectual wisdom, the individual would have to be able to recognize the sensually transferred similarities of the past situation that were remembered in intellectual coding and be able to pull from their intellectual memory the mind's book, chapter, and verse to draw a comparison to associate with an intellectually founded event, apply the intellectually stored wisdom to the current situation and act accordingly. It's not going to happen. This may work upon occasion, but an individual's intellectual files can only hold so much and stay fresh for only so long.

They're coded in intellectual media verbiage while those that trigger the experiential memory are coded sensually. It's like associating intellectually coded religious theology with sensually coded reality.

The individual has no waking conscious reference to their experiential memory library because they have no sensual history with the cause/effect relationship in a real-life situation as Lau Tzu did when making his inspired insightful understanding from which he derived the wisdom.

Lau Tzu's right thinking that inspired his insightful wisdom-enriched right understandings while gaining self-knowledge appear during his contemplative deliberations with his right concentration sustained in sensually witnessing the coming and going display of the "becoming" nature of our Source as manifested in his own flesh. Lau Tzu links self-discovery to one's enlightenment in verse 33 of *Tao Te Ching* when he writes how harmony will conquer the self and that in understanding the self, a truth seeker finds enlightenment.

In this verse, Lau Tzu gives a Cliffs Notes lesson on how to fish (find heavenly enlightenment). If this isn't detailed enough, a truth seeker's due diligence will uncover Siddhartha's expanded details on the process of self-training the ego-conquering harmony for an enlightened conscious awareness of this reality's impermanent nature.

Giving humanity an instruction book of relational etiquette that gives bits of wisdom about the dos and don'ts of how to think and behave to avoid being punished and maintain a level of expected morality might not be cheap. But, teaching them how to understand by their own means and in their own way why those actions are deemed to be "right or wrong"...to know why the Ten Commandments became commandments...is priceless.

Instead of giving an individual isolated bites of intellectual wisdom to ruminate over and put aside to be forgotten, it's better to teach them how cook up the wisdom themselves.

Spontaneous Self-Actualization

Not understanding that the scales of relational justice in this transforming cause/effect world are always set to the physical properties inherent to this reality's impermanent nature and that this lack of understanding is the seed for all human suffering, leaves an individual confused and suspended in wonder about their spiritual peace. All a religious believer has to battle this ignorance and the resulting fear of the unknown is the confidence they're putting in the blind faith they register intellectually in the cognitively drawn and filed account of an unverified religious promise made by a never-seen god. Its intellectual presence really isn't sufficient to settle the emotionally generated red flags arising from their unanswered inner sensual fear of the unknown they feel deep in their heart.

Not being content with what religion says about being saved from suffering and not having had any credible guidance in any other soul-saving philosophies only compounds an individual's day-to-day curious wonder. The majority of those living in this state of wonder will die in its spiritual confusion.

It's possible for an individual to self-train their awareness of the ways of an impermanent world through their own discovery. There's an intrinsic self-protective internal push from an individual's deeper conscious to heal their soul. Gaining an understanding of how the laws of impermanence affect the human condition's human experience will do this and is available to all who seek it. This discovery won't be recognized against the same sort of intellectually retained religious framework from one area to the next who've been introduced to different religious plans.

It has been said that self-healing can start spontaneously in an individual. There are those in different parts of the world who have, through self-examination, developed the wisdom enrichment needed for an enlightened awareness of what it was that caused their ignorance that led them to suffer to undo their prior faulty conditioning. Not realizing their discovery's spiritual significance and/or not having waking familiarity with any order of structure to their process, they fail in being able to share it to others.

With all the internalized prior conditioning from misleading claims that capture and mute their conscious awareness of any inborn connection to the primal truth of eternal peace, their idea of anything spiritual or religious gets classified and intellectually shelved in one way or another as being some shade of today's religious dogma, rites and rituals. It's very unlikely that a curious individual will relate the appearance of a real-time present moment sensual spiritual signpost of sorts to anything within the endless boundaries of their cerebrally sketched religious illusion of reality that describes what God's after-death heavenly kingdom or entourage might appear as. What Paul described Jesus's presence as being when he returns for his obedient souls when writing the Book of Revelations while imprisoned by the Romans, bears no resemblance to what's actually bringing life into this transforming present moment.

A truth seeker could be on the right track but still not associate what they're insightfully realizing with what a religious discipline would in any way classify as being something associated with finding an awareness of the truth. It would show no resemblance to what it should be as per their cognitive understanding of society's religious hoopla describing what suffering relief will be like after death. They cannot appreciate their present moment sensual signals as being the spiritual markers directing them toward gaining self-knowledge with the enlightened understanding of our reality's impermanent nature that will replace their present moment suffering with compassion, joy and happiness.

An individual could serendipitously feel the emanation of impermanence in real-time without cognitively linking it to the religious presence of our Source described in the highly edited biblical renditions of the stories of Jesus's teachings. The real-time incarnation as it's experienced and the illusionary idea of what intellectual media have it built up to be never really match up. The true spiritual significance of the sensually detected appearance of what their intellectually based mental images are supposed to be pointing at slides by unnoticed.

However, even though its sensual representation might not be recognized as being what their intellectually sketched take on spirituality is, the relational justice in this cause/effect reality still does its unalterable job and this brings the individual a level of peace of mind. Quiet right concentration of any kind has its benefits. It dampers mental disruption and brings some order to an unchartered mitote/maya state of mind that its social description has managed to camouflage.

Those that affect an enlightened understanding of impermanence serendipitously are fortunate if they never have to figure out what theological religious maxims their sensual discovery represents. They get the benefits of enlightenment without having to fend off the gut-felt uncertainty, guilt and social pressure that religious blind faith casts over a culture.

The primal truth's sensual detection wears a different colored outfit than its intellectual guise stands ready to recognize, associate and process as being such. Its sensual incarnation is imprinted in their personal present moment experiential understanding while they still consciously carry its cognitive image that was mentally sketched using mere intellectual ink. Its living presence is hand-drawn in sensual ink, but mentally processed and read through glasses blown with intellectual glass lenses.

The individual will gain a level of spiritual satisfaction that may never be consciously interpreted as being the spiritual thing that helps them find their way to their Sunday morning taught eternal Shangri-La with freedom from suffering. Bringing into focus an understanding that allows true spiritual growth that links the deeper and waking consciousness could slowly assume recognition and clarity as the individual's mind is self-trained to read the sensory language common to a sensual dialogue...or maybe they luck into finding some qualified guidance.

Path Recognition Nixes Pillaging for Answer

Individuals who have finally become at least superficially aware of the existence of the truth of our Source's nature and intended purpose have now had the longed-for answer that's been lurking in a subtle region of their deeper consciousness intellectually "linked" with their waking conscious mind that's been impatiently waiting, biding its time in its pool of addictions longing for the "answer" to their undoing. Now, they just need to sensually witness what they cognitively know is there...experientially from within.

With this, their longing for "what is not" stops forever. The endless groping of newly pillaged toys for the answer stops. The answer-bearing message from the subtle region of their deeper consciousness has finally been given the floor as it speaks its piece (sensually) describing exactly the details of how it feels.

With a truth seeker's fulfillment of their primal longing for the answer to find the antidote to the cause of their ignorance, they will give up religious ritualistic and ceremonial behavior. The religious dogma, rituals and rites lose their meaning. They retire their "on alert" hopeful, yet futile search for random hints and serendipitous discoveries to what the primal answer might be.

They no longer aimlessly fetter their daily energy away pillaging from toy to toy, idea to idea hoping to turn a new page that will at least give them a hint as to what the right question is to ask to catch scent of which direction to travel to find the answer. Waiting for this conscious realization to occur, the majority of Midwesterners wait their entire lifetime suspended in a fog of ritualistic uncertainty.

Whether stun-calmed or not, when an individual can visualize where their path to making a connection with their source is directed, they can drop being suspended in wonder. They can land with their feet hitting the ground running. Their spiritual quest shifts away from pillaging blindly from one religious claim to another while hoping to find the answer or to just better understand what the question is. It helps clear out mental cobwebs that set the pick for their ignorance to slide by again and rule their tilted perception of the situation.

They've now seen the truth and source of their ignorance and suddenly an unshakeable faith in the dependability of the consistency of the conditions that support and allow the truth's unchanging omnipresence that they've just sensually witnessed finds and comforts them. In satisfying their longing to understand our Source's nature and intended purpose, their steadfast faith in having intuitive insights that gives order to and strengthens their internal link of spirituality grows stronger. It's a feeling that an individual has to experience to understand.

As a truth seeker's sensual experiential understanding of what spiritual meaning was targeted by the rites, rituals, and ceremonies they've been practicing increases, their dependence on performing them will disappear. An unshakeable, steadfast faith in what they've experienced will form alongside the wisdom they self-train. Their enlightened understanding will conquer their self-ego and end their suffering.

Siddhartha's Three Jewels

Religious theology presents a reach in understanding to calm the mental conflicts coming from the ignorance of how the relational justice of present moment reality presents itself in the naked change of the flow of time. The ignorance is perpetuated by the lack of understanding of how to selftrain the development of the human mind to better understand the ways of nature that rule the cause/effect flow of the present moment.

People coagulate into groups of common seekers while still having their individual eyes open for a better, more satisfying answer to calm their dissonance. Whether truth seekers have chosen to follow the teachings of a self-proclaimed representative of a religion's god or a teacher of how to find their own way to an enlightened understanding of the source of their suffering, Siddhartha teaches of how truth seekers best approach this end.

Siddhartha spoke of the three jewels...the teacher, the teachings, and the community. A community is a group of individuals that have a common eye focused on a common end and way of enriching the development of their interpretation of what the truth describing this reality is. They gather to compare perceptions to help give shape and buoyancy to the repressed ideas that are trying to surface through the misguided internal white noise of misguided prior conditioning that feeds their ignorance and drowns out their understanding of their presence.

It can be beneficial for a truth seeker to meet with others who share the same forward focus, based on developing a better understanding of the ways of the nature of this reality. Siddhartha advises that for those seeking an inner recognition of the truth, that to intellectually discuss their experiential journeys helps to remove the layers of faulty misguided understandings and missed ideas to let surface insights recognizing the common truth of the ongoing interplay within the transforming nature of their right concentration.

5

Obeying the Ten Commandments

...Moral/Ethical Development Is Not An End In Itself

Religion's Fundamental Role in the Human Experience

Believing in a religious doctrine creates a pacifying downtime for those unaware of why they suffer. Until they realize that they need to understand how this reality's impermanent nature sets the rules for the cause/effect rhythm of each passing present moment, they will suffer through all the times when real causes and real effects of various situations don't match up with what they think they should be in their account of what reality appears to be. They can memorize the Bible, but this won't enlighten their awareness of our Source's nature of omnipresence which is what they need be aware of to undo their conditioned ignorance that distances their joy and happiness and allows their suffering.

Different religions provide different generic templates. They all stipulate a basic moral/ethical standard that adapts to the people of different cultures. It provides a means of outlining some order into a society's confusion and hidden unrest as their natural human curiosity longs to know the primal truth. A culturally shared religious belief can add order to an otherwise unruly mass.

Local statutes reflect the local religion's code of ethics. Atheists may not believe in a god, but they still have to live their lives by the moral/ethical influence coming from his list of commandments. Religions require their believers to have a faith that's blind to witnessing any evidence that in real-time demonstrates the participation of any member of the Holy Trinity in the making of the present moment.

Religions keep their projected philosophies updated to fit around emerging scientific discoveries that have made obsolete something that the believers have relied on their blind faith to verify. Religion's list of newly defined sinful behavior also gets updated to adapt to any social-scientific changes that are being recognized to help maintain its proclaimed plausibility.

The religious community panics in fear of the idea that what is here now in real-time may be all there really is. They may blame the status quo for not having what they need to make their suffering do away. They may think they need something that is not here in this status quo to find joy and happiness. They cannot see the heavenly beauty in the buzz of the present moment. They are not the meek who will inherit the present moment arrangement of the coming and going bits of energy that comprise the Earth that Jesus says the meek will inherit.

They have no sensual history reference of any tangible palace in the sky to go to after dying that has what they're missing in their living sensual cause/effect reality that they're longing for and just can't see in the status quo. Suffering individuals long for peace in the present moment, not peace after they die. They have no biblical guidance on how to understand and find in this lifetime what they're longing for.

All Disciplines Include Moral/ Ethical Standards

The different religious and spiritual disciplines all set moral/ethical standards that are expected by their respective gods or a primary step in being able to realize an enlightened awareness of how joy and happiness are replaced with suffering. This either satisfies a god demand or serves to anchor an individual's attempt to realize an inner heaven within their lifetime.

Midwestern Christianity sees obeying the moral/ethical standards set by the Ten Commandments as an end in itself that will please God and help avoid his wrath. It's not considered as a foundation for a calm mind that can then be used to self-train the mind control to enable realizing the inspired thinking to generate the wisdom-enriched insightful enlightened awareness about what they're ignorant about that left nothing for them to do but spend their present moments suffering.

When a religious believer can find the courage to shake off their blinders and revive their free will to satisfy their desire to find mental peace, they've taken the first step of a truth seeker doing the due diligence to become enlightened about what it was that convinced them to wear the blinders. They've realized that much of their present moment time is spent tied up suffering unexplained discomfort and frustration and they want to find effective relief from it now. Even though they may ask their god to deliver them from their suffering, they're going to try to help him by getting off the couch and gathering the information that he, this reality's source, has made available and figuring it out on their own.

When realizing the significance of their present moment unrest, they used the right thinking and right understanding described by Siddhartha in his *Eightfold Pathway to Enlightenment* to intellectually recognize that they have present moment suffering and that it's something that's within their power to end. Recognizing that they have felt this ongoing state of mental unrest as their primary problem satisfies the first of Siddhartha's *Four Noble Truths*.

After the second and third noble truths are realized...after they realize the problem has a cause and the cause has a solution...the truth seeker will realize the fourth noble truth by self-training the wisdom to find enlightened awareness about what it was that allowed them to suffer. The guidance offered in Siddhartha's, *The Noble Eightfold Pathway to Enlightenment* gives detail of how to strike the harmony that Lau Tzu discovered would defeat the ego and allow an enlightened awareness of what it was that they were ignorant about concerning this reality that caused them to spend their present moment in some sort of unrest.

In the first of Siddhartha's three levels of self-trainings outlined in his *Eightfold Pathway to Enlightenment*, the truth seeker self-trains their moral/ethical behavior. They self-train the first three of the noble eight folds...right speech, right actions, and right livelihood. (Establishing these moral/ethical standards is where the Bible stops telling its readers what to do to reach heavenly peace...a different kind of heaven.)

Moral/ethical standards are common protocol among the teachings of the different religious and spiritual beliefs. In recognizing the usefulness in having religion-stamped government standards for a social moral/ethical discipline meant to maintain social order and minimizing social conflict, Constantine's priests selected the books to comprise their Bible. They pulled the rug out for any truth seeker wanting to know what else they need to do to enlighten their wisdom-enriched awareness of the impermanent nature of this reality. They wanted all their Christians to look to Rome for guidance and not find it within themselves.

Mankind's collective waking awareness of the relational wisdom of not doing these negative things finally became clear to our ancient ancestors after many generations of noting the additional physical suffering to the offended and mental unrest to the offenders that accompanied these behaviors. It's said that God then wrote the warnings about committing ten certain behaviors that exceeded mankind's moral/ethical tolerance in stone around 3,000 years ago.

The Roman Catholic Church has been keeping the list of tabooed behaviors updated ever since. Today, the original list of things not to do continues to appear carved in stone throughout the United States. Look on any courthouse lawn, next to the lady holding the scales of relational justice.

The first agreement of the Toltec shaman Miguel Ruiz's *Four Agreements* is for an individual to be impeccable with their speech. This is the same starting point for those who are trying to understand and eliminate their suffering. Being impeccable with your speech is a personal agreement an individual makes within their belief system. Ruiz's first agreement is a Cliffs Notes summary of Siddhartha's first three folds on the way to enlightenment that describe how to self-train proper moral/ethical behavior and of the Ten Commandments list of sinful behaviors.

Buddhism goes on to suggest additional graduated levels of precepts, the less predominant behaviors that also tend to sidetrack or preoccupy a truth seeker's mental stability to go on to self-train the mind control to realize enlightenment. The number of Buddhist precepts observed depends on the purpose of intent of one's targeted spiritual application.

The first five Buddhist precepts include abstaining from killing, stealing, sexual misconduct, false speech and intoxicants. Observing eight precepts would add on abstention from all sex, untimely eating and sensual entertainment. Ten precepts would add abstention from taking pay and resting in high or luxurious places while others are suffering.

Siddhartha's *Eightfold Pathway to Enlightenment* identifies sufficient self-training in the moral/ethical standards as being a primary necessity before an individual can find the calmed mental capacity to proceed to self-train the mind control on their road to having a wisdom-enriched awareness, enlightened to what underlies their ignorance that allows their suffering. It's by not violating the behavioral guidelines that the mind stays cool from the agitation that results from any sins they might commit.

What Exactly is a Sin?

The proclamation that "Christ died for our sins" could easily be considered Christianity's logo. It is a totally unquestioned old established truth parroted anytime a minister takes a deep breath and needs a filler statement. Its repetition is used even when needed to substantiate the truth of its claim.

Even if a sinner knows what a sin is, what good does it do for Jesus to forgive them for their sins if they don't know what makes a sin a sin. It's assumed that God decrees what behaviors are sins, but what sets up the relational justice system that designates some behavior as being sins?

What is put to a disadvantage when a sin is committed? What good does it impede? It would be much easier not to repeat a behavior if it was known why it was wrong other than just because God says so.

What does this decree really mean? There's a plethora of interpretations of how the state of this right/wrong relationship represents itself in today's world with no real tie into how it actually plays into the sinner's quest for salvation. It's loosely applied and seems to be all-encompassing...a quick answer to just about any question. The quick answer buys time for thinking how to further substantiate the question. What exactly is it that makes a sin a sin anyway?

Jehovah told Moses on Mt. Sinai that to break any of his Ten Commandments is committing a sin. People make effort to obey the commandments because everybody else accepts the appropriateness, not asking what it is about the taboo behaviors that make them so bad and worthy of making commandment status.

There's at least one Hoosier who has never really heard the core meaning of this parroted statement even questioned, let alone meaningfully explained. The understanding of what a sin actually is in today's world and how the essence of that sin actually hinders the sinner's quest for mental deliverance from suffering or to gain enlightenment about why humans suffer is pretty sketchy. Maybe it gets lost in trying to figure out what the original sin is that all humans are born with?

The original sin dates back to Adam and Eve. The word is that we are born into this world bearing the eternal guilt of this primal sin. This Christian observation is similar to the Buddhist observation that being born is merely the birth phase in the cyclic process of suffering caused by a reaction, which is the result of ignorance. They both point to perpetual suffering. Could it only be a figment of one's language? Maybe it's a fundamentalist fear of stepping outside a written paper trail-fed state of stubbornness?

Christ died for our sins? If Christ died for our sins and after accepting Christ, we're forgiven, why do we still live in a reality in which devout Christians suffer? It's an easy thing to say, but what does it mean? The truth is that any individual suffers from their ignorance of understanding and dealing with the natural justice of this cause/effect impermanent reality.

Besides, there's at least one Hoosier that would refuse to be saved at the expense of someone else...Son of God or not. It's our First Amendment right! This is especially true when not being first asked or knowing what it was they were being saved from.

What is a sin, as stated in today's language dialect? What's a temptation as stated in today's language dialect? Look at the average Hoosier's waistline and compare that to the number of proclaimed-to-be good Christians that are thought to keep their sinning in check. We have a great imbalance here.

The first question someone who's being coaxed into taking the leap of blind faith to believe in God's plan to save the human from sin should be to know exactly what a sin is. Why are some behaviors or thought patterns considered wrong? What is wrong? When someone sins, what do they do? They suffer...but why?

The Bible says to get wisdom. Even though the Romans edited out the accounts of Jesus's teachings that might have better explained what a sin is and how sinning relates to the process of reaching heavenly enlightenment, the current edition doesn't. For all practical purposes, it could be said that anything that stands in the way of a truth seeker's process of developing this wisdom that undoes the ignorance that allows suffering is a sin?

When someone does something that hinders their progress in trying to calm their mind or hinders someone else's process to calm their mind to eventually self-train the wisdom to be enlightened about our Source's impermanent nature, they've committed a sin. When their mental activity is burdened with guilt, hate, envy, lust or any of these negative mental states, their mind will not be calm enough to self-train the mind control to find the body/mind harmony for any inspired thinking to allow the insightful awareness of this reality's impermanence to help undo their ignorance of what takes away their joy and happiness and makes them suffer.

A sin begins with any intention that interrupts the flow of the self-discovery process. A truth seeker has to work to have their mind free of or at least toward minimizing the confused guilt-like or negative feelings that clouds their attempts to self-train their control of their mind's thought direction of attention. They need this to self-train a wisdom-enriched understanding of their ignorance about the impermanent cause/effect justice of this reality that creates the hell that may define their present moment existence.

Ten Commandments Updated

The Bible offers no reason why the moral/ethical mandates of the Ten Commandments are needed to pursue wisdom or how acquiring wisdom brings one closer to reaching heaven as so described. So, to keep Christianity's sensitivity to nonacceptable behavior up to date, Christianity keeps a modernized updated list of banned behaviors. The Vatican has recently proclaimed an updated list of modern "thou shalt nots" to include "the new sins."

This thought train is centered mainly on an individual's behavior, which is actually just a symptom of the cause of the sinful expression. Behavior is just the resulting vibration of the effect the ignorance allowing the attachment to the various addictions reflecting the craving and aversion that cause people to suffer. It's in the process of the mind that the cause lays, not in the resultant behavior. Merely suppressing its behavioral symptom will not ease the suffering that originates from the cause of the symptom. Thought engineering is needed.

Even though the Bible says that man shall take care of the earth, one of the updates on the new list warns against environmental blight. Others include staying away from genetic manipulation and mind damaging drugs. These are just modern symptoms of the same root cause of addictions...not understanding why not to cling to imagined states of permanence...why recognizing and arresting the thought patterns that result in the fleeting reactions before they occur is needed to avert addictive reactionary behavior.

These mandated updates are temporary patches...thumbs in the dike. They will not uproot the source of the ignorance of the impermanent nature of this reality that allows the individual's resulting fleeting reactions coming from intentions aimed at attachment to addictive thoughts and behaviors originating from illusionary understandings of a reality thought to have a nature of continuity. This causes suffering and perpetuate the believer's misunderstanding between the impermanent nature of real causes and real effects that naturally occur in this multidimensional reality and those of an illusionary reality with a nature of permanence.

These Ten Commandments amendments forbid the behaviors that are only the symptoms resulting from purposes of intent that try to service wants or desires of an infected undefined belief system that wanders through the endless wants of the 1,000 random voices that rule the individual's or society's mitote/maya infested belief system and worldview. They leave the individual wandering/wondering through life suffering...waiting to die in hopes of making the team that rides the chariot into heaven, come Revelation's day of redemption, saved from suffering an eternity in hell.

Those paying heed to these updates don't know that to see the light and experience the promised joy and happiness it is necessary to understand the nature of the light and how to throw the switch now in the present moment, as now is the only present moment there will ever be. Their soul has to taste these states of suffering or not while alive to take the sensually stored record of their journey with them when they meet Saint Peter at the gate.

Bible Offers No Guidance on Selftraining the Mind Control to Gain Self-Knowledge to Undo Suffering

Religious and spiritual traditions agree that moral and ethical standards are needed to better manage any society and to maybe please a god. In Christianity, this is as far as biblical guidance goes toward developing a believer's spiritual maturity. Maintaining the behavioral standards needed for good ethical/moral behavior is offered as an end in itself in Christian Bible teachings.

Accept Christ and live a clean life and you're in. Just pray to God for relief of present moment unrest. Many Christians give God total credit for their successes. Not so many give him credit for their failures...that they usually blame on themselves or other people or things.

Religions offer no guidance on understanding the nature of the mind to enable controlling its host's behavioral intentions. They leave that to their god. They offer no lit pathway to unravel the anatomy of the belief system to be rid of the void of uncertainty and the effects of the resulting ignorance that allows their addictions to attachments that brings their suffering. There's no breakdown of how to form the mind/ body harmony Lau Tzu pointed to that's key to inheriting the Earth like Jesus said the meek would be able to do.

Describing someone as being a "good, devout Christian" implies about the same thing as describing them as being a God-fearing Christian and that suggests that the individual lives day to day while not breaking any of the commandments. They anticipate God's wrath if they sin. They can be trusted. They're good at keeping their job and family in order...good at keeping their word. Their compassion will afford them times when the help others.

But, reference to their spiritual maturity stops there. These complimentary critiques don't reference how spiritually mature they are. The compliments describe someone who knows how to follow the rules of behavior but hints at no higher spiritual plateau of aware understanding. This would possibly point to a higher level of altruism that complimented their human condition without being classified as being a saint?

What is it about the Pope that explains why he's thought by many to have a special connection to the god Jehovah? Maybe his fellow believers think God has given him superior wisdom and that's why what he says is what goes? It could be said that this is again where their blind faith kicks in.

Modern Christianity still requires obedience to the original Ten Commandments. This has served as an intellectual bookmark that's helped keep mankind's collective spiritual development stagnate for almost 3,000 years when God's list first appeared in stone. It reminds an individual of how they know they've been told how they should act and not so much how they feel they should act and understand why.

Beyond the point of moral/ethical training, religious groups hover in their required good behavior with their understanding of spiritual reality hinging mostly on an intellectually structured and retained order of unverified claims in a world they know and understand only intellectually. They have yet to consciously realize and acknowledge suffering moment-to-moment unrest to be their real-time problem for which there is a real-time solution and that freedom from what it is that allows this suffering is the universal freedom humanity longs for.

Any biblical guidance in the way to undoing addictions and suffering starts with the Commandments' order "Thou shalt not." This sets order to adopting the basic ethical/moral standards. The phrase "and this is why thou shalt not" is never offered.

There's no God-sent justification or reasoning as to the actual role good ethical/moral behavior plays in helping to stop the ignorance that allows the real-time suffering addressed in Christians' prayers that they seek relief from. The Bible leaves the impression that today's suffering is the effect of those tabooed behaviors and the way to stop suffering is to stop the behaviors. It doesn't address eliminating what it is that allows the ignorance of ongoing change that's responsible for the misguided direction that allows for the misaligned thinking that affects the sinful behaviors.

A deeper understanding of why the fruits of knowledge are condemned reveals that ignorance builds from believing in the unverified fruits promised by borrowed or received intellectual knowledge. The ignorance in doing this has allowed internalization of beliefs with natures that honor the existence of a continual reality that condone attachment to addictions to cravings and aversions as well as to imagined forms of life continuity. These infected claims result in the gradual formation of an individual's mitote/maya mental state and the menu of addictions that it feeds off of.

There is no biblical guidance on how to address what caused the ignorance that allowed the original sin of mankind when Adam and Eve ate from the tree of knowledge...of when an individual trusts their internalized intellectual knowledge to form their worldview. Without any guidance from the Bible, a Christian cannot effectively figure out how to self-train their mind to affect the inspired insightful wisdom the Bible says must be sought out. Good moral/ethical behavior is not an end in itself. It's just the beginning.

Of course, there's no biblical guidance leading a believer to see how the sought-after wisdom to help in living day by day in this cause/effect reality is actually the same wisdom that leads one to attaining an enlightened understanding of what causes human ignorance or what allows the cause to unfold. Real-time spiritual incarnations of our Source's living manifestation don't use the same communication format used when formatting the intellectually understood and remembered notions of the religious maxims like "God's way" or "holy." The real-life incarnation of what the Bible intellectually describes as the Holy Spirit is realized sensually. The biblical incarnation of the Holy Spirit originates from a written text...sensual recognition verses intellectual media recognition and retention. Do they ever really meet up?

A truth seeker must take the calmed mental state resulting from their moral/ethical lifestyle and self-train their mind and body to unite in harmony on the plateau of understanding and sensually witness the life manifesting within their body to enter into contemplative deliberation to be inspired by what they're being directly exposed to, to have insightful wisdom-enriched understandings of this impermanent reality. This resulting wisdom brings them closer to a full awareness of our Source's intended purpose of initiating ongoing change. Religions do not make this connection.

Religious Snake Oil Salesmen?

Training the mind control to then train the awareness-enriching wisdom to find heavenly enlightenment in the passing present moment lacks any religious guidance. There's no guidance on how to through humility-fueled mind/body harmony, develop the appropriate experiential latticework to support the protocol necessary to rediscover the sensual primal link gateway in between the human deeper and waking states of consciousness.

Religious groups and individuals deal with the real-time need to quiet present moment suffering in their own way. Many merchandise the need. Most try to benefit financially from it.

They craft their own recipe that segue from maintaining the biblical moral/ethical guidelines to achieving or better understanding their interpretation of the heavenly state of nonsuffering. They use their individual intellectual interpretations of their biblical references to present moment mental peace. They might say something like: "What he meant here was this." Still, finding the cause of present moment suffering isn't recognized as the key to heavenly enlightenment... Bible-style.

These religious sales methods are intellectually generated practices that attempt to disperse the significance of today's suffering and instill peace of mind based on the hope of future change for the better when a listening believer dies and goes to heaven. They do not address where to witness to then understand ongoing change to reach wisdom-enriched awareness of its truth. Training wisdom is not their end in sight. They live by their personal interpretation of the written biblical account of God's wisdom. They do not inspire having an eye directed at understanding the wisdom of our impermanent reality.

Supplemental Bible study step programs in tapes, CDs, DVDs, books and other media are available on most of the many Bible TV programs. These programs make their own sense in the illusionary world of their creator and probably do at least offer some placebo-effect relief of suffering or can at least momentarily displace the awareness of present moment suffering...providing about the same relief as counting to ten or transcendental meditation concentration focused into the illusion of the permanence of an object. Yet, they fail to train the wisdom to recognize and eradicate the misguided prior conditioning that will stop producing the fleeting intentions that cause the emotion-spawned reactions that continue to fortify the addictive attachments that rekindle their internal emotional fire.

Bible's Guidance Beyond the Ten Commandments

After a Christian sinner manages to finally stop breaking the Ten Commandments and their peace of mind has started to return, then what do they do? How can they spend the rest of their life getting to know their Source better?

The mitote/maya state of mental confusion is still there. How do they quell the hounding urge to satisfy one of the many wants from the many unrelated misguided beliefs that wait burning a hole in the pocket of their belief system? How do they recognize the bad in today's incarnations of the age-old cardinal sins? They are still out there.

They're given no direction on how or with what to replace the thoughts that delivered the deviant behavioral intentions to occupy their present moments. There is a way to train the mind to control those thoughts. After a while, most just drift back into the security of the familiar state of mind they had when generating their inappropriate (sinful) behaviors, like the majority of people who make New Year's resolutions.

They had nothing of primal significance to work toward. They lack a vision of direction. They've had no guidance on how to bring to their waking consciousness the right understanding to derive the relational wisdom that applies to the very living relationships they are having trouble understanding how to act in and not react to for the benefit of themselves and others.

There are no biblical suggestions on how to change the nature of one's mind to understand the ignorance that allows habit energy to form into the reactions that define their list of addictions. The Bible says to find wisdom, yet doesn't say how or how it relates to heaven as described. An individual needs to understand what the root of their addictions is to undo what causes their ignorance to put an end to the suffering it allows.

6

Guidance in Selftraining Mind Control

...Gaining Control of Your Mental Podium

Vision without action is a daydream.

—Japanese proverb

Guidance Beyond the Ten Commandment List of Sins

A truth seeker can self-train a wisdom-enriched waking awareness that enlightens them with the knowledge about what they don't understand about this reality that keeps them from living the present moment in the state of compassionate love that humans are capable of realizing. In the absence of this awareness about our reality that instills this state of mind, they suffer through all the misconceptions that can come from misjudging the nature of the environment they live in.

Christianity stops guiding an individual down the path to enlightenment at the point of living a moral and ethical lifestyle. Then there's the modern catchphrase of "doing unto others as you would have them do unto you." This golden rule is like a compassion-flavored chaser to help give the unexplained mandates a feeling of completeness. It sooths the bitter taste imposed by not being explained the why not about the Ten Commandments mandates. Some people change this golden rule to mean "Have others do unto you as you think you would do unto them."

Self-training acceptable moral/ethic behavior helps prep a truth seeker for advancing through the self-trainings in which they learn to understand how and why to self-train control of their mind. They can then obtain self-knowledge while enriching their waking consciousness with the wisdom to understand the relational truths that give definition to compassion. The compassionate state of mind emerges and the suffering disappears.

Our Kingdom Within...Find And Acknowledge It

Neither shall they say, lo here! or, lo there! for, behold,
the kingdom of God is within you.

—Luke 17:23, King James Version

Locating our Source's kingdom within and seeking the sensual understanding of how misguided prior-conditioning-inspired perceptions of cause/effect relationships fuel the miscued habit energy that generates the reactionary fleeting moods that hijack human freedom of thought is key to finding the strength to release its present moment deathgrip on the human free will. When an individual realizes that their suffering arises from their ignorance and can find the courage to recalibrate their mentally pictured biblical concept of heavenly bliss to mean the absence of that same present moment suffering that heavenly bliss is targeting to remove, they have become a truth-seeker.

They are ready for guidance in understanding the communication media of our Source as being the universal body-speak language of the human condition. Without associating a religiously accepted spiritual definer to its actual sensual incarnation when it appears, a truth seeker might have discovered the land of heavenly compassion and not realized it. Nothing lost though, really? It's the same pathway, guided or self-led, that will take someone from their suffering in ignorance to the heavenly enlightenment about what causes the ignorance and how to be rid of it.

When compiling the written accounts of Jesus's life and teachings that are found in today's Bible, the Romans edited out the written accounts of Jesus's teachings to groups of higher spiritual maturity where he provided the guidance on finding the heaven within oneself. Discoveries made in the past century have uncovered copies of a few of the written accounts that the Romans deemed unacceptable that were missed when Rome ordered burned all the unacceptable written accounts that tell of Jesus's teachings to those who could understand the more subtle levels of his intended message with all evidence of any other religious efforts that weren't Christian.

Another messenger of the one and only truth whose unedited guidance is becoming more readily available in the Midwest was Mr. Siddhartha Gautama. During his lifetime, Mr. Gautama was able to develop the supreme inner body/mind harmony to realize the Buddha kingdom within...he points out that this source of truth comes as part of the human condition and how its witnessing is available to all on equal terms.

Being that there's only one truth describing the nature and intended purpose of our Source, it becomes clear that it doesn't really matter who the messenger is or what language or time in history the message detailing the truth about the nature and purpose of our Source is in. There are different understandings and versions of Siddhartha's teachings. Every truth seeker should find the diligence to find and consider the teachings from all sources in finding their way to eliminate their ignorance that breeds their suffering. They should then extrapolate what they feel the teachers' intended meanings to be while experientially testing it out as they walk the pathway in their own way.

It's crucial that an individual feels worthy of attaining awareness. They must escape self-devaluation and feel that they have the capability and are equally worthy of realizing self-awareness. Some feel it's above their born-into social class... that they are not one of the chosen ones. They must discard self-doubt and realize that finding self-definition is equally available to all right now...in this lifetime.

When first finding the humility to strike up the right concentration needed for the mind/body harmony to effectively enter the interior factory of life transformation, most would look up to their teacher and ask what it feels like. Instead, tell them what it feels like. The change is the same in all, but an individual's intellectual description of that experience might vary. Discuss it and help each other hone down and enrich the understanding of life it offers. That assurance of familiarity with what was experienced is the start of a steadfast faith in the undeniable.

Today, anyone who goes to battle and dies fighting a country's wars has equal right to elect those who send them there. Anyone who can perceive pain and suffer has equal right to know why and how to be rid of it.

A truth seeker must find the courage to mentally step outside the search limits allowed by the dogma of their chosen religion and seek guidance on self-training their ability to find the sensitivity to follow their heart...to understand and control their mental activity to allow sustained focus within the arena of their heart. They must search through life's transforming present moment to piece together the puzzle and gain an aware primal understanding of the ongoing impermanence of this cause/effect world they must negotiate moment-by-moment.

Siddhartha Details Lau Tzu's Cliffs Note Clue to Bliss

> *Who understands the world is learned.*
> *Who understands the self is enlightened.*
> *Who conquers the world has strength.*
> *Who conquers the self has harmony.*
> —Lau Tzu, *Tao Te Ching* verse 33, 8

In one short verse in the book of wisdom *Tao Te Ching*, the ancient Chinese Taoist master Lau Tzu shares an ultrabrief summary of what's needed to overcome the ignorance guarded by the concept of the self and become enlightened about what caused it to develop. Lau Tzu insightfully points out the difference between the effects of intellectually knowing the world and experientially understanding the self...between honoring what's known in the head and what's felt in the heart. He implies how the harmonious discovery leading to self-knowledge or a wisdom-enriched understanding of what makes up the material body reveals an enlightened understanding of the nature and purpose of the reality that it is a part of.

It's a Cliffs Notes summary of the process that Mr. Siddhartha Gautama later offers a detailed description of. He offers guidance for any individual to self-train the ability to realize the harmony to attain the same enlightened understanding of this reality that Lau Tzu pointed toward. He shares with any truth seeker the method that worked for him. Lau Tzu depicts the strength gained in conquering the world. A truth seeker has to recognize any possible preoccupation that comes with worldly issues or the love of money…like Jesus teaches of in his parable of the sewer.

Thru faulty prior conditioning, an individual could have a worldview corrupted by a belief system that's internalized many experientially unverified claims that inspire misguided desires that point to no real end. Their worldview could end up being defensively focused in an illusionary state of reality that through their ignorance is believed to have a continual nature supporting the untruth that things and ideas have a nature of continuity.

Misunderstanding the most primal truth that everything is actually a transforming process in a state of impermanence brings friction between this actual cause/effect truth and what is believed to be the truth. The latter forms attachment to misguided thoughts of illusionary objects and ideas they might imagine to by permanent.

This creates a blindness that prevents an individual from recognizing the truth even if it were dangled in front of their face. This blindness prevents them from visualizing the way of self-training the calmness of mind to then self-train the mental control to find the body/mind harmony to sustain in an introspective contemplative detached deliberation that's focused into the essence of their flesh to find inspiration about the living truth they're awareness is focused into for the insightful understandings to conquer the ego-controlled ignorant self and derive the wisdom of enlightened awareness through this resurrected self-knowledge.

In *Tao Te Ching*, Lau Tzu's readers are being taught how to fish, instead of just intellectually memorizing individual bites of wisdom to be quoted when challenged. He's teaching how to develop the ability to generate wisdom while on the pathway to reaching heavenly enlightenment…instead of just reading it in quips from those who have.

Most truth seekers need guidance. They have to be mentally searching to feel the coming and going pulse of the truth and be able to harmonize their mind's awareness with their body's available presence to eventually eliminate the ignorance of this primal truth that allows their present moment suffering.

Those who have broken free from the intellectual lock of fear-inspired fundamentalist views to truly recognize that they suffer right now and want to eliminate its cause can follow the guidelines of Siddhartha's procedural strategy for self-training the same ego-defeating mind-body harmony that Lau Tzu pointed at in *Tao Te Ching* that worked for him. His strategy's teachings are summarized in *The Four Noble Truths* and the details for self-training the pathway to becoming enlightened about human ignorance are in *The Eightfold Path to Enlightenment*.

The Four Noble Truths give a basic four-phase order to the steps of becoming enlightened. Siddhartha's first noble truth is for a truth seeker to realize that suffering is alive and that it paralyzes their ongoing present moment. Next, a truth seeker sees that the suffering has a living cause. Thirdly, they visualize that the cause can be eliminated and lastly is the way to do just that.

The Eightfold Pathway to Enlightenment is intended for those who are ready to uncover the pathway toward an understanding of what causes their unrest. They at least intellectually realize that experientially understanding this reality will bring them relief from the suffering its ignorance allows. *The Eightfold Path to Enlightenment* is guidance in carrying out the fourth noble truth. It takes a truth seeker from the clutches of ongoing suffering down the pathway to liberation from the ignorance that allows it. *The Eightfold Pathway to Enlightenment* outlines a truth seeker's self-training process to understand their reality through gaining self-awareness.

The three self-training guidelines of Siddhartha's eightfold pathway to reaching enlightenment start with how a truth seeker trains their ethical/moral behavior to calm their mind. This allows self-training the mental control to sustain the right concentration to self-train the ability to derive the insightful wisdom while deliberating in the flesh arena targeted by their right concentration. Their vision is aimed toward their personal attainment of an enlightened understanding of their suffering as their real-time attention is aroused to search out and connect the dots to this end.

Different than a rehabilitative multistep plan that simply tells one to change what they think, Siddhartha's eightfold path tells one how they can get a conscious grasp on how the nature of what they think is tethered to the actual nature of this reality. When they change the nature of what they think, they change the nature of their mind that generates those thoughts and thus, the nature of their thinking.

Siddhartha's right ethical and moral behavioral training includes the first three folds of the eightfold pathway...right speech, right action, and right livelihood. This level of ethical/moral discipline coincides largely with the moral/ethical disciplines found in Moses's Ten Commandments.

This is pretty much the extent of what is heard preached about today throughout Bible Belt USA every Sunday morning...how to follow the Ten Commandments and not yield to temptation...the limits of ethical/moral standards. Any biblically inspired guidance on dealing with present moment emotional concerns that are not addressed in the Bible can be found on DVD's and books that reflect only the biblical interpretations of the person whose address is where to send the check to pay for the various publications.

Siddhartha's Plan Reaches Beyond the Ten Commandments

Siddhartha's process of self-training enlightenment about the cause of suffering offers guidance through and beyond the basic moral/ethical development stage of preparing a truth seeker's mind for spiritual maturity where Christianity's guidance stops and lets believers hover in blind faith praying to God for relief from their real-time suffering while waiting for a promised afterlife heaven...if they make the final cut on the day of judgment.

While looking to the biblically described heaven to escape eternal suffering, a believer's focus is more on controlling the sinful behavior that results in the mental unrest than on self-training the mind to understand and control the thoughts that resulted in the sinful behavior before it returns again in its existing form of a fleeting reaction the next time the situation arises.

Living by moral/ethical standards helps minimize the mental repercussions (guilt, regret, etc.) of sinful actions that interrupt and keep at bay a truth seeker's quest for an enlightened understanding of this impermanent reality. The behavior is a sin because of the unjust imbalanced mental agitation that's left in its wake.

These moral/ethical standards fall under the golden rule of doing unto others that seems to be the summarizing mantra of the Ten Commandments that answers any questions about any loose ends. This is the walking-in-theirshoes compassion of the Buddhist world that helps ease the frustrated mind to address finding peace.

Giving a truth seeker's waking attention to practicing Siddhartha's right speech, right action and right livelihood or Moses's Ten Commandments helps them minimize new mental disturbances resulting from inappropriate (sinful) thoughts and behaviors and helps to dampen the 1,000 unrelated voices from the believer's mitote/maya state of mind that are shouting inside their head all at once for their unrelated claims to be acted on right now in the individual's present moment. This creates a more calmed mental state of waking consciousness to proceed beyond establishing moral/ethical soundness on to self-training mind control.

After self-training ethical/moral behavior, the human ignorance remains that will return under the right circumstances that the individual hasn't prepared themselves to recognize and deal with. This ignorance and lack of guidance blinds Christian attempts at finding what Siddhartha describes as his second phase of self-training mind control with the right effort to sustain the right awareness to affect the right concentration to effectively advance to the third phase of self-training one's wisdom to understand what to do to release the ignorance that allows their suffering.

Rome selectively edited the accounts of Jesus's teachings and Siddhartha's teachings were passed down through human memory for hundreds of years before being recorded. His first sutra was the first recorded account of any religion or spiritual discipline. The divisions in understanding the intended message of Jesus's and Siddhartha's oral guidance for self-realization are numerous.

Neither of these enlightened teachers had a chance to write down their intended meaning themselves nor to later edit the efforts of others to record their accounts of the gospels or sutras.

After an individual has initially developed their own vision for experientially seeking the truth about this reality's impermanent nature and have managed to clean up their act to realize some peace of mind, they are ready to pursue Mr. Gautama's second phase of self-training their mind control to allow finding the needed mind/body harmony to achieve the right sustained concentration to then self-train their ability to have the inspired insights to generate the right understanding to decode the tree of wisdom that enriches their awareness of the impermanent nature of this reality to undo the ignorance that causes their suffering.

Self-training mind control includes the forth fifth and sixth folds of Mr. Gautama's behavioral guidelines that include how to unite in harmony the body with a sustained mental awareness (right effort and right awareness) to sensually give full attention (right concentration) to the then selftrain the wisdom to understand the ignorance that prevents joy and happiness and causes their suffering.

This is the process of self-training wisdom-enriched awareness that allows the individual to control the thought patterns that occupy their present moment and feed their mitote/ maya state of mental confusion. Mind control is nothing to be afraid of or intimidated by. Mind control is nothing we don't do every time we try to focus on doing anything. Anytime an individual concentrates to give mental instructions to their body is mind control...a five-year-old tying their shoestring... biting your tongue instead of shouting at someone.

This third and final self-training phase of Mr. Gautama's eightfold pathway to enlightenment requires a calmed mind with mind-controlled focus to self-train the process of developing a wisdom-enriched understanding of this reality's impermanent nature. After the ethical/moral discipline's been managed and the body/ mind focus and right concentration are united through hand-in-heart harmony it's possible to sensually witness in its place of origination, our Source's coming and going impermanent pulse of change to directly inspire the right thinking for the same insightful wisdom-enriched understandings that were recognized by Lau Tzu, Jesus, Siddhartha and many others who have attained enlightened knowledge about their ignorance but whose methods we have no written record of. Siddhartha's final guidelines deal with having the right inspired thinking based on the essence of the sustained right concentration that will give shape to or inspire the sought-after wisdom to see through the ignorance that allows human suffering.

What better place for a truth seeker to have their sustained mental awareness focused harmoniously with their body's presence than into its physical essence where they can sit heart in hand to sensual witness life itself being manifested, because that's exactly what they want to better understand? What could be a better source of inspiration to trigger insightful understandings about impermanence than to be sitting in the oven itself?

What better place could their harmonious mind/body awareness be while calmed in introspective deliberation to find inspiration to better understand this reality's impermanence than within their only connection to pure impermanence itself? Here, their awareness can best experience the pulse of life itself to instill sudden insightful wisdom-enriched understandings about what their awareness is 100 percent keyed into, to undo their ignorance of its ways that distances their joy and happiness and allows them to suffer.

And as long as the relational truths of our time-driven cause/effect reality haven't changed, a truth seeker can have the steadfast bone-felt faith that the derived wisdom that held water in the times of Lau Tzu, Jesus and Mr. Gautama will hold water now and continue to. This is having faith in the continued dependability of the omnipresence of the multidimensional cause/effect environment that maintained the sensually witnessed truth depicting the unavoidable and uncontrollable rhythm of ongoing change.

This is the process of gaining self-awareness through self-discovery where Mr. Gautama's eightfold pathway leads a truth seeker to the kingdom within. It's the subtle sensual truth that lives in everyone's ego-free deeper consciousness. They only need to clean up their act, calm down and humbly feel for the truth to have it float up through the sea of misguided endless claims they've internalized and will soon figure out and dismiss, into their waking consciousness. They change how they view the nature of this reality, and in so doing...they change the nature of their mind and their thinking. They begin spending their passing moments in a reality they actually feel the truth of.

The moral/ethical discipline and mind control self-trainings that inspire the right understanding lead to the training of the insightful wisdom. This undoes the ignorance that conceals the inborn human awareness of the fair justice invoked during the cause/effect interplay of all the tiny coming and going bits of energy that make up the metaphysical world and when combined give momentary material definition to the forms and objects for the human eye to perceive. This is the point where religious, spiritual and reality-tested scientific intended purposes intersect.

The four-section layout order of this book recognizes the same cause/effect rhythm as what Siddhartha used in ordering *The Four Noble Truths*. Siddhartha also recognized that an attention-getting effect of some cause is first presented to raise a listener's or reader's curiosity and increase their interest in wanting to next find out the cause. Suffering's existence and finding liberation from its cause, the two effects like in *The Four Noble Truths*, heads up sections one and three in this writing. Ignorance and the suffering's antidote are the causes of these effects and like in *The Four Noble Truths*, head up sections two and four. The reader would hopefully have the curiosity to investigate the causes for these effects.

7

Self-Train Mind Control

Right concentration (meditation or body/mind analysis) is not a behavior to copy...it's an individually unique process to nurture, train, and understand. Through self-training the ability to create a harmonious effort of sustained mind into body concentration, a truth seeker has all they need to dig for the needed self-knowledge.

Desire for Truth Must Be Genuine...Not Borrowed

For a truth seeker to undo the web of misguided prior conditioning that's left them unable to monitor their train of thought and direct its contents the desire must grow from an internal spark and they must consciously recognize this. The effects of present moment decisions should reflect intentions directed at understanding the truths that accompany an ever-changing reality. They will discover that this needs to be the nature shared between the purposes of the internalized claims that shape their worldview.

It will do them no good to be reaching for some sort of generic genie that other people say they have been able to find. Listening to suggestions on how to find their core is helpful, but there is no correct generic way to reach inside. Dogmatic rituals will leave a truth seeker trying to locate our Source with their mind centered on replicating another's technique instead of reaching the destination.

Living by a Ten Commandments behavioral code can help leave believers with minds calm enough to train, but it must be their primal curiosity that fuels their search engine. To self-teach themselves how to sustain the focus to check out what our Source is emitting as life manifests itself in their flesh, their indulgence must be energized by an internal flame and not from an outside plug-in. A truth seeker cannot maintain a harmonious mind/body state if their methodology requires thought patterns that interrupt the purpose of the concentration in their search to remind them of what should be done.

Any mental distraction can interrupt self-training mind control and leaves a truth seeker short of being able to generate the inspired insight needed to convey the self-knowledge to self-train the wisdom to undo the ignorant state of their belief system that bars their joy and happiness and allows their present moment suffering. Dogmatic ritual has a negative preoccupying side tracking effect on self-training mind control as does having the troublesome thought patterns an individual would have after wrongly killing someone, or breaking any of the Ten Commandments or by committing any of the cardinal sins.

The poor children of today that ingest pesticides on food and have to take medication for their acquired condition of attention deficit disorder that because of the chemicals, they can't maintain their attention where it should be. Will they ever be able to self-train mind control and wisdom even if they self-train the moral/ethical standards that might have sufficiently calmed their minds just a few years ago?

Must Get in the Pool to Learn How to Swim

Within human flesh is the only place where the human experience can find direct physical contact with the ways of the truth explaining the human condition. It's through ignorance about the transforming nature of this reality that an individual's evolving adaptation to change develops cravings and aversions to things that really don't exist. This unawareness underlies the addictions that feed their ongoing unrest. They must focus ahead on their sensual connection to the truth of things.

For any human to gather information about the outside world, there has to be sensual input through one of the five sensual ports. Anything that's not introduced to an individual's sensual arena will go unnoticed.

In order to develop an understanding awareness of the world, it must be experienced through the sensation that tells its story. If a truth seeker never takes their conscious awareness inside their inner world, they'll never be able to witness reality. They'll only have an intellectual picture of what's in there.

Sensation is the point at which mind and body meet. Sensual expression is the language our Source uses to tell its story. Our Source speaks its truth to us sensually through our hearts. Dispassionate attention is focused on the relaxed body with all senses awake and waiting. The deeper consciousness is finally getting to speak (sensually) its piece. It finally has somebody willing to listen (with sensual ears on).

For a truth seeker's ignorance to become nonignorance and for their mitote/ maya state of unrest and dissatisfaction it underwrites to disappear, they need to enter the theater of activity where the answer's found, alive and kicking. They must consciously experience it to understand it.

A sincere truth seeker, attending to their due diligence to satisfy their unfettered free will's demand to see a living sign to verify the realness of a claim's purpose, must feel the fire to know what it's like to be burnt. They must jump into the living essence of ongoing change to consciously understand its omnipresent relevance. In this truth seekers build steadfast faith in the certainty of reality's consistency to warranty the cause/effect factors to show the same living sign, time and time again for any human being whenever they want, to verify the experiential truth of the claim's purpose.

Ignorance-allowed suffering shows no prejudice to the human condition. It is the same for all. Its presence originates from the same place where joy and happiness are perceived.

Likewise, the antidote to the ignorance that allows the suffering is the same for all and is realized in the same pointin-time where suffering's found. It's found in the same present moment suffering has hijacked and terrorizes.

The awareness of the omnipresent truth about the nature of our Source that will enlighten an individual or save their soul has to come from where the nature of our Source or the bigger picture can be tested, experienced and witnessed sensually from within. Any other account of the nature and purpose of our Source is constructed intellectually...unique to each individual's imagination and void of any sensual testimony verifying its humankind truth.

There are Midwesterners that are on their way to heavenly enlightenment, realizing that their suffering does not originate from the outside. However, most people spend their entire life confused about where our Source originates. Do they look inward or upward when they think of their spiritual home?

Their present moments are spent with a fear-wrapped mind in denial waxed gross by the restrictive nature of fundamentalism while hovering in a real-time weekly display of pious ritual activity. They struggle with self-imposed demons of self-doubt and self-devaluation. They stumble down a path of unavoidable hypocrisy lost and confused silently feeling for a way out of a self-imposed apparent reality while suffering from frustrations and mental unrest.

An individual that has their moment-to-moment eye focused forward down the path to enlightenment in search of the truth about this ephemeral impermanent cause/ effect reality lives in a world they feel. They proceed purposefully down their daily path focusing on things and using their time-fueled present moments pursuing actions that lead them closer to undoing their ignorance. They proceed down their daily path focusing on having a present moment free from fleeting reactionary addictive behaviors that stem from the misguided prior conditioning that testifies to their ignorance.

While gaining awareness of our Source's nature to initiate ongoing change, the influence their ego has on their behavioral intentions is on the constant decline. They will learn to realize insightful waves of understanding at times other than when seated in full lotus position...maybe while standing in thought, waiting at a bus stop?

For a truth seeker to attain a wisdom-enriched awareness of ongoing change, their concentration must first be focused into the ongoing present moment manifestation of change itself. Then they can become more aware of the process of ongoing change and by sensually witnessing it, can undo their ignorance of it.

Everything Belongs to the Present Moment

There's no present. There's only the immediate future and the recent past.
—George Carlin

Today is yesterday's tomorrow and tomorrow's yesterday. The present moment is truly illusive. It can't be captured. Every coming and going bit of energy that constitutes everything in the universe(s?) belongs to the present moment. Memories of the past and projections into the future have no material substance or a transforming nature.

The present moment rides on the magic carpet of time that ushers on its spark of living change that transforms this present moment into its new never-before-seen incarnation that's in this living moment that's right now considered to be the next present moment. The present moment maintains the perception platform where all of our Source's bits of coming and going particles unite to reveal the newest arrangement of the 14-billion-year-old collection of energy bits that comprise today's reality.

Ever-change's steady touch can seem like a calm stillness as it creates the momentary stage for now to happen. The living waking conscious activity of humanity's free will lives and functions in this theater of perception. This ever-changing point in time is where the ongoing essence or spirit of the ultimate reality's intended purpose of initiating ongoing change lives and is showcased.

The present moment is the home of the Holy Spirit of our Source that carries the gift or spark of new life. It's the same spark of life today as it was 2,000-plus years ago.

The illusive ever-advancing present moment's where the energy of an individual's free will maintains its presence while weighing decisions on what to believe or what actions to initiate when expressing its host's intended purpose. Many people spend their current present moments wrapped up in dreaming about past or imagined future present moments while the current one slips by unnoticed. Many individuals have free wills that are choked up and deadened with fear of the unknown. Still, whatever the case may be, the human free will, active or passive, acts out being active or passive in the present moment.

It's in the ever-changing present moment that an individual's intended self-purpose, if infected with fear-inspired self-doubt, resigns from doing something the true inner nature is screaming needs to be done. The passing feeling of angst resulting from this inner felt conflict happens only in the present moment.

It's in the present moment where ignorance affects an individual's propensity to suffer. It's where suffering hides and flourishes, untouchable by people living in the past or dreaming about the future. It's in the space between the second that just ticked by and the one coming that the true essence of an individual's becoming personality resides.

It's the environment an individual must become familiar with. They must learn the relational customs of this illusive stratum of the human experience.

Our Source Lives Only in the Present Moment

To be omnipresent in fulfilling its role of initiating ongoing change, our Source has no available unused presence to be anywhere else. Our living Source can only be found in the present moment. That's the only place this reality's transformation can exist.

What the passage of time provides is the only thing that never changes in this impermanent reality. It's the existence of the process of the ongoing uncontrollable manifestation of new life that continues unchanged.

Having an aware understanding of this state of impermanence is what is referred to as having self-knowledge. By knowing what makes up the material self, a truth seeker gets in touch with what makes what makes up the rest of this world.

This is why truth seekers should spend their time living in the present moment to better understand our living Source. Gaining self-knowledge should be every human's life purpose. Devoting the present moment to worrying about the future or feeling regret and guilt over intellectual renditions of the past is a waste of time and leads nowhere but to more suffering.

An individual's present moment actions are what paint the picture of their future karma. They control their future by giving their attention to affecting the present. This future karma comes to light in future present moments. This is where their expressed talents unfold to reveal the fruits of their passion that are developed in the present.

An individual who's enlightened about this cause/effect reality has the humble vision to be thankful that the present moment is all there is and would be surprised at imagining how there could ever be anything any better...let alone righteously complete or holy. Jesus showed his appreciation for the spiritual value in what's here in the present moment when he said that the meek shall inherit the earth. To inherit the Earth, an individual is gaining awareness of the recognition of the arrangement of the coming and going bits of energy that unpredictability come and go but when they do, they create the essence of the Earth's present moment presence. The present moment is all there ever was and all there ever will ever be.

Concentrated Focus Can Only be in One Place at One Time

The waking human mind cannot multitask. True mental focus can only attend to one purpose at a time. It might be able to skip around quickly...especially when in a state of mitote/maya or when muscle memory is involved, but actual attention can only point to one thing at a time. When performing a martial arts form routine, to think about anything other than what the next physical movement will be, will result in messing up form.

The forward focus of a truth seeker looking for an enlightened understanding of their ignorance can advance their spiritual maturity as long as their focus on attaining that purpose isn't intermingled with any others. An eye focused on the truth of ongoing change cannot walk and chew gum at the same time. It's not possible to have mental presence in two theaters of awareness at the same time. Success is in mentally recognizing and releasing ties to the thought patterns resulting from the miscued cause/effect rationality of misguided prior conditioning that the fleeting reactions that cause suffering are related to.

This mental activity should surmise their right concentration...no more and no less. During their mind's attempted presence, their mental awareness and deliberation over the impermanent essence of their harmonious right concentration has to inspire their right thinking while letting both unpleasant and pleasant sensations pass. This is enough to fully occupy one's present moment mental attention. One must not try to have too many plates spinning at once as only one at a time can have the present moment mental podium.

The right effort to sustain right awareness can only find balance on one tight rope at a time. Any thought pattern that interrupts the focus on that lone wire will make the truth seeker fall from their straight and narrow path into the churning sea of endless purposes of nonrelated claims, to never develop an understanding awareness of the nature of the object of their concentrated focus.

Identify and Develop Trust in Personal Objectivity

It's an individual's birthright to become familiar with and respond to their intuitive feelings. Not learning how to develop the tools that come with the human condition is foolish. The purpose of any search for a final answer has to be rooted in pure self-determination and mature along with the steadfast faith in its resolve.

An individual has to take steps to let their inborn free will breathe. They need to give life to their suppressed childhood curiosity. It's still there. It's full of primal merit.

Once, a teenager sat in an auditorium before an electronic violinist live concert with a much-respected friend. One reason they enjoyed hanging out with their friend was that they admired them for their cool-good taste, hoping that maybe some would rub off?

During the concert, the teenager wondered what it was that qualified this show as being good. What was it that their friend saw in this artist that qualified it as being cool or good?

They should be able to think or act because they feel the need, not because their friend does or someone tells them that they should. For example, they can discover what their favorite tea is based on the reflective evaluation of their own taste buds.

Does an early riser drink English Breakfast Tea because the name on the box leads them to think it must be good because the English drink it and who would know better? Without assuming things, a person needs to Google "tea leaves" and read about what kinds of tealeaves are available. They do their due diligence. They'll find that the different teas all come from the same plant...the only difference is in the processing of the leaves.

Go to a tea café and ask. Then, follow Sandbox Etiquette Guideline Number 1, respectfully with all attention directed at the tea store employee...listen. Then, sensually experience a few different teas and decide which one actually best suit their taste buds.

Even if the taster's bloodline is stamped English, they still may not prefer the taste of English breakfast tea to that of another after gathering intellectual information and then testing it to sensually gain an inner felt knowledge through the experiential association gained through using the sensual feedback coming from their own taste buds.

The tea taster's free will is stretching its legs. It's a bit more awake. It will play more of a role in authorizing the next new claims they encounter before internalizing the belief of the encountered claim. They'll drink the tea's they truly like for the rest of their life.

A truth seeker should find contentment and be able to acknowledge confidence in what they are feeling...if they have developed the ability to detect it. It counts. They must realize the presence of their human condition draws equal importance to that of any living human past or present.

Note the feel of making the awareness transition from the mind's normal state into the essence of the body's flesh

The mind and body are naturally interlinked in 100 percent harmonious codependency, yet there're many individuals who never realize this natural fact or why or how to make use of the co-existence between their conscious awareness and the essence of their transforming flesh body. Awareness of this distinction helps an individual learn to use their natural harmony between the two, to better understand the inherent nature of both.

By recognizing the presence of the feel of the conscious mind (its awareness) and the sensually detected coming and going pulsations that emanate from the flesh of the body and with intentions pointed at sensing or recognizing the natural harmony that unites the two, the awareness of a truth seeker's thinking is suspended in the environment that's most likely to inspire the insightful understandings that will enrich their waking awareness with the wisdom of a more enlightened understanding of the nature of the same impermanent environment the mental awareness was suspended in.

It's interesting how the feel of arresting a busy mind to find the right concentration to set the stage to have insightful inspirations about the nature of this reality is similar to arresting the mind to slip into someone else's shoes. Having the mind control to have mental awareness interrupted to leave the mitote/maya mental state that can characterize the streamed thought patterns of the typical present moment to focus awareness into the essence of another's situation (instead of into the essence of their body's flesh) is rewarding.

Not yet having developed an experiential understanding of the process of understanding this reality's impermanence, it can be discouraging for a truth seeker when trying to build up faith in the intellectual idea that creating mind/body harmony will eventually bring them closer to freedom from suffering when they have something on their mind that seems so bad that nothing can make it better and this keeps interrupting their effort to sustain their focused awareness into the essence of their body parts. They try to focus their mental awareness to inside the essence of their body parts, and the imagined magnitude of this problem completely sidetracks their mind into body concentration efforts.

Instead of ruminating about this huge problem, the truth seeker needs to force their awareness back into the scan of the essence of the presence of their body parts, no matter how sloppy or interrupted it seems to be. Over time, with upcoming situations, it will become easier to put the huge worry aside and go back into their inner island of retreat.

The more times the uncontrollable mental preoccupation with a seemingly unbearable problem is interrupted for a sustained focused right awareness into the essence of the body parts, the easier it will become and the more steadfast the faith will become that the end goal of an eventual complete release of all desires attached to cravings and aversions will disappear, will eventually take on a sensual address and become more real and closer to reach.

The individual will become more familiar with the feeling of true security and home base it affords them. It becomes a regular thing for them, no matter what their perception of the outside circumstances they may be in appears to be. It will be this way all their life. They grow more comfortable with its familiarity the older they get. It's a solid place to stand and consider perceptions.

Self-training the mind control to realize effective mind/ body harmony helps develop a mental awareness based in compassion. Arresting the mind to recognize the essence of the body and with that the inspiration for insightful enrichment is wonderful practice for leaving the thought streaming of the present moment for a compassionate awareness.

This is the process Siddhartha taught and is how he self-trained the mind control to realize the right effort, right awareness and right concentration to then self-train the right wisdom (inspired right thinking, insightful right understanding) to become enlightened about his ignorance of the living harmony he finally became enlightened about.

Recognize Our Source's Living Presence...Gain Self-Knowledge

Each individual's reality consists of their present moment perceptions of the things and non-things made split-second real from the ongoing eruptions from the coming and going bits of energy displaying our Source's ever-changing presence. It's all this transforming world is. Its momentarily real perceived presence is here only to become a conditioned memory.

In Siddhartha's *Diamond Sutra*, the oldest surviving dated writing of any kind, he describes this as being how to contemplate the conditioned existence in this fleeting world. He suggests how it all momentarily comes together to form a drop of dew, a bubble floating in a stream, a flash of lightning, a flickering lamp, or even a dream. It's the conditioned perception of the real sensation where the mind and body meet.

These are just a few of the living emanations demonstrating our Source fulfilling its purpose to provide ongoing change. It's in the animated flick of the present moment where living transformation is abuzz. It's this same intertwined flow of life that, when the nature of its relationships is misinterpreted, allows the emergence of misguided illusionary expectations and disappointments.

What does it really mean to understand the self? Is it in knowing what one's favorite foods are? Is it in knowing if they're a night person or like to get up early?

To know the self, think more literally. Keep it physical. Don't feel the need to assume anything and read between any lines. To understand what makes up the self, a truth seeker must realize that like all other things, the physical self is not an object, but a transforming process. They must investigate the actual spark of life that touches the changing self during and between each passing present moment.

It's the same spark of life that our Source adds to bring about the change noted in Siddhartha's above observations.

Mr. Siddhartha Gautama discovered and grew to understand this with a totally wisdom-enriched awareness of our Source's presence. A truth seeker's understanding of the process of the self includes their acceptance of how their changing process of self is their only living connection with reality that actually emulates our Source's presence in this cause/effect reality.

Gaining self-knowledge or self-awareness is touted in Buddhism as a necessity in the process of gaining an enlightened understanding of the cause of the ignorance that allows human suffering. This self-knowledge involves more than knowing personal habits or preferences. Gaining self-knowledge includes understanding the nature and the process that the coming and going bits of energy provide in giving sustenance to their physical material self as a representative part of this material world.

8

Open Sensual Ears
and Know Mind/Body Harmony

...Stop Conscious Thought Streaming And Enter Nonverbal Experience Of Reality ...Our Source Speaks To Us On Ly Through Our Hearts

An intellectually engendered blind faith in the belief that there's a male god that created this reality and is in control of its fate only adds a numbing layer of abstract obscurity between how the believer perceives the ongoing sensual report they gather from the real world and what is intuitively projected from their sensual heart.

—Anonymous

Sandbox Etiquette 101:
Humble Attention Spawns Mind/Body Harmony

The state of humility is the human condition factory setting used for generating intentions grounded in altruistic compassion. The presence of this state of capacity subverts any ego-sent ulterior motive or agenda. It guards against the tempting urge to make assumptions or defensively take things personally. It reopens the door to childhood-like curiosity. Humility oils the wheels of understanding what makes up the self.

Even though our Source's presence encompasses all of the seemingly nonchanging material reality, try to visualize our Source as a separate entity...a subcontractor from the pool of available gods. Now imagine that on our Source's resume, its claim describing its nature and intended purpose is simply to initiate unchanging ongoing change. To manifest unyielding ongoing change our Source could only make its purpose true in the present moment living reality.

Humanity challenges our Source to provide an experiential real-time verification or living sign or self-evident proof to verify its claim describing its nature and intended purpose to initiate ongoing change. Humanity wants our Source to provide a living sign that all of humanity can recognize and share a common and unquestionable steadfast faith in.

As should be, any person hearing this claim should allow their unfettered free will to question and test this claim's purposed intention before allowing the purpose of its claim to be internalized into their belief system to shape their worldview. There will be no leap of blind faith here. It's a faith founded in a reality that's actually been experienced. Sandbox Etiquette Guideline Number 1 is a universal guideline from the age-old school of social experience. The proof of its effectiveness has been fashioned from years of exposing the human condition to the human experience. Its drive is tethered by humility and executed through mindful compassion.

Most Midwesterners are introduced to this social skill during their youth, back during their age of innocence. A common venue where many receive their first lessons in sandbox etiquette is at their preschool or kindergarten playground while relating to new friends during recess or maybe after school.

This life lesson deals with the ongoing presence of courtesy, respect and patience tempered through the presence of fundamental humility in the communication between two people. It's the "people art" used when asking someone for his or her name or to kindly hand over a shovel or sand bucket. It's the tactfully effective way to learn about something new that a friend knows or understands. Hopefully these early-learned life parameters of compassionate social grace will continue to prime the intentions of the young person's intended purpose throughout their life.

Sandbox Etiquette Guideline Number 1 says that the most effective way to have any entity share something, is to sincerely pose the question and then bow to them in humility while demonstrating patient respect with attentive listening and focused concentration while seeking a detailed understanding of the kindly-shared answer. They must choose to not be sidetracked by any crazy feeling of entitlement or social ranking. Out of courtesy to the questioned and to be able to accurately understand the object of the question, the questioner must not let their attention of their awareness to be captured by anything else.

Maybe it was through mankind's early discovering of the necessary protocol for gaining the original collective conscious awareness of this claim to the primal truth of our Source's ongoing intent to initiate ongoing change that Sandbox Etiquette Guideline Number 1 was derived? Without humility as the prime standard of overall intent, wisdom-enriched self-awareness is not possible.

Maybe humility surfaced into mankind's collective waking consciousness as one of mankind's unwritten social graces around 1000 BC when initial behavioral standards were first carved in stone? Maybe this paved the way for recognizing the need and appropriateness for the moral and ethical understandings represented by the Ten Commandments?

One's unfettered free will should question and test experientially when possible to validate the real-time performance or practicality of the intended purpose of any new claim before internalizing it into their belief system. The claim being tested here and now is that the ultimate reality's nature and purpose of intent is to initiate ongoing change. The venue the truth seeker's unfettered free will's claim-testing function will use to exercise Sandbox Etiquette Guideline Number 1 at this time is the only place they can...within the actual living flesh of their transforming body.

It's common to want to be shown a sign to verify the truth of a god's claim to salvation from the clutches of suffering. A sensual sign is exactly what the unfettered free will is asking for here. It's a sign that's perceivable to anyone to verify the truth of this claim to the nature and intended purpose of our Source's claim to initiate ongoing change in this cause/effect reality.

An individual's unfettered free will can actually only perceive the sign it's being showed by sensing it through the individual's sensual ports. The perceptual range of these five sensual inputs sets the perceptually defined limits of the human condition while physically confined in the human shell.

Of course, there are many who determinedly say that God told them in a dream or that they saw a sign in a vision. This may very well have happened or been perceived in their world. Who's really to say? But if the sign or message is not something available that everyone has equal opportunity to witness anytime or anywhere, it can't be coming from a fair god. It can't be a god that wants everyone to feel the comfort of his equally available-to-all presence.

Our Source doesn't need to send proof of its claim down from above where its ongoing purpose to initiate constant change is because the warmth of this ongoing presence manifests from within. Awareness through the touch sensual port is a proven and documented way the answer can be realized. Our Source speaks to us through our hearts.

This was the sensual port used by Mr. Siddhartha Gautama to achieve self-awareness and find liberation. Jesus meditated forty days and forty nights, but details of his methodology and targeted awareness state were not discussed in the books of the Bible that remained after Rome's 312 AD selection of which accounts of his life and story to include in the Bible.

What could Jesus have been doing in meditation for forty days and forty nights? Where was the attention of Siddhartha's mind focused for the night he sat under the Bodhi tree when he became enlightened? That's an awfully long time to verbally ask for blessings or forgiveness. If they were sitting there with their minds focused into the depths of their beings, they were doing exactly what is being described here. The ability to radiate humility into the depths of focus to strike sustained mind/body harmony to feel the truth radiated in the coming and going heartbeat of our Source must have been incredible.

To eliminate ignorance about something, it becomes necessary to go to where the subject of the related ignorance is on exhibition. Life manifests in the human flesh. That's where the curious can learn about the ways of change and undo their associated ignorance.

Intrapersonal Language of Body-Speak

For a truth seeker to consciously revitalize the primal link between their waking consciousness and the muted subtle region of their deeper consciousness, the common communication media must first be identified that is understandable by them both. Both of these states of consciousness are distinctive to the human condition and there has to be a language of body-speak that registers meaning in the subconscious as well as in the waking consciousness.

Sensual is the only language the human body knows. Intellectual media has a social presence. Feeling's presence is sensual.

It's in the sensation that the mind and body meet. The body senses it and the mind feels and perceives it. Its role as body-to-mind-to-body messenger is ageless. It's the only language any body and every mind can physiologically understand. Smiles and frowns are expressions of universally understood body-speak messages that need no verbal translations.

Sensual transmission is the only way to paint a four-dimensional picture of the outside world. It draws on the mind's sensually remembered and stored experiential understandings. It takes a 3-D illusion of stillness and interweaves the reality of time...our fourth dimension.

The deeper consciousness that orders the human heart to beat has no need for any verbal language. It draws on the only media that has the power to command undivided attention and deliver common meaning at both extremes of the human spectrum of consciousness. The communication vehicle that bridges over the interfering white noise mental static chatter that muffles messages of what the heart knows to be reality that attempt to travel up the primal link to correct what the waking consciousness might perceive to be reality is the language of sensuality.

This enables mind and body to meet in harmony and walk...sensual eyes open...heart in hand through the changing essence of human perception. The truth seeker can now sustain their focused awareness in the primal essence of life itself as cause/effect living change manifests from within. What better place could their thinking be for getting inspired to understand the relational justice of life that the activity in this environment demonstrates?

Detecting the Unchartered Cadence of Our Subtle Source Life Force... Crossing The Bridge of Sensual Communication

Mind/body harmony allows a truth seeker to feel Mother Nature's pulse of change.

A truth seeker must give their most humble attention in trying to receive our Source's answer to their free will's request for verification of our Source's basic primal claim that its nature and purpose of intent is to initiate ongoing change. Self-training the ability to harmonize the mental awareness and body presence to affect and sustain the right concentration will enable a truth seeker to bring to sensual ear the ongoing release of change as it manifests throughout their physical share of material reality. It resonates at the lowest decibel of primal audibility.

Total humility is needed for a truth seeker to snare and chain-down their ego and hold back the random unrelated thoughts that break the attempted sustained concentration needed to self-train thought-inspired insightful wisdom to undo the recipe of suffering that their ignorance stirs into each of their present moments. The truth seeker harmonizes their head with their heart to sustain focused concentration on our Source's sensual demonstration of its living presence.

It's the same transformation going on in everything everywhere to the outermost extension of this reality. Yet, what's in their human shell is all that any truth seeker will ever be able to actually draw experiential record from.

To be able to actually listen to and hear this message and understand our Source's answer would allow the truth seeker to align their expectations and intentions by the truth savvy discovered in the relational logic of that sensual answer... the derived wisdom. Over time, these insightful understandings hone a truth seeker's belief system to support a worldview with logic and reason that's in sync with the flowing justice found in the changing rhythm of the relational interactions of everyday life.

Ignorance about the relational justice of this cause/effect reality would gradually take the backseat and eventually disappear...along with the suffering it inspires. The illusionary expectations that justify thoughts inspiring clinging or aversion to seemingly real forms, objects and ideas that populate an individual's self-fashioned apparent reality where things don't change, would disappear. The suffering coming from illusions misaligned with reality would gradually disappear.

What means of looking besides sensually feeling could possibly be meant by saying to look inside? How else can a person learn about something inside other than to actually experience it? A truth seeker coordinates continued right physical and mental effort to affect a concentration that's focused on feeling the essence of what you've got systematically from head to toe and back again.

In a sustained concentration with the united coordination of physical effort and attentive mental awareness a truth seeker sensually absorbs the defining evidence of the effect of the body's sensual "causing" spark of life. All attention is focused on the sensually transmitted Sourceinitiated time-fueled cause that's repeated time and time again at lightning speed to perceive the collective effect felt as a very subtle ongoing stream of uncontrollable body-wide sensations.

The truth seeker feels the pulse of life's ongoing unchanging pace of change manifesting as new life. It finds traction in their flesh while humbly tiptoeing from one bubble of time to the next.

An individual sensually witnesses the truth of our Source's purpose to initiate change in real-time by catching our Source in the act, red handed, initiating the flow-of-life process of cause and effect or birth, death, and rebirth. Our Source's promise is channeled, present moment, real-time, through each individual's personal physical conduit of our mother-of-all Source during the sensually recognized coming and going of the sensations in the living matter of what's their own sprig-of-the-Source transforming human body.

As has finally been documented by today's science what was realized by Mr. Siddhartha Gautama and Jesus after reaching enlightenment 2,000-plus years ago, it's the cosmic dance of the totally unpredictable coming and going *kapalas*, what Siddhartha called the bits of energy that make up the metaphysical particles that make up the atoms that form into sensually perceivable human flesh. Their activity taps out the laws that set the scales of relational justice inherent to all interactions, regardless of scale of size. The energy dance gives the conceptual details to the changing image of an individual's transforming essence.

The sensual attempt will find the individual actually putting their right awareness inside the body part to feel the essence of its transforming presence as physical sensations arise from within. It's occupying a self-borrowed bit of space in the transition of time.

This is life in action, an individual's living presence. After locating their essence, they can really do no more than mentally step back and be a detached onlooker, as they can do nothing to alter or change it. (There's much wisdom that can come from this one observation in regards to many things like maybe control and involvement. This is an example of Siddhartha's right thinking inspiring the right understanding.) The nature of each of the bits of the coming and going energy particles is to uncontrollably come and go to write the recipe of change in the upcoming present moment. The truth seeker can then make right effort to sensually witness the characteristics of the sensual message and with the right thinking, inspire an insight from the relational order to secure a better understanding of the reality that tics by...that defines the existence of the physical self.

It's in this subtle sensual presence that an individual can eventually be inspired to insightfully realize the wisdom that things and non-things really are not and cannot be recognized as being solid with an existence of continuity. Their sanity will benefit from all the wisdom that can be deducted from the truth of this state of relational being.

It's in this present moment awareness steadied in the theater of change that the most basic primal living truth detailing our reality surfaces. As this wisdom unfolds, it becomes clear that nothing really is what it may appear to be based on its current presence and past history because the next-second reality is unpredictably different.

On one level the coming and going sensations represent a sensed cocktail of electromagnetic changes and biochemical reactions. Like ears of corn can actually be heard growing while breaking away from their supporting stocks on a hot day in mid-July, the cells of the human body are ever-dividing and creating their own ever-so-faint-to-human perception background buzz of new life.

At this more subtle level it's the coming and going of the bits of energy that make up the atoms of the blood that flow and the nerves that are sensing the electromagnetic current that links one microsecond to the next...the cause of this moment's reality to its effect in the next. Time is really indivisible plasma of sorts.

This is the buzz of the ultimate reality of time-initiated ongoing cause and effect that's totally safe from the threat of human modification. This body-deep presence is there all the time, just not realized by most as most have yet to develop and perfect their version of harmonious body/mind unity. Most have yet to realize this as an option to finding peace.

On a truth seeker's sensual plateau of common understanding the mind makes the right effort to tune in to perceptions of stimuli coming across the body's sensual port of feeling. Their material physical body makes the effort to relax into and be host to their sustained and focused mental awareness. The mind's goal is to ward off intruding unwholesome thoughts of any kind and find the body/mind harmony that will, as Lau Tzu said, conquer the concept of self and lead the truth seeker to becoming enlightened about the subject of ongoing change that their ignorance of has allowed them to suffer.

They've suffered ever since their earlier life decisions to internalize unverified claims into their belief system gave them a cumulative worldview that included miscued illusionary concepts relating to the continuity of life...stealing them away from their childhood innocence.

The Truth Seeker Taps into the Factory of Life Itself

A truth seeker has no better place to focus their isolated mental awareness to better understand the impermanent nature of life itself than where life itself is being manifested...for their focused awareness to just sit in the arena of change and listen and be inspired by its real-time demonstration. Self-training the mind control to ward off the interruptive thoughts to sustain an awareness focused in harmony with their body's physical presence into the essence of their physical flesh gives them a front row seat in the chamber where life is constantly being regenerated, to listen and be inspired.

Quiet contemplative deliberation while keeping the mental awareness focused will allow the coming and going pulse of life itself to inspire the truth seeker's right thinking to realize sudden wisdom-enriched insights about how things work that will eventually enlighten them with an aware understanding that will make them wise to their ignorance that's robbed them of their joy and happiness and allowed their suffering. It worked for Siddhartha, among others, and he tells of how he did it.

The "Sensation in the Tissue" is the "Writing on the Wall" ...Feel Consciousness Find Sync with the Moment-To-Moment Pulse Of Mother Nature

A truth seeker must "feel into focus" the void between hearing a claim and believing its purpose. They must realize change itself.

Self discovery fills the void of uncertainty of a confused or misguided belief system that misses the presence of or the feeling of the flame during the passing of the torch in the uniting of the relationship between the causing push of one present moment to its real effect in the next. It's the primal void of ignorance that breeds the uncertainty and misunderstanding that feeds their fear of the unknown.

The coming and going sensations that become the focus of a truth seeker's harmonious body/mind awareness provide the sensual evidence of change like holding a hand over the flame of a fire communicates the meaning of "hot." It's sensually witnessing the real-time process when the cause actually generates the effect that fills the void in the anatomy of their belief system that lacks that feeling for the true gut-felt understanding or at least familiarity with the transfer of cause/effect energy itself. This experienced event is retained in their sensory archives for a lifetime of future recall.

It's in a truth seeker's sensual experience that the right thinking is inspired to bring on the insightful right understanding. This documents our Source's material means of initiating change. It depicts how the littlest of things beyond human perception do nothing but come and go...transforming the seemingly constant material presence of what their united coming and going presence represents into something else. Just because everything does not necessarily breathe life, doesn't mean that everything's not alive with the motion of change.

This basic fact cannot be ignored as the relational truths of this primal coming and going activity write the book of relational wisdom that characterizes how all changing processes (things) relate to and are best integrated with other changing processes (things). It's the story of what's going on in one's Source-like human piece of transforming life that the inspirations for insights into the right understanding will decode our Source's life message revealing this wisdom that enlightens one to the truth of ongoing change and makes their waking consciousness wise to their self-ego's slide of hand and tricks of illusion.

Feel the buzz that connects one present moment to the next. Be familiar with what the static feels like during that time in between what happens after the cause of the upcoming present moment and its right-now Source. The synapse in between is what defines the sensual flavor of the present moment. Hang out where Father Time does his thing. Float with eyes closed in the plasma pool of time to better understand and sense from the feel to identify the characteristics of the factors/brain patterns that thread together the delay...the linger...the time to think.

Over time, familiarity with mind-into-body scanning instills a feeling of how much mind control has been selftrained. It's easier and quicker for a truth seeker to realize the sustained attention if their awareness has been interrupted. Visit often this arena of reverence because it can take a lifetime to finally understand it.

Find the savvy to match the intended purposes of the realized life truths with those described in theological lore that tell of the factors and players in our soul's salvation from future suffering during life after death. Size up what their present moment incarnation might actually be. Become able to recognize the spiritual significance of the mentally pictured religious icons of theology when what represents their living sensual emergence becomes a recognized part of the living present moment.

Vipassana...A Flash of Insight

The Buddhist form of right concentration that makes best use of Sandbox Etiquette Guideline Number 1 to establish the harmonious body/mind analysis to gain self-knowledge and eventual enlightenment comes from Buddhism's Theravada tradition. Its methodology includes Vipassanabhavana meditation. This is the style of right concentration (meditating) that Mr. S. N. Goenka teaches at his meditation seminars.

Vipassana meditation is a means of self-discovery that teaches self-training the ability to derive the wisdom of an enlightened understanding of the nature of this reality's impermanence...the subject of human ignorance. Through insightful inspiration found in giving attention to the coming and going sensations within one's body, a truth seeker can develop a wisdom-enriched understanding of the way things really are so their preconditioned misconceptions will disappear along with the unrest and dissatisfaction that steals away the compassion, joy and happiness of their present moment.

(This is the exact same means of self-trained harmonious mind/body self-analysis this author discovered when pushed by the intent of just knowing what life itself feels like. No association was made between this discovery and any intellectually stored religious theology for twenty-five years.)

"Vipassana" is translated in the Pali language as "insight." This is what Siddhartha Gautama self-trained his mind control to, then he self-trained his ability to generate the right thinking to inspire the insightful self-awareness to attain his enlightened understanding of his misunderstandings that brought on his suffering. Just like Lau Tzu briefed in his earlier writings, through the harmony Siddhartha was able to achieve through mind/body effort/awareness sustained coordination, he was able to understand and conquer his self-ego that managed his worldview in such a way that made him suffer when the causes and effects of his passing present moments didn't line up as he had been precondition to anticipate...basically speaking. Teaching his self-taught method of converting misunderstanding into an enlightened awareness of the truth to others is all he spent his post-enlightenment time and energy on doing.

Theravada Buddhism's conveyance of right concentration is spawned from the harmony a truth seeker establishes between the right effort of their body and right awareness of their mind to sustain the right concentration focused in the living essence of the truth being sought. It's with patience and through persistent mind-into-body self-analysis that a truth seeker's insightful right thinking inspires their sudden flashes of insightful truths for the right understanding that will continually sharpen and enrich their waking awareness with the wisdom that supports the truth of the sensually witnessed impermanence the right concentration is focused into.

Change happens constantly, and as it is manifested within the human body, it is recognized as a sensation. If an individual doesn't allow their attention to jump inside where the change is in action and observe it firsthand, they will remain ignorant about it and continue to react to life with various incarnations of attachment and aversion and continue to suffer in their ignorance. This process of gathering the experiential evidence that verifies and makes transparent the ways of the relational justice necessary to support the impermanent nature of this reality is Vipassana meditation.

Vipassana emphasizes the importance of being conscious of the physical aspect...the sensation. When a truth seeker displays a meditative concentration that dwells only in the mental thought patterns, they will miss out on the physical sensations that warn of the upcoming emotional unrest that follows their misinterpretation of reality as a result of their faulty prior conditioning. By directing attention into the sensations, the truth seeker will learn to detach themselves and realize through their monitoring their sensations what symptomatic feelings might precede what upcoming emotions. By catching themself before they react, they can learn how to not react.

Siddhartha stressed the importance of having awareness focused into the body. He realized how foolish it is to become attached to anything since nothing continues to be and how his desires hinged on his attachments to cravings and aversions. Through checking their development, they would stop and the suffering they inspired would disappear.

> But they whose whole watchfulness is always directed to their body, who do not follow what not to be done, and who stead-fastly do what ought to be done, the desires of such watchful and wise people will come to an end (*Dhammapada* XXI, 293).[9]

Vipassana meditation recognizes this reality's true state of emptiness and the nonexistence of life continuity by focusing the right physical effort and right mental awareness in harmony to have the right concentration within the essence of impermanence itself. To learn about something, it's necessary to experience it.

To gain waking awareness of the flowing reality that proves the nonexistence of the imagined, suspended-in-time concept of the self, an individual needs to, through body/ mind analysis, sensually tune into their physical arena where life is being manifested. While in introspective contemplative deliberation they can allow the very transformation being sensually witnessed to inspire their thinking with wisdom-enriched insights about that same impermanence for its right understanding.

During this entire self-training process, a steadfast faith in the reoccurance of the relational truths insightfully discovered finds the truth seeker. The heart of the teachings left by Siddhartha that have evolved into today's "Buddhism" is not founded in any sort of unverifiable blind faith in any unknown entity. It's not founded in a faith in the "Buddha". It's founded in a faith that stands steadfast in what an individual has experientially witnessed that contributes to creating the relational cause/effect laws of nature or the nature of this impermanent reality that has been opened up to the conscious understanding of the individual truth seeker.

Of the many different commercialized options available worldwide for guidance on practicing the right concentration when meditating or involved in introspective deliberation, Theravada Buddhism best channels Siddhartha's intended meaning for attaining an enlightened right understanding of the subject of human ignorance through personal self-discovery. Theravada Buddhism teaches a truth seeker how to fish for wisdom...to realize relational wisdom from within themselves. This eliminates the need to be ready to quote a book, chapter, and verse about what another source says about the way things are that may not even directly apply to the subject at hand.

Like no other "-ism" or "-anity" tradition, the Theravada interpretation of Siddhartha's intended message on finding freedom from suffering interprets an enlightened one's offered guidance on the process of self-training the wisdom to enrich self-awareness with the wisdom of the relational justice that supports the ways of this reality's impermanence. Self-training this wisdom undoes the ignorance of the changing flow of reality, allowing the soul-chaffing friction caused by this ignorance to disappear.

Mind Body Harmony Focus Can Start with Breathing

Theravada meditation practitioners maintain that focusing mind/body concentration on the living essence of one's breathing can serve as a place for a truth seeker to use to start developing their ability to attain clear mind/body concentration and not to have their efforts sidelined by the unrelated unwholesome thought patterns from the 1,000 shouting voices their mitote/maya mental state is continually trying to impose. Later when self-trained mind control is more developed, mental awareness can be more finely tuned into essence of the coming and going sensations throughout the body.

The right form of concentration (meditation) to bring awareness into the present moment is the target here, and being able to sustain a focused attention on respiration helps develop this kind of right concentration.

When the mind starts to wander, when unwholesome thought patterns interrupt the truth seeker's attempt to sustain mental awareness in the essence of the coming and going sensations in the body's flesh, breathing is easier to consciously locate and reconnect the mental awareness to than with the essence of the coming and going sensations of a body part. Breathing is a more tangible and familiar activity to the waking consciousness.

Breathing is a bridge between the waking conscious and the automatic nature of the deeper consciousness as we breathe whether we think about it or not. But it remains to be a body function that can be altered through waking intention.

Attention to breathing is not a breathing exercise it's an exercise in breathing awareness. It's pure and wholesome not involving any negativity. There's no imagined object or thought continuity found in attempts at right awareness focused into an illusionary apparent reality with a continual nature.

The breathing process is an activity that's constantly changing and not an imagined still mental image of a form or shape of imagined continual permanence. It seems like such a fine line to draw, but it makes a big difference. Imagining a still statue, or figure is illusionary and having mental awareness focused into the imagined essence of an imagined stillness will have little influence on inspiring insightful understandings of a transforming reality.

The coming and going sensations become easier to sustain awareness on as self-trained mind control becomes more developed. Wholesome thought patterns focused into the coming and going essence of the truth seeker's physical body mass presence puts their awareness in the furnace of change itself. What better place to gain inspiration about the nature of change than to be where it's in the process of being manifested?

With sustained awareness focused into breathing and with any thought activity consumed in removed contemplation, like with having mental awareness focused into the coming and going sensations of their flesh, the truth seeker's thinking can become inspired from their taste of reality's changing mood to generate insightful understandings. During future times of self-training body/mind right concentration when a truth seeker is focusing awareness into the essence of the coming and going sensations within their body's flesh and they should lose their sustained concentration to unwholesome thought patterns, they can still return to the more common sensation of breathing to regain focus until mind control is better self-trained.

Lau Tzu's Harmony Conquers the Self-Ego and Brings an Enlightened Understanding Of Impermanence

Who understands the world is learned.
Who understands the self is enlightened.
Who conquers the world has strength.
Who conquers the self has harmony.
—Lau Tzu, *Tao Te Ching*, verse 33, 10

A truth seeker focuses their mind's eye into the essence of their physical body's presence to harmoniously fuse mind into body to practice right concentration. Their mental awareness and physical presence cross over the bridge of communication, heart in hand, to the sensual plateau of understanding...the mirrored chamber of self-knowledge where the mind and body fuse into one purpose. Sensation serves as host for their perceptive interpretation.

With a truth seeker's self-trained ability to control the subject matter of their thought waves, focusing awareness on the different coming and going sensations can better be directed toward giving equal consideration into each body part. A truth seeker will perform a systematic pattern of full body-scan analysis. With time, their thinking will inspire an insightful better understanding of the wisdom that sorts out the relational justice that affects every part of an impermanent reality. Lau Tzu shares in his inspired insight above that in finding the harmony to gain the self-knowledge to understand the self is how an individual defeats the self-ego.

The individual does not show preference to any good sensations or avoidance to unpleasant ones. This balance of right awareness and equanimity toward sensations affects a truth seeker's ability to treat sensations objectively with impersonal deliberation and through their inspired right thinking and insightful right understanding, self-train wisdom to the objective truth of how things in this cause/effect reality exist...how they relate to each other in this whirlwind of ongoing transformation. Among the sensations they confront, over time they will recognize and learn to understand and dismiss the sensations that have developed into being the triggers for the emotional fleeting reactions that feed their addictions linked to their suffering from the ignorance thereof.

Without raised awareness, a truth seeker will continue to react the same to instances that cause their suffering. With too little equanimity, they become too sensitive to certain sensations and are likely to continue reacting, causing more suffering. One needs to be conscious of all the sensations within, but not to react, in knowing they will change. It's the nature of our Source creating life, initiating ongoing change, in their body.

The type of sensation should draw no preference as their essence is only to be observed objectively, while not bowing to any distractive thought patterns. The truth seeker's to have the same detachment as a scientist observing a laboratory experiment and to stop reacting and start acting after contemplative consideration.

The truth seeker must realize there's no unalterable core to their reality. Their essence is only an impersonal phenomenon with a nature to change that's totally beyond their waking control.

The truth seeker must uncover how to single out and ward off thought patterns that threaten to break up their focused mental direction. These are unwholesome thought patterns. They must discover how to slow down those complex cocktails of mood-destructive thought patterns and unravel them one misguided conditioning-inspired feeling by one misguided conditioning-inspired feeling to recognize and excuse their reoccurrence.

Establishing this primal harmony between a truth seeker's mental awareness and their physical presence that mirrors the harmony in reality itself allows them to better understand the natural flowing rhythm of what they don't understand. In the same verse, Lau Tzu's shares his inspired insight that the harmony that conquers the self brings enlightenment.

The truth seeker will realize that the cravings and attachments to illusionary thoughts and things of illusionary existence will only lead to disappointment and suffering. Lau Tzu understands how this reflects an individual's learned intellectual worldview with the strength to conquer the world while not understanding it.

This is the ignorance that brings suffering. Understanding the ego and breaking through the erroneous beliefs that it manages and protects will lead to an enlightened understanding of the ways of change. This undoes the human ignorance that allows it.

Only through establishing body/mind harmony is it possible to apprehend and understand the sensation trigger/ emotional reaction packages that rule a truth seeker's present moment state of mind and set their worldview. Through body/mind harmony, they will tame the mounting inertia of their human curiosity that longs to understand and conquer the self to find enlightenment to the ignorance that allows their suffering.

Body/Mind Analysis Calm Inspires Aura of Compassion

After a session of head-to-toe-to-head mind/body analysis, the mind's relaxed to an elevated degree of awareness of emptiness or lack of attachment to life continuity. It seems easier to put one's self into the other person's shoes. Unwholesome thought patterns have been recognized and rejected and replaced with a physical consciousness fueled by compassion-inspired wholesome thought patterns directed at attaining the intended goal where right concentration is focused. It brings the mind into a time of peaceful reflection. Empathy comes much easier.

With a free will poised in equanimity with a waking awareness of impermanence, it's easy for an individual to drift into thankful compassion for people or situations they know, good and bad...a compassionate loving-kindness. After mind/body analysis finding peace within their personal sliver of humanity, it becomes easier to see and will peace within the rest of humanity. It seems like the thing to do.

The truth seeker can start to understand the compassion that pulls their presence out of the pits of depression. There is no other individual slice of humanity that can take care of or help another slice of humanity connect their waking consciousness to the subtle level of their deeper consciousness to find enlightenment of the ignorance that causes them to suffer from depressive impulses.

This post body/mind analysis period is calming and satisfying. This is compassion at the primal altruistic level that's achievable by any color or gender variety of the human condition.

Any idea that right concentration nurtures a cold disregard for emotional involvement is said to be short-sided. Just the opposite is true. It's said in Theravada Buddhism that with right concentration, the absence of craving and aversion is not an attitude of callous indifference...it's a time of the active persuit of one's own liberation that does not come at the expense of others.

It's considered to be a state of holy indifference. One's mind can act with the good will and love that benefits others with nothing expected in return. Compassion for others in their failings or sufferings and sympathetic joy in their success and good fortune are said to be the inevitable outcome of practicing the body/mind analysis that's also common to Vipassana meditation.

Connect Through Compassion

Empathy is a seed from which compassion grows and matures. Standing in another's shoes works as the cleansing agent for selfpity and depression.

—Anonymous

Being alone and being lonely are two different things. Being lonely finds an individual with their worldview programmed to see their presence as the center of things. Trying to figure out what's best for "I am" separates in their mind the essence of their presence from the remaining part of this transforming interacting reality. It's a dead end with no real way to turn. It leaves the individual alone in its darkness.

At this point, if the individual steps back from this dead end and looks out to another individual's situation and takes their personal concerns out of the picture, they'll find an endless array of possibilities. Considering the other individual's situation and the forces that are affecting it will bring up experiential memories from their own life history.

These forces affect everyone. It's part of the human condition that's shared by all. There will arise a point of view on the emotions the forces evoke as well as ways of dealing with them.

Approach the other individual and ask them about these reflections. Strike up a new relationship. Leave loneliness in its dark corner.

An individual needs to form a personal presence that can be gifted to each person they come in contact with throughout the day. To be able to give each acquaintance the presence of an individual who has altruistic intentions of being free with a compassionate interpersonal exchange will leave them feeling better for the rest of their day. This is the type of gift that requires no national holiday to give.

Looking into the Sensual Mirror

It's only in visiting the sensual arena of our coming and going reality and witnessing it that a truth seeker can better understand this transitory state of change. This is where an individual can get to better know the essence of the only person they can never really meet or see in real life—themselves.

When people look into the mirror to see themselves, they only catch a visual impression of what the person's reversed image looked like a fraction of a second ago. Like a person's right hand will never touch their right elbow, from the outside they will never actually meet or see themselves. They can undo their ignorance of what bearing our reality's nature of impermanence has on their existence only by visiting it in its primal venue...the flesh arena of where transforming activity itself manifests...change as it actually happens.

The actual air of transformation alive in one's living essence is lacking in all the home movies, photographs, mirrored images and friends' verbal descriptions. This stuff serves as nothing but food for the ego to build on or base a defense. This real-time living process a truth seeker sensually witnesses while gaining self-awareness is the only mirror an individual can ever look into to get a nonreflective glimpse at the truth explaining their essence and a sensual look at the transforming muse of our Source's coming and going pulse that signs to all what they really are. The truth seeker gets a close sensual view of who and what they really are when they become familiar with what their mind entertains. This nonpausing process unfolds as time ticks by.

On the outside, it's this essence of a person that's the expression of the individual's intended purpose everyone else sees in the individual's transpiring moment-to-moment behavior to help form their impressions and define the individual's personality or intended purpose. These mental snapshots are what can get talked about around the cooler at work.

What Workout Instructors Could Be Doing

Many people select a basic workout regime from a wide variety of activities such as private trainers, weight lifting, running, swimming, spinning class, punching a heavy bag or maybe one of many available therapy/workout programs because their bodies need exercise and maybe it helps sidetrack their minds and find temporary relief from stress. There are gym workouts where the body becomes fatigued climbing a stationary mountain on a Stairmaster, while the mind becomes frustrated trying to focus on reading a book or trying to watch and listen to a wall-mounted TV. Finding a spot to peacefully direct one's train of thought can be a real task while sweating through a spinning class.

There are martial arts classes where the body becomes fatigued practicing technique while the mind becomes bored wondering why. There are ways of meditation where the body poises ready to contribute, while the mind is sidetracked while trying to fixate focus on an imagined object with a nonchanging nature that's continual presence really doesn't exist or maybe their awareness is stressed out while wondering if their pose is correct or one of a million other off-point things. These applications fail to understand what is needed for the human condition to truly rid itself of the unrest that they seek relief from. There's no mind/ body harmony realized to inspire the right thinking to self-train any insightful right understanding to wisdom-enrich the truth seeker's awareness of the truth of impermanence.

People do this while accepting it as a normal part of modern-day living and don't see it in any way associated with the process of eternal suffering relief that's targeted in church.

It's a healthy part of their daily living routine...not at all associated with the stoic nature of what their religious text has to say about finding eternal joy and happiness and relief from suffering. Forcing oneself to work out in this fashion might help develop some degree of self-control, but doesn't address the development of mind control.

They do this while acceptingly anticipating the underlying cause of their stressed-out psyche to soon again boil to the surface so they will have to return to their ritual of sorts to renew their temporary lease on mental quiet. It's OK. It's what their friends do. It's what they see pretty people do in TV ads. They tithe to this ritual by paying their monthly health club memberships dues.

Most Hoosier attempts at any of the modern-day relaxation techniques aren't recognized for having the potential to be a step in the spiritual process of becoming enlightened about what it is that robs them of their joy and happiness and is responsible for the stress over situations they don't quite know how to deal with like those that they are seeking relief from.

Their bodies and minds are both fatigued in their own ways, but don't get to work out together in harmony on a united front while gaining temporary relief. Neither the individuals nor their instructors have any idea of the possible reward if they only knew how to make this happen.

The mystical grandness of their intellectually sketched mental pictures of what salvation from suffering is occupies a religious/spiritual maxim page in their intellectual concept scrapbook that is only brought to attention while sitting on a Sunday-morning church pew. While, the truth is that each type of body/mind fitness activity occupies its own contributory niche somewhere along the continuum stretching from baseline suffering to realizing heavenly enlightenment. They each can help a truth seeker's spiritual awareness find its way or surface from the subtle regions of the deeper consciousness up the primal link to the individual's present moment waking awareness.

The true spiritual contributory/participatory potential hasn't been realized when this paradox hasn't even been pointed out with the guidance on how to develop a focused eye on eventually reaching an end of heavenly enlightenment. Their spiritual path is intellectually sketched, as there's been no waking taste of an understanding of our Source's intertwined nature and intended purpose. When the omnipresent coming and going vibration of the real-time expression of the intellectually known Holy Spirit are present, they aren't felt and regarded in that capacity. The connection just doesn't click. The true spiritual relevance slides by unrecognized.

They in no way attribute their physical/mental workout routine as playing a part of a on a quest to gain self-knowledge to permanently eradicate the cause behind their daily present moment fatigue and unrest. They just don't recognize it.

Even though the intent of modern-day methods of finding stress relief does not include achieving heavenly enlightenment, the task still includes the combining of body and mind effort and awareness in some fashion to find the temporary peace they are paying dues to find. The waking intent behind their stress relieving efforts doesn't intentionally include self-training the mind/body harmony to visit their inner theater featuring life-in-progress while knowing this to be a haven of introspection. They will have serendipitous flashes of unknowingly and unintentionally crossing this line and they will enjoy the peace if offers. Yet, they will recognize these brief moments as just being a part of their workout and any association that what they may be experiencing as being sensually tangible real-time spiritual signposts will slide by unrecognized.

When entering their workout facility, any idea of Sunday morning spirituality is left hanging in the closet with their Sunday goin'-to-meetin' clothes and set aside from these life-associated everyday activities. Why shouldn't it be? The relief they eagerly seek here differs from that they have in mind for Sunday morning...if they look forward to going to church in the first place.

This mental wall stands in the way of any present moment attempt at self-training internal spiritual maturity in this setting. The effectiveness is muffled by the internalized superimposed mentally imprinted notion of heavenly peace coming only externally in a godly manner and in this area, whether they're a religious believer or not. There aren't too many people who see anything holy about a workout environment.

They just don't make the connection that some common, ordinary and possibly modern-day activity in their culture could contribute to the process of something so spiritually monumental, of ancient Eastern origin, dating back to the days of sandals and togas. They don't relate the truth explaining our Source's (reality's) nature of impermanence to attaining happiness and joy in the passing present moment to the same truth that provides their eternal bliss, that's told of in the terms and language accent of the King James Bible translation.

Generally speaking, health club devotees have no expectant eye for detecting the age-old spiritual picture in a sensual dialogue that reveals the primal truth that's tied to the life of each passing present moment. As Jesus said in his parable about the sower, some can't see or hear the truth when it's right in their face due to being mesmerized by earthly concerns or by the lure of riches.

A Midwesterner can still unintentionally and unknowingly come one step closer to self-training their mind/body harmony to a higher degree than while in a gym lifting weights or while trying to read a book while sweating on a treadmill, still without having the waking intention of enriching their awareness of this reality's impermanence. Any sport that requires the mind to tell the body what to do and be there to make sure it performs as sensually instructed (hopefully as practiced many times) can accomplish this end...martial arts, yoga, ball sports, or anything involving hand-eye coordination.

The mind and body are working more as a united unit, yet still lack the waking visualization of finding the harmony in this to better understand the reality they live in and to eliminate their ignorance of the relational justice among the factors that defines the cause/effect design of this reality's process of transformation. The process isn't complicated. Each human's living condition is made up of this truth. The challenge is just finding a way for the spirit in that condition to understand it.

The Meek Shall Inherit the Earth...Jesus

Greed is a form of craving. Hatred is a form of aversion. Altruistically inspired giving and benevolence are their opposites. Gratitude negates entitlement.

Pride is thought to be the original and most serious of the seven deadly or cardinal sins. It's thought to be the source from which the others arise.

Because humility addresses intrinsic self-worth, it is thought to be the opposing virtue that balances out the vice of pride. Could it be that humility is the most primal of all the virtues?

It's only through humility the body/mind can shed their independent states of unparalleled attention and together as one find harmony in common focus to meet heart in hand in united analysis to cross the bridge of communication over the ego-land void of uncertainty to the plateau of understanding where in a total combine state of humility they wait and together, of one single purpose, listen to our Source sensually demonstrate the manifested truth of its intended purpose of always making readily available real-time present moment ongoing change.

The truth seeker's personal deliberation over the uncontrollable stream of bodily sensations leads to the accumulation of insight-inspired wisdom to reach liberation from its ignorance. Humility must turn the pages through the entire process of Sandbox Etiquette Guideline Number 1 while focusing concentration to sensually listen and not to talk with any composed mentally oral recitation of calculated wants or needs.

The personal relationship established between an individual and the truth that defines our Source during self-discovery is secured only through humility. Without a personal nature grounded by humility there would be no communication possible to form a waking conscious relationship with our Source in action.

Insightful contemplation while gaining self-knowledge reveals that humility is needed to live peacefully on this Earth without suffering. Through an insight gained from the dispassionate unattached patient contemplation over the cause/effect relationships among the factors of the uncontrollable stream of coming and going bodily sensations sensually witnessed while gaining self-knowledge it becomes clear how useless it would be for the individual to try to act out or try to control the coming and going of those sensations. It's pointless and foolish. Their unalterable presence must always be greeted by a truth seeker's most humble presence.

When applying this insight to other cause/effect life situations the reflective wisdom suggests that it's wise for an individual to live under the same principle of humility to effectively address the ever-renewed configuration of this reality's real-time present moment cause/effect presence. It's useless to act out and try to control things beyond their natural rhythm. It's true that when trying to unduly control situations, acting rude, inconsiderate or being deaf to reason, that this is when peaceful coexistence isn't possible and suffering results.

Maybe this is why Jesus said in the Beatitudes that the meek are blessed...that they will inherit the Earth. Maybe the meek are blessed for understanding the necessity for adherence to the facets of Sandbox Etiquette Guideline Number 1 used to gain self-knowledge, allowing the reflective wisdom to apply the observed insights of self-discovery to include and set the bar level for all their social behavior. The meek are on a level of awareness that allows them with the luxury of being ego-free for a more transparent perception of life to better enjoy, understand and appreciate what the transforming process called Earth has to offer.

Only through maintaining humility will any human being's perceptions share the wavelength savvy to recognize insightful wisdom among the cause/effect relationships of the passing moment. There's really something in remaining humble and nonassuming as time passes to allow ideas and inspirations to surface any time of day...not only when posed cross-legged in meditation.

9

Metacognition

...Recognize, Acknowledge, Own and Release
Unwholesome Thought Patterns

The Art of Contemplative Thought Control

Mankind's collective deeper consciousness has finally produced a word to describe the concept of thinking about what you're thinking about... metacognition. Like when long ago, mankind's social recognition of its accumulated dissonance coming from the effects of the repeated dabbling in the cardinal sins finally percolated and resulted in the fire-etching of the Ten Commandments' stone flyer, mankind's conscious recognition of another subtle concept finally takes form.

Metacognition...awareness and understanding of one's own thought process... modern terminology that further reflects how more enriched mankind's collective conscious grasp and understanding of humanity's involvement in understanding the present moment has become. When a truth seeker is driven to better understand the impermanent nature of this reality and is aware of how their belief system works, they can protect or change the nature of their mind to bring them closer to living their present moments in joy and happiness and put a stop to their suffering.

It's a necessary part of the spiritual development process of self-training the enriched wisdom that Siddhartha teaches of in his last two folds of his eightfold pathway to enlightenment that led hem to his enlightened understanding of his ignorance. This is a word that the Romans of 312 AD never would have allowed into their Bible. It's involved in finding direction and securing responsibility from within.

This modern-day term summarizes part of the preparatory process for self-training the mind control to then allow self-training a wisdom-enriched understanding of the ways of impermanence. Staying mentally focused on the coming and going sensations within the body to then deliberate and recognize and eventually remove unwholesome thought patterns associated with accumulated inner tensions and to dwell in their wholesome replacements is an important step in setting up the inspired thinking to open up the insightful understanding of an enlightened awareness.

As Mind Control Increases, So Does Wisdom Enrichment

With greater mind control that can sustain a longer span of contemplative deliberation, the thinking potential for inspiring the insights that self-train a more wisdom-enriched understanding of the impermanence that characterizes this reality's impermanent nature reaches deeper and broadens. Being able to sustain an uninterrupted awareness of one set of streamed thought patterns longer allows the truth seeker to settle into a more thought-out resolve.

The individual has more time to consider and analyze the subject of their thought. They have more time to ponder the subject. Their thoughts spiral deeper into the physical symptoms the thought patter triggers.

The Four Characteristics Of Making The Right Effort

...Recognize and Eliminate Unwholesome Thought Patterns...
Replace and Maintain with Wholesome...The Martial Arts Spiritual Tie-In

While attempting to self-train the mind control to create the mind/body harmony to wakingly grasp the meaning of the embedded enriched wisdom of self-knowledge while self-training a better understanding of the primal truth explaining the nature and intended purpose of our Source and ourselves, a truth seeker has to learn to sensually feel or understand the difference between wholesome and unwholesome thought patterns...that the difference doesn't necessarily relate to what they might subjectively think of as good or bad. It's more whether a factor is contributory or noncontributory in affecting the end purpose of their focused intention.

They need to learn to sensually detect the nature of their thought patterns... what characterizes those that are wholesome and fruitful toward reaching their intended goal and what characterizes those that are unwholesome and sidetrack their mental thought train toward the end purpose of what might be some needless want. This could possibly involve wholesome thought patterns that contribute to affecting an intended purpose directed at a bad goal or vice versa. Deeming the nature of thought intentions as good or bad can be subjectively judgmental and result in missing the point here.

Truth seekers need to sight forward their intended purpose of understanding their ignorance and finding their state of compassion, happiness and joy while they self-train the mind control that prevents unwholesome thought patterns that will stop them from reaching their sighted goal. Many stand wrapped up in a web of uncontrolled fleeting reactions, emotionally immersed in the resulting states of unrest while not even consciously realizing this to be suffering.

William Hart summarizes in *The Art of Living Vipassana Meditation*, what's been taught at S. N. Goenka Theravada Buddhist meditation seminars concerning what Siddhartha meant by right effort in his teachings on self-training mind control in *The Eightfold Pathway to Enlightenment*. It's divided into four objectives needed to minimize the unneeded interruptions in the right effort involved in the process of self-training the mind control to develop the mind/body harmony that enables the eventual understanding of human ignorance. This helps a truth seeker know how to better work through processing their thought patterns during their attempts at introspective deliberation while harmonizing their mind's awareness into their body's presence during right concentration that's focused into the physical theater of change (their flesh) to establish the right thinking to inspire their insightful wisdom-enriched right understanding.

An individual's right effort when used in the more outwardly visible physical process of learning a martial arts technique can be paralleled to the use of right effort in the more internally private process of mind/body analysis or meditation to illustrate Siddhartha's four objectives that characterize what he meant by the right effort that helps affect the mind/body harmony that will allow inspiring the right thinking to insightfully generate the wisdom-enriched right understanding of our reality's impermanent nature. The use of self-trained mind control in both of these processes enables an effective form of spiritual training as when compared to someone seeking the possible relaxation that might follow in the wake of trying to read a book or focus on a TV hanging on the wall while forcing their bodies through a half hour of the mentally detached vigorous activity used in a spinning class where self-training mind control isn't even considered a goal. In the same light of missing the point of training spirituality, a martial artist might think it's in some way "spiritual" to vent their day's built up frustrations by attacking a punching bag with no particular subject in mind to direct their thought activity at that will create a mind/body relationship that enables a more rapid development of their targeted technique.

The first objective Siddhartha taught is to learn to recognize the presence of any unwholesome thought patterns that threaten to interrupt the sustained wholesome thought pattern making up a truth seeker's harmonious right concentration as its focused into the essence of their body's presence during mind/body analysis. This can be the white noise from the untethered endless thoughts from their confused mitote/maya mental state.

The inappropriateness of these intrusive thought patterns parallel that of the wandering thoughts that cheat a martial artist's right concentration that's searching to feel what are the most appropriate physical components of their unique physical structure to most effectively train the targeted martial arts technique to accomplish the desired self-defense objective.

This subtle mental thought process can have interruptions of all kinds. The instructor's attitude, an upset stomach, a bad day at school, not wanting to be in class or maybe imagining how they look like Chuck Norris or Bruce Lee are only a few examples.

A martial artist's right concentration helps bring quicker success in developing an understanding of what muscle combination best affects the targeted technique (some effective and some not). Unwholesome thinking results in the same "lost purpose" type of mental effect to them as with a truth seeker who's thought process becomes interrupted by a nonassociated thought when attempting the focused breathing or body scan techniques of mind/body analysis.

In martial arts, there is no better demonstration of what the negative effects of the interruption from unwholesome thought patterns has on the martial artists right effort to maintain their sustained right concentration than when their mind wanders during a form exercise and they stop dead in their tracks with the embarrassed look of forgetful wonder on their face. Mind/body harmony is missing here. Mind drifting while doing forms is immediately punished with getting lost in the form...any form...any belt level. These could be the unwholesome thought patters of unrelated (unwholesome) thoughts like how well they might know their form or what people watching may think or anything that isn't directly related to what movement their body should make next and what a better way of making that move is that they've discovered through practice.

The second objective in Siddhartha's analysis as taught by Mr. Goenka to make the right effort is to recognize and abandon unwholesome thought patterns if and when they should arise again. Recognize their presence and move past them. With time, the martial artist and the meditator will become familiar with that feeling when their mind has wandered.

In body/mind analysis, after an unwholesome thought pattern is recognized, he says to just return to awareness focused in the breathing or body area. Don't allow any reactions or have emotions to whatever is inspired by whatever demons of disruption the unwholesome thought patterns might rekindle. This parallels recognizing and not repeating the nonproductive technique variations that don't positively affect shaping the targeted martial arts technique or with the floor forms, not allowing the mind to drift from what the improved incarnation of the next movement will be.

The third objective is to generate wholesome thought patterns that may even not yet exist that are wholesome toward reaching the intended goal. Maintain the positive halffull state of mind that replaces the nonproductive or unfruitful attitude and helps maintain the uninterrupted thought pattern to maintain the right effort. Sense the relieving feeling that lacks the anxiety or red flags of endless thinking that plague one's real-time spirit. This state parallels finding the effective and unique-to-the-individual muscle/bone structure coordination that positively affects honing the targeted goal of the martial arts technique.

Siddhartha's fourth objective in sustaining right effort is to maintain the wholesome states without lapse. Allow them to develop and reach full growth and perfection. This is like don Miguel Ruiz's fourth agreement that advises to just keep on trying to perform the right method of enforcing his first three agreements as just discussed at the end of this chapter ten.

Starting with an intellectually understood directive about purposes of mind controlling the body, martial arts participation develops the spirit. The mind becomes more aware of reality through developing a conscious awareness of the world through mind/body coordination. Self-training ability to ward of thoughts unassociated to striking the harmony of sustained focus of the mind presence to control body actions improves duration of concentration ability.

Sustain Harmonious Focus and Penetrate into Deeper Feelings

Mind/body harmony's essential for the mind to sensually witness the manifestation of life that's going on in the truth seeker's flesh that their mind's awareness is focusing into. If they've been successful at recognizing and filtering out any unwholesome thought patterns that interrupt their mind's focus, inspired insightful thinking is possible.

The deeper the unremitting focus of the mind into the body is, the deeper into the transforming abyss the mind can venture and the calmer it becomes. This can affect insights coming from the deeper echo of the deeper feelings of the truth seeker's living process. Deeper understandings can follow for a more enriched understanding of the impermanence that can build toward bringing back their joy and happiness and undoing their suffering.

The Intrinsic Pull to Establish Harmony

So many aspiring martial artists look to getting a black belt as being the main goal of attending classes. The power of the ego-engineered intention centered only on the subjective notoriety of wearing a black belt can be mentally blinding to a martial artist's conscious development of their spiritual growth. The black belt shows visible proof of something, yet they're not really sure of what it is.

Actively studying a martial art teases the inborn desire to find harmony with learning how to combine the more visible factors representing the body's presence in the coordination of body/mind harmony. It's common for students to become bored, quit and return to class years later without really knowing specifically what inner longing pulled them back.

Understanding and associating how a harmonious mind/body skill-learning process helps in actual spiritual growth slides by unnoticed and unrecognized. When the testing process for earning a black belt is complete, their classroom experiences could be summed up as a mixture of good workouts, boring moments and test-time nerves. At this level of appreciation, pride stands tall in representing the unspecified internal satisfaction in realizing some portion of some internal relational understanding that's calling out for conscious discovery.

Of course, the new friendships formed with fellow martial artists tend to have a deeper connection and the meaning seems a bit more transparent. Involvement in martial arts exposes a person more for what they can do without the aid of different props or while trying to wear different masks. A martial artist is what they bring with them. Evading the falseness of the ego can bring relief in itself.

The test time nerves can come from doubts about whether or not they had through their master's guidance, self-trained through mind/body harmony the most effective mind/body coordination to demonstrate their ability to perform the skill set needed to affect the techniques expected at their level of advancement. They're afraid unwholesome thought patterns might interrupt their present moment focus needed to best perform their technique at the particular present moment they are tested.

It's the same thing during times of competition. The martial artist is concerned that the uninterrupted wholesome thought patterns of right effort will be there to support their right concentration for the harmonious mind/body coordination to execute the martial arts technique best suited for them to win.

By passing the martial arts tests the martial artist can show that their body control has increased to where they can perform the martial art discipline's skills needed to get their black belt. The visible display of honed mind/body coordination in action is why the martial skills are considered an art. Buddhist monks offer public displays of their learned martial arts discipline to demonstrate in life-size proportion the product of their repeated use of self-trained mind/body harmony in perfecting their technique through their artistic coordination of its mind/body principles. They can't really demonstrate how they utilize their skill at maintaining a uninterrupted flow of wholesome thought patterns to create the mind/body harmony for providing the right effort to make possible their right concentration for the right thinking to inspire their self-training the wisdom-enriched insightful right understanding of their ignorance of the impermanent nature and intended purpose of our Source to undo that ignorance and relieve them of their suffering.

At least in the Midwest, the martial artist probably isn't aware exactly what the spiritual significance is that their repeated use of mind/body harmony accomplishes. But there's a strong intrinsic pull for the unidentifiable indefinable spiritual growth possible that keeps aspiring martial artists coming back to class.

1,000 Voices of the Mitote/Maya Shout in Protest

Most individuals spend their entire lifetime with their behavioral intentions managed by an ego that keeps their waking awareness prisoner, frozen up a mitote/maya state of consciousness. This ego becomes very wise to their ways. It never fails to remember the prior conditioning that influenced developing the addictions that help sustain their illusionary picture of this ever-changing reality. It's learned the right buttons to push to keep things safe and enforce obedience.

It knows how to push an individual's buttons before they have time to step back and think and so they mindlessly react. It can be extremely hard for them to pin their ego down to get a word in edgewise. It holds hostage their free will...forcing them to do things...to believe things before having a chance to experientially verify a new claim's level of truth. It's when the truth seeker receives the guidance and musters the strength to unite their body and mind in harmony and make the passage over the bridge of communication, heart in hand, united as one onto the sensual plateau of right understanding that the 1,000 mitote/maya unrelated voices shout in protest. Their every effort is to break into and interrupt the truth seeker's attempted steady thought design to sustain their right effort and right awareness into the right concentration the individual has suddenly and surprisingly managed to summons up.

The 1,000 voices of the endless claims that give the substance to their mental mitote/maya sense that their chameleon-like cover's about to be blown. They panic. They feel the primal link that stretches from the individual's truth-harboring deeper consciousness to their ego-managed answer-seeking waking consciousness is about to shake off layers of deadening faulty prior conditioning and resonate back to life. They raise the intensity of their misguided voices to a shrill sounding shout. They're up in full protest...the truth seeker's head is full of chatter...truly a sincere truth seeker's worst nightmare.

It's here during the truth seeker's right effort to focus their right awareness in the essence of present moment change in each of their body parts that the shouting 1,000 mitote/maya voices try to make the individual forget the tenants of humility spelled out in Sandbox Etiquette Guideline Number 1 to stop them from self-training their mind control. They encourage and want to see the individual ditch their humility and rudely turn their head from devotedly listening to our Source's message about impermanence and use their present moment thoughts to consider and weigh one of the endless pointless wants being shouted from their mitote/maya state of confusion. They hope just one injected thought from one needless want will for a short period of time catch the truth seeker's attention and put a stir into their efforts to focus their mind into contemplative deliberation over our Source's message.

They try to make the individual's mind wander with interrupting thoughts coming from any of the endless random unrelated topics up for grabs on the mitote/maya-controlled mental floor at the time. If successful, this disconnects the truth seeker's focus from the real-time sensual experience of the ongoing change within their own living flesh.

Mental thought patterns are always accompanied by a physical resonation. The truth seeker has to be strong enough not to become sidetracked by thinking about the thoughts that accompany the sensations. They need to be focused on the body area where the uncontrollable flow of sensations resides...the static from life's buzz.

A truth seeker needs to greet the flow of sensations with uninterrupted dispassionate indifference. They must learn to recognize these very unwholesome thought patterns, excuse their presence and learn to maintain the wholesome thought patterns they find to replace them that allow and encourage the sustained focus of their right concentration. This is a lifetime effort that even if the individual is aware of, most never learns to master.

Humble respect is shown to our Source by keeping an attentive relaxed quiet mind, while not breaking thought to attend to the subject of these attempts at disturbance. Breaking attention would be like rudely turning your head to listen to another friend while an individual just asked to share their secret for building sandcastles was kind enough to share their technique description.

It would be thoughtless and rude for someone to turn their head or attention from our Source as it demonstrates its intended purpose to listen to one of the mitote/maya voices shouting for their attention. They're trying to interrupt the truth seeker's effort to develop the sustained right concentration to focus on what will inspire the useful insight for the demise of the habit-energy reactions the mitote/maya had crafted to foster their addictions.

Maintaining the right concentration can really be tough. One's bond with the white noise of the misguided claims of internalized prior conditioning can be very strong. The primal fear of the unknown can easily step in and corrupt or at least sidetrack their right concentration. Out of fear, they might grab hold of and hold onto one of the pointless interrupting thought patterns.

Truth Seeker Executes Mitote/Maya Shakedown

It can be nearly impossible while trying to make the right effort with the right awareness to ignore the white noise of one's mitote/maya. It's difficult to find the courage to keep the white noise cocktail of different thought pattern incarnations designed to deal with guilt and fear out of the waking consciousness to sustain the right concentration focused into the sensual plateau of common understanding. The truth seeker will have had to have been successful in self-training their moral/ethical standards to even stand a chance at finding the mental calm to self-train their mind control.

Even though a truth seeker's current life experience may be one they ideally want to remove the present moment suffering from, it's the very ignorance of our Source's nature and purpose that causes their suffering that allows the uncertainty and latent fear that fills their belief system void that they manage to find safety in. They become accustomed to hovering in this familiar state of unrest. They build their social circles around its commonly shared symptoms. They've bore the suffering from their ignorance for so long, they're used to it. They consider it normal.

Clinging to the practiced mental patterns of past present moments can bring a feeling of security. Not understanding why it happens, an individual can become attached to this thinking style and cling to its misunderstood and misleading mental patterns.

It not only takes an intended purpose that projects the right effort and right awareness, but it also takes real genuine courage for an individual to try to turn off the familiar mind-chatter that devalues and mutes their use of the present moment. It takes individual character to leave it behind and step open-eyed and totally vulnerable into the essence of life as they sensually detect its changing manifestation. Religion dogma in no way supports this.

The individual's free will's going to finally be able to enforce the ageless primal law their belief system has been foolishly overlooking while indulging their ongoing suffering. Their free will's going to take to trial each of the 1,000 shouting unrelated voices, holding their shouted claims to blame for creating their mental mitote/maya state of mind and put on death row those claims responsible for the faulty prior conditioning that allowed the attachment to cravings and aversions to things or non-things.

The truth seeker will nab these infected claims as they try to break their right concentration while performing their sessions of harmonious mind/body analysis while they deliberate on the sensual plateau of understanding. They will be nabbed at other times throughout the day when the individual is confronted in situations similar to those the individual chose through ignorance to act in a way that through practiced repetition the actions assumed the habit energy to become the fleeting reactions that contribute to constituting the addictions that support their ongoing present moment suffering. The individual's self-trained mental awareness, thinking and understanding will be on call, looking for the sensual red flags.

The sensual proof of the falseness of these claims will be the undeniable omnipresent evidence noted during the right insightful understanding of the inspired right thinking they've had during sessions of harmonious body/ mind analysis viewed through right concentration since then. The steadfast faith in the omni-presence of the same cause/effect reality the condemning evidence was collected in to assure the continued presence of the proof and viability of the evidence would ensure the execution of the sentences.

They walk blindfolded with sensual eyes opened to realize their place in the Source-paced change of one present moment into a new one that's totally unchar-tered and new to this reality. They don't know what to expect when facing naked change head on. They have not yet developed any real steadfast faith-backed cour-age to back their venturing effort. This is why so many fail to make the switch.

Emotional Triggers Have Corresponding Sensations

What Siddhartha discovered that was of vital importance for him to gain his self-knowledge and a wisdom-enriched enlightened awareness of the subject of his ignorance, was where to go to experience firsthand. He grew to understand that anything that happens in the mind is a result of prior conditioned perceptions about inputs through his sensual ports. He saw that the conditioning of his emo-tional states was all realized in his sensations.

After it's initially understood what's gained from witnessing the truth, truth seekers will hang suspended in ignorance as long as their repeated attempts to focus right concentration into their physical theater of truth can't find an unin-terrupted platform on the plateau of understanding to work from. The repeated interruption of unwholesome thought patters that sidetrack the sustained focus of a truth seeker's right concentration will result in their difficulty in realizing spiri-tual growth from our Source's sensual message board of ongoing change.

Under the assault of continued interruptions and while meaning not to not give up and lose sight of the purpose of self-training a wisdom-enriched conscious awareness, their continued endeavors will prove to be ineffective and become rit-ualistic and dogmatic with no fruitful progress. They daydream while intending to affect mind control to park their awareness in the theater of ongoing change. They will lack the trained sensitivity to harness enough mind control to realize the right thinking needed to inspire the insights needed to effectively self-train the wisdom to undo the tree of intellectual knowledge that underlies their suffering. (The biblical story goes that mankind's been eating from the tree of knowledge since he was put on earth.)

Whether or not an individual knows it, a sensation, perception of that sensa-tion and emotional response to that perception react together. Coming and going sensations are coded with the thought patterns that influence the emotions that brew up the fleeting reactions that feed the list of personal addictions that lead to suffering. When something is perceived by the mind, the perception is always followed by a physical sensation signaling the emotion soon to follow.

The successful truth seeker attempts to sustain a focused awareness on the ever-present coming and going sensations, systematically and with equanimity, body part by body part, throughout their body. They don't grab at any pleasant sensations or try to squirm away from the unpleasant ones. They realize the sensations are going to manifest at their own rate regardless of anything they do.

During body/mind analysis, the sensual red flags coming in the wake of triggering perceptions, warning of upcoming reactionary behaviors are among those coded into the coming and going sensations that are receiving their impartial deliberation. Any red flag-causing thought wave could be the same one that affects several other different addictive behaviors.

During each present moment the truth seeker is attempting to find body/mind harmony, the thought-to-sensation-triggers are at the front of their focused mind where these triggering body sensations can eventually be recognized and not reacted to. They need to be met with equanimity to be eventually recognized, owned, waited out, and released. Along with recognizing and releasing the thought-to-sensation triggers that disrupt their mind control to sustain right concentration, the resulting related fleeting reactionary behaviors on the truth seeker's menu of interrelated addictions will not reappear.

The 1,000 voices of the individual's mitote/maya mental state that are shouting to interrupt the truth seeker's chain of thought, stand at the front of the individual's conscious mind where the reflective sensations that document their presence are detected as an unspecified part of the coming and going sensations. When starting to feel jealousy, ask if it's more fear-based or more anger-based and why? Recognize which body part is being affected. If it's a dropping or clutching sensation in the stomach, it's probably fear. If it's a burning, tight sensation in the shoulders and jaw, then it's likely anger. It might also be a combination of those sensations.

Thought and sensation go hand in hand. The sensation is the point where the mind and body meet. For a truth seeker to develop an understanding of what it is that their mind is ignorant about, it helps to observe the sensations that can signal the onset of the suffering their ignorance allows.

Siddhartha taught that to understand the totality of one's self, mind and body, it's necessary to observe the sensation. He said that the presence of sensations will be recognized as a contributing, yet indiscernible part of the uncontrollable pleasant and/or unpleasant sensations that appear only to disappear during body/mind analysis on the sensual plateau of right understanding where the mind and body meet.

It's by combining the essence of the body's presence with the mind's focused awareness at the same time together in harmony that it's possible to better understand the sensation trigger/emotional reaction packages that can dominate the present moment state of mind. Through body/mind harmony, they will tame the outer inertia of their human curiosity that longs to understand and conquer the self to become enlightened about the ignorance that allows their suffering.

Interrupt and Relax Reactionary Thought Pattern Chains... Contemplate the Appropriate Response

Think before reacting. Learn to hold the thoughts that lead to the moods, step back and deliberate. During repeated united body/mind analysis a truth seeker will learn to recognize the most significant tendencies or characteristics to eventually decide which tendencies or characteristics can be overlooked and which ones inspire relational insight among the interplay of those relationships in the flesh-felt sensual display. These realized tendencies, with the right understanding will inspire insights into this relational cause/ effect reality.

With patient contemplation and reflection during sustained concentration into the buzz of interplay among the uncontrollable streams of coming and going body sensations a focused individual is inspired to recognize insights relating to the interplay of what allows a cause to become or change into its effect during life's ongoing transformation.

While relaxed and focused in harmonious body/mind analysis on the plateau of understanding, the alert conscious mind has remained undisturbed by mitote/maya conscious thought interrupters and is sensually opened and tuned-in to strengthen the primal link with relational savvy from the deeper more subtle region of their consciousness. They concentrate uninterrupted while tuned into the sensually coded real-time exhibition of life manifested.

With their focused-right concentration they've confronted and with their ability to sustain that right concentration they've subdued what was once the uncontrollable thought pattern interference from their mitote/maya state of mind.

During a truth seeker's sessions of mind/body analysis while attempting to sustain a balanced mind/body harmony, they learn to step back mentally to not react to pleasant or unpleasant sensations coming from differing thought patterns that may represent the sensations that trigger clinging or aversive reactions. This helps eliminate the body's need to react to similar triggering sensations that inspire attachment to the craving or aversion common when seeking other endless wants simply because they may represent some form of short-term gratification for no worthy reason.

It can be understood why many of the triggering sensation-to-thought pattern packages that cause reactionary emotional suffering will become apparent even when not quietly practicing body/mind analysis. These triggering sensations will arise when confronting real-life situations in an environment similar to where the honing process enabling their faulty prior conditioning were first encountered... where the misguided understanding they allowed to shape their worldview was initially internalized and allowed to assume the habit energy that resulted in the continued unchecked reoccurrences of their suffering.

The increased sensitivity needed for effective deliberation will evolve along with a truth seeker's level of spiritual maturity to include times when they're not involved in quiet body/mind analysis. Just as in the method used by Siddhartha, they're progressively training their mind to recognize the inspired insights of right understanding that undoes their ignorance of the nature and purpose of our Source.

When thought patterns are considered with equanimity during impartial deliberation and waited out to naturally disappear, those concentration interruptions representing the misguided truisms forming the individual's mitote/maya that bring out the triggering sensations will subside. The individual's increasingly wisdom-enriched awareness of this relational cause/effect interplay will eliminate the need for an emotion-riddled mind to react to the sensations expressed during the body/mind analysis of naturally occurring coming and going sensations.

Mr. Geshe Rinchen sheds light on this process in his commentary book *Atisha's Lamp For the Path to Enlightenment*:

> Through prolonged familiarity with the understanding of reality, the disturbing emotions gradually come to an end. Then even if imprints of past actions with the potential to precipitate another ordinary rebirth no disturbing emotions are present to activate them. We will never again take rebirth through the force of compulsive actions and disturbing emotions and are free of the contaminated aggregates.[11]

With the proper balance of equanimity and awareness and the decrease in misguided influence originating from misguided prior conditioning, a truth seeker replaces letting their behaviors exhibiting their attachment to fleeting reactions run their life. They become capable of making and taking contemplated action. Instead of reacting to outside negativity, through their creativity they can opt for an action that is for the good.

As the damage from prior conditioning discontinues influencing the nature of the individual's mind, they develop a different worldview. As how their mind recognizes the nature of this reality changes, so does the nature of their worldview and the intentions addressed by their thought patterns.

Siddhartha teaches how when a truth seeker self-trains their right effort to achieve the sustained right awareness needed for their right concentration into a targeted arena of right focus to sensually witness the coming and going sensations, a truth-revealing bodily echo is felt pulsing from the plateau of understanding established by their mind and body working-walking together in harmony over the flesh-bound bridge of inspired insight. Through learning to observe the content of the thought design through displaced contemplation exercising fair and equal consideration of all thought patterns, the truth seeker picks apart the strands of intention that motivated the formation and appearance of these prior conditioned thought patterns.

They gradually become aware of which ones actually contribute to sustaining the wholesome right awareness that fuel the directed focus of right concentration and which ones or strands are unwholesome to staying focused on that targeted end. The truth seeker will begin to recognize the feeling of physical signs warning of their coming presence and excuse the ones that make good right effort bad right effort. Along with their disappearance, follows the suffering they inspire.

Deliberation designed to sense the unwholesome thought patterns that support satisfying an emotional hunger by overeating can lead to replacing them with wholesome ones supporting the contentment that can be realized from the positive side effects of the feel of having an tight empty stomach that doesn't feel like it's folding over the belt. There's a feel of reserved energy and of being well fed and thankful. A tight stomach line can remind an individual of times during their youth. A gut hanging over the belt becomes a constant justification for self-devaluation.

While stepping out of the circle of present moment suffering that's kept stoked by the conditioned repetition of what's developed into the fleeting thought patterns of addiction unique to each individual's mitote/maya state of mind, recognizing the reoccurrence of the thought patterns that define the states of consciousness described as the different types of joy and happiness experienced, can go unrecognized.

With many people, the thought patterns that bring on these wholesome states of mind have been long lost. They're no longer recognized for the joy and happiness they can bring. Many haven't experienced these thought waves sense they were coaxed out from their childhood innocence. After the truth seeker gets a mental whiff of the mental state leading to enlightenment from their ignorance, they will easily float back into the illusion of craving and attachment, only to settle back into their mitote/maya state of mind. But, this is still progress toward living in the present moment. Their consciously initiated purpose to reenter their theater of life manifested will reset their process of contemplative deliberation, which is where they will again find this peace.

Physiological Red Flags Precede Emotional Storms

A truth seeker must see through the thought patterns stirred by anger, distrust, shame, self-suspect, fears of the past, worries of the future, what to wear at the upcoming party or what was worn at the last one. As the truth seeker's wisdom grows, the unwholesome thought patterns will be more easily recognized for being what triggers the emotional unrest.

Fear's presence betrays itself physiologically to anyone attentive to its symptoms. Fear of the unknown will cause one's heart to beat faster, shorten their breath, make their hair stand on end and their muscles will tighten. Behavior to avoid fear is very natural when the human condition becomes cornered by a generated perception that its human experience may be cut short or altered in an unpleasant way.

First noticing the physiological symptoms signaling the reoccurrence of any of the basic emotions of anger, joy, surprise, fear, distress or disgust can allow an individual to develop a better understanding of the thought patterns that precede and bring on these emotions. The noted symptoms are the physiological red flags signing what has developed into some of the unmonitored fleeting reactions that precede their suffering.

Extended continuance and repetition strengthens the liking or disliking connection an individual retains toward any stimuli after their initial exposure. This will eventually result in future perceptions of the stimuli bringing out the brain wave patterns of conditioned addiction. The continued repetition of these parroted responses percolates the habit energy that eventually exhibits the fleeting nature of addictive behaviors.

Any sudden change a truth seeker notices in their physiology after perceiving any cause/effect interchange could be the physical signal preceding a developed habitual reactionary response. This signal warns of a reactionary response that's symptomatic of an addiction and the related emotions. When someone addicted to overeating has a friend that asks them if they'd like to go a buffet for lunch, like one of Pavlov's dogs, they will probably begin salivating at just the thought of it. The observance of body signals reveals the precursors of the soon-to-follow emotionally driven habit energy of what are the uncontrollable reactionary behaviors of addictions. One needs to open their eyes and feel cognitively comfortable with what their mind feels like when it's working to self-train the mind control to discover the relational cause/effect wisdom of how things relate to each other to understand and release the physiological triggers to their reactionary emotionally driven behaviors that define their addictions.

Whether during sessions of body/mind analysis or right before shouting profanities in frustration, maintaining a dispassionate and contemplative mind at the recognition of any sensual precursors in the coming and going sensations related to these behaviors can make possible the eventual control of the once too-quick-to-catch reactions that cause their suffering. It can stop the preconditioned emotion-driven addictive behaviors in their tracks before the reaction occurs. First, an individual needs to recognize that they are suffering from addictive behaviors. They then need to recognize and make mental note of their collective emotional status at the onset of addictive behaviors along with the resulting emotional minefield they seek relief from.

It might be that they become familiar with their state of mind at the onset of a feeding frenzy when they cannot overcome continued eating even after they know they feel full...a time when the term "portion size" has no meaning. The intellectually memorized reasons to discontinue eating pass through the mind, yet the reactionary push to eat more or maybe to be eating something known to be compromising to human health to gain temporary gratification has became too strong to stop eating...the draw to eat nutritionally empty white flour death bread sticks served at an Italian restaurant is just too strong to resist. There are too many overpowering reasons why it's OK to eat it or rather them at this time.

Before just reaching for something to eat when the urge to binge-eat arises, question where the hunger really comes from. Step back and deliberate. Realizing that the desire might really stem from the need to satisfy an emotional or spiritual and not a physical hunger is an important step in realizing peace of mind. Besides temporarily pacifying an unrealized emotional hunger, reaching for that bag of potato chips will do nothing but add inches to the waste.

Before each meal, set back in quiet contemplation and mentally review the state or rush of emotions at the onset of this acknowledged uncontrollable behavior. Picture being in this state and step back mentally as an onlooker and plan the desired actions of self-control. When the emotional state actually comes up that literally triggers a feeding frenzy, step back, recognize the emotion-signaling trigger and take the contemplated action, not the uncontrolled fleeting reaction of the much-repeated past that lead to an oversized waist.

The gradual development of addictive behaviors translates into the summation of many short-lived gratifications. This stands in opposition to the delayed gratification that can lead to present moment satisfaction. Are a few seconds of thinking "How good this tastes" worth having the rest of the day spent in self-disappointment every time your stomach comes into your view or your belly pushes its way over your too-tight belt? The shot of self-confidence following a contemplated turndown of any form of gluttonous behavior lasts all day and strengthens the internal faith in the future self-control. It's very relaxing and satisfying.

Short rapid breathing can signal the brewing up of what would normally be an uncontrolled blurting out of some hurt-intended insult at someone. Recognizing addictive behavior, isolating the thought pattern-sensual signals that trigger the emotions and planning for action when the trigger is recognized in the future before the reaction reoccurs allows control of its occurrence. This is what meditative body/mind analysis accomplishes in self-training the body/ mind harmony to use the mind to better understand the sensations in a more controlled environment. Self-training mind control is within everyone's capability and is a primal human right...if not responsibility.

Through the right awareness/mindfulness of right concentration during body/ mind analysis a truth seeker can through quiet deliberation meet the likable/dis-likable sensations representing the addiction triggers with equanimity to remain unattached and nonreactive to their presence. This helps condition the mind to operate in a similar fashion when not in the quiet-controlled environmental conditions of body/ mind analysis.

This waking presence of self-trained mind control bleeds over from meditative experience into normal waking hour behavior patterns. If they observe and dismiss the thought patterns signaling the urge to react, their new perception of the for-mally disruptive sensual triggers will replace the ignorance-spawned thinking that allowed their suffering. (Siddhartha's four objectives of right effort are in action here.) The reaction to the causing sensual trigger will stop arising if not fed the reactive habit energy of one's unmonitored response. (don Miguel Ruiz's parasite will starve and die out.)

The physiological symptoms signaling the emotional triggers resulting from the truth seeker's misguided prior conditioning are much more apt to arise at times when the truth seeker is not in full lotus position, but out in everyday environmental situations where the causing stimuli originally appeared. The red-flag sensations will arise during the situations typical of when they were initially encountered to have been many times repeated to have taken on the habit energy that led to their addictive behaviors that cause the individual's repeated suffering.

That's the time when the individual needs to be prepared to mentally step back and identify the thought pattern that triggers them to react. That's when they must be able to step back and deliberate on their presence and produce a more appropriate action to match to those stimuli.

By realizing that the seemingly permanent nature of the shapes and objects within the human sensual perception range is actually an undetectable process of continual change and accepting the truth that grasping at any notion of life con-tinuity is foolish, an individual has taken an early step in coming to terms with the ignorance that's the growing soil of their suffering. By better understanding the anatomy of their belief system and how it's effect on shaping the worldview relates to their perception of the nature this transforming reality, they can change the nature of their mind and the worldview it's developed to march to. Through understanding their mind, an individual changes its reactive nature to one capable of active dispassionate compassion-based action.

A truth seeker must find the courage to step outside the rut of safe repetitive behavior they've become used to and the security they've found living within its compromised decisions. It takes courage and renewed self-confidence to step outside that world to try out alternative behavior and find strength from a growing steadfast faith that the new behaviors are appropriate and in the omnipresence of the impermanent environmental dimensions necessary to keep that result constant when encountered in future present moments.

One Emotion Can Have Different Triggers...
One Sensual Trigger Can Inspire Different Emotions

The emotionally defined physiological reactions coming from the toxic mental states of greed, hatred, and delusion can come from a vast variety of sensual packages. The love of money touches us all from one source or another. Individuals hate to some degree anything that enlivens their individual fear of uncertainty. Seeing anything as having a nature of permanence that we can become attached to is just one example of delusion.

Looking back, an individual's first encounters with any sensation package is initially perceived and subconsciously labeled as being something liked or something disliked. Normal repetition of these split-second binary, yes/ no (like/dislike) perceptions will be slowly conditioned into unconsciously stored habit energy that eventually firms up into beliefs...some being that things have substance to become attached to...to crave or be aversive to. These develop into fleeting reactions that need no longer to be prompted by any consideration.

An individual can become attached or addicted to these responses, so over time they will happen automatically. This attachment defines the uncalculated addictive behaviors that cause much of their present moment suffering. These early like/dislike decisions grow to affect their judgment in everyday decisions. The early-learned liking/disliking attachments can later appear from other sensational triggers with similar emotional effects.

The ever-present coming and going sensations noted during the right concentration during body/mind analysis that accompany these liking or disliking perceptions can affect more than one resulting emotion. Having purposeful calmness in the presence of an ongoing unpleasant sensation can allow the individual to recognize or touch on the uncontrolled emotional ride of several different forms of related addictive thoughts or behaviors originating from the same class of sensational trigger.

A single sensation trigger can be a behavioral reaction trigger that's responsible for evoking several related addictive behaviors. Different reactions displaying similar intentions reacting to common relational interplay may involve different factors. It's not always necessary to identify one sensation trigger per addictive reaction. There's an overlapping humanistic relationship shared between all behaviors.

The same feeling of discomfort can originate from different causes. With different causing stimuli, the sensation triggers can bring on the same feeling of stress. They can result in different strains of the same emotional havoc. Similar physical symptoms of stress can trigger different combinations of emotions like worry, impatience or maybe anger.

By recognizing sensations that seem unpleasant while stepping back in introspective deliberation and not reacting, some degree of attachment to aversion can be eliminated. The same goes for eliminating attachment to craving by recognizing sensations that seem pleasant or likable without reacting to them. Sensation recognition helps a truth seeker eradicate the cause of their suffering.

When done in a controlled, balanced mental state of deliberation that sees sensations as being an equal occurrence and nothing more that a sensation to be considered and acted on, not as a sensation to be held on to and not released or a sensation to be ran away from and feared, a truth seeker is successfully eradicating their ignorance. They are approaching an enlightened understanding of their ignorance that causes their suffering.

Buddhist teacher Thich Nhat Hanh characterizes the unwholesome thought patterns:

> The basic unwholesome mental formations are greed, hatred, ignorance, pride, doubt and views. The secondary unwholesome mental formations, arising from the basic ones, are anger, malice, hypocrisy, malevolence, jealousy, selfishness, deception, guile, unwholesome excitement, the wish to harm, immodesty, arrogance, dullness, agitation, lack of faith, indolence, carelessness, forgetfulness, distraction, and lack of attention.[12]

During impartial deliberation of the coming and going sensations while self-training one's wisdom-enriched understanding of self-knowledge, the many different human mental formations that have their own corresponding physical sensation need to be dismissed by sensation type, not by intellectual reference to categorized emotion type. The different types of coming and going sensations can trigger more than one corresponding reactionary fleeting emotion. We don't want to miss seeing the forest by focusing only on the trees.

Sensation recognition changes in response to the environmental factors involved—i.e., more than one secondary unwholesome mental formation can be rooted in the same primary unwholesome mental formation. Recognize and dismiss one of the primary formations during the impartial deliberation over the corresponding coming and going sensations during right concentration by utilizing the right thinking and in the inspired insightful right understanding can influence the release of several secondary formations.

These noted mental formations reference the emotions that result from the habit-energy-formed fleeting reactions coming from the conditioned perceptions within one's worldview. They each have corresponding coming and going sensations to be experienced and confronted while the truth seeker gains self-awareness.

Recognizing and treating a basic unwholesome mental formation with the same dispassionate consideration and equanimity can affect the relief of suffering from more than one type of secondary mental formation.

Borrowed Perceptions Help Jumpstart Recognizing and Coping with Modern-Day Sensual Triggers

Using the perceptions of others (taking their experiential advice) to help minimize personal suffering allows an individual to first intellectually test drive the benefits coming from actively taking notice of a slight but planned alteration in their own worldview in how they perceive certain situations. They can then work toward experientially understanding the wisdom it offers while better internalizing and becoming familiar with the gut feeling of its strand of presence in the impermanent buzz of the coming and going sensations that its omnipresent pulse projects to them while sensually focused into their personal theater of life manifestation during their moments spent in mind/body analysis.

Lau Tzu's *Tao Te Ching* is a very famous and very old book that leaks of primal wisdom. It suggests ways of perceiving situations to avoid the suffering caused by misalignment between true reality and illusionary expectations that occupy the belief system of most people. Reading the brief witticisms of primal wisdom is why people like reading the book, even though the rather ancient air of its stiff wording style can make the intended message a bit more of a challenge to sort out.

However, being that these gathered quips of someone else's realized wisdom are remembered, stored and subject to the memory recall limits inherent to the intellectually based memory, it becomes less likely for a reader or listener to readily apply their newly borrowed wisdom to their everyday life situation even if they were quick to justify the relevance of its application. Its wisdom doesn't come to mind unless it's intentionally kept on ready call at the tip-of-thetongue quick recall memory list, which is short lived.

The likelihood of recalling useful, yet borrowed wisdom from the intellectual memory, not founded in experience, is like when an article is listed on Google and the less its subject is referenced, the farther down it slides from the top of Google's recall list until its resource becomes history. The intellectually filed borrowed wisdom drops in the memory recall order if there is no history of real-life application of its wise insight for its borrowed wisdom to have earned the heartfelt credibility to be used for generating the on-call intention rating to be added to their deep-seated sensually founded quick recall list file in the center of their brain.

For those who have realized what suffering is and that it has a curable cause and that they can find their way to understand and lessen that cause in this lifetime, a jump-start to help initiate the process of worldview realignment may be in order. This method of realignment is similar to the Mahayana Buddhist technique of intellectually stimulated practiced conditioning through repetition meant to instill a compassionate nature in the user. To use borrowed insightful wisdom on how to better perceive certain sensual stimuli-trigger packages is a way to possibly set up a pattern of recognizing the healthy mental states coming from a different way of focusing awareness using a new set of wholesome thought patterns. Practice brings experience and makes perfect.

Don Miguel Ruiz, a modern-day Toltec shaman, has done much writing on the subject of becoming enlightened about what causes human ignorance and the resulting suffering, and in his book *The Four Agreements*, he has left a spiritual jumpstart of sorts offering insightful guidelines appropriate for adapting to the self-training used in the process of stepping back to silently deliberate and to recognize and stop the reactionary behaviors stemming from faulty prior conditioning.

This frequency of needing to recall and use the intellectually stored and remembered belief system perception patches offered by don Miguel influences a truth seeker to more readily pull these bits of borrowed wisdom from their intellectual storage bins to more rapidly build the experience base for its desired effects to be stored in their deeper sensual memory. It offers an intellectual bridge, helping the individual to step back and better contemplate, to better recognize and regulate their sensation trigger/fleeting emotional reaction process and to not be so quick to thoughtlessly react to sensual cues in such a way that brings their suffering.

Don Miguel makes suggestions on ways for an individual to perceive very common everyday sensation triggers that many individuals have developed miscued reactions to that over time have synthesized into addictive reactions that result in their emotional episodes of suffering. He presents patches for a few of the most prevalent modern-day forms of misguided perception that signal the very common human emotional tailspins that most people spend their present moments wrapped up in to one degree or another.

He suggests how an individual can approach restructuring their misguided perceptions by injecting into their perception process a few personal agreements to achieve a different responding behavior and have less painful results. He offers guidance on how to minimize the suffering that can be caused by how an individual may choose to weigh, consider or mentally process what another person or entity says or does.

He offers four bits of wisdom in his book *The Four Agreements*. These are internal belief system agreements a truth seeker's muffled out free will makes with their ego-managed worldview with the twitchy trigger finger that's so quick to mindlessly react. These agreements will take a truth seeker's hand and help them take the first few steps across the bridge of communication over the primal void of experiential awareness. They're a wonderful jumpstart to developing an experiential awareness of understanding that will fill the user's belief system void in understanding what exists between the cause and effect in the events that occur during reality's flowing process of uninterrupted change.

In the beginning, similar to a religious claim explaining our Source, the purpose of the claims made by don Miguel's four agreements are founded merely in the truth seeker's blind faith in don Miguel's claims' unverified, untested, unexperienced promise. With enough real-life application and buildup of experiential history, the intellectually borrowed perceptions of don Miguel's experiential wisdom that aligns with the relational justice of impermanence will gain the individual's steadfast faith stamp of sensual truth verification.

Don Miguel has pried open mankind's collective ego-managed waking consciousness and picked through its collective mitote/maya. Mankind's mind-set is filled with an array of endless claims. He's identified two of the most prominent situational perceptions that lead to human suffering.

They originate from an individual's early-developed liking/disliking tendencies that have evolved into uncontrolled reactionary responses. To stop and analyze the perceptional makeup of mankind's collective emotional unrest, it's amazing how often the different forms of unrest are rooted in the same miscued understandings of the relational justice that these two perception patches involve.

The early development of the individual's tendency to make these miscued perceptions begins where the free will should stand up and ask "Why?" or shout "Prove It!" when confronted with a relationship concerning anything that they don't understand the nature of the claim being made. Are they going to just slide by on the blind faith that what's happening will adhere to the expectations that support their perception of what this reality apparently is? Do they stand there too uncertain to dig deeper into the intentions coming from the other side or do they just assume something? Have they developed self-justified feelings of self-devaluation to perceive something as being an attack of them personally that they feel to unsure about to mention?

The four agreements summarized:

1. Be impeccable with your word...applies to ethical/ moral self-training.

2. Don't take anything personally...applies to self-training mind control and wisdom.

3. Don't make assumptions...applies to self-training mind control and wisdom.

4. Always do your best...applies to staying focused on self-training mind control and wisdom.

Don Miguel's first agreement is for an individual to be impeccable with what they let come out of their mouth. This is a fundamental part of the Ten Commandments. The intent of this first agreement invokes the same self-training of moral/ethical behavior common to the first three folds of Siddhartha's *Eightfold Pathway to Enlightenment*. This level of self-development also sets the mood for the Buddhist behavioral precepts. It deals with helping to self-train a truth seeker's moral/ethical behavior to quiet their mitote/maya state of general unrest to allow them to tap into their stream of consciousness to self-train mind control to recognize and follow what don Miguel is offering as guidance in his middle two agreements.

When an individual watches what they say, it helps them watch what they do to hurt or shock a loved one in times of heated discussion on topics they don't really understand about themselves. It helps an individual think more about saying something constructive about another person or situation. Like in Siddhartha's first three folds of his eightfold pathway to enlightenment where he self-trains ethical/ moral standards, it allows an individual to maintain a peaceful mental status to allow their further self-development.

More considerate speech can help minimize the mental unrest that can follow the reactionary emotional storms generated from the sensual triggers following poorly chosen words that another individual might take personally or assume some terrible illusionary cause or effect about which is what the second and third agreements to perception substitution involve.

An individual's internal agreement between their free will and ego-managed worldview to not take things personally and not to assume things without investigating them first, represents the same type of wisdom affecting worldview reform achieved through following Siddhartha's guidance on self-training mind control. It tells an individual to slow down their thinking and observe their flow of consciousness and to try out don Miguel's suggested way of perceiving the situation and to stand aware to recognize any reactionary behaviors that just pop up uncontrollably.

It's similar to what a truth seeker does in right concentration. It melds together the needed right effort, right awareness into the right concentration. This process isn't premised in any Midwestern religious format.

By intellectually remembering don Miguel's borrowed wisdom and putting the four agreements into real-time practice, the individual is substituting their miscued way of perceiving situations for the borrowed perceptions drawn from a trusted entity who's kindly sharing their supposed experiential wisdom to be used to consider an alternative way of responding to a real-life situation. It comes from another individual's right understanding of how to better adjust the balance of relational justice realized by their perception of reality that was miscued from internalizing misguided prior conditioning.

When adopting don Miguel's second and third agreements, a truth seeker makes intellectual agreements between their free will and their prevailing ego-managed worldview to adjust their perception of incoming sensual signals in effort to interrupt and replace certain reactionary behavior that causes them to suffer. By following the rational of don Miguel's second and third agreements, they will act on new perceptions that come from using a borrowed understanding of the justice in relational interactions (cause/ effect event or happening) instead of reacting to their old misaligned perception.

The middle two agreements involve not taking things personally and not making assumptions without first performing the due diligence to substantiate any unwarranted assumptions made about questionable situational conclusions. By stepping back and reevaluating the package of sensations and trying out the new perceptions of don Miguel's borrowed wisdom instead of just reacting, as Siddhartha self-trained while learning right effort, awareness, concentration, thinking and right understanding, the individual can experience the lack of suffering from the normal mental dissonance of when a cause and effect don't match up. They can grow accustomed to recognizing the sensation triggers as they come up in future real-time present moments and in repeating the new replacement wholesome perceptions and along with the old perceptions, the associated emotions that kept the individual suffering will subside.

Instead of the individual entertaining thoughts like ruminating over how others might be judging them where they might calculate reasons why they are superior to that person for the sake of defensive security, the individual needs to recognize the futility of this and allow wholesome thought patterns to replace the troubling ones. Their thoughts should be focused on observing the other person and any contributions their productivity is making to make reality's state of ongoing change any better for themselves or for others. This makes for such a great win-win package of potential to walk up to and share with someone to start a productive mutually beneficial conversation.

Any sensation package that affects a feeling of guilt or regret needs to be recognized, considered and with choosing a different way of perceiving the situation, sidestepped. Recognize the coming of thought patterns that spawn the emotional displays of guilt, self-depreciation or deep regret. Perceive them differently. Replace thought patterns reflecting states of anger and resentment with those open to understanding. Eliminating unwholesome thought patterns opens an individual up to the creativity unique to their bundle of talents.

Their old worldview produced fleeting reactions to sensual triggers that represent an internal perceptual misinterpretation of the sensed relational justice that characterizes this cause/effect reality. Adoption of this intellectual perception-substitution helps with self-training one's mind control. They have opportunity to become familiar with what right thinking and right understanding actually feels like in real-time.

They will need to self-train themselves to develop the harmony between their body's physical presence and their mind's awareness of that presence to open the door to self-training the inspired insightful wisdom-enriched understanding of their ignorance of the field of ongoing change they have opened the door to. Hopefully, they'll correlate its significance and open up their intellectual lockbox of religious/spiritual maxims to make available to their free will for experiential verification, if possible.

Don Miguel's last agreement, to keep on trying and to always make the best possible effort echoes Siddhartha's suggestion for self-training the right effort to harness the right awareness to affect harmonious right concentration. Siddhartha suggests identifying the unwholesome thought patterns and to replace them with those that are wholesome. He suggests to then continue using the new wholesome thought patterns and to keep on trying to find new ones for other unwholesome thought patterns to successfully use his plan for the self-training the mind control to realize the ability to self-train wisdom.

After an individual consciously recognizes and understands the impermanent nature of this reality and wakingly realizes that if the actualization of any idea or belief depends on the assumed material permanence that allows human attachment, of any of the factors in its cause/effect relational flow, they will realize that their earlier understanding of that relationship was off track, founded on an illusion that something's nature is for it to not grow older or rot. In seeing this, the nature of their mind is beginning to change.

Maybe because the relational effect of impermanence is so self-evident and in-your-face as uncontrollable change files through real life that people miss wakingly seeing it, it seems that the importance of working within the recognized limits this truth's omnipresence seems to be minimized. People get sloppy in this part of how they think things through and they spend much time, banned to sit and do a time-out for a few hours a day in their resulting state of mused confusion.

If it's something somebody is saying, don't take it personally. Don't assume they mean something they didn't say. Ask them. Not doing so really crimps compassion and allows repeated suffering. Be aware of how this feels and try to keep repeating it is future similar situations.

If equipped with an eye to see and understand the truth about our impermanent reality, a truth seeker's adoption of these different sensation perception options will facilitate them in bridging the gap between self-training their mind and self-training their ability to see the wisdom that will reveal this end of unlocking the pent-up compassion-based state of awareness shadowed by their misperceptions. This is what changes the nature of their mind and their view of the world. This is how they undo their ignorance that allows their suffering.

10

Self-Training Mind Control
is Not an End in Itself

A Paradox in Self-Training Mind Control

For Hoosiers, the prevalent socially recognized stencil of sorts to corral spiritual subjective thinking that dares go beyond Christianity's guidance stopping point at the Ten Commandments moral/ethical standards was left by Siddhartha. He never was, but his followers choose to be called Buddhists.

There are differing interpretations of Siddhartha's intended message in his teachings about the eight folds in the pathway to becoming enlightened about the ignorance that allows human suffering by self-training a wisdom-enriched awareness. These differing interpretations of Siddhartha's intended meaning in his teachings have developed into different schools of thought of what Siddhartha meant in his guidance on self-training mind control and in self-training the wisdom that enlightens about human ignorance.

These differing interpretations center on Siddhartha's intended meaning of right effort and right awareness and how they are intergraded to affect harmonious right concentration and then how an enlightened understanding of human ignorance is eventually realized. The interpretations either affect the training of wisdom-enriched awareness or just result in the truth seeker's hovering in a calming, yet unsatisfied intellectual spin that only temporarily lessens the outer symptoms of inner suffering.

Siddhartha's Intended Message Divided Today

Christianity's OK with its claim to our Source's nature and purpose being experientially unverifiable. It's OK that it only needs to be intellectually satisfying before being internalized.

Believers consider the religious claim and then use their blind faith-backed visions to stitch together what they envision Jesus's intended plan to be. This sets up different Christian faiths (beliefs) and divides Christianity into its many sects.

Even though after Rome's 312 AD subjective edit of which writings were made available to its citizens in its Bible which leaves Christianity more spiritually undefined, the differing interpretations of Siddhartha's intended meaning in his teachings to gaining enlightenment have likewise mutated Buddhism into different sects. Over the years, a major split in the understanding of Siddhartha's intended meaning has formed into Buddhism's Theravada and Mahayana traditions.

These differences in interpretation of Siddhartha's intended meaning on how to reach heavenly enlightenment could be related to the differing levels of spiritual maturity of his followers. Differences in how truth seekers intellectually sketch the details laid out in Siddhartha's intellectual description of his sensual journey, like with Christianity's descriptions of Jesus's journey, will affect different pools of ideas that materialize into the different schools of belief.

Buddhism's Theravada school is the oldest, and its interpretation is taken from the older of the recordings of Siddhartha's teachings that are written in ancient Pali. The recordings used by the Mahayana tradition were written in ancient Sanskrit. The Pali recordings were not recorded until the passing of six hundred years after Siddhartha's death.

Of the many languages that have been involved in Bible translations, there were no written accounts found in Jesus's native Aramaic tongue. Like so, none of Buddhism's ancient recordings were found written in Siddhartha's native tongue. This has an effect on human understanding.

All of the accounts when finally recorded, hundreds of years later, were subject to the inherent problems of passing along intended meanings intellectually through the oral tradition as well as any passed along misinterpretations of Siddhartha's sutras in the first place by the individual who provided the accounts... the same human-enduced errors that plagued the first writings of the books of the Bible.

Different twists in Siddhartha's intended meaning could be rooted in the translations between languages. These are just a few more obvious reasons for the difference in the two traditions' differing interpretations of Siddhartha's original intended meaning.

It's not to say there is only one way to look at things, but it's true that there's only one network of relational wisdom to self-train that fits this cause/effect reality no matter what the name of the source may be that may claim its creation and ownership.

The two main Buddhist schools recognize no major difference in what Siddhartha teaches about waking up to become a truth seeker and realizing the problem has a living cause as specified in the first two noble truths in his teachings written in *The Four Noble Truths*. In the third and fourth truths of *The Four Noble Truths*, finding the cause and enlightenment from ignorance of the nature of impermanence, the difference in the interpretation of his intended message could lie in identifying specifically what the sought-after freedom is from...freedom from suffering or freedom from the ignorance that causes suffering...looking back or plotting forward.

The effects of these varying interpretations bleed down to affect the understanding of each of the contributing folds in Siddhartha's teachings of the way to enlightenment revealed in his *Eightfold Pathway to Enlightenment* that describes how he completed his pathway to enlightened self-awareness.

Buddhist Perceptions of Reaching the Plateau of Self-Understanding

The harmonious integration of a truth seeker's right effort with their right awareness will make possible their right concentration. In attempting right concentration, humility-primed harmony is the ticket to the plateau of self-understanding. Mahayana and Theravada Buddhism have different understandings on how to self-train the mind control and wisdom enrichment as taught in Siddhartha's *Eightfold Pathway to Enlightenment*.

Being on the plateau of self-understanding quiets the shouting from the 1,000 voice mitote/maya that tries to interrupt the sustained focus needed in the process of self-examination. The mitote/maya mental state streams a changing variety of purposes across the truth seeker's mental attention screen that are unwholesome to sustaining focus into the presence of the coming and going bits of energy during times of self-analysis. They will have interrupted thinking throughout their day at any other time they might try to focus on anything like trying to read a good novel.

Prolonged deliberation during right concentration allows a truth seeker to realize inspired insightful wisdom while absorbed into their internal cause/effect reality. They sensually witness the coming and going, give and take, cause/effect sensual essence of the change from one present moment to the next. Self-training a wisdom-enriched experiential understanding through self-analysis will undo the ignorance about the impermanent nature of reality and support liberation from its ignorance and the suffering it sponsors.

Buddhism's Theravada interpretation of Siddhartha's guidance offered in his *Eightfold Pathway to Enlightenment* in realizing the forth noble truth of finding the way to self-knowledge, points the truth seeker's concentration directly into the internal world of sensuality to catch our Source red-handed fulfilling its promise. This process directly challenges the uncertainties of the truth seeker's fundamental ignorance of the ways of impermanence.

Directing a truth seeker to wakingly experience the realtime present moment essence of the manifestation of life, will put them on the plateau of self-understanding to allow their inspired right thinking to insightfully learn how to become savvy to the natural laws of their state of being. This process allows them to end the foolishness of allowing fleeting reactions to signal their attachment to their imprinted cravings and aversions that characterize the addictions that control and neuter their current and future present moments of the human compassion that's inherently wired into the human condition.

With patience they will learn to visualize and purposefully release the potential stored in the genius of their unique special talents. The individual is learning what the enemy (the ignorance) is all about to understand the truth it conceals.

Mahayana Buddhism also believes the answer longed for by the human condition is found on the inside…they're just not sure where and exactly how to secure the mind/ body harmony to set up the hunt. The traditions vary in how they self-train the mind control needed to realize self-awareness. The focus of their right concentration remains locked into the intellectually obtained and processed wisdom of the cognitive world an individual intellectually knows the truth of, not from a world they feel the truth in.

After a truth seeker initially uses right thinking and right understanding to intellectually realize the existence of the problem of present moment suffering to satisfy the first noble truth, the Mahayana outlook fails to include the right thinking and right understanding back into Siddhartha's sequential order of self-trainings after establishing the mind control that he outlines in his eightfold pathway to enlightenment. It's untethered while offering no reference to any sort of protocol for how to generate the mind/body harmony for a sustained focus through their looking glass of right concentration into their theater of change to really listen to how the material self explains the presence of its essence.

With the Theravada interpretation, right thinking and right understanding are used again to satisfy the forth noble truth of finding the way to enlightenment where self-training is used to allow a truth seeker's wisdom enrichment.

Attention needs to be given to the delicate task of self-training the experiential wisdom to unlock the doors to one's primal link to allow the insightful right understanding in the deeper regions of their consciousness to rise to enlighten their waking conscious with the awareness and sensual understanding of the impermanence that defines its reality.

When satisfying Siddhartha's first noble truth on finding the pathway to enlightened awareness, right thinking and right understanding are used to intellectually realize the sensual problem that exists. When using right thinking and right understanding to satisfy the forth noble truth as with the Theravadists, newly inspired thought patterns with sensual roots inspire the insightful development of a wisdom-enriched waking understanding of the problem's cause and solution.

As a result of not using right thinking and right understanding to self-train the mind control necessary to extract wisdom, the Mahayana progression wanders through Siddhartha's eight folds with no real end in sight. The right thinking's not effectively set up to allow it to reach the plateau of right understanding where harmonious body/mind unity enters into right concentration that's tuned-into the sensual body language of our Source to humbly witness the story of life's manifestation...the sensual display of reality in a world one feels.

The Mahayana School doesn't prioritize self-training the sensual witnessing of the manifestation of ongoing change to lay the groundwork for understanding how to undo their ignorance of the ways of our Source's living omnipresent impermanent nature. During their attempted mind/body analysis, their focused attention can be directed at imaginative mental renditions like of a religious statue. Their effort of mentally picturing the statue as a permanent/continual object defeats their purpose by using an effort that breaks the rule that they're trying to better understand.

The Mahayana belief strategy resets or ignores Siddhartha's sequential order for undertaking the three self-trainings that guide a truth seeker to self-training the wisdom that defines their enlightenment. It keeps their search in the same ineffectual unending circular tailspin that's now became a part of the ritual that's been passed along for millennia.

Mahayana and Therevada Buddhist Teachers

The written teachings of two of today's exalted and honorable teachers of Buddhism, Mr. Thich Nhat Hanh, who teaches from the Mahayana school of thought, and Mr. S. N. Goenka, who teaches the Theravada tradition (Doctrine of the Elders), were closely considered and compared.

Mr. Thich Nhat Hanh is a world-renowned Vietnamese Buddhist monk. He has authored many books and offers guidance to several not-for-profit monastic communities around the world. Martin Luther King Jr. nominated him for the Noble Peace Prize back in the '60s. He is a student and teacher of the Mahayana Buddhist tradition.

Mr. S. N. Goenka is an Indian spiritualist teacher who teaches dharma worldwide...the natural law of liberation. He is not a monk, but a layman with family and a career history. He's a leading teacher of the Vipassana meditation technique of the Theravada school. He has not-for-profit programs set up worldwide to teach the method of attempting right concentration centered on sensual awareness.

Mr. Goenka has been authorized to teach the Theravada method. This process of mind/body analysis has been handed down through a progression of teachers that's said to reach clear back and touch Mr. Siddhartha Gautama himself.

The living-person-to-living-person passed-along style of attempting to maintain or keep alive a personalized transparent nature for the Theravada teaching subject matter is comparable to why the position of the Dalai Lama was created.

The Dalai Lama position was created as the best way to pass along the original intended meaning of the teachings of Atisha who reintroduced to Tibet the Mahayana Buddhist tradition at the end of the first millennia. Atisha's message is his interpretation of the 1,500-year-old incarnation of Siddhartha's original intended meaning in describing how he went from scratch, suffering, to a self-trained, wisdom-enriched enlightened understanding of his ignorance about our Source's ephemeral nature and intended purpose to initiate ongoing change.

Right Thinking and Right Understanding Used to First Recognize Suffering and Again Later to Understand Solution

Both Buddhist traditions teach Siddhartha's first noble truth that it is first necessary for an individual to realize that their big complaint with the status quo rests in the amount of time and energy wasted suffering through present moment unrest and dissatisfactions. A truth seeker must first have realized this on an intellectual level using the right thinking and the right understanding of what the problem is.

The Mahayana Buddhists believe this initial step of using the folds of right thinking and right understanding fulfills their functional purpose in the eightfold pathway. The Theravada Buddhists think right thinking and right understanding are again used in self-training wisdom in the seventh and eighth folds to reaching enlightenment. Theravada Buddhists also believe that the right thinking and right understanding are initially needed to intellectually realize the existence of the sensual problem, but are then again later needed to selftrain inspired right thinking from right concentration into the right wisdom-enriched waking understanding of this sensual reality. The first use satisfies an intellectual goal while the right thinking and right understanding fulfill a sensual goal when later used.

The Mahayana Buddhist interpretation of Siddhartha's intended message doesn't recognize the sequential inclusion of right thinking and right understanding after self-training the mind control as being the key to an enlightened understanding of their ignorance. They see Siddhartha's eightfold pathway as beginning with right thinking and right understanding, not to be used again after self-training the mind control to develop the right concentration to generate the right thinking that inspires an insightful wisdom-enriched understanding.

If a truth seeker wants to follow in the path to uncover the truth that lies inside that Siddhartha describes that worked for him, they need to self-train a peaceful frame of mind so they can then self-train the ability to control the direction of the thoughts generated in the mind. This selftrained mind control is then used to realize self-discovery and become enlightened about what makes the ephemeral reality that the physical self is a part of, work. Without using right thinking and right understanding to delve into the relational justice of this reality, a truth seeker could not arrive at the insights of enlightenment.

The Theravada school interprets Siddhartha's message to say that for a truth seeker to realize the suffering problem exists, they must use the right thinking and right understanding initially. After this the truth seeker discovers the second and third noble truths to self-train their moral ethical appreciation. Then, after the self-training of the mind control taught in next three folds, the right thinking and right understanding, seventh and eighth folds, sequentially follow. After self-training mind control, they incubate their sustained right concentration in self-discovery. Then the right thinking, used again, inspires the sudden insightful understandings that yield a wisdom-enriched enlightened sensual understanding of the ways of this impermanent reality. This allows the return of compassion, joy, and happiness as suffering subsides. Self-training wisdom-enriched awareness stifles the sensory synapse of suffering's interwoven network.

This second use is different than only using them to intellectually arouse interest in the search for the truth. The Theravada Buddhists teach that these last two folds in Siddhartha's pathway to enlightenment are used to self-train the truth seeker to derive the wisdom to understand and undo their ignorance that causes their suffering.

In Mahacattarisaka Sutta MN117, Siddhartha teaches of the stages in the self-training process that stretches from suffering to becoming enlightened about the cause of that suffering. Relative to the eightfold pathway, it's noted how that from right understanding (of the problem of suffering) comes the right thought (understanding suffering's cause). Then, from the right thought comes right speech and from that comes right action. From the right action comes having the right occupation and with this the self-training of moral/ethical appreciation is complete. It's time to self-train mind control.

Next, from right occupation comes right effort, and from right effort follows right awareness. Self-training the ability to sustain a harmonious focus of these two steps produces the right concentration, and with this the truth seeker is suited to self-train their wisdom.

Now, self-training a wisdom-rich enlightened understanding of the cause of suffering requires the sensual application of right thinking and right understanding. The sutta says that out of the self-trained right concentration comes wisdom and from the wisdom comes the right understanding. Mr. Hahn verifies that Siddhartha presented the eight-fold path to enlightenment in his first and last sutras in the following order: ...right view, right thinking, right speech, right action, right livelihood, right diligence, right mindfulness and right concentration.[13]

The Mahayana school interprets Siddhartha's intended message to be to only use the last two folds for bringing conscious awareness of present moment suffering to the attention of the truth seeker in fulfilling the first noble truth.

After self-training moral/ethical boundaries, self-training the mind control for right concentration, the guidance on how to self-train the wisdom that leads to liberation is missing in the Mahayana Buddhist tradition. By not having an eye focused on self-training the humility spawned mind/body harmony to experientially self-train wisdom, the truth seeker's right view (right thinking) and right thinking (right understanding) that Siddhartha described in his eightfold pathway to enlightenment remain chained to the tree of intellectual knowledge, blind to an enlightened self-awareness.

An Indistinct Approach to Self-Train Wisdom

For a truth seeker to self-train their own insightful self-awareness to undo their waking present moment ignorance of our Source's nature and intended purpose to initiate ongoing change, they must be in control of their mind enough to regulate where their thoughts are directed and what to anticipate finding when their focus is there long enough to see anything. With no intellectual eye self-trained for detecting the sensually registered experiential truth they are looking for, a truth seeker will not find it.

Mr. Hahn teaches to be cautious with our perceptions of what happens inside and outside of us. It's left undefined here in his Mahayana view about where to direct the mind to go to actually witness what it is that can undo human ignorance. He teaches that right view (right thinking) is not part of any path. Right concentration is not directly targeted at training wisdom.

The Theravada interpretation advocates that the path to enlightenment moves sequentially from one level of self-training to the next. Each fold's satisfaction is inclusively dependent on the preceding folds' development and realization. As interpreted in Siddhartha's sequential eightfold path to enlightenment the Theravada Buddhist tradition teaches that it's the right view (thinking) about the focused concentration into life's manifestation that inspires insightful right thinking (understanding) to self-train an individual's wisdom-enriched enlightened understanding. It's necessary to use right thinking and right understanding not only to intellectually see the problem...it must later be approached sensually to understand how to eradicate it.

In not recognizing the need to re-include right view (right understanding) again after satisfying the first noble truth of identifying suffering to then satisfy Siddhartha's forth noble truth to self-train the wisdom of enlightenment like with the Theravada tradition, Mr. Hahn's Mahayana teaching makes the claim that enlightenment follows one of the many Mahayana forms of right concentration.

There's no further Mahayana protocol aimed toward self-training the wisdom of enlightenment.

Mr. Hahn says:

> Our happiness and the happiness of those around us depend on our degree of right view (right thinking), touching reality deeply—knowing what is going on inside and outside of ourselves—is the way to liberate ourselves from the suffering that is caused by wrong perceptions. Right view (right thinking) is not an ideology, a system, or even a path. It is the insight we have into the reality of life, a living insight that fills us with understanding, peace, and love.[14]

Mr. Hahn adds:

> Right View (right thinking) cannot be described. We can only point in the correct direction. Right view (right thinking) cannot be transmitted by a teacher. A teacher can help us identify the seed of right view (right thinking) that is already in our garden, and help us have the confidence to practice, to entrust that seed to the soil of our daily life. But we are the gardener.[15]

Right view (right thinking) used synonymously with what the Theravada interpretation refers to as the first of two folds (seventh fold of eight) used in training wisdom is described by Mr. Hahn as a "living insight" that somehow fills us with the understanding, peace, and love that characterizes enlightened awareness. Theravada teaching describes how to enter into the arena of present moment life manifestation and where to place sustained concentration and what to look for to experientially learn the universal answer. Having mind/body's harmonious focus actively present where change itself manifests to experience its truth is what inspires the right thinking (seventh fold) to generate an insightful right understanding (eighth fold) is how wisdom is self-trained.

More than being a living insight as described by Mr. Hahn, self-trained wisdom really comes from insights into what's living to derive the self-understanding that bestows enlightenment about this reality's demonstrated impermanence to understand the cause of the fundamental or primal ignorance and in so doing allow the suffering caused by that ignorance to dissipate. It's only through one's wisdom-enriched right understanding of the relational interplay among the coming and going sensations apparent in our Source's sensual message that their once fear-shocked belief system fills with peace and love.

With Mr. Hahn's Mahayana interpretation, right view's (right thinking's) inclusion in the eightfold path has been sterilized of its association with training an individual's experiential wisdom and left to wander between the many different forms of concentration listed by Mahayana Buddhists. Siddhartha's intended meaning in self-training one's wisdom is being interpreted to be generalized thoughts that sound good and are true.

Yet the Mahayana interpretation uses words in such a politically safe way that their true focused meaning is lost and unfocused in the expanse of their spoken generality. Right view's relevance has been diluted and the description of its functional purpose hovers undiscovered. It's indiscriminate utility floats around in the circles of intellectual ponderment and cliché, unselectively bounding in and out of and complementing the other seven folds.

In the Mahayana teaching that right concentration is the final fold of the eightfold path to enlightenment, Mr. Hahn's interpretation describes the right view (right thinking) as being synonymous with an indescribable enlightenment. This assumed status creates the same sort of experiential-feeling void in the belief system anatomy as when taking the leap of blind faith by believing an unverifiable religious claim explaining the nature and intended purpose of our Source. Christianity's claim to suffering relief and the Mahayana interpretation miss having the experiential association that links the understood meaning from the individual's deeper egofree consciousness that's wise to their ever-changing nature to their waking conscious awareness.

The Mahayana interpretation fails to acknowledge that training the wisdom through right thinking (right understanding) is what decodes the tree of wisdom to enrich one's developing awareness with the understanding of the real-life truth of change that pushes a cause into becoming its effect. Right thinking inspires the insightful right understanding to derive the relational wisdom that explains the justice of what happens between the actual coming and going occurrence of this ongoing change.

It's true that a truth seeker has to wakingly self-train and realize the wisdom themselves. A requirement in the process of gaining self-awareness is that they personally realize the living truth of every step of Siddhartha's eightfold process that trains moral/ethical behavior to allow a calm mind to develop the concentrated control to inspire the right thinking for an insightful understanding capable of the wise applications of the detected truths to other of life's cause/ effect situations.

This Mahayana interpretation of Mr. Gautama's intended meaning is missing the re-inclusion of the right thinking and right understanding folds. It separates from the pathway by not self-training the mind control to realize the mind/body harmony that sets up the process to affect the need to re-include the right thinking and right understanding where the truth seeker self-trains their wisdom-enriched self-awareness.

The Mahayana idea of the right effort and right awareness needed to generate a harmonious right concentration is diffused into a kaleidoscope of alternative choices. Mind/ body harmony isn't a priority. A successful truth seeker humbly invokes the mental attention characterized by Sandbox Etiquette Guideline Number 1 with their mental attention focused on the sensual ports of their physical body patiently waiting to feel the flame of our Source's claim of ongoing change (impermanence) in any truth seeker's experiential sensual flesh minefield of sensitivity.

Compassion...From the Head or from the Heart?

Can a compassionate frame of mind be intellectually instilled or is it rooted in an understanding cultured in the heart? Can compassion be cognitively self-trained using the same habit energy development that morphs into the fleeting reactions of addiction? Can it be honed from association? Is there such a thing as intellectually cultivated compassion?

Is it realistic to think an individual could actually use a portion of their intellectual energy that would be normally used for tending to present moment concerns, instead as a mental bookmark for maintaining an alerted watch for situations where the use of compassion seems appropriate? Maybe so, but this would be done in hopes of gradually building a deeply felt appreciation for an intellectually understood concept of what compassion should be as described by another source? Can it be practiced frequently enough before its intellectual motivation loses its present moment priority to fade to where it's instant recall is missing when needed in making a split moment decision?

True compassion is thought to come from heart-sourced altruistic intentions. Can having the selfless presence that characterizes an altruistic presence be instilled intellectually? Isn't this like sensually recognizing a flame as being a flame when never having encountered one and having only heard a verbal description of what the heat of a flame feels like?

In effort to develop what they feel is an altruistic intention, Tibetan Buddhism (Mahayana school) suggests a self-taming method based in imagined empathy and repetition to train the mind into thinking in a compassionate way. This practiced behavior should eventually take root and become normal behavior with an altruistic nature.

In teaching how to cultivate an altruistic worldview they offer three conditionings an individual is to intellectually instruct themselves to choose from to best adapt while mentally repeating to themselves when they arise. Do they become attached/dependent on using those learned phrases? Is it good to have their present moment intentions focused in their intellectual order instead of being sensually aware to better allow intrinsically adapting to a new upcoming situation?

Tibetan Buddhism suggests that an individual interested in spawning compassion through rote training can, for one thing, see others as being their mother and focus on past kindness they've received. Or, they can practice great empathy and recognize that the other person too suffers from being consumed in a mitote/maya state and also suffers from the attachment resulting from ignorance and feel that they too should find freedom from this suffering. Thirdly, they suggest that an individual can reflect on how we all depend on each other and our belief systems are not naturally designed to emit the disturbing emotions an individual may be observing. They realize that the other individual too can benefit from the antidote to the primal/fundamental ignorance that all seek. Hence, empathy sparks compassion.

Is this really true compassion? Does it lack true altruism? Can someone really keep their conscious thinking continually preoccupied with achieving this goal? Are these truly altruistic intentions originating from a mind with a nature free of attachments? Is using these mind tricks as effective as using duct tape to quiet the mouths of the 1,000 shouting mitote/maya voices? Is there a difference?

Isn't this really an attempt at using force-cultured habit energy to transform an intellectually sketched notion of what compassionate behavior is into a perception that assumes altruism as the individual's present moment factory setting with the fleeting nature of an addiction? At what degree of wisdom-enriched awareness is it that an individual begins to act out of altruistic intentions?

Mixed Versus Sequencial Fold Order When Walking Down the Straight and Narrow Leading to Enlightenment?

It helps a truth seeker to generate the day-to-day motivation to spend their time trying to make spiritual progress if they have an end level in mind to target. If it's an end attainable in this lifetime, there will someday be no need to try to enrich their awareness with more wisdom.

Having an end theme to reference helps the individual see the mounting contribution as each step is completed. It threads the interconnection and cohesion that's passed on from one individual step in the process to the next...like the sequence involved in tying a shoelace or manufacturing a car.

On the pathway to enlightenment, it's after a truth seeker has reined in their inappropriate moral/ethical behavior that they might realize their mental state sufficiently calmed down and less likely to be bothered or preoccupied with disturbing thoughts in the wake of toxic behavior. They're then capable of self-training their mind control. This is the point in self-training an enlightened understanding of this reality's process of ongoing change at which the Mahayana and Theravada interpretations of Siddhartha's intended meaning in his teachings parts ways. Both Buddhist strains have paid common mind to the first three folds of Siddhartha's eightfold pathway to enlightenment that teaches self-training moral/ethical behavior...right action, right speech, and right livelihood.

To help show how Siddhartha's first self-training step is a common denominator shared between different religious/spiritual groups of truth seekers worldwide in the human pathway to enlightenment from humankind's primal ignorance, moral/ethical self-training is also the first step outlined in the process of gaining self-awareness found in the Toltec shaman don Miguel Ruiz's book *The Four Agreements*. It's a short modern-day, Cliffs Notes version of Siddhartha's guidance to self-training moral/ethical behavioral standards he writes how it's crucial to maintain impeccable speech.

At this point of self-training mind control, the Mahayana interpretation of Siddhartha's intended meaning diffuses into several directions. Their view ricochets between the eight tenants of the eightfold pathway...showing how the meaning of each fold is intertwined with the others.

The Mahayana interpretation emphasizes a revolving interdependent relationship between the eight folds of the pathway to enlightenment. It's a circular pathway, with no real end. It's not really one that begins at suffering and ends at enlightenment.

The Theravada interpretation proceeds forward from suffering to enlightenment. One level of self-training increases a truth seeker's spiritual maturity capacity to handle taking the next step to finally directing their right concentration directly into the arena of living change where they self-train the enriched wisdom to realize their joy and happiness and liberation from suffering.

It should be said that there may be more that one approach to right concentration, but it's true that there is only one coming and going presence for the right concentration to tune into. It has the same sensual presence in every human. It's the only message media available that our Source can use for broadcasting its exhibition that demonstrates its nature and intended purpose and inspire the insightful understanding of the cause of the human ignorance about all this that allows human joy, happiness and compassion to be overshadowed with human suffering.

The primal pathway to self-training a wisdom-enriched awareness of the ways of our Source's impermanence is sequential in nature. It's a linear path to seasoned spiritual maturity. It starts with a truth seeker's insipient suffering and ends where they understand and change the nature of their minds and have become enlightened about their ignorance concerning the ways of an impermanent reality. There's a cumulative push of focus that builds from calming one's mitote/maya mental state to finally self-training the wisdom to see the light.

The path is straight and narrow. Some have successfully traveled it and of those a few have left posted in various accounts the intellectually realized trail markers that pointed them down their experiential sensual pathway. This is a seemingly generic pathway suited for the human condition. Mr. Hahn of the Mahayana tradition writes how the eight folds of Siddhartha's *Eightfold Pathway To Enlightenment* are all interconnected on more of a give-and-take, fair exchange basis minimizing the importance of the sequential order Siddhartha gave to the process of self-discovery that worked for him. The Mahayana tradition approach cuts short the significance of the observed sequence in the order of the self-trained spiritual development.

After attempting to self-train mind control Mr. Hahn advises individuals to use their intelligence to apply the eightfold path to their lives. Experiential association is not prioritized as being what should be used to light a truth seeker's path of discovery down their road to enlightenment.

> Arya ashtangika marga ("a noble path of eight limbs") suggests the interbeing nature of these eight elements of the path. Each limb contains all the other seven. Please use your intelligence to apply the elements of the Noble eightfold Path in your daily life.[16]

The Mahayana tradition teaches that right concentration is the final phase of Siddhartha's *Noble Eightfold Path to Enlightenment*. This leaves the impression that a truth seeker's attempted right concentration is an end in itself and not that training right concentration is what prepares the truth seeker to personally have the inspired right thinking for the insightful understanding to self-train the wisdom-enriched awareness for their liberation.

In the Mahayana approach, the spiritual pathway for revealing the truth resident in the truth seeker's deeper consciousness to their waking consciousness is unchartered as compared to the Theravada approach and left to the truth seeker's intelligent application. It's as if it just happens, relatively unaddressed and not necessarily targeted.

Without having the end goal in mind of developing a wisdom-enriched self-awareness while using a self-training method of experiential discovery, a truth seeker's interpretation of the linking stages of development will not necessarily build progressively one on the other in a way to address an end of understanding the cause/effect ways of an impermanent reality. The truth seeker's conscious intention can reverberate in a mental haze that muddles the spiritual signposts along the Mahayana pathway to enlightenment.

This is a difference between the two main strands of Buddhism. Many Mahayana truth seekers lack a purpose alerted to reaching the end goal of freeing up from a subtle level of their deeper consciousness, their enlightened understanding of the unbridled change they don't understand.

Without focusing forward on self-training the harmonious mind/body right physical effort to strike the harmony with the right mental awareness to sustain the right concentration in anticipation of seeing what the essence of impermanence actually feels like in the new and upcoming present moment, the living nature of the next passing present moment will go by undetected. The truth seeker's mind will be occupied in thoughts elsewhere that will not be focused into the quiet deliberation needed for instilling the inspired right thinking to allow gaining insight from our Source's sensually spelled out message (sign from above) that demonstrates its impermanence will occur but will slide by unnoticed.

A Theravada student would address Siddhartha's final noble truth of using their due diligence to reach self-awareness by following the eight folds of Siddhartha's described pathway to enlightenment using the sequence Siddhartha suggested.

After self-training their moral/ethical standards, they would then self-train their mind control by learning how to sustain their harmonious right concentration focused into the essence of their flesh. They would then better appreciate the details of what's needed to have the right thinking to self-train their wisdom in the justice of the relationships that outline the cause/effect impermanence of this reality.

If used correctly, their right thinking could inspire the insightful right understanding that encompasses a wisdom-enriched self-awareness. These are the spiritual understandings that Siddhartha, Jesus and anyone else who's made the journey learned to appreciate. It's through the introduction of their self-developed approach to self-training their wisdom and liberation through the right thinking to find the inspiration for their insightful right understanding of our Source's nature and intended purpose. At this level of spiritual maturity, they affect the training of their wisdom to understand and undo their ignorance of this reality that creates the mental unrest that consumes their present moment. The Theravada school of thought believes that having a sound ethical/moral base and developing the ability to control and direct mental activity are important in the process of developing a wisdom-enriched understanding of the subject of human ignorance. Mental agitation is minimized, and the mind is honed into an effective device to enter into the flesh arena of ongoing change to gain the self-knowledge to eliminate all the conditioned ignorance.

At this point in Siddhartha's pathway to enlightenment after right thinking and right understanding had been initially used to intellectually realize the problem addressed in the first noble truth that suffering's here and that it's the underlying cause of present moment unrest, that right thinking and right understanding are used again to solve the problem. This step along the pathway requires a more spiritually mature mind capable of sustaining a focused awareness that could not be realized or addressed with the mental mess present when identifying the initial problem.

After using their right thinking and right understanding to gain sight of the problem as described by the first noble truth, the truth seeker experientially discovers spiritual signposts along the pathway to the solution for the problem of suffering. They need to think and understand again.

It's now time to reuse their right thinking and right understanding again to solve the problem. This allows developing their inspired insightful wisdom to enrich their waking awareness of relational nature of the truth of change to undo their ignorance of it and relieve its unpleasant symptoms.

The Theravada school of thought realizes that after the right thinking and right understanding have been used to gain an intellectual understanding of the goal to eliminate their suffering, the two folds need to be reused to enable the sensual right understanding to free them from the clutches of their conditioned ignorance. They will be able to see through or conquer their self-ego as Lau Tzu observed several millennia ago.

Walking uninterrupted down the sequential path to enlightenment would put the steps of right thinking and right understanding exactly where they also are needed...at the end of the eightfold path, to train a truth seeker to derive the wisdom. Through the three self-trainings of Siddhartha's eightfold pathway to enlightenment a truth seeker verifies and converts the intellectually understood claim to finding liberation from the cause of suffering to an experientially gained sensually verified right understanding of the truth.

With the right physical effort blended in harmony with the right mental awareness, the truth seeker directs their right concentration to open up the effective internal communication media, their primal link, to pick up, listen to and eventually decode the wisdom to understand the inspiring sensual messages they sense from within. Addressing this stage of development has its time and place while proceeding toward enlightenment. The personal advancement toward gaining this self-awareness must transpire one step at a time while reflecting the structural support from the self-trainings already addressed.

If a safe's tumblers don't fall in sequential succession, the tumbler-falling process will fail to unlock and open the safe to expose the riches stored inside.

Right Awareness Incohesively Unfocused

Mr. Hahn's Mahayana Buddhist interpretation of Siddhartha's intended meaning in his eightfold pathway to enlightenment lacks cohesion. There's no design to guide a truth seeker to first get their bearing on their moral/ethical conduct to find the mental peace to self-train the mind control to allow directing their body's effort and mind's awareness to unite in harmony to sustain a focused right concentration into the sensual porthole of their physical body to sensually witness the world of feeling to allow the inspired thinking to find the insightful wisdom to be enlightened about what causes their separation from happiness and joy.

Mr. Hahn asserts that the purpose of right mindfulness (right awareness) is to maintain the moral/ethical behavior guidelines of the Buddhist precepts. It's true that sufficient ethical/moral standards must become a maintained standard of behavior to keep a clear head to go on to self-train the mind control needed for the right concentration. However, even if the Mahayana tradition did teach of self-training harmony between right effort and right awareness in a way that focused harmonious concentration into the essence of their flesh, to attempt doing this while looking back on trying to maintain right moral/ethical behavior doesn't represent the forward tilted purpose of intent that right concentration must have to realize the harmony to prepare the truth seeker to self-train their wisdom to reach enlightenment. They make no real progress down the sequential pathway.

Besides, should the self-trained moral/ethical behavioral standard have been violated and mental unrest increased as a result, it would not be possible to advance to self-training mind control anyway. Self-training a disturbed mind into self-training the sustained mind control of right concentration would not be possible. Even so, should the moral/ethical behavior be maintained, what does a truth seeker do to advance if there is no forward sighted directive to follow?

Mr. Hahn teaches that right mindfulness (awareness) is simply being true to whatever set of commandments a truth seeker is following to achieve an adequate level of moral/ ethical behavior. Mr. Hahn teaches that:

> Right Mindfulness is the energy that brings us back to the present moment. To cultivate mindfulness in ourselves is to cultivate the Buddha within, to cultivate the Holy Spirit.[17]

These words sound good and who dares to deny them. But, they are giving too inflated and diffused of a meaning here to "right mindfulness" (synonymous with right awareness) and "cultivating the Buddha within" to attach any relevant understanding or action-based purpose to. It's true that right mindfulness (awareness) must be focused into the present moment, but it must further instruct as to where to sustain concentration and what one's mind should be focused on...looking for. Guidance needs to be given on what a truth seeker's harmonious mind/body concentration should be anticipating within the upcoming present moment while searching for the feeling that's suspended in the uncontrollable change that carries one causing present moment into its effect in the next.

Our Source is putting its flame under the finger of the individual. With the right concentration to inspire their right thinking to let sensually surface from a subtle level of their deeper consciousness up their primal link to inspire the right

thinking for the insightful right understanding in their waking conscious awareness to recognize what "hot" truly means to them in better-than-intellectual terms.
The way down the pathway to the end of self-enlightenment is so difficult that just
a few humans have been able to figure it out. The better described the sequential
flow of this process is, the better.

Conventional Attempts at Right Concentration Miss Target

There're quite a variety of styles of concentration with differing intended purposes...from modern-day relaxation techniques to ancient religious rituals. They
may share the same purposed intention of relieving some form of suffering, yet
still give their methods differing names and consider them from a different point
of view. For a truth seeker to realize what effective right effort and right awareness
really are and how to find relief from their present moment unrest they need to put
their mind and body on a harmonious present moment platform and this requires
a good teacher. It's a straight and narrow path.

Without understanding what heavenly enlightenment is and not having what
the pathway to heavenly enlightenment is made clear, the forward momentum of
a truth seeker's spiritual progression to reach wisdom-enriched enlightenment can
easily become stuck. This leaves the individual with nothing to do but pillage their
present moment looking under new toys and ideas to maybe catch a glimpse of the
answer to what's missing from their real-time human experience when they really
don't even know what they're looking to find or what the right question is to ask.

As long as what should be right thinking is actively sidetracked into some
derivative of wrong effort, from miscued focus resulting from their ignorance that
causes their present moment suffering, no progress will be made. This could be
when what's thought to be the right effort is actually the wrong effort to sustain
the right awareness. The concentration fades. The mental awareness drifts.

The ever-present but elusive truth inspiring present moment essence of life's
manifestation continues on undetected. With misdirected right effort and right
awareness, even though the coming and going sensations that through dispassionate deliberation can inspire the right thinking to recognize the insightful right
understanding to gain waking awareness of the wisdom that enriches their awareness of the truth of ongoing change will be occurring, the truth seeker will just
not be aware of it.

They will not be able to train their wisdom to the beat of the noted relationships in the pool of life-in-progress between the coming and going physical sensations. They will have to read accounts that parrot the wisdom they experientially
missed out on in books that can only intellectually describe the same experiential
wisdom. And because it's only stored in the intellectual memory, the accepted
logic of its intellectually instilled wisdom will soon fade. They have a void-of-feel-

ing spot in their belief system, around which they will, one way or another, fashion their worldview.

There are the Mahayana Buddhists that direct their right awareness to an imagined object such as the statue of some religious figure. Their internalized Buddhist claim has purpose to self-train mind control, yet their right concentration will not be directed into the deepest of wells where it needs to be to witness and contemplate the sensual signal of their body's coming and going sensations to inspire the insightful wisdom to undo their related ignorance. This leaves the truth seeker idling in attempted right concentration focused on an imagined object that doesn't actually exist while ignoring the fact that nothing stands still.

Doesn't the suggested means of concentration fail to consider the foolishness in searching for self-knowledge that reflects ongoing change with a separate mental agenda attempting to remain focused into the illusionary nonexistent life continuity that they want to become aware doesn't exist? This leaves them unable to self-train the right thinking that inspires the right understanding of the insightful wisdom that would lead them to the waking awareness of that truth.

Even though they might experience temporary stress relief from a seemingly deep state of relaxed transcendental trance or bliss, without addressing the unwholesome thought patterns, the suffering will later arise again. This thoughtology demonstrates, reinforces, and perpetuates the ignorance that allows it.

They will not have self-trained their minds to deliberate and to recognize the in-body signals and thought patterns brought on due to their inability to have detected the misguided nature of the unverified claims of faulty prior conditioning that's resulted in the reappearances of their fleeting reactionary behaviors... addictions. They'll never understand the nature of ongoing change if they've never personally been there to smell the air or squeeze the Charmin.

When considering different ways of gathering the inspirational insightful understanding of this reality's impermanence, Siddhartha taught that gaining the insights to wisdom enrichment was their common goal. He taught that developing the mind control was for this purpose. The purpose of training the mind control to meditate is not to experience some sort of blissful trance or elated high.

These states can be relaxing and calming to an individual, but any insightful realizations an individual might have in these states would be of the serendipitous type and not from an intention of gaining a direct understanding of impermanence.

From the vast assortment of modern-day ways to find mind and body relaxation, there are few that are directed at an end of gaining an enlightened understanding of this reality. Most of these processes fall short of inspiring thoughts to affect the right insightful understanding capable of deriving the relational wisdom to enrich the awareness of our impermanent reality to undo the conditioned ignorance of the truth. In some, concentration is misdirected while focused on an illusionary notion of nonchange like an object or some sort and not focused sensually, humbly waiting, attention poised while observing Sandbox Etiquette Guideline Number 1 with sensual ears on.

With just a slight refocus, the present moment mental effort spent fixated on modern stress reduction programs to search for relief to everyday problems could be re-coordinated and redirected through a state of body/mind harmony to eventually bring a truth seeker to the same enlightened state of total joy and happiness found in having developed an enlightened understanding like what was attained by a few of our ancient ancestors that are now recognized and worshipped by many as godly figures. Knowing that gaining the right understanding can be recognized as a goal attainable in this lifetime can stir up the motivation to do the due diligence to figure it out.

Self-Questioning Interrupts Self-Training Mind Control

Thinking without feeling is counterproductive for mind/ body analysis.

A truth seeker self-trains their wisdom to enrich their awareness and understanding of this transforming reality that they are ignorant about. With patience and persistence, this process exposes the nature of the underlying cause of their ignorance that shadows their passing present moment. To gain this enriched understanding, they have to find the mind/body harmony and pursue the inspired insights of right thinking and right understanding. If their thought patterns are anywhere else, they will not be harmonious zone of right concentration needed to gain enrichment.

Mr. Hahn teaches of four intellectual questions for an individual attempting right thinking (right understanding) to remember to mentally refer to when analyzing the appropriateness of their thoughts as per his understanding of the Mahayana school interpretation of Siddhartha's intended purpose:

> There are four practices related to right thinking: 1) Are you sure?
> 2) What am I doing? 3) Hello, habit energy 4) Bodhichitta—our
> mind of love is the deep wish to cultivate understanding in our-
> selves to bring happiness to many beings.[18]

However, if a truth seeker's present moment mental directive is preoccupied with self-questioning, their right awareness of their mind cannot be finding sync with their body's right effort to keep the essence of its presence directed at the needed mind/body harmony to affect their right concentration. Their awareness has to be gaining tenure in the essence of what it is they want to become aware of enough to understand.

It doesn't matter what intellectual venue a truth seeker's mind is visiting, Mahayana mental quizzing or the mental picture of a image mistakenly believed to have a nature of permanence or anything else unrelated. They are ignoring the reality that their lack of understanding or ignorance of is constantly punishing their present moment for. It corrupts their right awareness to be mentally wandering elsewhere. Right concentration should not be about sorting out intellectual considerations at the time of seeking experientially inspired insightful right thought (right understanding) of a sensual presence.

One loses their sustained right concentration if they start questioning their intention. In training their mind, they must secure confidence in what state of awareness their right effort and right awareness are harmonizing in while forming their right concentration. They must remain focused on coming and going sensations. If not, they've rudely turned their back on our Source during its live demonstration of the flame of its claim. They've not crossed the bridge of communication heart in hand for mind and body to meet harmoniously on the sensual plateau of understanding to experience the living essence of our Source.

Out of the common courtesy outlined in Sandbox Etiquette Guideline Number 1, a truth seeker's attention should not be averted to talking among or answering any of the 1,000 voices of their mitote/maya. They're not giving their total attention to sensually witnessing the details of impermanence that our Source is so kindly bringing to our attention. "Right thinking" (right understanding) isn't a thought generated by an individual; the "right thinking" (right understanding), as suggested by Siddhartha is really not about a truth seeker questioning their intentions as suggested by Mr. Hahn's Mahayana teaching, it's about deriving the wisdom from their insightful right thinking (right understanding) that was inspired by the right view (right thinking) of their right concentration on the unalterable coming and going manifestation of life in the present and soon-to-be upcoming, unexplored brand new passing present moment.

Self-questioning rudely interrupts the process of self-training wisdom. It disperses and deflects any attempt at a directly focused awareness to complete the progressive sequential order of actualizing Siddhartha's eight folds of guidance from sinner to being saved. It robs right concentration of being in the now of the present moment as it suffocated by unwholesome thought patterns of performing intellectual duties.

This awareness isn't right awareness. This questioning takes focused awareness out of the theater of change and puts it in the intellectual cavern of subjective consideration. Effective right effort at this point involves stopping the intellectual sidetracking and resuming the effort to sustain awareness in the area where the sensual display of the coming and going sensations as live manifests is in process.

Right Concentration Short-Circuited

Lack of recognized direction could be why there are so many forms of attempting right concentration in the Mahayana Buddhist tradition. As Mr. Hahn explains:

In Mahayana Buddhism, there are hundreds of other concentrations.[19]

Mr. Hahn lists nine levels of Mahayana meditative concentration, four on the form realm and five on the formless realm. On one level the individual still thinks and on the other eight levels, thinking gives way to other energies. The options involve a seemingly complex intertwining of intellectual ratings of the human condition. These would be subjective truths that stand relative to one's prior experience, different perceptions of truth for different people.

Mr. Hahn teaches of two different classifications of Siddhartha's right concentration. He says:

> The practice of Right Concentration (samyak Samadhi) is to cultivate a mind that is onepointed...There are two kinds of concentration, active and selective. In the active concentration, the mind dwells on whatever is happening in the present moment, even as it changes...When we practice "selective concentration," we choose one object and hold onto it.[20]

Both of these focuses will miss developing a wisdom-enhanced awareness by not focusing on what's being manifested within their human flesh. Besides, isn't holding onto the permanence of things illusionary?

The Theravada school of thought recognizes right concentration and offers the needed guidance on what spiritual sensual signposts to look for to inspire the right thinking to trigger the insightful understanding of the present moment manifestation of the coming and going impermanent energy the mind dwells or concentrates on within an individual's body.

It's a plateau of disclosure, a shade of simplicity closer to one's heart. It lies in a subtle layer of deeper consciousness just an inspired insight below one's waking mitote/ maya state of unrest.

The Tibetan strain of Mahayana Buddhism has several variations of meditating with two main types of meditation that are very similar to the two main Mahayana forms of active and selective concentration described by Mr. Hahn. These are on-point or placement meditation and analytical meditation.

In on-point meditation, the truth seeker tries to keep the mind focused on one single point such as a flower or a religious figure statue until a constant stare is obtained. In analytical meditation, they are allowed to think.

Selectively concentrating on, grasping at or clinging to the idea of an image that really doesn't exist is illusionary. This illusionary object of focus is in itself an imaginary display that is an example of the desired misguided understanding of the nature of things that's targeted for elimination...ignorance of the omnipresence of the truth of ongoing change. Actively dwelling on anything that's happening has to be selectively focused on the sensual theater within the human flesh with no intellectually imposed subtitles.

Tibetan Buddhism attempts right concentration with having the focused right awareness engaged in trying to synthesize thoughts into taking on an experientially realized history by first ingesting it intellectually and to then focus right concentration on its verbal repetition. This learning would be totally intellectual, void of any certificate of sensual understanding.

Can an individual understand the true meaning of "hot" by just repeating a description that others have discovered through experiencing the sensation? They have to hold their finger near a flame at some time to associate the sensual burn felt deep within with the intellectual description registered in the awareness of the intellectual mind.

It's true that through concentrated repetition, definitions can be memorized or learned intellectually. One can intellectually learn the definition of impermanence through repetition. However, impermanence defines our Source's nature and intended purpose. The human condition makes up a part of that source. The human deeper consciousness already knows this shared commonality. However, the working definition must be linked to their waking consciousness experientially, in the sensual body-talk language of the heart.

The variety of Mahayana forms of right concentration represent a collage of hit-or-miss attempts at combining unspecified effort and unspecified awareness hoping to strike up the right combination for the right concentration to realize the right thinking and right understanding that leads to the enlightenment about the object of their ignorance. These are intellectually guided attempts that might at best only affect temporary calming of a truth seeker's mitote/ maya state of mental unrest.

The roots of the unrest remain resident in the individual's belief system with the uncontrolled fleeting emotions to erupt again at a later time to similar stimuli that will re-agitate the perceptions that are uncontrollably reacted to. Feeling and detecting the essence of these coming and going sensations that warn of these emotion triggers should be the sole target of awareness during a truth seeker's right concentration.

Today's collection of styles of right concentration offers a methodology kaleidoscope of attempts at right effort and right awareness that don't exercise the right body/mind effort/awareness concentration that's harmoniously vested in recognizing the manifestation of ongoing change. The body and mind don't harmonize into a united cause to witness the life transformation that they want gain an enlightened understanding and awareness of.

The mind does not relax into the essence of the body's presence to sensually note the coming and going sensations. The body does not relax into the mind and make its physical presence readily accessible to the mind's attempted sensual visit into the physical display of what happens or what it feels like when one present moment changes into the next present moment.

How can a truth seeker expect to discover awareness of an impermanent reality from focusing their awareness on a nonexistent illusionary state of continuity? How can it inspire the right thinking for the insightful wisdom-enriched understanding of the nature of the reality relating to the coming and going definers of ongoing change if they're not there to sensually witness it? Their focus is not directed at the ongoing change that is needed to gain any inspiration related to its real-life relational truths.

Harmonious right concentration is necessary to sensually observe the ongoing change in action to have any truly inspired insights into the wisdom relative to the interplay of the real-time factors on display that actually define the nature and purpose of the observed transforming reality. An individual cannot rely merely on having blind faith in the same wisdom that's been memorized intellectually from a book of wisdom while not understanding through feeling how and from where it was derived. They will not be able to pop the bubble of their illusion.

The different Mahayana Buddhist attempts at making right effort and right awareness don't necessarily target their harmonious coexistence in right concentration. The forms of transcendental meditation, the meditation common to the different forms of Zen and Tibetan Buddhism are a few that don't target realizing body/mind harmony by attempting right awareness centered on an illusion of life continuity. They focus concentration on a mantra, on-point or analytical meditation. They make no right effort to unite in harmony the body and mind that allows the right understanding of the living communication media common to our Source to develop the wisdom-in-wait.

Using Sandbox Etiquette Guideline Number 1 to help create the humility based harmonious bonding of body/ mind (right effort and right awareness) to cross the bridge of communication hand-in-heart where one's waking consciousness is tuned-in to our Source's ever-present message of life's actual manifestation on the plateau of inspired right thinking and insightful right understanding that requires One's attention to be focused forward only to training more wisdom to further enrich One's awareness of the truth of ongoing change is what a truth seeker needs. Mental focus should not be consumed by any mental exercise or thought pattern spinning in any form of attachment to clinging or to aversive/ avoidance behaviors.

Cerebral Overload?

In considering Mahayana teachings, Mr. Hahn lists the Seven Miracles of Mindfulness and the Four Establishments of Mindfulness. In the third establishment of mindfulness, the mind, he lists from the Vijnanavada school of Buddhism fifty-one kinds of mental formations, including feelings that make up the second establishment of mindfulness. When one of the mental formations arises, the individual is to recognize them. He says this is also right mindfulness (right awareness). (Just to note in contrast, the Theravada school holds right awareness, Mahayana's right mindfulness, to indicate a truth seeker's mental attention to sustain having their mental awareness focused into their body's right effort to have its presence available to focus into and thus achieve the harmony needed to gain self-awareness.)

Under Mr. Hahn's noted Mahayanan fourth establishment of mindfulness, "phenomena of the objects of your mind," he lists the investigation of dharmas as being one of the Seven Factors of Awakening. He lists five kinds of meditation that can help individuals calm their minds. The fifth type, observing the different realms, lists eighteen elements that make the existence of the universe possible.

> If we look deeply into the Eighteen Elements and see their substance and their source, we will be able to go beyond ignorance and fears.[21]

There are a few other different lists of realms and appropriate meditations to benefit from. There are many other forms of analysis and categorizations of human behavior available in Mahayana Buddhism. The table of contents in *The Heart of the Buddha's Teaching* lists several:

The Two Truths, the Three Dharma Seals, the Three Doors of Liberation, the Three Bodies of Buddha, the Three Jewels, the Four Immeasurable Minds, the Five Aggregates, the Five Powers, the Six Parameters, the Seven Factors of Awakening, and the Twelve Links of Interdependent Co-Arising.

There's a countless number of insights into wisdom in these teachings. Still, to a reader or listener, this wisdom remains as being borrowed or intellectual wisdom. The originators of this wisdom were inspired by their insights during their introspective deliberation while tuned into the coming and going interplay among the same present moment factors observed by Siddhartha or others who personally selftrained wisdom while reaching the enlightening understanding of the cause of their ignorance.

Be warned about thinking that all of these wonderful insights into the human condition must be intellectually learned or memorized to pass experientially through to enlightenment. These lists of mental formations, elements and realms along with what over the centuries Buddhist schools have brought out and summarized about the human condition, help in developing a deep and revealing intellectual understanding of the human condition. This helps in directing one's insightful reasoning.

These should be read and considered. Maybe they'll help place one in better intellectual position to sensually expose the presence of their faulty prior conditioning to rise to the top during sessions of body/mind self-analysis and be eradicated. It may help point the way. However, a truth seeker can become completely bogged down trying to maintain reference to all the various lists. Siddhartha recognized the dangers of being handcuffed by the bondage of intellectual intrigue.

Its intellectual value is good only to help inspire the due diligence to realize liberation from the ignorance of our Source's impermanent nature. Intellectual knowledge cannot be called on to establish steadfast faith and give direction during their journey down the straight and narrow pathway.

This is why Siddhartha's eightfold pathway to enlightenment teaches a truth seeker to discover this liberation through the personal experience of getting to know the fiber of our Source within themselves...a transforming sliver of our Source's living truth.

When training the mind to know several different forms of meditation is seen as an end in itself, a truth seeker loses sight of self-training the mind control to then use the inspiring right thinking for the insightful right understanding to selftrain the experiential wisdom of an enlightened awareness. From one Midwestern point of view, the functional target of eliminating the fundamental ignorance seems to get lost in the Mahayana school's very detailed interdependent latticework of intellectually describing the human condition.

11

Self-Training Wisdom

Seek wisdom and ye shall find...Primal awareness

King James Version: "Wisdom is the principal thing; therefore get wisdom: and with all thy getting get understanding."

English Revised Version: "Wisdom is the principal thing; therefore get wisdom: yea, with all thou hast gotten get understanding."

World English Bible: "Wisdom is supreme. Get wisdom. Yes, though it costs all your possessions, get understanding."

Bible in Basic English: "The first sign of wisdom is to get wisdom; go, give all you have to get true knowledge."

—various translations of Proverbs, iv. 7

The biblically posted message to seek wisdom stands clear. Making the goal of this directive the leading motivation to rule a truth seeker's present moment will eventually be realized. The Bible says to seek and ye shall find. The continued effort at becoming enriched with the wisdom to identify and replace unwholesome thought patterns with wholesome ones will eventually pay off. If a diligent truth seeker sets their sights on understanding something, the answer will be found.

But, chances of getting the biblical author's original intended message could depend on which interpretation of Jehovah's intended message made public in Proverbs 4:7 is used among many, many other variables. It matters which of the many translations of the Bible an individual chooses to use in seeking direction. What God's intended meaning and theme of intention was in this directive of how and why to get wisdom varies, as per the translation of the Bible used.

Siddhartha's contribution to mankind's collective effort to secure a compassionate state of joy and happiness and eliminate suffering was that he was able to leave a record of the process that actually had worked for him. It centers around how to self-train the ability to calm the mind and then control the mind to be used as a tool to look inside a truth seeker's living flesh to then get the wisdom and its understanding that the Bible says to find.

Attaining a wisdom-enriched conscious awareness understanding how the interplay among the relational dynamics that transform causes into the effects that comprise the present moments of one's human condition under the ever-changing cosmos of the human experience is a worthy goal. Giving credit and unquestioned respect to the tiniest of role models is a must for any truth seeker who wants to become enlightened about the ignorance that makes them overlook the majesty of the statues of life tapped out by the wee masters of metaphysical wonder. The order of relational laws governing the coming and going bits of energy that make up the substance of our material reality are the primal source for all the ancient books of wisdom trying to make sense of the apparition of reality that exists within the perceptible range of the human condition that religions and science strive so hard to explain and/or claim credit for.

Self-training the ability to sustain contemplative deliberation centered in the coming and going sensations of our Source's subtle life-force during harmonious body/mind analysis enables the thinking to inspire the insightful understanding that brings into sight the relational wisdom to fully enrich a truth seeker's waking awareness. This is truly following the path to heavenly enlightenment about the subject of the ignorance that brings on suffering. To make sense of the relationships between the life forces of this reality is an inborn drive of all humankind... from the great philosophers to the best of the Monday night football announcers.

It could be said that it's insightful wisdom that critiques the true character and nature of the purpose of our Source. The relational truths that are summarized by the wisdom denoting how cause/effect factors relate to each other sets the bar for the wholesome thought patterns that replace the unwholesome thought patterns that had once easily sidetracked the truth seeker's present moment train of thought. Wisdom undoes an individual's ignorance to the life savvy of our Source's nature and intended purpose of ever-change.

Wisdom from Humanity's Collective Deeper Consciousness

Today, mankind gives worldwide recognition to those who manage to dig into the consciously undefined reservoirs of its collective deeper consciousness and allow the truth to be channeled through their work into society's waking recognition. The Nobel Peace Prize is awarded to those specializing in life's different disciplines that find the inspiration through their work for the insightful thinking to uncover and verify an unrecognized truth about the relational justice that defines this impermanent reality.

When Albert Einstein said that he wanted to learn to think like God thinks, maybe he just didn't realize that he was using the language of mathematics to bring a more focused understanding of how our Source thinks through his uncovering of the relational justice of E = MC2. Nobody taught it to him. The inspiration from his collective life experience pulled from the subtle regions of his deeper consciousness into his waking consciousness and put to definable order his insights revealing more of the specifics that further describe the nature of our dimensional reality. He offered newly realized insightful wisdom that better described the relational interplay between the coming and going bits of energy of our cause/effect reality.

He channeled to mankind's collective conscious awareness a more defined waking understanding of the relationship between time, mass and velocity that had been locked in the deeper regions of unrecognized unacknowledged truths that define the dimensional network of what holds together this environment. This newly recognized truth is one natural tenant that literally supports and makes possible our Source's omnipresent nature of impermanence that a truth seeker establishes their steadfast faith in.

Humanity now has a richer waking understanding of the relational interplay among the coming and going particles of this reality. It's now clearer how speed and mass and time affect each other. It's now intellectually realized that this interplay involves yet the predictable influence from an additional dimension known as time.

All the new books of physics chemistry and metaphysics will reflect this. This will surely help inspire more related insightful wisdom in the future as mankind's collective self-knowledge steps closer to undoing its ignorance about understanding ever-change.

Mr. Einstein's theory of relativity is an example of a product of the process of how our Source's wisdom surfaces to society's waking consciousness from under the layers of society's misguided illusions and superstitions that perpetuate the suffering caused by not understanding what is meant by the nature of our Source's truth of ongoing change. Many now intellectually understand Mr. Einstein's experiential wisdom.

Who taught the person years ago how to use the wheel?

What inspired their insight?

"All men are created equal" or "Thou shalt not lie, steal, or kill" are examples of insight-inspired wisdom that someone or group came to realize. Maybe these bits of relational wisdom came from the open discourse between individuals who were privately suffering from what over time came to be known as the cardinal sins? Through individuals sharing their feelings about the effects these behaviors caused, society's collective waking consciousness finally surmised how the relational justice of these behaviors brought on suffering. This process has removed many kinks from mankind's once much more barbaric understanding of the relational justice in this cause/effect reality.

A few of the above statements are inspired insightful wisdom that appeared written in stone as Commandments as far back as 1000 BC. The intended purpose of these claims had finally surfaced from mankind's collective deeper consciousness to be made public for mankind's spiritual advancement, even though mankind's still trying to get its collective head around each of them.

There are several religions with very old textbooks that voice time-proven claims of how to best please the deity they represent. They fail to describe to the multimillennia amassed collection of believers in these religious claims how to establish a personal relationship between their ego-managed waking consciousness and their understanding of this reality's impermanence. This process would allow them to tap into this subtle inner inspirational pool for wisdom while in quiet impersonal deliberation to acknowledge the insights.

They need to guide their believers toward consciously recognizing the primal truth of ongoing change to gain access to our Source's sensual lectures that inspire the right thinking to realize the truth-revealing wisdom that reveals the ways of our reality. It's everyone's path through the shady forest of misguided prior conditioning to the shining bright light describing the primal truth emitted from humanity's collective deeper consciousness that's reflected in every human sliver of it wholeness.

Many religious practitioners can recite this wisdom as spoken by prior enlightened souls they worship, as it's the same wisdom that comes from the different religions and science. They fail to recognize and describe the process of realizing insights from humble contemplative deliberation and introspective reflection during their right concentration into the present moment real-time interplay among the unalterable-by-man streams of coming and going inner-body sensations that the relational justice of this wisdom is deeply tied to.

Fount of Primal Wisdom

Modern society openly expresses the desire to analyze and understand the interplay between the interactions of the factors that makeup cause/effect situations clear down beyond the molecular level. Modern science, the representative of mankind's free will, insists on double blind studies in effort to surmount an experiential level of claim verification. Each individual can refer to their own personal arena of primal wisdom for their experiential verification.

Sports enthusiasts can really put their hearts into trying to analyze the game-related relational interplay between the athletes in last night's football game as well as prophesizing about the probable cause/effect sports relationships that might happen in tonight's game. It makes no difference. The strengths and weaknesses of the athletes or anything they can bring up to impress the other parties with the unusual depth and comprehensiveness of their inspired and insightful sports wisdom is open game. Yet, few Midwesterners ever talk about the art of living with this passion unless it's being shouted from a religious pulpit.

It's human nature to long for the understanding of the truth about what governs the gives and takes of this cause/ effect reality. The unknown scares people. Most just don't know where to look to truly satisfy this longing.

Instead of looking into the sports arena to understand the relational justice between the contributing factors of cause/effect interactions, they should look into their personal primal arena of ongoing change for this understanding. Bring into focus the tiny touchdown makers that pass the ball of time from on present moment to the next...the interactions between our itsy-bitsy now-you-see-them/ nowyou-don't primal role models that paint the picture of ongoing change. A truth seeker just needs to set their awareness to the low hum of life happening.

In the dimension where the interacting vibrations that comprise our little metaphysical role models takes on the shapes and forms that are perceivable by the human eye, their snap-in-time appearance takes on what the vast majority perceive to be continuous, while in reality, this snapshot of matter arrangement no longer exists. It's not a thing. It's a process that's spends its present moments coming and going...transforming into something else.

Truth seekers need to look for insights into cause/effect relationships in an environment where a cause receiving the spark of time transforms into an effect and where the effect becomes the cause of another effect making up the flow of the process of the ongoing cycle that affects uninterrupted moment-to-moment change. Decode the wisdom making sense of what happens that makes an effect stick to its cause or what it is that makes up the space in between a cause and its effect...the synapse that holds together each passing present moment that bonds together this ever-changing flow of reality.

Primal wisdom puts to poetry the just order supporting the coming and going interplay initiated by our Source. Primal wisdom unfolds from the right understanding of the inspired insights making sense of the noted sensations during body/mind analysis. This can be realized through reflective dispassionate observations made during sessions of the body/mind analysis of self-discovery while gaining self-knowledge...or wherever.

Basic Primal Wisdom is Selfevident...Yet Elusively Subtle

Through private deliberation during self-discovery a truth seeker will realize how useless it is to try to control the coming and going sensations they experience during their focused right concentration. They cannot increase or hold onto the pleasant sensations nor can they decrease the coming of the unpleasant sensations or make them leave any sooner. They can become unaware of them, but they will still be there.

No one can control the coming and going, totally unpredictable bits of energy that make up the shapes and forms that humans perceive that fill their world. This is the activity that humans will not understand the true nature of. It's this ignorance that they choose to suffer for. Science has just recently been able to digitally capture these wee messengers of truth in action.

Thus, one cause/effect insight made during self-discovery would be that in the dimensional parameters of this changing reality, as pounded out by our little role models, is that things come and go beyond any human's control. Whatever is perceived to come about also goes away. It changes. It becomes something else. Change is the plan.

The primal truth is, that it's foolish to cling to those recent perceptions as though they are still there. As it's pointless to crave and try to capture and take action on pleasant coming and going sensations or to strike up feelings to avoid sensations perceived as negative that an individual has no control or influence over.

The only aspect of this reality that has permanence is the unchanging, time-fueled presence of ongoing change.

The parameters of this truth should set the primal foundation supporting the uninhibited presence of an individual's free will...the artist of their belief system. The nature of any new claim's intended purpose being considered for internalization that violates the parameters of impermanence should not be believed and allowed entry into their belief system. It will not be allowed to infect their worldview with foolish notions of anything relating to a continuous reality.

An individual with the aptitude to recognize the pertinent wisdom in inspired insights is able to connect the dots. Siddhartha describes how this connecting of the dots took him to enlightenment in the seventh and eighth folds of the self-training wisdom phase of his eightfold pathway to enlightenment...right thought and right understanding.

First of all, they realize the experientially verified primal truth that our Source has a nature and intended purpose to initiate ongoing change. It's become clear to the individual that they cannot speed up or slow down the behavior of any of the coming and going sensations so they don't devote any purpose of intent at grasping at them or try to cling to them during sessions of self-discovery. They also realize that maybe it's not too wise to try to be so controlling or maybe even manipulating?

It follows that if all things change and the ever-changing essence of things cannot be influenced, it would be wise to conclude that there is no use to mentally cling to or grasp at the permanence of any thing or non-thing. Even though, visually, it looks like the shapes and forms don't change...they do. Anything's perceived permanence is really an illusion.

They cannot cling to something remembered that's perceived to be here now, when it's remembered presence does not exist. Clinging to any perceived thing is foolish. What one thinks they have is nothing but a perceived memory of a passing present moment in the passing lifetime of a process. They grasp at nothing but emptiness.

Clinging to material possessions or ideas and beliefs of any kind to make permanent their inherently impermanent nature is foolish. Attachment to anything beyond one's influence causes suffering. One who perceives they have everything has everything to maintain and has everything to lose.

There is a true cause/effect relational protocol of how the continual re-mixing of the universe's coming and going bits of energy relate to each other. Wisdom derived from inspired insights while in contemplative deliberations over the sensual feedback denoting the interplay among the bits of energy that comprise these sensations enriches one's awareness of our reality to where they have a waking understanding of the justice within the relational protocol of the ongoing cyclical process of a cause transforming into an effect only to become a cause that's transforming into another effect. Siddhartha would tell a truth seeker that they have to self-train being able to sustain their mind control to filter out unwholesome, thought-diverting thought impulses to allow the sustained chain of uninterrupted wholesome thought patterns of right thinking to inspire the insightful right understanding to see this.

The more often an individual makes the humble effort to seek self-definition through introspective contemplative deliberation while becoming consciously able to harmoniously unite a focused mind and body on the sensual egofree plateau of common understanding while sensually tasting the relational intermingling detectable in the ongoing stream of cause/effect interactions perceived as bodily sensations, the more life related insight-inspired wisdom they will accrue. This insightful wisdom is founded in sensual experience, not intellectual deduction or reasoning.

He Arena of Change...Home of the Aha Moment

What you are comes to you.

—Ralph Waldo Emerson

Wholesome thought waves inspire insightful understanding. Moments of insightful inspiration are unpredictable. The heartfelt truth describing our Source's nature of impermanence is something that's realized...that originates from inside.

It originates from the subtle region of the human core that's closer than from where words are formed.

The truth-in-action comes wired as part of the human DNA. Its awareness floats from an individual's deeper consciousness up their primal link into their present moment waking consciousness.

Much of the awareness of what it's all about dawns on an individual, bit by bit. While mentally absorbed in sustained contemplative deliberation with harmonious mind/body right concentration focused into the physical essence of the coming and going sensations within their flesh, a truth seeker's right thinking is primed to be influenced by the activity within where it's focused.

When a truth seeker is absorbed in introspective deliberation during mind/body analysis and their thinking becomes inspired by the ongoing change, their sudden insightful understanding that nothing stands still in time can suddenly appear to them like an auto stereogram does to a slightly altered visual focus. With an auto stereogram, when an observer looks at what appears to be a normal picture and they are able to overcome the normally automatic coordination between focusing and vergence, they can perceive a 3-D shape in what appeared to be the two-dimensional image of the stereogram. It's like it just dawns on them. It's an aha moment.

This method of self-training mind control leads to the inspired right thinking that feeds the insightful right understanding of the relational properties noted in the arena of focus to better recognize the cause/effect relational justice in this impermanent reality. It can be the sudden rush of insight where an individual suddenly gets it or sees the picture.

The expression "Oh yeah, that makes sense, I can see that" is a common mental acknowledgement supporting any small insight in the gradual unwrapping of the tree of wisdom while decoding the interconnected truth of ongoing change whether while in deep body/mind deliberation or while waiting for the check in a favorite restaurant.

This can be the same coming and going metronome that carries an individual through a moment of gazing off into the sky daydreaming during the last hour of the first day of sixth grade.

It can be like when a sudden intuitive insight changes the conditioned viewpoint of a teen-age girl about her boyfriend. Her thought pattern suddenly shifts just a bit and she sees what a jerk he actually is and her attitude toward him is forever changed. This initial realization can occur in less time that it takes for her to exhale her sigh of relief.

An individual never knows when the various sensations that combine to set the inspirational atmosphere for an intuitive insight will fuse into one sensual bookmark and an inspired insight will suddenly dawn on their conscious wakefulness. Maybe the living meaning of a real-life sensual incarnation of an age-old intellectually held religious maxim will stand out after some form of insightful association is realized to intermingle the intellectually defined theological persona with is real-time presence?

Sessions of body/mind analysis offering a controlled structured environment can help minimize outside interference in the process of quieting the mind to self-train the mind control to recognize inspiration that may feed insight. For many, sitting full-lotus, fingertip-to-thumb helps minimize interference in sustaining the right concentration to increase the probability of having the right thinking that will help inspire a dose of insightful understanding.

To others, they think about nothing but why are they striking this socially popular pose and find it difficult to sustain the wholesome right effort to find body/mind harmony...if they even have this as their intention. It at least allows them to work on self-training their mind control to stave off this unwholesome thought pattern to sustain awareness into the physical theater of change to better allow inspired thinking to give birth to insightful understanding at other times of day.

After a truth seeker has begun self-training their ability to control their mind, they gradually learn to stay increasingly focused throughout the day, when not in the full lotus position. This helps raise their awareness to the world of movement we are all a part of.

Some refer to this more developed state of right concentration when it's possible for a truth seeker to sustain it while out in the real world as walking meditation or maybe sitting meditation. The sustained right concentration will begin to underwrite an individual's intentions during their waking human experience.

Converting Our Metaphysical Role Models' Natural Laws into Parables

After self-training the mind control while seeking self-awareness in a controlled quiet area, a truth seeker eventually learns to more easily recognize the physical sensations common to the emotional triggers that cause suffering in their everyday life situations where the triggering sensations that correspond to their reactionary emotions are more likely to arise. Their spiritual sensitivity can grow to better identify and link these "red flag" sensations to the emotional distress they lead to.

When an individual can apply their insights involving the recognized relational tendencies to the cause/effect interplay of other cause/effect relationships involving other cause/effect components of the bigger picture from their mind/

body encounter with our Source's internal display of impermanence, they will have reached a higher level of enriched awareness.

It's the wisest of individuals that can recognize and associate the commonality in the factors of cause/effect relationships and apply the relational principles of the observed interplay of the insight-inspiring coming and going sensations into other of life's relational situations to transpose this understanding into parables, metaphors, similes or maybe analogies to help convey or parley the wisdom of the inspired insights in a way those individuals of lower spiritual maturity can better understand the intended meaning of the teaching. They can convert the relational principle into a simple story to better illustrate the broader moral or spiritual issue.

Their story incorporates the principle of wisdom in dynamics the crowd can better relate to. They tell of the truth in a way that translates and makes recognizable an intellectually maintained spiritual maxim into a present moment sensual dialogue that's encountered in their real-life situations on their level of spiritual maturity. The trick to this end is in understanding the color code or the stitch work that makes up and holds together the fabric of life.

The Bible sites many parables as told by Jesus. They were targeting the more basic levels of spiritual maturity as in the books the Romans allowed to populate their rendition of God's word that they wanted the Roman Christian population exposed to that wouldn't threaten the cohesiveness of their government in the same way that Jesus inspired with the whole of his teachings.

School of Hard Knocks

An individual's growing in experiential understanding extends far beyond the controlled confines used during planned body/mind analysis sessions. An individual's experiences coming from visits to the school of hard knocks also offer experiential insight-inspired wisdom. The school of hard knocks is an example of where serendipitously acquired wisdom of relational justice can originate.

Say an individual has miscalculated or underestimated a situation or maybe the situation worked out perfectly. It doesn't matter. Either way they've experienced the relational interplay of a time-fueled cause/effect situation. They deliberate on the interplay while feeling the effects.

If the interaction results didn't line up with what they had anticipated, there occurred an illusion-inspired miscue of cause and expected effect results in an actual cause/effect situation. After they deliberate over the interplay within the situational relationship, hopefully their thinking will inspire a wisdom-enriched insight that brings their understanding of the natural justice in that sort of cause and effect situation. Maybe their more wisdom-enriched understanding of the outcome will be wisely applied to similar future situations or be offered as sound advice to another person.

This derived experiential wisdom is from the same pool of wisdom as if realized during the controlled meditative environment used while gaining self-discovery. It's from the same tree of wisdom that the imperative of not to steal or not to tell a lie come from.

There is no required lotus position to realize this type of insightful wisdom. Living with humility helps allow one's frame of mind to become perceptive to realizing the insight among the interplay of relationships, no matter on what scale of perception, during each passing moment to then treat the observation of interplay with fair equanimity to find the wise understanding to enrich their awareness of ongoing change and its interplay in their cause/effect world.

Wisdom Aligns with Impermanence Truth Set in Consistent Environmental Conditions

This sets the foundation for steadfast faith.

This wisdom's savvy only applies to the dimensional makeup of this time-driven cause/effect reality. Should any of the dimensions that makeup this reality be changed or warped by anything like traveling at the speed of light which we're told changes the rate of reality's progression, the interplay between the cause/effect relationships would change and the observed insights about this new sort of relational interplay would generate a new book of wisdom relative to the nature of the rhythm of the new relational interplay among the factors that characterize the nature of what makes up the new reality. The same steadfast faith would exist like in this reality...only it would stand steadfast to a different configuration of experienced relational truths.

For example, the relational justice of the relational interplay establishing wisdom relative to what reality would be like in one of the black holes of our universe might pose some challenges to our book of wisdom describing relational justice in this reality. Gravity in a black hole is so great that light itself cannot escape. It would really be difficult to become attached to even the thought of becoming attached to anything. The concept of attachment wouldn't have enough of a presence to have earned the status of a concept in the first place.

The conscious realization of the insight-inspired wisdom that dwells in the network of justice in the life force that pushes a cause into becoming its effect is made possible through an individual's primal awareness of the primal truth describing the transient nature of the bigger picture. It serves as a cornerstone for the most respected of individual and collective public worldviews to grow from. Not all worldviews are based on a basic belief that offers that sort of potential.

Primal wisdom lines the aware individual's belief system to better feed and shape the development of the ever-maturing premise of their worldview. Attained primal wisdom eats away the residue of fear that lines the belief system of the unaware individual. It's the truth and those aware of it will quite wisely settle for nothing less.

It's in the confidence of the consistent alignment of the unswerving conditions of the environment that primal steadfast faith grows. These conditions have the back of our Source when making the claim that its nature and purpose is to initiate ever-change. The faith appears to the truth seeker and grows in strength alongside the revelation of the primal wisdom that lets its and their light shine through.

Spiritual Fusion Takes Time
...Compassion Slowly Assumes Default Status

Strengthening the spirituality link between the deeper consciousness and the waking consciousness is a gradual process. Spiritual fusion happens when an individual's waking mental awareness mirrors the life truths that radiate from every bit of their human condition.

Spiritual fusion materializes at different rates in different people. It's nurtured in different ways in different people. What sparks the insightful wisdom-enriched understandings that complete spiritual fusion can come from a variety of sources.

When an individual first develops an eye for the truth with sustained focus anchored only by an intellectual understanding of the truth, there's going to be unintended interruptions to their focused thinking coming from their gradually disappearing mitote/maya mental state of endless mental chatter. Only one of thing can occupy the mental floor of an individual's present moment attention at a time. This means the heartfelt security of their steadfast faith will come and go with their focused awareness on the truth of ongoing change...fading in between reality and illusion...in between moments of unwholesome mind wonder-inspiring and wholesome attention-sustaining thought patterns...in between reacting emotionally or stepping back to think first.

At times when their ego is in control and is managing the mental direction of an illusionary explanation for what reality apparently is, their present moments will pass with their free will unguarded from the misguiding effects of attachment to thought patterns invoking feelings based in cravings and aversions. Their passing present moment will be subject to the uncertainty-inspired fear that ruled their mind before getting their initial glimpse of the truth. The warmth of their steadfast faith that's felt in their heart will fade at these times.

As the individual's free will becomes increasingly freed from the mind-clogging thought patterns resulting from their internalized misguided prior conditioning with the many attachment-condoning claims and becomes increasingly enriched with the experientially realized relational wisdom inspired during their self-discovery, the more their eye for the truth will be supported by an unshakeable steadfast faith. Their steadfast faith will become increasingly less obstructed from the chatter of unwholesome mitote/maya interference. They will have the steadfast faith to guard and protect their intended purpose to spread the compassion they feel. They're approaching their goal of becoming enlightened about the details of what it is that they are ignorant about that allows their suffering.

The truth seeker has no way or reason to dream this steadfast faith up without first personally with their own sliver of our Source, tasting the awareness of the truth that pulses inside. It's not a blind faith of hope or wish that an unvalidated claim maker will be there to catch them if something grabs them as they take a leap of blind faith across the void of uncertainty created by the unsupported claim describing it's nature and intended purpose made through something read or what another individual says to be our Source and spiritual plan.

Science and Religion Fish from Same Pool of Wisdom

The common denominator for all the wisdom described in the different renditions of the Bible and other religious books, *Tao Te Ching*, Siddhartha's sutras, and science's accounts of reality is that they are all rooted in the same natural push and pull inherent to the relational interactions of those little coming and going role model bits of energy that bring to life in full living color what the unchanging parameters are that bridle our reality's self-defining process of omnipresent ongoing change. Religious theology may say that there is a god that turns the key, but science keeps updating its progressive verified understanding of how this world works.

The wisdom that gives order to the relational justice that determines the outcomes in all cause/effect relationships that support the impermanent infrastructure of this reality is all the same thing that all these different disciplines of thought are after. The relational justice in the wisdom that makes the "golden rule" the golden rule is the same for all considered.

To eliminate suffering, it's necessary to see things as they really are. The conceptions that are conditioned under the assumption of a reality with a continual nature need to be separated from conceptions that are forged under the understanding of there being an impermanent reality. When the truth is understood about the impermanent nature of this reality, it's going to be the same final answer truth that's defined by the same wisdom for anybody that's looking for it. Humanity will one day realize how this increasingly better-defined scientific truth is just the modern-day incarnation of what the enlightened ones described 2,000-plus years ago and how it harbors the answer to human suffering. It's the difference between a verbal language and sensual language...recognizing how science's digital signal and religion's analog signal can actually carry the exact same message.

Religions say that something happens or is true because their god says it's that way. Science tells why their god wants it that way. Over the years, when science has shown why something doesn't adhere to tradition or mankind's historic understanding, religions will alter their philosophies or become obsolete.

The unpredictable tendencies of those little bits of appearing/disappearing energy, the unobvious building blocks of the ever-transforming forms of the ever-transforming objects that can be seen in the human range of perception, establish the model for the unbendable laws in nature's rulebook. It follows that the primal cause/effect justice that governs those basic idiosyncrasies that characterize the inner nature of these forms and objects, continues up the ladder of perceivable size as these building blocks unite to assume the behavioral characteristics described in the table of elements to finally compose those very forms and objects that appear in the human field of perception when human perception connects those tiny coming and going dots of pure energy.

This living process humans perceive as reality is the only process humankind has available to interpret. No matter what language or point of focus used, it is only this process that any human could be trying to understand and describe. It's all there is to know.

The human range of perception seems to register and assign a more still and unchanging nature to those shapes and forms that make up nature's ever-changing picture show. The coming and going nature of everything doesn't really come into focus. Waking ignorance of this state of reality creates a primal wall that keeps an individual unwise to the self-evident tendencies of our transforming cause/ effect reality. They suffer as this reality rubs up against their illusionary notion of what the patchwork illusion of reality that they cling to must apparently be.

We strive to understand how to best connect those little coming and going dots of energy...what message they bear. Is it not true that the different religious/ spiritual wisdom substructures try to support the same wholesome moods that lead to the compassion, love and joy that are rooted in the insightful right human understandings that are derived from observations that are ultimately savvy to the relational truces of the tiny coming and going role models?

Don't human internal conflicts between what's illusionary and what's real originate from the same shoreless pool of misguided prior conditioning? Doesn't the targeted benefit of all the religious/spiritual/scientific spins extract and characterize its purposed cause using different ladles from the same pool of wisdom-enriched answers?

Fritjof Capra says in his book *The Tao of Physics*:

> Although the spiritual traditions described so far differ in many
> details, their view of the world is essentially the same. It is a view
> that is based on mystical experience—on a direct nonintellec-

tual experience of reality—and this experience has a number of fundamental characteristics that are independent of the mystic's geographical, historical, or cultural background. A Hindu and a Taoist may stress different aspects of the experience; a Japanese Buddhist may interpret his or her experience in terms that are very different from those used by an Indian Buddhist; but the basic elements of the world-view that has been developed in all these traditions are the same. These elements also seem to be the fundamental features of the worldview emerging from modern physics.[22]

Is it not possible that the religious claims are assuming ownership of the relational wisdom that really is generically founded in the relational laws of our living Source's nature of impermanence? Isn't it correct that in the King James Bible accounts of Jesus's message, that the heavenly trilogy claims credit for this natural law as wisdom from above or God's wisdom or God's way?

After Siddhartha became enlightened, it is said that he recognized the laws of nature's impermanence as nothing more than the natural laws available to all...the simple truth.

Siddhartha described what he had discovered as being nothing more than the simple truth. It wasn't his truth or a truth that had been divinely bestowed upon him. Others had discovered it, and others will in the future. It was simply the law of nature that he had experienced.

Lau Tzu tells of accumulating the wisdom of self-knowledge and its benefit in verse 33 of *Tao Te Ching* by finding the harmony to conquer the self. It's in coordinating the body and mind to work together to understand what the self is that an individual reaches this natural state of harmony necessary to be inspired to realize an insightful wisdom-enriched understanding of the ways of this reality.

This is the body/mind analysis experienced on the plateau of understanding that any truth seeker stands on when the state of their forward direction maintains the harmony of body and soul...sitting in full lotus position or standing in a bus station, a truth seeker can defeat the self. The wisdom that rings true for Lau Tzu, Jesus, and Siddhartha comes from the same pool of relational justice tapped out by the coming and going particles of energy that describe the nature of our reality.

This is the same relational wisdom that surfaced from mankind's collective deeper consciousness around 1000 BC. This insightful wisdom was inspired over time from mankind's collective observed consideration of the cause and effect of different behaviors alone and between individuals that seemed to consistently cause human suffering. These relational observations originate the wisdom that connects the causes to their effects...such as it is wise not to steal from others or it is wise not to tell a lie.

The results were finally burnt into stone tablets...the Ten Commandments. It was summarized in ten points that were appropriate to help minimize human suffering for those times. It helped establish the basis for society's behavioral/ ethical guidelines that might not have been so obvious to anyone of lower spiritual maturity. The tablets gave those of lower spiritual maturity a code of ethics to help them better manage their way through society's relational flow of unexpected naked change.

The Buddhist precepts run similar to the Ten Commandments for suggested best ethical/moral behavior. They voice the same wisdom outlining the same type of behavior for an individual who wants to quiet their mind to seek freedom from ignorance. Siddhartha teaches to then pursue self-training the mind to then self-train understanding this same wisdom. He claimed no credit for showing how to find the wisdom derived from the primal laws of nature that inherently belong to everyone.

Even with this being the case, different religions credit different incarnations of a god for being the source of wisdom as well as for being its enforcer. Science represents society's collective free will by asking "why" or "prove it" to the things religions just shout to be true because their god says so.

Science verifies newly uncovered bits of our reality's relational justice that surface through someone's inspired insightful understandings by documenting the suggested relationship(s) between the interplay of the cause/effect factors in question. Society appeases those who are fundamentalist religious believers by being politically correct and so be it that the believers have been offered no living proof associated with the truth of their claim to reaching a state of suffering-free heaven, they leave the door open for supreme intervention or influence to have been responsible for the creation of this planet. But still, it's all the same relational wisdom that brings the justice, to reward or punish the human condition as it struggles for balance on the high wire of human experience...blindfolded or not.

The Greek and Roman gods were credited for similar wisdom. Their Oscar was called back with the increase in mankind's awareness due to the questioning power of mankind's free will...modern science. This is exactly the same wisdom that answers to our Source's nature to initiate ongoing change.

Science's modern-day discoveries describing the tiny appearing and disappearing bits of energy that make up the metaphysical world are used as the titles for the books making up today's books of science. The truth detailing the relational justice among the interactions of the coming and going bits of energy that work together to make up the changing forms and objects viewable in the range of human perception creates the universally applicable principles that write the same infrastructure of wisdom that all religions, spirituality groups and science strive to understand or at least claim credit for. It's the truth that sets the limits for mankind's human experience.

Church Elders...Serendipitously Gained Experientially Inspired Wisdom

Church congregations often turn to their elders for their acquired wisdom. Is this borrowed, intellectual or experiential wisdom that's being valued?

It's the wisdom accumulated through the various life experiences of these people that they seek. It's their acquired wisdom that's rooted in their life experiences. It's not what they've read about or someone else has told them about, it's what they've learned that's based on where they've been, what they've seen and been physically involved in.

They might quote scriptures to backup their life insights or they might try to back up the wisdom of the scriptures by making applications to their own actual living experience. But either way, their life experience is always factored in.

It's about the wisdom coming from their insights about the interplay between the cause and effect factors of their life experience. Received and intellectual wisdom sources may play an important part in motivating or directing them into gaining their accumulated experiential wisdom, but it's the life experience that makes it stick and results in their valued insights based on a world full of relationships subject to the nature and ways of a changing, becoming and transforming environment.

Theater actors think back on past life experience when acting out their roles to bring back the emotions associated with those situations. It's the accumulated experience of young promising teachers and gifted young doctors that transforms or changes the promising and gifted into actually being a good teacher or a talented doctor. Experience is when the goodness has a chance to be released and the talents have the opportunity to expose the genius of the host.

As individuals that have their belief systems confined within the boundaries of an illusion grow older, they will gain experiential wisdom serendipitously. It accumulates regardless of their level of awareness as to how they acquire it or why they didn't acquire more. No matter how far apart the individual's theological island that's home to their religious maxims is from their conscious awareness of what happens during real life's present moment, they will acquire wisdom as they experience this cause/effect world.

It's the self-protective nature of the human condition to make sense of the environment it lives in. The click that registers the experience, as primary knowledge supporting a higher-level tier of faith not understood goes unnoticed, but it's there in the background, supported by its possibly unrecognized steadfast nature.

As one present moment changes into the next an individual's involvement in each cause/effect situation has some type of relational interplay potential to inspire the right thought waves to derive an insightful wisdom-enriched understanding from. Their deliberation over the relational interplay in a cause/effect relationship they had while they feel the effects has the potential for generating an insight about that interplay between the cause and effect that with sufficient inspired insight will register as wisdom.

They're self-training wisdom. Its significance as being a spiritual step toward their heavenly enlightenment will probably just go unrecognized. Even though it's following the same path of recognition that worked for Siddhartha and Jesus, they just aren't aware of its religious/spiritual association.

It's the experiential feeling of what went on between the cause and effect that sears the experience into the individual's sensual memory. The situation can inspire an insightful understanding of what happened between the factors involved in the interplay. It's the ability to access this life experience and then to reflect on the interplay and insightfully recognize applicable relational wisdom that will credit an elder as being wise. An individual is a wise person if they have the ability to take recognized insights into relational interplays and apply those insights to the factors of similar or even dissimilar cause/effect relationships, as Jesus did in his parables.

As they become elders in their congregation, there's a good chance they will be respected and possibly asked for their wisdom. In some cultures, it's a given. The development of the wisdom is rarely broken down and analyzed. Answers about how to allow joy, love and happiness to fill your life are within the experience of the living body. Understanding this pulse of reality is synonymous with being wise to life.

During the 2008 Republican Convention acceptance speech, the presidential nominee John McCain bared his account of what he had experienced during his five-year prisoner of war stay at the Hanoi Hotel prison camp during the Vietnam War. He described how one benefit of the experience was realized in how he had changed from a person with intentions to serve his ego to a person with intentions to serve those who saved his life. It's a switch toward spending the present moment with intentions coming from a more compassionate belief system.

Those five years of his life equipped his belief system with experientially verified sensual truths and the deeply seated insight-based wisdom resulting from these truths has made him wise to some of the misguided claims that had ruled his ego based illusionary worldview. His ability to be the messenger that channeled this wisdom has helped lead him to his position as a prominent leader of this country that's in pursuit of the source of that same wisdom. It's enabled him to recognize misguided ideas and beliefs that others are pursuing in their illusions of what apparent reality should be.

Knowing the anatomy of one's mind is possible. The mind can be conditioned to be in a state where insightful wisdom is realized for what it is and retained. It's much better to understand the process than gaining insightful wisdom only by chance or serendipitous discovery. Life's insights are available to everyone equally as life's truths are equally valid for everyone as is the pain associated with suffering. It's needless to say that anyone understanding how their mind works will be open to and accumulate at a more accelerated rate, a higher level of wisdom as they age.

Self-knowledge realized or not, is the common-to-all link between the inborn awareness of our nature and intended purpose present in the human deeper consciousness and its awareness in the waking conscious mind. It's the same ever-present, ever-changing life-giving message for everyone. Those who spend their time living moment to moment in an illusion will stumble across wisdom either from other sources that they may believe blindly or serendipitously.

They will not have benefited from understanding the process through self-training their mind to recognize and develop their only connection to the subtle reality from which inspired understanding about the interplay among cause/effect relationships resides...where creating a platform from where the recognition of relational wisdom becomes more apparent.

This is the Source-land for the insightful wisdom others have realized and written down. Other individuals struggle to memorize and store this wisdom in their intellectual memory files. It's through finding and maintaining the mental platform for this recognition to occur that leads to wisdom-enriched self-awareness.

Give Credit Where Credit Is Due

During an October 2013 broadcast of PBS's *Charlie Rose* show, Charlie Rose asked the baseball hall-of-famer Reggie Jackson what he attributed his happiness to. Reggie said that he thanks God up there for everything. If God is responsible for inspiring the thought waves that bring on happiness, who's responsible for the thought waves that initiate all the negative emotions?

Who's to blame for generating all the sadness, grief and hatred? Are life's bad events that bring on sorrow and loss staged by the Guy upstairs? Did God issue the perception to an individual or is it in how the individual was conditioned to perceive the situation? Is it the event package controlled by God, or how an individual is conditioned to perceive them that bring on joy or sadness? An individual doesn't have to think all that deep to answer this question.

Different people perceive the same event differently. What one sees as good, another may see as bad? Is it God who determines how each individual perceives things? What is good during one moment can quickly become bad the next, as perceived relative to everything else that pops up.

The thought waves that generate an individual's happiness were from the same origin as the ones that generate their sorrow. It's all tied up in how the individual chooses to interpret and perceive a situation. This will depend the conditioning from prior times of related experience. Maybe God preordained those happenings and how they are perceived? It doesn't have to be so iffy and complicated.

Christianity must give the process that makes up the transforming human condition credit for originating the intentions that generate their own directive thoughts. In the Ten Commandments, God gives mankind credit for generating their own thought waves when wrestling with any of the deadly sins that are bad enough to bring on his wrath. He lets them initiate harmful intentions before slapping their wrists. It's important that an individual gives credit for their thought waves to where the credit is due. Self-training the mind control to self-train the wholesome thought waves associated with the inspirational right thinking that leads into the insightful wisdom-enriched understanding on this impermanent reality allows an individual to advance spiritually while being consciously aware of it.

12

The Fruits of Harmonious Focus

...Primal Balance

Inner Compass Restored with a Faith to Die for

The atmospheric dimensions that support our reality's size shape and weight and assure the presence of the environmental conditions that allow the perception of its consistent flow are simply counted on to be there and taken for granted by most. This reality's supporting framework is just assumed to be always there.

While enriching their awareness of our Source's nature and intended purpose, a truth seeker's primal faith in this environment's unfading omnipresent consistency that sets the stage for our Source to continue initiating ongoing change resurfaces to conscious awareness. Their reverence to its newly realized self-evident truth becomes steadfast. This is primal level faith in the primal level truth.

This life circumstance is the only option humans have ever known for living out their human experience. Anyone who's realized the beauty of becoming consciously aware or at least putting into intellectual perspective the nature and purpose of our Source through sensually witnessing the truth of ongoing change simply cannot be persuaded from believing it's going to continue.

They find peace and comfort in having unshakeable confidence in its unfailing omnipresence. This realization sets the stencil, reassuring that the wisdom that applies to the relational justice of today also applies to the relational justice of tomorrow.

The steadfast faith that's available to all, now lines their belief system. The multidimensional infrastructure of the forces supporting these conditions assures the consistency of the presence of the inconsistent crazy antics of our tiny little coming and going role models as they demonstrate the impermanent nature of this reality.

Many individuals who've consciously planted this spiritual signpost will die before denying its truth or the truth related to one of the derivatives of its wisdom. "Give me liberty or give me death!" expresses total noncompromise for maintaining the same unbridled personal freedom that those bits of energy demonstrate in their unattached relational liberty dance, characterizing the true nature of what makes up this reality.

This represents an individual's applied wisdom inspired by an insight(s) possibly realized during careful reflection and humble detached deliberation during self-discovery. The right thinking was inspired while their harmonious mind/body awareness was focused into their sensual screening of the relational activity among their unalterable coming and going sensations.

A wise real-life application of an inspired insight the truth seeker might make during self-discovery could involve a situation where an overcontrolling leader's unreasonable mandates cause great suffering and oppression among those involved. While gaining self-knowledge at an earlier time an oppressed individual could have had the insight through humble detached deliberation and reflection during self-discovery that noted the ever-present state of liberty and freedom permeating the arena of sensual display beyond their control and the total freedom and uncensored nature of the coming and going of the streaming sensations.

One's freedom is a natural state. It originates from the most basic level of grass roots support. An individual's understanding and waking awareness of this natural freedom is their primal right that has to be realized. But, once it is, the overshadowing echo from its enduring truth cannot be dampened.

Their applied wisdom recognizes the prevailing relational justice in that if this is the way our Source presents reality, then that's the way it is and the way it should be. One entity should have no uncensored control over another. This freedom and liberty in the environment of cause and effect is being expressed and witnessed experientially through and from the changing transformation within their body. They realize that this is the nature and purpose of the bigger picture. The coming and going bits of energy are controlled by no one or any force common to this reality within the field of human perception.

Applied wisdom might suggest that the relational justice that assures metaphysical freedom from the unwarranted control of outside entities should also extend up the scale of size, through the range of perception where humans visualize their uniting to sculpt the shapes and forms that make up the bigger picture. It's a founding characteristic supporting the nature of ongoing change.

By the same stroke, a wisdom-enriched individual will also recognize that even when personal freedom can be denied during times of physical oppression, mental freedom from the ignorance that causes suffering can be denied to nobody. There's no outside switch to control.

Steadfast Primal Faith Finds Truth Seeker Naturally

A truth seeker's steadfast primal faith in the truth of our Source's nature and intended purpose to initiate ongoing change grows heart in hand alongside their wisdom-enriched understanding of its sensual presence while gaining self-awareness.

As a truth seeker realizes that the truth of ongoing change is coded into their primal core, their steadfast faith in its nature begins to grow. This sets foundation for the lifelong co-emergence of their wisdom-enriched awareness of the nature of this reality alongside their steadfast faith in its omnipresence.

Their confidence in the ongoing validation of the coming and going reality that has supported and inspired their new insightful understandings till this present moment will be there to validate their inspired insightful understandings of future present moments. This intuitive assurance seals their faith while making it personally steadfast.

The process where a truth seeker progressively cultures a process of self-training an increasingly richer understanding of life's impermanence from their deeper consciousness to experientially link it to their waking conscious awareness is met and supported by their steadfast faith. This faith lies in the dependability of the continual reemergence of the same physical indicators or our Source's signs from above that's presence verifies the living truth of the claim that our Source's nature and intended purpose is to initiate ongoing change anywhere anytime for anybody. Point is that this assures the continued and consistent validity of the wisdom-enriched understanding they inspired today.

Inner confidence that the relational wisdom derived during reflective deliberation over the relational interplay among the coming and going cause/effect factors involved in life's manifestation will remain valid throughout future present moments allows this to be a faith of vision and direction to a truth seeker's freedom from the ignorance that allows their suffering. The constant presence of the ongoing steady transformation of our Source's primal evidence is always there to make real the same natural laws and forces defining the changing presence of this present moment cause/effect reality. Our Source is always there, initiating change, perpetuating the same unchanging truth, stamping Father Time's warrantee on the continued applicability of any bit of its derived wisdom.

Individuals do not pick their faith. Their faith finds them. The truth surfaces from the individual's deeper consciousness to their waking conscious awareness. The truth seeker doesn't have to intellectually rationalize a reason to have growing confidence or faith in what they are self-training...they feel why.

They don't have to take someone's word as being so in deciding what they are faced with about what happens to their soul for all eternity...that's biting off quite a bit. They don't have to boast of having the courage to blindly follow the said purpose of a religious claim blindly. It's the self-generated light that illuminates the path of their vision. Before they blindly trust in a religious plan did the truth seeker first learn what faith really is or what it really means to have faith or how to tell the difference between today's varieties of faith born under the sign of today's technological faith buster? Today's technology allows a searcher easy rapid access to nearly endless information sources when searching out answers to help investigate blind faith-dependent claims of any kind. Technology's as exponentially beneficial to someone questioning a claim's validity as modern-day telescopes are in gathering light as when compared to the human eye.

After an individual first realizes intellectually what the omnipresence of the truth of ongoing change means, a steadfast faith in their vision to self-train their ability to experientially understand the truth of change will begin to fortify the new developing resolve of their waking consciousness. A faith primal to the truth describing what's primal about the nature and intended purpose of our Source will grow in step with the depth of the truth seeker's self-knowledge. The presence of this steadfast faith becomes unshakeable.

Primal Faith is a Selfsupporting Faith of Vision

It's not a faith of fashion nor do its practitioners need to make effort to stay politically correct. Having faith is not a decision...a truth seeker's free will earns it. It's a gift from our Source for listening fully focused and comprehensively to the living code unlocking and bringing into vision the means of eradicating the ignorance explaining the mystery about what connects a cause to its effect in life's ongoing transformation. Primal faith is the air of inner-felt confidence that is actualized in one's conscious display of self-responsibility as the individual knows it's up to them to shape their destiny. It underwrites the individual's confidence, tolerance and courage that welcomes for consideration other explanations or religious riddles explaining a different way of reaching the same final goal for all to have total eradication of the ignorance of impermanence that keeps their joy and happiness at bay and allows their suffering.

An individual can reach out and welcome a new untested claim that brings to air a previously unrecognized truth, as they understand the process of testing claims for truth savvy. There's no fear of new change as it's anticipated. The individual doesn't cling to an illusionary apparent reality they must defend against change, as its supporting logic is so fragile and easily upset. They need no written scripture to defend this faith.

Primal faith is a bone-deep heart-in-hand felt assurance seeded in the harmony felt during mind/body unification while gaining self-knowledge. It involves having confidence in the dimensional regularity supporting the conditions present when forming a personal relationship with our Source's sensually experienced truth defining its nature and intended purpose in generating the bigger picture. It's a faith in the lasting endurance of reality as when they consciously experienced the sensual burn of the truth.

There is only one ageless omnilingual tome of reference. It's found fused in between each set of present moment causing factors and their effects realized in the next present moment, defined in each dimension of this reality. Time-fueled ongoing constant change ensures the unalterable omnipresence of this dependable present moment input of life into living. In this, one can have steadfast faith.

This is much more spiritually rewarding than a forthright display of defiance made solely to publicly defend one's pride in being one of blind faith or to fulfill the need to pay one's dues to the martyred by barefacedly standing up, script in hand to be willingly persecuted just for the sake of being persecuted like many fabled forefathers who defended their blind faith.

Primal faith doesn't call for or require any unearned unwarranted trust. Primal faith is a faith of vision that's common to the human condition. It supports a vision of what can be based on true awareness of what is. It's a faith that's truth-finder-friendly.

A New Passion to Recognize and Defend Newfound Truth

After a truth seeker has had a sensual taste of our Source's most basic and primal truth they try to further cultivate insightful introspection to develop a better understanding of the relational interplay it's wisdom defines. It's the feeling of presence that links one present moment to the next that they sensually witness being channeled through their very body that they try to understand. Through the sustained right concentration, detached contemplation on the sensational flow of the essence of living change during their body/mind meeting on the plateau of understanding, a truth seeker realizes they have found their switch to the light that shines on everyone and warms the human soul.

They wake up, pull their head out of the sands of ignorant denial and seek the truth in and about all things. They begin to notice how the inspired insightful wisdom realized during contemplative deliberation while sensually witnessing the relational justice of the coming and going bodily sensations is enriching their awareness of our Source's truth of ongoing change and how it brings a new level of balance to everyday life situations.

They notice how the relational interplay between the living factors of situational relationships encountered during the passing present moments of their normal daily activities share common properties or principles with those encountered and sensually noted during their mind/body analysis sessions while gaining the experiential knowledge that brings self-awareness. Through impartial introspective deliberation with mind/body awareness focused into the object of their sustained right concentration, the coming and going sensations, they were inspired to have the right thinking to form wise insightful understandings of what's behind those thought patterns they're finally taking notice of.

They reap the benefits of their wisdom-enriched awareness of the truth more and more as they shake the static coming from misguided prior conditioning from their primal link allowing the truth resident in their deeper ego-free consciousness to migrate into their waking conscious awareness. Their vision of realizing total wisdom-enriched awareness is slowly popping their bubble of illusion and dissolving their ego they've needed to manage it.

A reawakened free will scrutinizes the nature of all newly encountered claims representing the intended purpose of ideas and beliefs coming from any borrowed, received or intellectual information source. If it's noted while verifying the nature of a new claim regarding the interplay between interrelated causes and effects that its intended purpose distorts the objective account of the interplay in a way that condones intentions of becoming attached to the idea of holding on to the cause or the effect of the situation, it will not be internalized. If the purpose of intent of a claim doesn't anticipate and appreciate the ephemeral nature of our reality, they will not believe the claim being made and allow it to influence their belief system to further shape their worldview.

They make effort to rekindle their self-preserving mental facilities that came as part of their human condition package at birth. With the right guidance they'll find the power to stop their habit energy from feeding the fleeting reactions they can't control to curb their eating habits. The ignorance causing their mismatching of real causes and real effects contributes to their inability to come to terms with their weight gain. The individual's realized of the truth of change to realize that real causes have real effects that will then go on to become real causes. They understand that real effects have real causes. They know that they can strongly influence what their future karma is going to be by how they affect the causes that make up their present moments.

Sniffing out personally what happens between the real cause and effect of passing present moments, the individuals stand confident and strong in their faith-guarded freedom to test, understand, and verify experientially or to witness a newly encountered claim's validation in action when possible for any new claim whose source is vying for its internalization into their belief system while aiming to influence their worldview. They'll test a sample of something before buying an entire case to test the advertised claim before they just go and buy it because the company said so and that's what most others do.

On the greater scale, this process can help distinguish and bring to social awareness the point where society should draw the line in the sand concerning any new or different arena of thought that is still in a foggy stage of social understanding. It only takes one person to recognize the relative truth of some unpopular or new-to-the-scene claim of social insight and have the primal faith inspired courage to, if necessary, solely support or stand against the intentions of the new claim's purpose. Steadfast faith accompanying a growing eye for the truth describing the continued presence of the ongoing nature of our Source gives an individual the strength that helps inspire and initiate needed change. "Four score and seven years ago...that all men are created equal."

With this core source of faith identified, the pressure and mental anxiety associated with an oncoming everyday confrontation dissolves. A confrontation can be felt to be a waste of time when an individual has the internal solace coming from having seen things to the core. A confrontation may be unavoidable, as the truth has to be defended so the natural flow of with the object of the misguided opposition can instead continue on, uninterrupted in its natural process of becoming.

Relationship with Our Source Within is Personal

As a truth seeker self-trains a wisdom-enriched self-awareness, they develop a very personal relationship with our Source. They try to teach themselves to take what they've intellectually captured as being the primal truth describing our Source's nature and intended purpose and sensually recognize its intellectually described spiritual markers that signal that targeted state of enlightened awareness.

They try to recognize the real-time sensual incarnation of the intellectual description they have of our Source's presence. This relationship between what they're trying to free from their deeper consciousness and their waking ability to absorb it encompasses a lifelong soul-saving personal experience. Their conscious mind is honing their mental awareness and physical essence into a sustained harmony that will recognize the sensual appearance of the intellectually sketched spiritual signposts.

It's an individual's human obligation to embark on a spirit-waking self-directed quest to realize fully an enriched conscious awareness of what's going on so they can better spread the compassion, joy and happiness that's all humans long for. The ongoing change is felt and found only in the space or void in between. It's what ties together the cause and effect of each elusive passing present moment of our time-fueled reality...what it feels like when this is changing into that. With humility a truth seeker sensually listens to our Source sign the story of this truth as it sensually presents its never-copyrighted impromptu present moment stage play.

As the coming and going sensations code out the address of where all of humanity comes from, it eliminates the need for any notion of individual loneliness. To be alone doesn't have to bring on a mental state of separation or loneliness. We all swim together in the same sea of humanity and share the same pulse of our Source's life rhythm.

The truth seeker accumulates an experiential history of their time spent in body/mind analysis, finding the mind/body harmony to cross the bridge of sensual communication to meet in introspective deliberation on the plateau of understanding. They stand ready on their sensual threshold where their focused mind and sensual body are united in harmony to witness the real-time present moment cause-and-effect cycle as they feel its speed-of-light manifestation unfold from the uncontrollable streams of bodily sensations as new life fills the tissue of their transforming physical flesh.

The spiritual link between the truth-savvy deeper consciousness and the ego-managed waking consciousness stands ready and open to channel an understanding of the truth of time into the truth seeker's waking consciousness.

In a religion's template solution to suffering, everyone is told that Jesus died for their sins so they could be saved through the grace of the outside entity that's making the promise and that they'll find out on the day of judgment if they're one the group of believers that will finally make it to a heaven where there's no suffering. Conversely, the process where a truth seeker self-trains their ability to self-discover the wisdom of self-knowledge till they've become enlightened about what it was that's replaced their joy and happiness with their suffering is a very personal and private process. They have to be personally responsible for walking the straight and narrow path to unmask the cause of their ignorance to end their misery.

Forming a waking understanding of the primal truth is a personal relationship between the depths of human evolvement that reaches back into the archives of time and an individual's waking purpose that points a living finger into the future. It's the real-time sensual incarnation of the intellectually conceptualized truth of change. Finding the strength to enter a new unchartered present moment, willingly exposed and vulnerable to the tides of the truth sets the foundation for the strong loving trust and maturing awareness from which steadfast faith grows.

When a truth seeker experiences body/mind harmony on the bridge of communication while sensually tuned into our Source's pulse of change, the introspective impartial contemplative deliberation that transpires will inspire their wholesome right thinking to insightfully better understand their state of presence. They sensually discover that their living essence is part of the same living essence that fills the air and everything else.

Their overshadowing humility helps keep in focus who they are and who they are not, should their egos be pushing the envelope of self-importance? It's the reference point from which an individual knows that another individual isn't superior to them as an individual and that they are superior to nobody else. This is an intrapersonal relationship that helps keep one's waking consciousness grounded in the humility that opens the world to their experience and allows them to, as Jesus says, inherit the earth.

Discovered Mind-Into-Body Purpose Inspires Eating to Live ...No Longer Living to Eat

Or do you not know that your body is a temple of the Holy Spirit within you, whom you have from God? You are not your own, for you were bought with a price. So glorify God in your body.
—1 Corinthians 6:19–20, English Standard Version (ESV)

What? Know ye not that your body is the temple of the Holy Ghost which is in you, which ye have of God, and ye are not your own? For ye are bought with a price: therefore glorify God in your body, and in your spirit, which are God's.
—1 Corinthians 6:19–20, King James Version

What an individual eats feeds and makes possible the different types of body chemistry that affects the present moment mood they're in which affects the types of thoughts they have.

While living suspended in ignorance, a religious believer's mind rides numb to the true intended use of their body that provides opportunity for both perception and expression. When body/mind harmony has been experienced in training the mental control to begin training wisdom, they will recognize the importance of letting one take care of the other.

Understanding that God's truth and the truth that holds the passing of the sensual reality of the present moment together should actually be the same truth will help bring the intellectual domain of theology and reality's sensual domain together. The new truths that science is continually revealing about how the human body reacts to different food constituents should be realized by religious fundamentalists as our Source's truth and regarded with the respect as should be for what they call God's truth.

The truths describing what radical food constituents do to destroy the body and what antioxidants do to defend the body are undeniable truths. However, when comparing the percentage of obese people in the Midwest with the number of people who attend church, it becomes clear that there are many Christians who pay little regard or have little respect for these hard facts. The facts are right in front of their faces. They don't equate these hard facts of reality with what they study and refer to as God's truth of theology. While using their energy to tread water in the ongoing river of change, they really just don't have enough left to care that much. Are they eating to satisfy their emotional hunger or their physical hunger?

The gratification coming from the feel of developing wisdom helps perpetuate a truth seeker's desire to maintain a lifestyle that keeps their material connection with our Source in tune. The aware individual sees the wisdom in eating to live and not living to eat. They see the vitalization that good nutrition gives them to better excel at their passion.

Their body/mind analysis continues to improve. In better understanding how things work, a deeper understanding grows for the expression that "your body's the temple of our Source." A healthy body draws them closer to feeling their Source's presence.

They realize that the devil is not the cause of their addiction to eating. Their food addiction is not just their karma for something they feel guilty over.

Their overeating grew from their conscious unfamiliarity with the working anatomy of their belief system. A deadened free will and the lack of feeling the truth of life between hearing a claim about something and believing it has infected their belief system with uncertainty inspired fear and doubt. They have generated an illusion to organize and defend their sanity from their personal mitote/maya of endless suffering. An individual with their mind hovering in the impending darkness of their unique illusion of reality with no direction identified for realizing their inborn potential cannot find reason to maintain care for the vehicle they will need to take them there. When they realize they can eventually understand the universe, starting with the introspective, impartial deliberation necessary to control their mind that's striving to sustain the mind/body harmony of right concentration focus into the essence of their living body as life manifests itself, they become more concerned about what food they stir into it to influence its sensitivity to its ever-changing process. It's just like not allowing information trash into their mental belief system; they don't want to allow nutritional trash into their material body. They want it to be in better shape to generate body/mind harmony.

As the nature of their mind changes, their awareness of digestive tract health, blood glucose levels, sun exposure, and cholesterol will all take on renewed significance. They will want the truth. They will soon know as much about the mechanics of their physical and mental anatomies as they do about the anatomy of their automobiles or the line-ups of their favorite sports teams.

They'll know more about what makes their blood healthy than what constitutes good motor oil. Those who had always offered grace before each meal, citing how "God is great and good and how they thank him for this food," will want to work in a line of appreciation for having the body to digest the food to allow better body/mind analysis sessions to be nearer to our Source. Their food has been selected in light of its nutritional value and not solely on how good it tastes.

Foodaholics will be recognized in the same light as alcoholics. They'll recognize their uncontrollable urges to eat as being what the modern-day incarnation of the temptations warned about in the Bible feels like.

Finding Sync with Our Source's Nature and Intended Purpose

Self-trained wisdom-enriched self-awareness fills the void of uncertainty created in an individual's belief system in between their hearing a religion's claim and believing it without personally verifying that the Holy Ghost it describes is what's here putting the life into each passing real-time present moment. Agreeing to believe a promise without it having a verified way to make it happen keeps an individual's need for experience-based verification compromised and at the mercy of an illusionary explanation of what reality apparently must be. Self-trained wisdom-enriched self-awareness will fill the void of uncertainty in an individual's belief system with the personally referenced experiential history of what the baseline essence of life really feels like as one present moment does its cause/effect dance and transforms into the next.

With this conscious understanding, this reality's nature of impermanence assumes the default setting within a truth seeker's worldview. They continue working to better understand the network of truth that supports it.

They now prioritize recognizing the nature of what makes up their worldview as being either impermanent or continual before retaining or internalizing the purpose of the claims about those things or ideas. They consciously realize that anything with a nature of continuity is illusionary.

Consciously realizing that the cause-initiating effect-allowing ephemeral status of this reality is what defines a claim's nature and intended purpose and that its omnipresence is what supports the day-after-day validity of the related wisdom will affect everything in a truth seeker's belief system. Their stifled free will resumes more of its unfettered status to sift out faulty beliefs and to stand guard against any future internalization of faulty claims that have a nature that condones time continuity. Their worldview is changing to reflect their self-trained insights and increased wisdom-enriched understanding of the impermanence of this reality.

Conscious appreciation for the impermanent state of this reality changes, cleanses and relines an individual's belief system. They excuse notions that relate to things and ideas as having a nature of continuity. This conscious recognition also changes the nature of their intentions that are reflected in their present moment point of view or the angle they choose to look at things from.

While adhering to the due diligence to realize enlightenment, over time, present moments spent in mental states of joy, happiness and love fueled by altruistic compassion become more common. The nature of the truth seeker's mind is changing from being one that causes their suffering by allowing attachment to different phases of craving and aversion to one that's self-trained to understand that our cause/effect reality has a tempo set at constant change and there's really nothing to get attached to.

What happens in real life becomes more acceptable. The haze dimming their understanding of the true relational justice that exists between situational causes and effects gradually becomes more transparent. The individual becomes more tolerant, more accepting, more settled. They release their fundamentalist attitude. They move forward.

Siddhartha's guidance offers a self-proven step-bystep outline to intellectually guide a truth seeker through self-training their spiritual maturation process from their selftrained physical and mental control onto self-training their insightful wisdom that touches the present moment reality of their life-story of transformation. It's through a truth seeker's attentive sustained awareness focused on the sensations that they feel in their body that inspires the right thinking and insightful right understanding that changes their way of perceiving and interpreting life situations. They understand how unnecessary any related emotional reaction is and let it pass. They anticipate and deal with the change that they are an included part of. They become proactive in having a positive effect on the present moment process that determines their future karma.

They feel better from one present moment of their journey through their human experience to the next. They feel better having their living hell lifted from their shoulders before they die.

A truth seeker can use their awakened understanding of the ephemeral nature of this reality as their springboard into their future. They've found compassion and love seeded in their ability to influence their future present moments through active control of what they do during the current ones.

They have regained the curiosity and unfettered free will from their childhood...only now it's seasoned with growing wisdom and protected by a steadfast faith of vision. They're beacons of the primal link that's written into the human code that ties each individual to the functional truth of our Source's nature and purpose of intent.

Their primal link bridges over and eliminates any possible void in experiential feeling that had separated their deeper conscious primal record of the truth describing the true nature of their human condition from their waking efforts to manage their human experience.

Their resurfaced compassion is greeted by their reborn interest in the details of the lives of their friends and family.

When a truth seeker changes what they recognize the nature and intended purpose of our Source and reality to be, they are changing the nature of their mind. By changing the nature of how they think, they will change what they think.

OK, suffering exists...It has a living cause and it has a living solution. How does that living solution fit into my living experience?

Siddhartha's fourth noble truth leads to the cessation of suffering...
Freedom from suffering is possible
...Now, find your own sensual pathway
for an enlightened understanding of its cause.

PART IV

FIND HARMONY
YOUR WAY

1

Standing at the Threshold

...Ask Yourself What it is You're Hungary For

Step into Your Own Shoes and Feel Others' Guidance

Atruth seeker must personally find and walk their own way to acquire an enlightened understanding of what happened to their happiness and joy and why they suffer as they do. They must consciously open up to the essence of the present moment to understand and own the source of their unrest.

Self-training the ability to sensually take the pulse of this reality's heartbeat of transformation gives an individual the means to make sense of the cause/effect relational justice that rules the passing present moment. Their inward felt familiarity anchors an unshakable steadfast faith that's rooted in the dependability of the omnipresence of the natural conditions that assure the continued consistency of that heartbeat. The wisdom that holds true for keeping that heartbeat healthy today will be the same tomorrow.

This is the experiential association that eliminates the doubt and uncertainty-ridden void in the belief system that originates from taking leaps of blind faith regarding the truth to any claim regarding any subject. Ungrounded faith allows for the internalization of unverified beliefs based only on unverified borrowed or intellectually founded unproven assurance of the newly internalized claim's truth. Can the claim's purpose find its truth in a transforming reality or does it need an illusionary one with a continual nature?

In trusting blind faith, they've eaten from the tree of intellectual knowledge... repeated the original sin. They've omitted opening their sensual ears to personally visit the claim's public demonstration. They miss what happens when forming an experiential association between present moment causes and their resulting effects.

The outside sources cited in the first three sections of this writing have been considered and selectively internalized to help shape the purpose of intent of a worldview focused by a belief system that has a passion to realize an enriched awareness of what actually defines the truth of ongoing change in real practical terms. It's a personal goal fueled by the burning desire to know what it really feels like to be alive.

This forth section presents ideas for self-training a wisdom-enriched understanding of the nature of this impermanent reality through using the sensual media dialogue appropriate for the version of ongoing change that our Source has maintained since the beginning of time. It points down the self-trained pathway that a truth seeker travels in attaining self-knowledge. As in Siddhartha's forth and last noble truth, the purpose of this step deals with how an individual personally feels out their own way of understanding the one and only sort of relational justice that works in an impermanent reality.

In this last section, there's less need for outside borrowed intellectual knowledge sources as done in the first three sections. This is aimed at allowing a truth seeker to understand in their heart each step they take down their pathway to the enlightened knowledge of what they are ignorant about that steals their joy and happiness and allows them to suffer. In coming this far, they should better understand their own sensual patterns and how to personnaly recognize and find the way from spiritual signpost to spiritual signpost that forms the infrastructure of the cause/effect bond supporting the life that manifests itself within their living flesh.

The previous sections' referenced advising guidance helped point the way. It gave the intellectual sighting to help the truth seeker take the sensual steps in their search for experiential satisfaction. Outside viewpoints help a truth seeker view the subject from the differing angles of differing platforms.

They can triangulate in to better understand the intended meaning of the subject of guidance described by the quoted information sources. Addressing a truth seeker's ability to experientially self-develop the right thinking to inspire the insightful right understanding that allows their conscious awareness to find sync with the relational justice of the truth of ongoing change is the objective of this fourth and final section.

2

Get Ready!

Respect Life's Simplicity

Look forward toward an end of discovering what it feels like to be alive and not back with thought patterns related to suffering. Consciously feeling the deep pulse of life can happen the first time it's tried, but making sense of what's being felt takes time to develop. Stay busy being born...not dying.

Many of the ingrained intellectual illusions that harbor religious/spiritual maxims originate from repeated exposure to the ancient religious/spiritual tomes that support the worldwide religious/spiritual movements of today. The truth seeker has to equate these descriptions to the sensual language imprinted on their real-time spiritual elevator buttons. The forward focus of any truth seeker needs to highlight and pull the intellectually modeled spiritual maxims outlining their notions of reaching an afterlife heavenly from their intellectually internalized and stored conceptualizations and equate them to the actual changing moods, states of mind and insightful revelations experienced in real-time.

These intellectually processed religious/spiritual maxims need to be recognized in light of the sensually recognized symptoms of a truth seeker's emotional suffering that they feel today. Any intuitively inspired insightful understanding that captures the same relational justice as the wisdom-enriched self-knowledge they target, has every bit as much spiritual significance as it would if they were sitting crosslegged rapt in the proper right concentration/right thinking/ right understanding common to the sustained harmonious deliberation of primal meditation. It could be said that any of these topics related to freeing up the congested space between an individual's deeper and waking consciousness deals with opening up their spirituality zip file.

Knock away the heavenly caste system of holy importance and the belief that certain material shapes and forms can be blessed or sacred when it's an undeniable fact that they don't continue to exist as perceived in some isolated snapshot remembered from the passage of time. Take the biased notion that certain things have a holy nature completely out of the picture. Every changing thing has the totally open potential to become something else. Don't limit its potential with a label.

Disrobe and wipe away any biased unverifiable ideas of eastern mysticism from any serious thoughts of finding the pathway to having an enlightened awareness of what allows the ignorance that steals away joy and happiness and spawns human suffering. Expose and consciously recognize things for what they really are and what they are becoming. A truth seeker can't minimize the significance of perceptions they're having because they mistakenly see them merely as passing observations they're having of life events of seemingly everyday importance.

Peel Away Labels and be Self-Reliant

Shouldering the label of Buddhist, Christian or member of any other "-ism" or "-anity" or anything placing any political correctness of where or how one's due diligence takes them or where or how their potential's to be realized, clouds their search to find the awareness that undoes their ignorance that allows them to behave in a way that they perceive as suffering.

Labels can give the false security of belonging. It's time to humbly step out and find the courage to consciously assume self-responsibility.

Labels can suggest allegiance, but this introduces the prejudice of what others might say or think. After an individual hears something that makes sense and is helpful but sees that it comes from someone of a controversial discipline, they might factor in their impression of that group and dismiss the positive idea.

Jesus of Nazareth was not a Christian and Siddhartha Gautama was not a Buddhist. Mr. Gautama left direct remarks addressing his intended position as not being considered the founder of a movement. What he experienced came as a natural law detailing an individual's perception of the relationship between the human condition and the human experience in the light of an impermanent reality.

Ask The Right Questions

Sometimes the questions are complicated and the answers are simple.

—Dr. Seuss

Dr. Seuss is right. Sometimes by the time an individual has figured out what they want to ask, they've jumbled around the factors enough that they've pieced together the answer.

A truth seeker must first, genuinely want to understand the spiritual enigma's entire process. As they try to connect the dots that make it happen as a process, it's where they don't feel intuitively justified that one thing will lead to the next that they should be asking why or why not. Until they feel intuitive comfort in the cause/effect connections between any of the involved steps in the process or between the factors in a situation, they need to investigate.

They need to verify or personally understand the involved factors to get that answer to eliminate their ignorance that's makes them suffer through not understanding the relational justice that applies to this step in the process. They're developing their experiential awareness in their intellectual knowledge.

The important point about getting started in the successful process of understanding the truth about anything is to know the right questions to ask. It's the first step after forming an intellectual understanding of the end goal. Let it be said again that these questions have to be generated from the burning desire to just know what it feels like to be alive.

They just want to consciously feel the life in the right now without following any necessary protocol. If they can't get it on their own, it's really not what they need.

Their internal unrest begs the first question why? With due diligence, they try one idea to answer it and it's answer will lead to the next question. These are questions coming from their gut feelings of uncertainty. The answers that can't be ruled out will form the foundation for an unshakeable steadfast faith that will grow with each nonnegotiable future answer that they witness the answer to.

One of Siddhartha's nonnegotiable answers was that his unrest was coming from his suffering caused by his ignorance. He spent over half of his life asking questions that all required answers that registered experientially. He spent the last half of his life telling listeners how he found the answers to these questions.

Siddhartha had the talent of being able to find the words to express his feelings. His feelings laid the pathway to understand why he couldn't find joy and happiness. His sutras describe the step-by-step process of how he reached his wisdom-enlightened state of consciously aware understanding.

There's no way to set up a truth seeker's schedule of answers. Too many become lost when enrapt with what their friends tell them the answers should be or what they may read somewhere. Their free will gets pushed to the background. The limits of spoken language dwarf new insightful understandings.

They must realize that since their suffering's coming from their own mental perception of the nature of this reality, it must be curable, like Siddhartha's third noble truth. This is the intellectual kindling that will light their fire to self-train their moral/ethical standards to then self-train their ability to self-train the mental control to allow self-training the wisdom to enrich their self-knowledge to experience undoing the ignorance that allows their addictions and the emotional firestorms that strip them of their joy and happiness and plague their lives with suffering.

When the truth is right in one's face (as it is right now) and if an individual doesn't have an eye to perceive the truth, they're not going to see or recognize the truth, no matter how plain it appears...as Jesus points out in his parable about the sower. Their attention has been sidetracked by thinking about the ways of the world and/or the love of money. There's a vast array of attitudes in the emotional storm of mankind's collective illusionary reality that's hijacked the present moment energy of most of our fellow human brothers and sisters.

To unlock a truth seeker's potential after they realize that they spend much of their lifetime in some form of suffering caused by their ignorance to the truth of ongoing change and that realizing the cause is within their own grasp they must focus on unraveling the relational wisdom describing the justice within each moment of passing time as an ever-present goal of each present moment.

The force that drives this questioning must be more than that needed to satisfy a simple cognitive task. It must command the priority that's needed to energize an inner drive. It has to be on the table more often than on Sunday morning or when reading the Bible before going to bed. Even though at first the direction to the final answer may be founded in intellectual knowledge, it remains being a most personal thing.

After the truth to each of these questions is recognized, the truth seeker's desire to understand this ignorance is felt so deeply that a truth seeker will defend the truth of these discovered undeniables, no matter who's attempting to convince them otherwise. It's just simply the undeniable and in-your-face truth. This testifies to the sprouting of a steadfast faith growing with the understood clarity of the omnipresence of our reality supporting the unconditional presence for our Source as it demonstrates its nature and intended purpose of initiating ongoing change. This growing faith is the shield that guards the free will and fortifies their purpose throughout the self-training during their search for self-knowledge.

They must understand that this state of suffering is not just a trick of fate, of destiny or of something predetermined and beyond their control. They must have the courage to know that the devil is not vexing them beyond their control. They must feel that the origin of what causes the ignorance that allows their suffering comes from within and that it's within their own power to understand and eliminate it within this lifetime.

The inner urge to ask the personal questions pushes them along from question to question. The guidance from past-enlightened souls can help light their way from self-defined answer to self-defined answer.

Internal Flame Needs Intellectual Rekindling

A truth seeker needs to have the right end in sight before they can focus their present moment on finding the right way to reach it. They must first know how to recognize the warmth emanating from the living truth of ongoing change to figure out what is needed to feed its flame.

It's acceptable that the right understanding in recognizing present moment suffering and the ignorance that causes it is first intellectually recognized before being able to experientially understand its meaning. To kick-start this process, the association of the real-time spiritual significance of this targeted present moment spiritual signpost with the intellectually catalogued religious maxim it represents more than likely has to be pointed out to the truth seeker by some borrowed or intellectual information source...how to connect intellectual expectations with sensual realities.

How to gain an enriched understanding of the human condition, sensually, then comes more into focus as a worthwhile end to work toward. Daily goals that contribute to this end receive passionate pursuit as over time their cumulative effect brings the truth seeker closer to attaining their self-awareness.

To overcome the state of affairs associated with taking a leap of blind faith and suffering the separation of their feeling heart from their logical head, the new believer must find the self-direction to step out of the free-will-stifling religious dogma and ask questions about their experience and realize that their present moment suffering is the true hell they seek relief from in an afterlife heaven. These are real factors that are experienced in the present moment. It doesn't matter how long ago the present moment first received the spark of life from Father Time, it will always be the same heaven and the same hell experience of the present moment. Steadfast faith in the regularity of our experientially witnessed transforming dimensional reality assures this.

To break from this religious dogma, religious followers of all disciplines must question the validity of their religious claim's means of gaining the promised eternal bliss and associate the maxims of the religious theories that define their religion's claim with the sensual signposts of the present moment that they feel while alive in this cause/effect reality. When they identify that it's the real-time suffering that causes their unrest and its understanding addresses their human longing for the spiritual satisfaction, they will be ready to learn of its truth.

Their initial phase of right thinking and their right understanding where they realize that suffering's their big problem, must at least intellectually recognize that this suffering comes from within the makings of their own worldview. It's locked up in and extends out no further than the flesh confines of the same human shell model that Jesus accused of imprisoning him and that he sought freedom from when talking with Judas in the Book of Thomas.

Those who are self-aware have no self-limiting filters of uncertainty and doubt that pull them from the comfort of their ego-free deeper consciousness into a waking reality where the link to their deeper consciousness has been snipped by the prior conditioning that's caused their uncertainty, doubt and fear of the unknown. Knowing this truth releases them from the ignorance of the truth that causes their suffering. It sets them free. It sets them free to inherit what the earth has to give as Jesus talks of in the Beatitudes.

After gaining waking awareness that there's a primal truth describing our Source's intent to initiate ongoing change in our cause/effect reality it becomes clear that this is the truth that will set them free from the ignorance that allows their suffering. Initially having only an intellectual awareness of this truth will light their fires to self-train their mind control to decode the tree of derived wisdom to enrich this awareness and become fully enlightened about the art of living.

The truth seeker must be asking questions and settling for nothing less than self-felt answers. They must be motivated to be healed and know what is missing from their status quo that they are longing to know about. They must focus forward, eyes opened for right answers...not back, ruminating over states of suffering.

Write Your Own Prescription

For a truth seeker to be establishing the mind/body harmony needed to put their conscious awareness in a living environment that can inspire their insightful thinking to understand the nature of that life-manifesting environment they're tuned into, they need to be working on developing the abilities that support that end. That end will not be met if their awareness is focused on how someone told them they should do it.

Even less productive is having their awareness circumvented by the wonder of a promised reality after death. They will never discover the humility inspired understanding of this reality's nature that Jesus said allows the meek to have conscious recognition and appreciation for what emanates from its Earthly expression.

3

Get Set!

Which Source of Causeeffect Relational Justice Balances Your Scales?

It's important for a truth seeker to know what they're seeking salvation from and how to deal with its cause. They must believe that by gaining conscious awareness of the truth they seek that explains it that its cause can be eliminated. In making decisions in this process, they must determine what sense of cause/effect relational justice balances the right/wrong, yin/yang scales in the worldview of their waking consciousness.

Is the destiny of their soul determined by the relational justice stemming from the unavoidable truth of the natural law of justice tapped out by the coming and going particles of energy defining the same relational give and take of our physical world that inspires the content of the books of science describing the unfolding knowledge detailing the nature of our reality? Or, do they entrust the destiny of their soul to the mystical undefined law of relational justice enforced by a never-before-seen entity that independently decides justice based on the guilt-guarded state of morality implied by a set of rules such as the Ten Commandments (including any periodic modern Papal-authorized updates) that offer no reason why the behaviors are considered bad and classified as a sin? Why should the two be different?

The Source of authority ruling this reality inconspicuously floats the balance of its scales of justice on these laws of reality that are tapped out by the coming and going particles of energy. As mankind learns to better understand these undeniable cause/effect relational laws through science's due diligence, the religious authority conforms to science's discovered truth or their theological creed disappears like so many have. From this, it would seem like using religion's scales of justice would be no more than making a subjective intellectual decision and that the relational justice of this impermanent reality would give consistency over time and be free of bias and prejudice.

This subjective God-imposed justice is not the same form of balanced, beautifully unbiased justice that has ruled this reality unquestioned as real-time judge and jury as every time-fueled coming and going bit of energy that serves as the most basic of causing factors in our expanding reality transforms, time-fueled, into its effect. God's justice is not Roman Bible described as being the same justice found in this coming and going pulse of impermanent change that has ruled our universe since he, the big bang, or whatever made it happen.

Should the fate of an individual's soul be decided according to the relational justice deemed proper by an unseen, unfelt entity or by the relational justice that rules the coming and going truths of this cause/effect living experience? The scripture's set of behavior guidelines looks up the same tree of wisdom, as does the vision of science. They point at the same end body of truth.

Find Balance Where Theology and Reality Meet...
Associate Intellectual Maxims with Their Sensual Incarnations

Present moment discontent is a state of mind that echoes throughout humanity. The ignorance that allows it is identifiable and correctable in this lifetime. Make reaching joy, happiness and compassion life's main goal and the ignorance that allows the suffering will subside. Consciously tuning into the inner heartbeat of change that exposes the solution is real.

A truth seeker must step outside their religious recipe to pop their illusionary bubble and redefine what their Hoosier heaven really is. They must begin to recognize spiritually significant occurrences when they present themselves during real-time for what they really are. Truth seekers need to know how to recognize and synthesize the real-time sensual incarnation of the spiritual signposts discussed at church, in books or on TV as part of their life-purpose recipe that will lead them to what is really meant by the concept of heaven in a believer's religious searching. The real-time appearances of intellectually stored religious maxims need to be recognized in their true present moment sensual dialogue.

Truth seekers must learn to associate their conceptual understanding of the biblically described Holy Spirit by the actual sensual physical characteristics that define the realtime Holy Spirit. The Holy Spirit injects the spark of life into this reality's process of transformation. Take the insight into introspective contemplative deliberation and further insights to a more enriched understanding will follow.

The truth seeker must self-train the insightful ability to recognize and associate the sensual texture of the present moment incarnations of intellectually stored religious maxims. These conceptualized religious maxims must gain sensual clarity and be appreciated as being a living part of the truth seeker's transforming human life experience.

4

Go!

I t's possible to self-train a calmed unruffled mind to sustain an uninterrupted intended thought pattern with purpose to better understand the essence of the transforming material body that houses it.

Wake Up And Engage Hell Now!

Religion is for people afraid of going to hell...
Spirituality is for those who see it and want out. . .
—Westside Indianapolis bumper sticker

Hell is associated in the Bible, the *Koran*, the *Torah* with words such as pain, anguish, loss, fear on up to unimaginable fire and brimstone that's coupled with eternal burning. This is promised to those who don't conform to God's commands. The religious claims to salvation from suffering warn and promise that if individuals do not follow the written-instone moral/ethical standards, this place hell is where their soul will be sent to spend eternity. It's quite inconceivable how all these forms of pain and anguish could burn simultaneously within the individual forever and ever. So stand warned and be frightened into having a blind faith, even though there's no transparency as to exactly why.

It's interesting how the Greek god Zeus no longer receives credit for ruling mankind. It's more interesting how many people still honor the place of eternal punishment named after the Olympian god Hades, Zeus's brother...the lord of the underworld and ruler of the dead. This Hades place of fire and brimstone is not mentioned in the Bible, yet to this day, it holds a reserved-for-after-death-point-ofdestination spot in the guilt-ridden minds of most of religious faith. It's the first thing on many people's minds when they think they may have broken a commandment... or maybe have done something wrong they don't even know about or understand.

The intended gravity meant to establish the magnitude of this threat's strength rests in the probability that individuals have wakingly experienced a present moment sensual taste of each of its threatened variety of hellish conditions, except maybe burning brimstone. These negative perceptions hold value to people because they're registered in their sensual menu of experiential history. Pain, anguish and other hurtful sensations naturally give signal for an individual's fleeting reaction to run for safety.

Their association with these states of being delves deeper than a mere intellectually registered association. The sensual memory associates the conditions of this threat with actuality...in sensually recorded memory...how hot the flame of this promised punishment actually would be.

If there were a worse state of sensual experience on some foreign planet that humanity has not sensually experienced, threatening with it would be ineffective. There's no way to describe and have sensually register solely through an intellectual description anything worse than what's actually been felt by the individual. Everything else is totally subjectively illusionary.

Intellectual cognitive memory and sensual memory don't use an interchangeable form of media communication. How can you make the sensual significance of hot register only through an intellectual description, if hot has never been sensually experienced? It's the difference between a state an individual intellectually knows and a state they sensually feel.

As believers pray to their god during their day-to-day human experience, they ask for relief from pain, sorrow and grief that's blind to nationality or social status. Pain is pain. Suffering lies at the heartbeat of the human experience. People pray to him for relief from suffering in the present hell and not so much to assure refuge from it after they die. The afterlife thing is a state they don't understand. They've yet to experience it.

Pain and suffering is an optional component of the present moment. Sensual participation in the passing present moment is all the living human condition knows. The passing present moment is all the human condition will ever know. It's the only arena hell can ever be related to. It's the only place our Source can be found. It's the only place it can be understood.

It's important to realize that the only time those horrible states of experience will be horrible is in the present moment. It can still be very scary to imagine them in a future present moment to be all bundled together and to last forever...yikes! That would be suffering to an illusionary nth degree. How intimidating.

Hell is a state of mind. The Toltec shaman don Miguel Ruiz summarizes his thoughts on the reality of actualizing hell:

> Religions say that hell is a place of punishment, a place of fear, pain and suffering, a place where the fire burns you. Fire is generated by emotions that come from fear. Whenever we feel the emotions of anger, jealousy, envy, or hate, we experience a fire burning within us. We are living in a dream of hell.[1]

The Theravada Buddhist tradition sees every present moment that an individual lives in conditioned ignorance as a present moment they create the suffering of hell. They believe that by gaining an enlightened understanding of the subject of their ignorance, what they experience is the compassion-based joy and happiness of heaven...free of suffering. They see heaven and hell as states that are experienced while the body is full of the impermanence of life.

Realizing this is so exciting! It puts affecting the process of hell's generation within the reach of the living human condition. It's a living state that can consume an individual's present moment. That means that it's something they can have control over. They can curb those things that allow its existence. They don't have to suffer from ignorance. If they set their sights on spending their present moments immersed in a state of compassion, they can eliminate the illusion that allows and feeds their ignorance and reach that end.

Thought patterns that support denial and intolerance help keep stoked the internal flame of an individual's personal hellfire. Out of their growing fear of uncertainty, an inspired stiffness to change shelters their waking consciousness and defends the internalized misguided claims of the prior conditioning that support their ongoing suffering. Their ego-managed waking consciousness blindly juggles the cause/effect realities of their passing present moments among the shouts of the 1,000 unrelated voices in their unique and lonely mitote/maya-ruled world. They're ignorant of what allows this state and they suffer.

Besides, aren't the concepts of heavenly enlightenment and hell both relative to an individual's spiritual maturity? It could be said that an ignorant man's state of mental suffering could be a wise man's mental state of tranquility.

Evict Resident "Heaven Above" Maxim From Belief System Void of Uncertainty...Let Curiosity Replace Fear of the Unknown

Release the cognitively sketched religious maxim "heaven above" that finds life in the human belief system where it feeds off the believer's fear of uncertainty to perpetuate the misguided notion that its unsubstantiated security is needed. The reality it finds its truth in has a nature of continuity that condones the attachment to the cravings and aversions that define the addictions and suffering that make life a living hell. It has a working arrangement with fear and guilt. The lack of fear-generated thinking will be replaced with curiosity that's not afraid to ask questions.

Spontaneous Evolvement

The time can arise where an individual is suddenly thrown into the spiritual fight-or-flight scare that can come from a traumatic life-or-death circumstance. In some, a sudden tragedy can stun-calm what was normally their unsettled mitote/maya state of mind.

An unexpected spiritual jolt that shakes up a person's need to secure a plan for their soul's future well being can lessen the need for guidance. They proceed to smell out for themselves what life really feels like, all guards down. They look for what and all that life really is and not what they've been told it should be about or how they've heard others try to find the answer.

In their mind at the time, it's not about any religious theology like their fix on spirituality is intellectually framed as being...it's about what's real and alive and what seems to really matter about the present moment. It's about what's in the heart, not what's in the head.

What does something that's really about the living flow of the present moment really have to do with the description of the god they have painted in their intellectual mind that's said to have lived in the time when there were no auto accidents or modern diseases like those that can threaten a person's mental balance in today's world?

They know they're alive and simply want to know what the living thing really is. Life's urgency can give them reason to re-prioritize giving their attention to realizing an enriched understanding of our primal basics over satisfying a needless ego want to stay aligned with today's social expectations.

The sudden feeling that none of the mental chatter that clogs up their present moment has anything to do with what really matters about witnessing life in action can keep their mitote/maya state of ongoing confusing mental chatter at bay. The individual force-shifts the mind control to focus their intent more on being a truth seeker even though they might not associate seeking what they're looking for in the simple truth of what the life in the present moment feels like when they've been conditioned to think that it's something about their cognitive fix on a God-provided, God-enforced eternal salvation from suffering that's the relevant thing when considering the spirituality of their human condition.

The stun-shocked state of mind that can come following a significant event has hotwired a calm moral/ethical state of mental presence sufficient to naturally begin a process like Siddhartha's process of self-training the mind control to sustain the focus of their mind into the essence of the body's presence to witness life's manifestation in their flesh...even if they've never heard of Siddhartha Gautama. The shock of the fight-or-flight stun factor pushes to the side the guilt and indecision of second-guessing an unsettled state of mitote/maya mental presence that normally sidetracks the intended purpose of an individual's regular thought intent that Siddhartha teaches needs to be settled to have a mind calm enough to self-train the ability to have a productive right concentration.

Unless they have guidance on what to do after reaching the point where they've directed their mental focus into the coming and going activity of their flesh and understand how it relates to their spiritual world they will probably not consciously recognize it as representing an increase in spiritual maturity from their having the right thinking to inspire the insightful right understandings of life's wisdom-enriched truths. They probably won't ever know that this would be appropriate for reaching any kind of heaven like they have intellectually pictured. They won't associate it with making contact with any sort of heavenly father.

They will not understand why or how to push away any unwholesome thought patterns to make the right effort to concentrate while deliberating introspectively with their focused concentration directed into the essence of their flesh that Siddhartha explains how he was able to do. Jesus had to have done the same thing while fixed in right concentration while meditating) as there's only so much the human condition can do, no matter how many languages there are to describe it in or times or cultures for it to have happened. In this individual's state of urgency, there's a very strong chance that the magnified intent behind their effort to make their body's presence available for their focused mental awareness will be so strong that any unwholesome thought pattern will know better than to even try to show its face?

With the sudden impulse to feel life and while not even considering it to be an option to label the impulse as being religious or spiritual, they would probably not try to associate their current intellectual theological understandings of religion or spirituality they may hear on Sunday morning at church or ponder over while sitting having a cup of coffee as being associated with its present moment sensual incarnation they're set to sensually experience.

Spiritual Slap in the Face...Copyright Infringement?

Atwenty-one-year-old Christian-raised Hoosier received a soul jarring slap in the face from a near fatal auto accident. After the crash he just wanted to know what life itself felt like. In the few years before the accident he'd been briefly introduced to a Zen meditation technique, yet had never felt it work for him, as he understood it should as described by others. He couldn't match what he was feeling to what others said to anticipate.

He really had no idea of what it was the meditation should achieve...no real idea of what the intellectual description of an end goal would sensually appear as. His intellectually scripted spiritualist maxim expectations of what calm might be like during meditation never materialized during the actual experience.

Even though he thought he was doing things right as instructed when attempting Zen-style meditation, he still had the 1,000 mitote/maya voices screaming for attention and stoning his efforts at calm concentration with an intellectually founded flow of uncontrollable unwholesome sidetracking thoughts. At this point of his life, he had no calm mental state from self-training the ethical/moral peace needed to control the mind to find harmony within his body.

His self-devaluation and mental chatter kept the technique's advertised plateau of calm beyond his reach. It left him feeling sure that he was one of those who were just not really capable of reaching that plateau of religious/spiritual calm that normal children could. He didn't feel like he was a member of the socially accepted group that it works for.

The applicability of what he'd learned during his prior eleven years of three-times-a-week church meetings never really kicked in to help him find relief or understanding about what was presently going on in his life. Earlier in his Christian upbringing, many times his unfettered free will won out when his uncertain ego-managed grasp on reality tried to push him into taking the leap of blind faith. There were many a Sunday morning that he tried to force himself to walk down the aisle to be baptized...but couldn't.

The uncertainty echoed too loudly in his inner ear. He couldn't get past thinking how what he had heard promised in church was nothing short of being untraceable hollow unbacked religious promises. There was no living proof. Instances of real-time heavenly communication never materialized.

Praying was like shouting out into the dark with flashes of the images of those who had told him that he should pray interrupting any possibility of focused result. God had been asked many times to show some tangible sign. He watched with eyes wide open for an outside sign, leaving his sensual ears completely deaf to the message pulsating from within. Besides, the physicality of living today's present moment had never really been tied into being a part of the ancient Holy plan.

Just happy to be alive and with the renewed gratitude for just having a physical body to perceive life through, his free will found the sincere personal conviction to disregard any thought of self-doubt or depreciation that was screaming from his mitote/maya state of mind and to feel for, to actually sensually touch the essence of life as it passed by. Not thinking of it being a religious sort of task, there was no ritualistic hubbub with intellectually formed religious maxims to steal away the energy of the purpose.

It was a personal mission, between him and the heartbeat of the present moment. With barebones humility, he mustered up some old self-respect and felt re-initiated as an equal part of the human condition and deserving of his First Amendment right to witness the essence of real-time life as it is.

He sensed the deep primal feeling that his living soul was equally alive and equally qualified and capable of realizing the peace offered through this meditation he'd heard so much about and that he'd seen at least one friend make such a regular part of their life. His self-devaluation was scared away by his strong desire to feel life right then, right where he sat.

He felt his sensual interpretation of the sensed activity was just as important and just as needed and valid in the interconnecting web of humanity as that of anyone else...guru or not. This slap in the spiritual face served to minimize the unsettled mind of his mitote/maya state that Siddhartha said a truth seeker needs to accomplish to be able to selftrain their mind control...the first of his three self-trainings in his eightfold pathway to enlightenment.

No coaching or intellectually stored notes guided him on his self-tailored technique. His Christian training gave no description or clue as to what real-time living reality was and his only introduction to Buddhism included his friend's brief instructions on Zen meditation and having once read Herman Hesse's book *Siddhartha*.

He set aside the protocol of the earlier formed intellectually sketched illusionary spiritual maxims depicting Zen meditation. He simply wanted to wakingly know what life itself, that he was now so grateful for, felt like, in present moment terms...no more...no less. He orchestrated an organic sustained focus of body/mind harmony stripped down to its mature simplicity. Finding the right concentration to sustain the body/mind harmony that enabled tapping into his personal sensual arena of ongoing change was a serendipitous discovery.

As he sat up in bed, he knew he was very alive in no uncertain terms. Unknowingly, there was a spontaneous revolvement of the primal link between his all-knowing, deeper consciousness and his ignorant-to-the-laws-ofongoing-change waking consciousness. Enough of the vision-clouding misconceptions from acquired misguided prior conditioning had been squelched while sitting in bed to realize wakingly that a more substantial awareness of what living felt like was present and lay in wait for rediscovery. He felt steadfastly certain that as sure as he could sit there and see the things around him, this inner life-to-life connection had to be there. It was only necessary to make the right effort to direct this new right awareness.

This is what he did. His efforts were guided by his desire to taste life...not to avoid suffering. His intentions were directed at a desired state of being, not away from an unpleasant state. He didn't put the two together and associate his technique's soul-saving relevance as the religious/ spiritual maxim signpost that it represented until its insight twenty-five years later.

He found a deep reservoir of humility to secure his right to this end and with no planned protocol observed the constructs of sandbox etiquette. He decided to offer his own style of respect for the gift of life. Through his entire body, he personally recognized the essence of its living presence.

This motivation for his conscious mind to witness what life felt like was free of any notion of association with any antiquated religious ritual or spiritual mysticism and was unrelated to any of his intellectually stored and unique to his illusion, religious or spiritual maxims. This was in itself refreshing and tempted further involvement. This was just one individual offering the living essence of their living body to the bigger picture in exchange for consciously feeling life manifest itself in the ongoing transformation of their material body, as it passes through time fully alive with change.

He sat up comfortably in bed in a relaxed lotus position thinking that that position somehow seemed to help the gurus concentrate. (So, there was bit of eastern copycat involved.) Instead of saying om and trying to concentrate on the stomach area, he fought off imposing thought interuptions and sensually listened quietly and respectfully hung suspended in the present moment while waiting for the focus of his sustained awareness to ring with the sensual verification of the presence of the essence of each part of his body in the space it occupies. This involved a smooth transition of focus from appreciated body area to appreciated body area. His body scan went from head to toe and back up again.

Equal time and consideration was given to each area and to the full range of the good or bad feelings associated to any of the sensations, just to stay free of any notion of prejudice. It was the feeling itself that was important. The sensations came and the sensations went away.

He continued this bedtime process for a while as it would frequently put him to sleep while his mind was in turmoil over how life causes and effects were matching up at twenty-one years old and all the changes imposed following a near fatal car crash. Performing the body scan process worked its way into remission as satisfaction was found in better knowing what life felt like.

Twenty-five years later he discovered that his designed process also depicts the "right concentration" described by Siddhartha in the publication of his sutras describing the eightfold pathway to enlightenment Siddhartha had self-designed to undo his ignorance of the ways of our reality's impermanence. Spiritual maxims were asleep in this individual's intellectually constructed illusion of what religion, God, and all that was about. The exercise was not even perceived really as being spiritual or religious. He just wanted to introduce the feel of life to his waking conscious awareness. There was no intellectual memory record of any prior similar behavior of this sort.

He was looking for the truth about what life itself felt like, but had no conception of being a truth seeker. There was no association between what he was doing and the spiritual maxims he had intellectually stamped in his worldview. He just wanted to feel and celebrate life itself.

After twenty-five years he recognized his technique being described on an obscure radio station as part of a book review critiquing the *Art of Living* by William Hart. This led to him recognizing the association between reality's sensual presentation of spiritual signposts and his intellectually sketched spiritual/religious theology maxims.

He put two and two together and stopped pillaging for the answer to the unknown question about his soul's welfare. There was no more skimming magazine or webpage articles, listening to religious/spiritual TV specials or maybe tuning in to radio programs featuring what could offer a grounded answer to his uncertainty-prompted questioning explaining his mortality. He finally had an idea of how to approach the question that he wanted an answer to. The end was finally in sight...intellectually, at least.

The auto accident slap-in-the-face helped open his spiritual eye to the safe place in his mind where he could step back into the neutral pool of the human condition and look at and consider anything that occupied his attention during passing present moments. No matter which bell of fear rang or the volume of its toll, this mental island in the stream of ongoing change made a perfect place to ward off uncontrolled reactions and plan a course of appropriate action.

Interestingly enough, when he was sleepy, he would easily fall to sleep when in this state of focused concentration.

5

Self-Train Moral/ Ethical Behavior

Find Peace of Mind in Ethical/Moral Affairs

Siddhartha points out that after he realized that the lack of joy and happiness and the presence of present moment suffering was his problem and that it was the effect of his ignorance and that it was something he could eliminate, the first thing he focused on was calming his mind. He makes clear how right speech, right actions and right occupation choice helped him to minimize mental distress to allow him to become familiar with his thought patterns and self-train his mind control.

Don Miguel Ruiz's first agreement in his book *The Four Agreements* is for an individual to strive to be impeccable with their speech for the same reasons given by Siddhartha. The thoughts that propel an individual's speech are the same ones that precede their actions and affect what they do to earn a living.

Christianity's Ten Commandments and periodic updates seek the same end. Their intention is to mandate initiating moral and ethical behavior standards to maintain a peaceful environment until the coming of Christ. That's also where religion's spiritual guidance stops. Rome only wanted to harness and calm its Romans.

Behaviors like robbing a liquor store or killing someone would be mentally debilitating and exemplify doing something that would greatly inhibit a truth seeker's success at securing the mental peace necessary to self-train the mind control to sustain the focus to find the body/mind harmony to the formulate inspired insights to self-train the wisdom to understand the relational justice in this cause/effect reality that their ignorance of allows their suffering. Their thought patterns would be too distressed to concentrate.

6

Self-Train Mind Control and Temper Mind/Body Harmony

...Understand Mood to Emotional Reaction Relationship

Individuals Live Before Their Thoughts or Emotions... They Make Them...They Don't Get Made by Them

After a truth seeker has gained sufficient control over what feeds their unruly mitote/maya mental state to demonstrate good moral/ethical standards, they can then work on self-training how to control where their mind maintains its awareness to allow uninterrupted contemplative, deliberative, unbiased introspection to self-train a sensually founded understanding of the wisdom that allows them to have their present moment awareness relate to the calm peace of altruistic compassion instead of having to deal with continual sword fights within the ignorance that causes their suffering.

They make the harmonious coordinated mind/body effort to sustain mental awareness within their personal physical realm of their physical life manifestation. What better place to be when wanting to better understand life, than where life itself is manifested? They ease into finding the pulsating echo detectable in the deep-body search. It's the sustained mental pinging for the sensations that accompany the corrosive signals that generate the emotional storms of painful confusion they recognize as suffering. They feel the body as the rebound of its manifestation diffuses unregulated into its surrounding reality to resonate in the cause of the effect to better understand the justice of the circular process of how one becomes the other.

They let their awareness resonate in the hollow emptiness of a body where in reality there truly is no solid mass. Inspired thinking will lead to the insightful understanding deriving the wisdom-enriched self-knowledge to undo the ignorance of ongoing change. Lau Tzu says this is the harmony that will defeat the stranglehold on their belief system their self-ego commands by eventually gaining an enlightened understanding of the life truths that clarify exactly what it is that ties their knots of ignorance that allows their suffering.

Cognitive control is important. Through controlling impulses, managing negative emotions, and delaying gratification while in pursuit of this long-term goal, an individual will eventually reach that end.

7

Self-Train Wisdom-Enriched Self-Knowledge

Integrate Self-Trained Mind Control Sensitivity Throughout Everyday Attention Span

A truth seeker has to learn to adapt the presence of their sustained right concentration (mind-controlled meditation) to the different environmental circumstances encountered throughout the day. Mind control is not limited only to the times of primal meditation where its resonance is more easily trained in a more controlled environment with fewer outside attention-grabbers.

Self-training mind control in the suggested quiet atmosphere of primal meditation is really just providing a controlled entry-level environment with minimal outside interruption to become familiar with the process of finding the right mind/body harmony to generate the right concentration. This prepares a truth seeker on how to confront each everyday present moment with the awareness to see through the unproductive nature of the thought patterns that bring on addictive behavior. This can be the thinking that resonates in suffering the unrest caused when what's expected doesn't line up with what is or vice versa.

This allows the gradual integration of a more controllable mind to adapt and acclimate the heightened awareness of a greater mental sensitivity throughout the day. Let it become the driving force fueling the individual's normal train of thought.

When self-training the harmony of mind control to sustain the right thinking (deliberation and dispassionate consideration) during body/mind analysis (primal meditation), a truth seeker must learn to deliberate or step back and notice and appreciate how with the flow of time their moods will flow and adapt to the uphill switchbacks of everyday life. They need to become aware of their body's perception of the sensations that accompany any mood changes at all times throughout the day...not just during times of mind/ body analysis.

A truth seeker must relax and identify the feel of the flow of perceptions that those sensation-triggers hitchhike a ride in on. It's this flowing thought process that carries the perceptions of the emotion-drawing sensation packages that trigger the recurring habit energy fueled reactions. Its appearance dons an ego mask to help hide its unfounded motivator from the wisdom locked in the deeper consciousness.

The truth seeker should become familiar with how they actually feel during the moments they perceive the real-life sensation packages that, after faulty prior conditioning have combined to trigger reactionary emotional distress. This is the same sort of self-trained mind control that's targeted during primal meditation while focused intently on the coming and going sensations while recognizing and eliminating any accompanying interruptive thought patterns while life manifests itself...filling their flesh with life...directly from the Holy Ghost.

This unchanging uncontrollable flow of sensation is always there. It provides texture to the human stream of consciousness. It's the unavoidable transformation into something else that defines the emptiness of form that everything in the realm of human perception really has.

This flow of consciousness is quite a suitable platform for sustaining an ongoing state of ignorance where the thought-shuffling input from a developed mitote/maya state sets the stage for ongoing confusion and frustration. It represents the state of reality for most people. On the other extreme, this stream of consciousness can support a state of wisdom-enriched awareness, proactively focused forward, that's too busy realizing ongoing love, compassion and happiness to fetter away time suffering over miscued understandings.

For a truth seeker to self-train their mind control, to have the conscious power to organize, manage and direct their thinking, they have to recognize their mind. They need to be able to single out and recognize the sensitivity of what the real-time expression of the ongoing process of thinking actually feels like. Then they can begin to slow down and identify the corresponding causing sensations associated with the affected reactionary emotions that overlay their waves of thought that seemingly slide in unchecked of their own accord. It's a beautiful feeling to recognize and realize that this state of mind doesn't have to be.

The truth seeker with a maturing spiritual awareness is learning to recognize and eliminate objectionable thinking patterns. This ability should continue to develop...whether silently positioned in full lotus position or not.

Anytime through the day a disturbing emotion takes over an individual's mental floor, the individual needs to become his or her own island of detached deliberation. Their recognition of sensually announced brain wave thought patterns becomes linked to the perceived mood they feel they are in. They learn to recognize its peculiar nature, step back and become familiar with the feeling of the type of mental unrest and its physical symptoms, understand its foreign nature and dismiss its noncontributory nonproductive no-end power. These sensual habit energy triggers affect the upcoming emotional anxiety allowing their suffering.

When the sensational trigger red flag appears again, the truth seeker can feel forewarned and with steadfast faith in their belief of this reality's same dimensional setup holding consistent, they can let it pass. They understand its foreign nature that recognizes attachment, ignorant of the relational wisdom of ongoing change.

It's while in waking awareness in the living sea of sensation-perception that a truth seeker can step back, consider and deliberate over what's going on that allows their reactionary response to the sensation's misguided perception. They recognize and attach or associate their perception of the ongoing sensation trigger package to the ongoing affected emotion/mood. They should learn to do this whether in the more controlled atmosphere of primal meditation or while driving down the highway or maybe while wrapped up in the arms of someone they really love.

They need to stand ready to adapt and integrate the trained or learned mind control methodology of primal meditation to real life's more uncontrolled environments where their perceptual triggers typically arise. They learn to give full attention to our reality's ephemeral essence.

Just like during the times of body/mind analysis of primal meditation, where they perceive the various waves of mind/ body sensations, their mind can now recognize those that trigger their moods of emotional havoc as well as relaxed joy, signaling present moment suffering or compassion that come in everyday life situations. The body/mind harmony protocol remains as during the more environmentally controlled primal meditation.

The timely migration of mind-flow protocol is what comes to a truth seeker as they change the nature of their mind. They're waking up to the truth savvy that accompanies the experientially associated relational wisdom undoing the ignorance of impermanence coming from their internalized misguided prior conditioning that entertains illusionary ideas of continual shapes, objects, beliefs and ideas having a nature of permanence or unchanging continuity that allows attachment. With this change in the truth seeker's nature of thought processing, there comes a change in their worldview...a change in their mind and in their thinking. Their emotionally reactive sensational triggers are in time recognized and acted on differently to no longer be a part of the present moment to cause them any suffering.

It's during normal daily life experience that the sensation triggers that sponsor reactionary mood swings are more likely to happen...not while sitting quiet in primal meditation. These are the same coming and going sensations targeted by the right concentration of self-trained mind control, only they are the different and in-your-face coming and going sensations associated with normal living that tag the different sensational triggers. A truth seeker trains their mind to have the awareness to withstand the distracting outside interference of everyday life.

It's within an individual's normal daily environment that situations that produce the sensation cocktails that trigger reactionary emotions present themselves. An unfettered free will must be well-nurtured and always on the alert. Right effort must be expended to sustain right awareness to find the right concentration needed for effective primal meditation when walking, sitting, riding a bus or eating in a restaurant.

The individual has to extend the effort and awareness of right concentration in primal meditation into their normal life to recognize the right thinking and right understanding to be available to decipher the cause/effect relational justice found in normal situations, not just limiting it to times when self-training mind control in quiet meditation. Normal life circumstances include the moments when the individual's real sensational red flag packages present themselves. This is when they must be acknowledged and dealt with.

Use Mind/Body Harmony...Exercise Primal Link

Mind-into-body concentration makes contact with our Source on the deepest of levels. It's like looking into the blue flame of life. That's as deep as it can go. Experientially witnessing our Source is not complicated and there are no special mantras or membership rituals required.

A truth seeker is making real progress in connecting the dots to understand life's purpose once the relationship in the theology-meets-reality concept is grasped. Gaining the waking capacity to associate how the present moment spirituality that this right concentration feeds and magnifies is actually the same neutered spirituality as that of the intellectually sketched model of spirituality of the described spiritual world of our biblical ancestors will in itself bring fervor to continue mind/body analysis. After this realization, the spirituality connection becomes more visible to the waking consciousness.

This means bringing to waking understanding how to intensify the enrichment of life wisdom through the inspired insightful experiential understanding of the network of relational justice in this cause/effect reality. Life's intentions have a clearer defined end purpose. Life is being lived on purpose.

To know that focusing concentration in this way means tapping into the same source of relational wisdom that relates to the situational justice in this cause/effect reality that's understood by many to be accessed only through devout reverence to the Almighty Above is huge. Theology meets reality on a more personal level.

Having this waking awareness unlocks the chains of apathy and encourages the pursuit of more wisdom. Knowing that this inner calm is the arena of inspiration for developing insightful life wisdom enables a truth seeker to purposefully accumulating more wisdom sooner than when waiting for the reservoir of experiential wisdom that can come with old age that has been accumulated serendipitously throughout life and maybe thought to be a different sort of wisdom than that posed biblically from God.

Everyone makes reference in one way or another to how good they feel and how they love it when they can get into a workout rhythm where they find some sort of mental cadence that enables their ability to find deep relaxation...like getting past "the wall" after about eighteen miles when running a marathon. Being in this harmonious mind/body awareness zone can help them enter into a calm introspection to reflect and think-out solutions to life's imbalances.

Having the mind control to sustain the right awareness in the essence of the body's presence found while exercising in the gym follows the same self-training ideology or profile as when seeking the body/mind harmony from the lotus position cross-legged under a Buddha tree. One difference is that it's much easier to focus sustained awareness on the coming and going sensations in the different body areas when they are burning fuel and heated up or their fuel depletion is being felt in some way. Their essence of their presence is magnified. The flesh within that space is sensually ignited.

When the heart rate increases to where it demands notice, the muscles begin crying for more glucose, sweat visibly seeps from skin pours and the lungs demand more oxygen, it is much easier for a truth seeker to sustain the wholesome thought patterns indicative of right effort with the focus of their mental right awareness into a harmonious right concentration into this more easily detectable excited physical state. The inspired right thinking generates insightful understanding of the savvy of the flame of life itself. This is the wonderful point where people become suspended in right concentration.

Some athletes will be sure to get plenty of sleep, eat carbs, buy new running shoes, a touring bicycle or maybe take a dose of their cannabis medication before challenging themselves with their chosen activity. Individuals anticipate and plan for a stretch of time where they can get lost in their thoughts and dig deep to decide how they really feel about something.

The tetrahydrocannabinol (THC) content of the cannabis plant triggers a seeming change in the rhythm and dynamism of thought patterns. The amount of change depends of course on the amount of THC involved and the person's level of tolerance.

THC-influenced thought patterns stand out in their own way. Like normal thought patterns, they too allow a truth seeker to quarry and consider their perceived mental state...forms of anxiety or euphoria for example. Something with the style of perception changes. The perceptual order of priority given to different sensual factors can vary.

Exercisers are setting themselves up for the flow of harmonious right thinking coming from their focused minds sensing the activity in their body parts to inspire the insightful understanding of the human condition that normally remains locked in the subtle level of the human deeper consciousness. They have opened the sensual pages of the living display of the relational savvy of our Source's tree of wisdom.

They are exercising and could be strengthening the primal link between their deeper consciousness and their waking awareness. They're probably not aware of it, but they are actualizing in real-time, the theological sketches they've made of the religious/spiritual concepts they've internalized to help support their comprised worldview. They probably don't realize this.

They're probably not thinking about their collection of intellectually stored accounts of what the Holy Spirit is...like the mind-imprinted visual of the Holy Spirit that crept silently through Egypt as a mist in the movie *The Ten Commandments*, as the tenth plague when killing all of Egypt's first-born sons. They probably don't sense the modern-day incarnation of the Holy Spirit as the spark of life in each of the coming and going bits of energy that melds the cause/effect rhythm of one present moment to the next as they ponder life's ways while peddling their stationary bicycle.

At that moment, if they are a believer, they are experiencing the real-life embodiment of their theological conceptions of what Christianity's Holy Spirit, God (source), and Christ (the message) are, unable to make the connection. They simply see their activity as modern-day working out, something unrelated to their spiritual development, which they really couldn't define if asked...a life-filled present moment unrelated to their mental sepia still shots of holy days long ago.

It's the intensified hard-to-forget feeling of this flame of life that propels the mental thought train into a relaxed state of introspection and effective problem-solving during times of physical exertion that people remember and is what keeps them coming back to their exercise forum for more. As they sweat and breath hard, they find relief in unlocking the deeper feelings they have when considering the relational justice among the causing factors in their reality. They are exercising the primal link stretching from the deeper to the waking consciousness and letting surface their inborn understanding of the human condition.

The desire for the thrill of adrenaline is different. The perception of the causal factors that results in the call for adrenaline involves more putting to test the coordination of learned mind/body harmony...like during a martial arts test. Breaking boards or getting the desired effect from exercising a technique, requires the harmonious timing of learned mind/body coordination coming from the mind/body muscle memory of prior conditioning. Right concentration has to be there to successfully coordinate the point of contact with the speed of the strike and best time for energy release. Their thought patterns shouldn't be sidetracked with thoughts of any other topics. Having the adrenaline increases their ability to focus.

Sensual Trigger Recognition is a Key to Mind Transformation

As an individual tries to understand and undo their ignorance of what's allowing their present moment suffering, they will become more familiar with how their mind operates. The process of making the right effort to perform perception rehab work to allow recognizing the sensual red flags and eliminating unwholesome nondirective thought patterns and replacing them with sustained directed wholesome thought patterns takes time.

Truth seekers develop a more alert recognition of things like the increased heartbeat, tightened muscles and possible short temper or the pressure between the temples that are the physical symptoms or the red-flag precursors of the sensation triggers that signal having a mental state paralyzed by the uncertainties that culminate in stress.

After catching this warning and stepping back in deliberation, they will realize that a solution to this arising state would be to instead focus attention on affecting productivity. They'll focus forward in a state of proactive attention. They'll sigh with recognized purpose. They'll move on.

They'll learn to replace the unwholesome thought patters associated with stress with the wholesome thought patterns that lead to productivity. Noxious ruminations of worry will be sharpened into present moment awareness. Needless shadows of guilt and regret will brightened up into rays of inspiration.

Unending crags of mental conflict will smooth into the give and take efforts of peaceful compassion. Fearinspired cognitions of self-doubt and uncertainty will turn into self-command.

Sensitize to Recognizing Association with Prior Lifetimes

While a truth seeker spiritually matures from their self-trainings needed to undo the ignorance that allows refreshing their joy and happiness, they need to learn to recognize and associate the reappearance of forgotten moods experienced during times of earlier lifetime contentment that have since been buried in the thought patterns related to the discontentment resulting from faulty prior conditioning.

With the expunging of unwholesome thought patterns, the implanted sensual perceptions from past occasions when they were sensually experienced that have faded into the deeper consciousness catacombs of accumulated experiential conditioning can make their way back into the present moment consciousness.

When freeing up a hijacked free will, there will be sudden reemergences of subtle emotions that were experienced during earlier times of their life. They might feel like shades of satisfaction or reassured contentment. These shades of lightened feeling are often accompanied by an unforced deep sigh of relief.

They can be accompanied by a feeling of déjà vu. Memories of similar thought patterns that generated emotions during times during an individual's time of childhood innocence might perplexingly reappear.

These renewed perceptions of reality were ones experienced before misguided conditioning was allowed to infiltrate the belief system to numb the worldview with the unregistered confusion over the nature of this reality and thus what system of relational justice to apply to the events that make up the present moment. These were times of perceiving things where frustrating thought patterns coming from unverified internalized claims smothered out the thought patterns experienced from appreciating things as they really are.

It's the reemergence of wholesome thought patterns long missed that have been subdued and shaded by the internalization of misguided claims that left the free will numbed with unsure doubt and question. Those long lost thought patterns quit making their appearance until undoing the ignorance that kept them shadowed.

Make Yourself an Island

An individual's focused mind and body can unite in harmony in the most quiet of places where the coming and going pulse of this reality's life percolation can deaden out all outside white noise. It's a private retreat for the individual to go to experience nothing but the sensual echo of the truth. An individual's mind and body when harmoniously united in right concentration is their sensual island of refuge.

It's the material platform from which their soul can explore the experience of living in the reality of this world to better understand the mystery of its nature of ever-change. They could be in no better place to learn about its ways of balancing the relational scales of justice.

It's a small part of a spiritual platform that everybody is an interconnected part of, but a piece that nobody else can stand on. Realize this and self-train the ability to tap into the solace and peace it offers.

The coming and going pulse of truth felt within the truth seeker's flesh is constant and their flesh is the only material site for sensual contact they have with this reality. Its charter follows the same set of rules no matter what social situation someone finds himself in. It can be consciously visited anytime things might seem to get too out of hand or intimidating. It's the perfect place to go when something seems too overpowering. It's a place that carries no mortgage and is just a thought away.

The truth of life's coming and going manifestation should also be consciously revisited any time things may seem to get a little too good. Any time, any place, the solace within one's human shell can be revisited to remind them that they aren't inferior to anyone else or that they are no better than anyone else...that they deserve fair treatment, and they must offer fair treatment. It's a place for an individual to consciously remind the unsure ego that manages the affairs of their worldview what balance really is...not to go manic/ depressive about whom or what they think they are.

The inner experience is ageless. It's timeless. The coming and going manifestation of life in the theater of peaceful retreat is the same at birth as it is at one hundred years old, passing time in a nursing home or meditating forty days and forty nights. The same pulse of the coming and going sensual media is always there. It gets more reassuring and sweeter each time it is visited.

It's the same coming and going sensual code tapping out the statutes of cause/ effect relational justice for every evolving form and shape in this reality. Each separate human body is a private personal wave in the all-inclusive sea of humanity.

While developing self-definition and undoing the ignorance of ever-change and finding the balance to break the rhythm of uncontrolled reactions to recognize, understand and act on perceived sensations, the mind develops freedom from attachment to thinking characterized by uncontrolled reactionary craving and aversive thought patterns. This develops the truth seeker's ability to recognize and retreat into their personal comfort zone.

In any situation, they can mentally step back, using their internal reality as an island to stand on, shake off developing stress and regain sight of their inner bearing. They can get a steroid injection of steadfast faith to help strengthen their resolve of self-confidence over the shadow of uncertainty. They can reconsider actions that might take a bigger piece of the pie than the individual really deserves.

With the right concentration, the 1,000 voices of the ego-managed mitote/ maya can be effectively squelched. The coming and going sensations are recognized with deliberating equanimity and impartial deliberation as to eliminate the mind jacking and overpowering emotionally triggered reactionary thought pattern displays. This zone can become a truth seeker's refuge any time and at any place for them to step back, weigh and consider options and to then act.

When an individual takes their thought stream back into a quiet idle zone of sensual deliberation, internal verbal dialogue is hushed. It's a slightly deeper shadow of consciousness. It's a zone of reflective feeling...massaging the free will... floating thoughts freely in the lake of rational relational possibilities. It's a time to seek and to find.

Conscious Appreciation of Primal Harmony

The process of becoming enlightened about the conditioned misinterpretations of the way reality works becomes self-perpetuating. With perseverance, the improvement in thought awareness and mind control is wakingly noticed. A foundation for growth has been established. It's supported and protected by a faith that's steadfast in what's been experienced.

To be able to wakingly see how sustaining the focus of mental awareness into the ongoing life manifestation within the body's flesh is, actually witnessing the most primal form of harmony, is invigorating. It's mentally lightening. It removes a load of sorts.

The deeper the understanding of this relationship settles into the conscious awareness, the more enlightened the truth seeker becomes. The more the feeling of true joy infiltrates their present moment. Realizing this sensual definition of the intellectual term gives a totally refreshed understanding of what harmony means. It can be seen how the word harmony is used so loosely with such a kaleidoscope of meaning.

It's completely simple and is defined from within. It sharpens the understanding of what's involved when more than one thing works together to accomplish a common goal.

Realizing that this wisdom-enriched understanding is free and present all the time creates an enlivening stir in the spirit. It's like getting a different feel for what's needed to create truly pure, uninterrupted, virgin harmony. It's the source of primal poetry. It's all that Siddhartha would talk about after it all finally made sense to him.

Yet, it's an awareness that just can't be put into words. It can be understood how this is the same present moment harmony that our enlightened ancestors had also sensually discovered and tried to put into words and teach. Understanding the sensual meaning of an intellectual message just doesn't happen.

It's a wonderful thing that can possibly be quicker understood when there are more people after the same goal and individual results from the efforts of the process are shared. To preserve its virgin nature, it's best if the field of its pursuit is maintained in the most pure and simple state possible, which happens only in the present moment. It has to be recognized in the place and time where it lives. Shadowing its truth with thought-taxing theological notions of different aspects of past figures in time and not what the message of those past figures in time was defeats the purpose.

The relational harmony that's sensually discovered is the present moment incarnation of what's intellectually depicted by religious theology. Including all the religious dogma, rites, and rituals of the past few millennia makes catching the present moment sense of how this harmony enables the inspired thinking for insightful wisdom-enriched self-understanding or self-awareness quite impossible.

Changing the Nature of the Human Mind

A truth seeker must be able to differentiate between a reality with an impermanent nature where all aspects of that reality are in a constant state of transformation and an illusionary reality with a nature that condones the notion of an object being in a state of continuity over the passage of time. The effects from how they recognize the nature of this reality will trickle down from the decisions they make and determine their present moment ratio of happiness to suffering.

Becoming wise enough to the suffering-related effects of thought patterns spawned from intentions chasing after any form of attachment to craving more or less of something to finding the resolution to give up the notion that something could have the permanence to become attached to in the first place is a big step forward in overcoming the primal ignorance of the human condition. It's coming one step closer to becoming enlightened about what keeps joy and happiness at a distance out of reach and allows suffering.

When an individual can differentiate between impermanence and continuity and can fittingly change what they recognize the nature of this reality to be and realize how, with their change in understanding, the relational justice between the cause/effect factors in any situation will change how they perceive what they experience in life, they have initiated change the nature of their mind and their worldview. Changing the nature of their mind, in turn changes the nature of their thinking.

Understanding the impermanent nature of this reality must be achieved now while still a living and contributing part of humanity's collective spiritual maturation process. It has to be achieved while living, when an individual can sensually register the feedback from actively tapping into the heartbeat of the whole of the living reality to introspectively contemplate and deliberate over what's being sensually communicated to understand what's wrong with their perspective on life that strips away their happiness and leaves them suffering.

When it makes sense to an individual that the same present moment suffering they pray to an outside entity to rid them of is actually rooted in their ignorance of the savvy of our Source's impermanent nature and that since the troubling effects of this cause materialize from their inner unrest, it becomes clear that this imbedded cause, would be better confronted from within where it festers in its highly contagious state.

Truth seekers must find the nerve to unchain their free will and place more trust in their ego-hushed intuitive questioning that often silently recoils to many of the things they decide to do in everyday situations. Their free will mutely queries many of their decisions while in the back of their mind they still silently bank on the mock dependability of earlier internalized misguided claims with purposes that the nature of were possibly never experientially verified. Hopefully, it will let them slide by again.

Their free will's built-in self-protection facet has for too long been left exposed to the corrosive influence coming from the gradual chipping away effect of their repeated unwarranted internalizing of under-verified claims in shaping their worldview. It gets to the point where some people will too easily grant the undeserved trust to believe just about anything they hear.

Having unverified cause-to-effect causal connections in what populates an individual's belief system, leaves an experience void or further widens the existing experience void in their belief system between hearing the claim made about the cause or the what/why of something and in perceiving it's effect. This experience void fills up with their doubt and uncertainty of the unknown. A fundamentalist scab forms to make the ends meet to ward off the present moment fear and suffering that always follows.

Their ego uses up much of their present moment energy trying to make fit or to cover up their inner misunderstanding of mismatching of causes and effects. It counters by building an impenetrable wall of denial. The cost of this fear-generated pride is time wasted and progress unmade. They, like modern science, need to witness the living proof of what they are told in the first place instead of blindly believing it.

Any claim that honors cause/effect relationships built on contributing causal factors having natures favoring any kind of permanence is misguided and based on an illusion that depends on the item's continuity over the passage of time. This includes illusions of things or ideas that remain as remembered to be that can become attached to. This type of claim represents a great proportion of the beliefs and ideas that people willingly believe and internalize to make their worldviews what they are.

When a truth seeker changes their perception of what they think the nature of things or ideas is or how something acts in response to this reality's impermanence, they are adjusting their perception of the nature and intended purpose of our primal Source that everything is a part of. Their ongoing thinking will reflect a matching change in the nature of their mind. When an individual changes the nature of their mind they are changing the nature of their worldview or how they think.

During this process when a truth seeker changes their perspective from ignorantly assuming the continual presence of things to recognizing present moment impermanence, the belief system is regaining its bearing. They have identified and filtered from the belief system the constructs of a worldview taken from the misguided beliefs internalized during prior conditioning that had been based on unverified claims where the purposes of many were designed to find their truth only in a reality with a nature allowing the continual permanence of its constituents.

Decoding the tree of wisdom that makes sense of the relational justice that exists among the factors making up the whole universal process of impermanence will bring a truth seeker to the point where their experiential knowledge frees them from the misconceptions of their prior conditioning that's robbed them of their joy and happiness and allowed their suffering.

A truth seeker needs to learn to recognize and associate the intellectually scored conceptions of theology's religious and spiritual maxims with their actual sensually coded living incarnations when they appear. A truth seeker must begin their journey to gaining self-knowledge from right where they stand at this very present moment without looking back.

Like Siddhartha said on his deathbed how everything changes and to do the due diligence to figure this out, developing a conscious understanding of this must become a life purpose. For the decades after his enlightenment, it's said that all he did was to help truth seekers find their pathway to gaining their enlightenment about their ignorance.

When a truth seeker finally understands and adjusts what they recognize the nature of our Source to be, they change the nature of how they see our Source's reality. By recognizing our reality's impermanence and rejecting notions tied to a reality with a nature of permanence, their worldview will not believe or originate intended purposes that deal with any kind of attachment. By changing the nature of their mind, they have changed the nature of how and what they think.

Develop Unsolicited Self-Perpetuating Compassion ...Practice Right Concentration Mind Control

Interrupting the conscious mind's streaming thought pattern to make the right effort to sustain the right awareness to enter into the right concentration where the mind is in the best ecosystem of sorts to inspire insightful wisdom enrichment is really the same thought control effort made when directing the mind into a state of compassion. Interrupting the waking mind's thought stream to purposefully redirect its intention of awareness into the essence of something else is the same.

In both cases, mental awareness is being consciously recognized and seized upon to be decisively redirected into the essence of the presence of something else's purpose. Practicing going into right concentration introduces and eases the way for allowing compassion to interrupt the ways of the conscious mind. It's a beneficial result of self-training the ability to control the mind to sustain an intended purpose of focus.

The mental pathway for compassionate thinking with a compassion-based worldview eventually becomes one within itself and with the protective strength of a matching steadfast faith, it regenerates its own existence. There becomes no need for the intellectual reminder designed to reopen the waking production of compassionate thought patterns. The Mahayana Buddhist mental conversations designed to remind one's self why another person deserves compassion or having to consciously invoke empathy for another person by changing from thinking about "me" or "I am" to slipping into the other person's shoes becomes unnecessary.

The present moment thought patterns confused by unrealized imbedded indecision about the nature of this reality's relational justice fail to reappear once they're recognized and understood. The pent up mental energy filling the truth seeker's belief system void of uncertainty is replaced by the thought waves that sponsor compassion. Childhood curiosity slowly resurfaces to replace their fear of uncertainty. The mental energy consciously servicing the uncertainty of what's in store for the "I am" that really doesn't exist can now dwell in the common-to-all field of relational justice this impermanent reality represents.

When taking the concept of "I" out of the conscious mind's thought stream, loneliness disappears and a feeling of shared commonality prevails. Altruism sponsors the intentions associated with proactivity. Altruism wraps itself around proactivity and compassion becomes well seated in the conscious mind.

The more often a truth seeker invokes their self-trained ability to control their mental awareness by interrupting their thought pattern stream to focus it into the essence of the presence of another purpose, they're experiencing what the transition's like to switch their awareness into a mental presence centered around compassion.

Okay Then...What Now?

Why does a religious believer seek protection from suffering via an outside separate entity...a god figure? Maybe it's matching to have an unknown protector on hand to pray to during the low times that will surely show up in the unavoidable unknown future. Is it just something that's common in their society? Are they afraid of going to hell, or does the all-inclusive stay in heaven that bans all the sinners appeal to them?

Not understanding what an existing presence in this reality might feel like after an individual's spirit parts from their body is very undefined and can be quite unsettling. The thought that all conscious perceptions might just cease and go blank at the time of death is too much of the unknown for many to face. The fear of the loneliness (the feeling of non-inclusion that comes with feeling left out) that can come with the thought of not being a consciously present part of the human condition in the stream of life instills fear in many.

Not knowing where the mind goes after the body dies is an important question to everyone. People seem to accept the change of having the mind part from the body when they die, but where would their sequestered concept that they recognize as "I," "me," or "self" (the ego that managed their worldview) go? Surely, the presence of awareness that they think with can't just stop. This uncertainty can bring paralyzing fear to an individual who has no direction on understanding the process it's a part of.

Is the imagined burn from the fire and brimstone that's stirred in with all the conceivable forms of suffering that Christianity threatens nonbelievers or erring believers with, really something an individual can understand and relate to in terms of their cumulative present moment sensual history? Is an individual appeased by the promise of an afterlife eternal joy and happiness even though until they die their life's full of the frustrating and wearisome present moments that they're promised afterlife protection from?

They live in a state of mind that causes them to suffer instead of developing the sensual history that supports the targeted niceties of the joy and happiness attained once up in heaven. Shouldn't they possibly condition their conscious awareness for the perception of joy and happiness while they're alive and have a window into seeing how to be able to actively influence the change that influences their future so after they die they'll be able to better recognize its presence up in heaven?

There has yet to be any real experiential testimony to critique the way the relational justice of this impermanent reality works for a spirit with no material body that's ventured out non-volunteer style to try out a new afterlife presence. Maybe there's a dimension of this reality with a nature that's continual?

Each individual can use their open imagination to ponder at how nice heaven can be as it's been tagged with no descriptive account in present moment terms. It's never been seen, felt, or even reported on by someone who's been there. Just its mention brings up a subjective state of perception that's adjusted to best complement the fears and desires in the environment any listening individual has reference to. One man's hell can be another man's heaven...depending on what their conditioned perspective is.

When a truth seeker in this lifetime self-trains a calm enough mental platform, they can find the humble cerebral focus to self-train their mind control. They can self-train the ability to develop and sustain the mind/body harmony to suspend their mental awareness in the essence of their body's coming and going material presence and become sensually familiar with the changing of life as it manifests itself. This can inspire their thinking to develop an insightful wisdom-enriched understanding of the relational justice that maintains balance in this sensually witnessed impermanent reality. They can eventually self-train an enlightened wisdom-enriched understanding of the nature of intended purpose of this reality.

Their ignorance that sponsored all their fears and uncertainty coming from the unknown would be gone.

This life path takes the unknown out the ignorance about the ways of the bigger picture that has created the individual's fear that panics them into looking for the answer to securing their mental peace through an all-knowing, all-powerful godly force residing up in the heavens. With the attainment of self-knowledge, their fear of the unknown disappears, as there's no unknown. After a wisdom-enriched awareness of reality is reached to enlighten the individual about the ignorance that causes their suffering and their self-defending ego is absolved, what do they have to seek protection from?

Endnotes

SECTION I

1. Ruiz, don Miguel. *The Four Agreements* 1997, Miguel Angel Ruiz, MD. 16.

2. Vigils, Bernadette and Arlene Broska. *The Mastery of Awareness: Living the Agreements*; foreword by don Miguel Ruiz. 22–23.

3. Ruiz, *Four Agreements*. 19.

4. Vigil, *Mastery of Awareness*. 11.

5. Ruiz, *Four Agreements*. 98.

6. Rinchen, Geshe Sonam. *Atisha's Lamp For the Path to Enlightenment*. 27 and 28.

7. Ibid., 38 and 48.

8. Ibid., 29.

9. Vigil, *Mastery of Awareness*. 38–40.

10. Ibid., 17.

11. Freud, Sigmund. *Moses and Monotheism*. 178–179.

12. http://en.wikipedia.org/wiki/affluenza.

13. Rinchen. *Atisha's Lamp For the Path to Enlightenment*. 31.

14. Ibid., 30.

15. Ibid., 43.

16. "Peter Merel's *Tao Te Ching* translation," verse 33, Alistair.Cockburn.us, accessed Oct. 24, 2014. http:// alistair.cockburn.us/Peter+Merel's+Tao+Te+Ching+translation.

SECTION II

1. Ruiz, don Miguel. From the book The Four Agreements 1997, Miguel Angel Ruiz, MD. 3.

2. Ibid., 4–5.

3. Ibid., 5.

4. Barber, Benjamin R. by *Consumed: How Markets Corrupt Children, Infantilize Adults, and Swallow Citizens Whole* Benjamin R. Barber. Copyright 2007 by Benjamin R. Barber 38.

5. Ibid., 41.

6. Ibid., 291.

7. Ibid., 81.

8. Ibid., 82. 11. Ibid., 212.

9. Hanh, Thich Nhat. *The Heart of the Buddha's Teaching. (1998)* by Thich Nhat Hanh 12.

10 Capra, Fritjof. *The Tao of Physics: An Exploration of the Parallels Between Modern Physics and Eastern Mysticism*, Third Edition, Updated. 32.

11 Ibid., 35.

12 Hanh. *Heart of the Buddha's Teaching.* 13.

13 Ibid., 13.

14 Ibid., 16.

15 Ibid., 14.

16 Ibid., 16.

17 "Peter Merel's *Tao Te Ching* translation," opening caveat, Alistair. Cockburn.us, accessed Oct. 24, 2014, http://alistair.cockburn.us/ Peter+Merel's+Tao+Te+Ching+translation.

18 Rinchen, Geshe Sonam. *Atisha's Lamp For the Path to Enlightenment.* 51.

19 Capra, *The Tao of Physics.* 86.

20 Notovitch translation. "The Lost Years of Jesus: The Life of Saint Issa." (http:// reluctant-messenger.com/ issa.htm), Chpt 6, verses 3–4.

21 Hanh. *Heart of the Buddha's Teaching.* 15.

22 Ibid., 16–17.

23 Ibid., 18.

24 Wikipedia contributors, "The Twilight Zone (1959 TV series)," *Wikipedia, The Free Encyclopedia,* http:// en.wikipedia.org/w/index.php?title=The_Twilight_ Zone_ (1959_TV_series) &oldid=630931410 (accessed October 24, 2014).

25 Hanh, Thich Nhat. *Interbeing: Fourteen Guidelines for Engaged Buddhism* by Thich Nhat Hanh. 123.

26 1   Rinchen. *Atisha's Lamp For the Path to Enlightenment.* 43.

27 Ruiz, *Four Agreements.* 13.

28. Wikipedia contributors, "Tanhā," *Wikipedia, The Free Encyclopedia.* http://en.wikipedia.org/w/ index. php?title=Ta%E1%B9%87h%C4%81&oldid=615113111. (Accessed 9-23-14.)

29 Rinchen. *Atisha's Lamp For the Path to Enlightenment.* 42.

30 Vigils, Bernadette and Arlene Broska. *The Mastery of Awareness: Living the Agreements*; foreword by don Miguel Ruiz. 24–25.

31 Ruiz, *Four Agreements.* (San Rafael, CA: Amber-Allen Publishing, Inc., 1997), 102.

32 Ibid., 110.

33 Ibid., 116.

34 Rinchen. *Atisha's Lamp For the Path to Enlightenment.* 32.

35 Ibid., 43–44.

36 Wikipedia contributors, "Tanhā," Wikipedia, The Free Encyclopedia. http:// en.wikipedia.org/w/index.php?ti-tle=Ta%E1%B9%87h%C4%81&oldid=615 113111 (Accessed 9-23-14.)

SECTION III

1. Chopra, Deepak. 1/1/2014 PBS fund drive.

2. Hanh, Thich Nhat. *The Heart of the Buddha's Teaching. (1998)* by Thich Nhat Hanh. 81.

3. Ruiz, don Miguel. From the book *The Four Agreements Companion Book* 2000, Miguel Angel Ruiz, MD. 119–120.

4. Hanh. *Heart of the Buddha's Teaching.* 53–54.

5. Smith, Jonah. "World Without Love." Los Angeles, CA, Voluptuary Music, 2009.

6. Capra, Fritjof. *The Tao of Physics: An Exploration of the Parallels Between Modern Physics and Eastern Mysticism*, Third Edition, Updated. 86.

7. Hanh. *Heart of the Buddha's Teaching.* 17.

8. "Peter Merel's *Tao Te Ching* translation," verse 33, Alistair. Cockburn.us, accessed Oct. 24, 2014, http:// alistair.cockburn.us/ Peter+Merel's+Tao+Te+Ching+translation.

9. *Dhammapada* XXI. (293) 16, BuddhismToday.com, Accessed 9-19-14, glish/texts/ khuddaka/dhp/21.html.

10. "Peter Merel's *Tao Te Ching* translation," verse 33, Alistair. Cockburn.us, accessed Oct. 24, 2014 http:// alistair.cockburn.us/ Peter+Merel's+Tao+Te+Ching+translation.

11. Rinchen. Geshe Sonam. *Atisha's Lamp For the Path to Enlightenment*. 39–40.

12. Hanh. *Heart of the Buddha's Teaching*. 74.

13. Ibid., 49.

14. Ibid., 54.

15. Ibid., 54–55.

16. Ibid., 50.

17. Ibid., 64.

18. Ibid., 60–62.

19. Ibid., 111.

20. Ibid., 105–106.

21. Ibid., 77.

22. Capra. *The Tao of Physics*. (Boston: Shambhala Publications), 116.

SECTION IV

1. Ruiz, don Miguel. From the book *the Four Agreements* 1997, Miguel Angel Ruiz, MD. 14.

Bibliography

Barber, Benjamin R. *Consumed: How Markets Corrupt Children, Infantilize Adults, and Swallow Citizens Whole* by Benjamin R. Barber.

Capra, Fritjof. *The Tao of Physics: An Exploration of the Parallels Between Modern Physics and Eastern Mysticism*, Third Edition, Updated.

Chopra, Deepak MD. *How to Know God: The Soul's Journey into the Mystery of Mysteries*. 2001.

Freud, Sigmund. *Moses and Monotheism*. 1939.

Frost, Robert. *Reluctance*. 1913.

Glickman, Marshall. *Beyond the Breath*. 2002.

Gunaratana, Bhante Henepola. *Mindfulness in Plain English*. 2002.

Hanh, Thich Nhat. *Interbeing: Fourteen Guidelines for Engaged Buddhism*. (1998) by Thich Nhat Hanh

Hanh, Thich Nhat. *The Heart of the Buddha's Teaching*. *(1998)* by Thich Nhat Hanh

Hart, William. *The Art of Living, Vipassana Meditation*: as taught by S. N. Goenka. 1987.

Isaacson, Walter. *Steve Jobs*. 2001.

King James Version. *The Holy Bible*. Cleveland, OH: The World Publishing Company.

Maoshing Ni Dr. *Longevity*. http://www.askdrmao.com/ category/ questions-and-answers/l/longevity/2014.

Notovitch translation. The Lost Years of Jesus: The Life of Saint Issa. http://reluctant-messenger.com/issa.htm.

"Peter Merel's *Tao Te Ching* translation," Alistair.Cockburn. us, accessed Oct. 24, 2014. http://alistair.cockburn. us/Peter+Merel's+Tao+Te+Ching+translation

Rinchen, Geshe Sonam. *Atisha's Lamp For the Path to Enlightenment*. Copyright 1997 by Ruth Sonam.

Ruiz, don Miguel. From the book *The Four Agreements* 1997, Miguel Angel Ruiz, MD.

Ruiz, don Miguel with Janet Mills. From the book *The Four Agreements Companion Book* 2000, Miguel Angel Ruiz, MD.

Smith, Jonah. "World Without Love." Los Angeles, CA, Voluptuary Music, 2009.

Vigil, Bernadette with Arlene Broska PhD. *The Mastery of Awareness: Living the Agreements*; foreword by Miguel Ruiz. 2001.

* This bibliography is a representative cross-section of the many sources used.

About the Author

Dave McCaslin was raised in central Indiana and from age 7 until graduating from New Castle's only high school, he attended a local church 3 times a week with his parents and three brothers. He was the only family member who never blindly accepted Christianity's templated claim that its god had a living presence in shaping the heartbeat of this ephemeral reality's ever-changing present moment flash-in-time.

He never took the blind leap to become a Christian.

Having been raised under semi-fundamental living circumstances may have left the author with somewhat of a chip-on-the-shoulder attitude towards Christian wisdom. The insights that surfaced in writing this text has exposed and helped bring clarity to the miscued rational those fundamental beliefs are founded in, bringing him closer to realizing emotional balance.

At age 21, he barely survived a car accident that left him weak and feeling quite grateful just to be alive. During recovery, out of innate curiosity and the gratitude for life itself, he wanted to consciously touch the buzz of life to intrinsically witness it in action.

He intuitively felt this living force had an intrinsic connection … that this could only be done where he had the capacity to actually feel or touch life itself and that was inside his living body.

At the time, he made no association between the intellectually sketched cognitive impressions left from the rather abstract religious theology's template he was taught at church and the living message he was seeking with his self-designed sensual method for reaching this end of consciously touching the living presence of life's essence.

Twenty-five years later, while hearing the end of a book review on an obscure internet radio station, describing how a certain strain of a spiritual discipline uses the same method he had engineered to feel the buzz of life that he made any conscious connection between an intellectually learned and remembered religious template and its present moment sensual incarnation.

Theravada Buddhism uses the act of feeling the buzz of life to self-train the mind control to develop a wisdom-enriched enlightened understanding about the nature of the ways of this impermanent reality to undo the human ignorance that causes human suffering.

... 2 years NFL debate finals, 1 year as high school tennis team captain, 16th in '75 New Castle, IN High sShool class of 354 students

... 4 years Snow Ski Instructor, 4 years National Ski Patrol Slope Leader Long Mountain & Nashville Alps Ski Resorts

... Indiana University Business Mgt/Admin degree, Bloomington campus

... Owned restaurant, land surveying company, real estate broker/appraiser/ investor company

... 6th Dan Master Tae Kwan Do ... Chung Park, Grandmaster 9th Dan

... Published 1st book ... *Hoosier Heaven*